Encyclopedia of Crime & Justice

Second Edition

EDITORIAL BOARD

Encyclopedia of Crime & Justice

Second Edition

Joshua Dressler, Editor in Chief

Volume 3
Juvenile Justice:
Juvenile Court—Rural Crime

MACMILLAN REFERENCE USA

GALE GROUP

THOMSON LEARNING

New York • Detroit • San Diego • San Francisco
Boston • New Haven, Conn. • Waterville, Maine
London • Munich

Macmillan Reference USA
An imprint of the Gale Group
300 Park Avenue South
New York, NY 10010

27500 Drake Road
Farmington Hills, MI 48331

Library of Congress Cataloging-in-Publication Data
Encyclopedia of crime and justice.—2nd ed. / Joshua Dressler, editor in chief.
     p. cm.
     Includes bibliographical references and index.
     ISBN 0-02-865319-X (set: alk. paper)—ISBN 0-02-865320-3 (v. 1: alk. paper)—ISBN 0-02-865321-1 (v. 2: alk. paper)—ISBN 0-02-865322-X (v. 3: alk. paper)—ISBN 0-02-865323-8 (v. 4: alk. paper)
     1. Criminology—Encyclopedias. 2. Criminal justice, Administration of—Encyclopedias. I. Title: Crime and justice. II. Dressler, Joshua.
HV6017 .E52 2002
364'.03—dc21   2001042707

Portions of "Delinquent and Criminal Subcultures" have been adapted in part from "The Code of the Street" by Elijah Anderson by permission of W. W. Norton & Company Inc.

Printed in the United States of America
Printing number
 2 3 4 5 6 7 8 9 10

J

(CONTINUED)

JUVENILE JUSTICE: JUVENILE COURT

Juvenile courts in the United States are legally responsible for young people who are arrested by the police or otherwise accused of breaking the criminal laws of their community. Some areas of the country do not have courts actually called juvenile courts. Law violations by young people may be handled by probate courts, juvenile divisions of a circuit court, or even comprehensive family courts. In every community, however, some form of court is charged with responding to cases in which a person under the age of adulthood (a juvenile) is suspected of breaking the law. Since these courts have jurisdiction over juveniles and they follow the same general principles of juvenile law, it is conventional to refer to them simply as juvenile courts.

Many juvenile courts handle other types of cases. They often handle dependency cases (or matters involving abused and neglected children) and youth charged with noncriminal acts (or status offenses) such as curfew violations, running away from home, and truancy. Other juvenile courts (especially those known as family courts) may handle domestic violence and child custody matters. Typically, however, a juvenile court's caseload is made up of law violations, status offenders, and dependency cases. Law violations usually account for about half of this workload.

Origins

Young people who violate the law before reaching the legal age of adulthood are referred to as *juveniles* in order to indicate that they are under the jurisdiction of the juvenile court rather than the criminal (or adult) court. Technically, juveniles cannot be arrested for committing crimes because the criminal code does not apply to young people under a certain age (usually age seventeen or eighteen). Rather than charging them with a crime, juveniles are usually arrested for committing acts of *delinquency*. A twenty-five year old who steals a car is arrested for the crime of auto theft. A fifteen year old who does the same thing is taken into custody for an act of delinquency that would have been considered auto theft if that youth had been an adult.

America's system of juvenile law was founded on the premise that, due to their immaturity, young people accused of crimes should be handled differently than adults. Ideally, the juvenile court is more responsive than an adult court would be to the social and developmental characteristics of children and youth. The services and sanctions imposed by juvenile courts should be designed to do more than punish wrongdoing. They should address the causes of the youth's misbehavior and eventually restore the youth to full and responsible membership in his or her family as well as the larger community. Some contemporary critics doubt whether this mission is achievable or even desirable in all cases.

Juvenile courts emerged during the late nineteenth and early twentieth century, the period in American history known as the Progressive era. Practitioners, policymakers, and historians often see the juvenile court's history quite differently. Some characterize the founding of the first juvenile court as the culmination of many years of effort to guard the safety and well-being of youth in the justice system. In this view, the invention of the juvenile court was sparked by so-

937

cial reformers and activists who understood that children are different from adults and should be held less culpable for their unlawful behavior. Reformers worked to create a separate juvenile court, both to protect youth from harm and to provide earlier and more rehabilitative interventions for young offenders.

There is another, entirely different explanation for the emergence of the juvenile court. Historians and sociologists have noted that despite the rhetoric of social reformers, many early proponents of the juvenile court were interested in crime control. Before the development of juvenile courts, young offenders appeared in criminal court alongside adult defendants. Judges and jurors found many youth innocent or simply dismissed the charges against them. Acquittal was preferable to sending a young defendant to a nineteenth-century prison, especially when the defendant appeared socially and physically immature. In the late 1800s, police and prosecutors in many of the nation's large cities were frustrated with the criminal court's inability to sanction young offenders. They welcomed the idea of a separate juvenile court system. Such a court, they argued, would be more capable of responding to juveniles on their own terms and more likely to intervene, even in cases of relatively minor offenses and very young defendants.

Expansion

The nation's first juvenile court opened in Chicago in 1899. By 1909, twenty states had established juvenile courts and all but a few had done so by the end of the 1920s. Although each jurisdiction established its juvenile court system with its own procedures and structure, juvenile courts across the United States were generally designed to focus on early intervention and rehabilitation and to emphasize an individualized approach to youth crime. Juvenile court judges based their decisions on the unique circumstances of each offender rather than simply the severity of the offense. The goal of criminal (adult) courts was to determine guilt and dispense the right punishment for each crime. Juvenile courts were asked to investigate the causes of bad behavior and then devise a package of sanctions and services to put juveniles back on the right track.

To give juvenile courts the flexibility they would need to fulfill this mission, lawmakers allowed the juvenile court process to meet a significantly lower standard of evidence and due process. Juvenile law was codified entirely separately from criminal law. The facts of a case were not used to establish guilt but to document the occurrence of delinquency. Judges were not required to follow detailed procedures or to adhere to complex legal rules. There were fewer legal formalities in order to free the juvenile court to intervene quickly and comprehensively with each youth accused of violating the law. Even when a juvenile was merely suspected of criminal involvement, a juvenile court judge could take jurisdiction over the matter, place the youth on probation, or even hold the youth in secure custody.

The juvenile court's expansive authority was derived from several concepts in English legal tradition. The most important of these was *parens patriae*, or roughly "the nation as parent." *Parens patriae* suggested that the government had an obligation and a duty to look after the interests of children when natural parents were unable to do so. Long before the concept was discovered by American reformers, England's Chancery Courts had been invoking *parens patriae* to take temporary custody of land and property that belonged to the orphaned children of wealthy families. In the mid-1800s, American courts had used *parens patriae* as a justification for placing recalcitrant children in "houses of refuge," an early type of reformatory. America's juvenile court founders argued that parens patriae also allowed the government to take charge of any child that was destitute, neglected, or ill behaved. This arrangement gave the juvenile court an unprecedented degree of power and discretion.

Retrenchment

Within a few decades of the juvenile court's founding, some observers began to wonder whether lawmakers' ambitions for the juvenile court had been excessive. Public criticism of the juvenile court intensified. Juvenile courts, especially those in urban areas, began to exhibit the worst features of criminal courts. Caseloads swelled, courtrooms fell into disrepair, and staff became disenchanted and disinterested. During the 1950s, legal activists began to challenge the sweeping discretion given to juvenile court judges. One influential law review article charged juvenile courts with violating important principles of equal protection and argued that "rehabilitation may be substituted for punishment, but a Star Chamber cannot be substituted for a trial"

(Mathew Beemsterboer, quoted in Manfredi, p. 39).

As with other social reform efforts, it is difficult to say whether frustration with the juvenile court was borne of faulty conceptualization or poor execution. The direction taken by juvenile justice policy, however, was unmistakable. During the latter half of the twentieth century, lawmakers began to infuse the juvenile court with the values and orientation of the criminal court. Many states altered their laws to reduce the confidentiality of juvenile court proceedings and juvenile court records. Most states increased the legal formalities used in juvenile court and shifted the focus of the juvenile justice process away from individualized intervention. Instead, juvenile courts and juvenile justice agencies began to focus on public safety and offender accountability. In addition, nearly all states enacted laws to send more youth to criminal court where they could be tried and punished as adults. In the span of a single century, the American justice system had enthusiastically embraced and then largely rejected the concept of viewing the illegal behaviors of young people as something other than crime.

Structure

By the end of the juvenile court's first century, it had been largely redesigned in the image of the criminal court. Yet, every jurisdiction in the United States continued to operate some form of juvenile court. The structure of juvenile courts across the country varied considerably. As the juvenile court concept spread across the United States in the early twentieth century, lawmakers invented a variety of structures for the new courts in order to incorporate juvenile court ideals into existing procedures and policies. Even today, the purposes and procedures of juvenile courts vary substantially from jurisdiction to jurisdiction.

Many communities in the United States do not even have actual juvenile courts. Frequently, the court responsible for handling young people accused of law violations is a division of some other court, such as a superior court or a circuit court (Rottman). In Connecticut, for example, the juvenile court is part of the Superior Court, which is a court of *general jurisdiction*. There are thirteen districts for handling juvenile matters in Connecticut although criminal and civil matters are organized into twenty-two separate geographic areas. In Georgia, the juvenile court is a separate court of *limited jurisdiction* and every one of Georgia's 159 counties has a juvenile court. Colorado handles delinquency cases in twenty-two district courts, which are courts of general jurisdiction. However, the city of Denver has its own separate juvenile court that is also a court of general jurisdiction. In contrast, Utah's juvenile courts are operated as a single, statewide structure of limited jurisdiction courts, and twenty different branches are divided among eight judicial districts.

In addition to differences in structure and organization, juvenile courts across the United States also vary considerably in their responsibilities and activities. Most states give their juvenile courts legal jurisdiction over cases involving delinquency, abuse and neglect, and status offense proceedings. Some juvenile courts also have jurisdiction over adoptions, terminations of parental rights, interstate compact matters, emancipation, and consent (i.e., to marry, enlist in the armed services, be employed, and so on). Occasionally, juvenile courts may even have jurisdiction over traffic violations and child support matters.

The scope of the juvenile court's responsibility for delinquency cases is generally defined by state law. In most jurisdictions, the juvenile court handles any act committed by a juvenile for which an adult could be prosecuted in criminal court. This would include everything from relatively minor offenses (e.g., loitering, disturbing the peace, and vandalism), to more serious offenses including weapons violations, drug offenses, arson, property offenses (e.g., shoplifting, theft, and burglary), and person offenses (e.g., assault, robbery, and homicide).

Most juvenile courts have responsibility for law violations committed by youth through the age of seventeen, but the upper age of the juvenile court's jurisdiction varies from state to state. In 1999, the upper age of juvenile court jurisdiction was fifteen in Connecticut, New York, and North Carolina, and age sixteen in ten states (Georgia, Illinois, Louisiana, Massachusetts, Michigan, Missouri, New Hampshire, South Carolina, Texas, and Wisconsin). In the remaining thirty-seven states and the District of Columbia, the upper age of juvenile court jurisdiction was seventeen. In every state, there are exceptions when a youth below the state's upper age of jurisdiction can be placed under the original jurisdiction of the adult criminal court. For example, in most states if a youth of a certain age is charged with an offense from a defined list of "excluded offenses," the case must originate in criminal court.

The formal goals and purposes of the juvenile court can be quite different from state to state. During the 1980s and 1990s, a number of states modified the formal missions of their juvenile court systems to incorporate a greater emphasis on punishment or accountability. In nine states, for example, lawmakers give the juvenile court an explicit mandate to hold young offenders accountable for their law violations by exacting proportionate retribution or punishment (Arkansas, Georgia, Hawaii, Illinois, Iowa, Louisiana, Michigan, Missouri, and Rhode Island). Other states emphasize prevention and rehabilitation as the formal goals of their juvenile courts (for example, Kentucky, Massachusetts, North Carolina, Ohio, South Carolina, Vermont, and West Virginia). In most states, the formal mission of the juvenile court is to achieve a combination of youth rehabilitation and public safety.

Personnel

The people who work in juvenile courts often include judges, attorneys (prosecution and defense), administrators, clerks, bailiffs, and a wide range of other staff such as secretaries, security guards, and maintenance workers. For the most part, however, when one thinks of juvenile court personnel, the primary categories are judges, attorneys, caseworkers (probation officers), and court administrative staff (executive and clerical).

Some juvenile courts focus primarily on fact finding. Juveniles brought before such courts are usually referred to other agencies following disposition. These courts are likely to have few employees—a judge, perhaps a court reporter, and a clerk. Other juvenile courts provide a full array of pretrial and postdisposition services and require large professional staffs. Juvenile courts in more than half of the states administer their own probation departments and many are responsible for their own juvenile detention centers as well. These full-service courts essentially function as social welfare agencies, correctional facilities, and collection agencies. Jurisdictions also vary in the extent of their pre-court screening of cases, partly because they vary in the degree to which law enforcement agencies divert youths from the juvenile justice system. If the local police send virtually all cases forward for court handling, the juvenile court's intake process must contend with a diverse population of youth and the court is required to employ more staff.

Many juvenile courts employ referees, masters, or commissioners to conduct juvenile court hearings. In some jurisdictions, these nonjudicial hearing officers handle a large portion of the juvenile court's workload. Their authority is often limited to entering findings and recommendations that require confirmation by a judge to become final. Because nonjudicial hearing officers usually earn less salary than judges, some courts rely heavily on referees and masters. Nonjudicial hearing officers may outnumber judges in a particular court by as much as seven to one. Some observers have expressed concern that the widespread use of nonjudicial hearing officers demonstrates a troublesome attitude among state legislatures and perhaps the public—that the juvenile court is an inferior forum and thus judges are not required (Rubin, 1981).

Another growing concern about personnel in the juvenile court is that too many juveniles still receive inadequate legal representation. Before the 1960s, there were few defense attorneys in juvenile courts. In many jurisdictions, however, the situation has not improved substantially. In the late 1990s, a joint study by the American Bar Association, the Youth Law Center of San Francisco, and the Juvenile Law Center of Philadelphia suggested improvements were still needed, including: (1) an increase in the number of defense attorneys and related support personnel; (2) greater equity in funding for juvenile defenders and prosecutors and for juvenile defenders in comparison with adult defenders; (3) more continuing legal training for juvenile defense attorneys; (4) abolition of the practice of using juvenile court as a training ground for new attorneys; (5) a policy to guarantee juveniles effective counsel at all stages of the juvenile court process; and (6) the creation of a training academy for juvenile defense attorneys equivalent to the federally funded training available to juvenile court judges and prosecutors.

Process

The official purpose of the juvenile court is to decide whether a youth should be *adjudicated* (or judged) as a delinquent. Part of this decision is based upon evidence of the youth's unlawful behavior, but the decision also involves an assessment of each youth's individual situation. When a youth is adjudicated delinquent, the juvenile court does not simply impose a sentence com-

Figure 1

To reflect their unique goals, juvenile courts use terminology that is different from the terms used in criminal (or adult) courts	
Criminal court	**Juvenile court**
Defendant	Juvenile or child
State v. John Doe	*In re John Doe*
Indictment	Petition of delinquency
Arraignment	Prelim/Intake hearing
Crime	Offense
Trial	Hearing or proceeding
Plead guilty	Admit to offense
Conviction	Adjudication
Sentence	Disposition
Jail	Detention center
Prison	Training school
Parole	Aftercare

mensurate with the severity of the offense. The court determines the best overall response to the entirety of the situation. This response—or *disposition*—may include elements of punishment and control, but it may also incorporate individual and family services, educational and vocational rehabilitation, and often restitution to the victim or community.

The actual process for handling delinquency cases can vary considerably from community to community. In some jurisdictions, all juvenile arrests are sent directly to the juvenile court where they are reviewed (or screened) by an *intake* unit within the juvenile court. The court's intake unit may then determine that the matter should be handled *informally* (or *diverted* from the official court process). If not diverted, the case matter may be *formally* charged (or *petitioned*) and proceed to an adjudication hearing. In other communities, the juvenile court may not be involved in delinquency cases until another agency (e.g., the prosecutor's office or a social service agency) has first screened the case. In other words, the intake function is performed outside the juvenile court. In Baltimore, Maryland, for example, juveniles arrested by the police are first screened by the Maryland Department of Juvenile Justice. The department decides whether to forward the case for prosecution in juvenile court or to refer the youth to some form of noncourt diversion program. In contrast, juveniles arrested in Phoenix, Arizona, go directly to the juvenile court and the juvenile court's intake unit decides whether

the case should proceed to adjudication or receive a diversion alternative instead.

Certain processing steps are common to most juvenile justice systems, regardless of terminology, the configuration of the court, or the allocation of service delivery responsibilities. Most juvenile justice systems have some form of intake or initial review of each case. Next there is a pretrial procedure to identify the appropriate charges and the prosecutor (or another agency) decides whether to file a formal petition in the case. Following the charging and petition decisions, the adjudication process begins. If the facts of the case are established, the youth may be formally adjudicated as a delinquent. Finally, a disposition process is used to impose sanctions and services.

Not all cases that merit formal handling are scheduled for adjudication hearings in juvenile court. Instead of filing a formal petition in juvenile court, the intake department (or prosecutor) may decide that a case should be removed from juvenile court and *waived* to criminal (adult) court. Cases are usually waived to criminal court because they involve serious or violent offenses, or because the youth has a lengthy record of prior offenses. In such cases, a petition is usually filed in juvenile court asking the juvenile court judge to waive jurisdiction over the case. The juvenile court judge then decides whether the case merits criminal prosecution. If a waiver request is denied, the matter is often immediately scheduled for an adjudication hearing in juvenile court.

At an adjudication hearing, the court hears the evidence and testimony pertaining to the case and the judge decides whether the youth should be adjudicated. If the proceeding results in a failure to adjudicate (analogous to an *acquittal*), the petition might be dismissed and the case could be considered closed at that point. Even if not adjudicated, a case may be *continued* in contemplation of dismissal. For instance, the court could recommend that a youth do something prior to dismissal of all charges, such as paying restitution or voluntarily attending drug counseling. Such a case would not be considered complete until the youth followed through as instructed and the charges were dismissed.

Cases that result in adjudication (analogous to *conviction*) are sent forward for a disposition hearing (analogous to *sentencing*). At the disposition hearing, the court determines the most appropriate package of services and sanctions for each youth. Options often include commitment

Figure 2

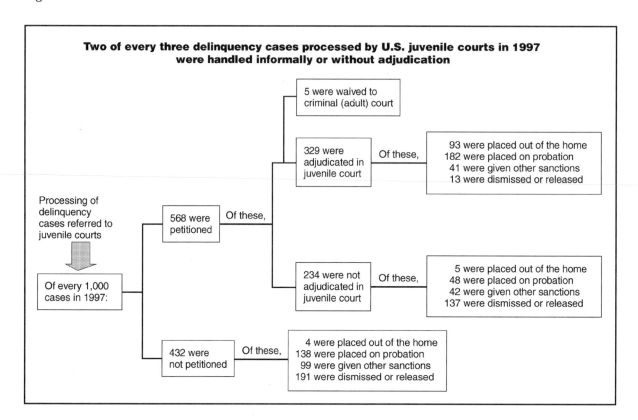

SOURCE: Melissa Sickmund, "Offenders in Juvenile Court, 1997." Juvenile Justice Bulletin. Washington, D.C.: U.S. Department of Justice, Office of Juvenile Justice and Delinquency Prevention, 2000.

to an institution, placement in a group home or other residential facility, probation (either regular or intensive), referral to an outside agency (for drug treatment, mental health services, etc.), community service, and fines or restitution payments. Ideally, the disposition is designed to protect the public safety as well as address each youth's individual needs and characteristics.

Caseload

In 1997 juvenile courts throughout the United States handled an estimated 1,755,100 delinquency cases. This was equivalent to nearly 5,000 cases per day. The national caseload in 1997 was more than double the number of cases handled by juvenile courts in 1970.

A property offense was the most serious charge involved in 48 percent of delinquency cases nationwide in 1997. The most serious charge was a person offense in 22 percent of the cases, a drug offense in 10 percent, and a public order offense in 19 percent (i.e., obstruction of justice, disorderly conduct, weapons offenses). Larceny-theft, simple assault, burglary, vandalism, and obstruction of justice were the most common delinquency offenses seen by juvenile courts in 1997. Together, these offenses accounted for 59 percent of all delinquency cases processed by juvenile courts during 1997.

More than half (57 percent) of the delinquency cases handled by U.S. courts with juvenile jurisdiction in 1997 were processed formally (i.e., a petition was filed charging the youth with delinquency). Of all the cases that were formally petitioned and scheduled for an adjudication or waiver hearing in juvenile court in 1997, 58 percent were adjudicated delinquent while less than 1 percent were transferred to adult court. Transfers to adult court were more common in cases involving formally handled person offenses (1.5 percent) and drug offenses (1.1 percent). Of the delinquency cases adjudicated in juvenile court in 1997, 28 percent resulted in out-of-home placement and 55 percent in probation.

Figure 3

Especially since the 1980s, U.S. lawmakers have increased the number of youthful offenders handled in criminal court

When juveniles are sent to adult court, they lose their legal status as minors and become fully culpable for unlawful behavior. The number of youths sent to adult court each year probably exceeds 200,000 but fewer than 10,000 are "waived" to adult court by juvenile court judges. Most youths sent to adult court are transferred by prosecutors or by state laws that make a trial in adult court automatic for certain types of offenses.

Juveniles generally follow 1 of 3 paths to adult court

Judicial waiver:
A juvenile court judge waives jurisdiction over the case after considering the merits of transfer for the individual youth.

Legislative exclusion:
A state legislature determines that an entire class of juvenile crimes should be sent to adult court automatically, usually serious offenses or repeat offenders.

Prosecutor discretion:
A state or local prosecutor has the authority to file charges against some juveniles directly in adult court, usually youths charged with serious offenses or those with lengthy arrest records.

SOURCE: Jeffrey Butts and Adele Harrell, *Delinquents or Criminals: Policy Options for Young Offenders.* Washington, D.C.: Urban Institute, 1998.

To examine changes in juvenile court caseloads while controlling for the size of the population, researchers often examine the per capita rate of delinquency cases (number of cases per 1,000 juveniles in the population). Juvenile population is defined as the number of youth age ten or older who were at or under the upper age of original jurisdiction of the juvenile court according to the laws of their state. Between 1987 and 1996, for example, the national delinquency case rate increased 34 percent, from 46 to 62 cases for every 1,000 youth at risk of referral to juvenile court. The steepest increases between 1987 and 1996 were seen among fifteen year olds (up 45 percent) and sixteen year olds (up 43 percent). The case rate for juveniles charged with drug offenses and person offenses also grew substantially, 120 percent and 80 percent, respectively.

Juvenile rights

Prior to the 1960s, juveniles accused of delinquent offenses had virtually no due process rights in American juvenile courts. Since the official purpose of the juvenile court process was to help rather than to punish, it was thought to be unnecessary to protect juveniles in the same ways that adult defendants were protected in criminal court. Juveniles arrested for delinquency had no right to an attorney unless they happened to live in a jurisdiction where this was granted to them by state or local law. They had no federal right to inspect or challenge evidence against them, or even be informed of the charges against them. The sweeping discretion of juvenile court judges had never been reviewed by the U.S. Supreme Court and local judges throughout the country were free to run their juvenile courts as they saw fit.

The situation changed suddenly and dramatically in 1967 when the U.S. Supreme Court announced its decision in a case known as *In re Gault*. An Arizona juvenile court judge had institutionalized fifteen-year-old Gerald Gault for making a mildly obscene telephone call to a neighbor. Based on the neighbor's complaint, Gerald was picked up by the local sheriff and placed in juvenile detention. The juvenile court did not bother to notify Gerald's family that he was in custody. It never heard testimony from the victim in the case, and it never established whether Gerald had actually made the call. Gerald was committed to a state institution for delinquent boys for the "period of his minority," or three years. If he had been an adult, his sentence would likely have been a small fine.

The Supreme Court's reaction to Gault's appeal was harsh and far-reaching. In any delinquency proceeding in which confinement was a possible outcome, the Court ruled, youth should have the right to formal notice of charges against them and the right to cross-examine prosecution witnesses, the right to assistance of counsel, and the protection against self-incrimination. The Supreme Court based its ruling on the fact that Gault had clearly been *punished* by the juvenile court, not *treated*. The opinion also explicitly rejected the doctrine of *parens patriae* as the founding principle of juvenile justice. The Supreme Court described the meaning of *parens patriae* as "murky" and characterized its "historic credentials" as of "dubious relevance."

Gault was one of a series of juvenile justice cases decided by the Supreme Court in the 1960s

Figure 4

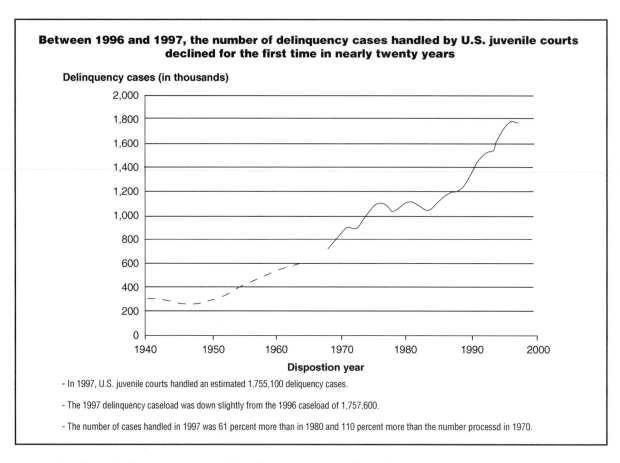

Between 1996 and 1997, the number of delinquency cases handled by U.S. juvenile courts declined for the first time in nearly twenty years

Delinquency cases (in thousands)

Disposition year

- In 1997, U.S. juvenile courts handled an estimated 1,755,100 delinquency cases.

- The 1997 delinquency caseload was down slightly from the 1996 caseload of 1,757,600.

- The number of cases handled in 1997 was 61 percent more than in 1980 and 110 percent more than the number processd in 1970.

SOURCE: C. P. Manfredi, *The Supreme Court and Juvenile Justice.* Lawrence: University Press of Kansas, 1998. P. 35. For the period 1941–1965. National Juvenile Court Data Archive, National Center for Juvenile Justice, Pittsburgh, Pa. 1999. For the period 1968–1997.

and 1970s. Together, the cases imposed significant procedural restrictions on U.S. juvenile courts. By the 1980s, juvenile courts had been "constitutionally domesticated." Juveniles charged with law violations had far more due process protections, although they were still denied the federal rights of bail, jury trial, and speedy trial. Juvenile courts were required to follow a higher standard of evidence ("reasonable doubt" rather than "preponderance") and juvenile court adjudication was considered equivalent to a criminal conviction in evaluating double jeopardy claims.

Some critics contend that the consequences of these reforms may not have been fully appreciated by youth advocates or even by the Supreme Court itself. As Justice Potter Stewart warned in his dissent to *Gault*, the introduction of greater due process for juveniles may have had the unin-

tended consequence of encouraging states to make their juvenile courts more like criminal courts:

The inflexible restrictions that the Constitution so wisely made applicable to adversary criminal trials have no inevitable place in the proceedings of those public social agencies known as juvenile or family courts. And to impose the Court's long catalog of requirements upon juvenile proceedings in every area of the country is to invite a long step backwards into the nineteenth century. In that era there were no juvenile proceedings, and a child was tried in a conventional criminal court with all the trappings of a conventional criminal trial. So it was that a 12-year-old boy named James Guild was tried in New Jersey for killing Catharine Beakes. A jury found him guilty of murder, and he was sentenced to death by hanging. The sentence was executed. It was all very constitutional (*In re Gault*, 387 U.S. 1, 1967, pp. 79–80).

Table 1

The number of delinquency cases handled by U.S. juvenile courts grew 48 percent from 1988 to 1997

Offense	Number of cases	Percent of total cases	Percent change: 1988–97
Total	**1,755,100**	**100%**	**48%**
Person offense	**390,800**	**22**	**97**
Criminal homicide	2,000	<1	31
Forcible rape	6,500	<1	48
Robbery	33,400	2	55
Aggravated assault	67,900	4	66
Simple assault	248,800	14	124
Other violent sex offense	10,200	1	59
Other person offense	22,000	1	72
Property offense	**841,800**	**48**	**19**
Burglary	135,900	8	2
Larceny-theft	401,300	23	23
Motor vehicle theft	48,800	3	–11
Arson	9,300	1	44
Vandalism	114,800	7	41
Trespassing	65,100	4	28
Stolen property offense	33,800	2	5
Other property offense	32,800	2	60
Drug law violation	**182,400**	**10**	**125**
Public order offense	**340,100**	**19**	**67**
Obstruction of justice	132,600	8	78
Disorderly conduct	92,300	5	107
Weapons offense	38,500	2	74
Liquor law violation	11,100	1	–31
Nonviolent sex offense	11,100	1	–4
Other public order	54,600	3	56
Violent Crime Index*	**109,800**	**6**	**61**
Property Crime Index**	**595,300**	**34**	**14**

* Homicide, forcible rape, robbery, and aggravated assault.
** Burglary, larceny-theft, motor vehicle theft, and arson.
Detail may not add to totals due to rounding.
Percent change based on unrounded numbers.

SOURCE: Melissa Sickmund, "Offenders in Juvenile Court, 1997." Juvenile Justice Bulletin. Washington, D.C.: U.S. Department of Justice, Office of Juvenile Justice and Delinquency Prevention, 2000.

Continuing controversies

Justice Stewart's comments seemed quite prescient as the twentieth century ended. For thirty years following the *Gault* decision, state legislatures across the U.S. continued the due process reforms endorsed by the Supreme Court. Using various mechanisms, lawmakers greatly limited the discretion of juvenile court judges and made the juvenile court process more evidence-driven and formalized. They also sent far more juveniles directly to criminal court, effectively abolishing the juvenile court's jurisdiction over many categories of young offenders.

The purposes and procedures of juvenile justice were becoming increasingly similar to those of criminal justice. Juvenile justice interventions that once targeted the depth of an offender's troubles were increasingly focused on the gravity of the offender's behavior. If the adequacy of intervention was once evaluated by its intensity, it was now to be judged by its duration as well.

As lawmakers reinvented the goals and procedures of juvenile courts in order to make them more like those of criminal courts, they became increasingly interested in new provisions for transferring juveniles to adult court. At first, transfer policies focused on a few exceptional cases, such as the most violent offenders. Soon, however, transfers were expanded to include drug offenders, juveniles accused of weapon charges, and even chronic property offenders. States first attempted merely to increase the number of youth waived to criminal court by judges. Later, the procedural difficulties involved in judicial waiver became burdensome and states began to experiment with other methods of increasing the level of punishment available for juvenile offenders.

New policy directions

Lawmakers throughout the country began to experiment with an array of new policy options for young offenders. For example, some states gave judges the power to "blend" criminal court sentences with juvenile court dispositions. Some jurisdictions passed blended sentencing laws that allowed judges to sentence juveniles directly to either juvenile or adult corrections. Other jurisdictions allowed judges to impose sentences that sequentially confined offenders to juvenile and adult correctional facilities. Young offenders would be confined in juvenile facilities until they reached a certain age and then they would be transferred to adult facilities to serve the remainder of their sentences. By the end of the 1990s, at least twenty states had enacted some form of blended sentencing (Arkansas, California, Colorado, Connecticut, Florida, Idaho, Iowa, Kansas, Massachusetts, Michigan, Minnesota, Mississippi, Montana, Missouri, New Mexico, Oklahoma, Rhode Island, South Carolina, Texas, Virginia, and West Virginia) (Torbet and Szymanski, 1998:6).

Sentencing guidelines and mandatory minimum policies for juveniles also began to proliferate during the 1990s. As of 1997, 17 states and the District of Columbia had enacted some type

Figure 5

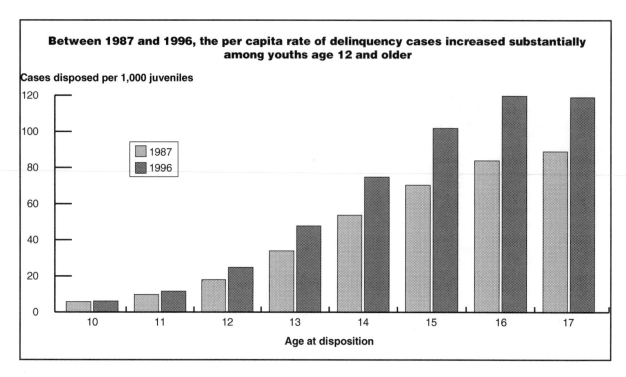

Between 1987 and 1996, the per capita rate of delinquency cases increased substantially among youths age 12 and older

Cases disposed per 1,000 juveniles

Age at disposition

SOURCE: Howard Snyder and Melissa Sickmund, *Juvenile Offenders and Victims: 1999 National Report*. Washington, D.C.: Office of Juvenile Justice and Delinquency Prevention, 1999. P. 146.

of mandatory minimum sentencing for at least some juvenile offenders (Torbet and Szymanski, pp. 7–8). Typically, sentencing guidelines apply only in cases involving violent or serious juvenile offenders as defined by statute. For example, Massachusetts adopted a law that required juveniles at least fourteen years of age who were found responsible for first-degree murder to serve a sentence of at least fifteen years in a correctional facility and juveniles found responsible for second-degree murder were required to serve at least ten years.

Some jurisdictions applied sentencing guidelines to young offenders by first requiring that they be tried in criminal court, but others (e.g., Arizona, Utah, and Wyoming) applied formal sentencing guidelines to the juvenile court. Juvenile dispositions were required to be consistent with a predefined sentencing menu based upon the most recent offense and prior record. The use of structured sentencing contradicted the basic premise of juvenile justice by making dispositions proportional to the severity of an offense rather than to the characteristics and life problems of an offender. Their existence highlights the extent to which the juvenile court has been replaced by a modified criminal court for youthful offenders.

Another significant departure from the traditional juvenile court concept is the growing popularity of allowing juvenile court records to follow young adults into criminal court. By allowing criminal court judges to consider a defendant's prior juvenile court record at the time of sentencing, states altered the terms of the agreement that created the juvenile court system in the first place. Originally, juveniles essentially agreed to receive less due process in juvenile court in exchange for a less formal, nonstigmatizing, and nonpermanent disposition. By the 1990s, however, the emergence of policies that permitted juvenile court records to enhance the severity of criminal court sentences revoked this arrangement. Defendants could now be imprisoned for many years as a direct result of a previous adjudication in juvenile court. As of 1997, all fifty states and the District of Columbia had statutes, court rules, or case law that allowed this practice (Sanborn, p. 209).

A remade juvenile court

Every jurisdiction in the United States continues to operate a separate juvenile court system, but many youth are ineligible for juvenile court and those that remain experience a juvenile court process that is far more *criminalized*. Juvenile court procedures are more complex and evidence-driven. Cases are more likely to be formally charged by prosecutors instead of being handled informally by probation workers. Juvenile court dispositions are increasingly governed by offense severity rather than by youth troubles. Defense attorneys are under pressure to defend juvenile clients more vigorously since adjudication may lead to more severe sanctions. Probation officers, prosecutors, and judges openly embrace the goals of retribution and incapacitation. In short, the similarities of the juvenile and adult justice systems are becoming greater than the differences between them. The primary challenge for lawmakers during the twenty-first century may be to decide whether to continue maintaining the separate juvenile court at all.

JEFFREY A. BUTTS

See also JUVENILE AND YOUTH GANGS; JUVENILE JUSTICE: HISTORY AND PHILOSOPHY; JUVENILE JUSTICE: COMMUNITY TREATMENT; JUVENILE JUSTICE: INSTITUTIONS; JUVENILES IN THE ADULT SYSTEM; JUVENILE STATUS OFFENDERS; JUVENILE VIOLENT OFFENDERS; POLICE: HANDLING OF JUVENILES; PREVENTION: JUVENILES AS POTENTIAL OFFENDERS; SCHOOLS AND CRIME.

BIBLIOGRAPHY

BERNARD, THOMAS J. *The Cycle of Juvenile Justice.* New York: Oxford University Press, 1992.
BUTTS, JEFFREY, and HARRELL, ADELE. *Delinquents or Criminals: Policy Options for Young Offenders.* Washington, D.C.: Urban Institute, 1998.
FELD, BARRY C. "Abolish the Juvenile Court: Youthfulness, Criminal Responsibility, and Sentencing Policy." *Journal of Criminal Law & Criminology* 88, no. 1 (1997): 68–136.
FOX, SANFORD J. "Juvenile Justice Reform: An Historical Perspective." *Stanford Law Review* 22 (June 1970): 1187–1239.
MANFREDI, CHRISTOPHER P. *The Supreme Court and Juvenile Justice.* Lawrence: University Press of Kansas, 1998.
PLATT, ANTHONY M. *The Child Savers: The Invention of Delinquency.* Chicago: University of Chicago Press, 1977.
ROTHMAN, DAVID J. *Conscience and Convenience: The Asylum and its Alternatives in Progressive America.* Glenview, Ill.: Scott, Foresman and Company, 1980.
ROTTMAN, DAVID, et al. *State Court Organization 1998.* Washington, D.C.: U.S. Department of Justice, Bureau of Justice Assistance, 2000.
RUBIN, H. TED. "Between Recommendations and Orders: The Limbo Status of Juvenile Court Referees." *Crime and Delinquency* 27, no. 3 (1981): 317–335.
———. "Role of Defense Attorneys in Juvenile Justice Proceedings." *Juvenile Justice Update* 2, no. 2 (1996): 1–2, 10, 11.
SANBORN, JOSEPH B., JR. "Second-Class Justice, First-Class Punishment: The Use of Juvenile Records in Sentencing Adults." *Judicature* 81, no. 5 (1998): 206–213.
SICKMUND, MELISSA. "Offenders in Juvenile Court, 1997." Juvenile Justice Bulletin. Washington, D.C.: U.S. Department of Justice, Office of Juvenile Justice and Delinquency Prevention, 2000.
SNYDER, HOWARD, and SICKMUND, MELISSA. *Juvenile Offenders and Victims: 1999 National Report.* Washington, D.C.: U.S. Department of Justice, Office of Juvenile Justice and Delinquency Prevention, 1999.
TORBET, PATRICIA, and SZYMANSKI, LINDA. "State Legislative Responses to Violent Juvenile Crime: 1996–97 Update." Juvenile Justice Bulletin. Washington, D.C.: U.S. Department of Justice, Office of Juvenile Justice and Delinquency Prevention, 1998.
WATKINS, JOHN C., JR. *The Juvenile Justice Century.* Durham, N.C.: Carolina Academic Press, 1998.

JUVENILES IN THE ADULT SYSTEM

Jurisdictional waiver constitutes a type of *sentencing* decision. Transfer of juvenile offenders for adult prosecution provides the nexus between the more deterministic and rehabilitative premises of the juvenile court and the free will and punishment assumptions of the adult criminal justice system. Mechanisms to prosecute some juveniles as adults provide a safety valve that permit the expiatory sacrifice of some youths, quiet political and public clamor about serious youth crime, and enable legislators to avoid otherwise irresistible pressures to lower further the maximum age of juvenile court jurisdiction. Waiver laws attempt to resolve fundamental crime control issues, reconcile the conflicted impulses engendered when the child is a criminal and the criminal is a child, and harmonize cultural contradictions between adolescent immaturity and criminal responsibility.

Since the mid-1980s, public frustration with crime, fear of youth violence, and the racial characteristics of violent young offenders have fueled a desire to "get tough" and provided political impetus to prosecute larger numbers of youths as adults. Some of these initiatives simplify transfer of young offenders to criminal courts by expediting judicial waiver, by excluding certain categories of offenses from juvenile court jurisdiction, or by allowing prosecutors directly to charge youths as adults. The offense exclusion and "direct file" approaches de-emphasize rehabilitation and individualized consideration of the offender, and instead stress youth's age and offenses, personal and justice system accountability, and punishment.

Every jurisdiction uses one or more statutory approaches to prosecute some juveniles as adults. Although technical and administrative details of states' transfer laws vary considerably, judicial waiver, legislative offense exclusion, and prosecutorial choice of forum represent the three generic approaches. They represent different ways to identify which serious young offenders to try as adults, emphasize a different balance of sentencing policy values, rely upon different organizational actors or administrative processes, and elicit different information to determine whether to try and sentence particular young offenders as adults or as children. These strategies allocate to different branches of government—judicial, executive, or legislative—the decision whether to try a youth as a criminal or as a delinquent.

Judicial waiver represents the most common transfer strategy. A juvenile court judge may waive jurisdiction on a discretionary basis after conducting a hearing to determine whether a youth is "amenable to treatment" or poses a threat to the public. These assessments reflect the traditional individualized sentencing discretion characteristic of juvenile courts.

Legislative offense exclusion frequently supplements judicial waiver provisions. This approach emphasizes the seriousness of the offense and reflects the retributive values of the criminal law. Because legislatures create juvenile courts, they freely can define their jurisdiction to exclude youths from juvenile court based on their age and offenses. A number of states, for example, exclude youths sixteen or older and charged with first-degree murder from juvenile court jurisdiction. Legislative line-drawing that sets the maximum age of juvenile court jurisdiction at fifteen or sixteen years of age, below the general eighteen-year-old age of majority, results in the criminal prosecution of the largest numbers of chronological juveniles.

Prosecutorial waiver or "direct file" constitutes the third method by which about ten states remove some young offenders from the juvenile justice system. With this strategy, juvenile and criminal courts share concurrent jurisdiction over certain ages and offenses, typically older youths and serious crimes, and a prosecutor decides in which forum to try the case.

Each type of waiver strategy has supporters and critics. Proponents of judicial waiver endorse juvenile courts' rehabilitative philosophy and argue that individualized decisions provide an appropriate balance of flexibility and severity. Critics object that judges lack valid or reliable clinical tools with which to accurately assess amenability to treatment or predict dangerousness, and that their exercises of standardless discretion results in abuses and inequalities. Proponents of offense exclusion favor just deserts sentencing policies, advocate sanctions based on relatively objective factors such as offense seriousness and criminal history, and value consistency, uniformity, and equality in the handling of similarly situated offenders. Critics question whether legislators can remove discretion without making the process rigid and over-inclusive, or simply delegating sentencing discretion to prosecutors who manipulate their charging decisions. Proponents of prosecutorial waiver claim that prosecutors can act as more neutral, balanced and objective gatekeepers than either "soft" judges or "get tough" legislators. Critics observe that prosecutors succumb to political pressures, exercise their discretion just as subjectively as do judges, and introduce extensive geographic variability into the justice process.

Judicial waiver and individualized sentencing

From the juvenile court's inception, judges could deny some young offenders its protective jurisdiction and transfer them to adult courts. Judicial waiver reflects juvenile courts' traditional offender-oriented approach to decide whether to treat a youth as a juvenile or to punish him as an adult. In *Kent v. United States* (1966), the U.S. Supreme Court required juvenile court judges to conduct a formal waiver hearing and to provide some procedural protections. Subsequently, in *Breed v. Jones* (1975), the Court applied the double jeopardy clause of the fifth amendment to delinquency convictions and required states to decide whether to try and sentence a youth as a juvenile or as an adult before proceeding to trial on the merits of the charge.

Kent and *Breed* provided the formal procedural framework within which judges make waiver sentencing decisions. But the substantive bases of waiver decisions pose the principal difficulty. Most states' waiver statutes allow judges to transfer jurisdiction based on their assessment of a youth's "amenability to treatment." The Court in *Kent*, for example, appended to its opinion a list of substantive criteria that juvenile court judges might consider. States' judicial decisions and waiver statutes specify "amenability" criteria with varying degrees of precision and frequently incorporate the list of *Kent* factors. Although some states limit judicial waiver to felony offenses and establish a minimum age for adult prosecution, other states provide neither offense nor minimum age restrictions.

In practice, judges appear to assess a youth's amenability to treatment and dangerousness by focusing on three sets of variables. The first consists of a youth's age and the length of time remaining within juvenile court jurisdiction. Juvenile court judges waive older youths more readily than younger offenders. A youth's age in relation to the maximum dispositional jurisdiction limits juvenile courts' sanctioning powers and provides the impetus to waive older juveniles if the seriousness of the offense deserves a much longer sentence than a juvenile court can impose. A second constellation of "amenability" factors include a youth's treatment prognosis as reflected in clinical evaluations and prior correctional interventions. Once a youth exhausts available juvenile correctional resources, transfer becomes increasingly more likely. Finally, judges assess a youth's dangerousness based on the seriousness of the present offense, whether the youth used a weapon, and the length of the prior record. Balancing dangerousness factors entails a trade-off between offense seriousness and offender persistence.

Judicial waiver criteria framed in terms of amenability to treatment or dangerousness give judges broad discretion. Long lists of factors, such as those appended in *Kent*, do not provide judges with adequate guidance, serve to reinforce their discretion, and allow them selectively to emphasize one variable or another to justify any decision. The subjective nature of waiver decisions, the absence of effective guidelines, and the lack of objective indicators or scientific tools with which to classify youths allows judges to make unequal and disparate rulings. Empirical evaluations provide compelling evidence that judges apply waiver statutes in an arbitrary, capricious, and even discriminatory manner. Different states' rates of judicial waiver for similar offenders vary considerably. Even within a single jurisdiction, judges do not interpret or apply waiver statutes consistently from county to county or from court to court. Research in several states report a contextual pattern of "justice by geography"—where youths lived, rather than what they did, determined their juvenile or adult status. Even within a single urban county, various judges in the same court decide cases of similarly situated offenders differently. A youth's race also affects waiver decisions. Studies consistently report that judges transfer minority juveniles at a higher rate than they do similarly situated white offenders. Differences in judicial philosophies, the locale of a waiver hearing, or a youth's race explain as much of the variance in transfer decisions as do a youth's offense or personal characteristics. Because assessments of "amenability" are so indeterminate, appellate courts give enormous deference to juvenile court judges' discretionary decisions.

Legislative offense exclusion and prosecutors' choice of forum

Legislative offense exclusion simply removes certain offenses from juvenile court jurisdiction—youths charged with those crimes are "automatic adults." Concurrent jurisdiction "direct file" laws grant to prosecutors the power to choose whether to charge a youth accused of a specified offense in either juvenile or criminal court without justifying that decision in a judicial hearing or with a formal record. Youths have no constitutional right to a juvenile court. State legislatures create juvenile courts and define their jurisdiction, powers, and purposes in many different ways. What they create, they also may modify or take away. States currently set juvenile courts' maximum age jurisdiction at seventeen, sixteen, or fifteen years old as a matter of state policy and without constitutional infirmity. If a legislature defines juvenile court jurisdiction to include only persons below a jurisdictional age and whom prosecutors charge with a nonexcluded offense, then by statutory definition all other chronological juveniles are adult criminal defendants.

Excluded youths tried in criminal courts have challenged their "automatic adulthood" as a denial of due process. Because courts decline to review prosecutors' discretionary charging decisions, excluded youths object that they do not receive the procedural safeguards required by *Kent*. Youths also contend that exclusion based on the offense charged constitutes an arbitrary legislative classification that violates equal protection. In *United States v. Bland* (1972), the leading case on the validity of legislative offense exclusion statutes, the court declined to review prosecutorial decisions because the constitutional separation of powers denies the judicial branch the power to compel or control the executive branch in essentially discretionary matters. In the absence of invidious discrimination on the basis of race, religion, or the like, a prosecutor's decisions about whether and whom to charge and with what remain beyond judicial review. Youths also have argued that offense-exclusion laws create an arbitrary and irrational statutory distinction—criminal or delinquent status—based on serious or minor offenses that violates equal protection. Courts uniformly reject such claims, noting that classification on the basis of offenses involves neither an inherently suspect class nor an invidious discrimination, and the loss of juvenile court treatment does not infringe any fundamental right.

Pure prosecutorial waiver statutes create concurrent jurisdiction in juvenile and criminal courts for certain offenses and give prosecutors discretion to charge youths of certain ages with the same offense in either forum. Unlike offense-exclusion where charges only for certain offenses can result in criminal prosecution, direct file legislation gives prosecutors greater latitude to choose the forum. Essentially, the prosecutor makes two types of decisions: whether probable cause exists to believe that the youth committed a particular offense and, if that offense is one for which concurrent jurisdiction exists, whether to charge the youth in either juvenile or criminal court. Although youths have challenged the validity of direct file laws that delegate to prosecutors discretion to choose a youth's juvenile or criminal status, appellate courts invoke the rationale of *Bland* and reject their claims.

Youth crime and "get tough" politics

The "baby boom" escalation in youth crime that began in the mid-1960s and peaked in the late 1970s provided a strong political impetus for "get tough" criminal sentencing and waiver policies. Beginning in the 1970s, juvenile waiver policies began to shift from rehabilitation to retribution, from offender to offense, from "amenability" to "public safety," and from the judicial to the legislative or executive branches. These statutory changes coincided with escalating youth crime rates and violence in the late 1970s and again in the late 1980s and early 1990s, and with public and political perception of youth crime primarily as an urban black male phenomenon. Two aspects of youth crime and violence have special relevance for understanding changes in waiver laws during the 1980s and 1990s. Since the mid-1960s, police have arrested black juveniles for all violent offenses—murder, rape, robbery, and assault—at a rate about five times greater than that of white youths, and for homicide at a rate more than seven times that of white youths. Secondly, while the number of homicide deaths that juveniles caused by means other than firearms fluctuated within a "normal range" of about plus or minus 10 percent during the 1980s and early 1990s, the number of deaths that juveniles caused with firearms quadrupled. Because of the disproportional involvement of black youths in violence and homicide, both as perpetrators and as victims, almost all of these "excess" homicides involving guns occurred within the urban, young black male population as a by-product of the "crack cocaine" epidemic. The intersection of race, guns, and homicide fanned a public "panic" and encouraged politicians to adopt "get tough" waiver policies.

The "crackdown" on youth crime of the early 1990s culminated the politicization of crime and waiver policies that began several decades earlier. In the 1960s, the civil rights movement created divisions within the Democratic Party between racial and social policy liberals and conservatives, northerners and southerners. Republican politicians seized crime control, affirmative action, and public welfare as racially tinged "wedge issues" with which to distinguish themselves from Democrats in order to woo southern white voters. For the first time, crime policies became a central issue in partisan politics. During the 1960s, conservative Republicans decried "crime in the streets" and advocated "law and order" in response to rising "baby boom" crime rates, civil rights marches and anti-war protests, and urban and campus turmoil. Since the 1960s, politicians' fear of being labeled by their opponents as "soft-on-crime" has led to a constant ratcheting-up of punitiveness as public officials avoid thoughtful discussions of complex crime policy issues in an era of thirty-second commercials. Efforts to "get tough" have supported a succession of "wars" on crime, drugs, and juveniles, longer criminal sentences, increased prison populations, and disproportional incarceration of racial minority offenders. The mass media depict and the public perceive the crime problem and juvenile courts' clientele primarily as poor, urban black males. Politicians manipulate and exploit these racially tinged perceptions for political advantage with demagogic pledges to "crack down" on youth crime, which has become a code word for young black males.

Legislative changes in waiver strategies

States made relatively limited use of offense-based strategies until *Kent* required a judicial waiver hearing and thereby provided the impetus for more streamlined and efficient transfer alternatives. A few states long had excluded from their juvenile courts older youths charged with capital offenses or crimes punishable by life imprisonment, such as murder. Some states also excluded youths charged with other serious crimes such as rape or armed robbery. But, reflecting the influences of "just deserts" jurisprudence, criminal career research, and "get tough" politics, two distinct legislative trends emerged between the 1970s and the early 1990s. First, more states excluded at least some offenses from their juvenile courts' jurisdiction, lowered the ages of juveniles' eligibility for criminal prosecution, and increased the numbers of offenses for which states may prosecute youths as adults. Second, the number of states that allow prosecutors, rather than judges, to select the forum via concurrent jurisdiction increased as did the offenses for which prosecutors may transfer youths.

A compilation and analysis of states' waiver laws in 1986 reported that eighteen states excluded at least some offenses from their juvenile courts' jurisdiction, typically capital crimes or murder by youths sixteen or older. One statutory compilation a decade later reported that twenty-six states excluded some offenses from their juvenile courts' jurisdiction, a 45 percent increase in less than a decade. A second statutory compilation in 1995 that included judicially waived youths previously convicted as adults in its excluded offense classification reported that thirty-eight states excluded at least some offenders from juvenile court jurisdiction. A third compilation that compared waiver statutes in 1979 with those in 1995 reported that during that period, eight additional states joined the excluded-offense ranks, a 35 percent increase. During the 1979–1995 period, almost half of the states also lowered the age of eligibility for adult prosecution and expanded the number of excluded offenses. Still another statutory survey reported that between 1992 and 1995, twenty-four states added some crimes to their excluded offense lists and six states lowered the minimum ages for some or all of their excluded offenses.

Transfer back or "reverse waiver"

In order to restore some flexibility to a prosecutor-dominated waiver process and to allow for appropriate dispositions of some "amenable" younger offenders, many states allow judges to "reverse waive" or "transfer back" to juvenile court cases that originated in criminal court either as a result of excluded offense or prosecutorial direct file decisions. About half of the prosecutor direct file and excluded offense jurisdictions allow a criminal court judge either to return a youth to juvenile court for trial or sentencing, or to impose a juvenile or youthful offender sentence in lieu of an adult criminal sentence. In some states, offense exclusion or direct file laws that place a youth initially in criminal court create a presumption of unfitness and shift the burden of proof to the juvenile to demonstrate why he should be returned to juvenile court for trial or disposition. In other excluded offense jurisdictions, the prosecutor may make a "reverse waiver" decision. In most states, however, a criminal court judge makes the "transfer back" decision to sentence a youth as a juvenile under provisions that recreate *Kent*-style proceedings. An evaluation of reverse waiver decisions reported that criminal court judges transferred back significantly more younger offenders, those who had fewer prior convictions and less previous exposure to juvenile correctional services, and those whom clinicians identified as "amenable to treatment." These reverse waiver findings correspond to comparable research on juvenile court waiver decisions, which report that judges typically transferred older youths, those with prior juvenile correctional experiences, and those whom clinicians deemed "unamenable to treatment." In short, the limited evidence on reverse waiver suggest that it closely replicates juvenile court judicial waiver.

Criminal court careers of waived juveniles

Juvenile and criminal courts' sentencing practices often work at cross-purposes and frustrate rather than harmonize the social control of serious and chronic young offenders as they move between the two systems. Until the recent amendments of waiver laws, criminal courts typically sentenced chronic younger offenders more leniently than they did older offenders because of the latter's cumulative adult prior records. The lenient responses to many young career offenders when they first appear in criminal courts occur because the criteria for removal from juvenile court and adult criminal sentencing practices often lack congruence. The "punishment gap" occurs because waiver decisions involve two, somewhat different but overlapping populations of young offenders—older chronic delinquent offenders currently charged with a property crime *and* violent youths, some of whom also are persistent offenders.

Criminal courts respond differently to chronic offenders currently charged with a property crimes and those charged with violence. Prior to 1993, juvenile court judges transferred the largest plurality of youths for property offenses (45 percent), rather than for crimes against the person (34 percent). The nature of the offenses for which juvenile courts transferred juveniles and their relative youthfulness compared with adult defendants affected their first criminal court sentences. Although several studies of dispositions of youths tried as adults report substantial variation in sentencing practices, a policy of leniency often prevailed. Earlier studies reported that urban criminal courts incarcerated younger offenders at a lower rate than they did older offenders, that youthful violent offenders received shorter sentences than did older violent offenders, and that for about two years after becoming adults, youths benefited from informal, lenient sentencing policies. A nationwide study of judicially waived youths sentenced as adults found that criminal courts fined or placed the majority (54 percent) of transferred juveniles on probation. Even among those confined, 40 percent received maximum sentences of one year or less and only about one-quarter (28 percent) received sentences of five years or more. More recent research reports that juvenile

court judges continue to waive primarily older chronic offenders charged with a property crime like burglary rather than with a violent crime, and criminal courts subsequently fined or placed on probation most transferred juveniles. Moreover, criminal court judges typically sentenced chronic property offenders convicted as adult first-time offenders more leniently than adults and often for shorter sentences than juvenile court judges imposed on comparable delinquents.

Unlike the criminal court sentences of chronic property offenders, the transfer decisions have profound consequences for waived violent youths. A study of the dispositions received by waived and retained youths whom prosecutors charged with a violent offense and who had a prior felony conviction reported that criminal courts incarcerated over 90 percent and imposed sentences five times longer than those given to youths with similar offense characteristics but who remained in juvenile court. Another study compared young robbery and burglary offenders in New York, whose excluded offenses placed them in criminal court, with a similar sample of fifteen- and sixteen-year-old youths in matched counties in New Jersey whose age and offenses placed them in juvenile courts. The New York criminal courts convicted and incarcerated a somewhat larger proportion of youths, but both justice systems imposed sentences of comparable length. Although burglary offenders in both jurisdictions recidivated at about the same rate, adult robbery offenders in New York reoffended more quickly and at a higher rate than did the juveniles in New Jersey. A study in Florida compared youths whom prosecutors direct-filed into criminal court with a matched sample of youths retained in juvenile court and found that by all measures, the youths whom prosecutors tried as adults did worse—they committed additional and more serious offenses more quickly than did those youths retained in juvenile jurisdiction. Several studies consistently indicate that criminal courts imprison more often and impose longer sentences on violent youths tried as adults than do juvenile court judges.

Because of differences in rates and types of offending by race, laws that target violent offenses indirectly have the effect of identifying larger proportions of black juveniles than white youths and exposing them to more severe adult penal consequences. As the number of waived cases increased from 1988 onward, and the proportion of violent offenses among waived cases increased, the percentage of black juveniles judicially waived to criminal court increased from 43 percent to 50 percent of all transferred youths. Although juvenile courts waived an equal proportion of black and white youths (49 percent) in 1989, by 1993 the proportion of waived white youths decreased to 45 percent while black youths comprised 52 percent of all waived juveniles.

The recent changes in waiver laws increase the numbers of chronological juveniles charged, tried, and sentenced in criminal courts. Despite legislative efforts to transfer more youths to criminal courts, surprisingly few analysts compare the rates of conviction or sentences of waived or excluded youths with those of retained juveniles or similar adult defendants. The few studies of waived juveniles' conviction rates in criminal courts suggest that criminal courts convict them at higher rates than do juvenile courts and perhaps more readily than they do other adult defendants. These higher conviction rates probably reflect prior prosecutorial and judicial screening decisions and the sample selection bias of youths waived to criminal court. A study in New York reports that criminal courts convicted youths charged with robbery at a significantly higher rate than did juvenile courts. A study in Hennepin County, Minnesota, reported higher rates of conviction and some type of incarceration for waived youths in criminal courts than for those retained in juvenile courts. A study of waived youths in seven states found that conviction rates varied from state to state and by type of offense, but that criminal courts convicted waived juveniles at about the same rates as other young adult offenders. Adult criminal courts sentence waived young offenders primarily on the basis of the seriousness of their present offense. The emphasis on the present offense reflects ordinary criminal sentencing practices as well as the failure systematically to include juvenile prior convictions in young adults' criminal histories. Criminal courts often sentence violent young offenders to substantial terms of imprisonment, including "life without parole" or the death penalty. Many studies report that waived violent youths receive sentences four or more times longer than do their retained juvenile counterparts. By contrast, waived chronic property offenders often receive more lenient sentences as adult first offenders than do their retained juvenile counterparts.

Youthfulness, proportional punishment, and the death penalty

Waiver of youths to criminal courts for sentencing as adults implicates legal and cultural understandings of juveniles' criminal responsibility. Waiver laws that exclude capital offenses from juvenile court jurisdiction expose some youths to the possibility of execution for offenses they committed as juveniles. Imposing sentences of "life without parole" on waived youths for crimes they committed at thirteen or fourteen years of age, and executing them for crimes they committed at sixteen or seventeen years of age, challenges the social construction of adolescence and the idea that juveniles are less criminally responsible than adults.

Both historically and at present, some states have executed people for crimes committed while they were children. States have executed nearly three hundred people for the crimes they committed as chronological juveniles, and courts currently impose about 2 percent of death penalties on minors. Since the reinitiation of capital punishment in 1973, states have executed nine offenders for crimes they committed as juveniles, six since 1990. Judges have pronounced death sentences on 140 offenders for crimes committed as juveniles, or 2.6 percent of all capital sentences.

The Supreme Court considered the culpability of young offenders in the context of death penalty litigation on several occasions in the 1980s. In *Thompson v. Oklahoma* (1988), the Court pondered whether a state violated the Eighth Amendment prohibition on "cruel and unusual punishments" by executing an offender for a heinous murder he committed when he was fifteen years old. A plurality of the Court overturned the capital sentence and concluded that "a young person is not capable of acting with the degree of culpability [as an adult] that can justify the ultimate penalty." The following year in *Stanford v. Kentucky* (1989), a different plurality of the Court upheld the death penalty for murders committed by juveniles aged sixteen or seventeen years at the time of their offense. Of the thirty-eight states and the federal government that authorize the death penalty, twenty-one allow the state to execute a youth for crimes committed at age sixteen and an additional four permit executions for crimes committed at age seventeen.

The Supreme Court gives even greater constitutional deference to states' sentencing policy decisions outside of the context of capital punishment, upholds mandatory life sentences even for drug crimes, and eschews proportionality analyses. The Court's deference to states' criminal policy judgments grants state legislatures virtually unreviewable authority to prescribe penalties for crimes. The Court's reluctance to limit states' criminal sentencing authority has special significance for juveniles tried as adults. "Sound-bites" of contemporary politics—"adult crime, adult time," or "old enough to do the crime, old enough to do the time"—convey current youth sentencing policy. Many of the most serious crimes for which criminal courts convict youths carry substantial sentences, mandatory minima, or even life without parole. Exclusion statutes without minimum age restrictions expose even very young offenders to such harsh penalties. The Federal Sentencing Guidelines explicitly reject "youthfulness" as a justification to mitigate sentences outside of the guidelines range, although several states' sentencing laws recognize "youthfulness" as a mitigating factor. However, statutes that include youthfulness among a number of aggravating-mitigating factors simply treat it as one element to weigh with other factors when sentencing. In most states, whether a judge treats youthfulness as a mitigating factor rests within her sound discretion. Appellate courts regularly affirm mandatory sentences of life without parole for thirteen-year-old juveniles convicted as adults.

As a result of recent changes in waiver laws, criminal courts sentence increasing numbers of youths to adult correctional facilities. Unfortunately, we lack reliable data on the number of imprisoned juveniles because most states do not classify young inmates on the basis of the process that brought them to prison. Many youths who committed their crimes as chronological juveniles may be adults by the time courts have waived, convicted, and sentenced them to prison. Because of the recency of many changes in waiver statutes, correctional administrators have not yet fully experienced the population or programming implications of these policy changes.

A 1991 survey of state correctional administrators reported that convicts aged seventeen or younger comprised less than one percent of 712,000 prisoners, but did not distinguish between waived or excluded youths and those in states in which juvenile court jurisdiction ended at fifteen or sixteen years of age. Another survey reported that offenders younger than eighteen years of age comprised about 2 percent of new commitments to prisons, and that about three-

quarters of those youths were seventeen at the time of their confinement. In 1993, criminal courts sentenced about 5,200 youths aged seventeen or younger to adult prisons.

Recall that criminal courts sentenced juveniles waived for property and for violent crimes differently as adults, and that recent waiver legislative amendments increasingly target violent youths. As a result, among persons sentenced to prison, a substantially larger proportion of younger offenders are committed for violent crimes than is true for adult prison commitments. For example, of youths under age eighteen sentenced to prison, 50 percent had been convicted of violent crimes, compared with 29 percent of adults admitted to prison. The percentages of youths committed to prison who had been convicted of violent crimes exceeded the proportions for sentenced adults for murder, robbery, and assault. Because of the disparities in rates of violent offending by race, criminal courts sentenced a majority of black youths (54 percent) to prison for violent offenses and a majority of white youths (57 percent) for property crimes. Because of the differences in sentence lengths imposed for violent and property crimes, the racial disparities in prison inmate populations will cumulate.

The infusion of juvenile offenders poses a challenge to corrections officials to develop age-appropriate programs and conditions of confinement for younger inmates. Correctional administrators anticipate increased pressure on already overburdened prison systems. Subject to variations in state laws and available facilities, correctional options for handling juveniles include straight adult incarceration with minimal differentiation between juveniles and adults other than routine inmate classification; graduated incarceration in which youths begin their sentences in a juvenile or separate adult facility and then serve the remainder of their sentence in the adult facility; or age-segregated incarceration either in separate facilities within the prison or in separate youth facilities for younger adults. Analyses of correctional practices in the mid-1990s reported that nearly all states confine juveniles sentenced as adults in adult correctional facilities either with younger adult offenders or in the general population if the juvenile is of a certain age, for example, sixteen. In 1994, thirty-six states dispersed young inmates with adult inmates, nine states housed younger inmates with those aged eighteen to twenty-one, and only six states segregated younger inmates from older prisoners either in juvenile training schools until they reached the age of majority or in age-segregated units within an adult prison. Prison officials generally regard juveniles convicted in criminal courts as adults and employ the same policies, programs, and conditions of confinement for them as for other adult inmates.

The influx of younger offenders poses management, programming, and control challenges for correctional administrators. Young peoples' dietary and exercise needs differ from those of older inmates. Younger inmates may engage in more institutional misconduct, and management techniques appropriate for adults may be less effective when applied to juveniles. Evaluations of the prison adjustment of serious or violent youthful offenders are mixed. A few states report that young offenders pose special management problems or commit more disciplinary infractions than do older inmates, while other states report few differences. One systematic study of the prison adjustment of young offenders compared a sample of waived youths convicted of violent crimes committed before the age of seventeen with a matched sample of incarcerated inmates aged seventeen to twenty-one at the time of their offenses. The waived violent youths adapted less well, experienced more difficulty adjusting to institutional life, accumulated more extensive disciplinary histories, and earned less good time. Juveniles in adult facilities are more likely to be victims of violent attacks and sexual assaults and more likely to commit suicide that those confined in juvenile facilities.

Conclusion

Since 1992, nearly half the states have expanded their lists of excluded offenses, lowered the ages of eligibility for exclusion from sixteen to fourteen or thirteen years of age, or granted prosecutors more authority to transfer cases to criminal court. Increasing numbers of younger offenders charged with serious crimes find themselves in criminal court. Excluded offense and direct file laws symbolize a fundamental change in juvenile justice jurisprudence and policies from rehabilitation to retribution. The overarching themes of the various legislative amendments include a shift from individualized justice to just deserts, from treatment to punishment, and from immature delinquent to responsible criminal. These trends in waiver policy reflect a legal reformulation of the social construction of "youth" from innocent, immature, and depen-

dent children to responsible, autonomous, and mature offenders. "Get tough" criminal sentencing policies provide no formal recognition of youthfulness as a mitigating factor. Once youths make the transition to criminal court, judges sentence them as if they are adults, impose the same sentences, send them to the same prisons, and even inflict capital punishment on them for the crimes they committed as children.

BARRY C. FELD

See also JUVENILE AND YOUTH GANGS; JUVENILE JUSTICE: HISTORY AND PHILOSOPHY; JUVENILE JUSTICE: COMMUNITY TREATMENT; JUVENILE JUSTICE: INSTITUTIONS; JUVENILE JUSTICE: JUVENILE COURT; JUVENILE STATUS OFFENDERS; JUVENILE VIOLENT OFFENDERS; POLICE: HANDLING OF JUVENILES; PREDICTION OF CRIME AND RECIDIVISM; PREVENTION: JUVENILES AS POTENTIAL OFFENDERS; SCHOOLS AND CRIME.

BIBLIOGRAPHY

BECKETT, KATHERINE. *Making Crime Pay: Law and Order in Contemporary American Politics.* New York: Oxford University Press, 1997.

BISHOP, DONNA M., and FRAZIER, CHARLES S. "Transfer of Juveniles To Criminal Court: A Case Study and Analysis of Prosecutorial Waiver." *Notre Dame Journal of Law, Ethics and Public Policy* 5 (1991): 281–302.

BLUMSTEIN, ALFRED. "Youth Violence, Guns, and the Illicit-Drug Industry." *Journal of Criminal Law and Criminology* 86 (1995): 10–36.

COOK, PHILIP J., and LAUB, JOHN H. "The Role of Youth in Violent Crime and Victimization." *Crime and Justice: A Review of Research* 24 (1998): 27–64.

FAGAN, JEFFREY. "Social and Legal Policy Dimensions of Violent Juvenile Crime." *Criminal Justice and Behavior* 17 (1990): 93–133.

FAGAN, JEFFREY, and DESCHENES, ELIZABETH PIPER. "Determinates of Judicial Waiver Decisions for Violent Juvenile Offenders." *Journal of Criminal Law and Criminology* 81 (1990): 314–347.

FAGAN, JEFFREY; FORST, MARTIN; and VIVONA, SCOTT. "Racial Determinants of the Judicial Transfer Decision: Prosecuting Violent Youth in Criminal Court." *Crime and Delinquency* 33 (1987): 259–286.

FELD, BARRY C. "Reference of Juvenile Offenders for Adult Prosecution: The Legislative Alternative to Asking Unanswerable Questions." *Minnesota Law Review* 62 (1978): 515–618.

———. "Juvenile Court Meets the Principle of Offense: Legislative Changes in Juvenile

Waiver Statutes." *Journal of Criminal Law and Criminology* 78 (1987): 471–533.

———. "Bad Law Makes Hard Cases: Reflections on Teen-Aged Axe-Murderers, Judicial Activism, and Legislative Default." *Journal of Law and Inequality* 8 (1990): 1–101.

———. "Violent Youth and Public Policy: A Case Study of Juvenile Justice Law Reform." *Minnesota Law Review* 79 (1995): 965–1128.

———. "Abolish the Juvenile Court: Youthfulness, Criminal Responsibility, and Sentencing Policy." *Journal of Criminal Law and Criminology* 88 (1998): 68–136.

———. "Juvenile and Criminal Justice Systems' Responses to Youth Violence." *Crime and Justice: An Annual Review* 24 (1998): 189–261.

———. *Bad Kids: Race and the Transformation of the Juvenile Court.* New York: Oxford University Press, 1999.

FRITSCH, ERIC, and HEMMENS, CRAIG. "Juvenile Waiver in the United States 1979–1995: A Comparison and Analysis of State Waiver Statutes." *Juvenile and Family Court Judges Journal* 46 (1995): 17–35.

GREENWOOD, PETER. "Differences in Criminal Behavior and Court Responses Among Juvenile and Young Adult Defendants." In *Crime and Justice*, vol. 7. Edited by Michael Tonry and Norval Morris. Chicago: University of Chicago Press, 1986.

GREENWOOD, PETER; PETERSILIA, JOAN; and ZIMRING, FRANKLIN. *Age, Crime, and Sanctions: The Transition from Juvenile to Adult Court.* Santa Monica, Calif.: RAND, 1980.

HAMPARIAN, DONNA; ESTEP, LINDA; MUNTEAN, SUSAN; PRIESTINO, RAMON; SWISHER, ROBERT; WALLACE, PAUL; and WHITE, JOSEPH. *Youth in Adult Courts: Between Two Worlds.* Washington, D.C.: Office of Juvenile Justice and Delinquency Prevention, 1982.

HOWELL, JAMES C. "The Transfer of Juvenile Offenders to the Criminal Justice System: State of the Art." *Law & Policy* 18 (1996): 17–60.

MAGUIRE, KATHLEEN, and PASTORE, ANN L., eds. *Sourcebook of Criminal Justice Statistics—1993.* Washington D.C.: Bureau of Justice Statistics, 1994.

MCCARTHY, FRANCIS BARRY. "The Serious Offender and Juvenile Court Reform: The Case for Prosecutorial Waiver of Juvenile Court Jurisdiction." *St. Louis University Law Journal* 389 (1994): 629–671.

PARENT, DALE G.; LIETER, VALIERIE; KENNEDY, STEPHEN; LIVENS, LISA; WENTWORTH, DANIEL; and WILCOX, SARAH. *Conditions of Confinement: Juvenile Detention and Corrections Facilities.* Washington, D.C.: U.S. Department of Justice, National Institute of Justice, 1994.

PODKOPACZ, MARCY RASMUSSEN, and FELD, BARRY C. "Judicial Waiver Policy and Practice: Persistence, Seriousness and Race." *Law and Inequality Journal* 14 (1995): 73–178.

———. "The End of the Line: An Empirical Study of Judicial Waiver." *Journal of Criminal Law and Criminology* 86 (1996): 449–492.

ROTHMAN, DAVID J. *Conscience and Convenience: The Asylum and Its Alternative in Progressive America.* Boston: Little, Brown, 1980.

SANBORN, JOSEPH B., JR. "Policies Regarding the Prosecution of Juvenile Murderers: Which System and Who Should Decide?" *Law and Policy* 18 (1996): 151–178.

SINGER, SIMON I. *Recriminalizing Delinquency: Violent Juvenile Crime and Juvenile Justice Reform.* New York: Cambridge University Press, 1996.

SNYDER, HOWARD N., and SICKMUND, MELISSA. *Juvenile Offenders and Victims: A National Report.* Washington, D.C.: Office of Juvenile Justice and Delinquency Prevention, 1995.

SNYDER, HOWARD N.; SICKMUND, MELISSA; and POE-YAMAGATA, EILEEN. *Juvenile Offenders and Victims: 1996 Update on Violence.* Washington, D.C.: Office of Juvenile Justice and Delinquency Prevention, National Center for Juvenile Justice, 1996.

TORBET, PATRICIA; GABLE, RICHARD; HURST IV, HUNTER; MONTGOMERY, IMOGENE; SZYMANSKI, LINDA; and THOMAS, DOUGLAS. *State Responses to Serious and Violent Juvenile Crime: Research Report.* Washington, D.C.: Office of Juvenile Justice and Delinquency Prevention, National Center for Juvenile Justice, 1996.

United States General Accounting Office. *Juvenile Justice: Juveniles Processed in Criminal Court and Case Dispositions.* Washington, D.C.: U.S. General Accounting Office, 1995.

ZIMRING, FRANKLIN. "Notes Toward a Jurisprudence of Waiver." In *Readings in Public Policy.* Edited by John C. Hall, Donna Martin Hamparian, John M. Pettibone, and Joseph L. White. Columbus, Ohio: Academy for Contemporary Problems, 1981.

———. "The Treatment of Hard Cases in American Juvenile Justice: In Defense of Discretionary Waiver." *Notre Dame Journal of Law, Ethics and Public Policy* 5 (1991): 267–280.

———. "Kids, Guns, and Homicide: Policy Notes on an Age-Specific Epidemic." *Law and Contemporary Problems* 59 (1996): 25–37.

———. *American Youth Violence.* New York: Oxford University Press, 1998.

Zimring, Franklin, and Hawkins, Gordon. *Crime is Not the Problem: Lethal Violence in America.* New York: Oxford University Press, 1997.

CASES

Breed v. Jones, 421 U.S. 519 (1975).
Kent v. United States, 383 U.S. 541 (1966).
Stanford v. Kentucky, 492 U.S. 361 (1989).
Thompson v. Oklahoma, 486 U.S. 815 (1988).
United States v. Bland, 472 F.2d 1329 (D.C. Cir. 1972), *cert. denied,* 412 U.S. 909 (1973).

JUVENILE STATUS OFFENDERS

One definition of a juvenile status offense is conduct "illegal only for children." A second is noncriminal misbehavior. Juvenile status offenders are youths of juvenile court age who violate laws that define how young people should behave. These misbehaviors are unlawful for children, but not unlawful for adults. It is the status of childhood that allows children to be the subject of a status offense.

Status offenders are habitual truants from school, runaways, or those considered incorrigible or beyond the control of their parents. They can be brought before a juvenile or family court judicial officer since state laws have proscribed these misbehaviors. Adults who drop out of college, drop out of society, or regularly flout their parents' rules or desires cannot be brought before a court. Laws do not ban such adult activities or allow for court sanctioning.

Juvenile status offenses also include the violation of a curfew hour that applies only to young people under a certain age. Their presence in a public setting after a certain hour, except when the activity is expressly permitted by a curfew law, subjects them to sanctioning. Another status offense is tobacco use or possession. Adults may smoke, juveniles may not. Alcohol possession or use is a status offense, as well, though this offense requires a partial redefinition. This ban applies to youths above juvenile court age and who are under twenty-one years of age. Adults may drink alcohol; young people under twenty-one may not.

Juvenile status offenders are distinguished from juvenile delinquent offenders. Status offenders have not committed an act that would be a crime if committed by an adult; delinquent youths have committed such an act. A theft or robbery by a juvenile is a violation of a criminal statute that applies to juveniles and adults. A juvenile violator is classified as a juvenile delinquent offender. An adult violator is classified as a criminal offender. A theft or robbery is a law violation, not a status offense.

A final status offense is gun possession by a minor. Adults may generally possess guns; juveniles may not. However, the use of a gun in the commission of a crime is an offense that applies to juveniles and adults.

Juvenile status offenses are distinguished from the child abuse, neglect, and dependency jurisdiction of a juvenile or family court. This type of matter requires judicial system protection for children receiving harmful care.

In 1997, status offenses constituted 13 percent of juvenile court case filings nationally, compared with 68 percent for delinquency filings, 15 percent for child-victim filings, and 4 percent for other filings.

Historical antecedents

The establishment of the juvenile court in 1899 reflected a recognition that children and youths were different from adults and should be treated differently by courts and correctional agencies. They were seen as immature, less capable of criminal intent in their lawbreaking, given to numerous violations that were natural to growing up in American society, and in need of disciplined guidance that could avert a criminal career. The expectation was that court-arranged interventions would protect dependent children from becoming delinquents, would prevent incorrigible youths from becoming delinquent, and constrain delinquents from becoming adult criminals.

Precepts directing children's obedience to parents go back to antiquity, to early Roman and Greek cultures, to the Fifth Commandment of the Hebrew Old Testament, and to directives of other Near Eastern civilizations. More recently, little solicitude was shown children in Europe and early America. Children were apprenticed at an early age, which often led to exploitation, beatings, and aborted opportunities to enter mainstream life. Children were loved or ignored, treated with care or harshly, without state or child advocacy organization interventions. A high death rate among children contributed to a certain history of indifference. With exceptions, the modern concept of childhood had not yet been discovered within a broad cross-section of society.

During the seventeenth and eighteenth centuries, interest in improving child-rearing practices began taking shape. Church and school officials promoted the dual precepts that children were special and fragile, but also corruptible and trying. The church, the family, the community, and the school were to join in fostering their development and controlling misbehaviors. Principles emerged that stressed discipline, modesty, chastity, hard work, and obedience to authority. Such Puritan values were very influential but not universal in the North American colonies. There was an interest in helping the poor who helped themselves, scorning others who were without motivation and urging a conforming, industrious life.

The Massachusetts "stubborn child" offense, still current into the 1970s, arose in the year 1654 when the House of Deputies of the Colony of the Massachusetts Bay in New England determined that children indeed misbehaved and treated authority figures with little or no respect, and the colony provided corporal punishment such as whipping for offenders.

The Massachusetts Constitution of 1780 authorized the incorporation of these and other early laws into the statutes of the Commonwealth. Over time, simplifying amendments were made, but as late as 1971, the state's Supreme Judicial Court upheld the stubborn child statute against a complaint that the statute was so vague and indefinite as to violate constitutional due process requirements (*Commonwealth v. Brother*, Supreme Court of Massachusetts, 270 N.E. 2d 389 (Mass.), 1971).

The creation of the U.S. Constitution, the nineteenth-century promulgation of Enlightenment philosophy, and the promise of human fulfillment and progress brought a more hopeful and positive attitude toward helping the downtrodden and the deviant, with greater focus on the conditions that contributed to poor adjustment. Nevertheless, children commonly were held, not helped, in impoverished almshouses and sentenced regularly to degrading jails where they lived side by side with adult inmates. Beginning about 1825 in more urban centers, specialized institutions were founded, such as orphan asylums for abandoned children and houses of refuge for runaway, disobedient, or vagrant young people and lesser juvenile criminals. Later, industrial (training) schools for young juvenile law violators and reformatories for youthful criminals were established often in rural areas. But jailing remained common. None of these approaches were found to be panaceas. Prior to 1899, juvenile law violators and status offenders were punishable as adults, though some institutions had been initiated to house juveniles only. The creation of the juvenile court in 1899 was intended to offer new hope for saving children. Juvenile court statutes defined delinquency to include numerous status offenses.

Accurate early data of official handling of status offense misbehaviors are difficult to come by. An examination of archival data of the offenses recorded for juveniles committed to the Wisconsin State Reform School in the pre-juvenile court decades of 1880–1889 and 1890–1899 found 50 percent and 40 percent of inmates, respectively, had been committed for "incorrigibility and vagrancy," the former offense far outnumbering the latter. Further, Milwaukee Juvenile Court records for 1908–1911 reflected significant numbers of incorrigibility, certain truancy and vagrancy, and considerable numbers of disorderly conduct and disorderly person offenses along with high percentages of larceny and burglary.

The first reports of the initial American juvenile court, in Cook county (Chicago), Illinois, found more than 50 percent of delinquency cases were in fact the status offenses of disorderly behavior, "immorality," vagrancy, truancy, and incorrigibility. Juvenile court data for Los Angeles for 1920 reported 220 petitions against girls, 90 percent of them for status or other noncriminal offenses. Interestingly, their working-class parents referred nearly half of the girls. Sixty-three percent of the girls were accused of sexual activity and more than half of these tested positive for venereal infection during their pre- or post-court stay in the detention center.

The breadth of proscribed behaviors

Early juvenile court codes enacted far more status offenses than those described above. The term "status offense" had not been created. The more contemporary distinction between a status offender and a delinquent had not been drawn. A status offense was a delinquent offense. There was no differentiation or restriction as to what a judge could do with a status offender compared with a delinquent. The judge could send an incorrigible child off to a state institution as readily as a chronic or severe law violator.

Code makers sought to regulate juvenile activities and bolster parental and societal control efforts with a juvenile court. Though the juvenile court was intended as a humane and rehabilitative instrument, its authority and powers were nonetheless awesome. The sweep of these codes was enormously wide.

For example, the South Dakota Juvenile Court Act, current for half a century and finally repealed in 1968, banned such juvenile misbehaviors as incorrigibility or intractability, association with "thieves, vicious, or immoral persons," absence from home, growing up in idleness or crime, repeated truancy, frequenting a house of ill repute, visiting a place where gaming devices are operated, frequenting a saloon, patronizing a billiard room, patronizing a wine-room or dance hall connected with or adjacent to a house of ill-fame or saloon, frequenting with a person of the opposite sex at a place where liquors may be purchased after 9 p.m., going to a secluded place with one of the opposite sex at nighttime, wandering about the streets in the nighttime without being on lawful business, writing or using vile, obscene, vulgar, profane or indecent language, smoking cigarettes or using tobacco in any form, drinking liquors other than at home, and being "guilty of indecent, immoral, or lascivious conduct."

These proscriptions constituted violations of law applicable to children. Juvenile violators of these status offenses were charged, along with juvenile violators of such crimes as burglary and larceny and assault, as juvenile delinquents. The violation of a status offense was perceived as a crime committed by a juvenile.

Other juvenile codes contained many of the banned misbehaviors set forth in the South Dakota code. The court's powers over conduct illegal only for children as well as juvenile law violations was meant to be exercised to provide the care, custody, and discipline nearly equivalent to that which should have been given by the parents. As the 1907 Colorado statute provided, any delinquent child "shall be treated, not as a criminal, but as misdirected and misguided, and needing aid, encouragement, help and assistance."

Juvenile court advocates, past and present, have contended that much good was done for young people and their communities by juvenile court interventions. However, court youths and their families in numerous juvenile courts, along with informed observers, have questioned for at least four decades whether the rhetoric of juvenile court was matched by the reality of implementation. Indeed, many youths were not helped, and some sustained harm from the intervention.

Juvenile courts early adopted informal handling approaches for use both with certain status and law violation offenders. The youths were placed on informal supervision or referred to external agency services in lieu of formal court handling. Status offenders represented a significant part of both informal and formal juvenile court workloads.

Juveniles court practices received little evaluation or critical examination until about 1960. These courts were informal hearing chambers. Lawyers found it difficult to practice in this judge-dominated setting, which was basically bereft of law or procedure. Many judges were not lawyers. Court probation officers held strong powers and were major influences on judicial decision-making. No serious questions were raised as to whether status offense youths should be differentiated from other youths who had violated criminal laws.

Separation of noncriminal conduct from delinquent conduct

In 1961, the California legislature was the first to remove noncriminal conduct from its delinquency definition. The new section 601 of its Welfare and Institutions Code, relating to the status offense child, was differentiated from section 602, the delinquent child. Section 601 sought to eliminate or otherwise make more difficult the commitment of a status offense youngster to a state delinquency institution.

Legislative reforms regarding status offenders often took place within a context of broader concerns and reforms of juvenile justice. The California legislature enacted copious code revisions due to concerns over the sweep of juvenile court jurisdiction, the unbridled discretion of officials, the absence of legal safeguards, excessive locking-up practices, and the stigma that flowed from being a court youth. California revisions were a harbinger of what was to follow.

A year later, New York took a related action. It created a new status offense category entitled "persons in need of supervision" (PINS), and prohibited commitment of these youths to delinquency institutions, though a shortage of alternative resources later led to an amendment that reauthorized such commitments.

Illinois created a separate category in 1965, "minor otherwise in need of supervision" (MINS). Colorado followed suit in 1967 with "child in need of supervision" (CHINS), joined by Florida, which chose the same title but the acronym CINS. In time, virtually every state moved in this direction. Georgia enacted the separate category of "unruly child," New Jersey followed suit with "juvenile in need of supervision" (JINS), and Montana named its new category "youth in need of supervision" (YINS). Several states, such as Pennsylvania and Florida, eliminated status offenses from their delinquency definition, rejected creation of a separate category, and placed these matters within the scope of the "dependent child" classification.

The dependency label, like the subsequently relabeled New Jersey category, "juvenile-family crisis," underscores the view that for status offenders, the family and home, not only the child, must be a focus of assessment and attention. It is known, for example, that numerous runaways escape for sexual or physical abuse; accordingly, they are better perceived as victims rather than as offenders.

Constraints on judicial powers

In 1965 a U.S. Children's Bureau compilation of local juvenile court cases in the mid-1960s found noncriminal cases constituted at least 26 percent of cases coming to court. Overall, a higher percentage of girls than boys had been charged in this fashion. The bureau's summary review of fifteen to twenty juvenile correctional institutions showed about 30 percent of residents had been committed on this basis. Its study of ten detention programs, local and state, showed that 48 percent of the 9,500 youths studied had not committed adult criminal acts. Of the 1,300 of these youths who had been held in adult jails pending hearings, 40 percent fell into the noncriminal category. Of the 8,200 of these youths who had been held in juvenile centers, 50 percent were in this category. One state reported in 1965 that 39 percent of children brought to its juvenile courts had been charged with noncriminal conduct.

Other studies reported that 45 to 55 percent of children committed to state delinquency institutions were status offenders, and that in the early 1970s, 60 to 70 percent of all girls ordered into these facilities had not committed criminal acts.

Reports such as these fueled concern that status offenders were being treated unfairly and should be handled differently than juvenile law violators. These concerns fused with the accelerating recognition that juvenile court intervention often failed, was not always benign, not infre-

quently led to abusive institutional or jail experiences, handicapped the way schools and employers and the military viewed these youths, was bereft of legal safeguards, and should be constrained.

In 1967 the U.S. Supreme Court issued a seminal decision that had immense impact on juvenile courts, including the handling of status offenders. In *In re Gault* it held that the juvenile court's procedures failed to meet constitutional standards of due process. Accordingly, children, like adults, must be afforded the right to counsel and to free counsel when a deprivation of freedom might occur. Other criminal court guarantees such as specific notice of charges, the privilege against self-incrimination, and the right to confront one's accusers, were mandated. One result of *Gault* was a sharp increase in defense lawyers in this setting. Attorneys proceeded to challenge numerous juvenile court practices, including those related to status offenders.

In the same year another major influence, the Report of the President's Commission on Law Enforcement and Administration of Justice, also sought to restructure juvenile courts to deal with more serious delinquency and to funnel less serious violations back to community agencies. It held special concern for the category of conduct considered illegal only for children. "This should be substantially circumscribed so that it ceases to include such acts as smoking, swearing, and disobedience to parents and comprehends only acts such as experimenting with drugs, repeatedly becoming pregnant out of wedlock, and being habitually truant from school. Serious consideration, at the least, should be given to complete elimination of the court's power over children for non-criminal conduct."

The commission embraced a consultant paper prepared for its delinquency task force that faulted the unexamined assumptions that these misbehaviors are precursors to delinquency, the lack of common meaning from one jurisdiction to another, or between different judges' ruling in the same jurisdiction, the absence of fixed criteria, and the assignment of criminal responsibility to children in many instances where blame or responsibility cannot be determined or where closer investigation would reveal their actions to have been reasonably normal responses to highly provocative or intolerable situations.

A second influential national report, promulgated in 1973 by the National Advisory Commission on Criminal Justice Standards and Goals, took two noteworthy positions: (1) the determination of delinquency should be reserved for a youth whose act, if committed by an adult, would constitute a criminal offense, and (2) only these delinquent youths should be eligible for commitment to institutions for delinquent children. The commission expressly avoided taking a position whether noncriminal conduct should be within the jurisdiction of a juvenile court.

These reports impacted the Federal Juvenile Justice and Delinquency Prevention Act (JJ&DP, Public Law 93–415, as amended) of 1974, which, following a grace period, banned states that accepted funding from institutionalizing status offense juveniles in state delinquency facilities. A second provision fundamentally banned their lock-up in pretrial detention facilities, although an allowance was made for brief detention under certain conditions. Most states entered into this program, and their legislatures responded to enact laws that complied overall with these requirements. Implementation of this act significantly changed court handling of status offenders.

The juvenile justice system underwent a process that has been described as the four Ds: (1) Decriminalization, that is, taking status offenders out from delinquency definitions and constraining court authority with these youths; (2) Diversion from the court of lesser offenders, including status offenders; (3) Due process implementations at all processing stages; and (4) Deinstitutionalization of status offenders and delinquents in concert with some expansion of community-based institutional alternative programs.

As states moved to constrain the locking-up of status offenders, both at pretrial and post-dispositional stages, related practices changed. Law enforcement officers were less willing to arrest runaways because the juvenile justice system would not lock up these youths, but instead would place them in a staff-secure, unlocked shelter care facility from which they could run away again. Police officers sometimes chose to apprehend a runaway not for that status, but upon the discovery of drug use or a petty theft, that is, a delinquency violation. Further, courts narrowed their entry doors since status offenders, if formally processed, could require the government to pay the cost of a lawyer and because secure institutionalization could not be an outcome of continuing defiance.

By 1980, there was growing interest in schools handling their own truancy problems, in families turning to community agency services and not to the courts, and, for example, in authorizations for courts other than juvenile courts to handle youthful alcohol violations. States reflected idiosyncratic approaches. Kentucky and Hawaii reported significantly higher rates of formal court handling of status offenders in 1993 than, for example, California and Illinois. With exceptions, urban juvenile courts increasingly confined their formal case processing to more chronic and more severe delinquents. Also with exceptions, suburban and rural juvenile courts often maintained significant status offender workloads, as other agency services were limited or did not particularly embrace these youths. Overall, community agencies did not pick up the slack of diminished court interest.

Over time, lawmakers shut down much of what juvenile courts had done earlier with status offenders. Pressures were placed on juvenile courts to find ways to use their authority to obtain control over these youths. One device known as "bootstrapping" gained currency in some courts. The initial status offense could not result in a freedom deprivation, but a judge would then prescribe rules of conduct. A status reoffense could, however, result in a civil contempt finding and placement in a nearby secure detention center. Bootstrapping was legitimated by amendment to the federal JJ&DP Act, and known as violation of a valid court order. States could still receive their federal moneys when secure detention was ordered via this mechanism.

Legal challenges to state jurisdiction over status offenders and juvenile court powers occurred in numerous states and resulted in conflicting outcomes. For example, a definition such as "beyond the control of his parents" was held to provide sufficient notice of impermissible behavior. Definitions of habitual disobedience and habitual truancy were upheld. Taking court jurisdiction for incorrigibility did not represent cruel and unusual punishment for children. Allowing status offense jurisdiction for girls up to an age older than for boys was disallowed. A single act of disobedience did not constitute beyond the control of one's parents. Curfew ordinances were approved or disapproved as to due process and equal protection of the laws depending upon their breadth and exceptions allowed. A parent in conflict with a child could not waive the child's right to counsel. A youth with fifty unauthorized school absences could not be committed to a state delinquency facility. While a status offender could not be committed to a delinquency institution, the youth could be committed to a training school designed exclusively for status offenders.

Senator Arlen Specter, the Chairman of the Subcommittee on Juvenile Justice of the U.S. Senate Committee on the Judiciary, wrote that at the time of the passage of the JJ&DP Act in 1974, close to 200,000 nondelinquent juveniles were held annually in secure confinement across the country. By 1981, however, this number had been reduced by 82 percent in the participating jurisdictions and 35 states were in full compliance with the deinstitutionalization mandate of the act.

There is some evidence that institutionalization of status offenders continues in a different form. Besides bootstrapping, two approaches are sometimes taken. The first involves a status offense by a delinquent youth who is on probation, since this misbehavior is proscribed by official probation conditions and the probation grant may be revoked. Data show this involves girls more often than boys. The second approach occurs with the substitution of other institutional settings, such as mental health institutions, treatment-oriented residential programs, and even drug treatment facilities. Data show that children of color are more often involved in the first approach, ending in public facilities, while white children more frequently end up in treatment in private facilities.

Status offender escalation to delinquent offender

There has been ongoing debate as to whether status offenders, with their defiance of authority or control, have more in common with law-violating delinquent youths, or with typical adolescents who experience conflict with authority figures in sorting out who they are becoming.

Examination of different studies of status offender careers has not found significant escalation into more serious law violations. Status offenders, like delinquent law violators, reoffend frequently, but their reoffenses are most often another status offense. Where there is an escalation, it is more often a charge of a misdemeanor, rather than a felony. Chronicity, rearrest five times or more, is very infrequent.

There is recognition that myriad delinquents have truancy backgrounds and that numerous delinquencies are committed by truants during the hours they should be in school. This is not to say there is a clear line of escalation from truancy to delinquency or serious delinquency.

In 1992, girls represented 42 percent of status offense cases, but just 15 percent of delinquency cases filed. Fifty-seven percent of arrests for running away from home during 1996 involved girls. While girls' delinquencies have increased in recent years, no study has shown a significant female escalation from status offender to delinquent. Male status offenders are more likely to reoffend and escalate, but "most of these males will not become hardened offenders" (Shelden et al.).

Current issues regarding status offenders

Status offense issues were not a prominent topic in juvenile justice in the early to mid 1990s. Violent crimes committed by youths, particularly homicides and other gun crimes, preempted debate and policy redirection. But certain areas remain a focus of attention.

On the surface, juvenile homicides appear to be a distant issue from noncriminal misbehaviors. But this is not so. Lawmaking bodies have expanded juvenile curfew laws. If juveniles are off the street, troubles are fewer. A violation provides justification for apprehension, if a police officer wants to make an arrest in the absence of a criminal-type law violation. Arrests of juvenile curfew violators increased 21 percent between 1995 and 1996, and 116 percent between 1992 and 1996; nearly three of four arrests involved a boy. What remains to be determined is the extent to which curfew laws reduce criminal conduct, and at what expense in police enforcement.

Another concentration is on the prevention of delinquency. The aftermath of school-related slayings by juveniles, such as the mass murders at Columbine High School in Littleton Colorado, brought a national soul-searching and determination to find ways to strengthen family life and the capabilities of children and youths to lead self- and community-fulfilling lives. Schools have been urged to counsel and refer young people with apparent adjustment problems to youth or family service agencies. Anti-truancy programs have accelerated and police interactions with truants are more visible. Assessment centers and other places where police can take truants, curfew violators, and runaway youths to reconnect with their parents or connect with human service agencies have became more popular. Court proceedings in some form are more likely with juvenile smokers due to extensive concerns over addiction to tobacco.

There is increased interest in early court intervention in the lives of delinquent youths and status offenders. There are more calls to relax the ban on secure confinement of status offenders. The perception that intervention with these youths is an inherent good and will prevent later serious offending is gaining currency again.

Returning to the four Ds, two may be in jeopardy. Diversion of status offenders may occur less. Since criminal courts now handle more serious delinquents, juvenile courts may reopen their doors to more status offenders as these courts search for a revised rehabilitation role. Deinstitutionalization may be jeopardized. Pressures to lock up these status offense youths "for their own good" are very strong. The counterargument—that instead of locking up status offenders, more resources are needed—is an attractive one. But throughout juvenile court history, there have never been enough, much less effective, resources.

H. TED RUBIN

See also JUVENILE AND YOUTH GANGS; JUVENILE JUSTICE: HISTORY AND PHILOSOPHY; JUVENILE JUSTICE: COMMUNITY TREATMENT; JUVENILE JUSTICE: INSTITUTIONS; JUVENILE JUSTICE: JUVENILE COURT; JUVENILES IN THE ADULT SYSTEM; JUVENILE VIOLENT OFFENDERS; POLICE: HANDLING OF JUVENILES; PREVENTION: JUVENILES AS POTENTIAL OFFENDERS; SCHOOLS AND CRIME.

BIBLIOGRAPHY

CHESNEY-LIND, MEDA. "Challenging Girls' Invisibility in Juvenile Court." *Annals of the American Academy of Political and Social Science* 564 (July 1999): 185–202.
EMPEY, LAMAR T., ed. *Juvenile Justice: The Progressive Legacy and Current Reforms.* Charlottesville: University Press of Virginia, 1979.
In re Gault, 387 U.S. 1 (1967).
LEMERT, EDWIN M. "The Juvenile Court—Quest and Realities." In *Task Force Report: Juvenile Delinquency and Youth Crime. President's Commission on Law Enforcement and Administration of Justice.* Washington, D.C.: Government Printing Office, 1967. Page 99.
———. *Social Action and Legal Change: Revolution within the Juvenile Court.* Chicago: Aldine, 1970.
Massachusetts Colony Laws, 1887.
MURRAY, JOHN P. *Status Offenders: A Sourcebook.* Includes foreword by Senator Arlen Specter. The Boys Town Center, Boys Town, NE: Boys Town Center, 1983.
National Advisory Committee on Criminal Justice Standards and Goals. *Courts.* Washington, D.C.: Government Printing Office, 1973.
ODEM, MARY E., and SCHLOSSMAN, STEVEN L. "Guardians of Virtue: The Juvenile Court and Female Delinquency in Early 20th-Century Los Angeles." *Crime and Delinquency* 37 (April 1991): 186–203.
Office of Juvenile Justice and Delinquency Prevention. Bulletins and Updates on Statistics. Washington, D.C.: U.S. Department of Justice, 1990–1999.
PLATT, ANTHONY M. *The Child Savers: The Invention of Delinquency.* 2d ed. Chicago: University of Chicago Press, 1977.
President's Commission on Law Enforcement and Administration of Justice. *The Challenge of Crime in a Free Society.* Washington, D.C.: Government Printing Office, 1967.
RUBIN, H. TED. *Juvenile Justice: Policy, Practice, and Law.* 2d ed. New York: Random House, 1985.
SCHLOSSMAN, STEVEN L. *Love and the American Delinquent: The Theory and Practice of "Progressive" Juvenile Justice.* Chicago: University of Chicago Press, 1977.
SHELDEN, RANDALL G.; HORVARTH, JOHN A.; and TRACY, SHARON. "Do Status Offenders Get Worse? Some Clarifications on the Question of Escalation." *Crime and Delinquency* 35, no. 2 (April 1989): 202–216.
SHERIDAN, WILLIAM H. "Juveniles Who Commit Noncriminal Acts: Why Treat in a Correctional System?" *Federal Probation* 31 (March 1967): 26–30.
South Dakota Revised Code, section 43.0301 (Repealed 1968).
STEINHART, DAVID J. "Status Offenses." *The Juvenile Court.* Los Altos, Calif.: David and Lucile Packard Foundation, 1996.
TEITELBAUM, LEE E., and GOUGH, AIDAN R. *Beyond Control: Status Offenders in the Juvenile Court.* Cambridge, Mass.: Bollinger, 1977.
U.S. Department of Health, Education, and Welfare. *Juvenile Court Statistics, 1965.* Statistical Series 85. Washington, D.C.: Government Printing Office, 1966. Page 85.

JUVENILE VIOLENT OFFENDERS

Most juveniles have committed a violent act, probably by the age of two. An objective observer spending a few minutes in a pre-school daycare center would likely see many incidents of physical assault and robbery. However, to classify an act as a crime (i.e., a behavior warranting severe sanctions by the justice system) is not as simple. Modern societies do not legally respond to the behaviors of young children as crimes because persons below the age of seven are generally considered unable to understand the implications of the actions. In fact, in most modern societies, it is common to assume that persons between the ages of seven and seventeen have a lesser degree of criminal responsibility for their actions than do adults.

Another complication in assessing the prevalence of juvenile violence is the varying definitions of what behaviors are violent. Most would include behaviors such as murder, forcible rape, assault with the intent to do serious bodily harm, and armed robbery. However, other behaviors are not as universally accepted as violent, behaviors such as the taking of a bicycle from another student on a school playground, fighting with a sibling, weapons possession in school, cruelty to animals, or drug selling. To some these behaviors are violent and justify strong sanctions for the perpetrators; to others the behaviors, while deserving attention, do not rise to the level of violent crime. In all, behaviors may or may not be classified as a violent crime depending on the age of the perpetrator and societal norms. Consequently, any attempt to assess the proportion of juveniles who commit violent crimes must acknowledge that the response is dependent on many assumptions.

Prevalence of juvenile violence

In recognition of these definitional issues, researchers who want to assess the prevalence of juvenile violence ask juveniles to report if they have ever committed a specific behavior, instead of simply asking the general question "Have you ever committed a violent crime?" The 1997 National Longitudinal Survey of Youth (NLSY97) asked a nationally representative sample of nearly nine thousand individuals between ages twelve and sixteen such questions. Conducted by the Bureau of Labor Statistics, the NLSY97 found that 22 percent of sixteen year olds in the United States admitted to committing an assault. Twelve percent of sixteen year olds admitted to having carried a handgun and six percent admitted to having been in a gang. The proportions of juveniles who admitted committing such acts were similar in urban and in rural areas and for white and nonwhite youth. However, the prevalence rates were greater for some groups of juveniles. Twice as many boys as girls admitted to having committed an assault or belonging to a gang. Five times as many boys as girls admitted to car-

rying a handgun. Youth ages twelve to sixteen who had been in gangs were far more likely to have carried a handgun (15%) than were youth who had not been in a gang (1%). In summary, based on the self-reports of juveniles in 1997, it is fair to conclude that about one-quarter of all juveniles in the United States in the late 1990s committed violent crimes before their eighteenth birthdays.

The prevalence of the violent behaviors can be placed in perspective by comparing it with the prevalence of other behaviors. Remembering that 22 percent of sixteen year olds in the NLSY97 admitted to committing an assault, larger proportions of sixteen year olds admitted to drinking alcohol (68%), smoking cigarettes (58%), having sex (43%), using marijuana (38%), or purposely destroying property (30%). Smaller proportions admitted to stealing something worth more than fifty dollars (11%), selling drugs (12%), or never being arrested for any crime (12%).

As this last statistic indicates, only a fraction of youth who admit to committing a violent act ever come to the attention of the justice system for a violent crime. Law enforcement agencies across the country report each year to the F.B.I.'s Uniform Crime Reporting (UCR) Program the number of arrests made of juveniles and adults for each of a long list of offenses. Since the 1930s, when the UCR Program was established, the F.B.I. has monitored violent crime trends with its own Violent Crime Index, four crimes that are usually considered to be violent and that are common across all parts of the country. These four crimes are murder, forcible rape, robbery, and aggravated assault. In 1998, the F.B.I. reported that 17 percent of all Violent Crime Index offense arrests, or 112,200 arrests, involved a person under age eighteen. More specifically, law enforcement made 2,100 juvenile arrests for murder, 5,300 juvenile arrests for forcible rape, 32,500 juvenile arrests for robbery, and 72,300 juvenile arrests for aggravated assault. Seventeen percent of juvenile arrests involved a female, 55 percent involved white youth, and 42 percent involved black youth.

From these arrest figures, it is possible to develop an estimate of the maximum proportion of the juvenile population arrested for a Violent Crime Index offense before turning age eighteen, if two assumptions are made. The first assumption is that no juvenile will be arrested more than once before his or her eighteenth birthday for a Violent Crime Index offense. The second assumption is that the number of arrests in each age group in 1998 (i.e., the arrests of ten year olds, the arrests of eleven year olds, etc.) were equal to the corresponding individual age group arrest estimates for persons who turned eighteen in 1998. With these two simplifying assumptions, it can be concluded that the 3.9 million persons who turned eighteen years of age in 1998 were involved in 112,200 arrests for a Violent Crime Index offense during their juvenile years. Therefore, no more than 3 percent (i.e., 112,200/3,900,000) of all juveniles who turned age eighteen in 1998 were ever arrested for a Violent Crime Index offense. This Violent Crime Index arrest prevalence estimate is a maximum estimate because the "one violent crime arrest per juvenile" assumption is certainly wrong. If it were assumed that the typical juvenile arrested for a Violent Crime Index offense was arrested twice for such crimes before his or her eighteenth birthday, then the estimated arrest prevalence rate would be cut in half, to 1.5 percent. In all, it is fair to conclude that at the end of the twentieth century in the United States about 2 percent of youth were arrested and entered the formal justice system charged with a Violent Crime Index offense during their juvenile years. In communities with juvenile Violent Crime Index arrest rates above the nation average, their officially recognized juvenile violent crime arrest prevalence rate was probably greater. In many communities, the rate was certainly lower.

The prevalence of juvenile violence based on arrest statistics is well below the self-report prevalence noted above. The difference between the prevalence of juvenile violence based on self-report and arrest data is due to several factors. First, the victims may not report the crime to law enforcement because they believe that the crime is not serious enough or that law enforcement will take no action in the matter. Second, some violent crimes are reported to and handled by other authorities, such as a school principal or a parent. And finally, once the crime is reported to law enforcement, only about one of every two violent crime reports result in an arrest. In all, juvenile violent crime prevalence rates will differ if based on self-report or official justice system statistics. This discrepancy is also why juvenile arrests can increase over time even though there is no change in juvenile behavior—when conditions change so that more juvenile crimes are reported to, or otherwise come to the attention of, law enforcement.

The growth in juvenile violence in the early 1990s

Since 1973, the U.S. Department of Justice has monitored the amount of violent crime committed by juveniles and adults in the United States through its National Crime Victimization Survey (or NCVS). Each year NCVS interviewers ask the residents ages twelve and above in tens of thousands of households about the crimes they have experienced and the offenders who committed these crimes. To monitor serious violent crime trends, the NCVS adds together reports of three specific crimes, which together act as a barometer of serious violence in the United States. These three crimes are sexual assault, aggravated assault, and robbery. (Note that the F.B.I. Violent Crime Index is similar to the set of crimes used by the NCVS to monitor serious violence with the exception of murder—which is difficult for victims to report to NCVS interviewers.)

The NCVS has found the rate of serious violent crimes committed by juvenile offenders (i.e., persons under age eighteen) changed little between 1973 and 1989. However, after these years of stability, the rate of serious juvenile violence increased nearly 40 percent in the short period between 1989 and 1993, focusing the nation's fears on the threat of juvenile violence. However, throughout this period of change, the percentage of all serious violent crimes committed by juveniles remained relatively constant, indicating the changes in juvenile crime were mirrored by similar changes in crimes committed by adult offenders—although throughout the period the media and others largely characterized the growth in serious violence as a juvenile crime problem.

The NCVS found that the proportion of juvenile serious violent crime reported to law enforcement changed little over the period between 1973 and 1997. Therefore, it is not surprising that trends in juvenile arrests for Violent Crime Index crimes have followed a similar pattern to victims' reports in the NCVS of juvenile serious violent crime. Following nearly fifteen years of consistency, the juvenile Violent Crime Index arrest rate increased more than 60 percent between 1988 and 1994. More dramatically, juvenile arrests for murder more than doubled between 1987 and 1993 after years of relative stability. The large growth in violent juveniles entering the juvenile justice system strained its resources and raised questions about the juvenile justice system's ability to protect public and control these youth.

The concept of the juvenile super predator

The large increase in violent crime arrests (and especially the increase in murder arrests) combined with the media's and the public's fascination with a few horrific incidents caused policymakers to ask in the early 1990s if juvenile justice policies and procedures should be changed. Surprisingly, the idea that today's juveniles are more troublesome and threatening than those of previous generations is not a new concern. Socrates made similar comments about the juveniles of his time. A juvenile court judge at the end of World War II wrote the following assessment of the teenagers of his time:

There is Teen-Age Trouble ahead. Plenty of it! We have just won a world war against the Axis enemies. Now we face a new critical war against a powerful enemy from within our gates. That enemy is juvenile delinquency. . . . [Juvenile delinquency] is an ever-growing evil, a shocking reality. It is a real and alarming menace to every city, borough, and township. It is a disease eating at the heart of America and gnawing at the vitals of our democracy. (Henry Ellenbogen, 1946)

There has always been a concern about the younger generation. In the past, adults generally attributed the deficiencies of juveniles to the poor quality of their education at home and in the schools and to poor acculturation. But in the early 1990s, other causes for the apparent differences in the younger generation were proposed. Due in part to the increase in crime and arrest trends, in part to the media obsession with juvenile violence, and in part to validation of the concept by a few high profile academics (e.g., John DiLulio of Princeton University and James Fox of Northeastern University), the phrase *juvenile super predator* entered the public consciousness. Juvenile super predators were characterized as ruthless sociopaths, youth with no moral conscience who see crime as a rite of passage, who are unconcerned about the consequences of their actions, and who are undeterred by the sanctions that could be leveled against them by the juvenile justice system. Some even argued that this new breed of offender had different DNA than their predecessors, changes caused by the alcohol and other drug abuse of their young, unmarried mothers. The argument went that violence juvenile crime was increasing and would continue to increase because this small group of juvenile super predators commits more vicious crimes

with higher frequency than delinquents of past generations. The supporters of this argument concluded that the rehabilitative approach of the juvenile justice system was wasted on these youth because their natures were largely unchangeable. Deficiencies of earlier generations were attributed to factors that could be changed with appropriate interventions; but this new breed of juvenile super predator was so disturbed that change was unlikely. As a result, rehabilitation would be ineffectual. Protecting the public from these vicious juvenile criminals became the primary concern of juvenile justice policymakers.

Many state legislators adopted the super predator explanation for the increase in juvenile violent crime in the early 1990s and responded appropriately. To insure the justice system had at its disposal the appropriate sanctions to handle this new breed of juvenile offender, nearly every state in the early 1990s changed in significant ways how their justice systems responded to violent juveniles. These changes were all designed to increase the flow of juveniles into the adult criminal justice system and they took many forms. Many states adopted legislation that required juveniles charged with certain violent crimes to be tried as adults or expanded the list of crimes that were excluded for juvenile court jurisdiction. Some states gave prosecutors the discretion to file certain juvenile cases in either juvenile or adult court. Some states broadened the range of offenses or lowered the age of a youth a juvenile court judge could transfer to the criminal court. Many states made multiple changes.

The importance of the super predator construct was that it focused the policy makers' attention on the offenders, and away from external social factors that could be causing violence by juveniles and adults to increase. If certain individuals were damaged beyond repair, the only solution was to incapacitate them to protect public safety. During this time period, the number of prison beds grew in the United States at unprecedented rates, while relatively few federal dollars were spent on delinquency prevention or rehabilitation programs. The simplicity of the super predator concept made it both attractive and harmful. It gave policymakers an easy answer to a complex social problem and an answer that permitted them to ignore (or discredit) many of the more complex social causes proposed for the increase in violent juvenile crime.

The decline in juvenile violence in the mid-1990s

But just as these fundamental changes were being made in the juvenile justice system in the United States, juvenile violent crime began to decline. Between 1993 and 1997 (the newest NCVS data available), the rate of serious violent crime committed by juveniles fell dramatically, to nearly the lowest level since 1973. By 1998, the juvenile Violent Crime Index arrest rate had fallen to the lowest levels in the 1990s, but still about 10 percent above the levels of the mid 1980s. Between 1993 and 1998 the juvenile arrest rate for murder also fell substantially, erasing all of the increase that occurred after 1987. Therefore, based on different measures, the rate of juvenile violence in the late 1990s was similar to or below the rates of the early 1980s. In the late 1990s the notion of juvenile super predators came under attack, loosing favor with legislators and policy-makers. But its legacy, the fundamental changes in how some juvenile offenders are handled by the justice systems in the United States, remained.

Causes for the growth and decline of juvenile violence

The period between 1988 and 1998 saw a rapid growth and then as rapid a decline in juvenile violence. The causes for these large changes after years of stability have been debated. With the concept of the juvenile super predator fading, other causes have been proposed. Alfred Blumstein from Carnegie-Mellon University proposed that much of the increase in juvenile and adult violence was linked to a change in the nature of the illegal drug markets during this period. In the late 1980s crack cocaine entered the urban centers of the United States. The drug market for crack differed in significant ways from other drugs. Crack was sold in small quantities. Users often made multiple purchases a day. Drug sellers, therefore, had to be available on nearly an around-the-clock basis on street corners, with money in their pockets and with guns to protect their businesses. Blumstein argued that the new competition among drug dealers and drug gangs and the presence of money and firearms caused a situation where violence would naturally increase. The decline in the crack market in the mid-1990s removed much of the drug's influence on the U.S. violent crime rate, with one exception. While crack left the inner cit-

ies, the weapons remained in the hands of juveniles and young adults.

A study of homicides by juveniles during this time period easily demonstrates the influence of firearms on juvenile violent crime trends. In the mid-1980s roughly half the juvenile homicide offenders killed with a firearm and half killed with other weapons (e.g., knives, clubs, hands, feet, etc.). The doubling of homicides by juveniles between 1987 and 1994 was all firearm related. During this period the number of juvenile homicides committed without firearms did not change, while the proportion of homicides committed with firearms increased by 82 percent. Correspondingly, the entire decline in juvenile homicides after 1994 was a decrease in firearm-related homicides. Clearly, between the mid-1980s and the late 1990s juvenile homicide trends were linked to firearms.

Many argue that juvenile gangs were responsible for much of the increase in juvenile violence in the late 1980s and early 1990s. There are no national statistics that can support or discredit such a statement. But national surveys of law enforcement agencies do show that the number of youth gangs did increase substantially during this period. In addition, research conducted by Terence Thornberry and his colleagues in Rochester, New York, found that while gang members reported less than one-third of the high-risk sample of youth they studied, they were responsible for more than two-thirds of the violent crimes committed by these youth. Thornberry and colleagues also found that the frequency with which juveniles commit violent crimes increases after entering a gang and declines after leaving a gang. Therefore, the growth of youth gangs and the increased number of juvenile gang members during this period may be the source of some of the increase in juvenile violence. However, based on reports from law enforcement agencies, the number of youth gangs and juvenile gang members did not decline during the mid-1990s while juvenile violence did. So the link between youth gangs and the trends in juvenile violence is not clear.

But why, after the large decline in juvenile violence as measured by the NCVS, were juvenile violent crime arrest rates in 1998 still above those of the early 1980s? The reason appears to be a policy change many states adopted in the early 1980s, a change that required law enforcement to make an arrest in domestic violence incidents. The evidence for this can be found in a study of arrest trends. Two high-volume violent crimes, robbery and aggravated assault, account for more than 90 percent of the Violent Crime Index. Their patterns control the overall Violent Crime Index arrest trends. If there were a general increase or decrease in violence (and in juvenile super predators), the expectation would be for parallel changes in juvenile robbery and aggravated assault. However, between 1980 and 1998 the juvenile arrest rate for robbery declined 35 percent, while the juvenile arrest rate for aggravated assault increased 64 percent. Therefore, the juvenile Violent Crime Index arrest rate in 1998 was above the 1980 rate because of the large increase in arrests for aggravated assault—even though the NCVS found similar rates of aggravated assault by juveniles in these two years. Another piece of evidence is the fact that the group with the greatest percent increase in arrests for aggravated assault was persons in the thirties and forties, not juveniles and youth adults—another fact that counters the juvenile super predator argument. Finally, from the early 1980s to the late 1990s female arrests for aggravated assault increased more than male arrests. Therefore, with no difference in juvenile violent crime, what could explain the large difference in juvenile violent crime arrests? One possibility is a change in public policy that targeted aggravated assaults and disproportionately targeted women and persons in their thirties and forties. The most likely candidate is the change in police response to domestic violence calls.

While not generally considered a juvenile issue, this change brought a large number of juveniles into the justice system charged with a violent crime. Fights with parents or siblings that had previously been ignored by law enforcement, or in which the youth had been charged with the status offense of incorrigibility or ungovernability, now resulted in an arrest for simple or aggravated assault. In 1998, it was not uncommon for as many as one-third of all juveniles referred to court for a violent crime to be charged with domestic violence. These youth with serious family problems present the juvenile justice system with a new type of juvenile offender, an offender type that has been around for years but largely ignored by the formal juvenile justice system, an offender with different service needs than other violent offenders.

Future predictions of juvenile violence

A part of the super predator rhetoric was the prediction of a coming bloodbath of juvenile violent crime as the number of juvenile super predators grew substantially with the expected growth in the general juvenile population into the twenty-first century. The events of the recent past show this argument to be flawed. In the period between the 1985 and 1998, when juvenile violence crime soared and then declined, when the number of murders by juveniles doubled and then fell back to its original level, the size of the juvenile population did not change significantly. Therefore, the level of juvenile violence can change substantially with no change in the juvenile population. The fact is that nothing in the juvenile population trends in the 1980s and 1990s predicted the growth and the decline in juvenile violence experienced during this period. The juvenile population in the United States is expected to grow by one percent per year in the first decade of the twenty-first century. Any effect of this small population change on the level of juvenile violence can easily be dwarfed by the influence of other factors, as was seen in the mid-1990s. The simple truth is, given our current knowledge of the processes that affect changes in the levels of juvenile violence, any attempt to predict the future of juvenile violence crime is foolhardy.

HOWARD N. SNYDER

See also GUNS, REGULATION OF; HOMICIDE: BEHAVIORAL ASPECTS; JUVENILE AND YOUTH GANGS; JUVENILE JUSTICE: HISTORY AND PHILOSOPHY; JUVENILE JUSTICE: JUVENILE COURT; JUVENILES IN THE ADULT SYSTEM; JUVENILE STATUS OFFENDERS; POLICE: HANDLING OF JUVENILES; PREVENTION: JUVENILES AS POTENTIAL OFFENDERS; SCHOOLS AND CRIME.

BIBLIOGRAPHY

BLUMSTEIN, ALFRED. "Youth Violence, Guns, and the Illicit-Drug Industry." *Journal of Criminal Law and Criminology* 86 (1995): 10–36.

Federal Bureau of Investigation. *Crime in the United States 1998.* Washington, D.C.: U.S. Department of Justice, Government Printing Office, 1999.

National Youth Gang Center. *1996 National Youth Gang Survey.* Washington, D.C.: U.S. Department of Justice, Office of Juvenile Justice and Delinquency Prevention, 1999.

SNYDER, HOWARD. *Juvenile Arrests 1998.* OJJDP Juvenile Justice Bulletin. Washington, D.C.: U.S. Department of Justice, Office of Juvenile Justice and Delinquency Prevention, 1999.

———. "Serious, Violent, and Chronic Juvenile Offenders: An Assessment of the Extent of and Trends in Officially Recognized Serious Criminal Behavior in a Delinquent Population." In *Serious and Violent Juvenile Offenders: Risk Factors and Successful Interventions*. Edited by Rolf Loeber and David Farrington. Thousand Oaks, Calif.: Sage, 1999.

SNYDER, HOWARD, and SICKMUND, MELISSA. *Juvenile Offenders and Victims: 1999 National Report*. Washington, D.C.: U.S. Department of Justice, Office of Juvenile Justice and Delinquency Prevention, 1999.

THORNBERRY, TERENCE, and BURCH, JAMES. *Gang Membership and Delinquent Behaviors*. OJJDP Juvenile Justice Bulletin. Washington, D.C.: U.S. Department of Justice, Office of Juvenile Justice and Delinquency Prevention, 1997.

THORNBERRY, TERENCE; KROHN, MARVIN.; LIZOTTE, A.; and CHARD-WIERSCHEM, D. "The Role of Juvenile Gangs in Facilitating Delinquent Behavior." *Journal of Research in Crime and Delinquency* 30 (1993): 55–87.

TORBET, PATRICIA; GABLE, RICHARD; HURST, HUNTER IV; MONTGOMERY, IMOGENE; SZYMANSKI, LINDA; and THOMAS, DOUGLAS. *State Responses to Serious and Violent Juvenile Crime*. Washington, D.C.: U.S. Department of Justice, Office of Juvenile Justice and Delinquency Prevention, 1996.

KIDNAPPING

Kidnapping is a widely known felony that may be described as the seizing and carrying away of another person against his or her will. The precise statutory definitions are much more elaborate than the foregoing, and occur in a variety of different forms. Most statutes also prohibit the unlawful restraint of anther person. Kidnapping is primarily regulated by state law, though certain federal laws may apply depending on the nature of the offense. In practice, a kidnapping may occur either by the use of force or by deception or enticement. Despite the connotation of the word "kidnapping," these statutes criminalize the taking of adults as well as children. Thus, a hostage-style holding or taking captive of an adult is prosecutable under kidnapping laws. Many kidnap attempts include requests for ransom money, though this is not necessarily an element of the offense. There are related laws for hostage-taking and ransom demands, and the elements of kidnapping may often overlap with these and other crimes.

Origins of the offense in English law

Kidnapping laws have been found as far back as three thousand years, where it was written in ancient Jewish law that "Anyone who kidnaps another and either sells him or still has him when he is caught must be put to death" (Exod. 21:16). The earliest ancient English kidnapping law was called "plagium," and was also punishable by death. The term "kidnapping" is said to have emerged in English law in the late 1600s, referring to the abduction of persons who were then transported to the North American colonies for slavery. William Blackstone, writing in the late 1700s, described the law of kidnapping as the "forcible abduction or stealing away of a man, woman, or child, from their own country, and sending them into another" (p. 955). "This is unquestionably a very heinous crime, as it robs the king of his subjects, banishes a man from his country, and may in its consequences be productive of the most cruel and disagreeable hardships; and therefore the common law of England has punished it with fine, imprisonment, and pillory" (pp. 955–956).

The focus of these early laws, at least in form if not practice, seems to be on the wrongfulness of transporting someone against their will to a different country or place. Given limits of transportation centuries ago, being carried off to a different country was likely to be permanent. Today, however, the law recognizes the additional evil of detaining someone against their will even without transporting him or her to a different region.

The old English common law also contained very similar laws against "abduction," such as "the forcible abduction and marriage" of a woman (Blackstone, p. 951). The stealing of children from a father was also criminal, as this was seen as not just the stealing of the father's children, but also his "heir" (pp. 696–697). By contrast, the rationale behind the modern American laws is based on liberty, even for children, as opposed to a loss on the part of their parents or anyone else. The terms "abduction" and "kidnapping" are often used interchangeably. Where they may have had different historical connotations, their use in modern parlance has gradually become synonymous.

Impact of the Lindbergh kidnapping

The details of the history of the American law of kidnapping are sparse at best, at least until the notorious kidnapping and murder of the one-year-old son of the famous aviator Charles A. Lindbergh. The capture and trial of the kidnapper, Bruno Richard Hauptmann, sparked great national attention in 1932. Hauptmann was not even tried for kidnapping, which would only have been a high misdemeanor under New Jersey law at the time. With inadequate evidence to prove premeditated murder, the prosecution eventually convicted Hauptmann under the felony murder doctrine for a death resulting during the course of a burglary. Stealing a child was not covered under the burglary laws, so Hauptmann was convicted (and eventually executed) for a death that resulted during the theft of the baby's clothes (*State v. Hauptmann*, 115 N.J.L. 412 (1935)).

This episode caught the nation's attention and sparked legislative action even before the trial was completed. The result was the so-called Lindbergh Law, adopted by Congress (18 U.S.C. §§ 1201–1202). The Lindbergh Law makes kidnapping a federal crime when the abducted individual is taken across state lines. Though not originally a capital offense, the law was later amended to give juries the discretion to recommend the death penalty in particularly heinous cases. The Supreme Court later declared the death penalty unconstitutional as it applied to the Lindbergh Law (*U.S. v. Jackson*, 390 U.S. 570 (1968)).

Elements of kidnapping and related offenses

As stated above, kidnapping statutes punish the taking or unlawful restraint of both minors and adults. Kidnapping and abduction laws may be triggered even if there is no carrying away. If the restraint is substantial enough to interfere with the victim's liberty, the perpetrator my be convicted under most kidnapping laws. A restraint occurring even in the victim's own home has been held to be a kidnapping where the rescue of the victim is unlikely (*Darrow v. Wyoming*, 824 P.2d 1269 (Wyoming, 1922)).

While kidnapping at common law was classified as a misdemeanor, almost every jurisdiction now lists it as a felony. The current punishment authorized by the federal Lindbergh Law is imprisonment from ten years to life. Some jurisdictions provide different degrees of kidnapping, with first-degree kidnapping being elevated from second-degree kidnapping based on any harm to the victim. While the Lindbergh Law does not separate kidnapping into degrees of severity, the Federal Sentencing Guidelines instruct a greater sentence based on the harm to the victim, or where a gun was used in the kidnapping.

The U.S. Sentencing Commission has provided various guidelines for the increase in punishment depending on the nature of the kidnapping. For example, when the victim is under the age of eighteen, and not a relative of the perpetrator, if the victim was intentionally mistreated (denied either food or medical care) to a life-threatening degree, the punishment is increased by four levels. If the victim was sexually exploited, the punishment is increased by three levels. The federal sentencing guidelines provide a two-level increase in the offense level for kidnapping if a defendant uses a gun or other dangerous weapon to commit the offense.

While the death penalty is no longer authorized by the Lindbergh Law, the death penalty is still applicable under federal law if the victim dies, which can trigger the felony murder doctrine and/or a conviction of first-degree murder. The death penalty with regards to state laws is almost certainly unconstitutional as well, absent the death of the victim. The Supreme Court has never held that a state law authorizing the death penalty for kidnapping alone is unconstitutional. But the Court has held that the death penalty for kidnapping and rape under state laws, where the victim is not killed, is cruel and unusual punishment under the Eighth Amendment, which is applied to the states via the Fourteenth Amendment (*Coker v. Georgia*, 433 U.S. 584 (1977)). One can easily surmise that if the death penalty were cruel and unusual in the context of a kidnap and rape, it would certainly be the same for kidnapping alone.

Many kidnapping statutes either have provisions covering ransom activity, or are construed in correlation with related ransom statutes. For example, 18 U.S.C. § 1202 is an extension of the Lindbergh Law (18 U.S.C. § 1201), and punishes the act of receiving or possessing money that was delivered as a ransom.

Legislative attention to parental kidnapping. Parents can be held liable for abducting their own children in violation of child custody orders, or even keeping their children too long beyond their legal visitation period. But note that absent a court order of custody rights, parents have equal rights to the custody of a child. A kidnapping or abduction statute is much less likely to cover acts of one parent taking a child from the custody of another unless there has been a court order dividing the custody rights. And, of course, a parent who "steals" a child from another parent will not be found guilty if the stealing parent was legally entitled to custody. These activities between parents are also regulated by child custody statutes of each state.

Because each state has its own child custody laws, there was predictably much confusion surrounding cases where a child was abducted by a parent and taken to a different state. The federal Lindbergh Law has long been held to be inapplicable to cases of parental kidnapping. Thus, in 1968 the National Conference of Commissioners on Uniform State Laws drafted the Uniform Child Custody Jurisdiction Act (UCCJA). The resolution provided standards for determining when a state may take jurisdiction of a child custody dispute, when other states are prohibited from intervening in such disputes, and when states must honor the custodial decisions of their sister states. Although most states adopted statutes enacting the UCCJA, there were many different versions and interpretations of the laws, resulting in further confusion. Congress responded in 1980 with the PKPA or Parental Kidnapping Prevention Act (28 U.S.C. § 1738A). The PKPA imposed a duty on states to enforce the decisions of a sister state, as long as the decision was consistent with the PKPA. The PKPA itself has guidelines very similar to the original UCCJA for when a state may or may not exercise custody jurisdiction over a child. The overall goal of preventing parents from kidnapping their children and taking them to other states in order to avoid child custody has been met with mixed results. (For a critique of these laws, see Goldstein.)

While the United States has struggled to regulate parents unlawfully taking children from state to state, international parental abductions—the act of one parent unlawfully taking a child to a foreign country—have increased dramatically in recent decades, perhaps due to the increases made in communication technology and transportation. In 1980, an international convention known as the Hague Convention on the Civil Aspects of International Law adopted a resolution regarding international parent abductions. In 1988, Congress finally passed the International Child Abduction Remedies Act (42 U.S.C. § 11601), which enacted provisions in compliance with the Hague Convention. Before this time, there was no remedy for a parent when his or her child was taken to a foreign country. Now, if the child is wrongfully held by a parent in a country that is a signatory to the Hague Convention, the aggrieved other parent may apply to the foreign country for prompt return of the child. Roughly forty-seven nations are signatories of this convention.

But because the Hague Convention does not authorize criminal punishment upon the abducting parent, and because many nations are not signatories to the Hague Convention, Congress passed the International Parental Kidnapping Crime Act of 1993 (18 U.S.C. § 1204). This act makes it a federal crime for a parent to wrongfully remove or retain his or her child outside the United States. This act also increases the remedies available for the left-behind parent to reacquire the child, at least in cases involving countries with which the United States has criminal extradition treaties. However, despite all the efforts of Congress and the international community, returning children that have been abducted to foreign countries remains an activity that is very difficult to regulate.

CHARLES H. WHITEBREAD

See also FAMILY RELATIONSHIPS AND CRIME; FEDERAL CRIMINAL JURISDICTION

BIBLIOGRAPHY

ALIX, ERNEST K. Ransom Kidnapping in America, 1874–1974: The Creation of a Capital Crime. Carbondale: Southern Illinois University Press, 1978.

AMERICAN JURISPRUDENCE. Kidnapping. West Publishing Group, 1964. Current through April 1999 Cumulative Supplement.

BLACKSTONE, WILLIAM. Commentaries on the Laws of England, 4th ed. Edited by George Chase. New York: Banks Law Publishing Co., 1926.

DAVIS, SAMUEL M.; SCOTT, ELIZABETH S.; WADLINGTON, WALTER; and WHITEBREAD, CHARLES H. Children in the Legal System. 2d ed. Westbury, N.Y.: Foundation Press, 1997.

GOLDSTEIN, ANNE B. "The Tragedy of the Interstate Child: A Critical Reexamination of the Uniform Child Custody Jurisdiction Act and the Parental Kidnapping Prevention Act." University of California–Davis Law Review 25 (1992): 845.

L

LIBEL, CRIMINAL

Criminal libel is a libel punishable criminally. It consists of a defamation of an individual (or group) made public by a printing or writing. The defamation must tend to excite a breach of the peace or damage the individual (or group) in reference to his character, reputation, or credit.

At common law, libel was recognized as a criminal misdemeanor as well as an individual injury justifying damages (a tort). Prosecutions of the offense had three goals: protection of government from seditious statements capable of weakening popular support and causing insurrection; reinforcement of public morals by requiring a "decent" mode of community discourse; and protection of the individual from writings likely to hold him up to hatred, contempt, or ridicule. The protection of the individual, a goal that is generally left to tort law, was justified by the criminal law's responsibility for outlawing statements likely to provoke breaches of peace.

Although contemporary criminal libel prosecutions are rare, development of the law in this area exposes a society's sense of the proper relationship between citizen and state as well as the proper balance between the community's need for avenues of communication and that for decency in discourse. The law of libel establishes the outer boundary set by interests in community and individual dignity on the processes of reason furthered by robust discussion. Libel, thus, is a perennial problem for a society that prizes uninhibited debate.

The history of criminal libel

The ecclesiastical courts. After the Norman conquest of England, William I established church courts that sentenced to public penance those found guilty of the canon-law crime of saying or writing a false allegation. The sinner, wrapped in a white shroud, holding a lighted candle, and kneeling, would acknowledge his "false witness" in the presence of the priest and parish wardens and beg the pardon of the injured party (Eldredge, p. 5). While this remedy gave the injured party vindication, its primary focus was absolution of the sinner.

By the sixteenth century, the king's courts, in efforts to wrest power from the church, competed increasingly with ecclesiastical courts for jurisdiction over defamation cases. Development of a mercantile class more concerned with the monetary impact of a defamatory statement than with saving the offender's soul further accelerated replacement of church courts by civil courts.

The Star Chamber. The invention of the printing press created a set of circumstances that heightened fear of seditious libel. The ponderous political folio written for the learned and given limited circulation in manuscript form was succeeded by the easily reproduced political tract and fly sheet addressed to the multitude. Consequently, in the early seventeenth century the Court of the Star Chamber, a court established to affirm and protect royal authority, began to punish political libel as a breach of the peace. Any criticism that the court felt was capable of causing the public to hold the government in disrepute constituted an offense. Since any such libel was thought to undermine public peace or legitimate government, its truth or falsity was immaterial.

In fact, "the greater the truth the greater the libel," since exposure of the truth was more likely to lead to the government's downfall or a breach of the peace than would false statements (Schofield, p. 516). To assure the conviction of governmental critics, all decisions of the Star Chamber were rendered, without aid of a jury, by officials of the very government being criticized. Guilt required no proof of any intent beyond intent to publish. Criminal libel, in essence, was a crime of strict liability.

To protect the public peace, the Star Chamber also recognized the libel of a private individual as deserving criminal punishment. It was feared that individual libels would provoke duels and family revenge, thus leading to bloodshed. A legal remedy was created to deter such behavior.

Development in the common law courts. In the late seventeenth century, after the abolition of the Star Chamber by Parliament, jurisdiction over criminal libel prosecutions was assumed by the common law courts. The law applied by the latter, however, was for the most part that earlier shaped in the Star Chamber. Typically, the legal system punishes criminally only the worst and most extreme forms of behavior but imposes civil damages on individuals for a wide range of less injurious conduct. The law of criminal libel reversed this norm. No tort cause of action exists for a libelous statement which is true, which libels only the dead, which is expressed only to the libeled individual, or which refers to a group so large that no individual member may justly feel tainted. In each of these situations, however, penalties for criminal libel existed at common law. The history of the Star Chamber, with its focus on preventing breaches of the peace and displays of disrespect toward the government, explains this aberration.

Assumption of jurisdiction over criminal libel by the common law courts nevertheless produced important consequences. Although prosecution for criminal libel remained a potent weapon of political oppression, the jury system developed as a curb on its abuse. Free-press proponents argued that the jury, in addition to finding fact, should decide the legal question of whether the writing constituted a libel. After a bitter struggle, this view was adopted by the Libel Act, 1792, 32 Geo. 3, c. 6o (Great Britain). Thereafter, by returning a verdict of not guilty, a jury could indicate indirectly its belief in the truth of the defamatory statement. Not until 1842, however, was evidence of truth expressly made ad-

missible at trial in England (Libel Act, 1843, 6 & 7 Vict., c. 96, § 6 (Great Britain)).

Development of the law in the United States

The use of criminal libel. Following the English example, the American Sedition Act of 1798, ch. 74, 1 Stat. 596, criminalized the publication of anything "false, scandalous and malicious" against the administration, Congress, or the President "with intent to defame . . . or to bring them . . . into contempt or disrepute . . . or to stir up sedition within the United States." Adverse public reaction to the statute led President Thomas Jefferson to pardon all convicted persons and Congress to pass statutes reimbursing all fines paid. Since that time, seditious libel has had little overt recognition in American jurisprudence. Statutory control of speech affecting government generally has been phrased in nonlibel terms.

Criminal libel statutes have wavered between an emphasis on the reputational injury that libelous statements create and the breach of the peace they threaten. The concern with breach of the peace, however, is more one of form than of substance, for courts have not required proof that the alleged libel was in fact likely to provoke a breach of peace. The public's general acceptance of the rule of law as a substitute for private revenge has significantly decreased the credibility of a "maintenance of peace" justification for prosecuting private defamation as a crime. Yet, the criminal libel law's historic peacekeeping function explains some of its current features, such as the lack of any requirement that anyone other than the injured party be aware of the libelous remark.

Defenses. Two major defenses to a defamation prosecution have developed: privilege and truth. Absolute and conditional privileges have evolved to protect societal values of discourse and communication. Absolute privileges prohibit prosecutions regardless of malice and generally are limited to official participants in the process of government, such as judges, legislators, and high public officials. The privilege is grounded on the belief that the public benefits by having officials at liberty to exercise their function with independence and without fear of litigation. A conditional privilege exists when the defendant publishes his statement to fulfill a public or private duty to speak, whether the duty is legally based (such as reporting a crime) or only morally grounded (such as answering a question of a business associate). Conditional privilege includes statements made to protect one's own legitimate interests. Such privileges, however, are vitiated by proof of publication with malice.

Although truth was not a defense in English common law, it has been accepted as such by most American states through judicial decision, statute, or state constitutional provision. Truth, under these provisions, usually has to be accompanied by good motives, however, before the defense is complete.

A concern for group libel. Public concern with libel has broadened from protection of individual reputation to include protection of respectful and tolerant discourse within the community. Twentieth-century history demonstrated that the poisonous atmosphere of the easy lie infects and degrades an entire society.

Yet, in spite of the group defamation tactics used by fascist organizations during the 1930s and 1940s, the common law tort of libel barred suit by any member of a defamed group who could not prove individual tainting and injury. Words against an indeterminate class, such as a race, were to be discounted by the hearer according to the size of the disparaged group. Discounting, however, presumes a rational hearer; group defamation often occurs in nonrational settings. The ineffectiveness of traditional tort law in combating the group libeler led many states to enact criminal laws prohibiting communications that were abusive, offensive, or derogative to a group or that tended to arouse public contempt, prejudice, or hatred toward a group.

In 1952 the U.S. Supreme Court upheld an Illinois statute criminalizing group libel (*Beauharnais v. Illinois*, 343 U.S. 250 (1952)). The Illinois legislature, wrote the Court, could reasonably believe group libel would jeopardize public peace. Group libel statutes have also been defended by some as a protection of pluralistic forces within a democratic society and of the individual members whose status derives from group affiliations. These laws, it is argued, protect the tone of society or the style and quality of life.

The constitutional protection of freedom of expression

The development of new doctrine. Before 1964 the Supreme Court largely avoided the dilemma between First Amendment (freedom of speech) and decency concerns. Libelous statements were simply excluded from First Amend-

ment protection, for they "by their very utterance inflict injury or tend to incite an immediate breach of the peace" (*Chaplinsky v. New Hampshire*, 315 U.S. 568, 571–572 (1942)).

In 1964, however, the Supreme Court acknowledged that civil suits for defamation could have an adverse impact on First Amendment values (*New York Times Co. v. Sullivan*, 376 U.S. 254 (1964)). The Court held that freedom of the press prohibited a public official from recovering tort damages for a defamatory falsehood relating to his official conduct without proof that the statement was made with "actual malice," defined as knowledge that the statement was false or as reckless disregard of whether it was false.

The Court equated libel suits by public officials with actions for seditious libel, and such actions were perceived as destructive of the public dialogue necessary for popular sovereignty. Critical speech must be protected if frank and forceful judgments are to be expressed. Accurate information is valued; consequently, truth must always be a defense from liability. The Court reasoned that although falsity has no value in a system of free expression, the difficulty and expense of proving truth, coupled with the uncertainty of the jury process, might cause critics to exercise caution at the expense of free debate. Falsehoods are protected only to avoid chilling potentially accurate expression. Intentional falsehoods, however, lack any redeeming social importance. Consequently, statements known or believed false by their utterer could give rise to liability. In a later decision, *Garrison v. Louisiana*, 379 U.S. 64 (1964), the Court extended to criminal libel the protections of its *New York Times* decision.

In 1967 the Supreme Court further expanded this doctrine by protecting the press against civil libel actions brought by prominent public figures (*Curtis Publishing Co. v. Butts*, 388 U.S. 130 (1967)). Although such plaintiffs were not public officials, the Justices recognized that they might be the subject of legitimate public interest or concern. Free speech included more than political expression or comment on public affairs.

Expansion of the application of the First Amendment to civil libel suits culminated in *Gertz v. Robert Welch, Inc.*, 418 U.S. 323 (1974)). The Court held that defamation actions brought by public persons (public officials and public figures) must meet the *New York Times* standard but that states could impose a lesser standard in actions brought by private individuals as long as at least negligence, but not necessarily actual malice, was demonstrated.

The crucial issue after *Gertz* is who qualifies as a public figure. That opinion suggested that the status of public figure could be established in one of two ways. First, an individual may achieve such fame and notoriety that he becomes a public figure for all purposes. Second, an individual may have injected himself or been drawn into a public controversy, thereby becoming a public figure for a limited range of issues.

Prior to *Gertz* the Court's emphasis was on protecting the press, as the public's guardian, from threat and limitation by the potentially stronger government and public figures. *Gertz*, however, recognized that the media themselves have become a vast repository of privilege and power that could be abused. *Gertz*, by facilitating civil suits by private figures, reserved some protection for individuals from abuses of a guardian grown too strong to disregard.

Constitutional impact on criminal libel. Although *Garrison* explicitly stated only that *New York Times* would apply to criminal libel prosecutions, there is no reason to assume that criminal defendants will not be protected at least as fully as civil defendants under *Butts* and *Gertz*. In fact, the stigma and deprivation of liberty associated with criminal prosecutions should make charges of criminal libel more subject to scrutiny under the First Amendment than are those of civil libel.

At minimum, therefore, the following should be clear: Truth, whether with good motives or otherwise, is always an absolute defense, and the burden of proving falsity is upon the prosecutor. Libelous statements concerning public officials or figures are criminally actionable only if "actual malice" on the part of the defendant can be proved. In all other cases negligence, at least, must be demonstrated.

While the decided cases all focus on media defendants, their scope would logically include nonmedia defendants. To exclude individual, but not institutional, communications from First Amendment protection would create a dangerous disequilibrium between the guarantee of freedom of speech and that of the press. Statements of the press may cause much greater damage than those of private persons because of the wider dissemination of press communications and the greater difficulty in effectively rebutting them. It is anomalous, therefore, that the press be held accountable only for negligence or malice while the private person, engaged in a casual private conversation with a single individual, be held liable for false statements regardless of fault or negligence.

Hate speech and group libel. In light of *New York Times* and its progeny, the continuing constitutionality of group libel laws is now unclear. *Beauharnais*, the 1952 decision that upheld such provisions, has been harshly criticized and has proven remarkably inert as a basis for further case law. Indeed, recent developments have only deepened the uncertainty surrounding this long-dormant decision.

Beginning in the 1980s, a few cities and an even greater number of colleges and universities considered or adopted prohibitions on speech conveying animus toward members of racial, ethnic, or religious minority groups and (in some cases) toward gays and lesbians. Civil libertarians challenged these "hate speech codes" as violations of the First Amendment. Defenders of them pointed to the approval of group libel provisions in *Beauharnais*, a case many thought weakened by subsequent decisions but one the Supreme Court had nevertheless refrained from ever overruling.

In *R.A.V. v. St. Paul*, 505 U.S. 377 (1992), the Supreme Court invalidated a city ordinance that prohibited cross burnings and like forms of racially or religiously motivated "fighting words." By proscribing only a select class of inflammatory behavior, the law in question, the Court held, impermissibly conditioned liability on the content of the message such conduct was thought to express. But while clearly intimating disapproval of "hate speech" provisions, the Court in *R.A.V.* again declined to overrule or limit *Beauharnais*; indeed, the opinion in *R.A.V.* cited *Beauharnais* approvingly for the proposition that certain "categories of expression are 'not within the area of constitutionally protected speech'" (p. 383). The constitutionality of "group libel laws," which can still be found on the books in several states, thus remains a mystery.

A critical analysis of criminal libel

Tort and criminal law: a difference of function. Although a defamatory statement may constitute both a tort and a crime, there are fundamental differences of purpose in the two systems of allocating responsibility. Whether the damage is to the individual's life, limbs, property, or reputation, the law of torts attempts to reduce the cost of injury through placement of liability. It employs deterrence and compensation to promote human dignity by using money damages to discourage the violation of an individual's integrity and to reduce the impact of those injuries that do occur. Tort law's concern with reducing the frequency, extent, and impact of injury results in a reluctance to set standards that, once attained, would cease to apply pressure for improvement. The tort of defamation vindicates a plaintiff's reputation, rebukes and economically penalizes the offenders and thus affects their behavior, and provides compensation for economic and personal loss caused by the defamatory statements.

Crime, on the other hand, is that deviance which society finds intolerable. Using the criminal process to respond to such behavior channels and reduces the emotive response—the passion—that the deviance engenders in those personally confronted by it. Without a system of criminal law, riot, vigilantism, and vendetta would be the only recourse for controlling deviance. As long as the criminal process retains a sufficient ritual representation of passion, these excesses may be deterred. To aid and restrict this release of passion, criminal law makes violation a moral issue by unifying legal and moral guilt, through use of articulated and knowable standards. Although criminal law serves other purposes as well, the potential for controlling passion often accounts for the choice of criminal, rather than civil, remedies in a given situation. Criminal law, thus, should be reserved for behavior that exceptionally disturbs the community's sense of security.

The role of the Constitution.

Unlike criminal law, which involves the expression of societal passion, the Bill of Rights of the United States Constitution is a document by which the populace, fearing the tyranny of a temporary majority, institutionalized a barrier to fulfillment of momentary whims. No document, constitutional or otherwise, can save liberty once it has been abandoned by the people, but it can retard the process of abandonment long enough to allow a deliberate, dispassionate reconsideration.

The First Amendment plays such a role. It is based on the premise that the individual and the community, rather than the government, should make the vital political, moral, and aesthetic decisions. Censorship, on the contrary, demands a difficult, if not impossible, decision on what the public should not know. If truth is viewed not as a fixed concept but as a transient one, any reduction of communication, no matter how abhorrent the communication, is detrimental to society. Even if some speech is in fact worthless, the risks

involved in censoring even offensive and obnoxious expression would significantly endanger uninhibited public debate, for there may be no principled stopping place.

First Amendment evaluations involve a tension between the values of free expression and those of public safety, morality, comfort, and convenience. This tension involves interests of society in general, and society bears the impact of the decision to sacrifice either. Traditionally, the societal benefits of a system of free expression are thought to outweigh the temporary societal dangers of false statements, at least so long as sufficient time exists for corrective discussion to take place.

In limiting civil suits for defamation, however, the impact of the First Amendment is not shared generally by the populace. Rather, it falls directly and immediately upon the defamed individual. If he is unable to obtain redress through the legal system because of First Amendment interests, the value of free speech is subsidized by the injured party rather than by the general populace that benefits from a system of free expression. Tort law, consequently, with its focus on individual injury reduction and impact minimization, is more solicitous of the defamation victim than is criminal law, with its focus on societal impact. This emphasis on individual over societal harm suggests that civil law, rather than criminal law, responses to libel should be the norm.

STANLEY INGBER

See also HATE CRIMES; PUBLICITY IN CRIMINAL CASES; SEDITION AND DOMESTIC TERRORISM.

BIBLIOGRAPHY

Annotation. "Libel and Slander: Criminal." *American Law Reports* 19 (1922): 1470–1543.
ELDREDGE, LAURENCE H. *The Law of Defamation*. Indianapolis: Bobbs-Merrill, 1978.
HOLDSWORTH, WILLIAM S. "Defamation in the Sixteenth and Seventeenth Centuries." *Law Quarterly Review* 40 (1924): 302–315.
INGBER, STANLEY. "Defamation: A Conflict between Reason and Decency." *Virginia Law Review* 65, no. 5 (1979): 785–858.
LOVELL, COLIN RHYS. "The 'Reception' of Defamation by the Common Law." *Vanderbilt Law Review* 15, no. 4 (1962): 1051–1071.
MATSUDA, MARI J. *Words that Wound: Critical Race Theory, Assaultive Speech, and the First Amendment*. Boulder, Colo.: Westview Press, 1993.

Note. "Constitutionality of the Law of Criminal Libel." *Columbia Law Review* 52 (1952): 521–534.

Note. "Group Vilification Reconsidered." *Yale Law Journal* 89, no. 2 (1979): 308–332.

POST, ROBERT C. "Racist Speech, Democracy, and the First Amendment." *William and Mary Law Review* 32 (1991): 267–327.

RIESMAN, DAVID. "Democracy and Defamation: Control of Group Libel." *Columbia Law Review* 42, no. 5 (1942): 727–780.

SCHOFIELD, HENRY. *Essays on Constitutional Law and Equity and Other Subjects,* vol. 2. Edited by the Faculty of Law. Northwestern University. Boston: Chipman Law, 1921.

SPENCER, J. R. "Criminal Libel: A Skeleton in the Cupboard." *Criminal Law Review* (1977): 383–394, 465–474.

STEPHEN, JAMES FITZJAMES. *A History of the Criminal Law of England,* vol. 2. London: Macmillan, 1883.

VEEDER, VAN VECHTEN. "The History and Theory of the Law of Defamation." *Columbia Law Review* 3 (1903): 547–573.

CASES

Beauharnais v. Illinois, 343 U.S. 250 (1952).
Chaplinsky v. New Hampshire, 315 U.S. 568 (1942).
Curtis Publishing Co. v. Butts, 388 U.S. 130 (1967).
Garrison v. Louisiana, 379 U.S. 64 (1964).
Gertz v. Robert Welch, Inc., 418 U.S. 323 (1974).
New York Times Co. v. Sullivan, 376 U.S. 254 (1964).

LITERATURE AND CRIME

Literature and crime live in happy symbiosis. Literature often depends on crime for a good story, and that story in turn frequently yields important insights about crime. If many of the Great Books involve crime, this comes as no surprise.

Some reasons why

To reveal something deep and timeless about human nature, a writer needs a special tension for the story's action and the characters' development. What better than a plot that involves a broken taboo; a violation of natural, religious, or human law; sin, punishment, guilt and redemption? That is one reason why crime, with all these perennial characteristics in abundance, often serves as useful grist for the literary mill.

Storytellers also find crime lends itself to an ideal literary device: the trial. A crucial part of the criminal process, the trial is custom-made for literature. The adversary legal system has conflict and resolution. Consider John Mortimer's stories about the veteran English criminal lawyer Rumpole of the Bailey. A criminal trial builds suspense and uncertainty, especially while the verdict is up in the air. Erle Stanley Gardner's Perry Mason books always have a criminal trial for a climax. "The Witness for the Prosecution," a story of a criminal trial by Agatha Christie, ends with a famous surprise. In *A Passage to India* by E. M. Forster, a man is acquitted of rape but we never know if the rape actually occurred. And we have to wait until the end of *Anatomy of a Murder* by Robert Travers to find out if the defendant wins because he could not help but yield to an "irresistible impulse."

A trial in literature showcases eloquence. Robert Bolt gives some unforgettable lines to Thomas More during his trial in the play *A Man for all Seasons.* Atticus Finch, the southern lawyer who defends a poor African American on trial for raping a white woman in Harper Lee's *To Kill a Mockingbird,* has moving courtroom lines. Ayn Rand makes Howard Roark a wonderful spokesman for individualism in his summation at the end of his trial for blowing up a housing project he designed in *The Fountainhead.*

There is drama too, as hopes are dashed or fulfilled, as serious penalties are imposed or escaped, as evil wins or loses, as the innocent or guilty get their not necessarily just rewards. Consider the military trials in Herman Wouk's *Caine Mutiny* and Herman Melville's *Billy Budd,* or the trial in Walter Scott's story "The Two Drovers." And there is symbolism, as each participant—prosecutor, accused, victim, judge, witness, defense counsel—represents a larger idea in society. Playwright Arthur Miller used this technique to great effect in *The Crucible,* in which the Salem witch trials were a metaphor for the communist witch hunt of McCarthyism.

Crime easily lends itself to literary calls for reform. Many gifted writers of fiction have seared the consciences of their readers by describing how poverty, parental abuse, bad living conditions, prejudice, and other societal factors lead to crime. Think of Charles Dickens's moving portraits in several of his novels, particularly *Oliver Twist,* or Jean Valjean, the hero of Victor Hugo's *Les Misérables,* driven by poverty to steal a loaf of bread for his family and for which he is sentenced to the gallows. E. L. Doctorow's *Billy Bathgate* tells the story of a boy's growing up amid Bronx gangsters in the 1930s.

Literature also shows how the legal system can err by convicting the innocent while following the forms of justice. Medieval justice, wrote Hugo in *The Hunchback of Notre Dame*, "had little concern for clarity and accuracy in criminal proceedings. The main thing was to see that the accused went to the gallows" (Victor Hugo, *The Hunchback of Notre Dame*, 179–180 (Lowell Bair, trans. Bantam Books, 1981)). A memorable example of this flaw is George Bernard Shaw's trial scene in *St. Joan*. No less memorable is the unjust conviction of Edmond Dantes in *The Count of Monte Cristo* by Alexandre Dumas. In the twentieth century, Franz Kafka wedged his way into our consciousness with *The Trial*, in which the hero, Joseph K., is convicted and imprisoned for unknown crimes.

Kafka's short story "In the Penal Colony" demonstrates how literature can display cruel, inhuman, and unacceptable prison conditions and how they can needlessly destroy without rehabilitating. Dantes's twenty years in the Chateau d'If island prison haunts every reader's mind, as do the unsettling scenes of prison life in Stalin's Russia by Alexander Solzhenitsyn in *The Gulag Archipelago*.

Equally important in explaining the literature-crime link is our ambivalence about criminals and the allure of evil. On the one hand, we occasionally, if paradoxically, admire those who break the law and, on the other, we often loathe them. One way to minimize the conflict is to endow criminals with virtues such as greatness or goodness. Robin Hood is a virtuous outlaw. The criminal can sometimes be attractive simply because he is an individual at odds with society, one against the many. And the successful criminal may, by definition, have superior mental or other powers, may be an evil genius. Arthur Conan Doyle had Sherlock Holmes respectfully call his nemesis Professor Moriarty the "Napoleon of Crime." A criminal may often have an outsized, unusual, and interesting, if warped, personality. The villains in many of Ian Fleming's James Bond books, such as Dr. No, Auric Goldfinger, and Ernst Blofeld, fit this description. Glamour may even be attached to an elegant rogue.

Another way to reduce the psychological tension is repression, whereby we bar from consciousness our admiration for criminals and replace it with loathing. But such apparent loathing is just another form of fascination, which can lead to obsession. The self-appointed censor who obsessively reviews books, magazines, and films

for obscenity falls into this category, as does Victor Hugo's dogged fictional policeman Javert in *Les Misérables*.

Reading about crime is a good thing for a society. Reading is not doing, although some have argued that a culture's portrayal of crime and violence in literary works (or on film or television) can breed more crime and violence. But this argument, so well portrayed in *The Seven Minutes*, Irving Wallace's 1970 novel about a rape-obscenity trial, ignores not only freedom of expression but also how much the experience of literature can serve as a psychological safety valve. Most people slake their thirst for crime vicariously.

Examples old and new

Whatever the reason, literature relies heavily on crime, but not always in the same way. Fiction writers use crime in their work in two different ways. In one type, represented by Fyodor Dostoyevsky's *Crime and Punishment* and Theodore Dreiser's *An American Tragedy*, crime and its consequences are the primary focus. In the other, crime is a subordinate though often crucial theme of the literary work. Examples of both kinds of crime literature abound and go far back in time.

The Bible brims over with disobedience and punishment. Adam and Eve committed the first crime by disobeying God's order not to eat the forbidden fruit. The first couple's son Cain murders his innocent brother Abel. Soon humans so degenerate into evil that God feels it necessary to wipe out the whole race except for one extended family, which He saves on the Ark. But in time a massive crime problem again blights whole cities, which God obliterates, leaving the names of Sodom and Gomorrah to echo evilly through the millennia. And on and on, including evil King Ahab and Jezebel, the genocidal Haman, and even great King David with his weakness for Bathsheba.

Ancient Greek culture also laced its literature with crime. *The Iliad* and *The Odyssey* grew out of Paris's crime of adultery and kidnapping of another man's wife. Picking up where Homer leaves off, Aeschylus's *Oresteia* and Sophocles's *Electra* portray first the murder of the Greek King Agamemnon by his unfaithful wife Clytemnestra and her draft-dodging lover Aegisthus, then Orestes's fatal revenge, and finally the forgiveness of Orestes after mental torture by the Furies.

The Greeks did not stop there. *Prometheus Bound* by Aeschylus concerns a crime like Adam and Eve's. Prometheus disobeys the gods by bringing fire to humans, which resembles the fire of knowledge Adam and Eve acquired from the forbidden fruit. For his violation, Prometheus earns eternal punishment. Sophocles's *Oedipus the King* portrays the crimes of parricide and incest, the struggle between fate and free will, and the guilt and expiation that follow. In *Antigone*, Sophocles raises the issue of civil disobedience, that is, when a higher law requires you to disobey the law of the state. In Euripides's *Medea* the main character murders her children because her husband has left her.

Dante's three-part *Divine Comedy*, completed shortly before the author's death in 1321, is an allegory about crime, punishment, and redemption. In *The Inferno*, Dante and his guide Virgil go through the horrors of the nine circles of Hell, where anguished men and women expiate earthly sins of lust and greed, violence, malice, fraud, and betrayal, in varying degrees of memorable punishment suited to each crime. It is a journey to the depths of evil. *Purgatorio* and *Paradiso* allow for the possibility (but not certainty) of redemption after penance, suffering, and atonement. But it is Dante's *Inferno*, with its vivid descriptions of sinners and their exquisite punishments, that stays in the mind (for example, the Envious have their eyes sewn shut, the Gluttonous starve).

Shakespeare's plays are a whole course in criminal law. At the core of *Measure for Measure*, for example, lies the question: How much should law be used to enforce morality? In the play, a strict law banning nonmarital sex is enforced against an engaged couple. Embedded in the discussion are basic issues of privacy. According to a character in the play, criminal laws need widespread public respect, lest they become "more mocked than feared," so that "liberty plucks Justice by the nose" (act 1, scene 3). But, as the play demonstrates, wooden enforcement of a bad law does not breed respect. One question in the play, which still nettles lawyers, is whether a criminal statute that has neither been enforced nor obeyed for many years can suddenly be resurrected and applied. Shakespeare's antifornication law carries a death penalty, so that *Measure for Measure* also raises the issue of appropriate punishment.

The most basic legal theme in *Hamlet* explores the struggle for the rule of law. *Hamlet* depicts the uncertain battle within human nature between the punitive passion for revenge and the more civilized law against individual retaliation. Hamlet's indecision about whether to kill Claudius for murdering Hamlet's father, for which Hamlet has been often criticized, can be seen as an effort not to yield to the passion for revenge. It is a step in the evolution of law.

Even the insanity defense is part of *Hamlet*. Hamlet pleads it when Laertes, unhampered by the hesitancy that so plagues Hamlet, seeks revenge for the death of Polonius, his father. Face to face with Laertes's wrath, Hamlet claims to be beset "with sore distraction" and "madness" (act 5, sc. 2). But Hamlet also at times feigns his "antic disposition" (act 1, sc. 5).

Richard III, as portrayed by Shakespeare, is almost everyone's favorite villain. No less hateful is Iago, who schemes and plots to destroy Othello and Desdemona. In *King Lear*, Edmund spends his life contriving treachery against his family. Macbeth, goaded by his ambitious wife, betrays and murders his king and benefactor. In *The Merchant of Venice*, Shakespeare shows us how law should be flexible rather than rigid, how hatred could lead a law-abiding man to criminal revenge, how pervasive prejudice could then mar his trial and lead to inappropriate punishments (such as forced religious conversion), and how an eloquent plea for "the quality of mercy" should not be rejected (act 4, sc. 1). *Julius Caesar* depends on a conspiracy to murder.

About fifty years after Shakespeare's death, John Milton wrote the only other epic poem to rival Dante's, and it also has crime and sin at its center. In *Paradise Lost*, Milton depicted disobedience on human and cosmic levels. The human disobedience was of course the fall of Adam and Eve, and in that regard Milton discusses free will and determinism. But the arch-criminal in *Paradise Lost* is not Adam or Eve; it is Satan, the apostate angel cast out of Heaven after leading an unsuccessful rebellion against God. Significantly, the poet makes Satan the strongest, most unforgettable, and most vital character in the poem. Milton's Satan is the predecessor of another literary fallen angel: the Romantic outlaw.

The Romantic outlaw came on the cultural scene in the early nineteenth century. He grew out of the fertile soil of Romanticism, with its stress on introspective individualism. The Romantic outlaw is an outcast, brooding, moody, wronged by society or flawed in some deep way but has, like Milton's fallen angel, redeeming qualities that fascinate us. The protagonists in Byron's great poems—*Manfred*, *Childe Harold*, and *Cain*, for instance—are the quintessential Romantic outlaws. Like Byron himself, the Byronic hero is often irresistible precisely because he is "mad, bad and dangerous to know" as Lady Caroline Lamb confided to her diary, quoted in Berjan Evans, *"Lord Byron's Pilgrimage,"* in *Byron's Poetry* 344 (Frank D. McConnell, ed. 1978)).

The mystery novel

In the mid-nineteenth century, a new form of crime literature arose: the detective or mystery novel. Invented by Edgar Allan Poe in America, this genre usually has a crime or mystery to be solved and a highly intelligent hero who, through logic or patient investigation or preternatural understanding of the criminal mind, finds the solution. Poe's stories "The Purloined Letter" and "The Gold Bug" and his clever detective Dupin started a popular literary trend that shows no sign of abating.

The mystery novel next flourished in England with *The Moonstone* and *The Woman in White*, both by Wilkie Collins. Arthur Conan Doyle's Sherlock Holmes tales are classics of the form, as are the works of Dorothy Sayers, Agatha Christie, and P. D. James. In the United States in the twentieth century, Raymond Chandler, Dashiell Hammett, Mickey Spillane, and Rex Stout made, with their tough, lean prose, enormous contributions to the modern crime novel.

In France, the prolific Georges Simenon wrote psychologically penetrating books about crime with his fictional police inspector Maigret at the center. Books such as *The Blue Knight* and *The Centurions* made former policeman Joseph Wambaugh the dean of American police novelists. From the genre of true crime, Meyer Levin's *Compulsion*, Truman Capote's *In Cold Blood*, Norman Mailer's *The Executioner's Song*, and Joe McGinniss's *Fatal Vision* are sterling books.

Prison

Writers have long described prison as a state of mind rather than a place of confinement. Hamlet tells his false friends Rosencrantz and Guildenstern that Denmark seems to be a prison. "We think not so, my lord," says Rosencrantz. Replies Hamlet insightfully, "why, then 'tis none to you, for there is nothing either good or bad but thinking makes it so. To me it is a prison." Shakespeare's melancholy but thoughtful Dane then adds: "I could be bounded in a nutshell and count myself a King of infinite space" (act 2, scene 2).

Such thoughts must have been in the English literary air in the seventeenth century. For Milton has Satan echo the same sentiment: "The mind is its own place, and in itself/Can make a heav'n of hell, a hell of heav'n." And of course Restoration poet Richard Lovelace, in "To Althea from Prison," famously said: "Stone walls do not a prison make,/Nor iron bars a cage" (*The Viking Book of Poetry of the English-speaking World* 445–446 (Richard Aldington, ed. 1958)).

Actual prison life rarely fares well in literature. The Bible describes Joseph's relatively easy prison sojourn in an Egyptian prison but makes us feel for the blind Samson imprisoned by the Philistines, "eyeless in Gaza." Drawing once again on the Bible, Milton used Samson's prison plight as the basis of his poem *Samson Agonistes*. Dickens's descriptions of imprisonment for debt are unforgettable, as are Solzhenitzyn's of the gulag. And Oscar Wilde used poetry to tell the world of his prison experience in *The Ballad of Reading Gaol*.

The criminal mind

Literature has a rich tapestry of criminal identities, and is particularly good at depicting the guilty conscience. In *Hamlet*, the Prince of Denmark has a play about a murder performed to see if Claudius will betray his guilt, which he does. Similarly, Macbeth strains out loud under the burden of his heavy conscience. And, of course, we have Dostoevsky's portrayal of Raskolnikov's eventual unburdening of his guilt-ridden conscience in *Crime and Punishment*.

Raskolnikov's confession comes after a series of interviews with the psychologically astute prosecutor Porfiry. In the most striking of those sessions, the young, intellectual murderer explains his distressing theory that great men—presumably including himself—are above the law and that they have the moral right to take the lives of others. Merely to be exposed to that theory is to glimpse how the mind of a criminal works in distorted ways.

No one theory explains the variety of the criminal mind. Robert Louis Stevenson gave the world *Dr. Jekyll and Mr. Hyde* and thereby tried to show that all human beings are simultaneously made up of good and evil. In Hugo's *The Hunchback of Notre Dame*, the sexually repressed priest Claude Frollo vents his passions: "when one does evil it's madness to stop halfway. The extremity of crime has a certain delirium of joy. . . . But an evil thought is inexorable and strives to become an action" (Victor Hugo, *The Hunchback of Notre Dame* 173–174 (Lowell Bair, trans. Bantam Books, 1981)). In *The Stranger*, Albert Camus depicts how the criminal mind may simply be alienated. In Balzac's *Père Goriot*, Vautrin is an articulate, intelligent escaped convict, full of practical experience and honorable to his own code.

The human condition

Crime in literature helps us better understand crime in life. "A crime is, in the first instance, a defect in the reasoning powers," wrote Balzac in *Cousin Bette*, and that mid-nineteenth century literary insight is both piercing and fruitful (Honore de Balzac, *Cousin Bette* 422 (James Waring, trans. Everyman's Library, 1991)). Much of crime can be explained by Balzac's theory—by reason losing control—with a few illustrations drawn from the vast body of crime literature.

Many crimes, for instance, are the result of sexual passion, where sound rational judgment flees, as demonstrated by Baron Hulot's exploits in *Cousin Bette*, Claude Frollo's in *The Hunchback of Notre Dame*, and Hester Prynne's in Nathaniel Hawthorne's *Scarlet Letter*. Closely related to crimes of sexual passion are crimes of irrational jealousy, such as Othello's murder of Desdemona and the murder in Somerset Maugham's short story "The Letter." Then we have crimes of revenge—for matters of pride or harm to friend or relative—that are reflected in a genre actually called revenge literature, exemplified by *Hamlet* and *The Oresteia*. Desire for money or what money can buy is another major cause of crime, whether resulting from poverty, hunger (Dickens, Hugo), or blind avarice (Balzac's *Eugénie Grandet*).

Other assaults on rationality that can cause crime are extreme political, social, or religious causes, and an inordinate need for power. Consider Shakespeare's various kings and warriors and *All the King's Men* by Robert Penn Warren. Ambition led Julian Sorel to murder in *The Red and the Black* by Stendhal. Then of course there is the sociopath or the insane person, whose mind is so defective, either temporarily or permanently, that he or she commits crime. We ought not to forget the temperamentally violent or the retarded who for those reasons commit crime, however unwittingly, like Lenny in John Steinbeck's *Of Mice and Men*. In short, crime literature has much of value to teach lawyers, judges, the police, criminologists, sociologists, and psychologists.

A reciprocal relationship

Thus, the close relationship between literature and crime, while at first a seeming paradox, is really mutually beneficial. True, one may be initially surprised by the unexpected nexus between high creative art and low antisocial behavior. But the relationship is indeed symbiotic and even synergistic. Literature draws on crime for subjects and stories. In their turn, criminology and criminal law—and the public—depend on literature for insights, criticism, and ideas needed for changes in outlook and attitude toward understanding, preventing, and punishing crime.

DANIEL J. KORNSTEIN

BIBLIOGRAPHY

DUNCAN, MARTHA GRACE. *Romantic Outlaws, Beloved Prison: The Unconscious Meaning of Crime and Punishment.* New York: New York University Press, 1996.

LADSWOON, LENORA, ed. *Law and Literature: Text and Theory.* New York: Garland, 1996.

POSNER, RICHARD A. *Law and Literature: A Misunderstood Relation.* Cambridge, Mass: Harvard University Press, 1988.

ROCKWOOD, BRUCE L., ed. *Law and Literature Perspectives.* New York: Peter Corp., 1996.

WEISBERG, RICHARD H. *The Failure of the Word.* New Haven: Yale University Press, 1984.

———. *Poethics: And Other Strategies of Law and Literature.* New York: Columbia University Press, 1992.

ZIOLKOWSKI, THEODORE. *The Mirror of Justice.* Princeton, N.J.: Princeton University Press, 1997.

M

MAIL: FEDERAL MAIL FRAUD ACT

Article I, section 8 of the Constitution authorizes Congress to "establish Post Offices and post Roads." This provision has been treated as authority for the continuing operation and regulation of the postal system (*McCulloch v. Maryland*, 17 U.S. (4 Wheat.) 316, 417 (1819)).

Adoption of the act

The first mail fraud legislation was adopted in 1872. As part of a general revision of the postal laws, Congress made it a crime to mail material intended to effectuate "any scheme or artifice to defraud" (An act to revise, consolidate and amend the statutes relating to the Post Office Department, ch. 335, § 301, 17 Stat. 283, 323 (1872) (repealed)). This provision evoked almost no discussion in Congress, so there is little legislative history to provide guidance to the courts.

The adoption of this statute, commonly known as the Mail Fraud Act, was an important turning point in the use of federal criminal sanctions, which previously had been reserved principally for conduct directly injurious to the federal government. The Mail Fraud Act, in contrast, extended federal jurisdiction to crimes clearly within the states' general jurisdiction and directly injurious only to private individuals, not to the central government. Federal mail fraud jurisdiction thus overlapped with, and was auxiliary to, state jurisdiction. The current version of the Mail Fraud Act is codified as 18 U.S.C. § 1341.

In 1952, following the pattern of the Mail Fraud Act, Congress adopted a wire fraud statute prohibiting "interstate wire, radio, or television" transmissions to effectuate "any scheme or artifice to defraud" (An act to further amend the Communications Act of 1934, ch. 879, § 18(a), 66 Stat. 711 (1952)). The Wire Fraud Act is now codified as 18 U.S.C. § 1343.

Challenges to the constitutionality of the act

The Supreme Court confirmed Congress's power to prohibit the mailing of material based upon its content. *Badders v. United States*, 240 U.S. 391, 393 (1916), held that Congress has the authority to regulate the act of mailing a letter, and to prohibit any act of mailing "done in furtherance of a scheme that [Congress] regards as contrary to public policy, whether it can forbid the scheme or not." Subsequently, *Parr v. United States*, 363 U.S. 370, 389 (1960), reemphasized that "the fact that a scheme may violate state laws does not exclude it from the proscriptions of the federal mail fraud statute." The Mail Fraud Act is an appropriate exercise of congressional power because it does not purport to displace the states' general jurisdiction over fraud; it reaches only schemes in which the mails are used.

The scope and application of the act. The twin elements of mail fraud—a scheme to defraud and a mailing—have been given a generous reading, and the Act has evolved into a flexible tool that reaches a remarkably wide range of conduct.

Scheme to defraud. No precise definition of the concept of fraud appears either in the mail fraud statute or in the cases construing it. In defining the statutory phrase "scheme to defraud," the courts have given the concept an extremely broad and flexible reading. In *Durland v. United*

States, 161 U.S. 306, 313 (1896), the Supreme Court rejected the contention that Congress had intended to limit the statute to fraud or false pretenses as defined by common law; the Court held that the statute prohibited "everything designed to defraud by representations as to the past or present, or suggestions and promises as to the future." Following the signal sent by the opinion in *Durland*, the lower courts have interpreted the term "defraud" in a broad nontechnical sense. Some courts have even said that the act "puts its imprimatur on the accepted moral standards and condemns conduct which fails to match the 'reflection of moral uprightness, of fundamental honesty, fair play and right dealing in the general and business life of members of society'" (*Blachly v. United States*, 380 F.2d 665, 671 (5th Cir. 1967)).

The Mail Fraud Act has become a favorite prosecutorial tool, and the act has been used to prosecute a wide variety of deceptive schemes designed to deprive victims of money or property, including check kiting, pyramid schemes, and welfare and insurance frauds. The act's flexible definition of fraud proved to be readily adaptable as new kinds of schemes were devised. Before more specific federal legislation was passed, the Mail Fraud Act served as the principal weapon against fraudulent securities transactions, extortionate credit transactions, real estate fraud, and credit card fraud. For this reason mail fraud has been called the federal government's "first line of defense" against fraud (*United States v. Maze*, 414 U.S. 395, 405 (1974) (Chief Justice Burger dissenting)). Even after the adoption of more specific legislation, the Mail Fraud Act continued to serve an important auxiliary function. Mail fraud charges continue to be combined with, or even used in lieu of, charges under more specialized statutes.

Perhaps even more important, the Mail Fraud Act has been extended to reach cases of public corruption, election fraud, and private breaches of fiduciary duty. What has come to be called the "intangible rights doctrine" developed in a series of cases in lower federal courts that extended the mail and wire fraud statutes to cases in which the victims were deprived of some intangible right or interest other than money or property. In the public sector, judges, governors, aldermen, congressmen, and many other state and federal officials were convicted of defrauding citizens of their right to the honest services of governmental officials. Generally these cases involved officials secretly making governmental

decisions with the objective of benefiting themselves or promoting their own interests, rather than looking to the interest of the citizens of the state or local government. Other intangible rights prosecutions involved the use of the mails to falsify votes, thus defrauding the citizenry of its right to an honest election. In the private sector, purchasing agents, brokers, union leaders, and others with fiduciary duties were convicted of defrauding their employers or unions by accepting kickbacks or selling confidential information.

The intangible rights cases substantially extended the concept of fraud. The cases typically involved neither an express misrepresentation, nor the loss of any property by the victim of the scheme. The courts found the element of deceit or misrepresentation satisfied by nondisclosure of dishonest or corrupt actions, and the loss of an intangible right obviated the necessity to determine whether the scheme caused any economic loss.

Although the Supreme Court called a temporary halt to the intangible rights doctrine, its decision was soon nullified by Congress. In *McNally v. United States*, 483 U.S. 350 (1987), the Supreme Court held that the mail fraud statute reaches only the deprivation of "property" rights. The Court declined to "construe the statute in a manner that leaves its outer boundaries ambiguous and involves the federal government in setting standards of disclosure and good government for local and state officials" in the absence of a clear statement from Congress indicating that it intended the Mail Fraud Act to apply in this context. Congress did not share the Supreme Court's concerns, and one year later it revived the intangible rights doctrine by enacting 18 U.S.C. § 1346, which provides that for purposes of the mail, wire, and bank fraud acts "the term 'scheme or artifice to defraud' includes a scheme or artifice to deprive another of the intangible right of honest services."

Intangible rights prosecutions raise serious concerns in both public and private sector cases. In the public sector the chief issues are the question whether it is appropriate for the federal government to police the integrity of state and local government officials, as well as concerns about fair warning and prosecutorial abuse that arise from the amorphous quality of the federal concepts of "fraud" and "honest services." Prosecutions in the private sector raise concerns that traditional matters of employment law and contract will be converted into issues of criminal liability.

The Supreme Court's reluctance to place its imprimatur on the intangible rights doctrine may reflect an uneasiness with what had become, in effect, a common law offense. A similar unease seems to be animating some of the lower courts, which are placing various restrictive glosses on the act, and may also provide an explanation for the Supreme Court's decision in *Neder v. United States*, 119 S.Ct. 1127 (1999). The precise holding in *Neder*—that materiality is an element of mail, wire, and bank fraud—is unsurprising, and it accords with most of the lower court decisions. In reaching this result, however, the Supreme Court emphasized that in interpreting the mail, wire, and bank fraud acts the courts should presume that Congress intended to incorporate the common law definition of fraud unless the statutory language rebuts that presumption. This is at odds with the general understanding of the Court's decision in *Durland* as cutting the Mail Fraud Act free from its common law moorings. While *Neder* may have little direct impact on the honest services prosecutions brought under the authority of 18 U.S.C. § 1346, it suggests that the federal courts may be prepared to rein in the Mail Fraud Act.

The history of the Mail Fraud Act illustrates both the institutional pressures that produce such broad open-textured laws, and the techniques the courts have used in responding to them. The difficulty of reaching agreement among hundreds of senators and members of Congress places practical limitations on the number and specificity of the federal laws that can be enacted. Congress has an incentive to enact broad and often incomplete legislation. This virtually guarantees that there will be various gaps in federal law, including federal criminal law. Federal prosecutors respond by asking the courts to extend broadly framed existing statutes—particularly the Mail Fraud Act—to new kinds of conduct. In other contexts, the common law role of the courts in making interstitial law under the authority of broadly worded statutes is relatively uncontroversial. But in the criminal context this common law role conflicts with the tradition of legislative supremacy in making criminal law, and it also raises concerns about due process and fair warning. Although the courts have often embraced their common law role, interpreting the mail fraud statute as a stopgap, other decisions reflect either a disagreement on the policy choice made by the courts, or a preference by individual judges for a return to greater fidelity to the rule of legislative supremacy.

Use of the mails. The second element of mail fraud is use of the mails "for the purpose of effectuating" a fraudulent scheme. As interpreted, this requirement is not difficult to meet. The defendant need not mail or receive anything himself. The statute applies to anyone who "causes" the mails to be used, and this requirement is met whenever the defendant acts with knowledge that use of the mails will ordinarily follow or is reasonably foreseeable. So long as the defendant causes a use of the mails that effectuates his scheme, the mailing itself need not contain any fraudulent representation, it need not be to or from the intended victim, and it need not be an essential element of the fraudulent scheme. In *Schmuck v. United States*, 489 U.S. 705, 710–11 (1989), the Supreme Court held that it is sufficient if a mailing is "incident to an essential part of the scheme . . . or a step in [the] plot." Under *Schmuck* a mailing that is quite peripheral to a fraudulent scheme may be sufficient to trigger federal jurisdiction under the Mail Fraud Act.

The Mail Fraud Act and the parallel wire fraud statute are so broad that they permit federal prosecution even where there is arguably no significant federal interest. A minor local fraud may involve the mailing of one letter or the placing of one interstate telephone call. To prevent federal prosecutions of petty local fraud, the Justice Department has adopted a policy that mail fraud prosecutions are ordinarily not appropriate for schemes involving isolated transactions or minor losses. There is, however, no real mechanism for enforcement of this limitation, and the local United States attorney exercises substantial discretion in deciding whether federal prosecution is appropriate in a particular case.

SARA SUN BEALE

See also FEDERAL CRIMINAL JURISDICTION; FEDERAL CRIMINAL LAW ENFORCEMENT; WHITE-COLLAR CRIME: HISTORY OF AN IDEA.

BIBLIOGRAPHY

BRADLEY, CRAIG M. "Foreword: Mail Fraud After *McNally* and *Carpenter*: The Essence of Fraud." *Journal of Criminal Law and Criminology* 79 (1988): 573–622.
BROWN, GEORGE D. "Should Federalism Shield Corruption?—Mail Fraud, State Law, and

Post-*Lopez* Analysis." *Cornell Law Review* 82 (1997): 225–300.

COFFEE, JOHN C., JR. "Hush!: The Criminal Status of Confidential Information After *McNally* and *Carpenter* and the Enduring Problem of Overcriminalization." *American Criminal Law Review* 26 (1988): 121–154.

———. "Modern Mail Fraud: The Restoration of the Public/Private Distinction." *American Criminal Law Review* 35 (1998): 427–465.

HENNING, PETER J. "Maybe It Should Just Be Called Federal Fraud: The Changing Nature of The Mail Fraud Statute." *Boston College Law Review* 36 (1995): 435–477.

KAHAN, DAN M. *Lenity and Federal Common Law Crimes.* Supreme Court Review. (1994) pp. 345–428.

MOOHR, GERALDINE SZOTT. "Mail Fraud and the Intangible Rights Doctrine: Someone to Watch Over Us." *Harvard Journal on Legislation* 31 (1994): 153–209.

———. "Mail Fraud Meets Criminal Theory." *University of Cincinnati Law Review* 67 (1998): 1–51.

RAKOFF, JED S. "The Federal Mail Fraud Statute (Part I)." *Duquesne Law Review* 18 (1998): 771.

WELLING, SARAH N.; BEALE, SARA SUN; and BUCY, PAMELA H. In *Federal Criminal Law and Related Civil Actions*, vol. 2. St. Paul, Minn.: West Group, 1998. Pages 1–73.

WILLIAMS, GREGORY H. "Good Government By Prosecutorial Decree: The Use and Abuse of the Mail Fraud Statute." *Arizona Law Review* 32 (1990): 137–171.

CASES

Badders v. United States, 240 U.S. 391, 393 (1916).

Blachly v. United States, 380 F.2d 665, 671 (5th Cir. 1967).

McCulloch v. Maryland, 17 U.S. (4 Wheat.) 316, 417 (1819).

McNally v. United States, 483 U.S. 350 (1987).

Neder v. United States, 119 S.Ct. 1127 (1999).

Parr v. United States, 363 U.S. 370, 389 (1960).

Schmuck v. United States, 489 U.S. 705, 710–11 (1989).

United States v. Maze, 414 U.S. 395, 405 (1974).

MASS MEDIA AND CRIME

The relationship between the criminal justice system and the media system has been the subject of research, speculation, and commentary throughout the twentieth century. This relationship may be understood in terms of dependency relations operative between these massive systems (Ball-Rokeach and De Fleur). Put most simply, neither the media nor the criminal justice system could operate effectively without the other. The criminal justice system is a resource for the media system in that it affords one of the common sources of news and entertainment stories. The classical surrogate scout role of the media, whereby they monitor the environment for actual and potential threats to individual and collective welfare, affords a powerful way for the media to attract their audiences. People must constantly update their understanding and ability to orient themselves to the environments in which they act. Media crime stories, whether the news or entertainment genre, instruct and update these understandings. Commercial media organizations translate this relationship with their audience into the profit that flows from advertisers. The media system's capacities to reach vast audiences of citizens and policymakers also positions it as an essential resource for the criminal justice system and all of its attendant judicial and law enforcement organizations. For the criminal justice system to operate effectively, it must have the authority that derives from people's willingness to grant it legitimacy, and media storytelling can profoundly affect this process. Allocation of scarce resources to the criminal justice system also depends upon success in the struggle to get "its" story positively framed and widely disseminated to media audiences. These macro dependency relations serve as context for examinations of specific aspects of media, criminal justice, public, and decision-maker relations.

Research attention has been given to the dependency relations between journalists and the police, courts, and jails. The impact of journalism on public perceptions of the criminal justice system, and on public attitudes toward specific cases—including the attitudes of potential and actual jurors—has been another frequent focus. The right of journalists to protect sources by not disclosing their names has also come under scrutiny from time to time.

While journalism may be the media profession with the most legitimate claim to exercise influence over the criminal justice system, it is by no means the only way the media exercise such influence. Entertainment media have also been studied and criticized for their influence over public perceptions of the people and institutions that comprise the criminal justice system. A striking amount of television programming has in one way or another (e.g., through comedy, mystery, drama, biography, docudrama, and soap opera) been centered on police, lawyers, judges, criminals, and victims of crime. The effects on public attitudes and behavior that these portrayals may have brought about have received considerable research attention. Media portrayals of violence, largely in television but also in movies and—increasingly in the 1990s—recorded music, have been studied in part for their potential to inspire real-life criminal behavior. Exposure to violent media content has been argued in criminal defenses as a mitigating factor in the guilt of defendants.

Since the early 1980s a television genre has emerged that is part journalism (in that it purports to deal with reality and with important subjects) and in no small part entertainment (in that it is dramatic, enhanced with music and special effects, and often includes actors playing various roles). Shows such as *Cops, America's Most Wanted,* and *Unsolved Mysteries* combine footage of actual arrests, interviews with people involved in crimes, and other documentary information with an assortment of dramatic elements to create a new sort of quasi-journalism scorned by professional journalists but very popular. While not yet the focus of much research attention, the emergence of such shows is occasionally credited for a perceived decline in the quality of broadcast journalism, which may have an indirect effect on the justice system.

Journalism

Only in the twentieth century did journalism attain the status of a profession, with professional schools, organizations, honors, norms, and the means of disciplining transgressors. Early conceptions of the journalist as an objective conduit of facts about the world have given way to more complex models of journalism in which the role of institutional imperatives and individual biases are recognized as highly influential, if not decisive, factors shaping the content of news (Bennett; McManus; Winch).

Various elements of the criminal justice system are among those most likely to influence journalism. Public interest in crime news is generally high, so there is a commercial incentive for newspapers and broadcasters to provide such information. Crimes are usually good stories; they can be told as morality plays, dramatic confrontations, and human-interest stories even when their value as hard news is not high. Demand for crime news produces close relationships between police, judicial officers, and reporters. The infor-

mation resources controlled by police, such as the identity of suspects, the status of cases, and the evidence assembled, are highly prized by reporters. Attorneys and (less frequently) judges may offer valuable information about ongoing (and even long-past) trials. Reporters do their best to cultivate close and reliable relations with the police, the courts, and the prosecuting attorneys on their beats. If a reporter is not on good terms with these people, he or she risks losing information necessary to tell a coherent or interesting story. A reporter may not be alerted to new discoveries of evidence, new legal strategies, or impending changes in the dates and times of public hearings. Often there is no source of this information other than the police, courts, and prosecutors.

Reporters control resources of their own, prized by the criminal justice system. The threat of adverse publicity can be potent, especially for elected officers of the court and (in some jurisdictions) police chiefs or sheriffs. Truly virulent public attacks on the police or the judiciary are rare, however, since the relationship between journalists and these institutions is ongoing and valuable; no newspaper or broadcast outlet can afford to burn such bridges. Apart from publicity, journalists can enhance the overall legitimacy of the justice system by covering its activities. Public confidence that the police are behaving appropriately or that the judicial system "works" can be maintained simply through routine coverage of crime. Stories that challenge that confidence may be presented as aberrations from an otherwise upbeat routine.

Pritchard and Hughes demonstrate the practical result of these dependency relations. They studied the newspaper coverage of a year's worth of homicides in Milwaukee, Wisconsin, with attention to the factors that determine whether a murder will merit coverage or not. They found that "reporters tended to take cues for evaluations of newsworthiness from race, gender, and age" (p. 52), information about both victims and suspects usually available from official sources. Deadline pressure seems to encourage reporters and editors to use such attributes to calculate the extent and nature of "deviance" the murder involves. While conventional wisdom describes newsworthiness in terms of "statistical deviance" (i.e., departure from the usual, as in "man bites dog"), Pritchard and Hughes show that "status deviance" (i.e., the death or suspect-status of high status citizens) and cultural deviance (i.e., murder of the "especially vulnerable," such as women, children, and the aged) explains the decision to cover or ignore a homicide (p. 52).

Pritchard had earlier (1986) demonstrated that coverage of homicides in Milwaukee was a strong predictor of whether or not the prosecuting attorney would plea-bargain the case. Murders that received more coverage in the newspapers were less likely to be bargained than low-publicity crimes. Pritchard notes that this finding is consistent with earlier research (Alschuler; Jones) regarding the decision-making of prosecutors that indicated that political considerations (e.g., fear of being seen as "soft on crime") exercised strong influence on prosecutors' decisions. Further, Pritchard, Dilts, and Berkowitz demonstrated that prosecution of pornography offenses in Indiana in the mid-1980s was influenced by the relative priority of pornography on the agendas of citizens and of the local newspapers.

The cumulative impact of Pritchard and others' work is to illustrate that reporters and editors are most likely to report crimes based on certain attributes of the victims and suspects, and that prosecutors monitor press coverage and choose which crimes to prosecute aggressively based in part on the level of press attention the crime has received. Since the criteria of reporters tend toward coverage of white victims and victims who are either female, very young, or very old (or some combination of those attributes), the least likely crime to be covered is one in which the victim is a black adult male. Thus the least likely crime to be aggressively prosecuted is one committed against a black adult male.

Defendants and defense attorneys are less likely to benefit from these relations of dependency. A guilty criminal defendant has no interest in sharing details of a crime, of course, and innocent defendants have no details to offer. Even if defendants do have valuable information, they are unlikely to have valuable information on a regular basis for years to come, the way police and judicial officers do. Defense attorneys are a bit more likely to be valuable sources in the future, but not nearly as likely as prosecutors. There is much more crime in the world than there is coverage of it, so most defense attorneys most times will not be defending newsworthy clients. But *all* newsworthy prosecutions are performed by a handful of offices, from city attorneys to federal prosecutors. Given a choice between developing close, mutually rewarding relationships with defendants or prosecutors, a

working reporter knows where his or her professional future is most safely insured. Robert Shapiro, a prominent defense attorney (and member of O.J. Simpson's "Dream Team") noted that "[t]he defense lawyer who has never dealt with the press, or has no pre-existing relationship with a particular reporter, is at a severe disadvantage. In order to overcome this, the lawyer must cultivate a line of communication with the reporter so the client's point of view can be expressed in the most favorable way" (p. 27).

One effect of crime coverage on the judicial process that has received considerable research attention is the influence of pretrial publicity on jurors. Partly due to the pattern of dependency relations described above, it has been noted that most coverage of crime is detrimental to the defendant, including the publication of information inadmissible at trial (Imrich, Mullin, and Linz; Dixon and Linz). Does this bad publicity produce predispositions in jurors one way or the other? A variety of experimental and quasi-experimental research studies have demonstrated consistent support for the hypothesis that at least mild antidefendant bias can be the result of exposure to pretrial publicity (Constantini and King; Dexter, Cutler, and Moran; Greene and Wade; Kramer, Kerr, and Carroll; Kerr, Kramer, Carroll, and Alfini; Moran and Cutler; Ogloff and Vidmar; Otto, Penrod, and Dexter). Judicial remedies such as voir dire, judges' instructions, and continuances are not guaranteed to overcome these effects (Kramer et al.; Carroll et al.; Vidmar and Melnitzer; Dexter et al.; Kerr et al.). Bruschke and Loges, however, found that the conviction rate for federal murder defendants whose cases received no discernible print coverage did not differ significantly from the conviction rate of defendants whose cases received high amounts of print coverage. In fact, Bruschke and Loges found that the highest conviction rate was observed among those who had between one and five stories written about their case. Once convicted, however, defendants with the most publicity received substantially longer prison sentences than those with little or no publicity.

The effect of pretrial (and during-trial) publicity on public opinion and jury bias can lead to policies such as gag rules (prohibiting trial participants from publicly discussing the case), restriction of court access to the press—particularly TV cameras—and changes of venue. Salwen and Driscoll point out that support for media regulation may spring from a "third-person effect" in which a person believes that others are prone to media influence while he or she is much less prone to the same effect. Studying public opinion regarding conflicting evidence and arguments during the murder trial of O.J. Simpson, Salwen and Driscoll found that there is a significant tendency for survey respondents to estimate higher media influence for others than for themselves, but that this belief is not strongly associated with calls for regulation of the press, particularly among well-educated respondents. While education in general may reduce one's willingness to endorse media regulation, it is not clear whether judges subject to the third-person effect might be more willing to impose restrictions given their unique role in the judicial process, despite their high levels of education. McLeod, Eveland, and Nathanson (1997) found that support for censorship of rap lyrics thought to incite misogyny and violence was associated with a third-person effect, although their college-student sample made it impossible to control for education.

Another approach to the study of news content and its effect on public opinion is framing. "Framing essentially involves *selection* and *salience*. To frame is to *select some aspects of a perceived reality and make them more salient in a communicating text, in such a way as to promote a particular problem definition, causal interpretation, moral evaluation, and/or treatment recommendation for the item described*" (Entman, 1993, p. 52, emphases in original). Research into the methods journalists use to reconstruct reality into "the news" has focused on the use of framing devices to turn events into coherent stories (Kahneman and Tversky; Graber; Sniderman, Brody, and Tetlock). Entman (1994) has argued that by showing visual images of black suspects and defendants in the grasp of white police officers, television news frames blacks as both more dangerous and under more direct physical control than whites (who are less likely to be shown in the physical grasp of an officer—especially a nonwhite officer). Dixon (1998) finds that black suspects are disproportionately shown on the news (compared to their proportion of arrested suspects in crime reports). The concept of framing suggests that such patterns of representation increase the salience of connections between blacks and crime in general, and thus perpetuate stereotypes of both black criminality and white authority.

Entertainment

The possibility that exposure to mass media entertainment—from comic books to the Internet—can inspire criminal behavior was the subject of research, speculation, and debate throughout the twentieth century. Some content is considered more suspect than others, particularly depictions of violence. Since 1950, violent television fare has been the subject of a great deal of research, and meta-analyses of this body of research tend to conclude that there is a consistent, moderate causal relationship between exposure to televised violence and aggressive behavior in the real world (Hearold; Paik and Comstock; Hogben). Various theoretical explanations for the link have been offered, notably including social learning (Bandura), excitation transfer (Zillmann, Hoyt, and Day), and disinhibition, or desensitization (Berkowitz and Rawlings; Thomas, Horton, Lippincott, and Drabman).

Not all aggressive behavior is criminal, of course. The laboratory studies that lead to the conclusion that exposure to televised violence causes more aggressive behavior in real life are frequently criticized for not being sufficiently realistic to be generalized to the potential for truly dangerous, criminal behavior outside the laboratory. This criticism is deflected somewhat by research using other methods, including large sample surveys, quasi-experiments (using a more realistic setting with naive subjects unaware that they are under observation) and "found experiments" (in which public records are searched for evidence of pre- and post-exposure effects) (Phillips), all of which tend to support the conclusion that a persistent but moderate effect on aggressive behavior can be traced to exposure to violent media.

Three particular subjects receive the bulk of research attention where entertainment-related effects are concerned: (1) the effects of any violent media on children; (2) the "cultivation" of beliefs about crime and the criminal justice system that results from viewing television; and (3) the effects of pornography on adults. It is frequently noted that by the time an American child reaches adolescence he or she is likely to have seen thousands of murders depicted on television (e.g., Huston et al's, calculation that by the time a child leaves elementary school he or she will have seen eight thousand murders) (cited in Bogart, p. 351). In the 1990s the increasing popularity of computer games that simulate wholesale slaughter of human beings (e.g., *Doom* and

Quake) has led to speculation that the wave of school shootings of the late 1990s has roots in part in the skills (such as arming, evaluating killed or wounded status, and strategizing) cultivated by playing such games and in the indifference toward suffering that leads to success in the games (Grossman).

Cultivation theory hypothesizes that television's depiction of the world leads heavy viewers of television to believe that the real world resembles the television world in key respects, including the likelihood of crime and the proportion of people involved in the criminal justice system (Gerbner, Gross, Morgan, and Signorielli). Carlson (1985) studied the content of crime shows in the late 1970s and the attitudes toward the criminal justice system held by viewers of these shows. He found that the crime shows on television in the late 1970s presented a very unrealistic view of the criminal justice system, specifically including the effectiveness of police, the rights of suspects and defendants, and the general level of criminal activity in the world. People who watch these shows report more support for authorities such as police, less support for civil liberties, and more political cynicism. Carlson notes that the consistent messages of crime shows may result in "an increase in demand for police protection" (p. 195) since police are portrayed as extraordinarily effective and crime as rampant. It should be noted, however, that the sort of crime shows Carlson examined were qualitatively different from the shows that emerged in the 1980s, beginning with *Hill Street Blues*. These later shows, many produced by Stephen Bochco, have featured flawed police who often fail to catch their suspects, and open criminals as recurring characters who appear immune to capture. The effects of such programs would, by Carlson's logic, result in mistrust of police and perhaps even more generalized cynicism.

Shrum and Mares each have attempted to explain the psychological processes by which cultivation occurs. Shrum points to the accessibility of heuristics, whereby it is easier for heavy viewers of television to rely on the impression TV makes on them when they answer questions about the real world than it would be for heavy viewers to search their minds and make a more elaborate—and perhaps accurate—calculation. Mares argues that respondents are not always aware of where their information comes from, and thus "source confusion" accounts for people's tendency to describe the real world in television terms. Potter, Warren, and others point out that even if viewers limit their exposure to non-fiction programs, such as news and news magazines (e.g., *20/20*), they are likely to end up with distorted impressions of the real world. The authors compare nonfiction TV depictions of antisocial behavior to real-world statistics. "If we rely on non-fiction programming to tell us about the parameters and nature of our society, that programming is constructing narratives that are not particularly useful for that purpose. Nonfictional television presents a very high rate of antisocial activity, and the most serious forms of that activity (physical violence and crime) are presented at rates far above the rates in the real world" (p. 86).

While fears regarding children's exposure to violent media are mostly centered on the likelihood that children will imitate or learn the criminal behavior they see, concerns about adults' exposure to pornography also include the impact of such exposure on such decisions as jury verdicts in rape trials (Linz, Donnerstein, and Penrod) and acceptance of "rape myths," for example, that women only pretend to resist rape (Allen, Emmers, Gebhardt, and Giery). Adults play many roles in the criminal justice system that make their attitudes toward crime important. If, as Linz and others demonstrate, exposure to pornography can affect jurors' decisions, voir dire in rape cases might benefit from questions about such exposure (if potential jurors could be counted on to respond to voir dire inquiries on this subject truthfully).

Conclusion

It is not always easy to define the ideal relationship between the media system and the criminal justice system. The goals and resources of the media do not mesh perfectly with those of prosecutors, defendants, judges, and police. The goals and resources that people possess as audiences and readers are different from the goals and resources those same people possess in other roles they play, as citizens, jurors, suspects, and consumers. The ongoing negotiation between the media, the justice system, and people in their various relevant roles produces the media effects observed in the research fields reviewed here (Ball-Rokeach). Many of these effects may be unintended or undesirable, but mitigating such effects as prejudicial pretrial publicity is often not possible without threatening goals that others consider paramount, such as press freedom or the desire of a prosecutor to try a case locally (i.e., avoiding a change of venue).

When goals are in conflict, and resources are scarce or fought over, the relative power of the parties to the conflict becomes the central issue. There is doubt that the ability of the media to influence the course of criminal justice is entirely legitimate or desirable, especially when that influence stems from the increasing dominance of the media's entertainment over its journalistic function. But the media are powerful enough to resist intrusive public policy and defend their resources (such as access to sources, control over their broadcast schedules, and use of information-gathering tactics such as hidden cameras). The justice system has powerful resources of its own to use to pursue its goals when they conflict with the media's. It is the public, particularly when the public is atomized, whose goals are least likely to receive support and benefit from rich resources when they are threatened by the goals of the media or the justice system. As Potter and Warren point out in their discussion of policies regarding the regulation of sex and violence on television, the political influence of the broadcasting industry allows the media to tie up regulators over definitional issues (What is sex? What is violence?), rendering public policy to limit such content ineffective.

We began and ended the twentieth century with a nervous tension of conflict and cooperation between the media and criminal justice systems. In nontotalitarian societies this tension is unavoidable as the goals and interests of these systems differ. A question for the twenty-first century is whether the delicate balance of power between these players will give way. A major concern is the trendline of increasing distrust of major social institutions, especially when combined with an apparent decline in the strength of commitment to civic society (Putnam, 1995). In other words, the relationship between the media and criminal justice systems is a dynamic one that reflects changes in the larger social and political environment where conceptions of justice and community are formed. For the criminal justice system to have legitimacy for its just administration of the criminal law and for the media system to have legitimacy for its contributions to civil society, each must be regarded as playing vital roles in furtherance of a democratic order that commands the allegiance of its citizens. In short, justice must remain part of the crime story, whether told by the criminal justice system or by the media.

BILL LOGES
SANDRA BALL-ROKEACH

See also CRIME CAUSATION: PSYCHOLOGICAL THEORIES; FEAR OF CRIME; PUBLICITY IN CRIMINAL CASES; PUBLIC OPINION AND CRIME.

BIBLIOGRAPHY

ALLEN, MIKE; EMMERS, TARA; GEBHARDT, LISA; and GIERY, MARY A. "Exposure to Pornography and Acceptance of Rape Myths." *Journal of Communication* 45, no. 1 (1995): 5–26.

ALSCHULER, A. "The Prosecutor's Role in Plea Bargaining." *University of Chicago Law Review* 36 (1968): 50–112.

BALL-ROKEACH, SANDRA J. "The Origins of Individual Media-System Dependency: A Sociological Framework." *Communication Research* 12, no. 4 (1985): 485–510.

BALL-ROKEACH, S. J., and DE FLEUR, L. B. "Media and Crime." In *Encyclopedia of Crime and Justice*. Edited by Sanford H. Kadish. New York: Macmillan, 1983. Pages 1021–1027.

BANDURA, ALBERT. "Social Cognitive Theory of Mass Communication." In *Media Effects: Advances in Theory and Research*. Edited by Jennings Bryant and Dolf Zillmann. Mahwah, N.J.: Lawrence Erlbaum Associates, 1994.

BENNETT, W. LANCE. *News: The Politics of Illusion*, 3d ed. White Plains, N.Y.: Longman, 1996.

BERKOWITZ, L., and RAWLINGS, E. "Effects of Film Violence on Inhibitions Against Subsequent Aggression." *Journal of Abnormal and Social Psychology* 66 (1963): 405–412.

BOGART, LEO. *Commercial Culture: The Media System and the Public Interest*. New York: Oxford University Press, 1995.

BRUSCHKE, JON, and LOGES, WILLIAM E. "The Relationship Between Pretrial Publicity and Trial Outcomes." *Journal of Communication* 49, no. 4 (1999): 104–120.

CARLSON, JAMES M. *Prime Time Law Enforcement: Crime Show Viewing and Attitudes toward the Criminal Justice System*. New York: Praeger, 1985.

CARROLL, J. S.; KERR, N. L.; ALFINI, J. J.; WEAVER, F. M.; MACCOUN, R. J.; and FELDMAN, V. "Free Press and Fair Trial: The Role of Behavioral Research." *Law and Human Behavior* 10 (1986): 187–201.

CONSTANTINI, E., and KING, J. "The Partial Juror: Correlates and Causes of Prejudgment." *Law and Society Review* 15 (1980–1981): 9–40.

DEXTER, H. R.; CUTLER, B. L.; and MORAN, G. "A Test of Voir Dire as a Remedy for the Prejudicial Effects of Pretrial Publicity." *Journal of Applied Social Psychology* 22 (1992): 819–832.

DIXON, TRAVIS L. *Overrepresentation and Underrepresentation of Blacks and Latinos as Lawbreakers on Television News.* Paper presented at the Meeting of the International Communication Association, Jerusalem, Israel (July, 1998).

DIXON, TRAVIS L., and LINZ, DANIEL. "Television News, Prejudicial Pretrial Publicity, and the Depiction of Race." Paper presented to the Annual Meeting of the International Communication Association, San Francisco, Calif., 1999.

ENTMAN, ROBERT M. "Framing: Toward Clarification of a Fractured Paradigm." *Journal of Communication* 43, no. 4 (1993): 51–58.

———. "Representation and Reality in the Portrayal of Blacks on Network Television News." *Journalism Quarterly* 71 (1994): 509–520.

GERBNER, GEORGE; GROSS, LARRY; MORGAN, MICHAEL; and SIGNORIELLI, NANCY. "Growing Up With Television: The Cultivation Perspective." In *Perspectives on Media Effects.* Edited by Jennings Bryant and Dolf Zillmann. Hillsdale, N.J.: Lawrence Erlbaum Associates, 1994.

GRABER, DORIS. *Processing the News: How People Tame the Information Tide,* 2d ed. New York: Longman, 1988.

GREENE, E. L., and WADE, R. "Of Private Talk and Public Print: General Pretrial Publicity and Juror Decision-Making." *Applied Cognitive Psychology* 1 (1988): 1–13.

GROSSMAN, DAVE. "We Are Training Our Kids to Kill." *Saturday Evening Post,* July–August 1999, pp. 64–72.

HEAROLD, SUSAN. "A Synthesis of 1043 Effects of Television on Social Behavior." *Public Communication and Behavior* 1 (1986): 65–134.

HOGBEN, MATTHEW. "Factors Moderating the Effect of Televised Aggression on Viewer Behavior." *Communication Research* 25, no. 2 (1998): 220–247.

IMRICH, DOROTHY J.; MULLIN, CHARLES; and LINZ, DANIEL. "Measuring the Extent of Prejudicial Pretrial Publicity in Major American Newspapers: A Content Analysis." *Journal of Communication* 45, no. 3 (1995): 94–117.

JONES, J. B. "Prosecutors and the Disposition of Criminal Cases: An Analysis of Plea Bargaining Rates." *Journal of Criminal Law and Criminology* 69 (1978): 402–412.

KAHNEMAN, D., and TVERSKY, A. "Choice, Values, and Frames." *American Psychologist* 39 (1984): 341–350.

KERR, N. L.; KRAMER, G. P.; CARROLL, J. S.; and ALFINI, J. J. "On the Effectiveness of Voir Dire in Criminal Cases with Prejudicial Pretrial Publicity: An Empirical Study." *The American University Law Review* 40 (1991): 665–693.

KRAMER, G. P.; KERR, N. L.; and CARROLL, J. S. "Pretrial Publicity, Judicial Remedies, and Jury Bias." *Law and Human Behavior* 14 (1990): 409–438.

LINZ, DANIEL; DONNERSTEIN, EDWARD; and PENROD, STEVEN. "The Effects of Multiple Exposures to Filmed Violence Against Women." *Journal of Communication* 34, no. 3 (1984): 130–147.

MARES, MARIE-LOUISE. "The Role of Source Confusion in Television's Cultivation of Social Reality Judgments." *Human Communication Research* 23, no. 2 (1996): 278–297.

McLEOD, DOUGLAS M.; EVELAND, WILLIAM P., JR.; and NATHANSON, AMY I. "Support for Censorship of Violent and Misogynic Rap Lyrics: An Analysis of the Third-Person Effect." *Communication Research* 24, no. 2 (1997): 153–174.

McMANUS, JOHN. "A Market-Based Model of News Production." *Communication Theory* 5, no. 4 (1995): 301–338.

MORAN, G., and CUTLER, B. L. "The Prejudicial Impact of Pretrial Publicity." *Journal of Applied Social Psychology* 21 (1991): 345–367.

OGLOFF, J. R. P., and VIDMAR, N. "The Impact of Pretrial Publicity on Jurors: A Study to Compare the Relative Effects of Television and Print Media in a Child Sex Abuse Case." *Law and Human Behavior* 5 (1994): 507–525.

OTTO, A. L.; PENROD, S. D.; and DEXTER, H. R. "The Biasing Impact of Pretrial Publicity on Juror Judgments." *Law and Human Behavior* 18 (1994): 453–469.

PAIK, HAEJUNG, and COMSTOCK, GEORGE. "The Effects of Television Violence on Antisocial Behavior: A Meta-Analysis." *Communication Research* 21, no. 4 (1994): 516–546.

PHILLIPS, DAVID P. "The Found Experiment: A New Technique for Assessing the Impact of Mass Media Violence on Real-World Aggressive Behavior." *Public Communication and Behavior* 1 (1986): 259–307.

POTTER, W. JAMES, and WARREN, RON. "Considering Policies to Protect Children from TV Violence." *Journal of Communication* 46, no. 4 (1996): 116–138.

POTTER, W. JAMES; WARREN, RON; VAUGHAN, MISHA; HOWLEY, KEVIN; LAND, ART; and HAGEMEYER, JEREMY. "Antisocial Acts in Reality Programming on Television." *Journal of Broadcasting and Electronic Media* 41, no. 1 (1997): 69–89.

PRITCHARD, DAVID. "Homicide and Bargained Justice: The Agenda-Setting Effect of Crime News on Prosecutors." *Public Opinion Quarterly* 50 (1986): 143–159.

PRITCHARD, DAVID; DILTS, PAUL; and BERKOWITZ, DAN. "Prosecutors' Use of External Agendas in Prosecuting Pornography Cases." *Journalism Quarterly* 64 (1985): 392–398.

PRITCHARD, DAVID, and HUGHES, KAREN D. "Patterns of Deviance in Crime News." *Journal of Communication* 47, no. 3 (1997): 49–67.

PUTNAM, R. D. "Tuning In, Tuning Out: The Strange Disappearance of Social Capital in America. The 1995 Ithiel de Sola Pool Lecture." *Political Science and Politics* 28 (1995): 664–683.

SALWEN, MICHAEL B., and DRISCOLL, PAUL D. "Consequences of Third-Person Perception in Support of Press Restrictions in the O.J. Simpson Trial." *Journal of Communication* 47, no. 2 (1997): 60–78.

SHAPIRO, ROBERT. "Secrets of a Celebrity Lawyer." *Columbia Journalism Review* 33, no. 3 (1994): 25–29.

SHRUM, L. J. "Assessing the Social Influence of Television: A Social Cognition Perspective on Cultivation Effects." *Communication Research* 22, no. 4 (1995): 402–429.

SNIDERMAN, P. M.; BRODY, R. A.; and TETLOCK, P. E. *Reasoning and Choice: Explorations in Political Psychology.* Cambridge, U.K.: Cambridge University Press, 1991.

THOMAS, M. H.; HORTON, R. W.; LIPPINCOTT, E. C.; and DRABMAN, R. S. "Desensitization to Portrayals of Real-Life Aggression as a Function of Exposure to Television Violence." *Journal of Personality and Social Psychology* 35 (1977): 450–458.

VIDMAR, N., and MELNITZER, J. "Juror Prejudice: An Empirical Study of a Challenge for Cause." *Osgoode Hall Law Journal* 22 (1984): 487–511.

WINCH, SAMUEL P. *Mapping the Cultural Space of Journalism: How Journalists Distinguish News from Entertainment.* Westport, Conn.: Praeger, 1997.

ZILLMANN, DOLF; HOYT, J.; and DAY, K. "Strength and Duration of the Effect of Aggressive, Violent, and Erotic Communications on Subsequent Aggressive Behavior." *Communication Research* 1 (1974): 286–306.

MENS REA

Mens rea, or "guilty mind," marks a central distinguishing feature of criminal law. An injury caused without mens rea might be grounds for civil liability but typically not for criminal. Criminal liability requires not only causing a prohibited harm or evil—the actus reus of an offense—but also a particular state of mind with regard to causing that harm or evil.

For a phrase so central to criminal law, *mens rea* suffers from a surprising degree of confusion in its meaning. One source of confusion arises from the two distinct ways in which the phrase is used, in a broad sense and in a narrow sense. In its broad sense, *mens rea* is synonymous with a person's blameworthiness, or more precisely, those conditions that make a person's violation sufficiently blameworthy to merit the condemnation of criminal conviction. In this broad sense, the phrase includes all criminal law doctrines of blameworthiness—mental requirements of an offense as well as excuse defenses such as insanity, immaturity, and duress, to name a few. This was a frequent usage of *mens rea* at common law. It remains common among nonlegal disciplines such as philosophy and psychology, perhaps because it captures in a single phrase criminal law's focus on personal culpability.

The modern meaning of mens rea, and the one common in legal usage today, is more narrow: mens rea describes the state of mind or inattention that, together with its accompanying conduct, the criminal law defines as an offense. In more technical terms, the mens rea of an offense consists of those elements of the offense definition that describe the required mental state of the defendant at the time of the offense, but does not include excuse defenses or other doctrines outside the offense definition. To help distinguish this more narrow conception from the broader, the Model Penal Code drafters substitute the term *culpability* for *mens rea*. Thus, Model Penal Code section 2.02, governing the Code's offense mental states, is titled "General Requirements of Culpability" and subsection (2), defining the offense mental elements employed by the Code, is titled "Kinds of Culpability." Unfortunately, the term *culpability* has come to suffer some of the same confusion between broad and narrow meanings as the term *mens rea*. While most frequently used in its narrow sense, as interchangeable with *offense mental elements*, *culpability* is sometimes used in a broad sense, as interchangeable with *blameworthiness*. The meaning of both *mens rea* and *culpability* must often be determined from their context.

The development of mens rea

The law did not always require mens rea for liability. Early Germanic tribes, it is suggested, imposed liability upon the causing of an injury, without regard to culpability. But this was during a period before tort law and criminal law divided. It seems likely that as the distinction between tort and crime appeared—that is, as the function of compensating victims became distinguished from the function of imposing punishment—the requirement of mens rea took on increasing importance.

The phrase *mens rea* appears in the Leges Henrici description of perjury—*reum non facit nisi mens rea*—which was taken from a sermon by St. Augustine concerning that crime. The sermon is also thought to be the source of the similar maxim in Coke's *Third Institutes*, the first major study of English criminal law: *"actus non facit reum nisi mens sit rea"* (the act is not guilty unless the mind is guilty). The Church had much influence on the development of this part of English law for several reasons. First, it preached the importance of spiritual values and mental states to a wide audience. Physical misconduct was significant only because it manifested spiritual failure; it was the inner weakness that was the essence of moral wrong. For example, "Whoever looketh on a woman to lust after her hath committed adultery with her already in his heart" (Matthew 5:27–28). Second, clerics were influential in the administration of government and governmental policy, both because they were among the few who could read and write and because of the Church's own political power. And third, the Church had its own courts, for trying clergy. In these courts new offenses were developed that put the new ideas of the importance of mental state into criminal law form.

While Christian thought on mens rea had a dominant influence over its development in English law, similar concepts are found in nearly all criminal laws, often without a history of Christian influence. The cross-cultural presence of concepts like mens rea provides some evidence that the notion of moral blameworthiness expressed by the broad conception of *mens rea* arises from shared human intuitions of justice and would have developed in English law through some other means, if not through the spread of Christian thought.

Once adopted as a basic principle of criminal law, the legal meaning of mens rea continued to evolve. The early stages of its development are illustrated by the decision in *Regina v. Prince* (13 Cox's Criminal Cases 138 (1875)). The defendant took an underage girl "out of the possession" of her father, reasonably believing she was over the age of consent. That the defendant's conduct was generally immoral was sufficient for Lord Bramwell to find that the defendant had the mens rea necessary for criminal liability. Lord Brett, on the other hand, would require that Prince at least have intended to do something that was criminal, not just immoral.

A somewhat more demanding requirement is expressed in *Regina v. Faulkner* (13 Cox's Criminal Cases 550 (1877)). In the process of stealing rum from the hold of a ship, a sailor named Faulkner accidentally set the ship afire, destroying it. Building upon Lord Brett's conception of a more specific and demanding mens rea, Lords Fitzgerald and Palles concluded that the mens rea requirement meant that Faulkner must have at least intended to do something criminal that might reasonably have been expected to have led to the actual harm for which he was charged. Thus, Faulkner ought not be liable for the offense of burning a ship when he intended only to steal rum from it; stealing in the normal course of things, does not lead one to reasonably foresee that a ship will be destroyed.

This last shift in the notion of mens rea marked not only a dramatic increase in the demand of the requirement, but also a significant qualitative change. No longer did there exist a single mens rea requirement for all offenses—the intention to do something immoral or, later, something criminal. Now each offense had a different mens rea requirement—the mens rea required for the offense of burning a ship was different from the mens rea required for the offense of theft. Liability now required that a person intend to do something that might reasonably be expected to lead to the harm of the particular offense charged. As some have expressed it, there is no longer a mens rea for criminal liability but rather *mentes reae*.

Common Law often grouped offenses according to whether an offense required a *specific intent* or a *general intent*. The categorization had practical significance. For a specific intent offense, a reasonable mistake often was a defense, while for a general intent offense only a reasonable mistake was a defense. Voluntary intoxication could provide a defense to a specific intent offense but not a general intent offense. The distinction has been largely abandoned, however, because it rested upon no coherent conception, which made it difficult to determine reliably into which category an offense fell. Further, it became apparent that the distinction assumed that each offense had a single kind of mens rea—a general intent or a specific intent—when in fact the law's practical operation showed increasingly that no such generalization could be made. Courts increasingly found that their desired mens rea formulations applied one kind of mens rea to one element of an offense and a different kind to other elements.

The Model Penal Code carried this insight to its logical conclusion. Section 2.02(1) requires the proof of culpability "with respect to each material element of the offense." In what might be termed a shift from *offense analysis* to *element analysis*, the Code expressly allows offense definitions in which a different level of culpability is required as to different elements of the same offense.

This element analysis approach—defining required culpability as to each offense element rather than as to each offense—provided, for the first time, a comprehensive statement of the culpability required for an offense. The early conceptions of mens rea were not simply undemanding, they were hopelessly vague and incomplete. They failed to tell courts enough about the required culpability for an offense to enable them to resolve the cases that commonly arose. For example, a prior case might tell a court that intentionally destroying a person's house was arson. But what results if the person intended the destruction but mistakenly believed she was destroying her own house? The previously announced intention requirement did not speak to what culpable state of mind was required as to the ownership of the building. A prior case might say intentionally killing a viable fetus was a crime. Was the defendant liable even if she reasonably (but mistakenly) believed the fetus was not viable? What culpable state of mind was required as to the viability of the fetus? When the mens rea requirement is unspecified or vague, it is left to the courts to decide ad hoc, and necessarily ex post facto, the precise culpability required for the offense. Element analysis permitted legislatures to reclaim from the courts the authority to define the conditions of criminal liability and, for the first time, to provide a comprehensive statement of the culpability required for an offense.

The shift to element analysis, then, was not so much an attempt to change the traditional offense requirements, as it was to make them complete. Common law lawyers and judges were wrong to think that their offense-analysis view of culpability requirements was adequate to describe the required culpability. Their misconception stemmed in part from their conceptualization of an independent "law of mistake," which they saw as supplementing the culpability requirements of an offense definition. Thus, a person might satisfy the requirements of theft by intentionally taking someone else's property, yet have a defense if the law of mistake allowed a defense in the situation, such as when the defendant reasonably believed the property was his. To the common law mind, offense culpability requirements and the "law of mistake" that governed when a mistake provided a defense could be separate and independent doctrines.

The Model Penal Code drafters, in contrast, recognized that a mistake defense and an offense culpability requirement are one and the same. To say that negligence is required as to the victim's age in statutory rape is the same as saying that only a reasonable mistake as to age will provide a mistake defense. To say that recklessness is required as to "another person's property" in theft is the same as saying that only a reasonable or a negligent mistake will provide a mistake defense. This interchangeability between mistake defenses and culpability requirements informs Model Penal Code section 2.04(l)(a), which provides simply that mistake is a defense if it negates an offense culpability requirement. This is sometimes called the *rule of logical relevance* because it makes a person's mistake relevant to the determination of criminal liability only if the mistake is inconsistent with the existence of an offense culpability requirement.

The mens rea–actus reus distinction

Common law doctrine traditionally paired mens rea with actus reus. Liability required both a guilty mind and a bad act. It is unclear, however, whether this most basic organizing distinction is coherent and useful to our understanding of offense requirements.

The actus reus of an offense typically is described as including the conduct constituting the offense, as well as any required circumstances or results of the conduct. The conduct must include a voluntary act. Where a result is an offense element, proof of the actus reus requires proof that the person's conduct and the result stand in a certain relation, as defined by the doctrine of causation: the conduct must have caused the result. Not every offense is defined in terms of conduct, however. In the absence of an act, liability may be based upon an omission to perform a legal duty of which the person is physically capable, or upon a person's knowing possession of contraband for a period of time sufficient to terminate the possession; these elements are part of the actus reus of the offenses. Thus, the actus reus of an offense commonly is said to include the doctrines of causation, voluntary act, omission, possession, and the conduct, circumstance, and result elements of the offense definition.

Undoubtedly, the actus reus–mens rea distinction is an extension of the obvious difference between a person's conduct, which we can directly observe, and the person's intention, which we cannot. In the simple case—the person shoots another person intending to injure him—both the person's conduct and intention are prerequisites to liability. The concepts of actus reus and mens rea adequately capture these two facts and note the empirical difference between them. It is natural to broaden the mens rea requirement beyond an intention to injure, to include recklessness or negligence as to injuring another person (as when a person target shoots in the woods without paying adequate attention to the possibility of campers in the overshoot zone). Similarly, it is natural to expand the actus reus requirement beyond an affirmative act of shooting another to include cases of injuring another by failing to perform a legal duty (as in failing to feed one's child) and cases of possession of contraband (such as illegal drugs), even though these may occur without an affirmative act.

While such an evolution is understandable, even logical, it does not follow that the resulting distinction is one around which criminal law is properly conceptualized, for the resulting concepts of actus reus and mens rea have limited usefulness.

First, there is no unifying internal characteristic among either the actus reus doctrines or the mens rea doctrines. Aspects of the actus reus requirements are not all "acts" or even all objective in nature. For example, a circumstance element of an offense may be entirely abstract, such as "being married" in bigamy or "without license" in trespass. Indeed, actus reus elements may include purely subjective states of mind, such as the requirement of causing "fear" in robbery or the necessary absence of "consent" in rape. Nor are

the mens rea doctrines all state of "mind" requirements, or even subjective in nature. The mens rea element of negligence, for example, is neither subjective nor a state of mind, but rather a failure to meet an objective standard of attentiveness. Mens rea elements seem no more common in form than actus reus elements.

Further, the mens rea requirements and actus reus requirements do not serve functions distinct from one another. Most mens rea elements go to assess whether a violation is blameworthy, but so do many aspects of the actus reus, such as the voluntariness portion of the voluntary act requirement in commission offenses, the physical capacity requirement in omission offenses, and the possession offense requirement that the person have possession for a period sufficient to terminate possession. Similarly, while many aspects of the actus reus define the conduct that is criminal—specifically, the conduct and circumstance elements of the offense definition—some aspects of mens rea, such as the culpability requirements in inchoate offenses, serve the same function of defining the conduct that is prohibited. (That is, the conduct that will constitute an inchoate offense cannot be defined without reference to the offense's mens rea requirement—an intention to commit the completed offense. Conduct that constitutes an attempt is not a violation of the rules of conduct in the absence of the defendant's intention to commit an offense.)

In large part because of these difficulties, modern usage tends to avoid the mens rea–actus reus distinction. The closest substitute is the more modest distinction between "culpability" requirements and "objective" requirements of an offense definition. The former include those elements that require the defendant have a particular state of mind or negligence; the latter refer to all other offense requirements, commonly grouped into conduct, circumstances, and results.

Modern culpability levels

Aside from their insight into the relation between mistake defenses and culpability requirements, the Model Penal Code drafters' greatest contribution in this area is their use of a limited number of defined culpability terms. This aspect of the Code's scheme has been adopted with variations in nearly every American jurisdiction with a modern criminal code, a majority of the states. Even in jurisdictions that still have not enacted a modern code, the Model Penal Code is of enormous influence. Judges rely upon the Code culpability definitions and its official commentaries in creating the judge-made law that the old codes require by their incomplete statements of offense culpability requirements.

In place of the plethora of common law terms—wantonly, heedlessly, maliciously, and so on—the Code defines four levels of culpability: purposely, knowingly, recklessly, and negligently (from highest to lowest). Ideally, all offenses are defined by designating one of these four levels of culpability as to each objective element. If the objective elements of an offense require that a person take the property of another, the culpability elements might require, for example, that the person *know* that she is taking property and that she is at least *reckless* as to it being someone else's property. In each instance, and for each element of an offense, the legislature may set the culpability level at the minimum they think appropriate either to establish liability or to set off one grade of an offense from another.

When an offense definition requires a particular level of culpability as to a particular element, it means that the required culpability as to that element must exist at the time of the conduct constituting the offense. (Culpability at the time of the result, rather than the offense conduct, is neither necessary nor sufficient. Changing one's mind after setting a bomb does not bar liability for deaths caused by the blast, if the intent to kill existed when the bomb was set.) This *concurrence requirement*, as it is called, reflects the law's interest in judging the culpability of the act rather than the general character of the actor. The required concurrence between act and culpability is implicit in the language of the Model Penal Code's section 2.02(2) culpability definitions.

Modern codes give detailed definitions of each of the four culpability levels. As the Model Penal Code commentary explains:

The purpose of articulating these distinctions in detail is to advance the clarity of draftsmanship in the delineation of the definitions of specific crimes, to provide a distinct framework against which those definitions may be tested, and to dispel the obscurity with which the culpability requirement is often treated when such concepts as 'general criminal intent,' 'mens rea,' 'presumed intent,' 'malice,' 'wilfulness,' 'scienter' and the like have been employed. What Justice Jackson called 'the variety, disparity and confusion' of judicial definitions of 'the requisite but elusive mental element' in crime should, insofar as possible, be rationalized by a criminal code. (Model Penal Code § 2.02 comment at 230 (1985))

Under the Code's culpability scheme, the objective building blocks of offense definitions are conduct, circumstance, and result elements (although many offenses have no result element). The culpable levels are defined slightly differently but generally analogously with regard to each of these kind of objective elements. For the sake of simplicity, the following discussion focuses on culpability as to causing a result, such as death.

Under the Code, the highest level of culpability is "purpose." A person acts "purposely" with respect to a result if her conscious object is to cause such a result. While the criminal law generally treats a person's motive as irrelevant, the requirement of "purpose" is essentially a requirement that the person have a particular motive for acting, albeit a narrowly defined motive. The requirement does not make motive generally relevant, but only asks whether one specific motive was present, such as the purpose to gain sexual satisfaction required by the offense of indecent exposure. Thus, "flashing" another in order to surprise or annoy would not satisfy the required purpose and would not support liability for the offense.

In contrast to "purpose," which requires the person's conscious object to cause the result, a person acts only "knowingly" if she does not hope for the result but is practically certain that her conduct will cause it. The antiwar activist who sets a bomb to destroy draft board offices may be practically certain that the bomb will kill the night watchman yet may wish that the watchman would go on coffee break and not be killed. The essence of the narrow distinction between purpose and knowledge is the presence of a positive desire to cause the result as opposed to knowledge of its near certainty. In the broader sense, the distinction divides the vague notion of maliciousness or viciousness from the slightly less objectionable callousness.

Most common law courts and modern codes make clear that a person's deliberate blindness to a fact does not protect her from being treated as "knowing" that fact. For example, it is a common case law rule that one who drives across the border in a car with a secret compartment but carefully avoids actually knowing what is hidden in it can be held liable for knowingly transporting marijuana if it can be shown that "his ignorance in this regard was solely and entirely the result of his having made a conscious purpose to disregard the nature of that which was in the vehicle, with a conscious purpose to avoid learning the truth" (*United States v. Jewell*, 532 F.2d 697 (9th Cir. 1976)).

The Model Penal Code resolves this problem of "wilful blindness" of circumstances in a slightly different way. Section 2.02(7) provides: "When knowledge of the existence of a particular fact is an element of an offense, such knowledge is established if a person is aware of a high probability of its existence, unless he actually believes that it does not exist." Thus, the smuggler is held to "know" of the marijuana if he is aware of a high probability that it is there. (Note that this standard requires something less than the "practically certain" standard that the Code uses when defining "knowingly" as to causing a result.)

In contrast to "knowingly," a person acts "recklessly" if she is aware only of a substantial risk of causing the result. The narrow distinction between knowledge and recklessness lies in the degree of risk—"practically certain" versus "substantial risk"—of which the person is aware. The distinction marks the dividing line between what we tend to scold as careless (recklessness and negligence) and what we condemn as intentional (purposely and knowingly). In a very rough sense, the distinction between purpose and knowing, on the one hand, and reckless and negligent, on the other, also appropriates the common law distinction between specific intent and general intent.

While knowing and reckless culpability focus on the likelihood of causing the result— "practically certain" vs. "substantial risk"— purposeful culpability pays no regard to the likelihood of the result. Even if the chance of killing another is slight, a killing is purposeful if nonetheless is the person's "conscious object." This characteristic of the purpose requirement reflects an instinct that trying to cause the harm, whatever its likelihood, is more condemnable than acting with the belief that the harm will or might result without desiring it. The practical effect is that reckless conduct can be elevated to purposeful conduct if the person hopes that the risk will come to fruition. This characteristic of purpose also illustrates how specially demanding it is. When determining whether knowing or reckless requirements are met, a jury might logically deduce those culpability levels from other facts. They may conclude that a person "must have known" the certainty or the risk of harm if she knew this fact or that. A purpose requirement, on the other hand, requires the jury to de-termine a person's object or goal, a somewhat more complex probing of a defendant's psychological state. To uncover a "purpose," a jury may have to dig deeper into the person's psyche, her general desires and motivations. If a jury is conscientious in adhering to the proof-beyond-a-reasonable-doubt standard constitutionally required for offense elements, this may be a difficult conclusion to reach.

In contrast to acting "recklessly," which requires a person consciously to disregard a substantial risk, a person acts only "negligently" if she is unaware of a substantial risk of which she should have been aware. If it never occurs to a person that her conduct creates a prohibited risk, such as causing death, she can at most be held negligent in causing the death. Nor can negligent culpability be elevated to recklessness if the person is only cognizant of a risk of causing lesser injury. Absent a special rule, causing death while being aware of a risk of injury, but not death, will result in liability for negligent homicide, but not reckless homicide.

One might think that "negligence" has something to do with omissions. An omission occurs when one "neglects" to act. The terms seem to share a common root. Older cases sometimes suggest or assume such a connection, but it has long since been agreed that "negligence," when used to refer to a level of culpability, can apply as easily to a commission as to an omission. The crux of negligent culpability is the failure to perceive a risk of which one should be aware while doing either an act or failing to perform a legal duty. It is equally clear that one can have any level of culpability as to an omission, not just negligence. Where a parent fails to obtain needed medical care for a child and as a result the child dies, the parent may have been purposeful, knowing, reckless, negligent, or faultless as to allowing the resulting death. The parent may have failed to get medical care because she desired to cause the child's death; or, she may not have desired to cause the death, but she may have been practically certain that her omission would result in the death; or, she may have been aware only of a substantial risk; or, she may have been unaware of a substantial risk but should have been aware. Generally, the culpability requirements apply to omissions in the same way that they do to commissions.

The distinction between negligence and the three higher levels of culpability is one of the most critical to criminal law. A person who acts purposely, knowingly, recklessly is aware of the circumstances that make her conduct criminal and therefore is by all accounts both blameworthy and deterrable. A defendant who acts negligently, in contrast, is unaware of the circumstances and therefore, some writers argue, is neither blameworthy nor deterrable. While writers disagree over whether negligence ought to be adequate to support criminal liability, it is agreed that negligence represents a lower level of culpability than, and is qualitatively different from, recklessness. For this reason, recklessness is considered the norm for criminal culpability, while negligence is punished only in exceptional situations, as where a death is caused.

Recklessness and negligence share an important quality that distinguishes them from purpose and knowledge. The latter asks a specific empirical question. Did the person have the required purpose or practical certainty of causing the prohibited result? The culpability requirement of recklessness and negligence, on the other hand, require a normative rather than an empirical determination. The recklessness inquiry admittedly begins by asking whether the defendant had a particular state of mind—awareness of a specific risk—but then shifts to an inquiry into whether the disregard of that known risk was sufficiently blameworthy to support criminal liability. In the language of the Model Penal Code, the disregard of a specific risk is reckless and the failure to perceive a specific risk is negligence only if the disregard or failure to perceive "involves a gross deviation from the standard of care that a reasonable person would observe in the person's situation" (Model Penal Code § 2.02 (2)(c)&(d)). A jury can come to this conclusion only after making a judgment about what the reasonable person (the law's objective standard) would do in the situation, comparing the defendant's conduct to that of the reasonable person's, and then assessing the extent of the difference.

Further, it is generally understood, and intended by the Model Penal Code drafters, that the reasonable person standard to which the defendant is compared when determining recklessness or negligence is a standard properly adjusted to take account of the defendant's "situation." This may include not only the physical conditions but also the facts known to the defendant and even personal characteristics of the defendant. Such individualization of the objective reasonable person standard gives decisionmakers some leeway in making what is essentially a general blameworthiness judgment, one that is not possible in judging purpose or knowing. That such a general blameworthiness assessment is permitted in judging recklessness is made all the more significant by the fact that recklessness, recall, is the norm, the most common level of culpability in modern codes. The common law was much less likely to individualize the objective standard of recklessness and negligence, tending instead to ignore differences in education, intelligence, age, background, and the like. In contrast, it is the characteristic of a modern code to attempt to assess what might reasonably have been expected of the particular defendant given the "situation."

Disagreements over the minimum culpability requirement

There is some disagreement over the appropriate minimum level of culpability for criminal liability. Some argue that recklessness should be the minimum, that neither negligence nor strict liability—liability in the absence of proof of negligence—should be tolerated. Others argue that negligence is an appropriate basis but that anything short of negligence is inappropriate. Still others argue that strict liability ought to be permitted in select instances. In practice, while recklessness is the norm in current criminal law, criminal liability for negligence is common in select instances, as is even strict liability on occasion. Why these differences in opinion?

Recall, first, the basic contours of recklessness and negligence. Recklessness requires that the person actually be aware of a substantial risk that the prohibited result will occur or that the required circumstance exists. And the risk must be of a sort that a law-abiding person would not disregard. That is, not every instance of conscious risk-taking is culpable. Every time one drives a car or builds a bridge, one is likely to be aware of risks that such conduct creates. But many risks are well worth the taking, for taking the risk creates a good that outweighs the danger. Other risk-taking is not necessarily beneficial, but neither is it condemnable. The law's definition of recklessness is its attempt to distinguish proper risk-taking, or risk-taking that is not so improper as to be criminal, from risk-taking that is condemnable.

A similar challenge for the law arises in the context of negligence. Negligence, recall, differs from recklessness in that the person is not, but should be, aware of a substantial risk. It is not negligent to be unaware of every risk, for no person could be so aware. In any case, it would be a waste of time and energy for people to try. In defining negligence, the law attempts to specify those risks to which one ought to pay attention, those risks that are likely enough and serious enough in their consequence to justify attention. In the language of the Model Penal Code, "the risk must be of such a nature and degree that the person's failure to perceive it, considering the nature and purpose of his conduct and the circumstances known to him, involves a gross deviation from the standard of care that a reasonable person would observe in the person's situation" (Model Penal Code § 2.02 (2)(d)). The "gross deviation" requirement helps distinguish the civil standard of negligence in tort law from that in criminal law: even a failure to meet the objective test will not support criminal liability, since the failure must be a "gross deviation" from the standard.

It is easy to confuse *creating* a risk of harm with *taking* a risk that an offense circumstance exists or that one's conduct will cause a prohibited result. Creating a risk is altering the circumstances of the world in such a way as to create the possibility of a harm that did not previously exist. Risk-taking, in contrast, is a mental process: acting in disregard of a known risk. One can create a risk of fire by leaving the stove on when leaving the house. One takes a risk of a fire starting by leaving the house knowing that the stove might start a fire. It is the latter that is a form of a culpable state of mind; risk-creation typically is an objective element of endangerment offenses. Also, one creates a risk of causing a result, but one cannot create a risk that a circumstance exists. One can create a risk that a fire will start, but one cannot create a risk that one is exceeding the speed limit. One is either exceeding the limit at the present or is not. In other words, while risk-creation, the objective issue, concerns only results, risk-taking, the culpability issue, concerns both results and circumstances.

Nearly all agree that recklessness is an appropriate basis for criminal liability and, for that reason, it is the default culpability level read in by most modern codes when an offense definition is silent as to the required culpability. Negligence, however, is controversial for some. One argument against liability for negligence focuses on what is said to be the law's inability to deter negligent conduct. Where there is awareness of risk, as with recklessness, the threat of punishment may cause a person to avoid the risk. The

threat of criminal sanction can make the person pause, perhaps reconsider, before choosing to disregard the risk. In the case of negligence, in contrast, a person cannot be deterred, it is said, because she has no awareness of the facts that make her conduct criminal. It is argued that imposing liability in such a case is a futile and wasteful use of sanctioning resources.

The same argument can be used to challenge the retributivist grounds for punishing negligence. If a person is unaware of the circumstances that make her conduct criminal, how can it be said that she has chosen to do something that is or may be criminal, and on what grounds can her moral blameworthiness be based?

One might respond to the impossible-deterrence argument by noting that it is too narrow, for it focuses only on special deterrence. Punishing the negligent person may well serve general deterrence goals: it may cause others to pay closer attention to possible risks. Indeed, punishing the person who is unaware of the risk she takes might well send a more powerful message than punishing those who consciously take the risk, for such punishment tells the potential offender that inattentiveness will not provide a defense to liability. One also can point to other utilitarian arguments, such as the crime control value of convicting negligent people for incapacitative or rehabilitative purposes. Such liability would bring within the jurisdiction of the correctional system people who are needlessly inattentive, thereby protecting society from them.

A more direct response, however, is to challenge the underlying assumption of the impossible-deterrence argument that inattentiveness in the individual at hand cannot be deterred in the future by punishment for the present lapse. The evidence suggests that people can chose to pay more (or less) attention to their surroundings and the consequences of their conduct. If speeding were punished with the death penalty in all cases, presumably people would pay more attention to their speedometers. Further, if inattentiveness can be deterred, if it is not hopelessly inevitable, then there can be moral blame in the failure to be attentive. If a person can choose how attentive he or she is to a particular kind of risk-taking, the person can be blamed for not being as attentive as the situation demands.

One might argue, however, that while some people can meet the law's objective standard of attentiveness, others cannot. To punish a person who cannot, especially for reasons beyond the person's control, is to impose a form of strict liability. There can be no blameworthiness in failing to meet a standard that the person is incapable of meeting. Further, to make the utilitarian argument, a person ought not be encouraged to be too attentive. To hold people criminally liable for risk-taking of which they are not aware could create fear of liability that would infect all action, thereby incurring societal costs through a pervasive timidity that hinders possibly beneficial risk-taking activity. The net effect of negligence liability might therefore be an overly deterred society.

But the response to these arguments is found in the restrictions commonly placed upon the imposition of negligence liability in modern codes. As illustrated by the Model Penal Code's definition of negligence quoted above, a person is held negligent only if she fails to be reasonably attentive to risks; the reasonableness of her attentiveness is judged in light of "the circumstances known to her" and in her "situation." That is, she can be held liable only if the jury finds that the situation was such that she reasonably could have been expected to have been aware of the risk. And, even under this individualized objective standard, the defendant's failure to perceive the risk must be a "gross deviation" from what reasonably could have been expected in the situation.

Many of these same arguments are echoed in the debate over strict liability, although the conclusion of the analysis is different. While strict liability is viewed with suspicion and used sparingly, even modern codes commonly use it in two kinds of cases. First, strict liability is common for offenses labeled as only a "violation" or some other term designed to distinguish them from true criminal "offenses." These are instances where the criminal law is performing an essentially regulatory function. The liability imposed for such quasi-criminal offenses typically is limited to civil-like sanctions, such as a fine. Traffic offenses are an example. In a second group of serious offenses, strict liability is provided as to one particular element of the offense. For example, strict liability is sometimes provided as to the age of the victim in statutory rape, especially when the victim is in fact very young. These are the instances of greatest controversy. (Recall that the interchangeability of culpability requirements and mistake defenses means an offense may be made one of strict liability either by explicitly providing that no culpability is required or by providing that a reasonable mistake is no defense.)

It is precisely the above arguments in support of the use of negligence that argue most strongly against the use of strict liability. The test for negligence is set carefully to mark the precise contours of moral blameworthiness that supports criminal conviction (and to provide for the degree of attentiveness that we reasonably expect and want, no more, no less). Of particular note are the individualization of the objective standard by which offenders will be judged and the requirement that the failure of attentiveness be a "gross deviation" from even this individualized objective standard.

Thus, to punish violators in the absence of negligence under this carefully crafted standard is to punish persons without sufficient blameworthiness—they could not have been reasonably expected to have avoided the violation—and to risk demanding a degree of attentiveness that would be more costly to societal interests than can be justified. Indeed, strict liability, by disregarding the circumstances or the person's situation, mental and physical, inflicts punishment even on the person who acts perfectly reasonably even by a purely objective, unindividualized standard, as the common law frequently imposed.

Three sorts of arguments typically are given in support of strict liability: that strict liability is limited in application to situations where the person probably is at least negligent, that the use of strict liability will lead people to be more careful, and that only civil-like penalties are imposed for strict liability, so that no serious injustice is done.

First, it is argued that strict liability typically is limited to instances where a person necessarily is at least negligent, especially where the negligence bar is lowered by the increased seriousness of the offense. It seems unlikely that a person would not be at least negligent as to whether a sexual partner is under the age of ten, for example. Similarly, many states impose strict liability in holding a person liable for murder when an accomplice kills a person in the course of a felony, the so-called felony-murder rule. Many accomplices to a felony will be negligent as to contributing to such a death. They should have been aware that, by engaging in a felony where one of them planned to have a gun, for example, a death might result.

It may be true that some of the people convicted under these strict liability doctrines do in fact satisfy the requirements of negligence, but this will not be true for all persons convicted. Indeed, if we sought only to convict those who in fact were negligent, a negligence requirement would serve the purpose. Presumably the point of adopting strict liability instead of negligence is to allow liability to be imposed even in the absence of negligence.

In some cases, "under the circumstances known to [the person]," a reasonable person "in the person's situation" might well make a mistake as to a sexual partner being under ten years old. Yet strict liability, as the Model Penal Code provides in this instance, will impose significant liability in the absence of negligence, and therefore in the absence of blameworthiness. Similarly, the felony-murder rule will impose murder liability even if in the situation at hand no one could have guessed that there was any chance that someone would be killed. Unless negligence is explicitly required, liability can be imposed even if a person is clearly nonnegligent as to the offense.

One might argue that we can rely on the discretion of prosecutors to forego prosecution in such cases of nonnegligence, but others would claim that such an expectation is unrealistic and misguided. If we care about the demands of the legality principle, we will have criminal liability depend on written rules, not personal discretion. Further, the "trust discretion" argument essentially concedes that the law itself, when it adopts strict liability, fails to make the distinctions necessary for a just result.

A further defense of this negligence per se argument for strict liability points to the significant burden placed on prosecutors to prove negligence. The difficulties of negligence prosecution create a danger that blameworthy and dangerous people will go free. Moreover, negligence prosecutions may incur costs that strict liability prosecutions avoid.

A possible response to these arguments is to shift the burden of persuasion to the defendant on some culpability issues, instead of dropping the culpability requirement altogether. If a case can be made for the special difficulties of prosecution together with the special need for effective prosecution, then a rebuttable presumption will be employed to help the prosecutor. It will, in any case, be preferable from the defendant's point of view than the irrebuttable presumption of negligence that strict liability provides.

While this approach is used in other countries to limit the use of strict liability, it is forbidden in the United States because of broad constitutional rules that require the state to carry the burden of persuasion on all offense elements. Although the underlying sentiment seems sound, in this instance the Supreme Court's rule—together with the Court's constitutional approval of the use of strict liability—has created an unfortunate and somewhat inconsistent state of affairs.

A second line of argument in support of strict liability is the claim that its use will cause people to be more careful. This may be true; strict liability may make people more careful. What is left unclear is whether strict liability is more effective in this regard than negligence. The negligence standard requires a person to do all that he or she reasonably can be expected to do to be careful. What can the use of strict liability add to this? Strict liability might be able to encourage people to be even more careful than the circumstances reasonably would require. But this seems a questionable goal. As noted above, some risks ought to be taken and it may be harmful to society to have a person unreasonably preoccupied with all potential risks.

One might argue that, in a few instances, the potential harm is sufficiently serious that the law ought to do everything within its power to avoid a violation, and strict liability provides that special "super-punch." But this argument does not explain the current use of strict liability, which is most common in minor offenses and less common in more serious offenses. More importantly, the argument misunderstands the nature of negligence. In judging a person's negligence, the seriousness of the harm is taken into account. One's inattentiveness as to whether one is speeding might be nonnegligent, but the same degree of inattentiveness to a risk of hitting a pedestrian would be negligence. The negligence assessment takes account of both the likelihood of the harm risked and its seriousness, among other things. As the potential harm becomes greater, a person's ability to avoid negligence liability for inattentiveness disappears.

A final argument in support of strict liability focuses on its use primarily in minor offenses with minor penalties. When liability is imposed in the absence of culpability, it is argued, the penalties at stake—typically fines—make the prosecution essentially civil in nature. The argument finds support in modern codes, which commonly limit to some extent the available penalties when strict liability is imposed. As the Model Penal Code provides, "Notwithstanding any other provision of existing law and unless a subsequent statute otherwise provides, when absolute liability is imposed with respect to any material element of an offense defined by a statute other than the Code and a conviction is based upon such liability, the offense constitutes a violation" (Model Penal Code § 2.05 (2)(a)). And violations are offenses for which imprisonment is not authorized.

There are two difficulties with the minor penalties argument. First, as has been noted, strict liability is not in fact limited to minor offenses. Note, for example, that the Model Penal Code limitation applies only to "an offense defined by a statute other than the [criminal code]," thus allowing the imposition of lengthy imprisonment for offenses defined by the code, such as statutory rape of a person under age ten. Even if the use of strict liability were limited to minor offenses, however, the minor penalties argument is problematic. If strict liability is to be justified on the grounds that only minor, civil penalties such as fines are imposed, one may reasonably ask, Why not use civil liability?

One might counter that criminal procedures are faster and have other enforcement advantages. But if special procedures are needed, the legislature has the authority to alter the procedures for civil actions or create special procedures for a special group of civil violations. In fact, a primary reason the criminal process is preferred in most cases is its potential to impose the stigma associated with criminal liability.

It is true that the stigma of criminal conviction can provide a deterrent threat that civil liability does not. But to impose criminal liability where the violation is morally blameless—where normally only civil liability would be appropriate—is to dilute the moral credibility of the criminal law, which can have serious consequences for the criminal law's crime control power. As the criminal law is used to punish blameless offenders under strict liability, its ability to stigmatize is increasingly weakened and, therefore, so is its ability to deter. Each time the system seeks to stigmatize where condemnation is not deserved, it reduces incrementally its ability to stigmatize even in cases where it is deserved. Any advantage gained from using criminal law to punish blameless violations is purchased at a serious cost. This result is particularly troublesome because social scientists increasingly suggest that the criminal law's moral credibility plays a large part in its ability to gain compliance.

PAUL H. ROBINSON

See also ACTUS REUS; CAUSATION; CIVIL AND CRIMINAL DIVIDE; DETERRENCE; EXCUSE: THEORY; MISTAKE; PUNISHMENT; STRICT LIABILITY; VICARIOUS LIABILITY.

BIBLIOGRAPHY

AMERICAN LAW INSTITUTE. *Model Penal Code and Official Commentaries*. Philadelphia: ALI, 1985.

ASHWORTH, ANDREW. *Principles of Criminal Law.* 2d ed. Oxford, U.K.: Clarendon Law Series, 1995.

COKE, EDWARD. *The Third Part of the Institutes of the Laws of England: Concerning High Treason, and Other Pleas of the Crown, and Criminal Causes.* (1644). London: E. and R. Brooke, 1797.

FLETCHER, GEORGE P. "The Theory of Criminal Negligence: A Comparative Analysis." *University of Pennsylvania Law Review* 119 (1971): 401–415.

———. *Rethinking Criminal Law.* Boston: Little, Brown, 1978.

HALL, JEROME. *General Principles of Criminal Law.* 2d ed. Indianapolis: Bobbs-Merrill, 1960.

KADISH, SANFORD H. "The Decline of Innocence." *Cambridge Law Journal* 26 (1968): 273–290.

KELMAN, MARK. "Interpretative Construction in the Substantive Criminal Law." *Stanford Law Review* 33 (1981): 591–673.

PACKER, HERBERT L. "Mens Rea and the Supreme Court." *Supreme Court Review, 1962.* Chicago: University of Chicago Press, 1962. Pages 107–152.

POLLOCK, FREDERICK, and MAITLAND, FREDERICK W. *The History of English Law before the Time of Edward I* (1895). 2d ed. 2 vols. With a new introduction and select bibliography by S. F. C. Milsom. London: Cambridge University Press, 1968.

ROBINSON, PAUL H. "A Brief History of Distinctions in Criminal Culpability." *Hastings Law Journal* 31 (1980): 815–853.

———. "Rules of Conduct and Principles of Adjudication." *University of Chicago Law Review* 57 (1990): 729–771.

———. "Should the Criminal Law Abandon the Actus Reus–Mens Rea Distinciton?" In *Action and Value in Criminal Law.* Edited by Stephen Shute, John Gardner, and Jeremy Horder. Oxford, U.K.: Oxford University Press, 1993.

———. "A Functional Analysis of the Criminal Law." *Northwestern University Law Review* 88 (1994): 857–913.

ROBINSON, PAUL H., and GRALL, JANE A. "Element Analysis in Defining Criminal Liability: The Model Penal Code and Beyond." *Stanford Law Review* 35 (1983): 681–762.

ROBINSON, PAUL H., and DARLEY, JOHN M. "The Utility of Desert." *Northwestern University Law Review* 91 (1997): 453–499.

SAYRE, FRANCIS BOWES. "The Present Significance of Mens Rea in the Criminal Law." *Harvard Legal Essays* (1934): 399–417.

STEPHEN, JAMES F. *A History of the Criminal Laws of England.* 3 vols. London: Macmillan, 1883.

STROUD, DOUGLAS. *Mens Rea; Or, Imputability under the Laws of England.* London: Sweet and Maxwell, 1914.

TURNER, J. W. C. "The Mental Element in Crimes at Common Law." *Cambridge Law Journal* 6 (1936): 31–66.

WILLIAMS, GLANVILLE. *Criminal Law: The General Part.* 2d ed. London: Stevens, 1961.

MENTAL HEALTH EXPERTS

See SCIENTIFIC EVIDENCE.

MENTALLY DISORDERED OFFENDERS

This entry covers the relationship of mental disorder to crime, the overlap between the criminal justice and mental health systems, and the nature and operation of institutions and programs that deal with mentally disordered criminals.

Crime and mental disorder

Crime is neither mental disorder nor necessarily evidence of such disorder. It is a misconception that all criminals are "sick," especially those who commit apparently senseless crimes or particularly serious crimes such as murder or rape. The concepts of crime and of mental disorder should be kept distinct. Crime is a violation of the criminal law, whereas mental disorder refers to behavior that is usually marked by some type of lack of the general capacity for rationality and accompanying distress or dysfunction. Conduct resulting from mental disorder may or may not be criminal and people with mental disorder may or may not be legally responsible for the behavior that mental disorder produces; criminal behavior, by contrast, is often highly rational. Thus, some crime is the product of mental disorder, but to consider all crime as a manifestation of such disorder would tend both to eliminate any sensible boundaries to the concept of mental disorder and to play havoc with generally accepted notions of morality and accountability.

The criminal behavior of people with mental disorders is difficult to estimate with precision because reliable data are hard to obtain. Many mentally disordered persons and many criminal acts never come to the attention of public authorities. Older studies of the issue, although suggestive, suffered from serious methodological flaws. Based on recent community-based studies that examine all criminal behavior, whether or not an offender is arrested and convicted, we can cautiously estimate that, in general, people with major mental disorders, such as schizophrenia or severe depression, are not at greater risk for criminal behavior than people without disorder. Drug use is much more closely correlated with criminal behavior than is mental disorder. People with and without major mental disorders who abuse illegal drugs and alcohol are equally and far more likely to engage in crime than people who do not use drugs, but people with mental disorders are about seven times more likely to abuse drugs and alcohol than people without disorders. Thus, although drug use independently accounts for more crime than does major mental disorder, the prevalence of criminal behavior among people with mental disorder may be greater because they are at much greater risk of drug use. People with less severe mental disorders, such as personality disorders, are at even greater risk for criminal behavior if they use illegal drugs and alcohol than people with major mental disorders or people without disorders.

The non-substance-related mental disorders that seem to have the strongest relation to crime are antisocial personality disorder (APD) and psychopathy, both of which are personality disorders. People with these disorders are generally in touch with reality and therefore are responsible for their behavior. APD is widely recognized as a mental disorder by its inclusion in the fourth edition of the American Psychiatric Association's *Diagnostic and Statistical Manual of Mental Disorders* (DSM-IV-TR), but its classification as a mental disorder is problematic. The criteria for APD, for example, are largely persistent, serious antisocial behaviors and do not include cognitive or affective psychopathology. These diagnostic criteria virtually guarantee that APD will be found to a great degree among offenders, but such criteria offer little reason per se to consider the condition a disorder. Psychopathy is also frequent among prisoners. Psychopathy is not an officially recognized diagnostic category in DSM-IV, but there are good data to validate the disorder and it is used by many clinicians. The condition is marked by a wide range of psychopathology, including extreme egocentricity and lack of the capacity to experience empathy and guilt, and many psychopaths violate the law. The criteria for psychopathy are more readily considered psychopathological than antisocial behavior alone, but many claim that psychopathy is simply a label for people we dislike and fear rather than a genuine disorder. There is substantial but imperfect overlap between psychopathy and APD: many people who engage in persistent, serious antisocial behavior are not psychopaths, and many psychopaths are able to avoid persistent, serious antisocial behavior.

Although older data indicated that prisoners had higher rates of mental disorder, including major mental disorders, than the population at large, more recent data on the rate of mental disorder among prisoners—clearly only a subset of people who commit crimes—indicates that convicted offenders appear to be no more mentally disordered than nonoffenders. Approximately 20 to 35 percent of the national population actively suffers from some form of mental disorder or has suffered from mental disorder at some time during their lives, a proportion that is almost identical in prison populations. The proportion of prisoners who suffer from major mental disorders is relatively small, much as it is in the population at large. Recent evidence indicates that about 16 percent of state prisoners suffer from a current disorder and almost one-third reported a current or past condition. State prison inmates with a mental condition are more likely than other inmates to be incarcerated for a violent offense, to have been under the influence of alcohol or drugs at the time of the offense, and more likely to have been homeless in the year prior to arrest. The data about prisoners may not be representative of the proportion of offenders who suffer from disorders for at least two reasons. Offenders with mental disorders may be in general less competent and more likely to be caught, and some offenders with disorders may be diverted to the mental health system.

The generally low rate of severe mental disorders among prisoners is reflected in the small percentage of felony defendants (probably less than 10%) for whom the question of incompetence to stand trial is raised and in the even smaller percentage (approximately 1–2%, although with substantial variance among jurisdictions) of those who raise the insanity defense. Defendants are rarely found incompetent to stand trial or not guilty by reason of insanity unless they are or have been suffering from a major mental disorder and seem grossly out of touch with reality.

It is a matter of common knowledge that the prison environment is highly stressful, particularly in ways that may tend to predispose persons to develop mental disorders. Inmates lack the usual range of stimuli; they are alienated from normal familial, affectionate, and sexual relationships and social supports; and they often are fearful for their safety. Consequently, it is predictable that some prisoners who were previously free of mental disorder will become seriously disordered while incarcerated.

The mental health and criminal justice systems

Much deviant or rule-breaking conduct falls within the purview of both the mental health and criminal justice systems. An assault, for example, may be treated as a misdemeanor, a symptom of mental disorder, or both. Serious crime may raise similar issues. A person who kills on the basis of a delusion may be seen as a candidate for criminal justice processing, during which an insanity defense may be raised and won. The same person may be viewed as primarily in need of mental health care and diverted from the criminal justice system.

Pre-arrest decision-making. A police officer is often the individual who decides whether a rule-breaker should be taken to a hospital or a jail. Some major mental disorder manifests itself as disorderly or frightening public behavior and consequently comes to the attention of the police. The mentally disordered person may also behave violently or disruptively in the home, again occasioning intervention. The police are quite expert at making quick determinations that a citizen is suffering from a mental disorder, but the decision to take a person to a hospital instead of a jail depends on a complex of factors going far beyond the simple assessment of whether mental disorder is present. Such factors include the seriousness of the criminal behavior, the seriousness of the perceived mental disorder (including whether the person has behaved self-injuriously or extremely bizarrely), the police officer's perception of the person's degree of responsibility for the behavior, the availability of cooperative psychiatric services, the desires of the family (if any), and the convenience of the officer, such as whether the officer will have to appear in court if the person is arrested.

A major factor that may influence the police officer's decision to arrest or commit is the existing criteria for involuntary commitment in the specific jurisdiction. At one time such criteria were quite broad, allowing hospitalization on a showing of mental disorder alone and consequent "need for treatment." In the late 1960s and throughout the 1970s, legislative reform and court decisions—the latter often based on constitutional principles—largely replaced vague, broad mental health standards with apparently narrower commitment criteria focused on dangerousness to self or others, as evidenced by a recent overt act or threat. Moreover, the terms of potential civil commitment were limited. Although the newer standards provided greater protection of liberty for people with disorders, at least in theory, mental health professionals criticized the new laws because they thought that they threatened to turn hospitals into jails by their criminal-justice-like criteria that focused on danger rather than disorder.

In reaction to these and related criticisms, many commitment laws were broadened somewhat in the late 1980s and 1990s. Nonetheless, concern for civil liberties and the expense of involuntary civil commitment have caused most involuntary civil commitment to be used in emergency situations and with limited terms of confinement for people with severe disorders. Thus, involuntary civil commitment is no longer a viable option either to incapacitate dangerous disordered people for long terms or to hospitalize disordered people whose condition does not present a major psychiatric emergency but who may engage in relatively nondangerous criminal offenses. The difficulty of hospitalizing the latter group has caused many such people to be processed through the criminal justice system. Such so-called criminalization of the mentally disordered has been decried by many because it seems unjust and inhumane to arrest and imprison persons whose nonserious criminal behavior is related to mental disorder and whose primary need is treatment.

These criticisms have merit, but they fail to address important issues. It is not always the case, for example, that disordered persons are not responsible for their behavior. Persons can be both "mad and bad," to use a popular locution, and to the extent that they are bad and responsible, they may fairly be arrested and punished. If treatment is required, it can and should be provided to prisoners. In addition, for all its faults, the criminal justice system provides greater due process protections than the legal protections in the mental health system. Moreover, public hospitals rarely provide fully adequate care and treatment, and hospitalization is not always in the disordered person's best interests.

Disordered prisoners in jail. When a mentally disordered person is arrested and formally charged by the prosecutor, or when a person becomes disordered after entering the criminal justice system, it is unlikely that he or she will be transferred entirely to the mental health system. If a prisoner is or becomes severely disordered in jail while awaiting trial, he or she will usually be treated in the jail itself or placed in the jail hospital ward. The prisoner will be transferred to a mental hospital only if the jail mental health facilities are incapable of providing minimal treatment and safety. Psychotropic medication is the treatment of choice for most people with major mental disorders, especially in the acute stage of disorder, and such medication can be prescribed and administered in jails. Unfortunately, mental health services in almost all jails—both urban and rural—are generally inadequate and inmates do not have access to services other than those provided by the jail authorities.

Incompetence to stand trial and to plead guilty procedures and commitments. A charged prisoner may be temporarily or, in some cases, permanently diverted into the mental health system if there is a question of competence to stand trial or to plead guilty. Due process requires that a criminal defendant must be competent, and it is the duty of the defense counsel, judge, and prosecutor to raise this issue if the defendant's mental condition seems to warrant it. Major mental disorder may produce incompetence, but the latter, which is a legal standard, is distinguishable from disorder itself. Most defendants with mental disorders are not incompetent.

A defendant is considered incompetent to stand trial or to plead guilty if he or she is unable to understand the nature of the proceedings or to assist counsel effectively. Although some commentators believe that pleading guilty requires higher or different competence than standing trial, the Court held in *Godinez v. Moran*, 509 U.S. 389 (1993) that the same standard of "rational understanding of the proceedings" could be applied for both purposes. A guilty plea must be knowing: the defendant must in fact understand that he or she is waiving constitutional rights, but the standard for judging competence is the same.

The proportion of cases in which this issue is considered varies enormously from one jurisdiction to another, even within a state, clearly indicating that the criminal justice system is not uniformly sensitive to the effect of mental disorder on competence to stand trial, and that factors other than the defendant's competence, such as the ready availability of evaluation facilities, play an important role. In general, however, the proportion of felony cases in which competence is questioned appears to be less than 10 percent.

The incompetence issue may be raised at any time before or during trial, but it is usually done shortly after arrest. When the defendant's competence is put at issue, the court will order an evaluation, which is usually performed by a psychiatrist or psychologist. A hearing will then be held to determine whether the defendant is incompetent. According to some studies, the defendant is actually found incompetent in only 25 to 30 percent of such cases.

If the defendant is found to be incompetent, a course of treatment will be ordered whose purpose is to restore the defendant to competence so that he or she can stand trial. Some jurisdictions allow the treatment to take place on an outpatient basis, but most incompetent defendants are committed either to civil hospitals or to hospitals for the criminally insane. The treatment of choice for incompetent defendants, most of whom are psychotic, is psychotropic medication, although some jurisdictions also provide psychoeducational therapy directed specifically at teaching the defendant the skills needed for competence to stand trial.

The U.S. Supreme Court held in *Jackson v. Indiana*, 406 U.S. 715 (1972), that incompetence to stand trial commitments could only be maintained for a reasonable length of time, and that if the defendant could not be restored to competence sufficiently to stand trial, either release or civil commitment was required. The length of time designated for incompetence commitments varies among jurisdictions, but it tends to be longer than is necessary for its purpose, which is not to "cure" the defendant but simply to restore competence. With proper medication and management, most disordered defendants can be restored to competence within a matter of months.

Although the *Jackson* decision prohibits lifelong incompetence commitments, defendants can still remain hospitalized for far longer than the few months needed if proper treatment is provided. Unfortunately, incompetence commitments are often made for other than mental health purposes; they may be used to delay proceedings or to incarcerate a defendant so that the prosecution can avoid the cost, strain, or uncertainty of trial. Moreover, hospitals for the criminally insane and other institutions that treat incompetent defendants often do not provide high-quality treatment that would ensure the success of brief incompetence commitments.

An interesting question is whether a defendant committed as incompetent to stand trial may refuse psychotropic medication treatment, which can create potentially unpleasant and serious side effects. It is clear that if such treatment is medically appropriate and there is a compelling reason, such as the defendant posing a danger to self or others, the state may medicate the defendant. Less clear is whether the state may medicate involuntarily solely for the purpose of restoring the defendant's competence in the absence of any other compelling reason. Most states assume and most courts have held that the state's interest in resolving the defendant's guilt outweighs the defendant's liberty interest. In *Riggins v. Nevada*, 504 U.S. 127 (1992), the Court implied that the state might be able to justify "medically appropriate" involuntary medication if it could not restore a defendant's competence with less intrusive means, but it did not decide the issue.

Another unresolved issue is whether a defendant who is competent only when he or she is being treated with psychotropic medication—so-called synthetic competence or synthetic sanity—may be fairly tried because such medication can alter a person's presentation of self and might give the finder of fact an inaccurate impression of the defendant. In *Riggins*, the Court held that an overmedicated defendant could not be fairly tried, but it has never decided whether an appropriately medicated defendant could be fairly tried. Courts have divided on this question and at least one Supreme Court Justice has indicated that trying synthetically competent defendants may be unconstitutional.

Sentencing.   In jurisdictions that give judges unguided or guided sentencing discretion, mental disorder is a factor traditionally used to argue for a reduced sentence. Many capital sentencing statutes explicitly mention mental abnormality as a mitigating condition and some even use the language of the insanity defense or the extreme emotional disturbance doctrine as the mitigation standard. The logic of such sentencing practices is straightforward. A criminally responsible defendant whose behavior satisfied all the elements of the offense charged, including the *mens rea*, and who has no affirmative defense, may nonetheless be less responsible because mental abnormality substantially impaired the defendant's rationality.

Mentally disordered prisoners. A disordered offender may have mental health treatment needs after being convicted and sentenced to prison. The U.S. Supreme Court held in *Estelle v. Gamble*, 429 U.S. 97 (1976), that the state must provide medical services to prisoners that are necessary to avoid "deliberate indifference" to prisoners' serious needs. In fact, mental health services, especially prescription of psychotropic medication, are widely available in state and federal prisons. Data from the 1990s indicate that about 50 percent of state and federal prisoners identified as mentally ill have taken a prescribed medication and about 60 percent have received some form of mental health service. Moreover, there are mental health units in prison hospitals to treat mentally disordered prisoners who cannot be safely treated or remain safely in the general prison population. Although prison mental health services are adequate and generally superior to such services in jail, they are seldom high-quality.

On occasion, prison mental health services are inadequate for a disordered inmate and the prison will seek to transfer the inmate to a mental hospital. In *Vitek v. Jones*, 445 U.S. 480 (1980), the Court held that inmates facing such transfers must be accorded due process protections because transfer to a mental hospital threatens to stigmatize the inmate and to expose the inmate to potentially intrusive forms of forced treatment. The Court held that a prisoner facing such a transfer is entitled to notice and a hearing before an independent administrator at which the inmate may present evidence and cross-examine witnesses called by the state. The prisoner is also entitled to the assistance of a qualified and independent adviser, although not necessarily an attorney. Further, the fact finder must furnish a written statement outlining the evidence relied on and the reason for transferring the inmate. If an inmate is transferred, the inmate may remain in hospital as long as it is necessary, but time in the hospital is credited toward the inmate's sentence. Transferred inmates are returned to the prison when this is indicated.

If an inmate is still disordered at the end of his or her sentence, whether serving time in prison or in hospital, and the state then wishes to involuntarily civilly commit the inmate, equal protection requires the state to use the same commitment standards and procedures it applies to citizens who are not serving a prison term (*Baxstrom v. Herold*, 383 U.S. 107 (1966). The logic of the *Baxstrom* case is compelling: At the end of a prison term, a prisoner is entitled to freedom and thus enjoys the same civil status as other free citizens. If the state then decides to deprive the ex-prisoner of liberty and to impose the stigma of involuntary hospitalization, the ex-prisoner should be entitled to the same protections granted other citizens.

Post-insanity defense commitments. Although incompetence proceedings affect a greater number of mentally disordered offenders, the insanity defense has claimed most of the attention devoted to offenders with mental disorder. Whereas the incompetence to stand trial standard addresses whether the defendant is at present unable to stand trial, the insanity defense standard concerns whether the defendant was mentally disordered and legally insane in the past, at the time of the offense. Thus there is no necessary relation between past and present mental status and between incompetence to stand trial and legal insanity: a defendant who was arguably legally insane at the time of the crime may be either competent or incompetent at the time of trial, and a currently incompetent defendant may not have been mentally disordered at the time of the crime. A defendant can only be tried if the defendant is currently competent, however, even if the insanity defense is raised. In some clear cases the prosecution will accept an insanity plea in order to divert the defendant quickly into a mental health facility.

The Court held in *Jones v. United States*, 463 U.S. 354 (1983), that if a defendant is acquitted by reason of insanity, the state is permitted automatically to commit the person to a hospital. Such hospitals may be administered by corrections departments or by mental health departments, but acquittees are virtually always committed to secure facilities. The justification for post-acquittal commitment is that an insanity acquittal represents a finding that the person is both dangerous and nonresponsible. Some jurisdictions treat the initial commitment for the purpose of evaluation of continuing dangerousness and nonresponsibility and soon have a hearing about whether the acquittee remains mentally disordered and dangerous and is therefore committable. Despite the possibility that the acquittee may no longer be dangerous or nonresponsible, other jurisdictions treat the insanity acquittal as a finding that commitment is immediately appropriate because dangerousness and nonresponsibility are conclusively presumed to continue. After commitment is authorized, an acquittee is entitled to periodic review of commitment.

The standard term of post-insanity acquittal commitment is indefinite because its primary purpose is protection of society from people who are both dangerous and nonresponsible, conditions that have no necessary limit. The term of post-insanity acquittal commitment is not limited by proportionality related to a guilty offender's deserved punishment because the acquittee was found not guilty, not responsible. The Court upheld such indefinite commitments in *Jones*, even for defendants who are acquitted for relatively nonserious crimes and who thus seem to pose little danger to the community.

In *Foucha v. Louisiana*, 504 U.S. 71 (1992), a closely divided Court held that once an acquittee was no longer mentally disordered or no longer dangerous, the justification for the commitment ends and the acquittee must be released. This holding makes great sense. If the acquittee is no longer dangerous, confinement for social safety is not required; if the acquittee is no longer suffering from mental disorder, the acquittee is then indistinguishable from any citizen who may be dangerous and responsible and hospital treatment is unnecessary. On the other hand, a vigorous dissent by four Justices seemed to suggest that although the acquittee had been found nonresponsible, a post-insanity acquittal commitment was a genuinely criminal commitment because the state was able to prove that the defendant committed the crime. Thus, commitment could continue indefinitely as long as the acquittee was dangerous, even if the acquittee no longer suffered from a mental disorder.

Insanity acquittees should be treated to permit release in the shortest possible time, but as in the case of incompetence commitments, adequate treatment is rarely provided and commitments often last for long periods. Once again, as in incompetence cases, lengthy commitments are rarely necessary or optimal on mental health grounds for insanity acquittees, few of whom are severely psychotic and disabled by the time of trial. Long-term hospitalization is not necessary for moderately disabled persons, and short-term hospitalization usually suffices for the treatment of acute serious disorders. Indeed, many insanity acquittees could benefit best from outpatient treatment, which is available in only a few jurisdictions. Moreover, it is generally agreed that

"dangerousness" is not a psychiatric condition per se that mental health professionals are competent to alleviate.

Some claim that insanity acquittees are committed to hospitals because society still wishes to "punish" them even though they have been acquitted. There is support for this claim: evidence from some jurisdictions shows that the length of insanity acquittal commitments is positively correlated with the seriousness of the crime charged, rather than with the acquittee's psychiatric condition, and insanity acquittees in general appear—although there are some problems with these data—to remain in the hospital about the same length of time as they would have been imprisoned for the crime charged. But custodial incarceration and "punishment" represent a misuse of mental health resources and professionals. Moreover, the integrity of mental health law and mental health care is undercut when treatment is not the primary focus of the commitment. Finally, a number of studies indicate that, contrary to popular belief, insanity acquittees are not particularly dangerous as a class. Even the custodial function of insanity acquittal commitments may be largely superfluous.

Quasi-criminal commitments. Some jurisdictions provide for mental health–related commitments for classes of offenders, such as so-called mentally abnormal sexually violent predators, who may be criminally responsible, but who are considered especially dangerous as a result of mental abnormality and who are thought to require specialized treatment. The primary goal of such commitments is undoubtedly public safety. These commitments were once common, but in response to intense criticism that such commitments were unfair and ineffective, they were largely abandoned in the 1960s by legislative repeal or lack of use. But motivated by continuing fears of alleged sexual predators and high-profile cases in which sexual offenders released from prison have committed horrendous offenses, since 1990 a substantial number of jurisdictions created new forms of commitment to respond to the danger some sexual offenders present.

Often termed "quasi-criminal" because they are a hybrid of criminal and mental health commitments, these commitments are usually triggered by conviction for a sexual offense and commitment proceedings begin after the sexual offender has completed his prison term. The criteria for commitment are commonly that the offender suffers from a mental abnormality and that the abnormality renders the offender a danger to society. If an offender is found to be a mentally abnormal sexual predator, commitment is for an indefinite term with periodic review. Modern quasi-criminal commitment laws do provide substantial procedural protections, including most of those required for criminal conviction, such as the right to counsel and proof beyond a reasonable doubt.

The Supreme Court upheld the constitutionality of such commitments in *Kansas v. Hendricks*, 521 U.S. 346 (1997). The Court reasoned that these commitments are not criminal and punitive. Rather, they are akin to ordinary involuntary commitment and similarly justifiable because the alleged predator poses a risk to the public and the necessary finding of mental abnormality implies both that the alleged sexual predator is unable to control his dangerous sexual behavior and is not responsible. In *Seling v. Young*, 2001 WL 37676 (U.S.), the Court reaffirmed that such statutes are non-punitive and therefore civil in nature, holding that an inmate could not obtain release on the ground that the commitment was punitive as applied because proper treatment and conditions of confinement were not being provided to him. The Court did say, however, that inmates may have state law and federal causes of action to determine if they are being treated in accord with state law and federal law and to provide necessary remedies. Citing *Foucha* and *Jackson*, the Court also reaffirmed that due process requires that the conditions and duration of sexual predator commitments must bear a reasonable relation to the purpose of the confinement, implying that treatment must be provided if treatment is at least one purpose of the commitment.

There were many problems with the reasoning in *Hendricks*. It is paradoxical to claim that a sexually violent predator is sufficiently responsible to deserve the stigma and punishment of criminal conviction and punishment, but is not sufficiently responsible to be permitted the usual freedom from involuntary civil commitment that even predictably dangerous but responsible agents retain. Every form of sexual aberration is not necessarily mental disorder or a symptom of it, and disordered sex offenders seldom manifest a psychosis or a severe behavioral disorder other than their offending sexual proclivities. If a state seriously believes that a mental abnormality is sufficient to justify potentially lifelong involuntary commitment, then such an abnormality should surely preclude criminal responsibility.

The Court also did not recognize that the criteria for the commitment, as defined by Kansas, were circular and overbroad. Indeed, the definitions of mental abnormality and dangerousness that the Court approved were sufficiently broad to permit commitment of virtually any offender as a dangerous predator with only minimal redrafting of the criteria. Finally, the Court assumed without argument that sexual predators cannot control their conduct, although such an assumption is subject to substantial conceptual and empirical criticism.

The public safety motivation behind sexual predator commitments is understandable. Some sexual offenders are indeed very dangerous. Penal incarceration is typically limited and thus many such predators may be released to prey on the community. Usually, however, custodial confinement in our legal order is justified only by criminal desert or by nonresponsible dangerousness. This leaves a gap because there is no means preventively to confine very dangerous but responsible people who have committed no crime or who have committed a crime but served their sentences and must be released. Quasi-criminal commitments attempt to fill this gap by requiring that predators be deemed abnormal and not responsible, which justifies permitting confinement for a longer period than ordinary criminal sentences, but the nonresponsibility assumption is unwarranted. Further, available evidence demonstrates that mental health treatment holds little promise of altering offensive sexual behavior and little genuine treatment is offered to committed predators. *Seling* describes various challenges to the conditions of sexual predator commitments in the lower courts that demonstrated that these conditions were unconstitutional and required improvement and monitoring to ensure that they met constitutional standards. Thus, these commitments appear simply to be an attempt to evade traditional constraints on the state's ability to confine citizens. If the dangers posed by sex offenders are perceived to be especially threatening, a logical response would be lengthier criminal punishment. Indeed, most of the nation's major mental health organizations argued that these quasi-criminal commitments are unwise and should be unconstitutional because they are a devious misuse of the mental health system to achieve essentially non-mental-health goals.

Competence to be sentenced and executed. A convicted defendant may become disordered in the interim between conviction and sentencing and, consequently, may also become incompetent to be sentenced because the defendant does not understand the nature of the proceedings. This rarely occurs, but the state must defer sentencing until the defendant is restored to competence. Virtually always, such defendants are psychotic and the treatment of choice would be psychotropic medication. Because such incompetence is rare, few decisions have considered the broader issues raised, such as whether such defendants may be forcibly medicated. Almost certainly, the same considerations that apply to incompetence to stand trial commitments would apply in this context.

More important, the Court held in *Ford v. Wainwright*, 477 U.S. 399 (1986) that it is unconstitutional to execute a prisoner who is incompetent because the prisoner does not understand the nature of the death penalty or why it is being imposed. The Court provided no consistent rationale for its decision, but it pointed to the uniform common law practice of barring execution of the insane. Most prisoners found incompetent to be executed will, again, be suffering from a psychotic disorder for which psychotropic medication will be the treatment of choice—but may the state forcibly medicate the prisoner so that he may be executed? The Court has not resolved this issue and at least one state has concluded that it is constitutionally impermissible forcibly to medicate an incompetent inmate for the purpose of executing that inmate. The problem has also divided mental health professionals, who disagree about whether it is ethical to offer healing services that will ultimately be used to permit the intentional killing of the patient.

The future treatment of disordered offenders

Concomitant with the proliferation during the nineteenth century of asylums to house the mentally disordered, there was an increasing perception that the so-called criminally insane were a distinct class with special needs that could best be met in separate institutions combining therapy with more secure custody for these allegedly dangerous persons. The result was the establishment of separate hospitals for the criminally insane that are more like prisons and that are often administered by corrections departments, rather than by mental health departments. They housed those found not guilty by reason of insanity, defendants found incompetent to stand trial, prisoners who had become severely disordered in prison, and, on occasion, civil patients who were so dangerous that a more secure institution seemed necessary.

In general, these institutions are highly custodial and do not offer high-quality mental health services. Long-term confinement in such institutions is frequently antitherapeutic. Much of the expensive, high-security custodial functioning of these institutions is probably unnecessary. Experience and studies have shown that many allegedly dangerous disordered offenders can be transferred to less secure hospitals where they can be treated like other patients or they may be safely released into the community, either outright or with outpatient treatment. When by court order and against hospital advice these transfers take place, the former inmates appear to make satisfactory adjustments, and only a small fraction later engage in serious criminal behavior.

The plight of inmates in institutions for the criminally insane has been ameliorated by legislative and judicial changes and by therapeutic advances. Newer psychotropic medications are more effective. Incompetence to stand trial and insanity acquittal commitments are much less likely to last for life or even for extremely long periods than in the past, and litigation has reformed some of the worst abuses of these institutions. Furthermore, some jurisdictions maintain a policy of placing selected mentally disordered offenders in special or general wards of civil hospitals or in special outpatient programs. These programs are oriented more toward therapy than custody and some succeed.

Amelioration of physical and emotional abuse and restrictions on the deprivation of liberty that attend secure confinement are surely welcome reforms. But too few resources are provided and therapeutic knowledge for dealing with severe mental disorders and criminal recidivism is still too limited to permit more than cautious therapeutic optimism. Despite criticism of separate treatment of the criminally insane and of treatment of disordered offenders generally, the combination of crime and mental disorder remains especially frightening and punitive responses to disordered offenders are common. As the new quasi-criminal commitments indicate, society's response to disordered offenders will not always be rational.

STEPHEN J. MORSE

See also COMPETENCY TO STAND TRIAL; CRIME CAUSATION: PSYCHOLOGICAL THEORIES; DIMINISHED CAPACITY; EXCUSE: INSANITY; PREDICTION OF CRIME AND RECIDIVISM; PSYCHOPATHY; SCIENTIFIC EVIDENCE; SEXUAL PREDATORS.

BIBLIOGRAPHY

American Psychiatric Association. *Diagnostic and Statistical Manual of Mental Disorders,* 4th ed. text revision. Washington, D.C.: American Psychiatric Association, 2000.

CONRAD, PETER, and SCHNEIDER, JOSEPH W. *Deviance and Medicalization: From Badness to Sickness (Expanded Edition).* Philadelphia, Pa.: Temple University Press, 1992.

DITTON, PAULA M. *Bureau of Justice Statistics Special Report: Mental Health and Treatment of Inmates and Probationers.* Washington, D.C.: United States Department of Justice, 1999.

FLEW, ANTONY. *Crime or Disease?* Reprint, London and Basingstoke, U.K.: Macmillan, 1975.

GUNN, JOHN, and TAYLOR, PAMELA J. *Forensic Psychiatry: Clinical, Legal & Ethical Issues.* Oxford, U.K.: Butterworth-Heinemann, 1993.

HODGINS, SHEILAGH, ed. *Mental Disorder and Crime.* Newbury Park, Calif.: Sage Publications, 1993.

KAPLAN, LEONARD V. "The Mad and the Bad: An Inquiry into the Disposition of the Criminally Insane." *Journal of Medicine and Philosophy* 2 (1977): 244–304.

LYKKEN, DAVID T. *The Antisocial Personalities.* Hillsdale, N.J.: Lawrence Erlbaum Associates, 1995.

MILLON, THEODOR; SIMONSEN, ERIK; BIRKET-SMITH, MORTEN; and DAVIS, ROGER D., eds. *Psychopathy: Antisocial, Criminal, and Violent Behavior.* New York: The Guilford Press, 1998.

MONAHAN, JOHN; STEADMAN, HENRY; SILVER, ERIC; APPELBAUM, PAUL; ROBBINS, PAMELA; MULVEY, EDWARD; ROTH, LOREN; GRISSO, THOMAS; and BANKS, STEPHEN. *Rethinking Risk Assessment: The MacArthur Study of Mental Disorder and Violence.* New York: Oxford University Press, 2001.

MONAHAN, JOHN, and STEADMAN, HENRY J., eds. *Violence and Mental Disorder: Developments in Risk Assessment.* Chicago: University of Chicago Press, 1994.

MORSE, STEPHEN J. "Fear of Danger, Flight from Culpability." *Psychology, Public Policy, and Law* 4 (1998): 250–267.

QUINSEY, VERNON L.; HARRIS, GRANT T.; RICE, MARIE E.; and CORMIER, CATHERINE A. *Violent Offenders: Appraising and Managing Risk.* Washington, D.C.: American Psychological Association, 1998.

RABKIN, JUDITH G. "Criminal Behavior of Discharged Mental Patients: A Critical Appraisal of the Research." *Psychological Bulletin* 86 (1979): 1–27.

ROBBINS, LEE N., and REGIER, DARREL A. *Psychiatric Disorders in America: The Epidemiologic Catchment Area Study.* New York: The Free Press, 1991.

STEADMAN, HENRY J. *Beating a Rap? Defendants Found Incompetent to Stand Trial.* Chicago: University of Chicago Press, 1979.

STEADMAN, HENRY J.; McCARTY, DENNIS W.; and MORRISSEY, JOSEPH P. *The Mentally Ill in Jail: Planning for Essential Services.* New York: The Guilford Press, 1989.

STEADMAN, HENRY J.; McGREEVEY, MARGARET A.; MORRISSEY, JOSEPH P.; CALLAHAN, LISA A.; ROBBINS, PAMELA C.; and CIRINCIONE, CARMEN. *Before and After Hinckley: Evaluating Insanity Defense Reform.* New York: The Guilford Press, 1993.

TEPLIN, LINDA A., ed. *Mental Health and Criminal Justice.* Beverly Hills Calif.: Sage Publications, 1984.

THORNBERRY, TERRENCE P., and JACOBY, JOSEPH E. *The Criminally Insane: A Community Follow-up of Mentally Ill Offenders.* Chicago: University of Chicago Press, 1979.

WALKER, NIGEL. *The Historical Perspective.* Crime and Insanity in England, vol. 1. Edinburgh: Edinburgh University Press, 1968.

WALKER, NIGEL, and McCABE, SARAH. *New Solutions and New Problems.* Crime and Insanity in England, vol. 2. Edinburgh: Edinburgh University Press, 1973.

CASES

Baxstrom v. Herold, 383 U.S. 107 (1966).
Estelle v. Gamble, 429 U.S. 97 (1976).
Ford v. Wainwright, 477 U.S. 399 (1986).
Foucha v. Louisiana, 504 U.S. 71 (1992).
Godinez v. Moran, 509 U.S. 389 (1993).
Jackson v. Indiana, 406 U.S. 715 (1972).
Jones v. United States, 463 U.S. 354 (1983).
Kansas v. Hendricks, 521 U.S. 346 (1997).
Riggins v. Nevada, 504 U.S. 127 (1992).
Seling v. Young, WL 37676 (U.S.) (2001).
Vitek v. Jones, 445 U.S. 480 (1980).

MISTAKE

The criminal law exists to prevent various kinds of harm, and those who violate its prohibitions are usually culpable because conduct that risks or causes harm is generally culpable conduct. For various reasons, however, a wedge can be driven between culpability and the causing or risking of harm. One can cause or risk harm without being culpable, and one can be culpable without causing or risking harm.

Mistakes illustrate the gap between culpability and harm. One can cause harm because one mistakenly believes her conduct is harmless. Conversely, she can mistakenly believe her conduct is harmful and thereby act culpably but not harmfully. Put succinctly, mistakes can *exculpate* one who causes or risks harm and can *inculpate* one who acts harmlessly or even beneficially. This entry will deal exclusively with exculpatory mistakes. Inculpatory mistakes are usually dealt with under the topic of Attempted Crimes, specifically under the doctrines of Factual Impossibility and Legal Impossibility.

The traditional approach

Traditionally, exculpatory mistakes have been treated in Anglo-American law as follows. If one engages in the prohibited conduct by mistake (as to what conduct one is engaging in), or causes the harm the law seeks to avoid by mistake (as to the riskiness of one's conduct), then, unless the crime requires the specific intent to engage in the particular conduct or cause the harm—in which case a mistake entails the absence of such an intent and therefore the absence of the crime—one is excused from criminal liability if, and only if, one's mistake is "reasonable." On the other hand, if one makes no mistake about what one is doing, or one's mistake is "unreasonable" (and no specific intent is required), then one is guilty of a criminal violation even if one does not realize the conduct is illegal, and even if that mistake is a reasonable one. In other words, although reasonable mistakes of fact will exculpate, mistakes over the existence or meaning of the criminal law itself, no matter how reasonable, will not. This last point is reflected in the aphorism "Ignorance of the law is no excuse."

The traditional approach is quite confusing and misleading in several respects. First, it treats a claim of mistake as an excuse for having committed a crime rather than as a denial that any crime has occurred. Secondly, and relatedly, it places the burden of proving the mistake on the defendant when it is the prosecution that must prove the crime. Third, and contrary to the popular aphorism, mistakes of law frequently exculpate and cannot be neatly distinguished from mistakes of fact.

To illustrate the first and second confusions in the traditional approach, consider Jane, who fires a fatal bullet at Joe and is charged with criminal homicide. Jane claims that she was hunting and believed Joe was a deer. On the traditional approach, Jane is guilty of homicide unless she proves that she made a *reasonable* mistake.

But suppose the criminal homicide she is charged with is "intentional homicide," which requires that she kill a human being knowingly or purposefully. Theoretically, the prosecution must prove that she knew or intended to kill a human being. This requirement is completely at odds with the requirement that Jane prove that she made a reasonable mistake regarding what she was shooting. If she made the mistake she claims, then whether or not her mistake was "reasonable," she did not commit the crime of intentional homicide in the first place and should not need to offer a defense to such a crime. Rather, the prosecution should have to prove—beyond a reasonable doubt—that Jane was not mistaken. For it is the prosecution's burden to prove the elements of the crime, one of which is an intent to kill. And Jane's claim of mistake is nothing more than a denial of that intent.

With respect to the third criticism of the traditional approach, which criticism is directed at the maxim that ignorance of the law is no excuse, consider the case of *Regina v. Smith (David)*, 2 Q.B. 354 (1974). The defendant there was charged with intentionally destroying the property of another. He had torn off some paneling that he himself had earlier affixed to the walls of his apartment. When he tore it off the walls, he believed he had a legal right to do so because he had installed it. He was unaware that the law of property makes items affixed by a tenant to a landlord's property the legal property of the landlord rather than the tenant. Assuming, however, that the criminal statute required knowledge that the property the defendant was destroying belonged to another, the defendant's ignorance of the law would render him not guilty of the crime, even under the traditional approach, and the court so held.

Moreover, the traditional approach to ignorance of law is tempered in the United States by various constitutional doctrines prohibiting ex post facto punishment and punishment under vague laws. And in one instance, *Lambert v. California*, 355 U.S. 225 (1957), involving a law requiring a specific action that almost no one would anticipate, the Supreme Court held punishment of one who was unaware of the requirement to be unconstitutional.

The elements approach

Due to the influence of the Model Penal Code (MPC), the traditional approach to exculpatory mistakes has been largely replaced by the "elements approach": a mistake exculpates if and only if it negates the *mens rea* (criminal mental state) that the legislature has required for the particular element of the crime. For example, if the legislature requires knowledge of X in its definition of the crime, any belief that X does not exist—any mistake, legal or factual, reasonable or not—will negate the crime, since belief in ~ X is legally inconsistent with "knowledge of" X. Similarly, if recklessness with respect to the existence of X is what the legislature has required, then the defendant's belief in ~ X will exculpate her unless she was reckless in believing ~ X (she was aware of a substantial and unjustifiable risk of X). (See MPC § 2.02(2)(c), definition of recklessness). If the legislature requires only negligence with respect to X, the defendant's belief in ~ X will exculpate only if the belief is not negligent. Finally, if the legislature makes the existence of X a matter of strict liability—no mens rea is required with respect to X—then the defendant's mistake regarding the existence of X is immaterial to her guilt under the statute. (The application of this approach to mistakes when the crime requires acting with the "purpose" of producing X or engaging in X is not as straightforward. Although some commentators have suggested that the defendant's belief in ~ X negates any purpose to produce or engage in X, the better analysis is that one can have a purpose to X in the criminal law sense even if one does not believe X will result. For example, if the Jackal takes what he knows is a one in one thousand shot at DeGaulle, hoping he will succeed in hitting him but believing he will not, he acts with criminal purpose. For if he hits DeGaulle and kills him, the homicide is surely purposeful. The Jackal will hardly be heard to claim that he lacked the required purpose merely because he believed his chances of success were poor.)

The reform here is really nothing more than the recognition that mens rea requirements logically entail certain treatment of mistakes, and that therefore there is no sense in treating exculpatory mistakes under a rubric separate from mens rea. The old approach is confusing and results in punishment for negligent, i.e., unreasonable, mistakes even though arguably a mens rea more culpable than negligence is statutorily required.

The new approach to exculpatory mistakes has also been extended beyond mistakes regarding elements of crimes to mistakes that bear on defense. Under the traditional approach, for example, a defendant who makes an unreasonable mistake regarding whether he is being attacked and thus may employ force in self-defense is deprived of the privilege of employing such defensive force. Under the new approach, exemplified by the Model Penal Code, the defendant retains the privilege except against a charge that reflects his actual culpability. Thus, if his mistake is only negligent, he may be convicted only of the negligent use of force. If it is a reckless mistake, he may be charged with reckless use of force. But if he has been genuinely mistaken, and he would have been entitled to use force had things been as he believed, he may not be charged with any degree of use of force higher than recklessness.

The Model Penal Code has also extended its elements approach to cover cases where the defendant's mistake exculpates him of the offense he otherwise committed but inculpates him in a different crime, one he mistakenly believed he was committing. Thus, if the defendant kills Polly, honestly mistaking her for a swan, and killing swans is itself prohibited, then the defendant may be held liable under the Model Penal Code § 2.04(2) for that degree of homicide that carries the same penalty as the crime (swanicide) he believed he was committing. In essence, the Model Penal Code constructs an artificial crime out of an attempt to commit one crime and commission of the *actus reus* (prohibited conduct) of another.

If the reforms above are basically analytic, the reformers were also prescriptive when it came to exculpatory mistakes about the existence or meaning of the criminal statutes themselves as opposed to mistakes about matters of fact or law that are elements of particular criminal statutes. They urged retention of the traditional position that ignorance of the criminal law did not in most cases excuse one from criminal liability. The Model Penal Code is illustrative. Section 2.02(9) prescribes that in interpreting a criminal statute, knowledge or belief regarding the existence or meaning of the criminal statute is not to be read into the statute as a required mental state. And section 2.04(3) lays down conditions for a quite narrow excuse of mistake of criminal law. (Basically, under MPC § 2.04(3), mistakes regarding the existence or meaning of a criminal statute excuse only when the statute has not been published or when the defendant has relied on an official but erroneous interpretation of the statute.)

Problems with mistakes of law

However, a problem surfaces at this point. Under the Model Penal Code and the approaches of most commentators, mistakes as to the meaning or existence of the criminal statute under which one is punished do not exculpate, whereas other mistakes of both law and fact may. But how is the line between these types of mistakes to be drawn? A legal positivist will regard law and its meaning as a species of fact. Whether there is a law against rape will depend upon facts about the legislature (whose existence and powers are themselves the product of other facts)— what it enacted, and so on—and the meaning of that law will depend upon facts about complex linguistic and judicial practices.

Moreover, at least for purposes of the criminal law, the proper jurisprudential stance arguably must be positivism: the principle of legality (i.e., that criminal laws must be enacted prior to the conduct they criminalize) and its corollary principle against vagueness can be viewed as demanding that the existence and meaning of criminal statutes be accessible to those subject to them in the manner that only facts, not values, can be.

Now what facts constitute the existence or meaning of the criminal law, mistakes as to which do not excuse, as opposed to those other facts, mistakes as to which do excuse? Let us consider some variations on the well-known hypothetical case of Lady Eldon, who returns to England from a visit to France with some French lace that she has purchased in her luggage. When asked at customs if she has any dutiable items to declare, she replies "no." French lace is a dutiable item. Has Lady Eldon committed a crime? (Wharton, p. 304). *See* F. Wharton, *Criminal Law* (1932): 304 n.9. (In the actual hypothetical, Lady Eldon's mistake is inculpatory, not exculpatory.)

Consider two variants of this hypothetical case. In the first variant, there is a law against failing to declare dutiable items. Those items are listed in regulations that are changed from time to time. Lady Eldon mistakenly believes French lace has been taken off the list. In the second variant, the criminal law itself states "it is a crime to fail to declare . . . French lace." Lady Eldon mistakenly believes that there is no such crime. In the latter case it seems clear that she has made a mistake about the existence and meaning of the criminal law. But how is this case different in any

material way from the former? Moreover, suppose she had read the regulations in the former case and misperceived the word "French" as "Flemish." How would that mistake be any different from, say, her perceiving the lace she is carrying as Flemish lace rather than as French lace, a mistake that would exculpate her if the statute requires a mental state of purpose, knowledge, or recklessness with respect to whether the lace one is failing to declare is French lace? Both mistakes are "factual."

Several approaches are taken to defining the boundary between those mistakes of law that do not excuse (except under rarefied conditions) and those mistakes of both law and fact that can excuse. The problem is usually formulated as distinguishing those mistakes of law that relate to the existence or meaning of the criminal statute and those mistakes of law that do not, with mistakes of fact being a third and nonproblematic kind of mistake. Because all mistakes of law are particular kinds of mistakes of fact, all three kinds of mistake are capable of collapsing into one another. But even if we accept that ordinary mistakes of fact are nonproblematic—they clearly can negate criminal liability by negating a required mental state—drawing the boundary between those mistakes of law that can negate criminal liability and those that rarely do is surely difficult conceptually.

Some identify the distinction as one between mistakes regarding the law under which one is prosecuted ("same law" mistakes) and mistakes regarding other laws ("different law" mistakes). Examples to illustrate the distinction include prosecution under a bigamy statute of one who knew about the proscription of bigamy but mistakenly believed his divorce from his first wife was legally valid; and prosecution under a theft statute of one who drives her car away from a garage after refusing to pay the mechanic what she regards as an excessive bill without realizing that under the law, the mechanic has a possessory lien on the car until the bill is paid; and the case in which defendant, unaware that under the law of property, the paneling he had put in his apartment had become the property of his landlord, tore up the paneling and was prosecuted for destroying the property of another.

The same law/different law approach requires that we have a theory about how to individuate laws. But no one has offered such a theory. Moreover, the prospects of coming up with one are bleak. How one individuates laws— for example, whether one considers the law of property, including the law regarding mechanics' liens or emblements, as separate from or as part of the law of theft or the law of destruction of others' property—looks to be quite arbitrary in the abstract without identifying the principles and policies that motivate the individuation. For example, different degrees of culpability might attach to different legal mistakes, though it is doubtful that differences in culpability will be consistent enough to make clear seams of individuation within the otherwise seamless web of the law.

The same criticism applies to other attempts to differentiate those mistakes of law that almost never negate criminal liability from those that frequently do. Some identify the distinction as one between mistakes of criminal law and mistakes of civil law. But mistakes of criminal law can be exculpatory when one criminal law refers to another. For example, conviction under a law criminalizing knowingly receiving stolen property can be defeated by the defendant's mistake, not as to the existence of that law, but as to whether the property he received is stolen. That mistake is one of criminal law.

Another proposed solution is to distinguish mistakes of law that relate to elements of a criminal offense and mistakes of law that relate to the existence and meaning of the criminal law governing the transaction. But this elements/governing-law distinction between mistakes of law requires that we be able to distinguish between the meaning of a criminal law and the meaning of its elements.

The analytic solution

Despite these problems in distinguishing mistakes of law that can exculpate from the mistakes of law that do not, the modern approach possesses the key to their solution. For the modern approach says that: (1) mistakes exculpate when they negate the mens rea required by the legislature; and (2) the legislature will be presumed not to require knowledge of the existence or meaning of the criminal law. If we put aside (2) and look at (1), we can avoid the problems of classification by asking what mental states with regard to what things did the legislature require. If, for example, the legislature requires knowledge of an element, then regardless how the defendant's mistake regarding that element is classified (reasonable or unreasonable), the mistake entails that she is not criminally liable.

This solution—the analytic solution—works so long as the legislature has been relatively clear about what mental states are required for various elements. But if the legislature has not been clear, and its intent must be interpreted through recourse to more basic policies and principles, matters become difficult. For example, ignorance of different aspects of the law will reveal varying degrees of culpability. The fact that one does not know it is illegal to take what belongs to another may not diminish one's culpability one whit, whereas the fact that one does not know that the paneling he installs in his apartment is the property of one's landlord does reduce or eliminate one's culpability for later destroying it. But the degree to which culpability is reduced by legal mistakes does not provide a fine enough instrument for separating those mistakes into two categories. There are countless criminal statutes, ignorance of which is widespread, and violation of which as a result of such ignorance is surely nonculpable. And there are many mistakes regarding civil law matters that, if they result in criminal violations, would not lead us to deem those violations nonculpable. (Consider someone who, in being prosecuted for fraud, claims he did not know that lying about the existence of the item promised was lying about a material term of the contract, the materiality of the lie being a component of criminal fraud.)

The only other consideration that might conceivably assist the individuation of law required when the legislature has been silent about mens rea is the claim, frequently voiced, that the criminal law cannot as a conceptual matter require mens rea as to its own existence. However, this argument is unsound. There is nothing in the least bit paradoxical about the law's being self-referential, especially if we separate the conduct that is proscribed from the mental state accompanying it. Indeed, as proof that requiring one to be aware of a criminal statute is an entirely possible condition for holding him liable under the statute, there are actual cases, such as *Ratzlaf v. United States*, 510 U.S. 135 (1994), interpreting criminal statutes to make awareness of their existence a necessary condition for violation.

A third policy that might aid in the individuation of mistakes of law required under the Model Penal Code and like approaches when the legislature is silent about mental state is that of not encouraging ignorance of law, which some believe allowing mistakes of law to exculpate would do. Now while it is true in some sense that we do not wish to encourage ignorance of law, it is also true that we do not realistically expect, nor do we wish to encourage, encyclopedic knowledge of law, even criminal law (to the extent it can be separated from law generally). It would be crazily obsessive even to want judges and lawyers to possess such encyclopedic knowledge, much less the general population. Indeed, one who attains such knowledge is more likely culpable for having done so at the expense of more pressing concerns than is one who in ignorance runs afoul of some recondite legal requirement.

To summarize, the law of exculpatory mistakes distinguishes between mistakes regarding the existence and meaning of the criminal laws themselves and other mistakes of both law and fact. Although the treatment of all mistakes in either category is controlled by the legislature's specification of mens rea, when the legislature has been silent or ambiguous regarding mens rea, the distinction between these categories of mistakes becomes important in interpreting the required mens rea. However, any line that can be drawn to separate these categories appears quite arbitrary: laws are constituted by facts, and the line between the criminal law and the rest of the law can be drawn at an indefinite number of places. Moreover, the principles and policies that might rescue us from arbitrariness in drawing such lines—for example, culpability concerns and concerns with not encouraging ignorance—fail to track any consistent boundary line that might be drawn.

LARRY ALEXANDER

See also ATTEMPT; EXCUSE: THEORY; MENS REA; STRICT LIABILITY.

BIBLIOGRAPHY

ALEXANDER, LARRY. "Inculpatory and Exculpatory Mistakes and the Fact/Law Distinction: An Essay in Memory of Myke Bayles." *Law and Philosophy* 12 (1993): 33–70.
American Law Institute. *Model Penal Code: Proposed Official Draft*. Philadelphia: ALI, 1962.
BAYLES, MYKE. *Principles of Law: A Normative Analysis*. Dordrecht, Netherlands: Kluwer Academic Publishers, 1987.
DRESSLER, JOSHUA. *Understanding Criminal Law*. 2d ed. New York: Matthew Bender/Irwin, 1995.
HUSAK, DOUGLAS, and VON HIRSCH, ANDREW. "Culpability and Mistake of Law." In *Action and Value in Criminal Law*. Edited by Stephen Shute, John Gardner, and Jeremy Horder. Oxford: Clarendon Press, 1993, Pages 157–174.
KADISH, SANFORD H., and SCHULHOFER, STEPHEN J. *Criminal Law and Its Processes*. Boston: Little, Brown, 1995.
Note. "Element Analysis in Defining Criminal Liability." *Stanford Law Review* 35, no. 4 (1983): 681–762.
SIMONS, KENNETH W. "Mistake and Impossibility, Law and Fact, and Culpability: A Speculative Essay." *Journal of Criminal Law & Criminology* 81 (1990): 447–517.
WHARTON, FRANCIS. *Criminal Law*. 12th ed. Rochester, N.Y.: Lawyer's Co-operative, 1932.

MODERNIZATION AND CRIME

Common beliefs often associate crime with features of modern society such as big cities, mass society, liberal democracy, capitalism, and modern mass media. In reality, the relationship between modernization and crime is highly complex. Modernization may be accompanied by declining, stable, or rapidly increasing crime rates, depending on the place, particular conditions, and time frame under consideration. A look at basic definitions provides a first understanding of the complexity of the relationship between modernization and crime.

Definitions: complex phenomena

First, crime is behavior defined as criminal by the law of the state. States typically undergo profound changes in modernization processes. So do criminal law and its enforcement. Thus, while behaviors change during modernization, so does their definition as criminal versus law-abiding. Both changes affect crime records.

Second, modernization is the replacement of traditional structural elements by modern ones. In the context of development theory, modernization is understood as a trend toward urbanization, mass communication, general political participation, and general education (Lerner). Classical sociologists have understood modernization as a movement from small social units (*Gemeinschaft*) toward mass society (*Gesellschaft*) (Ferdinand Toennies), toward functional differentiation (Émile Durkheim), toward high levels of rationality (Max Weber), or toward modern action orientations such as universalism, achievement, and affective-neutrality (Talcott Parsons). Closely related are recent debates on social networks and social capital that have also been applied to the understanding of crime (Hagan). Modernization is often thought to diminish the closure of social networks, and, as a consequence, social capital and social control. Finally, the term civilization is relevant for our theme. Civilization refers to people's growing capability of self-control, especially in the public sphere, in the context of evolving states and increasingly complex social configurations (Elias).

This terminological overview indicates the complexity of the phenomenon. First, modernization is obviously multidimensional. Second, not all dimensions—for example, urbanization, universalistic action orientation, or functional differentiation—necessarily progress at the same time or pace. We may thus, depending on place and time, face different constellations of components of modernization. Each of these constellations may have a specific effect on crime. Third, modernization may well not be unidirectional. For example, an increase in functional differentiation may cause problems of coordination and integration and these tradeoffs may initiate a trend toward dedifferentiation. These kinds of reversals are the underlying structural condition of what is often referred to as postmodernity.

It is thus not surprising that different empirical patterns can be observed depending on the researcher's focus on long-term European modernization, recent trends toward postindustrial society in the Western world, or modernization in post-Communist Europe or in countries of the third world.

The long-term European view

Social historians in recent decades have produced rich evidence regarding the relationship between modernization and crime in Europe since the Middle Ages (Johnson and Monkkonen, eds.). Long-term European history has indeed been characterized by numerous modernizing shifts: the building of modern nation-states, urbanization and industrialization, functional differentiation, rationalization, and the emergence of capitalist economies and of autonomous spheres of politics, economics, religion, and science. In general, this period was marked by major declines of violent crime and less unambiguous increases in property crime. While national statistics are obviously not available except for more recent periods, careful archival research in different localities provides a rather convincing picture.

Consider homicide: the rate of homicide in thirteenth-century England was at around twenty per 100,000 population. It declined to fifteen by 1600, between eight and two depending on location in the late 1600s, and further to 0.9 by the period 1780–1802 (see James A. Sharpe in Johnson and Monkkonen, eds.). Rates of homicide for Sweden declined from thirty-three per 100,000 during the fifteenth through seventeenth centuries, to sixteen during the first half of the eighteenth century, to 1.5 in the nineteenth century. The capital Stockholm experienced a decline from forty-three per 100,000 in the Middle Ages to below one in the second half of the eighteenth and, after an upturn to three in the nineteenth century, again declined to 0.6 in the first half of the twentieth century (Johnson and Monkkonen, eds., p. 9). The period of clearest decreases in violence coincided with a program of major reforms under King Gustav Adolf (1611–1632), including the foundation of many towns, the modernization of administration, and the systematic registration of Swedes by the clergy. Property crimes, however, showed an upward trend during this period (Eva Oesterberg in Johnson and Monkkonen, eds.; for similar trends for Amsterdam, see Pieter Spierenburg in the same volume).

Johnson and Monkkonen, in an introductory chapter to the above-cited collection, summarize the overall findings by these and other social historians. First, violent crime declined since the Middle Ages, especially between the 1600s and 1700s, until quite recently. Second, control emanated from the courts of the aristocracy. Third, urban centers tended to be more protected from violence than the countryside. And fourth, areas with less developed states tended to be more violent. These findings are consistent with sociological analyses of medium-term processes in nineteenth-century Europe. Using sophisticated statistical techniques, A. R. Gillis, for example, studies the effects of intensifying state surveillance through policing in France between 1865 and 1913. He concludes that the growth of policing deterred major property crimes while it increased charges for minor types of crime. Declines in major violent crime were better explained by urbanization than by intensified policing.

Social historians thus object to everyday beliefs and raise skepticism against arguments and findings by most sociologists and criminologists who, in a short-term view, associate violent and property crime with modernization. Instead they consider their findings to be in sync with the civilization theory developed during the 1930s by sociologist Norbert Elias. This theory would predict exactly what the cited historians have found, a dramatic decline in violence: European history since the Middle Ages has been characterized by peoples' growing capability of self-control, including constraint from violence, especially in the public sphere. This individual level change is, Elias argues, due to two conditions. First, the emerging modern nation-states claim the monopoly of the legitimate use of force. Violence as a means of dispute resolution thus becomes increasingly illegitimate and subject to penal law. Second, with urbanization and the growing division of labor, people are embedded in ever more complex social configurations. The use of brute force in the relationships that constitute these configurations is no longer suited to advance an individual's interests. More sophisticated action strategies are required. The result of these new constraints on individuals is growing self-control or civilization.

Rapid modernization in the twentieth century

Rapid modernization in the twentieth century led to different effects on crime. Examples include modernization in third world societies, especially after the end of authoritarian or dictatorial rule, and rapid modernization during periods of fundamental reform in societies with state-socialist forms of government.

Consider third world countries. Uncertainties of record keeping suggest that we focus on relatively reliable homicide and murder data. Dane Archer and Rosemary Gartner offer time series for a large number of third world countries, mostly through 1970. Some extend just through a decade, others through seven decades. Some countries show clear declines in violence. In Chile, for example, the homicide rate declined from above thirty per 100,000 during the first three decades of the twentieth century to below ten and as low as four during the 1960s and early 1970s. Egypt shows a 50 percent decline in murder rates between the early 1950s and mid 1960s. Ghana, Indonesia, and, for homicide, Mexico, Tunisia, and Israel show declines between 50 and 75 percent. Other countries are characterized by stable or cyclical rates of homicide or murder, respectively, including India, Kenya, Sudan, Tanzania, Lebanon, Pakistan, Korea, Philippines, and Sri Lanka. Countries with rising homicide or murder

rates include Taiwan, Bermuda, Thailand, and Turkey.

Other researchers study individual developing countries beyond 1970. In Nigeria, for example, urbanization after the end of colonial rule in 1960 appears to have been associated with massive increases in crime, even though crime figures follow a highly erratic course in a turbulent political environment (Olufunmilayo Olorun-timehin in Heiland, Shelley, and Katoh, eds.). Several studies are available for Caribbean and Latin American countries. For example, Barbados shows a threefold increase in crime rates between 1960 and 1980 (from 43 to 139 per 100,000 population) and Jamaica shows a more than 100 percent increase, while crime in Trinidad and Tobago is quite stable (Hyacinthe Ellis in Heiland et al., eds.). Ellis explains this increase in Jamaican rates of violence with a combination of massive economic crises and poverty and a disoriented state and law enforcement. While tough crime-fighting programs were pronounced, clearance and conviction rates declined to dismal levels. In Venezuela crime rates more than doubled between 1962 and 1987 (from 474 to 1,111 per 100,000 population). Homicide rates doubled between 1971 (6.2) and 1980 (12.5), then declined to 8.1 in 1987 (Christopher Bikbeck in Heiland et al., eds.), and increased again dramatically to reach a new peak of 24.4 in 1994 (Ana Maria Sanjuan in Pinheiro et al.). Rates for the city of Caracas were even higher with a level of 13.4 per 100,000 population in 1986, climbing to above eighty in 1993 and 1994, then declining more modestly to 64.5 in 1996 (Sanjuan in Pinheiro et al.).

Generally, then, crime statistics for developing societies show quite divergent trends through the beginning of the 1970s. This period is generally associated with decolonization, and globalization of political rule and economic trade. More recent studies on a smaller number of single countries point at an increase in crime rates. Clearly, simple conclusions on the relationship between development and crime cannot be drawn. Open questions include: Which sectors of the population are affected by which aspects of modernization and in which subpopulations is crime concentrated?

Other countries are of particular interest, as they underwent conscious and short-term modernizing reforms. Consider democratization and moves toward market economy. Both processes are generally considered aspects of modernization by development theorists. They also fit the more basic sociological understanding of modernization as they imply a replacement of particularistic action orientations by universalistic ones. Consider the People's Republic of China after the introduction of market reform. A period of highly stable official crime statistics is followed by a massive increase of serious crimes from 50,000 in 1980 to 366,000 in 1989. The vast majority of these crimes were committed by juveniles. In addition, economic crimes increased dramatically (see He Bingsong in Heiland et al., eds., and numerous media reports, e.g., *The New York Times*, 11 July 1996, pp. A1, A6). Or consider massive changes in political organization. South Africa, after the abolition of apartheid and following a period of deadly civil strife, experienced a massive increase in crime, including violent crime. Homicide rates reached above forty per 100,000 population by 1997 (John Aitchison in Pinheiro et al.). Another example of democratization is Brazil after two decades of military dictatorship (1964–1985). Homicide rates for São Paulo, Brazil's largest city, for example, increased from fourteen per 100,000 population in 1981 to above thirty-three by 1993. The increase, however, had already begun during the last years of dictatorship (Sergio Adorno, Maria Helena P. Jorge, both in Pinheiro et al.).

One of the most radical moves toward modernization was initiated near the end of the 1980s when the formerly state socialist countries of east, east central, and southeastern Europe introduced market reform and democratic political structures. Crime rates began to increase markedly during the 1980s, the decade of reform. The increases accelerated after the breakdown of state socialism in 1989 (Savelsberg, 1995) but leveled off in most countries by 1992 or 1993. Official police data show partly dramatic rate increases between the mid-1980s and the mid-1990s: for homicide, increases of 150 percent (Russia), 450 percent (Estonia), 250 percent (Lithuania), 100 percent (Poland), 100 percent (Czech Republic), 80 percent (Slovak Republic), and 50 percent (Hungary); for burglaries, increases of 270 percent (Russia), 300 percent (Estonia), 230 percent (Lithuania), and 300 percent (Slovak Republic); for robbery, increases of 300 percent (Russia), 500 percent (Estonia), 2,000 percent (Lithuania), 200 percent (Poland), 300 percent (Czech Republic), and 120 percent (Slovak Republic). Rates of assault and rape, on the other hand, were considerably more stable. Victimization research for eastern Germany, the area of the former German Democratic Republic, indicates that increases in the post–Communist era are not merely a reflection of changing control practices (see several contributions in Bilsky, Pfeiffer, and Wetzels, eds.). Crime rates apparently stabilized at levels comparable to those of mainstream west European countries, with some crime types at somewhat higher, others at somewhat lower levels (Van Dijk and Mayhew). Only countries emerging from the former Soviet Union reach considerably higher crime levels.

Theorizing crime increases during rapid modernization

How can we explain such trends in periods of rapid modernization? What accounts for the differences between these experiences and the decline in violence during the long-term European civilizing process? Classic sociological theorists and contemporary research suggest potential explanations.

Robert K. Merton's strain approach, recently revived for an explanation of newer U.S. crime trends (Messner and Rosenfeld), appears applicable to the post-Communist situation (Savelsberg, 1995). We expect rates of crime to increase with the proportion of people who have internalized material goals but do not have access to legitimate means of achieving them. The breakdown of communism (just like rapid development elsewhere) tends to be accompanied by intense hopes for economic improvement. Yet the economic situation has deteriorated for many groups in formerly state socialist societies. Basic goods have become much more expensive, unemployment rates have soared in some countries, and pension payments have been cut or fallen victim to high inflation rates (Gerber and Hout). In addition to material hopes, democracy and political liberty do not simply appear when so ordered by proclamation or constitutional change. Frustration with political conditions is widespread. John Hagan and others demonstrate in an empirical analysis of survey data on post-unification Berlin youths how East Berlin youths were much more exposed to anomic aspirations than their West Berlin counterparts. Related periods of rapid transformation are typically associated with a massive loss of legitimacy of major government and economic institutions. Recent research for the United States has provided evidence that such loss of legitimacy may result in increases in crime rates (LaFree).

Durkheim's classic argument and contemporary extensions provide further theoretical orientation. Durkheim discusses the trend of modernizing societies from segmentary to functional differentiation. He argues that segmentary differentiation is associated with mechanical solidarity, a fundamental agreement on norms and values shared by all members of society. This collective conscience is likely to be weakened in modernity. Individuality grows and traditional bonds loose their effectiveness. Yet, Durkheim does not assume a necessary breakdown of social order as mechanical solidarity is replaced by organic solidarity. Anomie, the lack of normative orientation, is only likely to occur under two conditions. First, functional differentiation is imposed by force. Second, modernization occurs at a speed that does not allow for new forms of association to develop (see Lewis Coser in his introduction to Durkheim, 1984). This argument is of particular interest for societies that undergo modernization as they emerge from autocratic rule. Totalitarian political systems typically repress civil society. They instead impose a set of organizations from professional associations to labor unions to youth organizations, all under the control of a centralized political leadership. The dissolution of such associations leaves a dramatic vacuum in social organization.

Only some elements of social organization prevail, some adverse, others welcoming to crime. Hagan et al. demonstrate how East Berlin youths are somewhat protected from engaging in excessive delinquency as they are, more than their western peers, embedded in tight social networks that provide massive social capital. Such networks were either an intended result of Communist policies, for example in schools that more strongly fostered community than western schools; or partly an unintended consequence of a state in which an omnipresent police, aided by secret police and informant systems (Shelley), played a central role. In a world characterized by mistrust in the public sphere, people withdrew into small social networks of trust, often centered on close kin. These networks continued to exert a sense of social control according to Hagan et al. (1995). They appear to initially dampen the crime wave that accompanied the end of communism.

Other survivals of the authoritarian, specifically Communist past direct our attention to the concept of partial modernization. From this perspective crime waves after totalitarianism may be less explained by the features of modernity but by surviving structural elements of the totalitarian past in the context of modern institutions. First, the demise of communism neither resulted in the eviction of the old elite (*nomenklatura*) from leading positions in politics and industry nor in the elimination of old networks between members of the former elite. The continuation of such networks provides fertile ground for corruption (see media reports, e.g., *The New York Times*, 9 September 1999, pp. A1, A14; 15 September 1999, p. A8; 7 October 1999, pp. A1, A6; 19 October 1999, pp. A1, A8). A second survival from the Communist era, especially in Russia, is organized crime. Under conditions of a centrally planned economy, segments of organized crime often played a central role in the shadow economy; they filled in where central plans could not satisfy demands. In the transformation period organized crime benefits from the insufficient functioning of new market institutions and from involvement with corrupt practices of members of the former *nomenklatura* (Handelman).

Increasing crime in late modernity

Another contrast with the declining rates of violent crime in the long-term European perspective is the recent increase in crime rates in most Western societies. Clearly, these countries have continued their development toward urbanization, general education, economic growth, and technological innovation.

Time series indicate that crime rates in Western industrialized countries increased in the post–World War II period, especially after 1960. Rates of homicide doubled in Denmark, Norway, and Sweden between 1950 and 1986 (Matti Joutsen in Heiland et al., eds.). Assault rates more than tripled in Denmark and Sweden. Robbery rates, in the average, increased around tenfold. In the former West Germany violent crime rates more than doubled between 1963 and 1980 and then stabilized at a high level. Burglary rates increased sixfold through 1987 and fraud rates about twofold (Heiland in Heiland et al.; for more countries up to 1974 see Archer and Gartner). Trends were most extreme in the United States during the 1960s and 1970s. Violent and property crimes more than doubled during the 1960s. They increased by almost another 50 percent during the 1970s and then stabilized on a high plateau during the 1980s (Louise Shelley in Heiland et al., eds.). American crime rates, however, decreased sharply during most of the 1990s.

Rosemary Gartner, in probably the most sophisticated analysis of homicide rates in eighteen developed countries for the period 1950 to 1980, describes trends and offers a theoretically guided statistical analysis of their conditions. While homicide declined slightly during the 1950s, it increased during the 1960s and 1970s, for the entire sample of eighteen countries by almost 50 percent for women and by 62 percent for males. Combining measurements over time and across countries, Gartner finds that risk factors predicting homicide include indicators of material deprivation, weak social integration, exposure to official violence (e.g., capital punishment), and—most strongly—divorce rates. Specifically for women, the ratio of female labor force to households constitutes a risk factor. Children seem to be more at risk in countries in which spending on social programs is more limited and in which more women work outside the home.

All of the factors identified by Gartner are exposed to the modernization process. Yet, very long-term trends in Europe between the Middle Ages and the early nineteenth century may well have affected these factors and those identified by social historians differently than modernization in the second half of the twentieth century. (1) The nation state, strengthening during the era studied by social historians, has been weakened by recent trends toward globalization. (2) Recent waves of economic modernization have contributed to a bifurcated labor market in which the lower segment has suffered considerable decreases in income and social security. This trend has hit particularly hard in countries such as the United States in which disadvantaged minorities were especially affected by economic restructuration. It may thus have contributed to the especially steep increases in crime rates in the United States (Sampson and Wilson). (3) The incorporation of an ever-larger percentage of the population into the labor market may have initially contributed to growing social control (Foucault), but has more recently turned into a risk factor as it increases opportunities for criminal behavior and decreases social integration. (4) The continuing growth of institutions such as work places, schools, and urban areas has further contributed to challenges to social control and integration. The larger these units are the less closure of those networks do we expect that link individuals and households with schools, workplaces, religious communities, and neighborhoods. Also, ever larger economic and government organizations have become increasingly alienated from the population. Alienation from these institutions has grown, as offenses against them have become more frequent and often accepted (Coleman, pp. 15ff). Many of the factors show the dialectic of modernization, which up to one point may contribute to decreasing crime but beyond that point to increasing rates. However, even highly developed industrial nations may not necessarily experience high and increasing crime rates in the late stages of modernity, as the Japanese case illustrates. The Japanese exception has been explained through control forms in that country that have been described as reintegrative shaming (Braithwaite).

The current wave of crime has, in some countries, contributed to punitive responses, a greater willingness to commit people to prison and (only in the United States) a revival of capital punishment. Yet in this entry we have seen that crime is associated with basic factors of social development. Solutions to high crime rates in late modernizing societies may be sought in the manipulation of those societal conditions that have contributed to dramatically varying crime rates over time such as value commitment, social integration, and embeddedness in legitimate exchange networks (Savelsberg, 1999). States, of course, also appear to play an important role as social historians have shown. Violent crime did decline as nation-states were built (on the risk of state violence in overly centralized states, though, see Cooney). Yet crime rates in fully developed nation-states vary considerably over time and by place. What features of states inhibit or contribute to crime has not been fully understood. More research is needed. One important area of research would have to examine the impact of weakening nation-states under pressures of globalization on crime. The establishment of political and legal authority at the supranational level and their impact on crime should attract more research attention in the future.

JOACHIM J. SAVELSBERG

See also CRIME CAUSATION: POLITICAL THEORIES; DEVELOPING COUNTRIES, CRIME IN.

BIBLIOGRAPHY

ARCHER, DANE, and GARTNER, ROSEMARY. *Violence and Crime in Cross-National Perspective.* New Haven, Conn.: Yale University Press, 1984.
BILSKY, WOLFGANG; PFEIFFER, CHRISTIAN; and WETZELS, PETER, eds. *Fear of Crime and Crimi-*

nal Victimization. Stuttgart, Germany: Enke, 1993.

BRAITHWAITE, JOHN. *Crime, Shame, and Reintegration*. Melbourne, Australia: Cambridge University Press, 1989.

COLEMAN, JAMES WILLIAM. *The Criminal Elite: Understanding White-Collar Crime*. New York: St. Martin's Press, 1998.

COONEY, MARK. "From Warre to Tyranny: Lethal Conflict and the State." *American Sociological Review* 62 (1997): 316–338.

DURKHEIM, ÉMILE. *The Division of Labor in Society*. New York: The Free Press, 1984.

ELIAS, NORBERT. *The Civilizing Process: The Development of Manners*. New York: Urizen Books, 1978.

FOUCAULT, MICHEL. *Discipline and Punish: The Birth of the Prison*. New York: Pantheon, 1977.

GARTNER, ROSEMARY. "The Victims of Homicide: A Temporal and Cross-National Comparison." *American Sociological Review* 55 (1990): 92–106.

GERBER, THEODORE P., and HOUT, MICHAEL. "More Shock than Therapy: Market Transition, Employment, and Income in Russia, 1991–1995." *American Journal of Sociology* 104 (1998): 1–50.

GILLIS, A. R. "Crime and State Surveillance in Nineteenth-Century France." *American Journal of Sociology* 95 (1989): 307–341.

HAGAN, JOHN. *Crime and Disrepute*. Thousand Oaks, Calif.: Pine Forge Press, 1994.

HAGAN JOHN; MERKENS, HANS; and BOEHNKE, KLAUS. "Delinquency and Disdain: Social Capital and the Role of Right-Wing Extremism among East and West Berlin Youth." *American Journal of Sociology* 100 (1995): 1028–1052.

HANDELMAN, STEPHEN. *Comrade Criminal: Russia's New Mafiya*. New Haven, Conn.: Yale University Press, 1995.

HEILAND, HANS GUENTHER; SHELLEY, LOUISE I.; and KATOH, HISAO, eds. *Crime and Control in International Perspectives*. New York: Walter de Gruyter, 1992.

JOHNSON, ERIC A., and MONKKONEN, ERIC H. *The Civilization of Crime: Violence in Town and Country since the Middle Ages*. Urbana: University of Illinois Press, 1996.

LERNER, DANIEL. *The Passing of Traditional Society*. New York: Free Press, 1958.

LAFREE, GARY. *Loosing Legitimacy: Street Crime and the Decline of Social Institutions in America*. Boulder, Colo.: Westview Press, 1998.

MESSNER, STEVEN F., and ROSENFELD, RICHARD. *Crime and the American Dream*. Belmont, Calif.: Wadsworth, 1994.

PINHEIRO, PAULO SÉRGIO, et al. *São Paulo Sem Medo: Un Diagnóstico da Violência Urbana*. Rio de Janeiro, Brazil: Garamond, 1998.

SAMPSON, ROBERT J., and WILSON, WILLIAM J. "Toward a Theory of Race, Crime, and Urban Inequality." In *Crime and Inequality*. Edited by John Hagan and Ruth Peterson. Stanford, Calif.: Stanford University Press, 1995. Pages 37–54.

SAVELSBERG, JOACHIM J. "Crime, Inequality, and Justice in Eastern Europe: Anomie, Domination, and Revolutionary Change." In *Crime and Inequality*. Edited by John Hagan and Ruth Peterson. Stanford, Calif.: Stanford University Press, 1995. Pages 206–224.

———. "Controlling Violence: Criminal Justice, Society, and Lessons from the U.S." *Crime, Law, and Social Change* 30 (1999): 185–203.

SHELLEY, LOUISE I. *Policing Soviet Society: The Evolution of State Control*. London, U.K.: Routledge, 1996.

VAN DIJK, JAN J. M., and MAYHEW, PATRICIA. *Criminal Victimization in the Industrialized World: Key Findings of the 1989 and 1992 International Crime Surveys*. The Hague, Netherlands: Ministry of Justice, 1993.

OBSCENITY AND PORNOGRAPHY: BEHAVIORAL ASPECTS

Portrayals of sexuality have existed in virtually every society for which we have historical records. At the same time, virtually every society (Denmark being an exception) has called for at least some limits to sexual material, leading to precarious balances between free expression and social control.

Sex is a deep and mysterious part of human nature, being intimately linked to many aspects of human behavior, including those with the potential for good and the potential for evil. Some thinkers believe that pornographic or obscene portrayals provide insight into the nature of life and sexuality, while others contend that such portrayals cause moral and physical harm. For example, the Report of the Commission on Obscenity and Pornography (1970) concluded that pornography is largely harmless, whereas the Attorney General's Commission on Pornography (1986) came to the opposite conclusion. The debate over the beneficial or harmful effects of pornography is as alive today as ever, and will probably never be fully resolved.

The controversy over the effects and meanings of pornography and obscenity is complicated by several factors that will be examined. First, many different types of sexual depictions are available, with each bearing different meanings and impact; furthermore, researchers disagree about which types are most prevalent in society. Some pornography contains substantial artistic value, while other material appeals predominantly to base prurient and aggressive emotions. Second, demonstrating effects has proved to be elusive because most of what we know is based on laboratory experiments rather than the real world, and the key concepts that govern research are unduly vague and elusive. Third, one's assessment of the impact of sexually oriented material is often at least somewhat dependent upon the political and moral values one brings to the table, and upon one's assumptions about human nature. The elusiveness of the concepts of research leave room for value judgments to enter one's assessment.

Finally, efforts to limit the availability of sexual materials have to be cognizant of constitutional limits that protect freedom of expression. Under the sway of the First Amendment in the United States, courts have attempted to balance free speech with the rights of the community to limit the most offensive and potentially harmful material.

Availability and spread of pornography

The availability of pornography and obscenity has increased steadily over the centuries, reaching a peak in the year 2000. The spread of such material has been associated with the growth of democracy (extending rights of expression to more citizens over time) and the rise of such new forms of technology as the printing press, photography, mass publishing, modes of transportation to deliver material over long distances, videos, cable television, and, more recently, the Internet. In 1992, Americans rented 490 million hard core videos, compared to 75 million in 1985; and in 1997, 10 percent of the money earned on the Internet (up to $1 billion) came from pornography that could be found on about 34,000 web sites. The easy international availability of pornography over the Internet increasingly poses and creates legal confusion, for the law differs in each country, and no authoritative international standard has been promulgated. Studies in the 1980s maintained that the production of pornography was often associated with organized and other forms of crime, such as prostitution; yet no consensus reigns on the extent of underworld complicity in the pornographic industry today, especially given the lowered barriers of entry into the market provided by videos and the Internet.

Obscenity and pornography defined

Although the terms *obscenity* and *pornography* are often used interchangeably, they are different. The *obscene* is something that is foul, filthy, or impure, especially when exposed to public view. *Obscenity* is a legal term of art that applies to certain depictions of sex that are not protected by the constitutional guarantee of free speech because they appeal to debased sexual desire rather than the intellect. In *Miller v. California*, 413 U.S. 15 (1973), the U.S. Supreme Court defined obscenity as material that is predominantly "prurient" (that is, appealing to impure sexual desire) according to contemporary community standards; is "patently offensive" in its portrayal of sexual acts; and lacks "serious literary, artistic, political, or social value" when considered as a whole. In essence, the concept of obscenity is limited to material depicting *hard core pornography*, which means graphic portrayals of ultimate sex acts or lewd exhibition of sexual organs.

Pornography is a nonlegal term with a broader meaning. It derives from the Greek words for "harlot" and "writing," and pertains to depictions of erotic and lewd behavior, including works with artistic or literary merit (by definition, obscenity lacks such merit). All obscenity is pornographic, but not all pornography is obscene.

The balance the Supreme Court has struck between hard core and non-hard core pornography in obscenity law assumes that hard core pornography is more harmful to society than non-hard core pornography. Yet studies conducted in the years since the Court created the present legal test for obscenity cast some doubt on this assumption, as many scientific studies have found some non-obscene material to be more harmful than obscene materials. The main reason for this problem is that the legal definition of obscenity in the United States does not include violence or the degradation of women.

In the 1980s a new, feminist-inspired notion of pornography emerged that took violence and the degradation of women into account. Unlike enforcement of obscenity law, which is based on criminal punishment, the new approach was based on civil rights actions (victims could sue pornographers for harms associated with pornography), and defined "pornography" in a new way: as the "sexually explicit subordination of women" that includes various scenes of violence, humiliation, and unequal treatment. Federal courts in the United States declared this civil rights approach unconstitutional in 1985 and 1986 (*American Booksellers Association v. Hudnut*) because its definition of pornography was too vague and sweeping, and because it represented censorship based on the ideas contained in the material (the main form of censorship the First Amendment does not allow). These concerns did not stop Canada from adopting this logic as the basis of its obscenity law in 1992 (*R. v. Butler*). Concerns about the negative effects of sexually explicit violence and the degradation of women in pornography have continued to be the subject of political, legal, and scientific debate.

Finally, we should note the special issue of *child pornography*, which is either pornography made with children as models, or computer simulations of children in sexually enticing poses. Child pornography is a special cottage industry, often consisting of photographs made by child abusers (pedophiles or organized crime) which are then shared with others. Child pornography was not considered a major social problem until the later 1970s, when the children's rights movement had gained headway, spawning new enforcement efforts and laws on the state and national levels prohibiting the making, distribution, and use of pornography made with children. In 1982, the Supreme Court upheld New York's child pornography law (*New York v. Ferber*), declaring that child pornography is not protected by the First Amendment. These laws have driven the child pornography market underground, requiring law enforcement to engage in undercover tactics that have occasionally given rise to concerns about entrapment (See *Jacobson v. United States*, 503 U.S. 540 (1992)). In 1996, Congress expanded prohibited expression by passing the Child Pornography Prevention Act, which prohibits the reproduction, possession, sale, or distribution of visual images depicting minors or those who "appear to be" minors ("virtual" child pornography) in sexually explicit conduct. This coverage is considerably broader than the exception to free speech authorized by *Ferber*, so the law has been challenged on First Amendment grounds. In 1999, lower Federal Courts upheld this act, which is surely headed for Supreme Court. (See *United States v. Hilton*, 167 F.3d 61 (1st Cir. 1999); *United States v. Acheson*, 195 F.3d 645 (11th Cir. 1999).)

For the rest of this entry primarily the term "pornography" will be used, as focus will be on the behavioral effects of all forms of sexual representations, not just the obscene.

Ideologies and estimates of harm

Although some believe that the question of the behavioral aspects of pornography is a straightforward scientific determination, the matter is not so simple. Anyone who studies the problem of pornography quickly notices how ideology is often a predictor of where a writer stands on the scientific evidence concerning harm. The most important ideologies in this domain are liberal, conservative, and feminist. The liberal view, which is epitomized by the American Civil Liberties Union (ACLU), is largely relativistic and individualistic: virtually any form of pornography should be permitted for consenting adults in the name of the sanctity of individual choice. Liberals are almost always skeptical of studies that purport to show how pornography causes harm. The conservative view supports legal controls and the claim that pornography causes moral and physical harm. Such conservative legal philosophers as Walter Berns and Roger Scruton maintain that sexual representations should be constrained in order to promote the interpersonal values of reason, responsibility, and commitment. Finally, the pro-censorship feminist view of such feminists as Catherine MacKinnon (as distinguished from the views of such anti-censorship feminists as Nadine Strossen, currently president of the ACLU) downplays the "moral" harms of pornography in favor of the argument that pornography depicting violence or the degradation of women causes actual violence and discrimination against women. Such feminists often endorse the distinction between "pornography" and "erotica" that feminist author Gloria Steinem made famous in 1983. Steinem argued that pornography is harmful, portraying women as the victims of male sexuality, while erotica is benign, showing women and men as equal partners in sexual interaction.

Types of pornography for research

Before we examine the evidence concerning the behavioral effects, we must look at the different classifications of pornography for purposes of research, because pornography encompasses a wide range of material (from James Joyce's novel *Ulysses* to the most unartful, sexually explicit video), and not all forms of pornography have the same effects. The most useful classification was provided by the Final Report of the Attorney General's Commission on Pornography, which posited three types: (1) *sexually violent material*, which portrays "unmistakably simulated or unmistakably threatened violence presented in a sexually explicit fashion," including sado-masochism, unwanted sexual aggression, and "slasher" films that depict violence along with sexual content; (2) nonviolent but *degrading* sexual material, which depicts "degradation, domination, subordination, or humiliation" (the commission decided what material is degrading based on what it thought "most people" would consider degrading, dominating, humiliating, and the like); (3) sexual material that is neither degrading nor violent.

The commission's findings concerning the predominant content of pornography were pessimistic and disturbing. It concluded that the vast majority of available pornography fits into categories 1 and 2. However, some more recent studies have looked more closely at content and concluded (at least tentatively) that the trend is away from violence and degradation. Furthermore, others have challenged the rather imprecise and impressionistic way the commission categorized material, casting doubt on its conclusion that violent and degrading material are predominant. (For example, the commission classified all sado-masochistic material as "violent," even though such sex is consensual, and it considered playful forms of "biting" to be violent.) While few question that the overall availability of pornography has increased (especially with videos, cable television, and the Internet), no one can say with any assurance what types or forms of pornography are most predominant.

Evidence concerning behavioral effects

At the most general level, many argue that pornography contributes to the decline of virtue and morality (it corrupts good character), and that it causes offense by its very presence (see *Paris Adult Theatre I v. Slaton*, 413 U.S. 49 (1973)).

The claim about offense is rather straightforward, but the contention of moral corruption is obviously more speculative, and has not been tested scientifically. But its supporters point to a commonsense assumption: if we are right to encourage the teaching of good literature because of its beneficial impact on readers' minds, then it makes sense to assume that bad and degrading literature will have the opposite effect. Furthermore, scientific evidence suggests that exposure to certain forms of pornography increases the likelihood of aggression or negative attitudes toward women, providing some support for the moral corruption theory (for such results reflect moral states), as do cross-cultural correlational studies that suggest that the extent of the availability of pornography is correlated with the extent of sex crimes. However, debate rages concerning the reliability and validity of such studies; and such countries as Japan provide counterexamples, as the high level of violent pornography in Japan is not matched by high incidents of sexual assault. Along these lines, researcher Robert Bauserman found in a review of the literature that sex offenders were not more likely than nonoffenders to have consumed pornography when they were young, though a minority of offenders were using pornography when engaging in their crimes (a finding consistent with police reports).

Harms can also arise in the making of pornography. The 1986 Attorney General's Commission stated that performers are sometimes coerced into appearing in pornography or performing acts for which they did not consent in their contracts. The commission also found that participants are often "young, previously abused, and financially strapped," and that participation in pornography often hurt their relationships and personal lives. Such concerns are most prevalent when it comes to child pornography. On the other hand, some women performers have espoused a new version of feminism and proclaimed their right to participate voluntarily in pornography. In addition, no one has conducted a serious empirical study of the harms associated with the making of pornography, leaving the matter to educated guesses.

The commission's conclusions concerning sexually violent pornography (based on its study of laboratory research conducted by other researchers) were strong and controversial: violent pornography "bears a causal relationship to antisocial acts of sexual violence." The commission was somewhat more qualified about the behavioral effects of significant exposure to nonviolent but degrading pornography, but it nonetheless maintained that exposure "bears some causal relationship to" violence, sexual aggression, and negative attitudes (e.g., viewers see rape as less serious than it is). The commission found far fewer negative effects for nonviolent, nondegrading pornography.

The research on the effects of violent, sexually explicit pornography conducted before and after the commission's 1986 report has been fairly consistent, giving some plausibility to the commission's conclusions about violent pornography, but less plausibility to its conclusions about degrading pornography. Experiments have shown that violent pornography coarsens male attitudes toward women, desensitizes them to sexual violence, and increases their aggression toward women (usually measured by their willingness to administer electric shocks to a female colleague of the researchers after being exposed to a film with the requisite content). Experiments control effects by exposing different sets of males (usually college students) to one of four types of films: violent and sexually explicit; violent without being sexually explicit; sexually explicit without being violent; neither sexually explicit or violent.

Studies indicate that the highest levels of aggression are recorded by those who viewed the violent and erotic films, followed by those who viewed the violent film. Perhaps surprisingly, some studies have found little affect on those who viewed the erotic but nonviolent film. The most important finding is that aggression levels are highest when women are portrayed as being sexually aroused by the violence perpetrated against them. Experimental psychologist Edward Donnerstein and two colleagues summed up their own research and that of others (this view has not been contradicted in the years since): "It is this unique feature of violent pornography—the presentation of the idea that women find sexual violence arousing—that plays an important role in producing violent pornography's harmful effects" (p. 88). Later work stressed that violence was the most important ingredient of the violence-sex link: even minor suggestions of sex will have effects similar to more sexually explicit depictions if violence is present. Sex appears to be less of a problem than violence.

Limits to the findings

Researchers and commentators have found flaws in the findings the commission and studies conducted before and after the commission's report. The most important criticisms boil down to the difficulty of extrapolating from the laboratory to the real world. The key criticisms include: (1) the evidence proves only correlation, not causation; (2) laboratory samples are artificial settings that do not reflect behavior in the real world. Aggression in the laboratory is not punished, and subjects perhaps perceive that the experimenters condone (or even encourage) aggression; and subjects might not believe they are inflicting real harm; (3) duration is not established. The effects of the violent pornography typically wear off after subjects leave the lab, as some studies have indeed indicated; (4) adequate operational definitions of aggression as a behavioral response and violence do not exist; (5) no longitudinal study (measuring the effects over a long period of time) has been conducted concerning the effects of pornography; and (6) the results show, at best, only "probable causation" (i.e., pornography increases the overall incidence of sexual violence, but is not shown to be causal in any particular case), not the type of direct cause that is most worrisome. Causation is least evident in the case of degrading, nonviolent pornography.

Thus, the evidence concerning the behavioral aspects of pornography is mixed. Legal scholar James Weinstein's assessment is apt. "The truth lies somewhere in between. Although there is some evidence that violent pornography (and perhaps 'degrading' pornography as well) causes violence against women, the evidence is far from conclusive" (p. 191).

Legal issues and enforcement

If the findings concerning violent and degrading pornography have merit, then there is a mismatch between law and reality, for the vast majority of potentially harmful material is not obscene, and therefore protected by the First Amendment. Yet the evidence concerning harmful effects is too speculative to merit a new exception to freedom of speech. In 1997 the Supreme Court struck down the national Communications Decency Act, a measure designed to protect children from exposure to pornography on the Internet, because of a host of free speech concerns that highlight the difficulty of enforcement posed by the First Amendment (*Reno v. American Civil Liberties Union*, 521 U.S. 844 (1997)). In addition, even the enforcement of traditional obscenity law has proved difficult to administer for reasons related to what legal scholar Herbert Packer has called the "limits of the legal sanction." The most important reasons for the underenforcement of obscenity law include: (1) low priority given to obscenity cases by prosecutors with limited resources; (2) relative public tolerance of freedom of choice when it comes to what can be portrayed as a "victimless crime"; (3) confusion over the key terms of obscenity law make juries reluctant to find defendants guilty beyond a reasonable doubt; (4) gifted defense attorneys know how to use the law and take advantage of jury sympathies and confusion.

Given the difficulties of enforcing laws prohibiting hard core pornography (obscenity), society should think carefully about criminalizing other forms of pornography as well, especially given dangers such efforts present to freedom of speech.

DONALD A. DOWNS

See also CRIMINALIZATION AND DECRIMINALIZATION; DEVIANCE; GENDER AND CRIME; HOMOSEXUALITY AND CRIME; MASS MEDIA AND CRIME; ORGANIZED CRIME; POLICE: POLICING COMPLAINANTLESS CRIMES; PROSTITUTION; RAPE: BEHAVIORAL ASPECTS; RAPE: LEGAL ASPECTS; SEX OFFENSES: CHILDREN; SEXUAL OFFENSES: CONSENSUAL; SEXUAL PREDATORS; VICTIMLESS CRIME.

BIBLIOGRAPHY

Attorney General's Commission on Pornography: Final Report. Washington, D.C.: U.S. Department of Justice, 1986.

BAUSERMAN, ROBERT. "Sexual Aggression and Pornography: A Review of Correlational Research." *Basic and Applied Social Psychology* 18 (1996): 405–427.

BERNS, WALTER. "Pornography and Democracy: The Case for Censorship." *The Public Interest* 22 (1971): 3–24.

DONNERSTEIN, EDWARD; LINZ, DANIEL; and PENROD, STEPHEN. *The Question of Pornography: Research Findings and Policy Implications*. New York: Free Press, 1987.

DOWNS, DONALD ALEXANDER. *The New Politics of Pornography*. Chicago: University of Chicago Press, 1989.

JANSMA, LAURA; LINZ, DANIEL; MULAC, ANTHONY; and IMRICH, DOROTHY. *Men's Interaction with Women After Viewing Sexually Explicit Films: Does*

Degradation Make a Difference? Communications–Monographs, 4: 1–24, 1997.

LYNN, BARRY. *Polluting the Censorship Debate: A Summary and Critique of the Final Report of the Attorney General's Commission on Pornography.* New York: ACLU Public Policy Report, 1986.

MACKINNON, CATHERINE. *Only Words.* Cambridge, Mass.: Harvard University Press, 1993.

MALAMUTH, NEIL. "Pornography's Impact on Male Adolescents." *Adolescent Medicine: State of the Art Reviews* 4 (1993): 563–571.

PACKER, HERBERT L. *The Limits of Criminal Sanction.* Stanford: Stanford University Press, 1968.

Report of the Commission on Obscenity and Pornography. New York: Bantam Books, 1970.

SCRUTON, ROGER. *Sexual Desire: A Moral Theory of the Erotic.* New York: Free Press, 1986.

STROSSEN, NADINE. *Defending Pornography: Free Speech, Sex, and the Fight for Women's Rights.* New York: Scribners, 1995.

WEINSTEIN, JAMES. *Hate Speech, Pornography, and the Radical Attack on Free Speech Doctrine.* Boulder, Colo.: Westview Press, 1999.

CASES

American Booksellers Association v. Hudnut, 771 F.2d 323 (7th Cir. 1985).

Jacobson v. United States, 503 U.S. 540 (1992).

Miller v. California, 413 U.S. 15 (1973).

New York v. Ferber, 458 U.S. 747 (1982).

Paris Adult Theatre I v. Slaton, 413 U.S. 49 (1973).

R. v. Butler, 89 D.L.R. (4th) 449 (1992).

Reno v. American Civil Liberties Union, 521 U.S. 844 (1997).

United States v. Acheson, 195 F.3d 645 (11th Cir. 1999).

United States v. Hilton, 167 F.3d 61 (1st Cir. 1999).

OBSTRUCTION OF JUSTICE

What brought down President Richard Nixon was not any involvement in planning the burglary of the Democrat National Committee's Watergate offices but his efforts, while president, to obstruct the investigation of that crime. In this instance, as in many others, Nixon's effort to cover up the burglary was not merely a separate criminal offense but an offense arguably even more serious than the crime he sought to cover up.

Obstruction of justice is a broad concept that extends to any effort to prevent the execution of lawful process or the administration of justice in either a criminal or civil matter. Obstructive conduct may include the destruction of evidence, the intimidation of potential witnesses or retaliation against actual witnesses, the preparation of false testimony or other evidence, or the interference with jurors or other court personnel. The purpose of criminal obstruction statutes—which every jurisdiction has, in one form or another—is thus to help protect the integrity of legal proceedings and, at the same time, protect those individuals who participate in such proceedings. Indeed, one of the earliest congressional enactments was a 1790 criminal statute that, among other things, established a number of obstruction offenses.

In keeping with the seriousness of the threat that obstructive conduct poses, and the myriad forms that obstruction takes, a broad array of federal criminal provisions (many overlapping) now target such activity. The principal statutes in this area are contained in chapter 73 of United States Code, Title 18. They are: section 1501 (misdemeanor to obstruct a federal process or writ server); section 1502 (misdemeanor to obstruct or resist an extradition agent); section 1503 (felony provision that targets efforts to influence or injure a court officer or juror, as well as other obstructionary efforts); section 1504 (misdemeanor to influence a juror by writing); section 1505 (felony to obstruct proceedings before departments, agencies, committees); section 1506 (felony to steal or alter a court record or provide a phony bail surety); section 1507 (misdemeanor to picket or parade with the intent of impeding or obstructing the administration of justice); section 1508 (misdemeanor to record or observe proceedings of grand or petit juries while deliberating or voting); section 1509 (misdemeanor to obstruct court orders); section 1510 (felony to obstruct criminal investigations); section 1511 (felony to obstruct state or local law enforcement with the intent to facilitate an illegal gambling business); section 1512 (felony to tamper with a witness, victim, or informant); section 1513 (felony to retaliate against a witness, victim, or informant); section 1516 (felony to obstruct a federal audit); section 1517 (felony to obstruct the examination of a financial institution); and section 1518 (felony to obstruct a criminal investigation of health care offenses).

General obstruction provision

The most frequently used of these federal provisions is section 1503, often called the "general" obstruction statute, which has its roots in a section of the act of 2 March 1831 ("An Act declaratory of the law concerning contempts of court"). Until recently, the first part of section 1503 targeted obstructive efforts aimed at witnesses, parties, jurors, or court officers and officials. The Victim and Witness Protection Act of 1982, however, removed the references to witnesses and parties; created new provisions to protect such individuals, and left the initial parts of section 1503 to focus only on jurors and court officers and officials. The 1982 act, however, did not eliminate section 1503's broad "omnibus clause," which focuses on no particular victim and reaches "[w]hoever . . . endeavors to influence, obstruct, or impede, the due administration of justice." The "due administration of justice" is defined to include grand jury proceedings, criminal prosecutions, and civil proceedings.

The omnibus clause's use of "endeavors" allows prosecutors to use the statute against obstructive effort that merely had a reasonable tendency to impede a legal proceeding. Whether or not the effort was successful does not matter. As the Supreme Court noted in *United States v. Aguilar* (1995), however, the effort must have some clear relationship "in time, causation or logic" to a legal proceeding. Thus, in *Aguilar*, the Court rejected the government's effort to use Section 1503 against a federal district judge alleged to have lied to agents from the Federal Bureau of Investigation investigating his ties to a labor racketeer. There was no proof, the Court found, that the agents had acted as an arm of the grand jury, or that the judge had known that his false statement would later be provided to a grand jury. Section 1503, the Court held, does not reach actions intended "to influence some ancillary proceeding, such as an investigation independent of the Court's or grand jury's authority."

Cases brought under section 1503's omnibus clause tend to fall into two general categories: those involving the concealment, alteration, or destruction of subpoenaed documents, and those involving the giving or encouraging of false testimony, either in the context of a grand jury investigation or in that of a criminal trial. Technically, the giving of false testimony, before a grand jury or at trial, will not support a prosecution under section 1503, in the absence of a specific intent to obstruct. As a practical matter, however, this additional element can usually be inferred. Thus there will be many cases in which perjury and ob-

struction charges will both apply and, because of their different elements, can both be brought. Other applications of section 1503 in the 1990s include its use against a grand juror who disclosed grand jury information to the target of the grand jury's investigation.

While federal prosecutors have occasionally used section 1503 to prosecute obstructive efforts in civil litigation, those cases are rather rare, even though practitioners often decry the frequency of such misconduct. There are at least two reasons for this. Not only is the perceived public interest in criminal litigation usually greater, but it is the prosecutors themselves who are stymied by the obstruction of criminal cases. Moreover, efforts to derail criminal proceedings are all the more dangerous and worthy of prosecution because, under double jeopardy doctrine, any acquittal obtained, however improperly, cannot be overturned on appeal.

Unless the obstruction charged under section 1503's omnibus clause is by "threats or force, or by any threatening letter or communication," the statute requires proof that the alleged obstructive endeavors have involved a "corrupt" purpose. The precise meaning of this term is somewhat unclear. Courts have held that the element is satisfied not only when a defendant has acted with the purpose of obstructing justice, but also when the obstruction of justice is a reasonably foreseeable consequence of his actions, and not his main purpose. Moreover, they have held, the corrupt intent may be inferred from the circumstances. Despite its breadth, however, the statute has withstood numerous challenges alleging unconstitutional vagueness, with courts often noting that the corrupt purpose requirement is actually what saves the omnibus clause from unconstitutionality in this regard.

The centrality of section 1503's scienter element (the element focusing on the offender's guilty state of mind) can raise some particularly difficult issues for lawyers, especially criminal defense lawyers. Defense attorneys' representational obligations have never immunized them from obstruction charges. Indeed, the cases are clear that the giving of otherwise lawful advice, like encouraging a client to assert his Fifth Amendment privilege, or the use of legal processes, like filing a complaint, can violate section 1503 if done with a corrupt intent to obstruct justice. The difference between zealous representation and obstruction can thus lie solely in intent. Although prosecutors have argued that this is a bright line analytically, defense counsel understandably have not always felt secure in the distinction. Ironically, the chief reason why the law is not more clearly developed on the difference between zealous advocacy and illegal obstruction is that prosecutorial self-restraint in this area has limited the number of cases.

The penalty for a violation of section 1503 is imprisonment for up to ten years, but the sentence may be far greater under certain circumstances. If the offense occurred in connection with a criminal case and involved physical force or the threat of it, the maximum term will be the maximum term that could have been imposed for any offense charged in the underlying case, or ten years, whichever is greater. If the section 1503 offense involved a killing, the punishment can be life imprisonment or death.

Witness tampering and retaliation

In contrast with the broad language of section 1503, sections 1512 and 1513 were designed to directly address efforts to tamper with or obstruct potential or actual witnesses or informants or to retaliate against witnesses, victims, or parties for their participation in federal investigations or legal proceedings. The range of conduct addressed by section 1512 is broad and includes intimidation, physical force, threats, misleading conduct, and harassment. Under prevailing case law, a defendant need not have realized that the witness he targeted was to be a *federal* witness.

These provisions of the Victim and Witness Protection Act filled some gaps in section 1503's coverage. They can, for instance, be used against an effort to tamper with a potential witness at a time when no official proceeding was pending. They are limited, however, by their concern with the welfare of witnesses, not the integrity of proceedings per se. The defendant who persuades a witness to mislead a grand jury, for example, has not violated section 1512, unless his conduct involves some effort to mislead the witness as well. In cases where the 1982 provisions and section 1503 both appear to apply, the result is somewhat unclear: Courts have disagreed on whether section 1503's omnibus clause can still be used to prosecute witness tampering and retaliation, now that sections 1512 and 1513 more specifically address such conduct.

In prosecutions under section 1512 for witness tampering, the government need not show that the witness was actually intimidated. It is enough that the defendant's threats had a tendency to intimidate. And while section 1512(b) requires a showing of specific intent to influence a witness, the prosecution only has to show that the defendant was aware of the natural and probable consequences of his conduct toward the witness. As with section 1503, the penalties for violations of sections 1512 and 1513 are keyed to the harm a defendant has inflicted and the nature of the proceedings.

Obstruction of agency proceedings and congressional inquiries

Addressing the gap left by section 1503's limitation to legal proceedings, section 1505 targets "corrupt" efforts to obstruct, impede, or influence the "due and proper administration of the law under which any pending proceeding is being had before any department or agency of the United States, or the due and proper exercise of the power inquiry" by a congressional body. Here, again, the definition of "corrupt" is critical, but in this instance, the term *has* been found unconstitutionally vague, at least when applied to lying to Congress. That was the ruling in 1991, by the Court of Appeals for the D.C. Circuit in *United States v. Poindexter* (an appeal arising out of the Iran-Contra affair). There, the court held section 1505's reference to "corrupt" to be "too vague to provide constitutionally adequate notice that it prohibits lying to Congress." Congress responded to *Poindexter* in 1996 by adding section 1515(b), which provides that, as used in section 1505, "'corruptly' means acting with an improper purpose, personally or by influencing another, including making a false or misleading statement, or withholding, concealing, altering, or destroying a document or other information." Extending to any "improper purpose," this definition remains quite broad, but has so far survived constitutional challenge. (Efforts to use the reasoning in *Poindexter* to challenge section 1503's omnibus clause have so far failed.)

Other obstruction provisions

Certain conduct that might be prosecuted under chapter 73 of title 18, as well as certain obstructive conduct that for technical reasons cannot be reached under those provisions, can be charged under various other statutes scattered throughout the criminal code and elsewhere. Thus, for example, even as the Supreme Court rejected the use of section 1503 against the federal district judge in *Aguilar*, it upheld his conviction under title 18, section 2232(c), which allows the prosecution of someone who reveals information about a federal electronic surveillance authorization or application "in order to obstruct, impede, or prevent such interception." Title 26, section 7212 reaches efforts to obstruct and impede the due administration of the Internal Revenue laws. The federal bribery, perjury, and contempt statutes may also be used against certain obstructive conduct, as can the criminal civil rights statutes, which have been invoked to prosecute efforts to deprive someone of his right to be a federal witness.

Even where a defendant has not been charged with any sort of an obstruction offense, he can, if convicted, still have his sentence increased under section 3C1.1 of the Federal Sentencing Guidelines for "obstructing or impeding the administration of justice during the investigation, prosecution, or sentencing" of his offense of conviction. This provision is frequently used by courts to enhance the sentence of defendants found to have perjured themselves while testifying at trial.

Federal evidentiary doctrine has also been designed to deter interested parties from using force, fraud, or intimidation to keep witnesses from testifying. If a defendant, in any sort of prosecution, is found by the trial judge (using a preponderance of the evidence standard) to be responsible for a witness's absence, the defendant will be deemed to have waived his constitutional right to confrontation and his hearsay objections with respect to the missing witness. This means, for example, that statements that the witness made to the government before he disappeared can now be used against the defendant.

DANIEL C. RICHMAN

See also BRIBERY; COUNSEL: ROLE OF COUNSEL; PERJURY.

BIBLIOGRAPHY

DE MARCO, JOSEPH V. "A Funny Thing Happened on the Way to Courthouse: Mens Rea, Document Destruction, and the Federal Obstruction of Justice Statute." *New York University Law Review* 67 (1992): 570–611.
GREEN, BRUCE A. "The Criminal Regulation of Lawyers." *Fordham Law Review* 67 (1998): 327–392.
LOU, GRACE, and RO, NANCY M. "Obstruction of Justice, in Fourteenth Survey of White Collar Crime." *American Criminal Law Review* 36 (1999): 929–956.

CASES

United States v. Aguilar, 515 U.S. 593 (1995).
United States v. Brenson, 104 F.3d 1267 (11th Cir. 1997).
United States v. Poindexter, 951 F.2d 369 (D.C.Cir. 1991), cert. denied, 506 U.S. 1021 (1992).

ORGANIZED CRIME

As with several terms in criminology, *organized crime* has been defined in a variety of ways and there is surprisingly little consensus regarding its meaning. In part this is because, unlike in the case of homicide or robbery or many other types of offenses, organized crime is a conceptual rather than a legal category. The issue of definition is an important one, however, since how we define organized crime has very important implications for how we attempt to explain it and for the steps we take as a society to prevent or control it.

Of course, all crime is organized to some degree. The criminal acts of juvenile delinquents, a small group of minor thieves, or a three-person team of con artists suggest at least minimal levels of social organization. Yet we do not usually intend the term "organized crime" to include such activities or groups. All crimes and criminals are located along a continuum of organizational sophistication that identifies differences with respect to factors such as the division of labor or stability over time. The importation, preparation, distribution, and sale of illegal drugs is a more organized crime than is a simple mugging; and a group of criminals who steal cars, modify them, and then ship them for sale outside of the United States requires more organization than a group of juveniles who commit the occasional act of convenience store theft. By implication, if not more explicitly, the term "organized crime" refers to groups and acts at the high rather than the low end of any continuum of organizational sophistication.

Unfortunately, the tendency to use the term "organized crime" to refer simultaneously to a type of behavior and a type of person often leads to circular reasoning. For instance, the phrase "'organized crime' is involved in narcotics distribution in New York" is tautological because narcotics distribution is an organized crime and whoever is involved in it is by definition in organized crime. Most typically, organized crime is defined in ways that emphasize high levels of cooperation among groups of professional criminals. In this way, the category organized crime is viewed as synonymous with the category organized criminals. In popular parlance, for instance, organized crime has been equated with "the mob," "the Mafia" or "The Syndicate."

Critics of definitions that tend to equate organized crime with criminal associations are quite correct in pointing out that such definitions discourage our potential understanding of the wide variety of other social actors involved in organized crime. Thus, they contend, there is more to organized crime than associations of professional criminals. There are victims, customers, regulators, suppliers, competitors, and innocent bystanders. Viewed this way, the criminal association is merely one component in a much more complex web of interrelationships that comprise organized crime. Moreover, the configurations among these various elements are always changing and these changes affect the ways in which any particular component (including the criminal association) is organized.

For these writers, organized crime is more usefully conceptualized as a set of market relationships rather than as criminal associations or secret societies. This position reflects the view that many of the kinds of activities with which we customarily associate organized crime—drug dealing, loan-sharking, gambling, the infiltration of legitimate business—are market activities and, therefore, the kinds of questions we need to ask about organized crime are the same kinds of questions we would need to ask about any kind of business. How are goods marketed? How are contractual obligations enforced? What sorts of relationships link criminal entrepreneurs to the general public as well as to those who seek to use state power to regulate their activities? Thus, organized crime involves an ongoing criminal conspiracy, ordered around market relationships that involve victims, offenders, customers, and corrupt officials among others.

To a considerable degree, criminological debates about how to best define organized crime (like debates about its history, structure, and most other matters) are fueled by the problems that plague efforts to undertake original research into organized crime. Many of the standard methodological tools of social science—the survey or the experiment, for instance—that are employed with effectiveness in addressing the nature of other forms of offending, lack real application in the study of organized crime. As a result, much of what we know, we have learned indirectly. Popular journalism, the findings of government investigations, and criminal and civil investigations have often substituted for firsthand observation by criminological researchers. For many critics, the lack of original research and the reliance on these other data sources make it difficult to separate fact from fiction. Moreover, when original research has been undertaken, such as the study by Francis Ianni and Elizabeth Reuss-Ianni of a New York Italian American crime family, it has often proven to be sharply critical of the official view of organized crime. Such studies have tended to reveal a considerably more complex picture than the one that often emerges in the pages of the "true crime" or fictional narrative or from the proceedings of government inquiries.

History

The pirates who plundered and looted merchant vessels in the seventeenth century and who undertook large-scale trade in stolen goods may be considered among the earliest organized crime groups to make their appearance in the Western world. Many of the activities that are associated with contemporary organized crime, such as prostitution, gambling, theft, and various forms of extortion, were also evident in the frontier communities of the nineteenth-century American West.

However, most observers locate the origins of the distinctly American style of organized crime in the urban centers of the late nineteenth and early twentieth centuries. In a fundamental way, urban conditions provided the kind of environment in which organized crime could flourish. The large population sizes provided a "critical mass" of offenders, customers, and victims and thereby facilitated the development of profitable markets in illicit goods and services. Moreover, the size and density of urban networks allowed criminal forms of organization to become diversified and encouraged the growth of essential support services (such as those offered by corrupt politicians or police).

These early forms of criminal organization were typically tied to local areas and because of the highly segregated character of the city, they had important ethnic dimensions. Irish neighborhoods, for instance, gave rise to street gangs with names like "The Bowery Boys" and the "O'Connell's Guards" and in Chinese, African

American, Italian, and Jewish neighborhoods criminal organization similarly reflected local cultural and economic circumstances. Neighborhood conditions provided ample opportunity for local criminal entrepreneurs who were willing and able to engage in a various forms of extortion or illicit marketeering.

During the first two decades of the twentieth century, residents of the "Little Italies" of many eastern industrialized urban areas had to contend with a crude form of protection racket known as "La Mano Nera" or "the Black Hand." Those members of the local community who were better off financially might receive an anonymous note demanding that a sum of money be paid to the writer. If payment was not forthcoming, victims were typically warned that they could expect to have their businesses bombed or the safety of their family members jeopardized. Customarily, the extortion demand was signed with a crude drawing of a black hand. While the receiver of the letter (as well as other members of the community) were led to believe that the Black Hand was a large and powerful organization, it is more likely that the extortion was the work of individuals or a small group of offenders who used their victims' fear of secret societies (and often their fear of the police) to coerce payment.

While most forms of criminal organization prior to World War I were relatively small-scale operations, the situation changed dramatically with the introduction of Prohibition. The Eighteenth Amendment to the U.S. Constitution was ratified on 16 January 1919 and went into effect one year later. The intention of the national experiment was to control alcohol use through the prevention of the manufacture, sale, and transportation of intoxicating liquors. In essence, national prohibition had created an illegal market unlike any that had existed before.

It can be argued that national prohibition facilitated the consolidation of the power of criminal organizations. Although pre-Prohibition criminal enterprises had often been profitable, the revenue potential of Prohibition was unprecedented. While precise estimates of the amount of money that flowed through organized crime groups are difficult to make, it is clear that the manufacture and sale of illegal alcohol had become a major industry. In 1927, for instance, the U.S. Attorney's Office estimated that the criminal organization of the notorious Chicago gangster Al Capone had an annual income of $105 million. In subsequent years, the profits from the sale of illegal alcohol in Chicago and other cities funded the movement of criminal organizations into diverse sectors of both the licit and the illicit economies.

The importation and distribution of illegal alcohol also encouraged national and international linkages between criminal groups. For instance, the involvement of Canadian organized crime figures in smuggling operations that moved alcohol to the United States facilitated the eventual control by American organized crime groups of Canadian criminal operations in cities such as Toronto and Montreal. On a national level, intergroup cooperation was evidenced by regional conferences of those involved in the illicit liquor business. One such major gathering of crime figures was held in Atlantic City in 1929 and was attended by representatives from criminal organizations located in several major urban areas.

Importantly, the profitability of those industries that subverted national prohibition fostered an environment of widespread corruption in several cities. For many members of the general public as well as many law enforcement and elected officials, prohibition lacked any real moral authority. The relationships between criminal organizations and the political machines that held sway in many cities were stabilized during Prohibition, and the intricate connections between these sectors of the urban social fabric were maintained for decades to come.

The Great Depression of the 1930s did not affect the business of organized crime to the degree it affected many aspects of the legitimate economy. After Prohibition ended in 1933, major criminal organizations diversified and became increasingly powerful in the process. Gambling, loan-sharking, and the growth industry of narcotics distribution became important sources of criminal revenue as repeal threatened the proceeds from the illegal sale of alcohol.

An increasingly significant area of enterprise during this period was "racketeering." While the term may be defined many different ways, it generally refers to the variety of means by which organized crime groups, through the use of violence (actual or implied), gain control of labor unions or legitimate businesses. Often, though, the relationships that joined organized crime groups to unions or legitimate business were mutually advantageous. The leadership of a labor union, for example, might seek to exploit the violent reputation of those involved in organized crime in order to pressure an employer to meet a demand for concessions. Similarly, a business owner might attempt to control the competitive character of the legitimate marketplace or to avert labor troubles through affiliation with those willing to use violence and intimidation in the pursuit of economic goals. The International Longshoremen's Association and the International Brotherhood of Teamsters are among the best known examples of labor organizations affected by racketeering.

In 1950, organized crime became a highly visible part of American popular culture. A series of televised congressional hearings chaired by Senator Estes Kefauver sought not only the testimony of law enforcement experts but also of supposed members of organized crime networks. In general, the latter type of witness tended to remain silent or to otherwise express an unwillingness to provide evidence. These refusals made for startling television viewing and were interpreted by many observers as unambiguous proof of the sinister character of the problem of organized crime.

In its final report the Kefauver committee concluded that organized crime in America was largely under the control of an alien conspiracy known as "the Mafia." The Kefauver committee argued that the organization, which was said to have its origins in Sicily, was firmly in control of gambling, narcotics, political corruption, and labor racketeering in America. The Mafia, it was suggested, cemented its power through the use of violence, intimidation, and corruption.

The influence of the Kefauver committee in shaping postwar perceptions of organized crime as the product of an alien conspiracy, which subverts American social structure rather than emerging from it, cannot be underestimated. Its findings influenced significantly the ways in which policymakers, journalists, academics, and members of the general public would think about the problem of organized crime for decades to come. However, critics have charged that the committee was more engaged by the process of public drama than by a search for the truth. In this respect, it can be argued that the committee had very little proof upon which to base the startling conclusions that it reached about the nationwide conspiracy of ethnic criminals.

A number of developments in subsequent decades nevertheless appeared to be consistent with the findings of the Kefauver committee. In 1957, an apparent conclave of Mafia members was raided in the small upstate town of Apalachin, New York. In 1963, another congressional investigation of organized crime (known popularly as the McClellan committee) heard testimony from a supposed Mafia insider, named Joseph Valachi. According to Valachi, the control of organized crime in America rested with an organization known as "La Cosa Nostra" rather than the Mafia. Valachi described the character of the organization, the oaths that its members took, and recounted the historical process by which the modern La Cosa Nostra was formed after a purge of the older and more traditional Mafia leadership of the 1930s. Once again, critics pointed out that very little of what Valachi had to say could be corroborated independently and that he himself had a record of lying to law enforcement authorities when it suited his purpose. Still, Valachi's testimony helped strengthen a kind of ideological and moral consensus around the view of organized crime as an alien parasitic conspiracy rather than as a problem indigenous to American social life. Moreover, his testimony and the work of the McClellan committee more generally legitimated the subsequent development of investigative approaches to organized crime, including the widespread use of wiretaps, witness immunity, and other strategies facilitated by the passage of the Organized Crime Control Act of 1970.

In 1967, President Lyndon Johnson appointed the President's Commission on Law Enforcement and Administration of Justice to examine all aspects of crime and justice in America. One of the task forces associated with this commission was charged with the responsibility of investigating the nature and dimensions of organized crime. The report of that task force, shaped principally by the well-known criminologist Donald Cressey, reinforced and extended the view of organized crime as an alien ethnic conspiracy. According to the task force, La Cosa Nostra was comprised of approximately five thousand members organized within twenty-four "families" each of which was associated with a particular regional sphere of influence. Moreover, these families were said to be organized in terms of a rigid hierarchical chain of command. The highest level of decision-making in the organization was a "National Commission" that served as a combination legislature, supreme court, and board of directors.

While a number of critics dissented, there was a widespread consensus by the 1970s that organized crime did indeed reflect an Italian American hegemony. The apparent findings of investigative commissions and task forces were underwritten by films such as *The Godfather, The Valachi Papers,* and *Mean Streets* as well as by other elements of popular culture. At the same time, it was increasingly acknowledged that other groups were beginning to make significant inroads in organized crime. Typically described in terms of their ethnicity, such groups were said to include African Americans, Hispanics, Asians, and Russians. The powerful character of earlier organized crime imagery affected the ways in which such groups were labeled by the mass media and by relevant policy communities and it became common to speak of the growing power of the black, Mexican, or Russian "Mafias."

By the 1980s many observers had come to the conclusion that whatever control La Cosa Nostra exerted over organized crime was in decline. The systems of widespread corruption that had emerged out of Prohibition typically involved well-articulated relationships between organized crime groups on the one hand and established political machines on the other. These machines, which facilitated the centralization of police and urban political corruption, had largely disappeared by the 1970s. Moreover, because municipal policing had become more professionalized and because federal agencies had begun to develop an increasing interest in the activities of organized crime, the bases of large-scale, long-term corruption had been undermined.

The passage of new legislation aimed at the control of organized crime and the aggressive prosecution of cases involving Italian organized crime figures also did much to weaken the hold that La Cosa Nostra had on licit and illicit businesses. Perhaps most important in this respect was the passage of the RICO (Racketeer Influenced and Corrupt Organizations) Act and related statutes. The members of Italian American organizations in Philadelphia, Kansas City, Boston, and elsewhere were effectively prosecuted and high-visibility cases were brought against well-known figures such as John Gotti and the heads of the five New York crime families were seen as clear proof of the power of the prosecutorial assault.

It is also worth noting that the decline within urban areas of traditional Italian communities and the movement of second and third generations to the suburbs removed from cities much of the popular support that many organized crime figures had previously enjoyed. In addition, it has been suggested that the continued tendency of the Mafia (or La Cosa Nostra) to recruit new members from a dwindling pool of uneducated and violent felons did little to ensure the adaptability of the organization as the business of organized crime became more complex at the end of the twentieth century. In addition, the gains made by other ethnic groups often came at the expense of the Italian American crime syndicate's interests. The traditional control of the heroin markets was lost to Mexican and Asian groups whose strategies for importation of the drug did not depend on the muscle that the Mafia may have been able to exert for so long against the New York waterfront. Similarly, the very lucrative cocaine business was under the control of Colombian cartels rather than Cosa Nostra families. The cartels required neither the financing nor the private violence that the Italian syndicate might have been able to lend to the operation of an illicit market. Such groups were themselves well financed and in possession of their own fearsome reputations regarding the use of violence to settle disputes or to threaten competition.

The concern in the 1980s and 1990s about the emergence of new organized groups was accompanied by a concern about the increasingly transnational character of organized crime. This crime trend has been understood, in large part, as an outcome of the post–cold war reconfiguration of national and economic boundaries. The reduction in trade restrictions, the development of global systems of finance and telecommunications, the increasingly transparent nature of national borders, and the dramatic internal changes in many nations (such as those in the former Soviet Union) made it easier for criminal conspirators to expand their operations internationally. Such operations are tracked, investigated, and prosecuted with great difficulty since effective enforcement requires levels of international cooperation among policing agencies from different nations that often vary markedly regarding their enforcement priorities and the resources available to them.

Police intelligence during the period suggested, for instance, that organized crime groups from the former Soviet Union, Asia, and Italy were forming partnerships among themselves as well as with drug merchants in Central and South America. As in the case of legitimate business, such foreign expansions resulted from the desire to engage new markets. The links between Colombian drug cartels and the Sicilian Mafia, for example, reflected an interest on the part of the cartels to enter European markets where, as compared to the United States, cocaine could be sold at a higher price and where drug enforcement activity was less aggressive. Estimates of the economic impact of transnational crime are difficult to make and run as high as several hundred billion dollars annually.

The international context

Particularly salient aspects of organized crime in the United States are its apparent durability and the degree to which it has permeated popular culture. Over the decades it has evolved in ways that suggest both an endemic social problem and a distinctly American cultural mythology. Such considerations do not imply, however, that the phenomenon of organized crime is in any sense unique to the United States.

Of course, cross-national comparisons of organized crime levels and activities are exceptionally difficult to make, given considerable variation in legal codes, and the quantity and quality of intelligence information. As a result, generalizations about the kinds of national characteristics that do or do not provide the environment in which organized crime will flourish are always tentative. However, several factors do seem to have real relevance in this respect.

One such factor is the gap that exists between the goods and services which citizens demand and the legal codes that attempt to regulate supply. The experience with alcohol prohibition in the United States (as well as with current drug policies) has convinced many that when laws are designed to regulate illicit markets, organized crime is an inevitability. In the former Soviet Union, an extremely large black market thrived as all forms of individual economic enterprise were illegal. It has been argued that the personnel, who comprise the organized crime groups that have come to be seen as an extremely serious problem in the post-Soviet societies of Eastern Europe, developed their entrepreneurial skills in the context of such market economies.

Traditions and political structures conducive to corruption are also very important to the development of organized crime. The role attributed to American urban political machines is not unique in this respect. The historically authoritarian character of Soviet society encouraged the subversion of the legal control of many forms of entrepreneurial activity and fostered widespread disrespect for the law and political authority. It can be suggested that the immense wealth accumulated by drug cartels in Mexico, Colombia,

and other countries when combined with political traditions of one-party rule (as in Mexico or Nigeria, for example) and an immense gap between rich and poor, make political and law enforcement corruption, and as a consequence, organized crime, likely outcomes.

The development of organized crime is also related to geographic location. The proximity of Mexico and Canada to the United States, for instance, has affected the growth of organized crime in both countries. For Mexican crime groups, proximity to the United States provides access to a sizeable and relatively easily penetrable drug market. In the Canadian case, the cultural and social similarities to the United States, and a relatively open border, in addition to several other factors, facilitated the movement northward of major organized crime groups in the 1950s and 1960s. In a different way, according to the U.S. State Department, Chile had avoided, until the closing years of the twentieth century, many of the problems with organized crime that are characteristic of other South American countries due largely to its geographic isolation.

While it is clear that organized crime can emerge out of many different sorts of political contexts, perhaps it is most secure in nations with liberal democratic traditions that emphasize upward mobility and individual achievement. In the United States, cultural approval of the upwardly bound is pervasive and an important part of national ideology. It has often been the case that cultural support of the organized criminal has been no less extensive than for those who have made fortunes in more conventional ways. Not only within their own ethnic communities but also within the wider society, organized crime figures such as Al Capone and John Gotti have emerged as folk heroes and media celebrities.

Ethnic succession and organized crime

The role that ethnicity plays in shaping American organized crime has long been at the center of a heated debate among criminologists. Two broad schools of thought may be identified in this regard. The first, which many critics label the "alien conspiracy theory," assigns primary significance to the role played by Italian American groups in organized crime from the early days of this century until at least the 1980s. From this point of view, large scale American organized crime emerged out of earlier forms of Italian criminal organization such as the "Black Hand" gangs discussed earlier. Such gangs were themselves thought by advocates of this position to have reflected criminal styles and organizational forms imported to America from Sicily and other areas of southern Italy during the large-scale immigration of the late nineteenth and early twentieth centuries. While small-scale forms of criminal organization may have predated the importation of the Mafia, advocates of this view maintain that the history of organized crime in America really is the history of the American Mafia. It is claimed that internecine struggles among groups of Italian American gangsters in the 1930s (known as the Castellammarese War) led to the Americanization of the Mafia and the emergence of a new and dynamic leadership that is associated with such well-known organized crime figures of the 1940s and 1950s as Charles "Lucky" Luciano, Frank Costello, and Vito Genovese. As the Americanized "La Cosa Nostra" replaced the more traditional organizational form of the Mafia, Italian American hegemony over organized crime was firmly established for several decades. From this point of view, it is not ethnicity as a variable that matters so much as the distinctive ethnicity of Mafia members. By implication, there is something very unique about the cultural character of southern Italy that has frequently predisposed immigrants from those regions to become involved in organized crime. Not surprisingly, Italian Americans have long complained about the Mafia stereotype and about the suggestion that organized crime is exclusively or largely the domain of those with Italian ancestry.

While the alien conspiracy theory has been legitimated by journalists, government inquiries, and many scholars, its critics argue that it too often substitutes myth for fact. There is, for instance, very little evidence to suggest that Italian American crime was characterized by a unilinear evolution or even that certain of the pivotal events (such as the Castellammarese War) even took place. However, critics charge, the most serious limitation of this argument may be that it tends to treat organized crime as a "special case." Because it attributes organized crime to a small number of criminal conspirators and to unique secret societies, the perspective asks few questions to which general answers can be given. By conceptualizing organized crime as the product of "evil" groups and by conceptualizing these groups as the product of singular social circumstances and powerful personalities, the argument

blocks the way to a more abstract understanding of the problem. Moreover, by viewing organized crime as something that is imported to America, rather than as an indigenous product, the perspective does not seek to explain the relationships that link such crime to elements of American social structure.

A second perspective attempts to provide a historical context for the Italian American experience by arguing that it is part of a much broader process of "ethnic succession" in organized crime. This argument maintains that organized crime is not the exclusive domain of any one ethnic group. Rather, groups move into organized crime when other channels of upward social mobility are not open to them, and move out as more legitimate means of attaining wealth, power, and prestige become available. According to the sociologist Daniel Bell, who originally made this argument in the 1950s, organized crime functions as a "queer ladder of social mobility."

Thus, advocates of the ethnic succession argument maintain that in the burgeoning cities of the late nineteenth and early twentieth centuries, organized crime was dominated by the Irish. As Irish gangs formed, they became connected to urban political machines that were also under Irish control. As the legitimate power structure became increasingly available to Irish Americans, however, they began to view organized crime as less attractive, and as they moved out of such activity, other groups—most notably Jewish and Italian organized criminals—assumed an increasingly important presence. However, because the Italian domination of organized crime coincided with the rise of mass media, and the investigative activities of the Keafauver committee and other government bodies, the one-to-one correspondence between organized crime and Italian ethnicity became fixed in public discourse.

As Italian dominance in organized crime declined in the 1970s and 1980s, the process of ethnic succession continued. African American, Hispanics, Asians, Russians, and others, it is said, have each in turn replaced their predecessors as changes in the legitimate structures of opportunity have accommodated—often grudgingly—groups who previously played significant roles in organized crime.

The ethnic succession argument presents a more complicated picture of the relationships involving organized crime, ethnicity, and American social structure than the one suggested by theories of alien conspiracies. It contends that organized crime is not imported to America but is instead a logical product of the distinctly American character of minority group stratification and of the restrictions on legitimate opportunities that minorities face. Organized crime is not the property of any particular group but rather a means of social mobility that the existence of illicit markets makes available. As such it has been intertwined historically with other semilegitimate channels of upward mobility, such as entertainment, boxing, and union and urban politics. Like organized crime, these channels of upward mobility do not depend on credentials or family status and, as a result, have also been characterized by processes of ethnic succession.

Analytically, the ethnic succession argument encourages a focus on the variable character of ethnic group experiences in organized crime. Not all groups have been involved in such crime and those that have been involved have tended, often, to specialize in particular forms of illicit activity. By recognizing the differing experiences that groups have with organized crime, it is possible to develop a more general understanding of how ethnicity and historical circumstance interact. Some groups, such as the Germans and Scandinavians, were more likely to settle in rural areas of the Midwest rather than in urban areas of the east, and as a result their involvement in organized crime was less typical. In a consistent way, the cultural backgrounds of other groups have influenced the kinds of illegal activities in which they did become involved. Early in the twentieth century, for instance, the Irish specialized in gambling and labor racketeering. The latter choice reflected their more general involvement in the leadership of the labor movement. It has also been argued that the large-scale involvement of Italian organized criminals in the illegal alcohol business during prohibition represented an attempt to enter an illicit market that was new and thus not under Irish control. Much later in the twentieth century, Vietnamese and Chinese organized crime groups have specialized in extortion and the importation of drugs, while Russian groups have specialized in various forms of fraud, forgery, and counterfeiting.

Aspects of organized crime other than market specialization may also be related to ethnicity. Cultural experience, for instance, may relate to the level of mistrust of government, the degree of community tolerance for particular types of organized crime activities, the willingness to use violence, and to the forms that criminal organizations assume.

Some critics have charged that the theory of ethnic succession is too simplistic. In short, it is suggested that the image of ethnic groups as, in some sense, lined up and waiting their turn to enter organized crime and then neatly exiting when legitimate opportunities present themselves is not consistent with the historical record. There are several strands to this criticism. First, there is historical evidence to support the conclusion that in many cities—including, for example, Philadelphia, Minneapolis, and Cleveland— organized crime has not been under the control of any particular ethnic group but has been run instead by multiethnic hierarchies.

Second, it may be erroneous to assume that organized crime is a channel of upward mobility readily available to those who are at the bottom of the social hierarchy and who lack access to more conventional channels. Rather, the process has been more complicated such that success in large-scale organized crime appears to be possible only after at least some gains have been made in the conventional order. As stated, the success of the Irish in organized crime early in the century depended on their collaborative relationships with the police, labor unions, and political machines. Thus, prior success in more conformist spheres seems to make success at organized crime possible.

Third, the ethnic succession argument appears to assume that organized crime is a zero-sum game such that movement into this activity is only possible when other groups move out. This need not be the case. If particular markets (for instance, the market in marijuana) do not tend toward monopolization, then clearly groups can move in without pushing anyone else out. Another line of criticism maintains that the major weakness of the argument concerns its failure to explain why, within any ethnic group, some individuals rather than others involve themselves in organized crime. This criticism rightly alerts us to the observation that, with respect to any ethnic group, it is only a very small minority who engage in organized crime. Most ethnic group members remain hardworking, develop legitimate entrepreneurial enterprises, and in general strive to make effective use of those opportunities that do present themselves. According to this view, movement into organized crime is not a response to a reduction in opportunity but a rationally chosen style of life that exploits subterranean American values regarding "easy money" and "the fast life." The General Theory of Crime, developed by Michael Gottfredson and Travis Hirschi, suggests that those who engage in organized crime, like those who engage in other forms of crime, do so because they lack high levels of "self control" rather than because they experience the frustration borne of blocked opportunity. A corresponding point can be made regarding the tenet of ethnic succession theory that those who are forced into organized crime move out when legitimate opportunities present themselves. Some observers, such as Peter Lupsha, have noted that movement out often seems more a matter of defeat or attrition than of any effort to gain real respectability. The Italian American organized crime figures who had risen to prominence by the middle of the twentieth century left organized crime principally as a result of death or prosecution. Many of those who remained faced vigorous opponents who sought a share of the businesses that they controlled.

Structure

Questions about the structure of organized crime usually involve a consideration of two distinct yet related issues. The first concerns the form and level of organization that characterize criminal associations. The second involves a consideration of the structure of the various markets within which these associations operate.

With respect to the first question, debate has centered around the level of rationality of organized crime groups. In simple terms, the concept of rationality refers to the degree of "organizational sophistication." To the extent that organized crime groups are highly rational, they possess a well-defined division of labor, formal authority relations, and a structural permanence which implies that the organization exists independently of the people that comprise it at any particular point in time. Those descriptions of La Cosa Nostra, for instance, as a relatively formalized bureaucracy with positions for "bosses," "underbosses," and "soldiers" suggest a highly formalized model.

In contrast, it has been argued that organized crime groups more closely resemble informal rather than formal organizations. In this model, organized crime groups are said to consist principally of localized sets of loosely structured relationships that derive from kin and other forms of intimate association. The organizational context is seen to be based less on bureaucratic formality and more on shared cultural understandings and cooperation. Analyses by James O. Finckenauer and Elin K. Waring of the structure of the "Russian Mafia" in America, for instance, reveal that criminal associations typically resemble informal networks and as such are not centralized or dominated by any small group of individuals. Moreover, those individuals who do exert particular influence in these networks do so because of personal influence rather than because of positions that they occupy. There is also little evidence to support the view that these organizational structures outlive the involvement of their central participants.

Some critics of the more formalized model, such as historian Mark Haller, maintain that it is incorrect—at least in the case of Italian American crime organizations—to equate an association of organized criminals with a business enterprise. Rather, the members of such associations are relatively independent entrepreneurs who run their own illegal businesses from which they derive income. The organization does not provide "jobs" but serves the needs of its members in a variety of ways, not the least of which is the establishment of relationships and partnerships that facilitate the exploitation of illicit opportunities. Of course, not all groups operate this way and it is important to distinguish those that function like businessmen's associations from those that are themselves business enterprises. The Cosa Nostra differs from a Colombian drug cartel in that the former is a type of social group that serves the interests of its members while the latter is a business group that is concerned with the sale and distribution of illicit goods. To group them together would be to confuse organizations like the Rotary Club with businesses like department stores.

It is also possible that differing views about the level of rationality of organized crime are not so much in conflict as they are differentially applicable. It may be that at certain (higher) levels of some crime organizations, authority is relatively formalized and, to some degree, structure exists quite independently of the activities in which the group is involved at any particular time. At the same time, relationships involving those at lower levels of the organization—or involving those in the organization and those beyond it—function in much more informal ways. Thus, rationality may not only vary between crime organizations but within them as well.

With respect to the structure of the markets in which organized crime is engaged, a key structural issue concerns what is sometimes assumed to be the inevitability of market monopolization. From one point of view, the trend toward monopoly is the central and defining feature of organized crime. Through the provision of "protection" to those involved in illicit businesses (such as bookmakers), through the establishment of trade associations involving legitimate sectors of the economy (such as the laundry business), or through other extortionate practices, organized crime groups are able to monopolize the delivery of particular goods and services.

In contrast, others have argued that the tendency of illicit markets associated with organized crime is to resist monopolization. Based on an analysis of gambling and loan-sharking operations in the New York City area, for instance, Peter Reuter (1983) concluded that the fear of police intervention and a lack of court-enforceable contracts tend to make markets fragmented and localized. Moreover, entry into such markets was relatively easy and prices for illegal services were set by the competitive power of the marketplace rather than by any sort of central pricing authority. While violence might be expected to facilitate monopolies, it has been found that it is used less frequently (and is less useful) than is sometimes believed. Not only does the use of violence invite police scrutiny, it also suggests a rather unstable mechanism for market control. By implication, any such monopoly is always vulnerable to groups as willing or more willing to use violence.

Activities

The range of activities in which organized crime groups are said to be involved is vast indeed. Traditionally, it has been argued that these activities are of two major types. The first involves the distribution and sale of illicit goods and services. Specifically such illicit enterprises might include prostitution, drugs, gambling, pornography, and loan-sharking. Extortion, the other major form of activity, is undertaken as an end in itself or as the means to other ends. These extortionate practices include various forms of business and labor racketeering and, it is argued, they have often provided the point of entry by which organized crime groups "infiltrate" legitimate businesses. While infiltration may in some cases be the appropriate word, in other cases, it obscures the role played by business interests that knowingly engage with organized crime groups because they believe it is in their best interests to do so. Such cases suggest collaboration

rather than infiltration since the relationship is more symbiotic than parasitic. Thus, a legitimate business might use the relationship with an organized crime group as a source of investment capital while the organized crime group might view the relationship as an effective way to launder funds, diversify risk, or achieve some level of public respectability.

What illicit marketeering and extortion share in common, to some degree, is the potential for organization and routinization. In all such cases, not only collaborators but also victims understand the nature of the relationships in which they are involved. However, both groups may be unwilling to share the task of preventing or controlling the prohibited conduct. This may be because of their own profit-sharing, in the case of collaborators, or because they fear that such action could put them in danger, as in the case of victims.

Other forms of activities associated with organized crime groups—such as the use of violence or political corruption—must be understood in terms that stress the instrumental character of such practices. By definition, the businesses of organized crime operate beyond the reach of law and therefore conflicts that arise among participants cannot be resolved using the state-approved legal apparatus. Under such conditions, violence (and more importantly the threat of violence) assume some significance as techniques of conflict resolution. In a related way, organized crime groups need to be able to evade or to neutralize those state agencies charged with their control. Traditionally, corruption has proven to be an important mechanism by which this task is accomplished. As in the case of the infiltration of legitimate business, however, corruption is more often a form of symbiotic relationship than a form of victimization.

By the 1980s and 1990s, policymakers and academics alike had begun to argue that it would be misleading to think about organized crime activities in traditionally narrow terms. While various forms of extortion and marketeering continued to be important income sources, organized crime had become much more sophisticated. Of particular interest in this respect was the increasingly important role that criminal associations were thought to play in various financial markets. In the late 1990s, for instance, it was claimed that organized crime groups owned or controlled several New York brokerage firms.

During this period, attention also focused on the crime of money laundering. As cash businesses, drug trafficking, gambling, and other organized crimes generate huge amounts of money that is vulnerable to seizure by state authorities. The movement of these funds through international money markets not only launders the money but also in many cases extends criminal enterprises and facilitates corruption and bribery. It has been estimated that over $750 billion in illicit funds is laundered worldwide annually of which $300 billion is laundered through the United States.

Controlling organized crime

For many observers, organized crime is not only an object of academic study but also a practical problem about which something needs to be done. Policies aimed at the control of organized crime have tended to emphasize one of two types of strategies. The first targets the members of organized crime groups while the second focuses on the structural characteristics and market relationships that make organized crime possible. It is important to stress that these two broad strategies are not in conflict with each other. However, they do reflect quite different assumptions about how the human and economic resources available for the control of organized crime should be employed.

Strategies that focus on the members of organized crime groups tend to involve the use of the criminal justice system for the purpose of prosecuting offenders. Local state and federal agencies have used a wide arsenal of investigative and prosecutorial weapons to this end. These have included the extensive use of wiretaps, witness immunity and witness protection programs, and special grand juries. Perhaps the most important prosecutorial tool is the Racketeer Influenced and Corrupt Organizations (RICO) Act, which was passed in 1970. The act makes it a crime to acquire an interest in, to participate in the affairs of, or to invest the profits acquired from an enterprise through a pattern of racketeering activity. In the period after 1980, most significant organized crime prosecutions involved the use of the RICO statutes, and the decimation of the traditional Cosa Nostra organization has been attributed to RICO prosecutions.

Critics, however, maintain that all such policies have an inherent limitation in that they proceed from the assumption that the control—through prosecution—of members of organized crime groups is somehow synonymous with the control of organized crime. Such "headhunting"

approaches, it is argued, confuse the arrest and prosecution of offenders with the control of the activities in which offenders engage. It has been suggested that even when they are successful, these strategies remove only some illicit entrepreneurs from the marketplace and thereby strengthen the rewards for those who remain. This outcome may be made more likely by the tendency of law enforcement to prosecute most successfully those operators who are smallest and weakest. Historically, it has been the case, critics argue, that the response to criminal prosecution is often adaptation on the part of organized crime groups. In the latter years of the twentieth century, for instance, the transparency of many national borders, and the growth of the Internet and of international money markets facilitated such adaptations by posing complex jurisdictional problems to enforcement agencies.

Rather than focus on the members of organized crime groups as the object of policy attention, many analysts argue, it is necessary to focus on the environments within which the businesses that comprise organized crime operate. Seen in this way, organized crime may require market rather than law enforcement interventions. One such intervention aims to decriminalize or legalize those goods and services that form the basis for many organized crime markets. Thus, state lotteries and legalized gambling in places like Las Vegas and Atlantic City provide alternatives to a service that would otherwise only be available in illicit markets. However, the approach poses risks since it is not necessarily the case that legalization results in the destruction of illegal markets. It can instead create a social climate that proves to be even more supportive of illegal conduct.

Another strategy involves efforts to "follow the money." The recognition that organized crime activity facilitates the accumulation of large amounts of cash that must be laundered implies a need to make the money itself the object of policy attention. Money laundering by organized crime groups in the 1980s and 1990s (particularly the profits from the drug trade) has facilitated the relationships between organized crime groups and organizations in the more legitimate economy as well as between such groups and the governments of states for which such money is an important source of revenue. Thus, increasing attention has focused on the development of "money laundering" laws and policies that take the profits away from offenders by seizing or freezing assets derived from organized crimes.

Indeed, in the United States, money laundering prosecutions rose 400 percent between 1991 and 1993. Effective money laundering policies necessitate a degree of international cooperation that cannot always be achieved either because of differences in enforcement resources or in political will. Such strategies also depend heavily on long-term undercover operations, stings, and the use of informants, all of which pose difficult ethical problems.

VINCENT F. SACCO

See also ALCOHOL AND CRIME: THE PROHIBITION EXPERIMENT; CRIMINAL CAREERS; GAMBLING; RICO (RACKETEER INFLUENCED AND CORRUPT ORGANIZATIONS ACT).

BIBLIOGRAPHY

ABADINSKY, HOWARD. *Organized Crime,* 5th ed. Chicago: Nelson-Hall, 1977.

ALBANESE, JAY. *Organized Crime in America,* 3d ed. Cincinnati, Ohio: Anderson, 1998.

ALBINI, JOSEPH. *The American Mafia: Genesis of a Legend.* New York: Appleton-Century Crofts, 1971.

BEARE, MARGARET E. *Criminal Conspiracies: Organized Crime in Canada.* Scarborough, Ontario: Nelson Canada, 1996.

BERGREEN, LAURENCE. *Capone: The Man and the Era.* New York: Simon and Schuster, 1994.

BEST, JOEL, and LUCKENBILL, DAVID. *Organizing Deviance,* 2d ed. Englewood Cliffs, N.J.: Prentice-Hall, 1994.

BLOCK, ALAN. *East Side–West Side: Organizing Crime in New York 1930–1950.* Swansea, Wales: University College Cardiff Press, 1980.

CARTER, DAVID L. "International Organized Crime: Emerging Trends in Entrepreneurial Crime." *Journal of Contemporary Criminal Justice* 10 (4) (1994): 239–266.

CRESSEY, DONALD R. *Theft of the Nation.* New York: Harper and Row, 1969.

FINCKENAUER, JAMES O., and WARING, ELIN K. *Russian Mafia in America: Immigration, Culture and Crime.* Boston: Northeastern University Press, 1998.

GODSON, ROY, and OLSON, WILLIAM J. "International Organized Crime." *Society* 32, no. 2 (1995): 18–29.

GOTTFREDSON, MICHAEL R., and HIRSCHI, TRAVIS. *A General Theory of Crime.* Stanford, Calif.: Stanford University Press, 1990.

HALLER, MARK H. "Bureaucracy and the Mafia: An Alternative View." *Journal of Contemporary Criminal Justice* 8 (1982): 1–10.

——. "Illegal Enterprise: A Theoretical and Historical Interpretation." *Criminology* 28 (1990): 207–235.

IANNI, FRANCIS A. J., and REUSS-IANNI, ELIZABETH. *A Family Business: Kinship and Social Control in Organized Crime.* New York: New American Library, 1973.

——. *The Crime Society: Organized Crime and Corruption in America.* New York: New American Library, 1976.

JACOBS, JAMES B., and GOULDIN, LAURYN P. "Cosa Nostra: The Final Chapter?" In *Crime and Justice: A Review of Research,* vol. 25. Edited by Michael Tonry. Chicago: The University of Chicago Press, 1999. Pages 129–189.

JENKINS, PHILIP, and POTTER, GARY. "The Politics and Mythology of Organized Crime: A Philadelphia Case Study." *Journal of Criminal Justice* 15: 473–484.

KAPPELER, VICTOR E.; BLUMBERG, MARK; and POTTER, GARY W. *The Mythology of Crime and Criminal Justice,* 2d ed. Prospect Heights, Ill.: Waveland Press Inc., 1996.

KENNEY, DENNIS J., and FINCKENAUER, JAMES O. *Organized Crime in America.* Belmont, Calif.: Wadsworth Publishing Company, 1995.

LIGHT, IVAN. "The Ethnic Vice Industry, 1880–1944." *American Sociological Review* 42 (June 1977): 464–479.

LUPSHA, PETER. "Individual Choice, Material Culture, and Organized Crime." *Criminology* 19 (1981): 3–24.

MCINTOSH, MARY. *The Organization of Crime.* London: The Macmillan Press Ltd, 1975.

MOORE, WILLIAM HOWARD. *The Kefauver Committee and the Politics of Crime 1950–1952.* Columbia: University of Missouri Press, 1974.

MYERS, WILLARD H., III. "The Emerging Threat of Transnational Crime from the East." *Crime, Law and Social Change* 24 (1996): 181–222.

NELLI, HUMBERT. *The Business of Crime: Italians and Syndicate Crime in the United States.* New York: Oxford University Press, 1976.

O'KANE, JAMES M. *The Crooked Ladder: Gangsters, Ethnicity and the American Dream.* New Brunswick, N.J.: Transaction Publishers, 1992.

PEARCE, FRANK, and WOODIWISS, MICHAEL. *Global Crime Connections.* Toronto: University of Toronto Press, 1993.

REUTER, PETER. *Disorganized Crime: Economics of the Invisible Hand.* Cambridge, Mass.: MIT Press, 1983.

——. "The Decline of the American Mafia." *The Public Interest* 120 (1995): 89–99.

RICHARDS, JAMES R. *Transnational Criminal Organizations, Cybercrime, and Money Laundering: A Handbook for Law Enforcement Officers, Auditors and Financial Investigators.* Boca Raton, Fla.: CRC Press, 1999.

SCHATZBERG, RUFUS, and KELLY, ROBERT J. *African American Organized Crime.* New Brunswick, N.J.: Rutgers University Press, 1997.

SMITH, DWIGHT. *The Mafia Mystique.* New York: Basic Books, 1975.

TYLER, GUS. *Organized Crime in America: A Book of Readings.* Ann Arbor: The University of Michigan Press, 1967.

P

PERJURY

The American legal system, like most legal systems, relies heavily on the testimony of witnesses. Juries rely on witness testimony to reach verdicts in criminal and civil trials; grand juries rely on witness testimony to investigate crimes and to bring criminal charges; Congress relies on witness testimony in its legislative hearings; and a wide range of administrative agencies rely on witness testimony in making both policy decisions and rulings in specific matters. The decisions of each of these bodies are only as reliable as the witnesses appearing before them. The law making perjury a crime is one effort to encourage witnesses to be truthful.

Perjury at common law

Although false swearing or "bearing false witness" has been considered a spiritual offense since at least biblical times, perjury did not become a secular crime in England until much more recently. In the Middle Ages, witnesses as we know them did not exist. The witnesses were the jurors, and so it was the verdict, not a particular witness, that was either true or false. Correspondingly, it was the jurors, not the witnesses, who would be punished for a "false" or "perjurious" verdict. By the sixteenth century, when the modern trial by an independent and impartial jury began to emerge, perjury by witnesses also came to be punished separately, first by the Court of Star Chamber and later by English common law courts. By the mid-seventeenth century, common law perjury was defined as swearing falsely, under oath, in a judicial proceeding, about a material issue. This same definition of perjury was generally incorporated into early American common law and statutes.

Modern perjury statutes

Each of the fifty states has its own perjury statute, and federal law contains two general perjury provisions (18 U.S.C. §§ 1621, 1623). Although differences abound among these statutes, most modern perjury statutes have four elements: (1) the statement must be made under oath; (2) the statement must be false; (3) the speaker must intend to make a false statement; and (4) the statement must be material to the proceeding. Each element must be proven by the prosecution beyond a reasonable doubt.

Oath. The oath may take many different forms, so long as it contains a solemn declaration to tell the truth. It must, however, be administered by a person legally authorized to do so and in a setting in which the oath is authorized to be administered. The oath can apply both to oral testimony and to written declarations made under the penalties of perjury.

Falsity. To be perjurious, a statement made under oath must be false. Thus, a perjury conviction cannot be based upon a statement that is so vague or ambiguous that it cannot be considered affirmatively false. Similarly, as the Supreme Court held in *Bronston v. United States*, (409 U.S. 352 (1973)), a statement that is misleading, but not actually false, cannot lead to a perjury conviction. In that case, the defendant Bronston had testified under oath in a bankruptcy hearing, during which he was asked whether he had ever had any Swiss bank accounts. Bronston responded that his company had once had a Swiss bank account. Although Bronston's response was literally true, it was misleading because it suggested that Bronston had not had a personal Swiss bank account, which he had. The Supreme Court nevertheless held that Bronston could not be prosecuted for perjury because his answer, even if deliberately deceptive, was not actually false. While the Court did not condone Bronston's misleading testimony, it reasoned that it was the questioner's responsibility to ensure that Bronston's answers were not ambiguous or non-responsive.

Intent.   To be guilty of perjury, a defendant must do more than make a false statement under oath. The defendant must also intend to do so. Sometimes referred to as "scienter," this intent requirement is expressed in various ways. The federal perjury statutes require the false statement to be made "willfully" or "knowingly." Other state statutes require the statement to be made with an intent to mislead or with a belief that the statement was untrue. The intent requirement means that an "honest mistake" or an unknowing falsehood cannot be perjurious.

Materiality.   The final element of most perjury statutes is the requirement that the false statement be "material" to the proceeding in which it is made. To be material, a statement must have the tendency or capacity to influence the court or other body before which the statement is made. Materiality is a broad concept, and a statement will be considered material not only if it directly relates to the matters at issue in the proceeding, but also if it could lead to the discovery of other relevant evidence or if it could enhance (or detract from) the credibility of a witness.

Materiality was traditionally considered to be an issue of law to be decided by the judge presiding over a perjury prosecution. In 1995, however, in addressing the related crime of making an unsworn false statement, the Supreme Court ruled that the materiality of a false statement was an issue for the jury. Shortly thereafter, the Supreme Court applied the same reasoning to the materiality element in perjury prosecutions. Thus, as with the other elements of the crime, the materiality element in a perjury case must be proven by the prosecution to the jury beyond a reasonable doubt.

Perjury prosecutions

Perjurious testimony or declarations can be given in a wide variety of contexts. Perjury prosecutions, however, most often result from false testimony given in a criminal trial or before a grand jury. Less frequently, a perjury prosecution will be based on false testimony given in a civil trial. In rare cases, false testimony in a civil deposition can lead to a perjury prosecution. Under federal law and in most states, perjury is a felony.

In many cases, perjury charges are brought when a prosecution for other criminal conduct is not possible—for example, when the defendant has already been acquitted of the other criminal conduct, or the statute of limitations on that conduct has expired, or there simply is not enough evidence of the other criminal conduct. The perjury conviction of Alger Hiss in 1950 is perhaps the most famous modern example of such a prosecution. Although Hiss was never charged with spying, he was prosecuted for perjury for lying to the federal grand jury that was investigating the spying allegations.

Related offenses

Subornation.   Willfully procuring another person to commit perjury was traditionally considered to be a separate offense called subornation of perjury. This separate offense is largely superfluous, however, because one who causes or induces another to commit a crime is punishable under general principles of accomplice liability or solicitation. Although some states and the federal government still recognize subornation as a separate offense, the Model Penal Code recommends that the separate offense be eliminated.

False statement.   Federal law (18 U.S.C. § 1001) makes it a crime to make a false statement to the government. The elements of this offense are substantially similar to the elements of perjury. The statement must be false, it must be made "knowingly and willfully," and it must be material. Unlike with perjury, the statement need not be made under oath; however, it must be made in a matter within the jurisdiction of the executive, legislative, or judicial branches of the federal government. The jurisdictional element is construed broadly and includes not only false statements made directly to the government (for example, statements to an F.B.I. agent about an ongoing investigation), but also false statements made indirectly to the government (for example, statements to a defense contractor that will be relied upon by the government).

A few states have enacted general laws against making false statements to public officials or agencies, but most of those laws are limited to written statements, and some require that the statement be made after written notice that a false statement is punishable as a crime.

MICHAEL A. SIMONS

See also COUNSEL: ROLE OF COUNSEL; JURY: LEGAL ASPECTS; OBSTRUCTION OF JUSTICE.

BIBLIOGRAPHY

American Law Institute. *Model Penal Code and Commentaries: Official Draft and Revised Comments,* part 2, article 241. Philadelphia: ALI, 1980.

BLACKSTONE, WILLIAM. *Commentaries on the Laws of England,* vol. 4. Oxford, U.K.: Clarendon Press, 1769. Reprint, New York: Oceana, 1966.

FITZPATRICK, BRIDGET, and TORRACO, JOHN. "False Statements." *American Criminal Law Review* 36 (Summer 1999): 607–627.

GORDON, MICHAEL D. "The Invention of a Common Law Crime: Perjury and the Elizabethan Courts." *The American Journal of Legal History* 24 (1980): 145–170.

HOLDSWORTH, WILLIAM. *A History of English Law,* vol. 4. 3d ed. London: Methuen, 1977.

KISLAK, REBECCA, and DONOGHUE, JOHN J. "Perjury." *American Criminal Law Review* 36 (1999): 957–982.

NESLAND, JAMES, and GODWARD, COOLEY. "Perjury and False Declarations." In Otto G. Obermaier and Robert G. Morvillo, eds., *White Collar Crime: Business and Regulatory Offenses.* New York: Law Journal Seminars-Press, 1990. Pages 10–1 to 10–81.

PERKINS, ROLLIN M., and BOYCE, RONALD N. *Criminal Law,* 3d ed. Mineola, N.Y.: Foundation Press, 1982.

POLICE: HISTORY

Throughout the history of civilization, societies have sought protection for their members and possessions. In early civilizations, members of one's family provided this protection. Richard Lundman has suggested that the development of formal policing resulted from a process of three developmental stages. The first stage involves *informal policing,* where all members of a society share equally in the responsibility for providing protection and keeping order. The second stage, *transitional policing,* occurs when police functions are informally assigned to particular members of the society. This stage serves as a transition into *formal policing,* where specific members of the community assume formal responsibility for protection and social control. Lundman suggests that the history of police involved a shift from informal to formal policing. Indeed, as societies have evolved from *mechanical* (members share similar beliefs and values but meet their basic needs independently) to *organic* (members are dependent upon one another as a result of specialization) societies, social control became more complex. Whereas there was little need for formal, specialized policing in mechanical societies, organic societies require more specialization to ensure public order.

Over time, organic societies developed into states and governments. A *state* is defined as "a political creation that has the recognized authority to use and maintain a monopoly on the use of force within a clearly defined jurisdiction," while a *government* is a "political institution of the state that uses organization, bureaucracy, and formality to regulate social interactions" (Gaines et al., p. 1). The origins of formal policing began with the organization of societies into states and governments.

The form of government heavily influences the structure of police organizations. As Langworthy and Travis have argued, "since all police systems rely on state authority, the source of state power ultimately represents the basis of police authority as well" (p. 42). Different forms of government have established different types of police forces. Shelley suggests that there are four different models of policing (i.e., communist, Anglo-Saxon, continental, and colonial) that differ based on their sources of legitimacy, organizational structure, and police function. The present author suggests that the communist model of policing obtains legitimacy through the communist political party, is organized as a centralized, armed militarized force, and performs the functions of crime control and enforcement of state ideology. The continental and colonial models have similar organizational structures and functions as the communist model, however the continental model obtains its legitimacy through the central government while the colonial model establishes legitimacy through the colonial authority. In comparison, the Anglo-Saxon model obtains legitimacy through local governments and is based in law. This model is organized as a decentralized force that is armed in some countries (United States) and not in others (England). Finally, police functions in this model include crime control, order maintenance, and welfare and administrative responsibilities.

In this entry, a historical description of the Anglo-Saxon model of policing is presented. The changes in the mission, strategies, and organizational structures of policing through different time periods are examined. A particular emphasis is placed on the historical roots of policing in England and their influence on modern policing in America. This entry will also detail the changes of American police forces since their establishment in the 1800s as organizations of social control. Current debate about recent changes in the mission, strategies, and organizational structures of police will be described and the future of police organizations will be examined.

Early policing in England

Until the mid-1800s, law enforcement in England was a local responsibility of citizens. From 1066 (invasion and conquering of England by William Duke of Normandy) to the 1300s, police services were provided through the *frankpledge* system. Under this system, citizens were appointed with the responsibility of maintaining order and controlling crime. Men were formed into groups of ten, called a *tything*. Ten tythings were grouped into a *hundred* and were supervised by a *constable*. Groups of ten hundreds created a *shire*, controlled by *reeves*. The word *shire-reeve* is the derivative of our current term *sheriff* (Uchida). In 1215, King John was forced to sign the *Magna Carta*, a document that guaranteed basic civil rights to citizens. The rights guaranteed under the Magna Carta limited the power of the throne and their appointees, and greatly contributed to many of the liberties citizens of England and America enjoy today.

During the 1500s, England increased its participation in world trade and through the 1700s more citizens moved into the cities and crime began to rise. Although England had one of the harshest criminal justice systems of its time, including death sentences for minor crimes, crime and disorder continued to rise. Many began to hire their own private police, and the king began a system of night watch for the large cities. In 1737, the first formal taxation system for the purpose of law enforcement was introduced. City councils were allowed to levy taxes to pay for a night watch system (Gaines et al.). Despite these

efforts, crime continued to rise and the need for a different system of policing was evident.

The beginning of "modern" policing in England

Three names are generally associated with the development of the first modern police forces in England—Henry Fielding, Patrick Colquhoun, and Sir Robert Peel. Henry Fielding was a playwright and novelist who accepted a position as magistrate deputy of Bow Street Court in 1748. He is credited with two major contributions to the field of policing (Gaines et al.). First, Fielding advocated change and spread awareness about social and criminal problems through his writings. Second, he organized a group of paid nonuniformed citizens who were responsible for investigating crimes and prosecuting offenders. This group, called the Bow Street Runners, was the first group paid through public funds that emphasized crime prevention in addition to crime investigation and apprehension of criminals. While citizens responsible for social control used to simply react to crimes, the Bow Street Runners added the responsibility of preventing crime through preventive patrol, changing the system of policing considerably.

Despite the Bow Street Runners' efforts, most English citizens were opposed to the development of a police force. Their opposition was based on two related factors: (1) the importance placed on individual liberties, and (2) the English tradition of local government (Langworthy and Travis). To reconcile these issues with the development of a police force, a Scottish magistrate, Patrick Colquhoun, developed the *science of policing* in the late 1700s (Langworthy and Travis). Colquhoun suggested that police functions must include detection of crime, apprehension of offenders, and prevention of crime through their presence in public. The function of crime prevention was supported by other influential scholars at the time. In his 1763 essay *On Crimes and Punishment*, Italian theorist Cesare Beccaria proposed that "it is better to prevent crimes than to punish them" (p. 93).

Colquhoun also argued that highly regulated police forces should form their own separate unit within the government. Furthermore, he argued that judicial officers could provide oversight and control police powers if they were organized as a separate unit within the government, in effect proposing the *separation of powers* controlled through a system of *checks and balances*

(Langworthy and Travis). The ideas expressed in the science of policing were consistent with political theorists' descriptions of the *social contract*. Political philosophers in the seventeenth and eighteenth centuries (particularly John Locke, Thomas Hobbes, and Jean-Jacques Rousseau) speculated about the relationship between societies, states, and governments. The theory of the social contract suggests that individual members of a society enter into a contract with their government where governments are responsible for providing protection and maintaining social order. In exchange for this protection, members of the society agree to relinquish some of their rights, including the right to protect their own interests through the use of force. Democratic societies are structured systems based on the balance between individual rights and the collective needs of those societies. In modern societies, the police are the agents responsible for maintaining that balance.

Despite the virtues of the science of policing, issues regarding the English tradition of local governmental control remained. This issue was addressed by Sir Robert Peel. Peel is credited for establishing the first modern police force in England under the Metropolitan Police Act, a bill passed in Parliament in 1829. This act created a single authority responsible for policing within the city limits of London. The force began with one thousand officers divided into six divisions, headquartered at Scotland Yard. These officers (known as "Bobbies" for their founder) were uniformed and introduced new elements into policing that became the basis for modern police. The County Police Act of 1839 allowed for the creation of similar police forces in other localities, where responsibility and costs for the agencies were shared by the central and local governments (Walker and Richards).

Walker (1999) described three new elements of the English police forces as particularly important for modern policing. First, borrowing from the Bow Street Runners, their mission was crime prevention and control. The philosophy that it was better to prevent crime than simply respond to it greatly influenced the role of modern police officers. Second, their strategy was to maintain a visible presence through preventive patrol. Finally, the third element was that of a quasi-military organizational structure. As described by Walker, "Peel borrowed the organizational structure of the London police from the military, including uniforms, rank designations, and the authoritarian system of command and disci-

pline" (1999, p. 21). These three elements of policing developed in the early 1800s in the London police department had a significant impact on modern policing.

Early policing in colonial America

The development of law enforcement in colonial America was similar to that of England during the same time period. Law enforcement in colonial America was considered a local responsibility. As in England, the colonies established a system of night watch to guard cities against fire, crime, and disorder. In addition to night watch systems, there were *sheriffs* appointed by the governor and *constables* elected by the people. These individuals were responsible for maintaining order and providing other services. Nalla and Newman have described the following as problems plaguing colonial cities that were considered the responsibility of police: controlling slaves and Indians; maintaining order; regulating specialized functions such as selling in the market and delivering goods; maintaining health and sanitation; managing pests and other animals; ensuring the orderly use of streets by vehicles; controlling liquor, gambling, vice, and weapons; and keeping watch for fires.

While night watch groups were established in the northern colonies, groups of white men organized into *slave patrols* in the southern colonies. These slave patrols were responsible for controlling, returning, and punishing runaway slaves. The slave patrols helped to maintain the economic order in the southern colonies. These slave patrols are generally considered to be the first "modern" police organizations in this country. In 1837, Charleston, South Carolina, had a slave patrol with over one hundred officers, which was far larger than any northern city police force at that time (Walker, 1999).

Policing on the western frontier varied widely. According to Langworthy and Travis, settlers originally from northern colonies created *marshals* and police forces similar to those in northern colonies, while settlers from southern colonies developed systems with sheriffs and *posses*. In many western settlements, however, there was no formal organized law enforcement. In these areas, groups of *vigilantes* were formed by volunteer citizens to combat any threat to the order of the settlements. These groups of self-appointed law enforcers had a significant influence on collective social norms, including the lack of respect for the law, which had been haphazardly enforced primarily through vigilante violence.

In the 1800s, changes in American society forced changes in law enforcement. Specifically, the processes of industrialization, urbanization, and immigration changed this country from a primarily homogenous, agrarian society to a heterogeneous, urban one. Citizens left rural areas and flocked to the cities in search of employment. Hundreds of thousands of immigrants came to reside in America. Unsanitary living conditions and poverty characterized American cities. The poor, predominantly immigrant urban areas were plagued with increases in crime and disorder. As a direct result, a series of riots occurred throughout the 1830s in numerous American cities. Many of these riots were the result of poor living conditions, poverty, and conflicts between ethnic groups. These riots directly illustrated the need for larger and better organized law enforcement. Both the watch systems in the north and the slave patrols in the south began to evolve into modern police organizations that were heavily influenced by modern departments developing in England during the same time (Walker, 1999).

"Modern" policing in America

The first modern police forces in America borrowed heavily from those established in England. In particular, American law enforcement agencies adopted the mission of crime prevention and control, the strategy of preventive patrol, and the quasi-military organizational design of the first modern police department established in London. In addition to these three elements, American policing borrowed other features from the British system, for example, the tradition that police have some limitations on their authority (Walker, 1999). The protection of individual liberties was highly emphasized in both England and America, therefore limits were placed on governmental and police authority. This was not the case in other European countries, where, as Walker notes, police agencies were given broader powers and citizens had fewer individual liberties. Another feature borrowed from the English heritage is that of local control of police agencies. Although many other countries have one centralized, national law enforcement agency, the English and American systems do not. In the American system of law enforcement, police are controlled at the local, state, and federal level, although the majority of

departments are local municipalities. A related defining feature of American policing adopted from English heritage is that of a highly decentralized and fragmented system of law enforcement. According to 1993 figures, there are nearly twenty thousand different law enforcement agencies within the United States (Maguire et al.). Lack of coordination and cooperation among local law enforcement agencies is generally characteristic of the American system of law enforcement. These three elements (limited police power, lack of centralized control, and a decentralized and fragmented structure), combined with the quasi-military organizational structure of modern departments in England, describe the Anglo-Saxon model of policing.

There were differences, however, between the British and American systems of law enforcement. One of the most significant differences is the absence of strong political influences over police organizations in England, compared to the strong relationship between politics and policing that existed in American policing (Walker, 1999). While police administrators in England were protected from political influence, politics heavily influenced American police agencies. In fact, policing during the nineteenth century in America has been described as inefficient, ineffective, lacking professionalism, and highly corrupt (Walker, 1999).

Numerous scholars have described the evolution of policing in America. Although the historical facts are generally not disputed, the interpretation of these events does raise some debate. Within this entry, the evolution of policing in America will be presented loosely following the framework devised by Kelling and Moore, which describes three distinct eras (political, reform, and community). These eras are summarized in Table 1.

Policing nineteenth-century America—the political era

As previously noted, American policing in the late nineteenth century was plagued with political influence. Local politicians used positions on the police force to reward their supporters after election. Therefore the ethnic and religious composition of police forces often reflected the groups who had local political influence. In addition, positions and promotions on local police forces could be bought. For example, Walker (1999) notes that in New York City, "a $300 payment to the Tammany Hall political machine was

Table 1

Three eras of policing in America

	Political era 1840s–1900s	Reform era 1920s–1970s	Community era 1970s–present
Authorization	Political	Law and professionalism	Community support (political), law, professionalism
Function	Crime control, order maintenance, broad social services	Crime control	Crime control, crime prevention, problem-solving
Organizational design	Decentralized and geographic	Centralized, classical	Decentralized, task forces, matrices
Relationship to environment	Close and personal	Professionally remote	Consultative, police defend values of law and professionalism, but listen to community concerns
Demand	Managed through links between politicians and commanders, along with face-to-face contacts between citizens and patrol officers	Channeled through central dispatching activities	Channeled through analysis of underlying concerns
Tactics and technology	Foot patrol and rudimentary investigations	Preventive patrol and rapid response to calls for service	Foot patrol, problem-solving
Outcome	Political and citizen satisfaction with social order	Crime control	Quality of life and citizen satisfaction

SOURCE: George L. Kelling and Mark H. Moore. "The Evolving Strategy of Policing." *Perspectives on Policing* 4. Washington, D.C.: National Institute of Justice, 1988.

the only requirement for appointment to the force" (p. 24). There was little or no training given to officers, no recruitment standards to speak of, and no job security because officers could be hired or fired at will. Corruption was a major characteristic of policing during this time period. Low-ranking officers, high-ranking police officials, and sometimes even entire departments were involved in corruption and misconduct. Patrol officers often accepted bribes to not enforce laws controlling moral crimes (e.g., drinking, gambling, and prostitution). This type of corruption was well known and pervasive.

Police work during this time period has been described as hopelessly inefficient due to officers' reliance on foot patrol with no effective communication system and little direct supervision. Officers often evaded work due to the lack of official oversight and citizens had difficulty contacting the police because the officers could not be located on their beats. However, police did provide a variety of social services to citizens, including feeding the hungry and housing the homeless. For example, Whitehouse reports that the Boston Police Department during the 1800s was re-

sponsible for a variety of public services, which included lodging the homeless, removing dirt and garbage, and checking every household daily for cases of cholera. Other urban departments also routinely housed the homeless and looked after wayward youths (Monkkonen).

Walker, however, cautions readers against the "myth that officers were friendly, knowledgeable about the neighborhood, and helpful" (1999, p. 25). He suggests that due to the high turnover of police officers and residential mobility, officers were unlikely to have close relations with people in the neighborhood. Furthermore, he suggests that police frequently used physical force and enjoyed little citizen respect. During this time period, increases in citizen violence finally led to the adoption of weapons carried by police officers. The nostalgic interpretation of police as friendly neighborhood characters walking the beat has led some scholars to caution that the good old days were not that good (Walker, 1984).

Surprisingly, the daily duties of patrol officers during this time did not differ significantly from activities performed by patrol officers today. The diary of a patrol officer from the Boston Police Department in 1895 describes most of his time spent responding to minor problems in the neighborhood and handling many problems informally (von Hoffman, 1992). It appears that officers during the political era spent little time handling major problems or serious incidents and rarely invoked the legal system. This is also true of patrol officers today.

Policing twentieth-century America—the reform era

Police in America changed dramatically during the twentieth century. According to Walker (1999), three principle forces were underlying this change: the police professionalism movement, modern technologies, and the civil rights movement. Other scholars suggest that police reform was the result of investigative commissions, reform initiated by police administrators, and political reform in general (Gaines et al.).

In the early 1900s, a broad social and political movement in America, *progressivism,* was bringing attention to and demanding reform across a broad spectrum of social problems. Progressives believed it was the government's responsibility to improve the living conditions of citizens. They called for the regulation of big business and corrupt local politics, changes in labor laws, and improvements across all social welfare services. Included in this larger reform effort was the professionalization of police forces. The professionalization movement sought to reform the inefficient and corrupt police agencies that had developed during the nineteenth century. During this reform era, there was a total restructuring of police departments and a redefinition of the police role due to the perceived failure of police to enforce the law (Walker, 1977). Reformers sought to eliminate political influences, hire qualified leaders, and raise personnel standards. In addition, the reform agenda called for a mission of nonpartisan public service and restructuring of police organizations through the use of the principles of scientific management and the development of specialized units (Walker, 1999).

Several prominent police reforms had a significant influence on policing during this time period. Richard Sylvester, superintendent of the Washington, D.C., Police Department from 1898 to 1915, became the national voice for police reform. He served as president of the International Association of Chiefs of Police (IACP) and had a significant impact on acceptance of the reform agenda across numerous departments. Similarly, August Vollmer, police chief in Berkeley, California, from 1905 to 1932, advocated the hiring of college graduates and offered the first collegiate course in police science at the University of California. Vollmer is also famous for the development of the principles of modern police administration. Advocates of the concepts of administrative efficiency sought to "centralize the authority within police departments" and to "rationalize the procedures of command control" (Walker, 1977).

The reform of police agencies during the first part of the twentieth century was very slow to develop, and in some cities the impact of early reform efforts was nonexistent. Although considerable gains were made in agencies of cities such as Cincinnati and Berkeley, reform efforts were largely ineffective in other agencies, such as those of Los Angeles and Chicago (Walker, 1977). Efforts to professionalize the police increased after the 1931 reports by the Wickersham Commission, which contained vivid descriptions of police misconduct and use of force. The Wickersham Commission Report was the first national study of the criminal justice system in America and had a significant impact on the revitalization of the reform movement.

Professionalization continued under the direction of O. W. Wilson, one of Vollmer's protégés. Wilson was the chief of police in Wichita, Kansas, from 1928 to 1935, a professor of criminology at the University of California, and chief of the Chicago Police Department in the 1960s. Wilson had a significant impact on organizational changes within police departments during this time, largely through his textbook *Police Administration* (1950). Utilizing scientific principles of management, Wilson emphasized workload distributions based on calls for service and efficient management of personnel through bureaucratic design. Wilson also encouraged departments to gauge their success through measurable outcomes (numbers of arrests, citations, etc.) and rapid response to calls for service.

Also influential during this time period was J. Edgar Hoover, director of the Federal Bureau of Investigations (F.B.I.). Hoover's leadership of the F.B.I. had a direct influence on local police agencies because of his portrayal of agents under his command as highly trained and educated, professional, and honest. In addition, he instituted the F.B.I.'s Top Ten Most Wanted List, controlled the Uniform Crime Report (UCR) system, and effectively communicated to citizens that his organization was involved in a "war on crime." Most local departments wanted to emulate the professional F.B.I. agents and thus perpetuated the "crime fighter" image.

New technologies also had a significant influence on policing in the early to mid-twentieth century. Three technologies in particular have revolutionized policing: the two-way radio, the patrol car, and the telephone. As previously noted, policing in the nineteenth century was characterized as ineffective and inefficient, in part because officers could not be contacted on their beats. With the advent of the two-way radio, officers could be notified about calls for service and police supervisors could contact their officers directly. This change in technology had a significant impact on the provision of services to the public and the supervision of police personnel. Likewise, the use of patrol cars in the 1920s greatly enhanced the mobility of police officers and significantly reduced their response time to calls for service from citizens. Finally, the use of the telephone allowed citizens to have direct contact with the police department. Citizens were encouraged to call the police for any type of situation and the police promised a rapid response.

These new technologies also had unintended consequences on policing, the effect of which was not fully understood until much later. For example, the patrol car served to isolate patrol officers from the community. Previously, when officers patrolled on foot, they had an opportunity to engage citizens in conversations and had a familiarity with the neighborhood that was lost once officers patrolled in cars. When officers drove through neighborhoods with their windows rolled up, citizens perceived officers as outsiders in their communities. Encouraging citizens to call the police for service and promising a rapid response dramatically increased the workload of officers. Citizens began to call police for minor problems and the police continued to respond. In addition, police were called to handle private matters that they had not been responsible for in the past. The interactions between citizens and police took on a more personal nature as police responded to citizens' homes rather than simply patrolling and engaging citizens on the street. As described by Walker, the result of these new technologies "was a complex and contradictory change in police-citizen contacts. Whereas the patrol car isolated the police from the people on the streets, the telephone brought police officers into peoples' living rooms, kitchens, and bedrooms. There, officers became involved in the most intimate domestic problems" (1999, p. 32).

To summarize, policing during the reform era changed as organizations characterized by inefficiency, corruption, and low personnel standards were transformed into "professional" departments. The professionalization movement stressed changes in the levels of officer education and training, appointment of qualified reform-minded administrators, and adherence to scientific principles of management. Police organizational structures during this time were centralized, specialized, and bureaucratic. Professional officers emphasized their functions of law enforcement and crime prevention through random motorized patrol and rapid response to calls for service.

The police-citizen crisis of the 1960s

The 1960s were a period characterized by much civil unrest. Citizens were dissatisfied with the social and political conditions, and particularly with the treatment of minorities. During this time, the U.S. Supreme Court decided a series of landmark cases that limited the investigative techniques used by police officers. For example, the court decided in *Mapp v. Ohio* (367 U.S. 643 (1961)), that evidence obtained during a search and seizure that violated citizens' Fourth Amendment rights could not be used against them in a court of law. Dubbed the *exclusionary rule, Mapp* guaranteed that the fruits of an unconstitutional search could not be used during prosecution. In 1966, the court ruled in *Miranda v. Arizona*, 384 U.S. 436, that a suspect must be advised of his or her right against self-incrimination (protected by the Fifth Amendment) and the right to council (protected by the Sixth Amendment) before police can interrogate that suspect. Any admission of guilt obtained prior to giving the *Miranda* warnings cannot be used against the suspect during prosecution. Critics of these and other decisions claimed that the Supreme Court was "handcuffing" police. Most studies have shown, however, that these rulings did not have the substantial influence that either side believed would result (Leo).

During this time, the civil rights movement was gaining momentum and becoming more militant. Protestors gathered to demonstrate against race discrimination and injustice within the criminal justice system. White male police officers became the symbol of all the political and social ills of American society. Police officers across the country responded to protestors with physical brutality, which served to increase the tension between minority groups and the police. This tension exploded in the form of riots and civil disobedience, often sparked by incidents involving the police (Walker, 1999).

In response, a series of presidential commissions were ordered to investigate these issues. The most famous, the Kerner Commission investigated the causes of the nearly two hundred disorders that had taken place in 1967. The Kerner Commission reported that there was deep hostility and distrust between minorities and the police. The report recommended the hiring of more minority officers and that police practices be changed significantly. Interestingly, the commission reported that those departments that were believed to be the most "professional" were in fact those that had the most serious disturbances and civil unrest. This challenged many of the assumptions of the professionalism movement (National Advisory Commission on Civil Disorders).

Findings from social-scientific research further raised concern about the effectiveness of "professional" police departments. The American Bar Foundation's (ABF) field observation of police in 1956–1957 reported that officers exercised large amounts of discretion during encounters with citizens. Contrary to the popular conception of police officers as "crime fighters," studies found that officers spent most of the time maintaining order, providing services, and performing administrative tasks (Wilson; Bittner). The Kansas City Preventive Patrol Experiment found that increasing the level of preventive patrol within an area did not have a significant influence on the level of crime or reduce citizens' fear of crime (Kelling et al.). A study examining the effectiveness of criminal investigations reported that the percentage of crimes cleared by arrest is relatively low, that follow-up work is often unproductive, and that most detective work involves mundane tasks and paperwork (Greenwood and Petersilia). Another study showed that increases in the response time of officers did not increase the likelihood of obtaining an arrest (Pate et al.). Finally, evaluations of the effects of *team policing* (a police tactic that involved the creation of specialized teams responsible for policing particular geographic areas) showed no influence on the level of crime (Sherman, Milton, and Kelly). Collectively, these studies suggested that current police practices were not effective in preventing crime or satisfying citizens.

Policing in America from the 1970s to the present—the community era?

The 1960s police-citizen crisis, coupled with research findings from the 1970s, questioned the core philosophies underlying policing in America. In a seminal article on policing, Wilson and Kelling proposed the *broken windows* thesis. They argued that a broken window in an abandoned building or car is a symbol that no one cares about the property, making it ripe for criminal activity. Wilson and Kelling stressed the importance of controlling minor crimes and disorders in an effort to curb more serious crime. Making citizens feel safer and improving their quality of life should be the goal of police. This idea sparked the development of a number of different police strategies and tactics designed to improve police-community relations. The philosophy of *community policing* is built upon the premise that reducing citizens' fear of crime while forming a partnership between the police and the community is a worthwhile goal of police organizations. Particular tactics utilized in this philosophy include foot patrol, problem solving, police substations, and community groups, among others. These tactics stress citizen satisfaction and improvements in citizens' quality of life. In addition to changes in tactics, changes in organizational design must also accompany community policing. Police organizations are to become decentralized, flatter hierarchies with less bureaucratic control. Patrol officers at the lowest levels are encouraged to be creative in their responses to problems and are given more discretion to advance their problem-solving efforts.

Kelling and Moore have described the 1970s and 1980s as an era in which a shift toward community policing occurred. They suggest that community policing is a strategic change complete with changes in organizational structures, tactics, and outcomes (see Table 1). However, changes in organizational design appear to be more theoretical than practical. Maguire's examination of organizational change in a sample of large departments shows that there were no significant changes in the bureaucratic structures of police agencies practicing community policing in the 1990s compared to those who were not.

Although community policing and problem solving have been popular policing strategies, some departments are utilizing *zero-tolerance* policies. Zero-tolerance policies encourage the use of aggressive police tactics and full enforcement of minor offenses. For example, the New York Police Department instituted zero-tolerance policies in the mid-1990s in an effort to reduce minor disorders and control crime. Based on the "broken windows" hypothesis, aggressive enforcement of minor crimes is predicted to produce the same outcomes of increasing citizen satisfaction and improving quality of life that are sought under the models of community policing. However, the tactics are very different. Community policing encourages partnership development, less frequent use of arrest, and more creative responses to particular problems. Zero-tolerance policies encourage the use of arrest and other get-tough policies. Furthermore, trends in the militarization of police have been well documented. The number of police agencies that use police paramilitary units (PPUs) and special weapons and tactical teams (SWATs) have increased by over 80 percent since the 1970s (Kraska and Kappeler).

It is clear that the idea of the existence of a "community era" in policing is not without critics. Walker (1984) claims that scholars have misinterpreted and misused history in their descriptions of the "community era." Williams and Murphy suggest that scholars have not attended to the obvious influences of slavery, segregation, and discrimination on policing throughout history. Somewhat surprisingly, the description and interpretation of the history of police continues to be a matter of great debate. Perhaps this is due to our need to fully understand the events of the past to effectively guide the events of the future.

ROBIN SHEPARD ENGEL

See also FEDERAL BUREAU OF INVESTIGATION: HISTORY; POLICE: COMMUNITY POLICING; POLICE: CRIMINAL INVESTIGATIONS; POLICE: HANDLING OF JUVENILES; POLICE: ORGANIZATION AND MANAGEMENT; POLICE: POLICE OFFICER BEHAVIOR; POLICE: POLICING COMPLAINANTLESS CRIMES; POLICE: PRIVATE POLICE AND INDUSTRIAL SECURITY; POLICE: SPECIAL WEAPONS AND TACTICS (SWAT) TEAMS; URBAN POLICE.

BIBLIOGRAPHY

BECCARIA, C. *On Crimes and Punishment.* (1763). Translated by H. Paolucci. New York: Bobbs-Merill, 1963.

BITTNER, EGON. *The Functions of the Police in Modern Society.* Rockville, Md.: National Institute for Mental Health, 1970.

GAINES, LARRY K.; KAPPELER, VICTOR E.; and VAUGHN, JOSEPH B. *Policing in America.* Cincinnati, Ohio: Anderson Publishing, 1999.

GREENWOOD, PETER W., and PETERSILIA, JOAN. *The Criminal Investigation Process,* Vol. 1, *Summary and Policy Implications.* Santa Monica, Calif.: RAND, 1975.

KELLING, GEORGE L., and MOORE, MARK H. "The Evolving Strategy of Policing." *Perspectives on Policing* 4. Washington, D.C.: National Institute of Justice, 1988.

KELLING, GEORGE L., et al. *Kansas City Preventive Patrol Experiment: A Summary Report.* Washington, D.C.: The Police Foundation, 1974.

KRASKA, PETER B., and KAPPELER, VICTOR E. "Militarizing American Police: The Rise and Normalization of Paramilitary Units." *Social Problems* 44, no. 1 (1997): 1–18.

LANGWORTHY, ROBERT H., and TRAVIS, LAWRENCE P., III. *Policing in America: A Balance of Forces.* 2d ed. Upper Saddle River, N.J.: Prentice Hall, 1999.

LEO, RICHARD. "The Impact of *Miranda* Revisited." *Journal of Criminal Law and Criminology* 86, no. 3 (1996): 621–692.

LUNDMAN, RICHARD J. *Police and Policing: An Introduction.* New York: Holt, Rinehart & Winston, 1980.

MAGUIRE, EDWARD. "Structural Change in Large Municipal Police Organizations during the Community Policing Era." *Justice Quarterly* 14, no. 3 (1997): 547–576.

MAGUIRE, EDWARD R.; SNIPES, JEFFREY B.; UCHIDA, CRAIG D.; and TOWNSEND, MARGARET. "Counting Cops: Estimating the Number of Police Departments and Police Officers in the USA." *Policing: An International Journal of Police Strategies & Management* 21, no. 1 (1998): 97–120.

MONKKONEN, ERIC H. *Police in Urban America, 1860–1920.* Cambridge, Mass.: Cambridge University Press, 1981.

NALLA, M. K., and NEWMAN, G. R. "Is White-Collar Policing, Policing?" *Policing and Society* 3 (1994): 303–318.

National Advisory Commission on Civil Disorders. *Report of the National Advisory Commission on Civil Disorders.* Washington, D.C.: U.S. Government Printing Office, 1968.

PATE, TONY; FERRARA, AMY; BOWERS, ROBERT A.; and LORENCE, JON. *Police Response Time: Its Determinants and Effects.* Washington, D.C.: Police Foundation, 1976.

SHELLEY, LOUISE. "The Sources of Soviet Policing." *Police Studies* 17, no. 2 (1994): 49–66.

SHERMAN, LAWRENCE W.; MILTON, CATHERINE H.; and KELLY, THOMAS V. *Team Policing: Seven Case Studies*. Washington, D.C.: Police Foundation, 1973.

UCHIDA, CRAIG D. "The Development of American Police: A Historical Overview." In *Critical Issues in Policing: Contemporary Readings*. Edited by R. G. Dunham and G. P. Alpert. Prospect Heights, Ill.: Waveland Press, 1993. Pages 14–30.

VON HOFFMAN, ALEXANDER. "An Officer of the Neighborhood: A Boston Patrolman on the Beat in 1895." *Journal of Social History* 26 (1992): 309–330.

WALKER, SAMUEL. *A Critical History of Police Reform*. Lexington, Mass: D.C. Heath and Co., 1977.

———. "'Broken Windows' and Fractured History: The Use and Misuse of History in Recent Police Patrol Analysis." *Justice Quarterly* 1, no. 1 (1984): 75–90.

———. *The Police in America*. 3d ed. Boston, Mass.: McGraw-Hill College, 1999.

WALKER, SAMUEL, and RICHARDS, M. "A Service under Change: Current Issues in Policing in England and Wales." *Police Studies* 19, no. 1 (1996): 53–74.

WHITEHOUSE, J. "Historical Perspectives on the Police Community Service Function." *Journal of Police Science and Administration* 1, no. 1 (1973): 87–92.

WILLIAMS, HUBERT, and MURPHY, PATRICK V. "The Evolving Strategy of Police: A Minority Perspective." *Perspectives on Policing* 13. Washington, D.C.: National Institute of Justice, 1990.

WILSON, JAMES Q. *Varieties of Police Behavior: The Management of Law and Order in Eight Communities*. Cambridge, Mass.: Harvard University Press, 1968.

WILSON, JAMES Q., and KELLING, GEORGE L. "Broken Windows: The Police and Neighborhood Safety." *The Atlantic Monthly* no. 249 (1982): 29–38.

CASES

Mapp v. Ohio, 367 U.S. 643 (1961).
Miranda v. Arizona, 384 U.S. 436 (1966).

POLICE: COMMUNITY POLICING

Some police experts would argue that over the last twenty-five years the concept of community policing has quietly revolutionized law enforcement in America (Kelling). The precise nature and scope of this transformation is still the source of much debate, but what is clear is that community policing has captured the attention of the nation's government and police departments. In 1994, Congress passed the Violent Crime Control and Law Enforcement Act, which provided over $8 billion to hire 100,000 additional community police officers over a six-year period. In addition, a new agency, the Office of Community Oriented Police Services (COPS), was created to carry out this mission, and to administer extensive funding and implementation of community policing programs across the country. According to the latest estimates, community policing is widespread, with approximately 80 percent of larger municipal and county police departments employing an average of twenty or more community policing officers (LEMAS, pp. 2–3).

Definition of community policing

Since community policing is a difficult concept to define, a helpful way to understand exactly what it encompasses is to identify its key philosophical, tactical, and organizational characteristics.

Philosophical characteristics of community policing. At its core, community policing fundamentally challenges the underlying assumptions that have shaped American policing for most of the twentieth century. Since the 1930s, the traditional law-enforcement approach to policing has emphasized the independence of police agencies from the communities they serve, the importance of an individual officer's professional and dispassionate treatment of all citizens, and the close association between police work and fighting crime. In contrast, community policing significantly broadens the traditional role and function of the police. It takes the view that the police and citizens are co-producers of police services, jointly responsible for reducing crime and improving the quality of life in local neighborhoods.

According to the philosophy of community policing, local police should provide citizens with formal access to the department's decision- and policy-making process. Neighborhood residents are encouraged to voice their concerns to the police, and it is the responsibility of the police to thoughtfully address these concerns (Cordner). While police professionalism remains important, this quality is no longer equated with officers' being detached and aloof from local citizens. Under community policing, police officers are expected to initiate frequent personal contacts with community members on their beats, and to interact in an attentive, friendly, and compassionate manner. Enforcing the law and fighting crime remain important elements of policing, but community policing recognizes that, in reality, most police work is oriented toward nonenforcement tasks such as maintaining order and providing social services (Eck and Rosenbaum). Consequently, reducing community disorder, helping to mitigate residents' fears about crime, solving problems, and caring for individual victims, are all regarded as equally important to making arrests and solving crimes.

Tactical characteristics of community policing. Community policing demands that police departments reform their relationship with local communities, and that police officers change their attitudes and behaviors toward citizens and police work. The following interrelated programs and activities are oriented toward fostering a closer rapport between the community and the local police department, increasing the quantity and quality of police-citizen interactions, and enhancing the capacity of the police to engage in problem-solving partnerships.

Relationship between the police department and the community. In order to foster police-community cooperation in tackling community problems, police agencies must first elicit community input. This can be achieved via a variety of methods, including door-to-door visits conducted by police officers, mail-out surveys, and residential block meetings. The gathering of this information helps the police identify and prioritize community concerns. In their attempts to reduce crime and disorder, the police can enlist the help of community members by encouraging citizens to report illegal or suspicious behavior. In return, the police can educate citizens on how to avoid becoming victims of crime through crime prevention programs such as Neighborhood Watch. More importantly, continued cooperation between the police and community requires the establishment of trust.

Even though most of the decision-making authority is reserved by the police, a long-term relationship between the police and local residents can be created if police departments are responsive to community needs and accountable to the community for any actions they take (Goldstein, 1987). Police departments might demon-

strate this commitment and accountability by evaluating how well they have satisfied public concerns, and by providing community members with frequent updates on a particular case. Police departments could use follow-up surveys mailed to residences, neighborhood meetings, or telephone interviews with community members, to gauge "customer satisfaction" with the quality of police service delivered (Skogan and Hartnett). Feedback might be provided through newspaper reports, flyers, or community announcements.

Quantity and quality of police-citizen interactions. One of the cornerstones of community policing is the attempt to improve the frequency and the quality of interactions between individual police officers and members of the public. Assigning police officers to foot or bicycle patrols in specific geographical areas facilitates more frequent and personal contacts between the police and citizens than motorized patrol (the hallmark of traditional policing).

Police-community cooperation is cultivated by police officers getting to know residents on their beat. In addition, the removal of officers from their patrol cars gives them greater opportunity to engage in order maintenance and social service tasks. The visible presence of officers, who are easily accessible and caring in their encounters with residents, may help reduce citizens' fears of crime, and the improved rapport between the police and local citizens can improve officer morale and job satisfaction. Finally, an officer's assignment to a permanent beat helps create an officer's sense of responsibility toward the overall improvement of community life.

Problem-solving partnerships. The notion that the police and the public should collaborate in solving neighborhood problems helps move community policing past the criticism that it is just an exercise in improving community relations. In fact, as Goldstein makes clear, the creation of problem-solving partnerships between the police and the communities they serve is a radical departure from traditional policing (Goldstein, 1990). Rather than reacting to specific incidents and resorting primarily to law enforcement as a means of controlling crime, the police are encouraged to let communities identify local problems and to work with the community to find the most effective solution.

What it is so innovative about this approach is that the onus is on police officers to discover and carefully analyze the underlying cause(s) of concern. It is then their responsibility to focus all their efforts on a solution specifically tailored toward solving the problem at hand. Law enforcement is still recognized as one of the means available, but effective problem-solving demands that police officers should search for alternative methods of social control, and be guided by community preferences (Mastrofski et al., 1995). This might require that the officer draw upon resources beyond the confines of the police department, such as coordinating between citizens and other local government and community organizations. In sum, problem solving does not only rely upon greater familiarity between the police and the community, but on the ability of the police to recognize patterns or relationships between incidents, and on the willingness of the police to choose long-term, judicious, and highly selective solutions over short-term, cumbersome, and universal responses.

Organizational characteristics of community policing.   Given its shift away from reactive patrol and incident-based responses (the principal tactics of traditional policing), it is clear that the effective implementation of community policing requires significant organizational change. Under the traditional model of policing, U.S. police departments were highly centralized and bureaucratized. The paramilitary structure of the police department was organized hierarchically, with key operational decisions being made by those at the upper levels in the organization. These decisions were then transmitted down the organization in the form of rules and orders, and enforced via a rigid chain of command. Since supervisors were directly responsible for the decisions made by line officers, decision-making authority at the street level was, in theory, subject to their direct control. However, given that a great deal of police work takes place outside of any form of direct supervision, it is not surprising that line officers continued to exercise a great deal of discretion.

In contrast to the traditional model, community policing recognizes that the knowledge and experience of line officers is of critical importance to the police organization. In order to be responsive to community problems and engage in problem solving, the rank and file must have greater autonomy in making decisions (Sparrow). The independence and freedom of line officers to respond to local community problems is encouraged by the decentralization of the police structure, and the formal recognition that police work is, by its very nature, highly discretionary. The creation of community substations in local neighborhoods and the organization's attempt to provide line officers with continuous access to resources, increases organizational flexibility and the capacity of the police officer for solving problems (Goldstein, 1987). Less emphasis is placed upon written rules as a means of managing officers, and a higher premium is attached to developing an organizational culture that values mentorship and guidance, and which encourages line officers to be innovative in their attempts to find solutions to problems of neighborhood crime and disorder (Cordner). Finally, those departments committed to a community-policing model must develop alternative measures of police effectiveness and accountability. The number of department arrests, or citations, can no longer be regarded as the sine qua non of a police organization that considers order maintenance and social service as of equal importance to crime control.

In addition to crime rates, measures that focus on the quality of police service and the effectiveness of problem-solving strategies are useful indicators of how well the police are performing, and to what extent the police are accountable to the community. Are citizens less fearful of neighborhood crime? Are the police responsive to community problems? When interacting with neighborhood residents, are the police courteous and helpful? Have problem-solving strategies been effective?

Without changes in the structure of the organization, its management style, and its measures of effectiveness and accountability, community policing cannot be implemented successfully.

Origins and evolution of community policing

Community policing has been evolving slowly since the civil rights movement in the 1960s exposed the weaknesses of the traditional policing model. Even though its origin can be traced to this crisis in police-community relations, its development has been influenced by a wide variety of factors over the course of the past forty years.

The Civil Rights Movement (1960s). Individual elements of community policing, such as improvements in police-community relations, emerged slowly from the political and social upheavals surrounding the civil rights movement in the 1960s. Widespread riots and protests against racial injustices brought government attention to sources of racial discrimination and tension, including the police. As visible symbols of political authority, the police were exposed to a great deal of public criticism. Not only were minorities underrepresented in police departments, but studies suggested that the police treated minorities more harshly than white citizens (Walker). In response to this civil unrest, the President's Commission on Law Enforcement and the Administration of Justice (1967) recommended that the police become more responsive to the challenges of a rapidly changing society.

One of the areas that needed the most improvement was the hostile relationship separating the police from minorities, and in particular the police from African Americans. Team policing, tried in the late 1960s and early 1970s, developed from this concern, and was the earliest manifestation of community policing (Rosenbaum). In an attempt to facilitate a closer police-community relationship, police operations were restructured according to geographical boundaries (community beats). In addition, line officers were granted greater decision-making authority to help them be more responsive to neighborhood problems. Innovative though it was, staunch opposition from police managers to decentralization severely hampered successful team implementation, and team policing was soon abandoned.

Academic interest (1970s). All the attention surrounding the police and the increased availability of government funds for police research spawned a great deal of academic interest. Researchers began to examine the role of the police and the effectiveness of traditional police strategies much more closely. In 1974 the Kansas City Patrol Experiment demonstrated that increasing routine preventive patrol and police response time had a very limited impact on reducing crime levels, allaying citizens' fear of crime, and increasing community satisfaction with police service. Similarly, a study on the criminal investigation process revealed the limitations of routine investigative actions and suggested that the crime-solving ability of the police could be enhanced through programs that fostered greater cooperation between the police and the community (Chaiken, Greenwood, and Petersilia).

The idea that a closer partnership between the police and local residents could help reduce crime and disorder began to emerge throughout the 1970s. One of the reasons why this consideration was appealing to police departments was because the recognition that the police and the community were co-producers of police services spread the blame for increasing crime rates (Sko-

gan and Hartnett). An innovative project in San Diego specifically recognized this developing theme by encouraging line officers to identify and solve community problems on their beats (Boydstun and Sherry).

The importance of foot patrol. It is clear that challenges to the traditional policing model and the assumption that the police could reduce crime on their own, helped generate interest in policing alternatives. However, it was not until the late 1970s that both researchers and police practitioners began to focus more intently on the specific elements associated with community-oriented policing. The major catalyst for this change was the reimplementation of foot patrol in U.S. cities. In 1978, Flint, Michigan, became the first city in a generation to create a city-wide program that took officers out of their patrol cars and assigned them to walking beats (Kelling and Moore). Meanwhile, a similar foot patrol program was launched in Newark, New Jersey.

The difference between these two lay primarily in their implementation. In Flint, foot patrol was part of a much broader program designed to involve officers in community problem-solving (Trojanowicz). In contrast, the *Newark Foot Patrol Experiment*, which was modeled on the study of preventive patrol in Kansas City, focused specifically on whether the increased visibility of officers patrolling on foot helped deter crime. Results from these innovative programs were encouraging. It appeared that foot patrol in Flint significantly reduced citizens' fear of crime, increased officer morale, and reduced crime. In Newark, citizens were actually able to recognize whether they were receiving higher or lower levels of foot patrol in their neighborhoods. In areas where foot patrol was increased, citizens believed that their crime problems had diminished in relation to other neighborhoods. In addition, they reported more positive attitudes toward the police. Similarly, those officers in Newark who were assigned to foot patrol experienced a more positive relationship with community members, but, in contrast to Flint, foot patrol did not appear to reduce crime. The finding that foot patrol reduced citizen fear of crime demonstrated the importance of a policing tactic that fostered a closer relationship between the police and the community.

As foot patrol was capturing national attention, Herman Goldstein proposed a new approach to policing that helped synthesize some of the key elements of community policing into a broader and more innovative framework. Foot patrol and police-community cooperation were integral parts of Goldstein's approach, but what distinguished problem-oriented policing (POP) was its focus on how these factors could contribute to a police officer's capacity to identify and solve neighborhood problems. By delineating a clear series of steps, from identifying community problems to choosing among a broad array of alternative solutions to law enforcement, Goldstein showed how increased cooperation between the police and community could do more than reduce fear of crime. An intimate familiarity with local residents could also provide the police with an invaluable resource for identifying and solving the underlying causes of seemingly unrelated and intractable community problems. With its common emphasis on police-community partnerships, parts of the philosophy of problem-oriented policing were readily incorporated into ideas about community policing.

The beginnings of a coherent community policing approach (1980s).   Interest in the development of community policing accelerated with the 1982 publication of an article entitled "Broken Windows." Published in a national magazine, *The Atlantic Monthly*, the article received a great deal of public exposure. Drawing upon the findings of the *Newark Foot Patrol Experiment*, James Q. Wilson and George L. Kelling constructed a compelling and highly readable argument challenging the traditional crime-fighting role of the police, and exploring the relationship between social disorder, neighborhood decline, and crime.

According to Wilson and Kelling, officers on foot patrol should focus on problems such as aggressive panhandling or teenagers loitering on street corners that reduce the quality of neighborhood life. Similar to a broken window, the aggressive panhandler, or the rowdy group of teenagers, represent the initial signs of social disorder. Left unchecked they can make citizens fearful for their personal safety and create the impression that nobody cares about the neighborhood. Over time, this untended behavior increases the level of fear experienced by law-abiding citizens, who begin to withdraw from neighborhood life. As residents retreat inside their homes, or even choose to leave the area altogether, local community controls enervate and disorderly elements take over the neighborhood. Eventually, this process of neighborhood deterioration can lead to an increase in predatory crime. Wilson and Kelling argue that by patrolling beats on foot and focusing on initial problems of social disorder, the police can reduce fear of crime and stop the process of neighborhood decay.

Goldstein's work and Wilson and Kelling's article sparked widespread interest in problem solving, foot patrol, and the relationship between the police and the community, all of which were becoming broadly associated with community policing. Police departments were quick to seize upon the ideas and publicity generated by these scholars, and in the 1980s they experimented with numerous problem- and community-oriented initiatives. In 1986 problem-oriented policing programs were implemented in Baltimore County, Maryland, and Newport News, Virginia (Taft; Eck and Spelman). In Baltimore County, small units composed of fifteen police officers were assigned to specific problems and responsible for their successful resolution. In Newport News, the police worked with the community to identify burglaries as a serious problem in the area. The solution involved the police acting as community organizers and brokering between citizens and other agencies to address the poor physical condition of the buildings. Ultimately the buildings were demolished and residents relocated, but more importantly problem-oriented policing demonstrated that the police were capable of adopting a new role, and it did appear to reduce crime (Eck and Spelman).

An initiative to reduce the fear of crime in Newark and Houston through different police strategies, such as storefront community police stations and a community-organizing police response team, was successful in reducing citizens' fear of crime (Pate et al.). Interestingly, the results in Houston suggested that generally the program was more successful in the areas that needed it least. Whites, middle-class residents, and homeowners in low-crime neighborhoods were more likely to visit or call community substations than minorities, those with low incomes, and renters (Brown and Wycoff).

These studies further catalyzed interest in community policing and problem solving, and from 1988 to 1990 the National Institute of Justice sponsored the *Perspectives on Policing Seminars* at Harvard University's Kennedy School of Government. Not only did this help popularize these innovations in policing, but it helped scholars and practitioners refine and synthesize the mixture of ideas and approaches labeled community- and problem-oriented policing. One policing seminar paper in particular received a great deal of scholarly attention. *The Evolving Strategy of*

Policing, by George Kelling and Mark Moore, summarized the history of policing and identified what was unique about recent developments in the field. In contrasting three different policing approaches and finishing with the advent of the "community problem-solving era," Kelling and Moore appeared to be sounding a clarion call, announcing the arrival of a complete paradigm shift in law enforcement.

In the face of such bold proclamations, it is unsurprising that scholars began to examine community policing more critically, and queried whether it could fulfill its advocates' many promises. Contributors to an edited volume on community policing entitled *Community Policing: Rhetoric or Reality?* noted that without a workable definition of community policing, its successful implementation was difficult. They also suggested that community policing might just be "old wine in new bottles," or even a community-relations exercise employed by police departments to boost their legitimacy in the eyes of the public (Greene and Mastrofski). The outgrowth of these thoughtful criticisms was to encourage researchers to design more rigorous methodological studies that could evaluate the effects of community policing more clearly.

Community policing as a national reform movement (1990s and beyond). By the 1990s, community policing had become a powerful national movement and part of everyday policing parlance. Encouraged by the federal funds made available through the Office of Community Oriented Policing Services (COPS), police departments across the country shifted their attention toward implementing community policing reforms. Annual conferences on community policing became commonplace, and researchers began to study community-policing programs in cities all over America. Besides the availability of funds and promising research findings, the political appeal of community policing and its close affinity to long-term trends in societal organization contributed to the widespread acceptance of community policing (Skogan and Hartnett).

Given the large concentration of African Americans and Hispanics in American cities, groups who have historically been engaged in a hostile relationship with the police, an approach to law enforcement that promised to improve police-community relations by working with, rather than targeting, racial and ethnic minorities held great appeal for local politicians concerned with pleasing their constituents. In addition, community policing reflected a more general underlying trend in the structure, management, and marketing practices of large organizations. In contrast to rigid bureaucracies and their dependence on standard rules and policies, decentralization created smaller, more flexible units to facilitate a speedier and more specialized response to the unique conditions of different organizational environments. Rather than emphasizing control through a strict organizational hierarchy, management layers were reduced, organizational resources were made more accessible, and both supervisors and their subordinates were encouraged to exercise autonomy and independence in the decision-making process. Finally, the extent to which consumers were satisfied with the market produce, in this case police services, became an important criteria for measuring police performance (Skogan and Hartnett).

At the outset of the twenty-first century, the momentum behind community policing shows no signs of slowing down. Even though police departments may have been slow to adopt all the philosophical precepts, tactical elements, and organizational changes commensurate with the entire community-policing model, its slow and steady evolution suggests that it is a permanent fixture on the landscape of American policing (Zhao and Thurman).

The theory and practice of community policing

Community policing promises that closer alliances between the police and the community will help reduce citizen fear of crime, improve police-community relations, and facilitate more effective responses to community problems. But there are also drawbacks associated with community policing: hostility between the police and neighborhood residents can hinder productive partnerships; increases in officers' decision-making autonomy can lead to greater opportunities for police corruption; and resistance within the police organization can hamper community policing's successful implementation. Drawing upon empirical research, this section will focus on the merits and problems associated with community policing.

Effect on crime. Evidence that community policing reduces crime is mixed. Early studies showed that crime declined in Flint, Michigan, as a consequence of foot patrol, but in Newark, New Jersey, crime levels remained unaffected. In a detailed examination of the implementation of a community-policing program in Chicago (the Chicago Alternative Policing Strategy), the authors concluded that crime went down in those districts exposed to community policing (Skogan and Hartnett, p. 18). Similarly, after nearly two years of community- and problem-oriented policing in Joliet, Illinois, the total number of reported index crimes dropped precipitously (Rosenbaum et al.).

In terms of citizens' fear of crime the evidence is also mixed, but it weighs more heavily in a positive direction. In both Flint and Newark, foot patrol contributed to increased feelings of neighborhood safety, and recent studies generally support this conclusion. In Indianapolis, people felt safer in those neighborhoods where the police and local residents cooperated in problem solving (Mastrofski et al., 1998). Even though the benefit of fear reduction appears widespread, its impact is inconsistent across different groups. For instance, in Chicago, in contrast to whites and African Americans, Hispanics did not appear to experience an increase in perceived public safety (Skogan and Hartnett).

Police-community relations. Under community policing the relationship between citizens and the police is supposed to improve. It does appear that increased cooperation between the police and local residents increases satisfaction with police services on both sides, although this is not universal. In Flint, residents were so pleased with neighborhood foot patrols that they agreed to a tax increase in order that the program might continue, and in St. Petersburg, Florida, 85 percent of those residents who lived in community-policing areas of the city reported being "very" or "somewhat" satisfied with their neighborhood police services (Mastrofski et al., 1999).

However, recent evaluations of community policing suggest that the level of community satisfaction with police services varies according to how it is implemented, and the social characteristics of community members. Even though community policing promises to benefit everyone, specific programs may favor particular community interests (such as those of local business owners) and dominant (white, middle-class) groups (Skogan; Lyons). In poor and high-crime neighborhoods, residents may be distrusting of the police and rates of community participation may be very low. The benefits of community policing may be highest in these areas, but the challenges the police face in convincing citizens that they are committed to the long-term improvement of the local neighborhood, in creating productive partnerships, and in mobilizing citizens to get involved in local organizations, are also greatest.

Goldstein argues that police officers who work more closely with community members and are granted more autonomy in making decisions, experience more positive feelings toward citizens and higher job satisfaction. There is considerable evidence to support this assertion, but it is still unclear whether this effect is long-term, and whether it applies to all officers rather than just those selected for community-policing assignments (Wycoff and Skogan). Even though community policing emphasizes the importance of nonenforcement alternatives, police officers do show some ambivalence toward their increasingly community-oriented role. In one survey of line officers in a police department with community policing, 98 percent of officers agreed that assisting citizens is as important as enforcing the law, but 88 percent also said that enforcing the law was an officer's most important responsibility. Similarly, almost all officers agreed that citizen input about neighborhood problems is important, but 25 percent said they have reason to distrust most citizens (Mastrofski et al., 1998). Researchers and police practitioners are well aware that the police subculture is resistant to innovations that challenge the role of police officers as crime fighters. It is clear that some police officers do label community policing as merely "social work," or an exercise in community relations. One of the crucial challenges community policing faces will be to help officers recognize the benefits of reducing social disorder and encouraging public involvement in neighborhood problems in relation to solving crimes and making arrests.

An additional concern is that an increase in the decision-making autonomy of line officers and closer police-community relations will provide the police with greater opportunities for abusing their authority and corruption. Little work has been done on this, but the high levels of patronage and corruption that plagued the police in the nineteenth century (an era characterized by close ties between the police, community members, and local politicians) is a clear reminder of the danger of implicating the police directly in community life.

Police-community problem solving. One of the promises of community policing is that increased police-community cooperation will facilitate problem solving. Research in this area is still in its infancy, but initial findings are encouraging. A comparison of community policing officers to officers engaged in traditional reactive patrol demonstrated that community-policing officers were substantially more involved in problem-solving activities (Mastrofski et al., 1999). Furthermore, several studies suggest that police officers are willing to explore alternatives to law enforcement in order to tackle the underlying causes of community problems. An important element of this process is that the police work closely with other local government and community organizations. A project funded by the National Institute of Justice on community responses to drug abuse found that the police and local community organizations worked effectively together at both the level of enforcement and youth-oriented prevention (Rosenbaum et al.). In Oakland, California, the police department worked closely with other agencies and used noncriminal justice strategies to tackle drug-related problems in the city. Police officers targeted suspected drug houses and collaborated with city inspectors to cite these houses for breaking building code violations. Police enforcement of building regulations reduced drug activity, and this positive benefit diffused into surrounding areas (Green).

Conclusion

Community policing represents a major development in the history of American law enforcement, but the extent to which this approach is a success and dominates contemporary policing still remains a source of debate. At its core, it challenges the traditional concept of the police as crime-fighters by drawing attention to the complexities of the police role and function. Reducing crime remains an important element of police work, but community policing demands that police officers function as community organizers and problem solvers to help reduce citizens' fear of crime and improve the overall quality of neighborhood life. It is unsurprising that such a radical redefinition of policing has encountered some opposition from police officers who are committed to their traditional police role. Nonetheless, the fact that the majority of police departments across the country have implemented some kind of community-oriented policing program is testament to the pervasive influence of this new approach.

Despite widespread support for community policing, it is still prudent to be cautious regarding its potential for improving the state of the country's neighborhoods. It is still unclear whether communities that are poor and socially disorganized, or rapidly developing, can benefit from community policing. If there is not a viable community already in place, how can the police contribute to improving neighborhood life?

Furthermore, it is important not to lose sight of the ethical and legal problems that can emerge as a consequence of this expansion of the police role into the nation's communities. Encouraging officers to foster closer ties with neighborhood residents and granting them greater decision-making autonomy increases opportunities for corruption, and raises questions about the limits on government power. There is a danger that the police will serve the interests of powerful community members and/or will use their authority to interfere in the lives of law-abiding citizens who have not requested their service.

Despite these concerns and limitations, it is clear that the philosophical, tactical, and organizational characteristics of community policing have generated a great deal of innovation in how we think about the police and how police work is done. With this creative energy driving us forward, there is every reason to be optimistic about the possibility of improving policing in the decades ahead.

JAMES J. WILLIS

See also FEDERAL BUREAU OF INVESTIGATION: HISTORY; POLICE: HISTORY; POLICE: CRIMINAL INVESTIGATIONS; POLICE: HANDLING OF JUVENILES; POLICE: ORGANIZATION AND MANAGEMENT; POLICE: POLICE OFFICER BEHAVIOR; POLICE: POLICING COMPLAINANTLESS CRIMES; POLICE: PRIVATE POLICE AND INDUSTRIAL SECURITY; POLICE: SPECIAL WEAPONS AND TACTICS (SWAT) TEAMS; SCIENTIFIC EVIDENCE; URBAN POLICE.

BIBLIOGRAPHY

BOYDSTUN, JOHN, and SHERRY, MICHAEL. *San Diego Community Profile: Final Report.* Washington, D.C.: Police Foundation, 1975.

BROWN, LEE P., and WYCOFF, MARY ANN. "Policing Houston: Reducing Fear and Improving Service." *Crime and Delinquency* 33 (1986): 71–89.

CHAIKEN, JAN M.; GREENWOOD, PETER W.; and PETERSILIA, JOAN. "The Criminal Investigation Process: A Summary Report." *Policy Analysis* 3, no. 2 (1977): 187–217.

CORDNER, GARY W. "Community Policing: Elements and Effects." In *Community Policing:*

Contemporary Readings. Edited by Geoffrey P. Alpert and Alex Piquero. Prospect Heights, Ill.: Waveland Press, 1997. Pages 45–62.

ECK, JOHN E., and SPELMAN, WILLIAM. *Problem-Solving: Problem-Oriented Policing in Newport News.* Washington, D.C.: Police Executive Research Forum, 1987.

ECK, JOHN E., and ROSENBAUM, DENNIS P. "The New Police Order, Effectiveness, Equity, and Efficiency in Community Policing." In *The Challenges of Community Policing: Testing the Promises.* Edited by Dennis P. Rosenbaum. Thousand Oaks, Calif.: Sage, 1994. Pages 3–23.

GOLDSTEIN, HERMAN. "Toward Community-Oriented Policing: Potential, Base Requirements and Threshold Questions." *Crime and Delinquency* 33, no. 1 (1987): 6–30.

———. *Problem-Oriented Policing.* New York: McGraw-Hill, 1990.

GREENE, JACK R., and MASTROFSKI, STEPHEN D., eds. *Community Policing: Rhetoric or Reality?* New York: Praeger, 1988.

GREEN, LORRAINE. "Cleaning Up Drug Hotspots in Oakland, California: The Displacement and Diffusion Effects." *Justice Quarterly* 12, no. 4 (1995): 737–754.

KELLING, GEORGE L. *Police and Communities: The Quiet Revolution.* Perspectives on Policing, no. 1. Washington, D.C.: Government Printing Office, 1988.

KELLING, GEORGE L., and MOORE, MARK H. *The Evolving Strategy of Policing.* Perspectives on Policing, no. 4. Washington, D.C.: Government Printing Office, 1988.

Law Enforcement Management and Administration Statistics (LEMAS). Washington, D.C.: Government Printing Office, 1997.

LYONS, WILLIAM. *The Politics of Community Policing: Rearranging the Power to Punish.* Ann Arbor: University of Michigan Press, 1999.

MASTROFSKI, STEPHEN D.; WORDEN, ROBERT F.; and SNIPES, JEFFREY B. "Law Enforcement in a Time of Community Policing." *Criminology* 33, no. 1 (1995): 539–563.

MASTROFSKI, STEPHEN D.; PARKS, ROGER B.; REISS, ALBERT J., JR.; and WORDEN, ROBERT F. *Policing Neighborhoods: A Report from Indianapolis. Research in Brief Preview.* Washington, D.C.: National Institute of Justice, 1998.

———. *Policing Neighborhoods: A Report from St. Petersburg. Research in Brief Preview.* Washington, D.C.: National Institute of Justice, 1999.

The Newark Foot Patrol Experiment. Washington, D.C.: The Police Foundation, 1981.

PATE, ANTHONY M.; WYCOFF, MARY ANN; SKOGAN, WESLEY G.; and SHERMAN, LAWRENCE W. *Reducing Fear of Crime in Houston and Newark: A Summary Report.* Washington, D.C.: The Police Foundation, 1986.

ROSENBAUM, DENNIS P. "The Changing Role of the Police: Assessing the Current Transition to Community Policing." In *Policing Communities: Understanding Crime and Solving Problems, An Anthology.* Edited by Ronald W. Glensor, Mark E. Correia, and Kenneth J. Peak. Los Angeles, Calif.: Roxbury Publishing Company, 1998. Pages 46–63.

ROSENBAUM, D. P.; BENNETT, S. F.; LINDSAY, B.; and WILKINSON, D. L. *Community Responses to Drug Abuse: A Program Evaluation.* Washington, D.C.: National Institute of Justice, 1994.

SKOGAN, WESLEY G. *Disorder and Decline: Crime and the Spiral of Decay in American Neighborhoods.* New York: Free Press, 1990.

SKOGAN, WESLEY G., and HARTNETT, SUSAN M. *Community Policing, Chicago Style.* New York: Oxford University Press, 1997.

SPARROW, MALCOLM K. *Implementing Community Policing.* Perspectives on Policing, no. 9. Washington, D.C.: Government Printing Office, 1988.

TAFT, PHILIP B., JR. *Fighting Fear: The Baltimore County C.O.P.E. Project.* Washington, D.C.: Police Executive Research Forum, 1986.

TROJANOWICZ, R. *An Exploration of the Neighborhood Foot Patrol Experiment in Flint, Michigan.* East Lansing: Michigan State University, 1982.

WALKER, SAMUEL. *The Police in America: An Introduction,* 3d ed. New York: McGraw-Hill, 1998.

WILSON, JAMES Q., and KELLING, GEORGE. "Broken Windows: The Police and Neighborhood Safety." *The Atlantic Monthly* 249 (1982): 29–38.

WYCOFF, MARY ANN, and SKOGAN, WESLEY G. *Community Policing in Madison: Quality from the Inside Out.* Washington, D.C.: National Institute of Justice, 1993.

ZHAO, JIHONG, and THURMAN, QUINT C. "Community Policing: Where Are We Now?" *Crime and Delinquency* 43, no. 3 (1997): 345–357.

POLICE: CRIMINAL INVESTIGATIONS

This entry provides an overview of the criminal investigation process and investigative methods. The focus of the discussion is on definitional issues along with the identification and evaluation of the types and sources of information often used in criminal investigations.

Criminal investigation defined

An investigation refers to the process of collecting information in order to reach some goal; for example, collecting information about the reliability and performance of a vehicle prior to purchase in order to enhance the likelihood of buying a good car. Applied to the criminal realm, a *criminal* investigation refers to the process of collecting information (or evidence) about a crime in order to: (1) determine if a crime has been committed; (2) identify the perpetrator; (3) apprehend the perpetrator; and (4) provide evidence to support a conviction in court. If the first three objectives are successfully attained, then the crime can be said to be solved. Several other outcomes such as recovering stolen property, deterring individuals from engaging in criminal behaviors, and satisfying crime victims have also been associated with the process.

A useful perspective on the criminal investigation process is provided by information theory (Willmer). According to information theory, the criminal investigation process resembles a battle between the police and the perpetrator over crime-related information. In committing the crime, the offender emits "signals," or leaves behind information of various sorts (fingerprints, eyewitness descriptions, murder weapon, etc.), which the police attempt to collect through investigative activities. If the perpetrator is able to minimize the amount of information available for the police to collect, or if the police are unable to recognize the information left behind, then the perpetrator will not be apprehended and therefore, the perpetrator will win the battle. If the police are able to collect a significant number of signals from the perpetrator, then the perpetrator will be identified and apprehended, and the police win. This perspective clearly underscores the importance of information in a criminal investigation.

The major problem for the police in conducting a criminal investigation is that not only is there potentially massive amounts of information available, but the relevance of the information is often unknown, the information is often incomplete, and the information is often inaccurate. Further, to be useful in proving guilt in court (where beyond a reasonable doubt is the standard), the evidence must have certain other qualities, and certain rules and procedures must be followed in collecting the evidence.

The structure of criminal investigations

Criminal investigations can be either reactive, where the police respond to a crime that has already occurred, or proactive, where the investigation may go on before and during the commission of the offense.

The reactive criminal investigation process can be organized into several stages. The first stage is initial discovery and response. Of course, before the criminal investigation process can begin, the police must discover that a crime occurred or the victim (or witness) must realize that a crime occurred and notify the police. In the vast majority of cases it is the victim that first realizes a crime occurred and notifies the police. Then, most often, a patrol officer is dispatched to the crime scene or the location of the victim.

The second stage, the initial investigation, consists of the immediate post-crime activities of the patrol officer who arrives at the crime scene. The tasks of the patrol officer during the initial investigation are to arrest the culprit (if known and present), locate and interview witnesses, and collect and preserve other evidence.

If the perpetrator is not arrested during the initial investigation, then the case may be selected for a follow-up investigation, the third stage of the reactive investigation process. The follow-up investigation consists of additional investigative activities performed on a case, and these activities are usually performed by a detective. The process of deciding which cases should receive additional investigative effort is referred to as *case screening*. This decision is most often made by a detective supervisor and is most often guided by consideration of the seriousness of the crime (e.g., the amount of property loss or injury to the victim) and solvability factors (key pieces of crime-related information that, if present, enhance the probability of an arrest being made) (Brandl; Brandl and Frank).

Finally, at any time in the process the case may be closed and investigative activities terminated (e.g., victim cancels the investigation, the crime is unfounded, there are no more leads available, or an arrest is made). If an arrest is made, or an arrest warrant is issued, primary responsibility for the case typically shifts to the prosecutor's office. The detective then assists the prosecutor in preparing the case for further processing.

With regard to proactive criminal investigations, undercover investigations are of most significance (Marx). Perhaps the most well-known type of undercover strategy is the *sting* or *buy-bust* strategy that usually involves a police officer posing as someone who wishes to buy some illicit goods (e.g., sex, drugs). Once a seller is identified and the particulars of the illicit transaction are determined, police officers waiting nearby can execute an arrest. Another common strategy involves undercover police officers acting as *decoys* where the attempt is to attract street crime by presenting an opportunity to an offender to commit such crime (e.g., a police officer poses as a stranded motorist in a high crime area; when a robbery attempt is made, nearby officers can make an arrest). Undercover strategies are controversial primarily because of the possibility of entrapment. Although a multitude of court cases have dealt with this issue, the basic rule is that the police can provide the opportunity or can encourage the offender to act but cannot compel the behavior—a fine line indeed.

Sources of information and evidence in criminal investigations

As noted earlier, the major problem for the police in conducting criminal investigations is determining the utility of the information (evidence) collected. While much information may be discovered or otherwise available to the police, only a small portion of it may be accurate, complete, and relevant, and hence useful, in establishing the identity (and/or whereabouts) of the culprit. As discussed below, not all types of information are equal in this regard—some types of evidence are usually more useful than others.

Information from physical evidence. Physical evidence is evidence of a tangible nature relating directly to the crime. Physical evidence includes such items as fingerprints, blood, fibers, and crime tools (knife, gun, crowbar, etc.). Physical evidence is sometimes referred to as forensic or scientific evidence, implying that the evidence must be scientifically analyzed and the results interpreted in order to be useful.

Physical evidence can serve at least two important functions in the investigative or judicial process (Peterson et al.). First, physical evidence can help establish the elements of a crime. For example, pry marks left on a window (physical evidence) may help establish the occurrence of a burglary. Second, physical evidence can associate or link victims to crime scenes, offenders to crime scenes, victims to victims, instruments to crime scenes, offenders to instruments, and so on. For example, in a homicide case, a body of a young

female was found along a rural road. Knotted around her neck was a black electrical cord (physical evidence). The cause of death was determined to be ligature strangulation via the electrical cord. Upon searching the area for evidence, an abandoned farmhouse was located and searched, and a piece of a similar electrical cord was found. This evidence led the investigators to believe that the farmhouse may have been where the murder actually occurred. Further examination of the scene revealed tire impressions from an automobile (more physical evidence). These tire impressions were subsequently linked to the suspect's vehicle.

Most forensic or physical evidence submitted for analysis is intended to establish associations. It is important to note that physical evidence is generally not very effective at identifying a culprit when one is not already known. Typically the identity of the culprit is developed in some other way and then physical evidence is used to help establish proof of guilt. Possible exceptions to this pattern are fingerprints (when analyzed through AFIS or Automated Fingerprint Identification System technology) and DNA banks. With AFIS technology, fingerprints recovered from a crime scene can be compared with thousands of other prints on file in the computer system at the law enforcement agency. Through a computerized matching process, the computer can select fingerprints that are close in characteristics. In this way a match may be made and a suspect's name produced.

DNA printing allows for the comparison of DNA obtained from human cells (most commonly blood and semen) in order to obtain a match between at least two samples. In order for traditional DNA analysis to be useful, a suspect must first be identified through some other means, so that a comparison of samples can be made. However, emerging technology involves the creation of DNA banks, similar to the computerized fingerprint systems, in order to compare and match DNA structures. There is little question, as technological capabilities advance, so too will the value of physical evidence.

Information from people. Beside physical evidence, another major source of information in a criminal investigation is people, namely witnesses and suspects. Witnesses can be classified as either primary or secondary. Primary witnesses are individuals who have direct knowledge of the crime because they overheard or observed its occurrence. This classification would include crime victims who observed or who were otherwise involved in the offense. Eyewitnesses would also be included here. Secondary witnesses possess information about related events before or after the crime. Informants (or *street sources*) and victims who did not observe the crime would be best classified as secondary witnesses.

A suspect can be defined as any individual within the scope of the investigation who may be responsible for the crime. Note that a witness may be initially considered a suspect by the police because information is not available to rule him or her out as the one responsible for the crime.

Besides the basic information about the particulars of the criminal event and possibly the actions of the perpetrator (to establish a modus operandi), another important type of information often provided by witnesses is eyewitness descriptions and identifications. Such information is quite powerful in establishing proof—for the police, prosecutor, judge, and jury—but the problem is that eyewitness identifications are often quite inaccurate and unreliable (Loftus et al.). Research has shown that many factors—such as environmental conditions, physical and emotional conditions of the observer, expectancies of the observer, perceived significance of the event, and knowledge of the item or person being described—can significantly influence the accuracy of eyewitness statements.

Hypnosis and cognitive interviews are two investigative tools available in the interview setting for the purpose of enhancing memory recall, and thus enhancing the accuracy of eyewitness information. Hypnosis is typically viewed as an altered state of consciousness that is characterized by heightened suggestibility (Niehaus). For the police, hypnosis is used as a method of stimulating memory in an attempt to increase memory recall greater than that achieved otherwise. While the use of hypnosis has increased sharply in the 1990s many courts have refused to admit such testimony because of accuracy concerns, or have established strict procedures under which hypnotically elicited testimony must be obtained (e.g., interview must be videotaped, the hypnotist should know little or nothing about the particulars of the case, no other persons are to be present during the interview, etc.). Most problematic is that under hypnosis, one is more responsive to suggestions (by definition) and thus, the hypnotist (intentionally or not) may lead the subject and inaccurate information may result. Once again then, information

is produced but it is unknown whether the information is accurate.

Another method used to enhance memory recall among witnesses involves the use of the cognitive interview (Niehaus). A cognitive interview is designed to fully immerse the subject in the situation once again, but through freedom of description not hypnosis. The subject is instructed to report everything he or she can think of no matter how trivial it may seem. The witness may be instructed to recount the incident in more than one order. The intent is to allow for a much deeper level of recollection than the traditional interview. Research has shown that the cognitive interview approach elicits significantly more accurate information than a standard police interview, which typically involves frequent interruptions of explanations and descriptions, includes many closed-ended and short answer questions, and involves the inappropriate or overly strict ordering of questions (Niehaus).

In contrast to interviews of witnesses, interrogations of suspects are often more accusatory in nature. Usually interrogations are more of a process of testing already developed information than of actually developing information. The ultimate objective in an interrogation is to obtain a confession (Zulawski and Wicklander).

For obvious reasons, offenders have great incentive to deceive investigators. Understanding this, there are several tools available to investigators who wish to separate truthful from deceptive information. First is the understanding of kinesic behavior, the use of body movement and posture to convey meaning (Walters). Although not admissible in court, information derived from an understanding and interpretation of body language can be quite useful in an investigation. The theory behind the study of nonverbal behavior is that lying is stressful and individuals try to cope with this stress through body positioning and movement.

Although no single behavior is always indicative of deception, there are patterns (Zulawski and Wicklander). For example, a deceptive subject will tend not to sit facing the interrogator with shoulders squared but will protect the abdominal region of the body (angled posture, crossed arms). Major body shifts are typical especially when asked incriminating questions; and use of *manipulators* (or created jobs) are also common among deceptive subjects (e.g., grooming gestures), as are particular eye movements (Zulawski and Wicklander).

Much like nonverbal behavior, verbal behavior can also provide information about the truthfulness of a suspect. For example, deceptive subjects tend to provide vague and confusing statements, talk very soft or mumble, provide premature explanations, focus on irrelevant (but truthful) points in an explanation, or may claim memory problems or have a selectively good memory. Of course, interpretations of nonverbal and verbal behaviors in terms of deception must consider individual, gender, and cultural differences in personal interaction.

The polygraph is a mechanical means of detecting deception. The polygraph is a machine that measures physiological responses to psychological phenomenon. The polygraph records blood pressure, pulse, breathing rate, and electro-dermal reactivity and changes in these factors when questioned. Interpretation of the resulting chart serves as the basis for a judgment about truthfulness. Once again, the theory is that a person experiences increased stress when providing deceptive information and the corresponding physiological responses can be detected, measured, and interpreted. While this general theory is well founded, the accuracy of the polygraph depends largely on the skill of the operator and the individual who interprets the results of the polygraph examination (Raskin). No one can be forced to take a polygraph and polygraph results are seldom admissible in court. Often investigators threaten suspects with a polygraph examination in order to judge the nature of their reaction to it, or to induce a confession (Raskin).

Other sources of information

Along with physical evidence, witnesses, and suspects, there are a number of other sources that can provide useful information in a criminal investigation. These include psychological profiling, crime analysis, and the general public.

In the last two decades, psychological profiling has received much media attention. It is often portrayed as a complicated yet foolproof method of crime solving. In reality, psychological profiling is not all that mysterious. Psychological profiling is a technique for identifying the major personality, behavioral, and background characteristics of an individual based upon an analysis of the crime(s) he or she has committed. The basic theory behind psychological profiling is that the crime reflects the personality and characteristics of the offender much like how clothes, home decorations, and the car you drive reflects,

to some degree, your personality. And these preferences do not change, or do not change very much over time.

In constructing a psychological profile, the characteristics of the offender are inferred from the nature of the crime and the behaviors displayed. The elements of a psychological profile are essentially statements of probability as determined from previous crimes and crime patterns (Holmes). Profiles are best suited and most easily constructed in cases where the perpetrator shows indications of psychopathology such as lust and mutilation murder, sadistic rape, and motiveless fire setting.

The value of a psychological profile is that it can help focus an investigation or reduce the number of suspects being considered. In this respect, a psychological profile is much like most physical evidence; a psychological profile cannot identify a suspect when one is not already known. There has been very little systematic research that has documented the actual impact of psychological profiles on criminal investigations. In an internal examination by the F.B.I. (as reported in Pinizzotto, 1984), analysts examined 192 cases where profiling was conducted. Of these, 88 were solved. Of these 88 solved cases, in only 17 percent did a profile offer significant help. Given the limitations of psychological profiles, it is clear that they are not as useful as media depictions might suggest.

Crime analysis is another potentially powerful source of information in a criminal investigation. Simply defined, crime analysis is the process of identifying patterns or trends in criminal incidents. Various means can be used to reach such ends, from computer mapping technology to computer data banks. The Violent Criminal Apprehension Program (VI-CAP) of the Federal Bureau of Investigation is an example of an elaborate and sophisticated crime analysis system. When police departments are confronted with unsolved homicides, missing persons, or unidentified dead bodies, personnel in the department may complete a VI-CAP questionnaire, which asks for detailed information regarding the nature of the incident. These data are then sent to the F.B.I. and entered into the VI-CAP computer system, which is able to collate the data and possibly link crimes that occurred in different jurisdictions based on similarities in the crimes. This system, and similar intrastate systems, are designed to facilitate communication and sharing of information across agencies.

Finally, the general public is a potentially useful source of information in criminal investigations. As defined here, the public consists of people who have information relating to a particular crime or criminal but often cannot be identified through traditional methods (like a neighborhood canvass). Crime Solvers (or Crime Stoppers) tip lines and television shows such as *America's Most Wanted* provide a method of disseminating information and encouraging individuals to come forward with information relating to particular crimes. Although once again, little systematic research has examined the actual effects of such strategies, information that has come from the general public through these sources has led to the solving of many crimes across the county (Rosenbaum; Nelson).

Conclusion

This discussion has provided an overview of the criminal investigation process and the role, function, and utility of various types and sources of evidence within the process. With these understandings, one may be able to better appreciate the complexities of criminal evidence and the criminal investigation process.

STEVEN G. BRANDL

See also CRIMINAL PROCEDURE: CONSTITUTIONAL ASPECTS; ENTRAPMENT; FEDERAL BUREAU OF INVESTIGATION: HISTORY; POLICE: HANDLING OF JUVENILES; POLICE: HISTORY; POLICE: ORGANIZATION AND MANAGEMENT; POLICE: POLICE OFFICER BEHAVIOR; POLICE: POLICING COMPLAINANTLESS CRIMES; POLICE: PRIVATE POLICE AND INDUSTRIAL SECURITY; POLICE: SPECIAL WEAPONS AND TACTICS (SWAT) TEAMS; SCIENTIFIC EVIDENCE; URBAN POLICE.

BIBLIOGRAPHY

BRANDL, STEVEN G. "The Impact of Case Characteristics on Detectives' Decision Making." *Justice Quarterly* 10 (1993): 395–415.

BRANDL, STEVEN G., and FRANK, JAMES. "The Relationship Between Evidence, Detective Effort, and the Disposition of Burglary and Robbery Investigations." *American Journal of Police* 13 (1994): 149–168.

HOLMES, RONALD. *Profiling Violent Crimes: An Investigative Tool.* Newbury Park, Calif.: Sage, 1989.

LOFTUS, ELIZABETH F.; GREENE, EDITH L.; and DOYLE, JAMES M. "The Psychology of Eyewitness Testimony." In *Psychological Methods in Criminal Investigation and Evidence.* Edited by David C. Raskin. New York: Springer, 1989. Pages 3–45.

MARX, GARY. *Undercover: Police Surveillance in America.* Berkeley: University of California Press, 1988.

NELSON, SCOTT A. "Crime-Time Television." *F.B.I. Law Enforcement Bulletin,* August 1989, pp. 1–9.

NIEHAUS, JOE. *Investigative Forensic Hypnosis.* New York: CRC Press, 1998.

PETERSON, JOSEPH L.; MIHAJLOVIC, STEVEN; and GILLILAND, MICHAEL. *Forensic Evidence and the Police: The Effects of Scientific Evidence on Criminal Investigations.* Washington, D.C.: U.S. Department of Justice, 1984.

PINIZZOTTO, ANTHONY. "Forensic Psychology: Criminal Personality Profiling." *Journal of Police Science and Administration* 12 (1984): 32–40.

RASKIN, D. C. *Psychological Methods in Criminal Investigation and Evidence.* New York: Springer, 1989.

ROSENBAUM, DENNIS. "Enhancing Citizen Participation and Solving Serious Crime: A National Evaluation of Crime Stoppers Program." *Crime and Delinquency* 35 (1990): 401–420.

WALTERS, STAN B. *Principles of Kinesic Interview and Interrogation.* New York: CRC Press, 1996.

WILLMER, M. *Crime and Information Theory.* Edinburgh, Scotland: University of Edinburgh Press, 1970.

ZULAWSKI, DAVID E., and WICKLANDER, DOUGLAS E. *Practical Aspects of Interview and Interrogation.* New York: Elsevier, 1992.

POLICE: HANDLING OF JUVENILES

The juvenile justice system mirrors the adult system of criminal justice in that it has three basic components: police, courts, and corrections. More likely than not, whether or not a juvenile is processed into this system is dependent upon the outcome of an encounter with the police. It is accurate to say that the police serve as the "gatekeepers" to the juvenile justice system—they serve this function in the adult system as well. The police in turn begin the criminal justice process by making initial decisions about how to handle incidents involving juveniles. Indeed, the role of the police in juvenile justice is an important one.

Police officers have many contacts with juveniles that are for the most part unknown. For this reason, the cases that reach the juvenile courts are only a small fraction of the interactions that police have with juvenile suspects and offenders. In deciding how to handle incidents involving youth, the police have a wide range of responses available to them. This latitude is a necessary element to police work as patrol officers are presented with various and often complex situations (Whitaker). However, in light of this discretion, one should be concerned with how police make decisions involving juveniles as it is an important decision, one that may formally classify juveniles (correctly or incorrectly) as delinquents and introduce them to the juvenile justice system.

This entry will focus on the police part of juvenile justice and will provide an overview of policing juveniles. It will briefly review the police role in juvenile justice from a historical perspective and it will review the organizational structures existing in policing today to handle juveniles as well as the legal rights of juveniles who are accused of some wrongdoing. This entry will then review what we know about police-juvenile interactions, including a discussion of how police dispose of their encounters with youth, and what factors shape their decision-making. Finally, ideas for future research on policing juveniles are discussed.

Historical overview and organizational structure

The focus and purpose of "juvenile justice" has undergone considerable change in the past century. Juvenile justice systems were originally formed to protect youth from the adult systems of justice and to allow discretion in decision-making involving youth so that juvenile justice actors could make decisions that were in the best interest of the child. The ideals behind the formation of the juvenile court, for example, revolved around rehabilitation and helping juveniles who might have problematic home lives or who were psychologically immature or troubled (Scott and Grisso). Troubled and delinquent youth were not thought to be fully capable of guilty intentions, rather they were thought to be in need of help and guidance. However, the idea that juveniles should be handled with "kid gloves" and that they should be protected from the adult system of justice has changed—particularly since the mid-1970s. These changes have not, however, had many direct implications for police handling of juveniles; they more often have altered the context of the juvenile courts.

Remarkably, the police role in juvenile justice has remained much the same. One of the central reasons for this has to do with the occupation of policing. Police officers work alone, without direct supervision, and they bear the burden of much discretion. It is difficult to know what officers do during their shifts and many of their contacts with youth (and adults) go without documentation in official records. When the creation of juvenile justice systems occurred (and this happened sporadically throughout the states), police handling of juveniles was not of much concern.

Prior to the early twentieth century, police had the authority to arrest juveniles (possibly more authority than with adults because juveniles had no procedural protections) but juveniles were usually dealt with informally. That is to say, police officers would warn kids, bring them home to their parents or guardians, or maybe relinquish them to a community agency (i.e., a local church or school) (Bartollas and Miller). It is important to put this within the context of policing during this period. Policing in America prior to the 1920s and 1930s was very political. Patrol officers campaigned for local politicians and as a reward were allowed to keep their jobs or to begin a job as a patrol officer. Patrol officers were politically recruited from the neighborhoods in which they lived, and as a result they knew many of the juveniles living in their assigned areas. Kelling notes that many cases of youth crime and disorder were settled with the end of a nightstick. The youths' families and their political connections would more than likely influence the outcome of a police-juvenile interaction. These police practices with juveniles (and adults) came under scrutiny during the Progressive era, which marked a period of professionalization for police.

The professionalization movement in policing occurred in response to a movement to establish professional standards in policing and it occurred as the result of increased technology in America (see Walker, 1992). The professionalization movement sought, among other things, to eliminate political control of the police, raise personnel standards, appoint qualified chiefs to lead police departments, refocus the police toward fighting crime, and create specialized units to handle special problems. When policing underwent this reform in the early twentieth century, some of the changes were targeted at policing juveniles. Police departments began acknowledging the problem of juvenile crime and began to address this issue as part of an overall policing strategy (Miller). Moreover, reforms targeted at policing juveniles called on police to prevent juvenile delinquency—rather than merely attempting to make arrests. Police attention to juvenile crime before the mid-twentieth century was focused on crime prevention rather than on apprehension, deterrence, and punishment.

With this new attention to juvenile crime came the hiring of female officers. Female police officers were introduced to the policing occupation during the early twentieth century and they were initially hired to work with juvenile delinquents and runaways. They were labeled juvenile "specialists" because it was thought that women had a "special capacity for child care" and that handling juveniles was in fact women's work (see Walker, 1977, pp. 84–85).

During the early 1900s larger police agencies began instituting some organizational structure to handle juveniles. In the 1920s August Vollmer, the father of police professionalism, who was at the time chief of police in Berkley, California, formed one of the first juvenile bureaus (Walker; Bartollas and Miller). Vollmer advocated for increased training and specialized training for juvenile officers. He wanted juvenile officers to be educated on the causes of juvenile delinquency and to develop programs that would help keep juveniles out of trouble. Specialized juvenile units and bureaus would be found in most metropolitan agencies by the mid 1900s, their primary focus on crime prevention. Police agencies that did not have the manpower (or need) for an entire juvenile unit or bureau would often have at least one "juvenile specialist" who focused his or her efforts on keeping kids out of trouble and preventing juvenile crime. The establishment of these organized juvenile units and bureaus spawned the development of police athletic leagues and youth diversion programs— some of which still exist today. Police athletic leagues were created to help foster a relationship between police and kids. Diversion programs divert youth from the criminal justice system by using counseling and other tactics to teach kids about accountability and the consequences of delinquency. In the 1960s these were formal programs designed to avoid labeling youth as criminals and to lighten the load of the criminal justice system.

Today most police agencies have juvenile units or juvenile specialists, but the focus of the juvenile officer in metropolitan agencies has evolved over time. Juvenile specialists now operate as detectives, and are called juvenile unit detectives, juvenile specialists, and so on. They are embraced as an essential part of police departments and are no longer viewed as the add-on that they once were. Juvenile officers spend much of their day doing investigative work, following up on juvenile crimes and on juvenile victimization. This is not to say that juvenile officers never spend time involved in crime prevention, that crime prevention can no longer be their sole focus. In terms of prevention, juvenile officers still spend some time forming police athletic leagues and youth diversion programs that began in the middle of the twentieth century. It is also common for juvenile detectives to make appearances at elementary, middle, and high schools to deter juvenile crime and to speak out against drug use and gang formation. In fact, many metropolitan departments train one or more officers to work directly with schoolchildren of all ages, educating students on the consequences of delinquency and drug use. One particular prevention program, DARE (Drug Abuse Resistance Education), became very popular nationwide during the 1990s.

During the 1990s many police departments hired officers to work specifically on the DARE project. DARE, which was developed in the Los Angeles, California, police department as a drug prevention program for school children, uses uniformed patrol officers to educate school children on the dangers of drug use. DARE officers often had offices within public schools, where kids could easily access information or ask questions. Early evaluations suggested that DARE worked and as a result many departments in the 1990s assigned uniformed officers to the DARE project. Unfortunately, extended evaluations of this program now suggests that the long-term effects of project DARE are not as beneficial as once thought; in fact they may be nonexistent (see, for example, Rosenbaum et al.; Rosenbaum and Hanson). For this reason, many departments are phasing out DARE as a preventive measure or are at least restructuring the program. The role of the juvenile officer or detective continues to evolve, and with time involvement in investigation has taken precedence over prevention, although this may change with new reforms in policing. Under the umbrella of community and problem-oriented policing, police departments nationwide are beginning to form partnerships with communities so that they can be more efficient at preventing crime. This new approach to policing will surely influence how police address issues of juvenile crime. In 1998 and 1999 President Bill Clinton awarded millions of dollars in School-Based Partnership grants, which funded partnerships between the police, schoolchildren, and the community. The goal of these partnerships was to target specific problems of school crime and violence and to develop a link between kids and cops. Evaluations of these projects are ongoing.

Is juvenile crime on the rise? There has been an increased concern about the incidence and seriousness of juvenile offending over the past few decades. Local and national media regularly alert American families to instances of juvenile crime. This growing awareness and concern has prompted renewed attention to the juvenile justice system, with particular concern over how juveniles are processed in to and out of the system. Whether or not this growing concern is warranted is debatable. While policy makers and public opinion call for "get tough" approaches with juveniles, some argue that there are no justifications for such an approach (see Bernard, for an example). In 1996, juvenile arrests accounted for almost 20 percent of the arrests tabulated for the F.B.I.'s Uniform Crime Reports. The number of juvenile arrests in 1996 represented a 35 percent increase over the preceding ten years, while arrests overall during that period increased only 13 percent. Further, the number of juvenile arrests for violent personal offenses represented a 60 percent increase (see Worden and Myers). Statistics of this kind along with well-publicized incidents of youth violence over the past decade have prompted policy makers to call for measures that would make the juvenile justice system more punitive. Bernard argues that the statistics do not justify such an approach. A deeper analysis reveals that the number of juvenile arrests (with the exception of homicide arrests) has basically paralleled the rise and fall in the number of juveniles of crime-prone age (p. 342). In fact, juvenile crime has been on a decline, down by one-third since 1975 (Bernard). One might logically infer or hypothesize that the increase in the number of police arrests of juveniles could reflect police adoption of the "get tough" movement.

Legal rights of juveniles

The creation of juvenile justice systems was based on conceptions of rehabilitation and treatment, not on punishment. For this reason, up until the 1960s persons working in the juvenile justice system and those working in criminal justice generally were allowed an enormous amount of discretion when making decisions about youth. Discretion exists when a person of authority can choose several types of formal and informal actions, or inaction. With increased discretion and no formal procedures to handle juveniles, criminal justice agents could then act in the best interest of the child. For this reason, punishment policies and procedural safeguards that existed in the adult criminal justice system were not regularly required or operating in juvenile justice systems (Feld). The idea was that juvenile justice would be individualized for each youth and it would be based on a rehabilitative and treatment philosophy. Police were to formally process youth into the system only if it appeared necessary to curb future misconduct or if it were necessary given the seriousness of the suspected offense.

In a landmark case, *In re Gault*, 387 U.S. 1 (1967), the Supreme Court sparked the beginning of a juvenile justice reform that remains ongoing. The legal response to juvenile delinquency has changed dramatically since the *Gault* decision. In *Gault*, the Court began, unintentionally, the process of criminalizing the juvenile justice system and transforming it into what many regard as a near mirror image of the adult criminal justice system (see Feld; Bartollas and Miller). The decision in *Gault* required states to give juveniles many procedural safeguards that were previously only required for adult suspects. Before this time, juveniles had no regulated rights from state to state (Scott and Grisso), though some states did allocate rights to juveniles before *Gault*, even though they were not required to do so by Supreme Court standards. Two Supreme Court rulings directly affected police handling of juveniles. In *Gault*, the Supreme Court clarified that juveniles were protected from self-incrimination and that they had a right to counsel (though it is not clear if juveniles, like adults, can waive these rights). In *State v. Lowery*, 230 A.2d 907 (1967), the Supreme Court ruled that juveniles were also protected from unlawful searches and seizures (Bartollas and Miller). The assignment of these and other legal rights to juveniles, many of which pertain to procedural issues in the juvenile court, was supposed to protect juveniles from procedural injustice within the system. One unintended result was that the assignment of procedural protections became the impetus for changing the juvenile justice system into what we see today—a system that closely resembles the adult criminal justice system. The assignment of rights to juveniles varies from state to state, with some states providing more than others, as the Supreme Court only establishes the minimum protections required.

To confuse matters, the age at which one is legally considered an adult also varies from state to state. Most states consider a person to be an adult at the eighteenth birthday, ten states use the age of seventeen, and three states determine adulthood at sixteen. However, this is not the end of the "legal age" issue. As a result of the public's concern over juvenile crime in the late 1990s, many legislative reforms within states targeted the juvenile justice system. Many states have passed offense-specific legislation that allows police and prosecutors to charge juveniles as adults if the offense is serious. While this legislation does not effect policing day to day, it does speak to the current trend of juvenile justice and the desire to get tough on America's youth. These types of legislation are emerging sporadically throughout the states and they are in direct conflict with the initial goals and purpose of juvenile justice. Social science research suggests that youth are not cognitively, socially, or psychologically mature—and are thus unable to process decisions in a mature, adult manner (Scott and Grisso). This "get tough" on kids approach allows the seriousness of the offense to determine a child's maturity—as if the seriousness of the act itself implies adulthood. It is unclear whether this movement to get tough on juveniles has affected police handling of juveniles, or if it will in the future. Research on the connection between "get tough" policy and police behavior needs to accumulate, but one might hypothesize that police might be more lenient with juveniles because they realize that any formal action on their part might have serious consequences for youth.

Police-juvenile interactions

As Walker (1992) notes, juveniles represent a special set of problems for the police. First, police have more contact with juveniles, who are hanging out on the streets, and this might cause some anxiety for other citizens in the area. Second, juveniles have more negative attitudes toward the police, possibly because of their increased contacts with police (Walker, 1992).

Police interact with juveniles in many ways. Street level patrol officers interact with many youth who are suspects and victims, only a fraction of whom are formally processed into the juvenile justice system. These interactions occur either as police respond to dispatched calls for police service or as police initiate encounters with youth, who may or may not be involved in mischief, during the work day. Although many police departments have specialized juvenile units or bureaus to handle juveniles, these officers usually do not play a role in juvenile justice until a patrol officer decides to formally process a youth (this only occurs approximately 15% of the time) or refers an incident report involving a youth to the juvenile unit. Juvenile specialists usually do not respond to calls for police service that involve juveniles and they are not involved in most police-juvenile interactions.

Research on police-juvenile interactions conducted in the 1960s and 1970s reported that two-thirds to three-quarters of the encounters were more likely than not the result of a complainant's request for police assistance and that police initiated only a small fraction of their encounters with youth (see Black and Reiss, 1970; Lundman et al.). Research undertaken in the late 1990s suggests that police were initiating about half of their encounters with juveniles (Worden and Myers). This is in line with what we might expect from contemporary police officers working in the community policing era, where they are expected to pay greater attention to the less serious quality-of-life offenses, in which juveniles are likely to be involved. Other police interactions with juveniles are the result of a citizen's request—either by calling the department and requesting service or by flagging down an officer who happens to be in the neighborhood.

These interactions tend to be of a minor legal nature (Black and Reiss, 1970; Lundman et al.; Worden and Myers). They rarely involve serious, personal offenses and more likely the encounters involve public disorder offenses, nonviolent offenses, or suspicious circumstances that do not require any formal action be taken by the police. Evidence from the 1990s reveals that police encounters with youth typically involve only one juvenile and usually there is not a victim or complainant present during the encounter. When a victim is present, they rarely request that the police arrest the juvenile—they are more likely to request other police actions (not to arrest, to warn, and the like). Further, police generally do not have any prior knowledge of the youth with whom they interact, and as a result they must make decisions with the limited information available (see Worden and Myers).

Police handling of juveniles: outcomes

Extant research on police patrol officers repeatedly suggests that officers utilize a variety of actions to handle the citizens and situations with which they are presented (Black, 1980; McIver and Parks; Bayley; Worden; Klinger). An inquiry into police actions with juveniles reveals the same variation; juvenile arrest rates appear to be similar to adult arrest rates, around 15 percent (Black and Reiss, 1970; Lundman et al.; Black, 1980; Smith and Visher; Bayley; Worden; Klinger). This leaves, on average, an estimated 85 percent of encounters where no arrest occurs, but in which police utilize their authority in other ways to curb the future misconduct of juveniles.

If police practices with juveniles are at all similar to practices with adults, most police-juvenile interactions are handled informally (Wordes and Bynum). That is not to say, however, that formal courses of action are never taken. Formal police actions might include taking a juvenile into custody, taking a report, referring to a social service agency or juvenile court, giving a citation, or making an arrest (Walker). Previous research indicates that informal courses of action are more common (Piliavin and Briar; Black and Reiss, 1970; Lundman et al.). However, this does not mean that the police do nothing with the majority of juvenile suspects they encounter; this would imply that informal actions taken by the police are insignificant. Rather, the police utilize their authority in other ways: by questioning a juvenile about a particular offense; conducting searches for evidence; negotiating for a particular outcome; asking for information; requesting that a juvenile leave the area or cease disorderly/illegal behavior; or threatening to charge or make an arrest if the problem persists. While these courses of action might be considered informal in nature, as there may be no written record of the chosen outcome, they still represent officers' "use of authority" and they should be considered in discussions of police outcomes in juvenile cases. These actions represent officers' attempts to handle the problem.

Research conducted in 1996 and 1997 through systematic social observation of police officers in the field captured information on police contacts with 604 juvenile suspects (see Worden and Myers). This research reveals that police are much more likely to dispose of their encounters with youth informally. Only 13 percent of juvenile suspects were arrested and 3.6 percent received a formal citation. However, juveniles were likely to be subjected to other forms of police authority. Police investigated juvenile suspects by interrogating or questioning almost half, and searching either the juvenile or the area around the juvenile over a quarter of the time. A small fraction of the juveniles (one tenth) were commanded by police to cease disorderly or illegal behavior, to leave the premises, or to provide information related to some criminal offense. One quarter of the juvenile suspects were threatened to be charged or cited for their wrongdoing. Only 14 percent of these juveniles were outright released without receiving formal or informal sanctions. Most juveniles who encounter the police are not arrested or cited (and are thus not processed into the juvenile justice system), but they are subject to police authority in some other form.

Explaining police decision-making (outcomes) with juveniles

A large volume of research has accumulated on police decision-making with suspects generally, with particular attention to how the arrest decision is shaped by the characteristics of the situation. Some of this research has addressed the effect of suspect age (i.e., are juveniles more likely to be arrested than adults?) (see, for example, Mastrofski, Worden, and Snipes; Smith and Visher). One might suppose that police decision-making with juvenile suspects turns on different factors than decisions regarding adults. Police might feel they have even more latitude with juveniles and they may, for example, rely less on situational factors of a legal nature to inform their decisions. Further, inasmuch as police make decisions based on their own sense of what ought to be done, they may be even more inclined to do so when the citizen with whom they interact is a juvenile.

Other research has looked strictly at police-juvenile interactions. There is currently a paucity of research on how the police behave and the choices they make while interacting with juveniles. Some research has examined specialized juvenile officers, either as they patrolled streets or as they made decisions after a juvenile had been referred to their unit (Piliavin and Briar; Hohenstein; McEachern and Bauzer; Terry; Wordes, Bynum, and Corley). These examinations mostly looked at officers' use of authority as police made decisions about arrest, detention, and referrals to other social service and social control agencies.

One might expect that the decision-making patterns of juvenile specialists might vary from those of patrol officers inasmuch as juvenile specialists make decisions in a situational context that differs from that of patrol officers. While patrol officers make decisions on the street with little information available and with added pressure to make a quick judgment, juvenile officers make their decisions after a case has been referred to them with possibly more information and more time available for assessment. For example, the juvenile specialist might be more able to obtain information on juveniles' family lives, the amount of parental supervision they receive, and their previous infractions of the law. Finally, juvenile specialists presumably have more training on handling juveniles, particularly on making decisions that are in the best interest of the youth.

Some research has examined patrol officers' encounters with juvenile suspects, employing a method of systematic social observation. Research on police that employs a method of systematic social observation reveals the variety of actions officers take, including but not limited to arrest, in their attempts to resolve problems with juveniles. It also reveals a clearer picture of the types of offenses and problems in which juveniles are involved and under what circumstances a juvenile enters the juvenile justice system. This method enables researchers to examine dispositions that police do not systematically record and that would not normally be accounted for in official police records (Black and Reiss, 1970; Lundman et al.; Worden and Myers). Research by Black and Reiss (1970) and Lundman and colleagues focuses on the arrest decision in police-juvenile encounters; the study by Worden and Myers examines police arrest practices with juveniles as well as officers' use of other forms of authority (commands, threats, investigative tactics, and advising). One other study utilizes police-juvenile contact records from 1968 to 1975 to analyze police arrest practices with juveniles (Sealock and Simpson). All of the above studies typically took a situational approach to explaining police decision-making with juveniles in that they looked to factors available in the officers' immediate situation to see if they had a bearing on police outcomes. More specifically, the focus was on the influence of both legal and extralegal factors.

It is widely known and accepted that police officers have high degrees of discretion and autonomy from supervisory and organizational authority (Lipsky; Brown). Patrol officers tend to work in isolation, not necessarily by choice but by the nature of the work itself, where there is no immediate supervision. While police agencies provide a demanding set of rules and guidelines to follow, it is the officer who must make on-the-spot decisions to resolve situations. Laws, statutes, and ordinances are often vague or inapplicable and, subsequently, do not provide much guidance for decision-making on the street. In addition, the handling of juvenile problems adds more uncertainty to police work. Police have to manage the application of laws specific to juveniles where juveniles are at times treated as adults and other times not (McNamara). This might even be cause at times for police to shy away from handling juvenile problems.

In turn, individual officers decide who will and will not be arrested, who will receive a citation, and who will and will not be informed about another agency that may offer assistance with a particular problem. How do officers make these decisions? On what do they base their decisions?

We know that police behavior varies. We know, for example, that all officers would not utilize the same level of authority in a given situation. Theorizing about what affects police behavior has generally taken three approaches, either independently or in combination: psychological; sociological; and organizational. Psychological theories of police behavior rest on the proposition that officers' actions are influenced by their own outlooks and background characteristics (e.g., education level achieved, training, length of service, attitudes about policing and about the people they serve, and so on) (Worden). Sociological theories rest on the proposition that officer behavior is influenced, at least in part, by the situation they confront and the distribution of different aspects of social life (e.g., the race and socioeconomic status of the suspect and complainant, demeanor of the suspect or complainant, how many other officers are present, and so on) (Black, 1976; Black and Reiss, 1967, 1970). Proponents of organizational theories believe that the police organization (the chief, supervisors, organizational rules and procedures, etc.) influences officer behavior.

These theoretical orientations have been used in the past to explain choices that police officers make while handling problems with suspects. To date there has been little research examining police decision-making with juveniles. Extant research in this area utilizes a sociological approach and examines the influence of situational factors on police discretion—that is, the extent to which police behavior is patterned, for example, by victim preferences, seriousness of the offense, evidentiary strength, and juvenile demeanor.

Sociological approach.   Sociological or situational theories of police behavior turn to factors in the officers' immediate situation to explain their behavior. The underlying assumption is that people respond to the social structure of the situation. There are an infinite number of possibly influential factors in one's environment. A large body of research has accumulated on this subject and this research supports the hypothesis that police respond to the situation with which they are presented (see Smith and Visher for an example).

In police-citizen encounters, there are some situational cues that we expect officers to be attuned to when making decisions, for example, offense seriousness and the amount of evidence; this grouping of factors has been labeled *legal* factors. Other factors that might reflect a suspect's social status or what police might perceive as their "subversive capability," and for which effects on police decision-making are undesirable, are *extralegal* factors (Black and Reiss, 1967). A person's social status includes those characteristics that "one carries with them from situation to situation, such as their sex, age, race, demeanor, ethnic, or social class status" (Black and Reiss, 1967, p. 9).

Legal factors.   A significant amount of research has focused on the influence of legal factors on police behavior with juveniles. Legal factors might include the seriousness of the offense, the amount of evidence available to the officer, whether or not the juvenile appears to be under the influence of alcohol or drugs, and whether or not the victim requests that the police take, or not take, some kind of action. Research testing hypotheses on the influence of these factors confirm that they do have a significant impact on police decision-making.

The influence of the seriousness of the offense and the amount of evidence available to the officer is well documented in extant research. Research on police-juvenile interactions suggest that these events are more likely than not of a minor legal nature and that when the offense is a serious one (e.g., a felony) and the evidence is strong, police are more likely to make an arrest (Black and Reiss, 1970; Lundman et al.; Sealock and Simpson; Worden and Myers). Likewise, when juvenile specialists make decisions other

than arrest (detention decisions, referral decisions, and so on) and when patrol officers make decisions (for example, detention decisions) regarding juveniles that occur later in the process than the decision to arrest, they too tend to be influenced by offense seriousness (Hohenstein; Piliavin and Briar; Terry; Wordes et al.).

Police also tend to consider and respond to complainants' preferences when making decisions—in fact, one study finds that when police initiate an encounter with a juvenile they are significantly less likely to arrest than when they are responding to a complainant's request for police assistance (see Worden and Myers). As one might expect, when complainants request that a juvenile be arrested, the police are more likely to make an arrest (Black and Reiss, 1970; Lundman et al.). One interesting finding is that there is strong evidence that when the complainant is a minority the police utilize more authority not only in the form of arrest but also in investigation (searches, questioning) and commands or threats (see Worden and Myers). Also, when complainants request that the police do not make an arrest, police are less likely to take this action. This might be partly explained by the fact that when an offense is of a minor legal nature, the police may need complainants to sign a formal complaint in order to make an arrest. Police do not always make an arrest, even if the offense is a serious one; the decision might still be left to the complainant—or at least open to input from the complainant.

Especially in cases involving juveniles, officers might be expected to consider whether or not a suspect appears to be under the influence of alcohol or drugs. While possession of drugs is an offense for both younger and older persons, possession of alcohol is an offense only for persons under the age of twenty-one. There has been little research on this matter. Worden and Myers report that when the suspects are juveniles under the age of eighteen, and when they appear to be under the influence of alcohol or drugs, the police are not more likely to make an arrest than they are to simply release the juveniles. Further, police are not any more likely to employ investigative tactics or use commands and threats under these circumstances; this too is unexpected. It could be that police officers are more likely to offer assistance and comfort in these situations, or at least when a juvenile is in need of assistance. Or maybe police officers do not view underage drinking as a serious offense, as they are aware that the majority of teens experiment with drinking and it is usually unrelated to more serious criminal acts.

Research on the role that legal factors play in police decision-making confirms that in cases involving adults and juveniles alike, police are influenced by these factors. Police are more likely to use authority and make an arrest when the offense is a serious one, when the evidence is strong, and when the victim prefers that an arrest be made. However, these legal factors do not determine police decisions. While they may play a substantial role, it is sometimes the case that when the offense is serious and the evidence strong, the police do not arrest. Likewise, at times, when the offense is of a less serious nature and the evidence is weak, the police use their discretion and make an arrest. Researchers look to extralegal factors to help further explain police decision-making.

Extralegal factors. The absence of concrete decision-making rules and guidelines to structure officer behavior, along with the observation that legal factors do not determine the use of police discretion, has focused social scientists on the role that extralegal factors play in decision-making. Attention to this issue has come about due to the realization that police officers bear the burden of an enormous amount of discretion and that they make decisions in a context with few informational cues available. It is in this light that one might expect situational characteristics that are readily observable to the officer—such as the suspect's demeanor, race, sex, and level of wealth—to play a role in decision-making.

As patrol officers exercise their authority and handle situations "they are in an important sense dependent for cooperation upon those whom they have control" (Black and Reiss, 1967 p. 11). Research examining the influence of suspect demeanor, a reflection of cooperation, has produced consistent evidence that it has a substantial influence on police behavior. Police researchers have consistently found support for the expectation that citizens who are disrespectful toward the police are more likely to be arrested and more likely to have force used against them than those who are respectful or simply deferential. This finding is uniform across studies of police-juvenile encounters as well as police encounters with adults (Black and Reiss, 1967; Black and Reiss, 1970).

While one's demeanor is termed an extralegal factor, one should, from an officer's perspective, give some consideration to what it really means to be disrespectful toward the police. We

know that police use their arrest powers infrequently and that they do not arrest everyone that they legally could. If an officer is trying to decide which action is going to prevent a reoccurrence of a problem he may very well decide that the disrespectful person should be arrested more often than the respectful person under the same (or even more serious) circumstances. If someone is not deferring to police authority while the police are in their presence, why would the police believe that the person would defer when they leave—or that anything other than arrest will end the problem? In such a case, arrest may be used as a tactic to handle the situation because the police feel that any other outcome may not end the problem.

Observational studies done by Black and Reiss and Lundman and others in the 1960s and 1970s suggest that police arrest minority juveniles at a higher rate than white juveniles. And more recent research that analyzes official records paints a similar picture, suggesting that minorities are more likely to be arrested as well as detained and referred to other agencies (Wordes and Bynum; Wordes et al.; Sealock and Simpson). At least one study's findings suggest that juveniles of lower socioeconomic status are more likely to be arrested (Sealock and Simpson). However, each of these findings were born out of analyses where complainant preference and suspect demeanor could not be accounted for—two factors that have proven to be important predictors in other studies. More recent observational research, which controls for demeanor and victim preference, as well as other legal factors like offense seriousness and evidence strength, suggests that race does not play a role in determining arrest, or other authoritative actions by the police (Worden and Myers). It also suggests that police are not more likely to arrest juveniles who appear to be of lower socioeconomic status than those from the middle class. It does, however, provide evidence of a different police bias—a gender bias. Females are significantly less likely to be arrested by police than their male counterparts—even when controlling for offense seriousness, evidence strength, and victim preference.

Future of policing juveniles

In light of the enormous amount of discretion that police have with juveniles, one should be concerned with how these decisions are made as they are important decisions, which may formally classify juveniles (correctly or incorrectly) as delinquents and introduce them to the juvenile justice system. The sociological approach to understanding the use of police discretion with juveniles only explains so much. Researchers must look to other factors and take different approaches to explaining behavior with juveniles (as they have with adults, that is, psychological and organizational approaches). Future research on policing juveniles should try and increase our knowledge of the kinds of troubles in which juveniles are involved. Further, research should be directed at examining the effect of police outcomes on future juvenile delinquency. Do formal actions by the police have positive or negative effects on future misconduct? Little is still known about police juvenile interactions, and less is known about what effect police decisions have on future delinquency. Further research in these areas might improve the fairness and the effectiveness of the police role in juvenile justice.

STEPHANIE M. MYERS

See also JUVENILE AND YOUTH GANGS; JUVENILE JUSTICE: HISTORY AND PHILOSOPHY; JUVENILE JUSTICE: COMMUNITY TREATMENT; JUVENILE JUSTICE: INSTITUTIONS; JUVENILE JUSTICE: JUVENILE COURT; JUVENILES IN THE ADULT SYSTEM; JUVENILE STATUS OFFENDERS; JUVENILE VIOLENT OFFENDERS; POLICE: HISTORY; POLICE: COMMUNITY POLICING; POLICE: CRIMINAL INVESTIGATIONS; POLICE: ORGANIZATION AND MANAGEMENT; POLICE: POLICE OFFICER BEHAVIOR; POLICE: POLICING COMPLAINTANTLESS CRIMES; POLICE: SPECIAL WEAPONS AND TACTICS (SWAT) TEAMS; PREVENTION: JUVENILES AS POTENTIAL OFFENDERS; SCHOOLS AND CRIME; URBAN POLICE.

BIBLIOGRAPHY

BARTOLLAS, CLEMENS, and STUART, J. MILLER. *Juvenile Justice in America.* Upper Saddle River, N.J.: Prentice Hall, 2000.

BAYLEY, DAVID. "The Tactical Choices of Patrol Officers." *Journal of Criminal Justice.* 14 (1986): 329–348.

BERNARD, THOMAS. "Juvenile Crime and the Transformation of Juvenile Justice: Is There a Juvenile Crime Wave?" *Justice Quarterly* 16, no. 2 (1999): 337–356.

BLACK, DONALD. *The Behavior of Law.* San Diego, Calif.: Academic Press, Inc., 1967.

———. "Dispute Settlement by the Police." In *The Manners and Customs of the Police.* New York: Academic Press, 1980. Pages 109–192.

BLACK, DONALD, and REISS, ALBERT J. *Studies in Crime and Law Enforcement in Major Metropoli-tan Areas.* Report submitted to the President's Commission on Law Enforcement and Administration of Justice. Washington, D.C.: U.S. Government Printing Office, 1967.

BLACK, DONALD, and REISS, ALBERT J. "Police Control of Juveniles." *American Sociological Review* 35 (1970): 63.

BROWN, MICHAEL K. *Working the Street: Police Discretion and Dilemmas of Reform.* New York: Russell Sage Foundation, 1988.

FELD, BARRY C. "Abolish the Juvenile Court: Youthfulness, Criminal Responsibility, and Sentencing Policy." *The Journal of Criminal Law and Criminology* 88 (1997): 68–137.

HOHENSTEIN, WILLIAM. "Factors Influencing the Police Disposition of Juvenile Offenders." In *Delinquency: Selected Studies.* Edited by Thorstein Selling and Marvin Wolfgang. New York: Wiley, 1969.

KELLING, GEORGE. "Juveniles and Police: The End of the Nightstick." In *From Children to Citizens: The Role of the Juvenile Court.* Vol. 2. Edited by Francis Hatman. New York: Springer-Verlag, 1987. Pages 203–218.

KLINGER, DAVID A. "Quantifying Law in Police-Citizen Encounters." *Journal of Quantitative Criminology* 12, no. 4 (1996): 391–415.

LIPSKY, MICHAEL. *Street-Level Bureaucracy: Dilemmas of the Individual in Public Services.* New York: Russell Sage Foundation, 1980.

LUNDMAN, RICHARD; SYKES, RICHARD; and CLARK, JOHN P. "Police Control of Juveniles." *Journal of Research in Crime and Delinquency* (January 1978): 74–91.

MASTROFSKI, STEPHEN D.; WORDEN, ROBERT E.; and SNIPES, JEFFREY B. "Law Enforcement in a Time of Community Policing," *Criminology* 33: (1995): 539–563.

MCEACHERN, A. W., and BAUZER, RIVA. "Factors Related to Disposition in Juvenile Police Contacts." In *Juvenile Gangs in Context.* Edited by Malcolm W. Klein and Myerhoff. Engelwood Cliffs, N.J.: Prentice Hall, 1967.

MCIVER, JOHN, and PARKS, ROGER B. "Evaluating Police Performance: Identification of Effective and Ineffective Police Actions." In *Police Violence.* Edited by William Geller and Hans Toch. New Haven, Conn.: Yale University Press, 1983. Pages 21–43.

MCNAMARA, JOHN H. "Uncertainties in Police Work: The Relevance of Police Recruits' Background and Training." In *The Police: Six Sociological Essays.* Edited by David J. Bordura. New York: Wiley, 1967. Pages 163–252.

PILIAVIN, IRVING, and BRIAR, SCOTT. "Police Encounters with Juveniles." *American Journal of Sociology* 70 (1964): 206–214.

ROSENBAUM, D., and HANSON, GORDON. "Assessing the Effects of School-based Drug Education: A Six Year Multilevel Analysis of Project DARE." *Journal of Research in Crime and Delinquency* 35, no. 4 (1998): 381–412.

ROSENBAUM, D.; FLEWELLING, R.; and BAYLEY, S. "Cops in the Classroom: A Longitudinal Evaluation of Drug Abuse Resistance Education (DARE)." *Journal of Research in Crime and Delinquency* 31, no. 1: (1994): 3–31.

SCOTT, ELIZABETH, and GRISSO, THOMAS. "The Evolution of Adolescence: A Developmental Perspective on Juvenile Justice." *The Journal of Criminal Law and Criminology* 88 (1997): 138–189.

SEALOCK, MIRIAM D., and SIMPSON, SALLY S. "Unraveling Bias in Arrest Decisions: The Role of Juvenile Offender Type-Scripts." *Justice Quarterly* 15 (1998): 427–457.

SMITH, DOUGLAS, and VISHER, CHRISTY. "Street Level Justice: Situational Determinants of Police Arrest Decisions." *Social Problems* 29 (1981): 167–177.

TERRY, ROBERT. "The Screening of Juvenile Offenders." *The Journal of Criminal Law, Criminology, and Police Science* 58, no. 2 (1967): 173.

WALKER, SAMUEL. *The Police in America*, 2d ed. New York: McGraw Hill, 1992.

———. *A Critical History of Police Reform: The Emergence of Professionalism*. Lexington, Mass.: U.C. and Heath, 1977.

WESTLEY, WILLIAM. "Violence and the Police: A Sociological Study of Law, Custom, and Morality." Boston, Mass.: MIT Press, 1970.

WHITAKER, GORDON P. "What Is Patrol Work?" *Police Studies* 4 (1982): 13–22.

WILSON, JAMES Q. *Varieties of Police Behavior*. Cambridge, Mass.: Harvard University Press, 1968.

WORDEN, ROBERT E. "Situational and Attitudinal Explanations of Police Behavior: A Theoretical Reappraisal and Empirical Assessment." *Law & Society Review* 23 (1980): 667–711.

WORDEN, ROBERT E., and MYERS, STEPHANIE M. "Police Encounters with Juvenile Suspects." *Report to the National Research Council's Panel on Juvenile Crime: Prevention, Treatment and Control*. This report has also been submitted to the National Institute of Justice (pursuant to Grant 95-IJ-CX-0071). Washington, D.C.: U.S. Government Printing Office, 1999.

WORDES, MADELINE, and BYNUM, TIMOTHY S. "Policing Juveniles: Is There Bias Against Youths of Color?" In *Minorities in Juvenile Justice*. Edited by Kimberly Kempf Leonard, Carl E. Pope, and William H. Feyerherm. Thousand Oaks, Calif.: Sage, 1995. Pages 47–65.

WORDES, MADELINE; BYNUM, TIMOTHY S.; and CORLEY, CHARLES J. "Locking Up Youth: The Impact of Race on Detention Decisions." *Journal of Research in Crime and Delinquency* 31 (1994): 149.

CASES

In re Gault, 387 U.S. 1 (1967).
State v. Lowery, 230 A.2d 907 (1967).

POLICE: ORGANIZATION AND MANAGEMENT

Discovering the best way to organize and manage the police is a popular topic among police managers and administrators, researchers, reformers, and others interested in improving the American police. Over the past century, police organization and management have changed tremendously. Many of these changes can be attributed to changes in the environment of policing: the development of new technologies, the emergence of new offense types, differences in public opinion about the police, and managerial innovations in the public and private sectors. This entry highlights some of the important changes that have taken place in the organization and management of American police agencies, explains briefly why these changes occurred, and discusses some of the current trends that provide a hint of changes to come.

The American system of policing

The American system of policing is unique by world standards. There are approximately twenty thousand state and local police agencies in the United States (Maguire, et al.; Reaves and Goldberg, 1999). Other English-speaking democracies have a much smaller number: Canada has 461, England has forty-three, India has twenty-two, and Australia has eight (Bayley). Furthermore, the majority of police agencies in the United States are only loosely connected to one another. Many have overlapping jurisdictions at multiple levels of government, including city or town, township, county, state, and federal agencies. The majority are general-purpose agencies with responsibility for patrolling a certain area, responding to calls from citizens, and investigating certain offenses. Most of the general-purpose local police departments are small, with 81 percent (11,015) employing fewer than twenty-five full-time sworn officers, 42 percent

(5,737) employing fewer than five officers, and 7.5 percent (1,022) relying on only part-time officers (Reaves and Goldberg, 1999). Others are special-purpose agencies with responsibility for a specific territory (such as a park or an airport) or function (such as enforcing alcoholic beverage laws or wildlife regulations). Some agencies do not fall neatly within these categories. For instance, sheriffs' agencies in some states do not provide police patrol, but do provide a variety of other related services: running jails, guarding courtrooms, or providing canine service, undercover deputies, or investigative assistance to local police agencies. These variations in the size, type, and function of American police agencies make it difficult to establish an ideal method of organization and management applicable to all agencies.

A number of influential critics have claimed that because the American system of policing is so fragmented and loosely coordinated, it is ineffective and inefficient. For instance, Patrick Murphy, former police commissioner in several American cities, once wrote that many communities

are policed by a farcical little collection of untrained individuals who are really nothing more than guards. These genuinely small departments (fewer than twenty-five sworn officers), to begin with, tend not to have much of a franchise by and large; with small territory and limited clientele, they do not face much of a crime problem. (Murphy and Plate, pp. 71–72)

Murphy was one of several reformers to suggest that these small police agencies should be eliminated or consolidated into larger and more professional departments. For instance, one of the major recommendations made in 1967 by the President's Commission on Law Enforcement and Administration of Justice was the coordination and consolidation of police services (p. 67).

Supporters of police consolidation tend to focus on two themes. First, they claim that larger police organizations can make more efficient use of resources by taking advantage of the economies of scale resulting from eliminating redundant functions. Second, many believe that the fragmented nature of the American policing system results in poor communication, coordination, and cooperation between police agencies. This results in an information-gap that allows victims and offenders to "slip between the cracks."

Research by Elinor Ostrom and her colleagues casts at least some doubt on both of these concerns. They studied patterns of police service delivery in eighty mid-sized metropolitan areas throughout the United States, containing 1,827 "police service producers." In a series of publications, Ostrom showed that when it comes to the size of a police organization, bigger is not necessarily better (Ostrom and Smith; Ostrom, Parks and Whitaker). Ostrom and other researchers have found that smaller police agencies often deliver more personalized services, have higher clearance rates, and are able to deploy a higher proportion of their personnel "on the streets" (Weisheit et al.).

Ostrom also found that while metropolitan areas in the United States are policed by a patchwork of agencies, they have developed locally cooperative networks for delivering public safety across jurisdictional lines. These networks are glued together with an array of formal (contractual) and informal (handshake) agreements between agencies. Two techniques used to minimize the fragmentation are contracting services out between law enforcement agencies and forming mutual aid agreements that allow officers from neighboring agencies to render assistance as needed. A 1997 study suggests that police consolidation may not be economically beneficial to communities (Finney, 1997). While consolidation may be a good solution for some communities, evidence suggests that it may not be a universal cure for police fragmentation.

Cooperation also occurs among agencies at different levels of government. Many state police and highway patrol agencies provide patrol services on state roads, even when those roads traverse a community with its own police force. State and county agencies also routinely provide investigative assistance to smaller agencies, especially in the case of more serious offenses such as homicide or rape. The formality of these agreements ranges from written legal contracts to verbal agreements. During the 1990s, there also was a proliferation of multijurisdictional "task forces" to combat offenses such as drug-trafficking. According to one study, many were formed based on "the realization that drug sellers did not respect jurisdictional boundaries. Law enforcement agencies serving contiguous jurisdictions therefore needed to coordinate enforcement activities both to share information and resources and to avoid overlapping investigations" (Jefferis et al., p. 86). These task forces often contain representatives from agencies at the city or town, county, state, and/or federal levels.

The Federal Bureau of Investigation (F.B.I.) allows state and local law enforcement agencies to access the National Crime Information Center (NCIC) database and the Automated Fingerprints Identification System (AFIS). It is also common practice for federal law enforcement agencies (such as the Drug Enforcement Administration (DEA), the Bureau of Alcohol, Tobacco, and Firearms (ATF), and the Immigration and Naturalization Service (INS)) to be called into local and state jurisdictions to collaborate in solving certain offenses, especially those that cross jurisdictional boundaries. While newsworthy cases such as the 1995 Oklahoma City bombing highlight the collaboration between local and federal authorities, more routine collaboration occurs regularly in police agencies around the nation.

Cooperation between agencies also exists at an international level. The International Criminal Police Organization (INTERPOL) "enables law enforcement information to flow easily from officer to officer across borders, language barriers, time zones, and terrains in the basic service of justice" (Imhoff and Cutler, p. 10). INTERPOL was established in 1914 to respond to criminal activity that transcends international boundaries. Although INTERPOL is not an international police force and does not have police powers, it serves as a means of communication between law enforcement agencies across the world. INTERPOL membership consists of 176 countries. Each member nation has a central headquarters called a National Central Bureau (NCB) that is managed by law enforcement officials from that country. The NCBs serve as hosts for information that is transmitted between INTERPOL members, as well as for information sent directly from INTERPOL's main headquarters, or the "General Secretariat," in Lyon, France (United States Department of Justice). INTERPOL has been responsible for solving international crimes dealing with religious cult groups, drug-trafficking, art thefts, the child sex trade, computer software fraud, organized crime, counterfeit pharmaceuticals, and money scams.

To foreign observers, the American system of policing seems disorganized and perhaps a bit chaotic. Despite the large number of agencies, a variety of mechanisms have been developed to seal the gaps between agencies. Thus, while law enforcement agencies at different levels of government do experience poor communication with other agencies and an occasional squabble over jurisdiction, they also cooperate with one another frequently. Some critics of the present system continue to suggest that the proliferation of small agencies results in a less efficient and effective system. Others find the American policing system to be the epitome of decentralized government, with local governments able to exert control over the kind of policing they receive. One consequence of having so many police agencies of different sizes and types is that there are important differences between them. The following section examines two of these: variations in the styles and structures of American police organizations.

Variation in style and structure

Until the early 1960s, American policing was a "closed" institution. State and federal politicians did not routinely run for elective office on platforms related to crime and policing. The average American citizen probably had little knowledge of what police work entailed. Courts did not devote much energy toward scrutiny of the police. In all, policing remained closed to the eyes and ears of the public and their representatives.

Several circumstances in the 1960s converged to open up American policing to external audiences. Police use of force and discriminatory treatment of minority citizens became a prominent theme during protests over civil rights and the war in Vietnam. Several of the riots that engulfed American cities occurred in the aftermath of police actions such as shootings, traffic stops, or raids (Walker). Classic news stories of the era captured images of police officers using excessive force against citizens. The National Advisory Commission on Civil Disorders (1968) found that "deep hostility between police and ghetto communities" was a primary determinant of the urban riots that it studied. The U.S. Supreme Court, under Chief Justice Earl Warren, began to closely scrutinize the activities of the police. In several landmark cases, the Court restricted the powers of the police to conduct searches (e.g., *Mapp v. Ohio*, 367 U.S. 643 (1961)), obtain confessions (e.g., *Miranda v. Arizona*, 348 U.S. 436 (1966)), or prevent detainees from consulting with an attorney (e.g., *Escobedo v. Illinois*, 378 U.S. 478 (1964)). Finally, rising crime rates during the 1960s also began to cast doubts on the effectiveness of the police. From 1968 to 1971, three national commissions recommended sweeping reforms of the American police: the National Advisory Commission on Civil Disorders, the National Advisory Commission on Criminal Justice

Standards and Goals, and the President's Commission on Law Enforcement and the Administration of Justice.

Research since the early 1970s has shown that police officers have a great deal of discretion in their day-to-day work. They must regularly make decisions about conducting searches, making arrests, using force, stopping vehicles, issuing warnings, and many other discretionary activities in which police engage daily. While the criminal law structures some of the decisions that police officers make, it does not, in most cases, dictate what they must do. Therefore, police officers are frequently left to their own devices in making decisions. Since the 1960s, however, a number of controls have been instituted to reduce the amount of discretion that police officers have to make certain decisions. For instance, many agencies have formal written policies governing the conditions under which police officers can pursue a fleeing vehicle or use deadly force against a suspect. Some state legislatures and police agencies have instituted statutes or policies that require police officers to make an arrest when they see evidence of domestic violence. Despite these types of controls, the conditions under which police officers do their work make it difficult to curtail their discretion very much. As long as they continue to work alone in low-visibility settings in the absence of direct supervision, police officers will need to rely on some degree of discretionary decision-making.

Because they have so much discretion, police officers develop different styles of policing. Some are aggressive, busily making arrests, stopping vehicles, and seeking out offenders. Others prefer a more laid-back approach, counseling juveniles and issuing warnings rather than making arrests whenever possible. Even when police agencies try to constrain discretion by declaring "zero-tolerance" policies for offenses such as drug possession, officers sometimes prefer not to make an arrest in certain situations. The notion that a police officer develops his or her own "working personality" is in stark contrast to the image of a police officer as an automaton, responding impartially to every situation according to the letter of the law.

In 1968, James Q. Wilson observed patterns of discretionary behavior in eight police departments. He found that police organizations, like the individuals within them, also tend to develop unique styles of policing. Wilson developed a taxonomy to describe three prominent styles of policing that he observed: legalistic, service, and watchman. In legalistic-style departments, officers initiate formal contact with citizens and structure their work according to the criminal law. For many years, the Los Angeles Police Department was regarded as the prototypical legalistic police agency, with its reputation for neatly pressed uniforms and the "just the facts, ma'am" reputation popularized by Sergeant Joe Friday on the television series *Dragnet*. In service-style departments, officers initiate informal contact with citizens and rely less on the criminal law. In watchman-style departments, officers neither initiate contact with citizens as frequently, nor rely as much on the criminal law.

Wilson argued that the social and political environment in which a police organization is situated has an effect on the style of policing that it adopts. Cities adopting the legalistic style tend to have more heterogeneous (mixed) populations and professionalized, nonpartisan, "good governments" (exemplified by the city manager form of government). Service-style departments tend to be located in cities with more homogeneous populations and professional, nonpartisan governments. Cities with watchman-style departments tend to have more heterogeneous populations and a more partisan political tradition (exemplified by the mayor-council form of government).

Police agencies are not only defined by their styles, but also by their structures. According to Robert Langworthy, structure is "the framework on which a police organization arranges its resources to conduct its activities" (p. 17). The following seven elements are the core dimensions of a police organization's structure (adapted from Langworthy and from Maguire):

1. *Vertical Differentiation:* The nature of the hierarchy, including the number of command layers and the social distance between layers.
2. *Occupational Differentiation:* The extent to which the organization relies on employees with specialized occupational skills.
3. *Functional Differentiation:* The degree to which the organization divides its work into specialized functions. Nearly all police agencies have separate divisions for patrol, investigations, and administration. The further they divide these divisions into more specialized subunits, the more functionally differentiated they are.
4. *Spatial Differentiation:* The spread of the organization within its jurisdiction. Police agencies with a single headquarters facility

are less spatially differentiated than those with precinct houses, substations, and other offices located within neighborhoods.

5. *Administrative Intensity:* The proportion of employees assigned to administrative support functions (like human resources or computing) as opposed to core tasks such as patrol or investigations.

6. *Formalization:* The extent to which an organization relies on formal written policies and procedures rather than informal guidelines such as tradition or friendship.

7. *Centralization:* The extent to which decisions within an organization are concentrated at the top of the hierarchy.

Police organizations adopt different structural configurations. Some have up to twelve levels of command, while others have as few as four. Some are centralized, with decisions flowing down from the chief's office, while others are more decentralized, with decisions flowing up from patrol officers.

For much of the 1990s, police reformers debated the best ways to structure a police organization. Following trends in the private sector, police management textbooks for much of the twentieth century urged police executives to adopt formalized, centralized, specialized, and hierarchical structures. Community policing seeks to reverse this trend, urging decentralized, less hierarchical, more generalized, and less formal structures. Research has shown that police organizations are changing their structures slowly, but not as radically as urged by community policing reformers. Nevertheless, there is a small but growing trend among police agencies to reject traditional structures.

Managing police organizations

Given the variations in the styles and structures of police organizations, is there one best way to manage and administer them? Most experts in management do not think so. They draw on one of the iron rules of organizing: that successful organizations adapt to the specific circumstances (or contingencies) of their environments. This is known as contingency theory, and it is the framework for the following discussion.

Traditional methods of police management emerged from two sources: a militaristic view of policing, and management concepts from the private sector that were established in the beginning of the twentieth century. The most influential writer on police management from about 1950 to the early 1970s was Orlando W. Wilson, former superintendent of the Chicago Police Department. Wilson's popular textbook on police administration reinforced classic managerial principles: span-of-control (having a limited number of subordinates per supervisor or manager), an unambiguous hierarchy (so everybody knows to whom they must report), and centralization of command (in which decisions are made at the top and flow down). This school of police management has become known as the "military" or "professional" model.

Since the early 1970s, reformers have urged police administrators to adopt more democratic styles of management. As Egon Bittner wrote "The core of the police mandate is profoundly incompatible with the military posture. On balance, the military bureaucratic organization of the police is a serious handicap" (p. 51). Reformers argue that policing is ill-suited for military management strategies because the vast majority of police work involves dealing with citizens in ambiguous "low visibility" settings. In other words, since so much of what the police do is discretionary, a military model of management stifles the ability of police officers to make on-the-spot decisions.

For much of the 1970s and 1980s, discussion about the faults of the military/professional model was little more than rhetoric. Other than a few documented attempts to change styles of police management, the movement to change basically picked up momentum over that two-decade period. Those efforts that did attempt to change police management failed in many ways, although their experiences provided lessons for designing strategies for change in the future. For example, in 1971, the Dallas Police Department attempted to implement a comprehensive strategy "intended to produce vast organizational change and personnel enhancement" (Wycoff and Kelling, p.). While there were some successes, the process of change has been described as painful and tumultuous: many people involved in the change process experienced negative psychological, physiological, and professional consequences.

During the 1990s, various reform efforts that had been gathering steam over the past two decades began to coalesce into a single movement known as community policing. Community policing is a comprehensive reform movement that has been defined a number of ways. One definition, used by the Justice Department's Office of Community Oriented Policing Services, contains three elements: organizational and managerial change, problem-solving, and community partnerships. Most relevant for this discussion is the focus on organizational change as a distinct component of community policing. As the managerial change agenda became associated with community policing, it was taken more seriously than when it was a stand-alone movement. Now, police agencies all over the country are experimenting with new management styles such as Total Quality Management (TQM). Police administrators now obtain degrees in business administration and public administration. Some are more likely to read the *Harvard Business Review* than *Law and Order*.

The community policing movement emerged at the same time as other significant movements in business and government. Hammer and Champy's *Reengineering the Corporation* (1993) had a dramatic effect on corporate management styles and strategies. Similarly, Osborne and Gaebler's *Reinventing Government* (1992) and Vice President Al Gore's *National Performance Review* (1994) have led many government agencies to adopt similar strategies. These ideas are influencing police administrators. For instance, former New York Police Commissioner William Bratton, one of the most well known police executives in the nation, claims that he had "become a staunch advocate of using private-sector business practices and principles for the management of the NYPD, even using the business term 'reengineered' rather than the public policy term 'reinventing' government" (p. 224). The confluence of the community policing movement with the emergence of these popular management strategies has led to changes in the management of police organizations. The changes are not yet evident in every police agency, and even those agencies that have experimented the most with new strategies still have vestiges of the military or professional model. However glacial these changes may be, it is apparent at national meetings of police executives that change is in the air.

One of the most well known innovations in police management during the 1990s is Compstat (computer comparison statistics). Compstat was initiated in the New York City Police Department by former Commissioner William Bratton, who used computerized databases to track crime and disorder in each precinct. Bratton held meetings in which precinct commanders were expected to be familiar with the trends in their jurisdiction and have formulated a plan to respond to those trends. Compstat was the cornerstone of Bratton's crime reduction strategy. Many attribute the dramatic reductions in New York's crime rate to Compstat, though criminologists have expressed some reservations about this claim. At a minimum, Compstat is an interesting example of how to use technology as a management tool. Agencies around the nation are now embracing Compstat, adopting sophisticated information technologies that allow them to track data on crime, disorder, calls for service from the public, and the nature of the police response. The following section explores the impact of information technologies on police organization and management.

Information technologies and the police

Police organizations collect and store a vast amount of information. Traditionally, this information resided on sheets of paper stored in file cabinets. Today, police organizations are being transformed by the information age. Most have implemented management information systems (MIS) to record, store, access, and analyze data on calls-for-service from citizens, the nature of the police response to these calls, reported crimes, arrests, gun permits, motor vehicle stops, and many other types of data. Some agencies maintain centralized control over access to information, while others have adopted integrated management systems that can be accessed by law enforcement officials at any level (from patrol officer to chief). This "all access" approach allows employees with different needs to access the data without having to wait or file a formal request. Some agencies store and access data electronically, but do not use it as a means for improving the organization. Others use data as a tool to improve management and operations. While most large police agencies today have made enormous improvements in their capacity to collect and store large amounts of data, many have made little progress in using the data they collect. Developing the ability to use data for improving operations and management represents an important challenge for police organizations today. This section introduces some of the information technologies used by police and discusses their potential for improving police management.

Computer Aided Dispatch systems (CAD) are now commonly used by many police departments. CAD systems prioritize calls-for-service received by the communications center, "stacking" less urgent calls so that police officers can respond to those calls requiring more immediate attention. Once a call is prioritized by the CAD system, it can be broadcast to an officer in a patrol car through either the radio or a computer. CAD makes it easier for human call-takers and dispatchers to remain abreast of what calls are being answered, where officers are located, and how long they have been out on a call. This reduces the likelihood of dispatching errors and enhances officer safety (George). CAD systems are also useful for collecting and storing data. Once a call is received at the communications center, it is categorized by the CAD system. Depending on the agency's information storage capacity, the data are then integrated into the information system for some period of time, after which they are archived for long-term storage.

Many police agencies in the United States now have Mobile Digital Terminals (MDTs) or Computers (MDCs) installed in their patrol cars (hereafter referred to as MDTs). MDTs have a number of uses, not all of which are available in all jurisdictions. First, they allow an officer to receive "silent dispatches" over the computer rather than through the radio, so that police scanners can not be used to monitor police communications. Second, officers can check motor vehicle registrations, drivers' licenses, and outstanding warrants directly, without having to wait for a dispatcher to run a computer check. Third, officers can enter police reports into the computer while out in the field, rather than having to return to the police station early to complete paperwork. Fourth, officers can send e-mail to other officers, including those who are not on duty at the time. Finally, officers can sometimes retrieve information on arrests, criminal backgrounds, and calls for service from databases that are networked between agencies at local, state, or federal levels. According to the 1997 Law Enforcement Management and Administrative Statistics (LEMAS) survey, 78 percent of large municipal law enforcement agencies in the United States use some type of mobile digital terminal or computer (Reaves and Goldberg).

Using statistical methods and geographic mapping techniques to analyze trends in crime, disorder, arrests, and calls-for-service (hereafter called crime analysis) is now becoming popular in many agencies. Geographic Information Systems (GIS) are useful for visually plotting the occurrence of particular offenses within a jurisdiction. By combining statistics on crime, disorder, arrests, or calls-for-service with de-scriptions of land areas, crime analysts are able to "map-out" those areas in the community with concentrations of particular problems. The police can then focus their efforts within these relatively small "hot spots." The maps produced by GIS are more than a fancy replacement for the old-fashioned "pin maps" used by police for years. Ideally, they should be able to track crime trends (or trends in calls or disorder) as they evolve. Thus, if a police sting operation in a particular neighborhood results in the displacement of offenders to the surrounding areas, the GIS maps should reflect this movement. Few agencies have reached this ideal state yet due to problems in linking separate databases and computer systems. Once these problems are ironed out, crime mapping will represent an increasingly important tool used by the police to analyze and respond to crime trends. According to the 1997 LEMAS survey, 60 percent of local law enforcement agencies with one hundred or more officers use computers for crime mapping (Reaves and Goldberg).

Other information technologies have more direct application for conducting investigations and tracking offenders. For example, digital imaging allows "mug shots," suspect composites, and other photographs or images to be stored electronically and transmitted to other police agencies. The Automated Fingerprints Identification System (AFIS) stores pictures of fingerprints in a national database of over 30 million fingerprint cards (Peak). AFIS allows investigators to solve criminal cases that are several months or even several years old. According to the 1997 LEMAS survey, most local and state law enforcement agencies that employed one hundred or more police officers had access to AFIS in 1997 (Reaves and Goldberg).

Because management information technology has become so valuable to police departments across the country, the International Association of Chiefs of Police (IACP) has created the Law Enforcement Information Management Section (LEIM) to create long- and short-term goals for the use of computerized information systems in law enforcement agencies. Members of LEIM believe that the dramatic increase in the use of computers by law enforcement officials will also increase the need for computer training at every level of law enforcement in the future (International Association of Chiefs of Police). Police agencies face a number of hurdles as they struggle to embrace the information age. Finding qualified   and   trustworthy   information-technology professionals is often difficult for police agencies. Those who are qualified can usually find much higher-paying positions in the private sector. Analyzing information for operational purposes (such as crime analysis) is one step above simply collecting and storing it. Analyzing information for management purposes—to enhance accountability and improve the responsiveness of the organization—represents a much more dramatic step. Both steps are necessary before police organizations can truly become "learning organizations" (Senge).

Police recruitment and training

So far, much of the discussion has involved changes in the police organization: its structure, style, management, or technology. Yet many police administrators think it is at least as important to change the people within the organization. This means developing recruitment and training strategies that produce a new breed of police officer. For instance, Baltimore Police Commissioner Thomas Frazier suggests that police organizations need to recruit officers with "a spirit of service rather than a spirit of adventure." For community policing to take root, officers will need to be as interested in serving the community as in fighting crime. Others believe that while recruitment may be one strategy for changing police organizations, it is not the only answer. Furthermore, many police agencies have little control over their recruitment strategies due to civil service hiring restrictions. Nonetheless, there have been some changes in recruitment since the 1970s.

One of the major changes in police recruitment has been the effort to attract individuals who represent the population they will serve, including females and minorities (Langworthy et al.). To carry out their sensitive role, police officers must be able communicate effectively and compassionately with a diverse population. Policing has historically been a white male institution. Since the Civil Rights Act of 1964 (specifically Title VII) and the Equal Employment Opportunity Act of 1972, this trend has started to change. A series of court cases in the 1970s and 1980s further defined the legal guidelines for hiring minority and female police officers. Over the past twenty years, there has been an increase in the number of females and minorities in large police departments (Reaves).

Police departments use a variety of techniques to recruit applicants: they place ads in newspapers and on Internet sites, post flyers and brochures, contact criminal justice programs in colleges and universities, and attend career fairs. They also attract potential applicants through a variety of programs such as citizens' police academies, "Explorer" groups for young adults, reserve or auxiliary officer programs, and college internships. In 1998, the U.S. Department of Justice established the Police Corps, a scholarship program for college students who agree to work as police officers for at least four years after graduating. The Police Corps program is expected to increase the pool of educated applicants to police departments, while at the same time reducing the cost of recruiting and training new officers (Office of the Police Corps and Law Enforcement Education).

In addition to selective recruitment efforts, a sound and well-balanced training curriculum is another method for improving the quality of police personnel. While the importance of police training was recognized by police reformers at the beginning of the century, it was not until the early 1960s that it became more accepted by police administrators (Langworthy et al). Although there are variations across the country, there are three core types of police training: (1) basic training, (2) field training, and (3) in-service training. Basic training teaches basic skills and techniques necessary to conduct day-to-day police work. General topics covered in basic training include police procedure, criminal law, use of force, emergency response, ethnic and cultural diversity, interacting with citizens, and numerous other specialized topics. After basic training is completed in the academy, rookie officers (or "boots") sometimes participate in a field-training program in which they accompany field training officers (FTOs) on patrol. In field training, rookie officers apply the knowledge and skills acquired in basic training to real-life situations on the streets. FTOs assess whether recruits are able to conduct routine police activities skillfully and independently. Also, it is during field training that rookie officers are socialized into the police subculture, a force that exerts considerable influence over police officer's behavior (Van Maanen).

Police training continues over the course of a police officer's career with in-service training that takes place for a required number of hours per year (determined by individual police departments). Workshops, classes, and conferences on specialized topics can teach seasoned officers new techniques, as well as provide them with valuable information that can be incorporated into daily police activities (Haley). Some current topics taught during in-service training include community and problem-oriented policing, dealing with youth gangs, new types of drugs, and a variety of other specialized topics.

Training is a double-edged sword. Some amount of police training is necessary to ensure that officers have a core body of knowledge and certain skills. Although it is common for citizens and politicians to request more and better police training, it is a tired remedy for fixing whatever is wrong with the police. Mastrofski claims that "Training can be very useful for when trying to give officers new skills, but it is decidedly ineffective in changing officers' attitudes and motivations" (p. 6). Furthermore, many police agencies (especially smaller ones) send their officers to regional training academies whose curriculum they have little control over. Once again, training may be one answer to improving police organization and management, but it is not a miracle cure.

Conclusion

Throughout the twentieth century, police administrators, politicians, reformers, and scholars have sought out the best ways to organize and manage the police. Perhaps the biggest lesson learned is that there is no one best way. Although the American policing system is unique by world standards, it contains fascinating differences in style, structure, management, technology, and personnel. In their quest to improve the organization and management of American police agencies, police administrators continue to experiment with innovations in each of these areas.

EDWARD R. MAGUIRE
CAROL ARCHBOLD

See also CONFESSIONS; POLICE: COMMUNITY POLICING; POLICE: CRIMINAL INVESTIGATIONS; POLICE: HANDLING OF JUVENILES; POLICE: POLICE OFFICER BEHAVIOR; POLICE: POLICING COMPLAINANTLESS CRIMES; POLICE: PRIVATE POLICE AND INDUSTRIAL SECURITY; POLICE: SPECIAL WEAPONS AND TACTICS (SWAT) TEAMS; SEARCH AND SEIZURE; URBAN POLICE.

BIBLIOGRAPHY

BAYLEY, DAVID H. *Police for the Future.* New York: Oxford University Press, 1994.

BITTNER, EGON. *The Functions of Police in Modern Society.* Chevy Chase, Md.: National Institute of Mental Health, 1970.

BRATTON, WILLIAM J., with KNOBLER, PETER. *Turnaround: How America's Top Cop Reversed the Crime Epidemic.* New York: Random House, 1998.

FINNEY, MILES. "Scale Economies and Police Department Consolidation." *Contemporary Economic Policy* 15, no. 2 (1997): 121–128.

———. "Constituency Preference and Police Consolidation: The Case of West Hollywood." *Contemporary Economic Policy* 17, no. 2 (1999): 235–243.

FRAZIER, THOMAS. "Comments Delivered at the First Meeting of the National Community Oriented Policing Resource Board." Washington, D.C., 22 February 1996.

GEORGE, D. "Computer-Assisted Report Entry: Toward a Paperless Police Department." *Police Chief* March 1990, pp. 46–47.

GORE, AL. *Common Sense Government Works Better and Costs Less: Third Report of the National Performance Review.* Washington, D.C.: Government Printing Office, 1994.

HALEY, KEITH. "Training." In *What Works in Policing: Operations and Administration Examined.* Edited by Gary Cordner and Donna Hale. Cincinnati, Ohio: Anderson Publishing, 1992. Pages 143–155.

HAMMER, MICHAEL, and CHAMPY, JAMES. *Reengineering the Corporation.* New York: HarperCollins Publishing, 1993.

IMHOFF, JOHN J., and CUTLER, STEPHEN P. "INTERPOL." *FBI Law Enforcement Bulletin* 67 (1998): 10–17.

International Association of Chiefs of Police. http://www.iacptechnology.org (1999).

JEFFERIS, ERIC S.; FRANK, JAMES; SMITH, BRAD W.; NOVAK, KENNETH J.; and TRAVIS, LAWRENCE F., III. "An Examination of the Perceived Effectiveness of Drug Task Forces." *Police Quarterly* 1 (1998): 85–107.

LANGWORTHY, ROBERT H. *The Structure of Police Organizations.* New York: Praeger, 1986.

LANGWORTHY, ROBERT; HUGHES, THOMAS; and SANDERS, BETH. *Law Enforcement Recruitment, Selection, and Training: A Survey of Major Police Departments in the U.S.* Washington, D.C.: Academy of Criminal Justice Sciences, Police Section, 1995.

MAGUIRE, EDWARD R. *Context, Complexity and Control: Organizational Structure in American Police Agencies.* Albany, N.Y.: SUNY Press, 1999.

MAGUIRE, EDWARD R.; SNIPES, JEFFREY B.; UCHIDA, CRAIG D.; and TOWNSEND, MARGARET. "Counting Cops: Estimating the Number of Police Departments and Police Officers in the USA." *Policing: An International Journal of Po-*

lice Strategies & Management 21, no. 1 (1998): 97–120.

MASTROFSKI, STEPHEN D. *Policing for People*. Ideas in American Policing Lecture series. Washington, D.C.: Police Foundation, 1999.

MURPHY, PATRICK V., and PLATE, THOMAS. *Commissioner: A View from the Top of American Law Enforcement*. New York: Simon and Schuster, 1977.

National Advisory Commission on Civil Disorders. *Report of the National Advisory Commission on Civil Disorders*. Washington, D.C.: U.S. Government Printing Office, 1968.

Office of the Police Corps and Law Enforcement Education. http://www.ojp.usdoj.gov/opclee (1999).

OSBORNE, DAVID, and GAEBLER, TED. *Reinventing Government*. New York: Addison-Wesley, 1992.

OSTROM, ELINOR; PARKS, ROGER B.; and WHITAKER, GORDON P. *Patterns of Metropolitan Policing*. Cambridge, Mass.: Ballinger Publishing Co., 1978.

OSTROM, ELINOR, and SMITH, DENNIS C. "On the Fate of 'Lilliputs' in Metropolitan Policing." *Public Administration Review* 36, no. 2 (1976): 192–200.

PEAK, KENNETH, J. *Policing America: Methods, Issues, Challenges*. Upper Saddle River, N.J.: Prentice Hall, 1997.

President's Commission on Law Enforcement and Administration of Justice. *Task Force Report: The Police*. Washington, D.C.: U.S. Government Printing Office, 1967.

REAVES, BRIAN A. *Local Police Departments, 1993*. Washington, D.C.: Bureau of Justice Statistics, 1996.

REAVES, BRIAN A., and GOLDBERG, ANDREW L. *Census of State and Local Law Enforcement Agencies, 1996*. Washington, D.C.: Bureau of Justice Statistics, 1999.

———. *Law Enforcement Management and Administrative Statistics, 1997: Data for Individual State and Local Agencies with 100 or More Sworn Officers*. Washington, D.C.: Bureau of Justice Statistics, 1999.

SENGE, PETER M. *The Fifth Discipline: The Art and Practice of the Learning Organization*. New York: Doubleday, 1990.

United States Department of Justice. "INTERPOL—United States National Central Bureau." http://www.usdoj.gov/usncb (1999).

VAN MAANEN, JOHN. "Observations on the Makings of a Policeman." *Human Organization* 32 (1973): 407–418.

WALKER, SAMUEL. *Popular Justice*. New York: Oxford University Press, 1980.

WEISHEIT, RALPH A.; WELLS, L. EDWARD; and FALCONE, DAVID N. *Crime and Policing in Rural and Small-Town America: An Overview of the Issues*. Washington, D.C.: National Institute of Justice, 1995.

WILSON, JAMES Q. *Varieties of Police Behavior*. Cambridge, Mass.: Harvard University Press, 1968.

WILSON, ORLANDO W. *Police Administration*, 2d ed. New York: McGraw Hill, 1963.

WYCOFF, MARY ANN, and KELLING, GEORGE L. *The Dallas Experience: Organizational Reform*. Washington, D.C.: Police Foundation, 1978.

CASES

Escobedo v. Illinois, 378 U.S. 478 (1964).
Mapp v. Ohio, 367 U.S. 643 (1961).
Miranda v. Arizona, 384 U.S. 436 (1966).

POLICE: POLICE OFFICER BEHAVIOR

In the 1950s, The American Bar Foundation sponsored a series of observational studies that spanned the criminal justice system. The researchers observed an astounding array of incompetence and corruption in criminal justice practices, due in part to the pervasive discretion inherent in the system. *Discretion* can be described as official action taken by criminal justice professionals based on their individual judgments. The American Bar Foundation's "discovery" of discretion was particularly important in the field of policing, where it was generally recognized that the lowest level workers within police departments' organizational hierarchies have the greatest amount of discretion over critical decisions. According to Samuel Walker, several factors account for the existence of pervasive police discretion: the ambiguous nature of criminal law, the working environment of police officers, and limited police resources. Researchers have attempted to explain how, when, and why criminal justice officials make discretionary decisions that affect the lives of citizens. Indeed, much of the research in policing has attempted to explain officers' decision-making.

Some people speculate that officers make decisions based on *extralegal* variables; that is, officers' decision-making is based on factors that are not considered legitimate in a democratic society (e.g., suspects' race, sex, age, etc.). In the 1990s, for example, some police agencies have been accused of using racial profiling policies (i.e., making decisions to conduct field interrogation and traffic stops based solely on a citizen's race), which leads to important questions. Do police officers in our society make decisions based on legal or extralegal factors? How and why do police officers use their discretion? These are the questions that underlie nearly fifty years of police research. The findings from this body of research will be summarized in this entry. Four specific categories of explanatory factors are identified, the relative explanatory power of these factors is described, and the research findings are summarized. The entry concludes with a description of the need for additional research to better understand how, when, and why police officers use their discretion.

Explaining police behavior

In general, police research has focused on explaining four particular types of police officer behavior: detection activities, service activities, the use of arrest/citations, and the use of force (Sherman, 1980). Detection activities include field interrogation and traffic stops, investigative techniques, etc. Service activities include mediating disputes, assisting citizens, and engaging in problem solving and community policing activities. Official police action is examined through the use of arrest or citations. It is through these actions that police invoke the criminal justice system and bring the power of the state to bear on individuals. Finally, police use of force, although statistically a rare event, has been extensively examined. In the 1960s and early 1970s, much of the research focused on examining the relationship between one predictor variable (e.g., suspects' race) and one outcome variable (e.g., police use of arrest). As research advanced, however, more refined statistical techniques enabled researchers to examine the influence of multiple explanations of police behavior simultaneously.

The factors that explain police behavior have also been generally grouped in four categories: situational, individual, organizational. and community (Sherman; Riksheim and Chermak). Situational factors refer to the characteristics of police-citizen encounters that may influence how an officer acts during that situation. These situational factors include the characteristics of the suspect (e.g., race, sex, age, demeanor, etc.), characteristics of the victim (e.g., race, sex, age, relationship to the suspect, etc.), characteristics of the situation (e.g., location, number of bystanders present, etc.), and legal characteristics

(e.g., presence and amount of evidence, seriousness of the offense, etc.). Individual factors refer to the characteristics of individual officers that may influence their behavior (e.g., officers' sex, race, age, attitudes, education, training, etc.). Organizational factors include any characteristics of the police organization that might influence officer behavior (e.g., administrators' preferences, formal and informal policies, departmental size, levels of supervision, etc.). Finally, researchers have also speculated that community factors (e.g., public expectations and preferences, crime rates, demographic characteristics, political characteristics, etc.) may influence officer decision-making. The research findings regarding the relative influence of specific factors over police behavior from each of these four groups (situational, individual, organizational, and community) are described below.

Situational/legal characteristics. Situational factors that explain police behavior can be subdivided into four categories: (1) suspect characteristics; (2) victim characteristics; (3) characteristics of the police-citizen encounter; and (4) legal characteristics. As a whole, situational characteristics—particularly legal characteristics—have a relatively strong influence over officer behavior.

Suspect characteristics. Suspect characteristics are perhaps the most controversial potential influences over officer behavior. Do officers make decisions in whole or in part due to the sex, race, age, socioeconomic status, or demeanor of suspects? There has been a particularly strong focus in quantitative research to examine the effects of nonlegal variables on officer behavior. It has been reported that these nonlegal variables typically explain a relatively small portion of the variance in comparison to legally relevant variables, but they have been accorded a great deal of attention. The reason for that attention is that nonlegal variables should not influence the behavior of criminal justice agents if the U.S. system is to be considered legitimate, fair, and just.

Suspects' race/ethnicity. Some minority groups allege that they are singled out by police. They argue that officers often make decisions—field interrogation stops, traffic stops, arrest, and use of force—based on racial considerations. This belief is so widespread among minority communities that the phenomenon has been labeled DWB or "driving while black." A large body of research has accumulated that examines whether or not officers' behavior is influenced by a suspect's race. Collectively, these findings have been somewhat mixed based on the type of officer behavior that is examined.

Studies that have considered officers' decision-making during detection activities (e.g., field interrogation stops, pat down searches, and traffic stops) have generally found that suspects' race does have an influence over officer behavior. For example, the San Diego field interrogation study in the early 1970s reported that 66 percent of citizens stopped for questioning by police were African American and Mexican American males, but they only represent 30 percent of the local population. Likewise, a lawsuit filed in 1993 by the American Civil Liberties Union (ACLU) against the Maryland State Police cited evidence that 73 percent of drivers stopped by officers were African American even though they represent only 17 percent of all drivers (*Wilkins v. Maryland State Police*; see Walker). In 2000, internal documents from the New Jersey State Police (NJSP) indicated that officers were trained to identify potential drug traffickers based on race.

Disparities and discrimination in field interrogations are a major cause of tension between police and minority communities. While many officers believe aggressive field interrogations and traffic stops are legitimate, effective crime-fighting tactics, they are perceived as harassment by some segments of the population. Aggressive anticrime tactics may result in the racial stereotyping of possible suspects, which is often reinforced by departmental policies. For example, the Christopher Commission in 1991 concluded that the aggressive style of the Los Angeles Police Department (LAPD) constituted an attack on minorities and their communities.

Minority suspects are arrested at disproportional rates to their representation in the population. For example, African Americans represented 31 percent of all arrests, 38 percent of all index crime arrests, and 44 percent of all violent crime arrests, however, they represented just 12 percent of the U.S. population (Walker, Spohn, and DeLone, p. 88). While these figures certainly display disparity in arrest, the larger question is whether this disparity is based on race—that is, whether or not there is discrimination. Some studies utilizing data collected in the late 1970s reported that officers did make arrest decisions based, in part, on the suspect's race (Smith and Visher; Robert Worden, 1989). Nevertheless, in their review of studies examining police behavior, Riksheim and Chermak concluded "utilizing a variety of data sets and examining various offenses, most of these studies found that race had no effect on police arrest decisions" (p. 365). Some have speculated that while suspects' race does not have a direct influence over officers' behavior, it may have an indirect effect operating through other factors such as suspects' demeanor, offense seriousness, and the preference of the victim (Walker et al).

Although police use of force against suspects occurs relatively infrequently, researchers have studied the phenomenon extensively. This attention is most likely due to the severe implications the behavior has for individuals, communities, and the society at large. The use of excessive force—or brutality—by police officers is a source or great strain in police-community relations, particularly in minority communities. Widely publicized examples of police brutality in the 1990s—including the beating of Rodney King in Los Angeles, the physical and sexual assault of Abner Louima in New York City, and the killing of Amadou Diallo, also in New York City—have led to a renewed police-community crisis similar to that experienced in the 1960s. Studies routinely show that minorities are overrepresented as suspects who have force used against them, and who are shot or killed by officers. Robert Worden's (1996) analysis of 1977 data showed that police were more likely to use both reasonable and unreasonable force against black male suspects. Research conducted prior to the U.S. Supreme Court ruling in *Tennessee v. Garner*, 471 U.S. 1 (1985), which placed constitutional limits on the use of deadly force by police, concluded that officers were more likely to use force, particularly deadly force, against African American suspects (Fyfe). Changes in administrative policies guiding the use of deadly force, however, led to decreases in the use of deadly force. Specifically, adopting the defense-of-life rule significantly reduced the racial disparity in police shootings and reduced firearm discharges in both Memphis and New York City (Fyfe). Other data showed that the ratio of African Americans to whites who had deadly force used against them decreased from seven-to-one to three-to-one from 1970 to 1984. Current studies have reported mixed results regarding the influence of suspects' race over police use of force (for review, see Riksheim and Chermak; Robert Worden, 1996).

Suspects' sex. Several theorists have speculated that female suspects are less likely to be arrested than male suspects because officers are more likely to act in a chivalrous manner by protecting women from criminal sanction (Visher). Research prior to 1980 did indicate that female suspects were less likely to be arrested compared to males (Sherman). A review of the more recent empirical research, however, concluded, "gender was not an important predictor of arrest" (Riksheim and Chermak, p. 365; also see Visher). Of the twenty-six empirical studies reviewed by these researchers, twenty-one reported no relationship between gender and arrest when other factors were controlled. Some research on the use of force, however, has reported that male suspects are at a slightly higher risk to have force used against them compared to female suspects (Robert Worden, 1996).

Other researchers have speculated that the chivalry hypothesis applied only to women who act in a stereotypically feminine manner. Those women who break this stereotype (by engaging in prostitution, or acting in a hostile or aggressive fashion, or simply because they are part of a minority group) are more likely to be arrested. As a result, hostile women, particularly hostile women of color, may be at increased risk of coercive police action relative to hostile male suspects. This hypothesis, however, was not supported when tested empirically (Visher; Engel, Sobol, and Worden).

Suspects' age. Although handling juvenile incidents is believed to be a special problem, researchers know very little about actual street interactions between police and juveniles. Research conducted in the 1960s suggests that officers are more likely to initiate contact with juveniles than with adults and that officers have a large amount of discretion during these encounters. This research also shows that taking no official action is the most likely outcome of encounters with juveniles. When arrest is used, it is more likely in situations that are more serious, when victims request arrest, and the juvenile suspect acts in a hostile manner toward police (Black and Reiss).

Much of the research that has empirically examined arrest and the use of force indicated that suspects' age is not a significant predictor of police decision-making (Riksheim and Chermak). Findings from the most recent systematic observation data set—the Project on Policing Neighborhoods (1996–1997)—also indicated that suspects' age is not a significant predictor of arrest (Engel and Silver).

Suspects' socioeconomic status. Early qualitative studies suggested that suspects' socioeconomic status had an influence over police behavior and bivariate results from studies prior to the 1980s consistently found that lower class suspects were more likely to be arrested (Sherman). Since an individual's socioeconomic status is highly correlated with race in American society, multivariate statistical models are needed to disentangle this relationship. Multivariate studies have found that suspects' level of wealth has no independent influence over officers' decision to arrest (Engel and Silver). Another study has reported that the influence of suspects' class is contingent upon officers' attitudes toward community policing (Mastrofski, Worden, and Snipes). One of the few studies to consider the effect of suspects' class over police use of force found that this variable had no influence after other factors were controlled in a statistical model (Friedrich). Collectively, the evidence regarding the influence of suspects' socioeconomic status is best described as mixed.

Other suspect characteristics: mental status, demeanor, intoxication. Several other suspect characteristics—mental status, demeanor, and intoxication—have widely been considered strong predictors of police behavior. For each of these variables, however, recent studies have challenged conventional wisdom regarding their influence over officer behavior.

As a result of deinstitutionalization, police calls to incidents involving citizens with mental disorders have increased significantly, leading to increases in criminal justice processing of these citizens. It is unclear, however, how a suspect's mental status influences police behavior. Few empirical studies have examined the relative probabilities of arrest for mentally ill versus non-mentally ill suspects. Teplin's study of police discretion toward mentally ill citizens in Chicago found the probability of being arrested was approximately 20 percent higher for mentally ill suspects compared to non-mentally ill suspects. This study, however, reported bivariate relationships and did not adequately control for other factors that could influence police decisions to arrest. After controlling for other situational and legal factors known to influence police decision-making, Engel and Silver found that mentally disordered suspects were significantly less likely to be arrested. Police have a large amount of discretion available to them when deciding what course to take regarding mentally ill suspects. Observations of the police suggest that they are more likely to use informal means to handle situations involving mentally ill citizens. For example, officers often use "psychiatric first aid" as an alternative to hospitalization or arrest (Teplin).

A large body of research has indicated that suspects who acted in a hostile or disrespectful manner toward police were significantly more likely to be the recipients of coercive police actions. This body of research, however, was strongly criticized by David Klinger (1994) for not adequately controlling for the seriousness of the offense and for interpreting illegal offenses (for which suspects could be arrested) as displays of a disrespectful demeanor. After taking these criticisms into account, current research continues to show a strong relationship between suspect demeanor and officer behavior (Worden and Shepard). Suspects who act in a disrespectful or hostile manner toward police are significantly more likely to be arrested, issued citations, and have force used against them.

Suspects who are under the influence of alcohol and/or drugs are also significantly more likely to be the recipients of coercive police actions. Research findings have consistently shown that intoxicated suspects are more likely to be stopped and questioned, arrested, issued citations, and have force used against them (Robert Worden, 1989; Riksheim and Chermak). Recent research, however, has suggested that the sobriety of a suspect does not have an independent effect on arrest when the sobriety and demeanor of a suspect are considered together (Engel et al.). This research suggested that intoxication itself does not lead to arrest but that intoxication combined with displays of disrespect place suspects in greater risk for coercive police action.

Victims' characteristics.   The bulk of empirical research examining the influence of victims' characteristics on police behavior have focused on the victims' preference (or request) for an arrest, and the relationship between the victim and the suspect. Research findings have consistently reported that victim preference has a strong influence over officers' decisions to arrest. If a victim requests that the offender be arrested, officers are more likely to arrest; conversely, if a victim requests that the offender not be arrested, officers are significantly less likely to arrest (Smith and Visher). Visher reported that female victims requesting arrest have a stronger influence over officer behavior than male victims who request arrest. In a recent study of police behavior, Mastrofski and colleagues reported that officers granted complainants' requests for the most restrictive form of control in 70 percent of the incidents observed.

The relationship between the victim and the suspect has also consistently predicted officer behavior. Studies prior to the 1980s consistently reported a bivariate relationship between the victim-offender relationship and officer behavior; officers were more likely to arrest if the relationship was more distant (Sherman). Multivariate findings have confirmed these early findings. For example, Smith and Visher have found that if the victim and suspect are strangers, officers are significantly more likely to arrest the offender. Alternatively, if the victim and suspect are well-acquainted, officers are significantly less likely to arrest.

Only a few studies have considered the influence of individual characteristics of the victim. The majority of findings indicated that the complainants' race had no influence over officers' detection activities and decisions to arrest. For example, one study found that the race of domestic violence victims had no influence over police behavior in those disturbances (for review see Sherman; Riksheim and Chermak). Mastrofski and his colleagues reported that officers were significantly less likely to grant citizens' requests to control another citizen when the complainant was disrespectful to the police, intoxicated, mentally disordered, or involved in a close relationship with the other citizen.

Characteristics of the police-citizen encounter.   Research regarding the influence of the characteristics of situations have produced mixed results. Research reviewed by Sherman showed that police were more likely to arrest suspects in situations where the police entered the encounter proactively (i.e., not in response to a citizen or dispatched request for service). More recent research, however, has shown that police entry does not have a significant influence over arrest behavior (Mastrofski et al., 1995; Engel and Silver). Likewise, the location of a police-citizen encounter as either public or private does not have an influence over police decisions to arrest or use force (Worden and Shepard; Engel et al.). Other factors, such as the presence of bystanders and the presence of additional officers, have been shown to increase police use of force, but not the use of arrest (Engel et al.). However, as noted by Riksheim and Chermak, "the influence of most situational characteristics on arrest behavior remains unresolved" (p. 365).

Legal characteristics.   Legal considerations appear to have the strongest and most consistent influence over police behaviors (i.e., detection activities, arrest/citations, and use of force). Legal factors include the seriousness of the offense, amount and type of evidence, injury of the victim, presence of a weapon, suspect's prior record, and if the suspect is currently wanted for a prior offense. While researchers' initial measures of legal variables were rather crude, more precise measures continue to show a strong relationship to police behavior. For example, offense seriousness was routinely measured as a dichotomous variable representing a felony or misdemeanor offense; however, this variable is measured as an ordinal scale to capture greater variation in levels of seriousness (Klinger, 1994).

Most studies of police arrest behavior have confirmed that legal factors have the strongest influence over police arrest decisions. Mastrofski and his colleagues (2000) reported that legal considerations (e.g., evidence of suspects' and complainants' wrongdoing, citizens' requests for arrest) were the most influential factors explaining officers' decisions to respond to citizens' requests to control another citizen. Earlier work by Mastrofski and others (1995) showed that legal factors accounted for 70 percent of the explained variance in officers' decisions to arrest—the majority of this explanatory power was from the strength of the evidence. Likewise, other studies have found that legal considerations strongly and consistently predict officers' use of force (Robert Worden, 1996). Klinger also found that legal considerations had a stronger influence over police behavior than suspects' demeanor, and concluded that researchers must make greater efforts to consider the influence of legal factors in their studies of arrest and other officer discretionary action.

To summarize, there is some evidence that particular types of citizens—racial and ethnic minorities, particularly African American males—are subject to differential treatment by police officers. Legal factors, however, play a much greater role in explaining officer behavior. Nevertheless, widely publicized incidents have accumulated over time and created a perception of systematic police harassment of minority citizens. As noted by Walker, this evidence, combined with citizens' perceptions of discrimination and disparity, created a police-citizen relations crisis in the 1980s and 1990s.

Individual characteristics of officers

Individual explanations refer to the influence of police officers' own characteristics over their behavior. In the 1960s, tensions between

police and citizens exploded in the form of riots and civil disobedience (Walker). In response, a series of presidential commissions were ordered to investigate these issues. The most famous, the Kerner Commission, investigated the causes of the hundreds of disorders that had taken place in late 1960s. The Kerner Commission reported that there was deep hostility and distrust between minorities and the police. The report recommended the hiring of more minority officers and that police practices be changed significantly. As a direct result of the police-community crisis of the 1960s, police organizations sought to hire officers that were more representative of the communities they serve, including the hiring of more minorities and women. In addition, higher standards for recruitment combined with the educational opportunities provided through the LEAA (Law Enforcement Education Program) raised the education level of police officers from 20 percent of officers with a college degree in 1960, to 65 percent in 1988 (Walker, p. 37).

One of the assumptions of these reforms is that officers who are minorities, women, better educated, and better trained, will act differently than their white, male, less educated, less well-trained counterparts. Specifically it was assumed that: (1) minority officers will relate better to minority citizens; (2) female officers will be less aggressive and therefore less violent than male officers; (3) college-educated officers will be better able to deal with the complex demands of policing; and (4) increased officer training will better prepare officers for handling situations on the street. Research has attempted to determine if these assumptions are accurate. Contrary to expectations, with but a few exceptions, the bulk of the research suggests the behavior of officers who are female, minority, educated, and better trained is not significantly different from that of male, white, less educated, less well-trained officers.

Officer gender.   Since the 1970s, there has been a gradual increase in the number of female officers. By the mid-1990s, women represented about 13 percent of officers in large city departments (Walker). There have been many hypotheses suggested regarding the attitudes and behavior of females compared to male officers. Those in support of hiring more female officers argued that females would be less aggressive than male officers and better able to handle difficult situations verbally. Those opposed to hiring female officers suggested that female officers would not be able to handle aggressive situations and would ultimately create an officer safety problem. Furthermore, they argued that female officers would act more like social workers and not actively enforce the law.

Studies have shown that officers' attitudes toward their role, their departments, and toward citizens do not differ between men and women (Alissa Worden, 1993). More recent investigations of officers' attitudes toward community policing and problem solving policies, however, have shown that female officers have more positive attitudes toward citizens and community policing initiatives than do male officers (Skogan and Hartnett).

Despite some differences in attitudes, research findings confirm that there are only very slight differences in on-the-job behavior between the sexes. Studies of police officers in several agencies have revealed that female and male officers responded to similar calls for service and encountered similar proportions of problem citizens (e.g., citizens who are intoxicated, angry, violent, etc.). Only slight—and nonstatistically significant—differences existed in the proportion of arrest and citations issued by male and female officers (for review, see Walker).

Findings regarding officers' use of deadly force, however, have been somewhat mixed. Studies have shown that male officers are involved in deadly force incidents more often than female officers, but female officers who are partnered with a male officer reacted similarly to their male partners when responding to violent confrontations (Walker). In addition, a study of police officers in Indianapolis Police Department and St. Petersburg Police Department during 1996–1997 found that male officers are more likely than female officers to respond positively to citizens' requests to control another citizen (Mastrofski et al., 2000).

Officers' race. Since the reforms noted above in the 1970s, there has been a steady increase in minority officers. By 1993, African American officers were the majority in Detroit, Washington, D.C., and Atlanta, while in Miami, Hispanic officers represent 48 percent of force and African Americans represent another 17 percent (Walker, 1999). Proponents of the reform effort suggested that minority officers would have a better rapport with minority citizens, would be less likely to discriminate against minority citizens in arrest or other police actions, and would be less likely to use force against suspects (particularly minority suspects). Again, however, few of these hypotheses have been sup-

ported by research. In general, research has found a strong difference in the attitudes of minority and white officers, but few differences in actual behavior and performance.

Research has found significant differences in the attitudes of minority and white officers toward citizens and community policing policies. For example, a survey of officers assigned to minority districts in New York City found that minority officers were more likely to have positive attitudes toward their assigned districts and citizens within those districts. In addition, Skogan and Hartnett found that minority officers had more positive attitudes toward citizens and community policing initiatives compared to white officers.

As with gender differences, however, differences in officers' race do not translate into differences in behavior. While studies have shown that officers' race has a weak influence on officers' arrest behavior, the relationship is complex. Studies have shown that African American officers arrest African American suspects more frequently than white officers, however these differences may reflect more responsiveness to requests of African American victims (Walker). In addition, some research has shown that minority officers are more likely to use force on minority suspects than white officers. Research has also shown, however, that minority officers are more likely to be assigned to patrol neighborhoods that are predominantly minority. After controlling for differences in assigned patrol areas, differences in the arrest and use of force patterns between white and minority officers does not remain significant (Fyfe).

Officers' education. Reform efforts also called for an increase in the educational standards among police officers. Police reformers argued that officers with college degrees would be better able to deal with complexities of the job, more likely to use alternatives to arrest, and less likely to use force against citizens. Yet, contrary to conventional wisdom, there is no strong evidence that officers with a college education behave differently than those without. A study of police behavior in twenty-four police departments in 1977 showed that officers with a college education were just as likely to arrest or use force against suspects as were officers without a college degree (Robert Worden, 1990). As with female and minority officers, however, officers with more education have more positive views toward citizens and community policing policies (Skogan and Hartnett). These attitudes, however, do not appear to translate into behavior.

Officers' attitudes. The theory that attitudes influence behavior is intuitively compelling. As Worden suggests, "to maintain that people act in ways that are inconsistent with their attitudes seems patently absurd" (1989, p. 670). Nevertheless, empirical findings suggest that police officer attitudes and behavior are only weakly correlated. Beginning with research in the 1960s, scholars have speculated about the influence of police officers' attitudes on their behavior. For example, policing scholars described the "authoritarian police personality," and often suggested that officers' attitudes (e.g., cynicism) influenced their behavior.

Over time, this description of a monolithic police personality was replaced with more compelling descriptions of varying attitudes—and behaviors—among police officers. Attitudinal explanations of police behavior often took the form of typologies. For example, William Muir identified four different types of officers based on the relationship between two separate attitudinal dimensions. These types of officers were expected to vary not only in their attitudes, but also in their "styles" of policing—that is, Muir speculated that differences in officers' attitudes led to differences in their behavior.

Most quantitative research on police behavior, however, has found only weak relationships between officers' attitudes and their behavior. Mastrofski, Ritti, and Snipes found that officers' attitudes, including their individual enforcement priorities, bore weak relationships to their patterns of DUI enforcement. In analyses of dispute resolution, traffic enforcement, and proactive patrol or "aggressiveness," Worden (1989) found that officers' attitudes also did not account for variations in their behavior. Only two quantitative studies have found a significant relationship between officers' attitudes and their behavior. Mastrofski, Worden, and Snipes reported that officers with more positive attitudes toward community policing were significantly less likely to arrest suspects, and Mastrofski and colleagues (2000) found that officers with positive attitudes toward community policing were more likely to grant citizens' requests to control another citizen. Nevertheless, this small body of quantitative research is consistent wit a much larger body of social-psychological research on attitude-behavior consistency, which has suggested the estimated relationships between attitudes and behavior are counterintuitively small.

To summarize, research findings suggest that officer characteristics have a very limited impact on their behavior. Yet, it is unclear if citizens alter their behavior based on officers' characteristics. That is, research has addressed differences in officers' behavior based on officers' characteristics, but not changes in citizens' behavior toward officers' based on these characteristics. Without knowing this information, one cannot assess the true impact of reform efforts that have changed the look of American police.

Organizational factors. One possible explanation for the findings that officers' characteristics have very little impact on their behavior is that the recruitment, selection, and training processes screen out individuals with attitudes and characteristics that are inconsistent with the dominant values of police officers. A second possibility is that peer pressure to conform to organizational values and behaviors exerts a powerful influence. Individuals who begin with slightly different attitudes (and who may behave differently) are socialized into the attitudes and behavior of the group. As a result, rookie African American officers are socialized into thinking and acting like the other (predominately white) officers, and female officers adopt attitudes and behavior of the dominant male police culture. This explanation suggests that police socialization, subculture, and other organizational factors have a strong influence over officer behavior.

Police subculture. Early qualitative research identified and described police subcultures in American police organizations. As described above, some researchers described the "police personality," while others identified different individual policing styles. The existence of a subculture suggests that officers share a number of attitudes, values, and beliefs that separate them from other members of society. These attitudes, values, and beliefs are transmitted from one generation to the next through a process of socialization. Van Maanen has described the recruitment, training, and on-the-street experiences of new patrol officers that socialize them into the police subculture. These officers develop a "working personality" or police view of the world. This view is often an "us versus them" orientation that allows officers to identify themselves as different from citizens. The ethos of police culture has been described as including bravery, autonomy, secrecy, isolation, and solidarity (Reuss-Ianni and Ianni). It has been suggested that multiple and competing subcultures exist in a single department, that subcultures differ across departments, and that officers' behaviors are influenced by socialization processes and police subcultures (Reuss-Ianni and Ianni; Van Maanen). These propositions, however, have not been supported with systematic empirical research.

Structural characteristics: department size/ levels of bureaucratization.   Research from observational studies and survey research have reported that officers from smaller departments tend to initiate more traffic stops and were more likely to arrest suspects compared to officers in larger departments (Mastrofski, Ritti, and Hoffmaster). Other research, however, reported that department size had no effect on arrest behavior (Liska and Chamlin). Examining police behavior across twenty-four different departments, researchers found that officers in more bureaucratized departments were more likely to arrest suspects and use force against them (Smith and Klein, 1983; Robert Worden, 1996). Crank has also reported that officers in more bureaucratized departments in both urban and rural areas were more likely to arrest.

Policing strategies and tactics.   There has been great debate over the effectiveness of innovative policing strategies and tactics. It has generally been acknowledged that changes in patrol officers' behavior are necessary for the successful implementation of any new policing strategy. Several examinations of the use of increased police personnel focused on specific target areas or offenders (i.e., policing "hot spots," or "crackdowns") have reported that officers are significantly more likely to arrest in these areas during periods of intensive, aggressive enforcement (Sherman, Gartin, and Buerger). As noted by Walker, these policies influence arrest rates in the short term, but often do not have a long-term effect.

Debate over the effectiveness of community policing has led to recent examinations of the behavior of community policing officers compared to regular beat officers. Parks and others reported that community policing officers in Indianapolis and St. Petersburg spent less time interacting with citizens—particularly problem citizens—compared to beat officers. Preliminary findings from the research collected in 1998 in Cincinnati suggests that officer assignment (as a community policing or beat officer) does not have a direct influence on arrest decision-making, however it appears there are some different decision-making processes being employed. More research is needed in this area before any firm con-

clusions can be reached regarding the influence of community policing policies over officer behavior.

Formal and informal policies.   Formal policies refer to the rules and regulations of departments that are written by administrators and placed on officers. Some examples of formal policies that have been thought to influence police behavior include domestic violence (mandatory arrest) policies, use of force policies, and policies regulating the use of high-speed pursuits. Research has shown that some formal policies do have a significant effect on police behavior. For example, as previously noted, changes in use of force policies from the fleeing felon standard to defense-of-life policies have been shown to reduce the numbers of police shootings. Generally, formal policies are more likely to influence police behavior if they are clearly communicated and enforced by administrators (Walker).

Informal policies or guidelines are not specifically written, but are nonetheless understood by officers within the department. Some examples of informal policies that may affect police behavior are those regarding the policing of juveniles, minorities, the homeless, and traffic violators. Little empirical research has examined the influence of formal and informal policies over police behavior. Mastrofski, Ritti, and Snipes reported that officers' perceptions of the DUI enforcement preferences of their supervisors and administrators did not significantly predict arrest behavior.

Department styles.   In 1968, James Q. Wilson published his now classic work, *Varieties of Police Behavior*, which argued that the six police departments studied differed greatly in their policing styles. Specifically, he suggested that three distinct policing styles existed: watchman, legalistic, and service. In watchman style departments, officers treated order maintenance rather than law enforcement as their primary function. Officers ignored many common minor violations, especially traffic and juvenile offenses, and would also tolerate a certain amount of vice and gambling. As a result of handling situations more informally, officers were more likely to use force rather than arrest, and perhaps more likely to engage in corruption. In contrast, legalistic departments emphasized law enforcement over order maintenance. Officers were expected to issue large numbers of traffic tickets, detain and arrest a high proportion of juvenile offenders, make large numbers of misdemeanor arrests, and act vigorously against illicit enterprises.

Since police handled situations formally, they produced larger numbers of arrests and citations than officers in departments with other styles. Service style departments emphasized providing service to their communities by handling all citizen requests (unlike the watchman style), but were less likely to respond with an arrest or otherwise formal sanction (unlike the legalistic style). Officers in service departments were expected to have good community relations, aggressively handling all serious crime, while informally handling less serious crime.

There has been little empirical testing of Wilson's propositions regarding the different styles of police departments and their influence over officer behavior. In empirical examination of police behavior in twenty-four police agencies, Smith and Klein reported that officers in more legalistic departments were significantly more likely to arrest.

Supervision. Many have speculated about the potential influence field supervision has over subordinate behavior. Although most scholars and practitioners agree that one role of police field supervisors is to control the behavior of their officers, the degree of control that supervisors actually have continues to be a matter of debate. Most of the empirical research exploring the influence of supervision over patrol behavior has focused on three general types of behavior: the frequency and duration of encounters with citizens, patrol officer discretionary decision-making toward citizens, including decisions to arrest or issue tickets, and officer misbehavior, including work shirking and departmental violations (for review, see Engel). The findings from this body of literature have been mixed, although studies that have reported a significant relationship between field supervision and officer behavior have found that the relationship is relatively weak. In a critique of this literature, Engel notes that the research lacked rigorous methodological designs, advanced statistical techniques, and valid measures of supervision. This research showed that particular supervisory styles did significantly influence patrol officers' use of force and engagement in problem solving activities.

To summarize, the body of research examining the effects of organizational factors over police behavior is not substantial, despite being a potential source of great explanatory power. Riksheim and Chermak have characterized the limited findings on organizational level variables as

encouraging, but clearly more research needs to be conducted in this area.

Community factors. In Riksheim and Chermak's review of the literature on police behavior, they note that "arrest is the only area of police behavior that has generated a substantial number of findings on the influence of community-level variables" (p. 369). Community level factors include political variables (e.g., measures of political context, type and strength of local governments, constituents' political views, etc.), economic variables (e.g., measures of wealth and poverty, unemployment, female-headed households, etc.), and demographic variables (e.g., aggregate measures of age, race, cultural heterogeneity, etc.). Police have been heavily criticized within minority communities for providing a perceived different level of enforcement in their neighborhoods.

The influence of political environments over police behavior has been infrequently tested and the limited empirical evidence available has been mixed. For example, a city-manager type government increased the likelihood of arrest for some types of offenses arid not others (Langworthy). Economic and demographic variables are highly correlated. Some studies have reported that aggregate level economic and demographic variables do have a significant influence over police behavior, however the findings are somewhat mixed. For example, while Liska and Chamlin found that the percentage of nonwhite residents significantly increased the arrest rate, Crank reported different results based on the measure of cultural heterogeneity used. Other research has also reported that neighborhood crime rates did not have an effect on arrest. A recent study, however, found a relationship between police killings and racial and economic inequality, density, and overcrowding (Jacobs and O'Brien 1998).

Klinger (1997) has proposed a theory to explain how the levels of crime in communities affect police behavior. He suggested that police will respond more punitively (or with more "vigor") toward less serious crimes in lower crime rate districts compared to higher crime rate districts. That is, Klinger proposed that with the exception of very serious offenses, as district-level rates of crime increase, officers are less likely to arrest. This theory has not been empirically tested. While recent increased attention toward community-level explanations of police behavior is encouraging, this body of research needs to be further developed and adequately tested.

Conclusion

It is clear that much effort has been devoted to attempts to explain police behavior. Since the 1950s, these efforts have evolved from research that was primarily qualitative in nature to current research that utilizes more complicated methodologies and analyses. This latter research has given scholars the tools to thoroughly explore police behavior by enabling comparisons that analyze characteristics of each observed police-citizen encounter. The four broad areas of factors that have been examined are situational/legal characteristics (e.g., suspect, victim, police-encounter, and legal features), individual officer characteristics (e.g., gender, race, education, and attitudes), organizational characteristics (e.g., police subculture, strategies, formal and informal policies, department styles, and supervision), and community characteristics (e.g., political, economic, and demographic).

Clearly, some of these factors exert a greater degree of influence over police behavior than others. For instance, it is generally agreed that individual officers' characteristics have little or no causal effect on police behavior, whereas legal factors are considered to be very strong predictors of police behavior. While extralegal variables usually have a smaller effect, they are important nonetheless because one would not expect these factors to influence behavior if police organizations are to be considered legitimate. The bulk of police research in the 1970s and 1980s focused on the explanatory power of situational and individual characteristics over police behavior. Much of the research in the 1990s has refined these earlier findings through more careful measurement and better data collection techniques. Unfortunately, less is known about the potential influence of organizational and community factors over police behavior; the range and level of explanatory power of these factors is not fully known.

Future police research should consider not only the influence of organizational and community factors, but also needs to examine a wider range of behavior. Currently, most research attempts to explain police use of arrest and force. More research is needed that examines other police actions that may not be as punitive as arrest and use of force, but nonetheless have a significant influence over the lives of citizens. Finally, police researchers need to explore alternative methods of data collection in an effort to better understand not just the decisions officers make, but why they make those decisions.

ROBIN SHEPARD ENGEL

See also FEDERAL BUREAU OF INVESTIGATION: HISTORY; POLICE: COMMUNITY POLICING; POLICE: CRIMINAL INVESTIGATIONS; POLICE: HANDLING OF JUVENILES; POLICE: ORGANIZATION AND MANAGEMENT; POLICE: POLICING COMPLAINANTLESS CRIMES; POLICE: PRIVATE POLICE AND INDUSTRIAL SECURITY; POLICE: SPECIAL WEAPONS AND TACTICS (SWAT) TEAMS; URBAN POLICE.

BIBLIOGRAPHY

BLACK, DONALD, and REISS, ALBERT J., JR. "Police Control of Juveniles." *American Sociological Review* 35, no. 1 (1970): 63–77.

CRANK, JOHN P. "The Influence of Environmental and Organizational Factors on Police Style in Urban and Rural Environments." *Journal of Research in Crime and Delinquency* 27 (1990): 166–189.

ENGEL, ROBIN SHEPARD. "The Effects of Supervisory Styles on Patrol Officer Behavior." *Police Quarterly* 3, no. 3 (2000): 262–293.

ENGEL, ROBIN SHEPARD, and SILVER, ERIC. "Policing Mentally Disordered Suspects: A Reexamination of the Criminalization Hypothesis." *Criminology* (2001).

ENGEL, ROBIN SHEPARD; SOBOL, JAMES J.; and WORDEN, ROBERT E. "Further Exploration of the Demeanor Hypothesis: The Interaction Effects of Suspects' Characteristics and Demeanor on Police Behavior." *Justice Quarterly* 17, no. 2 (2000): 235–258.

FRIEDRICH, ROBERT J. "Police Use of Force: Individuals, Situations, and Organizations." *Annals of the American Academy of Political and Social Science* 452 (1980): 82–97.

FYFE, JAMES J. "Police Use of Deadly Force: Research and Reform." *Justice Quarterly* 5 (1998): 165–205.

JACOBS, DAVID, and O'BRIEN, ROBERT M. "The Determinants of Deadly Force: A Structural Analysis of Police Violence." *American Journal of Sociology* 103 (1998): 837–862.

KLINGER, DAVID A. "Demeanor or Crime? Why 'Hostile' Citizens Are More Likely to Be Arrested." *Criminology* 32 (1994): 475–493.

———. "Negotiating Order in Patrol Work: An Ecological Theory of Police Response to Deviance." *Criminology* 35, no. 2 (1997): 277–306.

LANGWORTHY, ROBERT H. "Wilson's Theory of Police Behavior: A Replication of the Constraint Theory." *Justice Quarterly* 3 (1985): 89–98.

LISKA, A. E., and CHAMLIN, M. B. "Social Structure and Crime Control among Macrosocial

Units." *American Journal of Sociology* 90 (1984): 383–395.

MASTROFSKI, STEPHEN D.; RITTI, RICHARD R.; and HOFFMASTER, DEBRA. "Organizational Determinants of Police Discretion: The Case of Drinking-Driving." *Journal of Criminal Justice* 15 (1987): 387-402.

MASTROFSKI, STEPHEN D.; RITTI, R. RICHARD; and SNIPES, JEFFREY B. "Expectancy Theory and Police Productivity in DUI Enforcement." *Law & Society Review* 28, no. 1 (1994): 113–148.

MASTROFSKI, STEPHEN D.; SNIPES, JEFFREY B.; PARKS, ROGER B.; and MAXWELL, CHRISTOPHER D. "The Helping Hand of the Law: Police Control of Citizens on Request." *Criminology* 38, no. 2 (2000): 307–342.

MASTROFSKI, STEPHEN D.; WORDEN, ROBERT E.; and SNIPES, JEFFREY B. "Law Enforcement in a Time of Community Policing." *Criminology* 33 (1995) 539–563.

MUIR, WILLIAM K., JR. *Police: Streetcorner Politicians*. Chicago: University of Chicago Press, 1977.

PARKS, ROGER B.; MASTROFSKI, STEPHEN D.; DE-JONG, CHRISTINA; and GRAY, M. KEVIN. "How Officers Spend Their Time with the Community." *Justice Quarterly* 16, no. 3 (1999): 483–519.

REUSS-IANNI, ELIZABETH, and IANNI, FRANK. "Street Cops and Management Cops: Two Cultures of Policing." In *Control in the Police Organization*. Edited by Maurice Punch. Cambridge, Mass.: MIT Press, 1983. Pages 251–274.

RIKSHEIM, ERIC, and CHERMAK, STEVEN M. "Causes of Police Behavior Revisited." *Journal of Criminal Justice* 21 (1993): 353–382.

SHERMAN, LAWRENCE W. "Causes of Police Behavior: The Current State of Quantitative Research." *Journal of Research in Crime and Delinquency* 17 (1980): 69–100.

SHERMAN, LAWRENCE W.; GARTIN, PATRICK R.; and BUERGER, MICHAEL E. "Hot Spots of Predatory Crime: Routine Activities and the Criminology of Place." *Criminology* 27, no. 1 (1989): 27–55.

SKOGAN, WESLEY G., and HARTNETT, SUSAN M. *Community Policing, Chicago Style*. New York: Oxford University Press, 1997.

SMITH, DOUGLAS A., and KLEIN, JODY R. "Police Control of Interpersonal Disputes." *Social Problems* 31 (1984): 468–481.

SMITH, DOUGLAS A., and KLEIN, JODY R. "Police Agency Characteristics and Arrest Decisions." In *Evaluation Performance of Criminal Justice Agencies*. Edited by G. P. Whitaker and C. D.

Phillips. Thousand Oaks, Calif.: Sage, 1983. Pages 63–97.

SMITH, DOUGLAS A., and VISHER, CHRISTY A. "Street-Level Justice: Situational Determinants of Police Arrest Decisions." *Social Problems* 29 (1981): 167–177.

TEPLIN, LINDA A. "Criminalizing Mental Disorder: The Comparative Arrest Rates of the Mentally Ill." *American Psychologist* 39 (1984): 794–803.

VAN MAANEN, JOHN. "Working the Street: A Developmental View of Police Behavior." In *The Potential for Reform of Criminal Justice*. Edited by H. Jacob. Beverly Hills, Calif.: Sage, 1974. Pages 83–129.

VISHER, CHRISTY A. "Gender, Police Arrest Decisions, and Notions of Chivalry." *Criminology* 21 (1983): 5–28.

WALKER, SAMUEL. *The Police in America*, 3d ed. Boston, Mass.: McGraw-Hill College, 1999.

WALKER, SAMUEL; SPOHN, CASSIA; and DeLONE, MIRIAM. *The Color of Justice: Race Ethnicity and Crime in America*, 2d ed. Belmont, Calif.: Wadsworth Thomson Learning, 2000.

WILSON, JAMES Q. *Varieties of Police Behavior: The Management of Law and Order in Eight Communities*. Cambridge, Mass.: Harvard University Press, 1968.

WORDEN, ALISSA POLLITZ. "The Attitudes of Women and Men in Policing: Testing Conventional and Contemporary Wisdom." *Criminology* 31, no. 2 (1993): 203–242.

WORDEN, ROBERT E. "Situational and Attitudinal Explanation of Police Behavior: A Theoretical Reappraisal and Empirical Assessment." *Law & Society Review* 23 (1989): 667–711.

———. "A Badge and a Baccalaureate: Policies, Hypothesis, and Further Evidence." *Justice Quarterly* 7 (1990): 565–592.

———. "The Causes of Police Brutality: Theory and Evidence on Police Use of Force." In *Police Violence: Understanding and Controlling Police Abuse of Force*. Edited by William A. Geller and Hans Toch. New Haven, Conn.: Yale University Press, 1996. Pages 23–51.

WORDEN, ROBERT E., and SHEPARD, ROBIN L. "Demeanor, Crime, and Police Behavior: A Reexamination of the Police Services Study Data." *Criminology* 34 (1996): 83–105.

CASES

Tennessee v. Garner, 471 U.S. 1 (1985).

Wilkins v. Maryland State Police, Maryland Civil Action No. CLB–93–483 (1993).

POLICE: POLICING COMPLAINANTLESS CRIMES

Certain types of criminal offenses, such as some forms of commercialized consensual sex (e.g. prostitution), nongovernmentally sanctioned gambling, public drunkenness, and drug addiction, are said to generate no complaints. These offenses are often designated as *victimless crimes* because of a perception that these crimes involve no specific objects of attack, which is one of the defining characteristics of larcenies, assaults, and other common law crimes. The term "victimless crimes" also assumes that the participants are adults and fully capable of making informed decisions about their participation in these activities and that they are engaged in these activities through their own volition.

The term victimless crime, when used to describe various activities that constitute a class of illegal behaviors, has been a source of considerable controversy because these crimes do cause substantial human suffering, not in the direct way that common law crimes produce clear injury to the victims, but indirectly through damaged lives and communities. For many who look at the fallout created by victimless crimes, it seems obvious that the activities forbidden by the relevant criminal laws should indeed be outlawed. They should be treated as crimes, observers argue, for they are too damaging to go unregulated. Those who hold this position argue further that victimless offenses violate various community standards and propriety that have been codified into law to protect the moral welfare of the public and the physical health of its citizens. Consequently, proponents of this position argue that law enforcement officers should police such activity in order to promote and reinforce the social order.

On the other side of the debate are those who say that the formal machinations of the criminal justice system should not be alerted or activated to respond to the activities currently known as victimless crimes. Those who maintain this position argue that because the selling and purchasing of these services is consensual, such crimes do not warrant the attention of the criminal justice system. In other words, because those who participate directly in these proscribed activities do not report the illicit behavior to the authorities, the government should not intervene. From this perspective, law enforcement activity directed at victimless crimes is unjustified and constitutes an unreasonable intrusion into the private lives of citizens. Proponents of this reasoning further argue that governmental attention to these activities greatly burdens the police, the courts, and the correctional system by diverting funds and energy away from serious crimes that directly affect their victims (Territo, Halstead, and Bromley).

This entry will not discuss the legal and philosophical issues relating to the criminalization versus decriminalization debate often associated with so-called victimless crimes, but instead focuses on the fact that participants engage in such crimes voluntarily. The point that participants in victimless crimes do not report the illicit behavior to the authorities has several crucial implications for understanding the nature of crime and social control. This entry addresses those implications and the law enforcement actions directed toward them.

The crime of prostitution is illustrative of the various rationales for taking law enforcement action against victimless crimes and addresses generally the methods that police agencies employ to combat such crimes. Other sorts of victimless crimes will be addressed in passing as a means of demonstrating the similarities manifest in this category of crime.

Why law enforcement action is requested for victimless crimes

There is a substantial assortment of activities that constitute each classification of victimless crime. Diversity is clearly the case in the chosen exemplar, because prostitution varies widely in terms of types of services rendered, prices charged, location of operation, and, consequently, official attention from law enforcement. In order to understand the differences in police dealings with various sorts of prostitution, it is necessary to describe briefly the range of the commercial sex trade.

While there are male prostitutes and female customers, most of those who trade sexual favors for monetary compensation are female and most of their customers are males. Consequently, most of the ensuing discussion of this vice crime and the law enforcement response to it will focus on female prostitution involving male customers. The high end of the continuum of female prostitution entails the services of escorts (also known as call girls) that men solicit for an afternoon sexual diversion or for an expensive evening (often during professional conventions). Call-girl operations are generally far removed from public view because in most instances the initial contact and the arrangements are made by telephone or, increasingly, by computer, thus allowing the customer (commonly known as the john) to specify the physical characteristics of the woman he wishes to procure and the services he desires. Escort services are businesses where satisfied repeat customers are highly desired because they are safer and more profitable. Thus, every effort is made to ensure confidentiality and safety of both the prostitute and the client. Consequently, the actual exchange of money and the provision of sexual services are conducted behind closed doors, usually in an upscale hotel room. Unless the act is accompanied by some sort of extreme irregularity such as a heart attack during the encounter, the entire incident is relatively unremarkable. Because the nature of such transactions rarely includes either uninvolved witnesses or complainants who might be offended or injured, law enforcement officials are seldom called to come into contact with those who participate in this type of prostitution. Without an official witness to the act or a complainant, law enforcement rarely comes into contact with either of the participants.

In the middle of the economic spectrum of prostitution are women who frequent public gatherings such as bars and dance halls in order to pick up customers. Prostitutes working this aspect of the trade typically contact their potential clients from the array of patrons, often with the approval and occasional support from a bartender or other legitimate employee of the establishment. They then engage in a brief period of social drinking, suggest some form of additional intimacy, and present a proposed fee for specified services. After reaching an agreement, prostitute and client retire to a nearby hotel or motel room where the deal is consummated.

With this type of prostitution, the initial contact, negotiation, and agreement takes place in a low visibility environment in which only a few people might take notice of the criminal activity. Unless the prostitute mistakenly approaches an unwilling person as a client, or the pickup is made in a location where such activity is unwanted, or there is an assault perpetrated by either party, police involvement is unlikely. (The likelihood of an assault tends to increase with two factors. As the price of the transaction decreases and as the instability and lack of permanence in the location of the event increases, the likelihood of an associated assault increases. The assault may be perpetrated by a dissatisfied john or it may be perpetrated by confederates of the prostitute

who may be lying in wait at a prearranged location. In the latter instance, the offer of sex is merely a ruse to gain the confidence of the john who is subsequently attacked and robbed, often left for dead. Such a situation is often referred to as a "Murphy Game.") Similarly, because the sexual activity that occurs between prostitute and client takes place in private confines, it is not likely that the police will be alerted to the transaction.

At the lowest end of the spectrum of the commercial sex trade are the street prostitutes (often referred to as hookers) who typically work in the open in areas known as "strolls" located on main streets of mixed use and commercial neighborhoods. The street prostitute is usually dressed provocatively and can be seen waving at traffic (flagging) or walking very slowly with the flow of traffic and stooping to make eye-contact with drivers approaching her slowly from the rear ("trolling"). When a driver stops and rolls down a window, the hooker typically leans into the car and engages in a brief negotiation with the ostensible customer. While conducting this negotiation neither party initially knows the true identity of the other and each often suspects the other of being an undercover police officer. Usually the negotiation will continue until the prostitute is convinced that the john actually wants to procure sexual services. Such convincing requires the john to describe what sort of activity is desired in the most specific and graphic terms. If the prostitute and the customer reach an agreement, they consummate the transaction nearby—in a room at a cheap motel that the prostitute frequents, in the customer's vehicle, or even in public view in places such as alleys, sidewalks, and driveways or front yards of local residents.

The public nature of the contact, bargaining, and consummation that constitute street prostitution places it under considerable law enforcement scrutiny. Such scrutiny results not only from the visibility to police officers on patrol, but because prostitution itself fosters a climate where other sorts of criminal activity can thrive. Some of this additional criminality is part and parcel of the prostitution trade, while other components emerge as crimes of opportunity. Perhaps the single biggest reason for both sorts of ancillary crimes is that street prostitution is a trade that operates strictly on a cash basis.

Street prostitutes sometimes try "scamming" potential customers, deceiving them into parting with their money without having provided any sexual favors—by literally grabbing the money and running away. Another common deception is to convince the customer either to remove his trousers and underwear or to lower them around his ankles, sexually arouse the customer as a distraction, grab the customer's wallet and quickly depart the area.

Many other people in the locales where street prostitutes work are also aware of the large amounts of cash carried into the area by those who come to procure sex. For those inclined to take things from others through force or fear, the ready supply of cash is a tempting target. Consequently, robbery is a problem that plagues many strolls as criminals seek to get cash from the potential customers before contact with a prostitute is made. This sort of robbery—often referred to as "rolling"—can also be done in concert with prostitutes who lure customers to some secluded spot where accomplices steal his money and other valuables. If the customer decides to report the crime, the police become involved to the same degree they normally would when robberies occur. (Customers usually do not report their victimization because they do not want friends and family to know of their involvement with prostitutes.) In rare instances, "rolling" victims end up dead and the high degree of police involvement that is routine in homicide investigations ensues. In sum, the predatory criminality that accompanies street prostitution is a major source of police attention to this so-called victimless crime.

A second reason why police attention is directed toward street prostitution comes from the display of sexual activity in public places. Payment for all forms of prostitution is based on how many customers they can service in a given time frame. Because street hustling is the least lucrative form of prostitution, the time taken to acquire the privacy of a hotel or motel room is time away from the next customer. Consequently, customers usually never leave their cars in a substantial portion of street hustling encounters. In some cases the prostitute enters the car and the customer drives away from the main thoroughfare onto a quieter street—often a residential area—to consummate the deal at curbside or even in the driveway of a local resident. In other cases the prostitute directs the customer into a nearby alley or parking lot, where she then meets him. It is not unusual for the entire transaction to take place during daylight hours in the midst of passersby. Whatever the particular details, citizens who live and work in the areas where prostitutes and customers carry on in public often call the police to report the illicit activity.

A third source of complaints comes from the parents of missing children. Street hustling is an easy form of prostitution and provides fast cash to those who participate. As a consequence, teenage runaways can be easily drawn into the business (Lyman). While the parents of many of the youngsters who become involved in street prostitution are not aware of what their children are doing, some parents do inform the police of their children's involvement. In a related vein, because the police are aware of the runaway–street prostitution nexus, officers looking for female runaways often check the local street hustling scene in their attempts to locate missing children.

Finally, and perhaps most importantly, the primary source of complaints about prostitution in many communities is the women who live, shop, and work in legitimate businesses located in and around the strolls where other females ply their illegal trade. These women, weary of being approached—and sometimes accosted—by men who wish to employ the services of a prostitute, will call the police to complain. Women at the lower end of the economic ladder, who either must walk or use public transportation, suffer disproportionately from unwanted solicitations by men who are unable to differentiate prostitutes from those women who are not prostitutes.

Police tactics employed in victimless crimes

Once the police receive a complaint related to the commercial sex trade from either a willing participant who has been somehow harmed or, more typically, from an unwilling bystander, they may respond in several ways. If the complaint involves a specific crime (e.g., a robbery), the police will investigate the crime if warranted. If the complaint alleges some broader pattern of criminality (e.g., an active stroll), detectives may conduct a surveillance operation to ascertain the scope of the problem while the patrol officers on the beat direct more attention to the location. Beat officers have at their disposal a variety of options to dissuade prostitutes and their customers from continuing their activities in the area. One option employed as an initial strategy is to make frequent stops at commercial establishments and other places where prostitutes loiter and provide their services. Doing so discourages prostitutes and customers from making contact and consummating deals. It also produces a feeling of security among the general public and shows that the police are sensitive to community concerns.

If the increased presence of uniformed law enforcement officers does not serve as a deterrent, officers may initiate progressively more proactive measures with increasingly more severe consequences for the offenders. Officers may, for example, enforce traffic violations more rigorously, for example, by issuing summons to johns who block traffic lanes while chatting with known prostitutes. Police often lecture suspected customers about the impropriety of cruising for prostitutes and offer stern warnings that they not return to the area. Likewise, officers may cite streetwalkers for illegal hitchhiking or for impeding pedestrian traffic on sidewalks.

Expanded police presence and an increase in enforcement of illegal activities associated with prostitution sometimes prove insufficient methods of controlling the problem. When more drastic measures are necessary, the police will often institute a variation of the "sting" operation where officers, men or women, will pose as participants in the prostitution trade—as either prostitutes or johns—in order to make criminal cases against the real participants. This tactic generally involves the use of decoys in a two-stage effort. The first stage, directed at the prostitutes, involves undercover officers posing as potential customers who attempt to elicit an offer of sex for money. This method presents legal barriers because entrapment laws require that the prostitute herself (or himself) offer sex for money. Moreover, the law requires that the prostitute explicitly state the sexual services being offered and the exact amount of money to be exchanged. If these requirements are not met, the police will not make an arrest because they realize that their case will not stand up in court.

Even when the police make successful cases, prostitution stings often have little long-term impact on the overall level of commercial sexual activity in a given community because prostitutes view arrest and incarceration as little more than a minor inconvenience, a part of the cost of doing business. Prostitutes respond by laying low for a period or changing locations until the police ease enforcement efforts. They rarely leave the business altogether.

The second stage of prostitution sting operations is directed at customers. In this phase, female officers posing as prostitutes will loiter in the area of the stroll. When customers approach and offer money for sex, they are arrested. Be-

cause being arrested is extremely embarrassing for many customers, the police anticipate that a substantial portion of them will resist arrest. Consequently, decoys are supported by other officers who perform the actual arrest and convey the customer to a detention facility. The decoy is then free to prepare the proper reports for prosecution.

Modern technology has improved prosecution in both types of sting operations with sensory-enhancing technology such as night vision optics and audio amplification equipment. Video and audio recordings have been introduced in many court proceedings. In some cases the people legitimately living and working in the affected areas have been allowed to state in open court how the neighboring street hustling has negatively affected their quality of life. In an increasing number of municipalities, the names and even pictures of arrested participants have been published by the local news media.

The efficacy of all of these enforcement techniques has been augmented through the assistance of officers whose primary assignment is the investigation of juvenile crime and status offenses (runaways). These officers will check the areas frequented by street hookers and their pimps in an attempt to locate curfew violators, investigate child exploitation in sexually oriented businesses (nude model studios, massage parlors, and cabarets featuring topless and nude dancers), and return runaways to their parents or guardians. Any adults present with juveniles will be investigated and prosecuted when appropriate.

With some minor modifications the same law enforcement tactics can also be applied to the upper and middle segments of the prostitution spectrum. However, because the call girl and, to a lesser degree, the mid-range bar hustler are less likely to conduct business in the open, complaints to the police and subsequent enforcement responses are less frequent.

Extrapolation to other types of criminality

Although this entry has emphasized prostitution, the principles discussed can be extrapolated and applied to other areas of "complainantless" crimes such as gambling, illegal drug use, or public intoxication. Even enforcement actions directed toward other criminal activities unrelated to traditional vice crimes can be rationalized on the same basis; that is, the true victims are not the participants but are innocent bystanders.

For example, traffic offenses that do not involve vehicle-to-vehicle or vehicle-to-pedestrian contact are included in the rubric of complaintantless crime. Because there are no victims in the traditional sense and because the only witness is a police officer, traffic offenses are not perceived to be malum in se by a large section of the public. At best, the enforcement of traffic laws is viewed as an inefficient use of a police officer's time when other types of criminal violations are more deserving of attention. Unless an actual collision has taken place many members of the public feel that police attention to traffic violations is unwarranted. At worst the enforcement of traffic laws is incorrectly viewed as a dubious means of providing local revenue and as an unnecessary limitation of freedom.

However, prompting by the public is also evident even in traffic offenses. As a case in point, when motorists speed through areas near schools where children walk, parents will direct complaints to the police. Similarly, when lanes are blocked by illegally parked delivery trucks, complaints to the local police will follow. However, citizen outrage and a demand for instant and vigorous police action usually takes place when there has been an increase in the severity and frequency of traffic accidents. Traffic accidents where children are the victims tend to draw the fastest and most vigorous police response.

The most effective response to a rapid rise in traffic accidents comes through a program known as *selective enforcement*. It is an accepted reality that the police simply cannot respond to every traffic law violation. Selective enforcement entails a four-step process that allows the officers to focus their attention on the most serious offenses. First, the formal reports of the most frequent and severe forms of traffic accidents are reviewed and analyzed to determine patterns (such as time, day, location) and common hazardous driving actions. Second, officers who are normally assigned to patrol the areas in question are briefed on the situation and advised of the interrelated variables causing the accidents. Third, the officers are directed to issue traffic citations only for the specific hazardous driving behaviors leading to the accidents. Fourth, the efficacy of the enforcement program is reviewed and a decision is made to continue, reduce, expand or alter the enforcement efforts accordingly.

Whether the criminal activity is prostitution or some other form of so-called victimless crime, involvement of the formal machinations of the criminal justice system may never completely eliminate the offending behavior. However, agents of the criminal justice system, particularly the police, are ethically bound to respond to the needs and desires of the affected citizens who live and work in the area, and are legally bound to take the appropriate action against the perpetrators. They are also required to do so with procedures in compliance with established legislation and judicial review.

TOMAS C. MIJARES
DAVID A. KLINGER

See also CRIMINALIZATION AND DECRIMINALIZATION; DOMESTIC VIOLENCE; FEDERAL BUREAU OF INVESTIGATION: HISTORY; POLICE: COMMUNITY POLICING; POLICE: CRIMINAL INVESTIGATIONS; POLICE: HANDLING OF JUVENILES; POLICE: ORGANIZATION AND MANAGEMENT; POLICE: POLICE OFFICER BEHAVIOR; POLICE: PRIVATE POLICE AND INDUSTRIAL SECURITY; POLICE: SPECIAL WEAPONS AND TACTICS (SWAT) TEAMS; SCIENTIFIC EVIDENCE; SEX OFFENSES: CONSENSUAL; VICTIMLESS CRIME.

BIBLIOGRAPHY

LYMAN, MICHAEL D. *Criminal Investigation: The Art and the Science.* Upper Saddle River, N.J.: Prentice-Hall, 1999.
TERRITO, LEONARD; HALSTEAD, JAMES; and BROMLEY, MAX. *Crime and Justice in America: A Human Perspective.* St. Paul, Minn.: West Publishing, 1992.

POLICE: PRIVATE POLICE AND INDUSTRIAL SECURITY

In this entry the terms *private security* and *private police* are used interchangeably. However, private security more often refers to *in-house security* (personnel who conduct policing activities within an organization), and private policing refers to *contract security* (security guards/officers hired by organizations to secure and protect assets and personnel). These terms are used synonymously because the history and functioning of in-house and contract personnel is fairly similar. Contract personnel (typically uniformed) do policing more often than in-house personnel, but there are circumstances and contexts in which in-house personnel, although not uniformed, conduct policing activities very similar to those of public police and contract personnel.

The growth of the private security industry is generally perceived as a twentieth-century phenomenon. However, policing by private organizations can be traced back far into history. This is particularly the case with market economies in which competing interest groups influence the growth of private policing in contrast to single party societies, or single order religious or political societies, where competing policing organizations are generally not tolerated. The history of private and public policing is intertwined. In England, it is likely that private policing (rather narrowly defined historically) both preceded and necessitated the introduction of public police.

The emergence of state-controlled law enforcement, particularly in England, grew out of private organizations that were established to maintain public order, as well as to enhance private interests. Earlier work on private policing in London during the 1800s suggests that Jonathan Wild was one of the first private police agents to contribute to maintaining social order. During this period, property crime was rampant in London; Wild, who was labeled "thief taker," retrieved stolen goods and helped police to solve many cases for a fee. Even the first forerunners of public police, the Bow Street Runners, were funded by prosperous merchants and business interests. Many competing organizations arose during this time. Wealthy merchants hired armed guards to secure private property.

In the United States, private policing in the form of contract services essentially grew out of a public policing, paramilitary model. New York was the first city to establish a police force in 1844; in 1855 Allan Pinkerton, Chicago's first public detective and Cook County Deputy Sheriff, established the first private police organization, called the NorthWest Police Agency, in Chicago. By the end of the century there were fifteen private policing agencies in Chicago and twenty in New York. Private police organizations probably grew not because of the inadequacy of the public forces, but rather because the demand for policing exceeded the supply, and because the private agencies could be manipulated more effectively than the public.

The Pinkerton, Burns, and Wackenhut agencies are some of the more well known private policing agencies, and they still exist today under the same names. Both Pinkerton and Burns, as former U.S. Secret Service Agents, adopted that agency's organizational style. The highly centralized operations of the Secret Service were characterized by the collection of information, dossiers on suspects, extensive case files, methods of surveillance, and undercover operations. They went to great lengths to separate themselves from private investigators whose reputations were unfavorable in the popular culture of the time.

These agencies supplied contract security guards in large numbers to major industrial establishments. The activities of private police agencies as strikebreakers during the early part of the twentieth century helped earn private police a tarnished image. Of particular interest were personnel involved in security functions within companies. Referred to as in-house security, their origins are of considerable interest, but are little studied. The industrial giant Ford Motor Company employed as many as 3,500 persons in the early 1930s in a private police force, which was known as the "The Ford Service."

In the 1950s and 1960s there was a steady increase in the number of people employed in the private security industry, particularly in the contract-security services. Today, private security industry employees far outnumber those employed in public policing. Private security companies in the United States number over ten thousand, with estimated annual revenues exceeding $15 billion. Conservative employment estimates for the United States suggest that there are about 67,000 registered private investigators, over 27,600 in-house store detectives, 371,300 security officers, and 95,800 managers and staff representing in total well over 500,000 personnel. The 1999 Contract Security Industry data reveal that there are over 719,000 contract guards. Employment of guards is expected to grow faster than the average growth for other industries.

Scope of security work

Specific occupations within the security profession are diverse. They include security officers, asset protection personnel, security directors of businesses, security supervisors, vendors of alarm services, investigators (e.g., those involved in pre-employment screening, background checks), technology services (e.g., access control systems), and guard services. Both contract and in-house security personnel can be found in a range of industries that include utilities, transportation, manufacturing, oil, pharmaceutical, health care, banking, insurance, retail, hotel, food services, and sports. In-house security departments in certain industries employ hundreds of people to coordinate security for thousands of employees. Some service industry security units monitor several hundred thousands of clients. In certain large industries, in-house security operations typically have departmental budgets exceeding $15 million. These figures generally exclude budgetary allocations for contract security, security performed by non-security units, and security consultants.

Despite significant differences in the scope of work between law enforcement officers and private police, security professionals as a group are in various ways similar to law enforcement officers. First, they are similar in the sense that both organizations serve like interests. Though private security serves the narrow interests of the organization for which it works both groups strive to reduce crime and prevent client losses. Thus, each organization's goals include order maintenance functions and protecting their respective clients. Interestingly, while the client base of private security is arguably smaller, the fact remains that with the expansion of large, privately owned property—where much of public life takes place—the role of private and public policing has become increasingly blurred. Consequently, private security is not only concerned with corporate interests but also the public who constitute a significant client base.

Second, security professionals often are former law enforcement or military personnel who join the private sector upon retirement. The presence of a large number of such personnel in private security has had considerable influence on the organizational culture of security departments. The military model has served as the framework for instilling professionalism in private policing through militarization, a process that has fostered such attributes as obedience, physical training, education, and the display of uniforms. At the same time, historically, law enforcement agencies hired individuals with prior military experience. Law enforcement remains the primary occupation for military retirees and military "wannabees," as it provides all the trappings, such as uniforms, caps, and brass, available to military professionals.

Finally, the observable behavior of personnel in both organizations is often identical. For example, security personnel wear uniforms and drive vehicles similar to those of law enforcement. Further, some of the functions such as securing premises, patrols, and crowd management are very similar for both organizations.

The fact that personnel employed in private security, especially in recent years, far outnumber law enforcement officers and that they engage in pursuits similar to those of law enforcement, suggests that the police could have willing partners in cooperative efforts to achieve common goals.

Nature of security work

Very little is written about the nature of private police work. Public perceptions of private security attest to the assumption that security work is done by "rent-a-cops" who lack the requisite training and education. The nature of private policing involves more than patrol and guard duties. Activities may include establishing perimeter security through such elements as guard services, signs and notices, fence design criteria, protective barriers, locks, alarms, and protective lighting. While most of these responsibilities are tied to asset protection, these activities are also designed to prevent insiders and outsiders from committing crimes. Employee theft is a major concern for all workplace organizations. Measures are designed to prevent other detrimental activities such as workplace violence, drugs in the workplace, and white-collar crime.

Security work includes fire protection with attention focused on the causes of fire, fire brigades, fire control surveys, fire alarm technology, and fire protection plans. Security departments are also concerned with access control issues including swipe cards and badge systems, personnel movement, automated access systems, degrees of restriction, and other classification systems that support access control.

It is not uncommon for security departments to be involved in the planning stages of developing business environments. Security analysts interface with architects to ensure security features, such as electronic surveillance equipment, in the design stage. Personnel security is another feature of security departments. Some of the tasks included within this area include employee crime, employee suitability, preemployment screening, executive protection, and other evaluation programs relating to personnel.

Another major function of most security departments is risk management, disaster management, and emergency preparedness. Some of these tasks include risk identification, risk analysis, risk reduction, and program evaluation. Risk management includes defining vulnerabilities, and planning and conducting security surveys. Emergency planning and the management of both natural and human-induced disasters constitute the core of a security department's functions. Within this framework of risk, insurance plays an important role for security managers, who must consider the application of varieties of insurance such as bonds, federal crime insurance, kidnap and ransom insurance, fire insurance, and liability insurance.

Security managers are also concerned with computer crime and information security. One of the major tasks for large corporations is securing proprietary information from unwanted disclosures. Other functions include legal and liability issues.

Security managers have to be concerned with developing strategic alliances and relationships within the organization to maintain security effectiveness. In addition, security managers have to develop relations with the media, public law enforcement, fire departments, and other security organizations.

Legal authority

Typically, security officers have no more authority to act than private citizens, except when they are deputized by local enactment or are provided with special powers. Private police (citizens) enjoy arrest powers, which are typically similar across all the states.

One of the primary concerns of security management is to ascertain by what legal authority security officers can investigate suspected shoplifters, embezzlers, and the like. This may help management determine the level of training security officers should receive to accomplish their objective of protecting the business environment. The potential legal bases include (1) security officers with citizen powers; (2) security officers with special legislatively authorized power; and (3) security officers who are also police officers. In the case of security officers working under the authority vested in them through state legislation or local ordinances, their legal authority is the same as that of public law enforcement officers. However, in most instances, particularly in private enterprise, private security personnel operate in the capacity of ordinary citizens. Therefore, the focus of this section will be on citizens' legal powers.

Under common law every citizen, like the law enforcement officer, has a right to make an arrest. A private citizen can make an arrest for a criminal offense without a warrant if the arrested person has committed a felony in his/her presence or if the arrested person has committed a felony offense outside the presence of the citizen but the arresting person has reasonable cause to believe that a felony has been committed. The scope of a citizen's arrest power is similar to that of a law enforcement officer. However, a citizen's arrest is always made at the arrestor's own risk. That is, if the arrest proves to be unlawful, the arrestor is exposed to the risk of criminal or civil liability. A private police officer is subject to these limitations and must balance the need to protect the interests of his employer with the need to avoid making false arrests.

Many states do not authorize citizens' arrests for misdemeanors. Among those states that do have such provisions, the rules regarding misdemeanor arrests are not uniform. Some state statutes are narrow and limit misdemeanor arrests to "public offenses," which refers to disturbing the public peace or violating the public order. In most states, however, a private person may arrest one without a warrant who commits a misdemeanor in his presence.

In addition to the provisions of various statutes on misdemeanor arrests, some states provide special legislation enabling merchants and their agents to deal with shoplifters and other offenders. It is clear that these statutes have originated from the need to prevent the large losses that occur each year in this industry. Once again, there is no uniformity in these statutes.

The amount of force a private citizen or a government officer can use in making an arrest depends on the type of offense and the status of the arresting person. A general rule is that the amount of force used to arrest a person cannot exceed the extent of resistance offered. Again, if the arrest is for a felony offense, the authority of a private citizen is that of a law enforcement officer.

Regarding searches and seizures, the Fourth Amendment guarantees every citizen "to be secure in their persons, houses, papers." The amendment, however, only protects against intrusions from governmental officials, not from private citizens. Therefore, if evidence is seized from a suspect without any official knowledge, or without collusion with a law enforcement officer, the evidence is admissible in a prosecution and does not violate the Fourth Amendment. This is not to imply that a private citizen can seize evidence from any person at any time with impunity. Persons who enter private premises without authority or improperly seize the property of others may be subject to civil liability. Furthermore, one may be guilty of violating a criminal law and may be subject to prosecution for unauthorized entries and seizures that are not consensual. If a private citizen is in any way acting as an instrumentality of the police, or the police have knowledge of the citizen's action, there is a good possibility that the exclusionary rule will apply in any future prosecution and the evidence seized will be suppressed.

Thus, when a private security officer working in the capacity of a private citizen seizes evidence, even if the evidence is seized unlawfully, such evidence can be used for prosecution. However, if the security officer is given legal status through the states' required licensing or deputation process, the security officer would lose his status as a private person and illegally obtained evidence would be inadmissible in the court. This does not rule out the possibility, however, that a private security officer could also be sued for illegally obtaining evidence from a suspect. In general, the most conservative approach is to abide by the rules that apply to the public law enforcement officer. This also helps make the case that the private officer has acted in a professional manner (i.e., like a public law enforcement officer). Abiding by the constraints and requirements of public law enforcement will avoid any mistakes that might jeopardize the case.

It is clear that public law enforcement officers have a right to search persons upon a lawful arrest, but the private security officer may enjoy a broader privilege to search beyond the immediate suspect. What about searching employees who are not arrested? Can a security officer search employees' lockers or desks on suspicion of some misconduct? These questions are significant in view of current concerns about use of drugs in the workplace and employee theft. Generally, employers reserve the right to search employees' lockers or desks either as a preemployment condition or as post-employment consent to search. In some instances, employers have duplicate keys to lockers and desks. Where there is no reasonable expectation of privacy, that is, the employee does not enjoy the privilege of calling the space his own; the employer, through the security personnel, generally reserves the right to examine the contents at any time.

Public vis-à-vis private police

In recent years there has been an increase in the attention paid to developing working relationships between seemingly similar but fundamentally different organizations that regulate public life. There are numerous examples of established relationships between law enforcement and private security organizations at the city, state, and federal levels. Some of these cooperative efforts date to the early 1980s. However, very little research has addressed the attitudes of law enforcement officers and security professionals toward each other. Findings from earlier research in general suggest that security professionals believe that law enforcement officers do not respect them. The findings also suggest that law enforcement officers are primarily concerned with arrests and less concerned with crime prevention. In addition, it has been found that law enforcement agencies solicit information from security agencies but do not reciprocate in kind. Another common finding is that police officers believe that private security forces are not professional, that they are client-oriented, and that they are reluctant to prosecute. Other studies have found that security professionals rated their relationship with the police as good to excellent, while the police rated their relationship with security professionals as good to poor. Cross-national research on law enforcement and security relationships in Singapore, Brazil, China, India, Russia, and South Africa also suggest similar findings.

Recent work in the United States on the relationship between law enforcement officers and security professionals' suggests that security professionals believe law enforcement officers have a negative view of security professionals, while law enforcement officers believe that security professionals view police positively. Law enforcement officers typically have a neutral view of security, while security personnel hold the police in relatively high regard. On the issue of working relationships, interestingly, police officers believe that the existing working relationship between the two sectors is good. Conversely, security personnel view the state of the working relationship as poor. Not surprisingly, the results also suggest that police officers perceive security personnel as unequal partners in crime prevention, though security professionals were more likely to believe that they are coproducers of crime prevention efforts with policing agencies. Despite these differences, both groups acknowledged that there are at least some cooperative efforts between the two sectors, and that they could do more to foster and encourage a better working relationship with the other.

Due to the changing nature of security work, the distinction between public and private policing is becoming blurred. For example, public law enforcement officers often moonlight as security officers. While in some instances these officers wear official police uniforms and drive police cruisers while working at off-duty jobs, police officers working as security officers often act in a manner similar to private security officers. Private security forces in some areas are vested with full police powers. Examples from South Carolina (Sea Pines and Hilton Head Plantation), Virginia (Aquia Harbor), Oregon (Sun River), Tennessee (Fairfield Glade), and Pennsylvania (Poconos) suggest that their security forces remain privately controlled, paid, and attired, but are court sworn with the full capacity to arrest, search, and seize. In the Poconos, private communities have their security patrols deputized under Pennsylvania's dormant 1895 Night Watchman Act, originally adopted to enable coal companies to create their own union-busting police. In Michigan, similar legislation recently vested private security at certain malls and hospitals with total police power. Frenchman's Creek, a wealthy gated enclave in Florida's Palm Beach Gardens, boasts its own five-man Special Tactical Operation Patrol (STOP), which does not have full police powers but is equipped with camouflage clothing, night-vision scopes, infrared heat detectors, high-speed vehicles, and specially trained dogs.

In some types of police/security relationships, the distinction between public and private police is even further blurred. If one examines the nature of public and private police relationships, one can use the metaphor of cold-fusion to describe the complex and legally blurred relationships between law enforcement and security. An example of this type of interaction involves a joint police/security interaction where the recording industry contributed $100,000 to assist the Federal Bureau of Investigation (F.B.I.) in investigating pirated tapes and records. In another example, the F.B.I. and IBM Corporation jointly participated in a sting operation involving the sale of computer secrets in Silicon Valley. In yet another example, the Law Enforcement Intelligent Unit (LEIU) was founded as a private organization for local and state police to share intelligence files. Its membership is restricted to public police. The nature of the organizational culture permits the exchange of information that would not otherwise be possible by agents acting strictly in a public capacity. Thus these relationships provide opportunities for blending, but they blur boundaries between law enforcement and security organizations.

The future of private police

Despite great increases in the number of people employed in the private security industry, researchers know very little about what they do, how they do it, and what it means to the general public and the employees who come in contact with them. The popular culture clearly portrays an image that is not complimentary. Newspaper and magazines in the 1980s and early 1990s often described the lack of professionalism and inappropriate training among security officers.

While private policing involves more than just security officers, the public in general, and even students who major in criminal justice, only think of security officers when the term "private security" is uttered. Further, it is not uncommon for college students, both criminal justice and noncriminal justice majors, to describe security officers as "rent-a-cops," "toy cops," "unintelligent," "paid baby-sitters," and "overweight and unskilled." While both law enforcement and security professionals envision increased cooperation between the two groups in the future, security professionals have greater hope than public police for a relatively equal relationship.

The official society for security professionals, the American Society for Industrial Security (ASIS), has over twenty thousand members worldwide. In conjunction with some universities, the ASIS is working toward developing model course curriculum and program offerings. Many criminal justice programs in the United States offer course work or a concentration in security management as part of their programs. Some universities even offer degree programs in security. Security programs are typically housed in criminal justice departments and their course work is generally modeled after traditional law enforcement/police administration curricula. To make security education more relevant to academics and practitioners, changes in security curricula are needed in order to broaden its scope by incorporating methodology-based business and social science courses. ASIS membership has also supported programmatic and curricular changes, calling for the inclusion of social science and business-related courses in security education.

MAHESH K. NALLA

See also FEDERAL BUREAU OF INVESTIGATION: HISTORY; POLICE: HISTORY; POLICE: COMMUNITY POLICING; PO-LICE: CRIMINAL INVESTIGATIONS; POLICE: HANDLING OF JUVENILES; POLICE: ORGANIZATION AND MANAGEMENT; POLICE: POLICE OFFICER BEHAVIOR; POLICE: POLICING COMPLAINANTLESS CRIMES; POLICE: SPECIAL WEAPONS AND TACTICS (SWAT) TEAMS; SCIENTIFIC EVIDENCE; URBAN CRIME; URBAN POLICE; VAGRANCY AND DISOR-DERLY CONDUCT.

BIBLIOGRAPHY

BAILIN, PAUL S. *Private Security Services to 2004.* Cleveland, Ohio: The Freedonia Group, Inc., 2000.

CUNNINGHAM, WILLIAM C., and STRAUCHS, JOHN J. "Security Industry Trends: 1993 and Beyond." *Security Management* 36, no. 12 (1992): 27–30, 32, 34–36.

HENRY, STUART. *Private Justice: Towards Integrated Theorizing in the Sociology of Law.* London: Routledge and Kegan Paul, 1993.

INBAU, FRED E.; FARBER, BERNARD J.; and AR-NOLD, DAVID W. *Protective Security Law.* Boston: Butterworth-Heineman, 1996.

MARX, GARY T. "The Interweaving of Public and Private Police in Undercover Work." In *Private Policing.* Edited by C. D. Shearing and P. C. Stenning. Newbury Park, Calif.: Sage, 1987.

McCRIE, ROBERT D. "A Brief History of the Security Industry in the United States." In *Business and Crime Prevention.* Edited by M. Felson and R. V. Clarke. Monsey, N.Y.: Criminal Justice Press, 1997. Pages 197–218.

NALLA, MAHESH K. "Opportunities in an Emerging Market." *Security Journal* 10 (1998): 15–21.

NALLA, MAHESH K., and HUMMER, DONALD. "Relations between Police Officers and Security Professionals: A Study of Perceptions." *Security Journal* 12 (1999): 31–40.

NALLA, MAHESH K.; HOFFMAN, VINCENT J.; and CHRISTIAN, KENNETH E. "Security Guards Perceptions of Their Relationship with Police Officers and the Public in Singapore." *Security Journal* 7 (1996): 287–293.

NALLA, MAHESH K.; MORASH, M. A.; VITARATOS, BARBARA; and LINDHAL, SCOTT. "A Study of Security Challenges and Practices in Emerging Markets." *Security Journal* 8 (1997): 247–253.

NALLA, MAHESH K., and NEWMAN, GRAEME R. *A Primer in Private Security.* New York: Harrow and Heston, 1990.

NALLA, MAHESH K., and NEWMAN, GRAEME R. "Public Versus Private Control: A Reassessment." *Journal of Criminal Justice* 19 (1991): 537–547.

SHEARING, CLIFFORD, and STENNING, PHILIP C. "Private Security: Implications for Social Control." *Social Problems* 30 (1983): 493–508.

SKLANSKY, DAVID A. "The Private Police." *UCLA-Law-Review* 46, no. 4 (1999): 1165–1287.

STARK, ANDREW. "Arresting Developments: When Police Power Goes Private." *The American Prospect* 42 (January/February 1999): 41–48.

SOUTH, NIGEL. "Law, Profit, and 'Private Persons': Private and Public Policing in English History." In *Private Policing.* Edited by Clifford Shearing and Philip C. Stenning. Beverly Hills, Calif.: Sage, 1990. Pages 72–109.

WEISS, ROBERT P. "From 'Slugging Detectives' to 'Labor Relations': Policing Labor at Ford, 1930–1947." In *Private Policing.* Edited by Clifford Shearing and Philip Stenning. Beverly Hills, Calif.: Sage, 1987. Pages 110–130.

POLICE: SPECIAL WEAPONS AND TACTICS (SWAT) TEAMS

Until the late 1960s police agencies throughout the United States responded to crisis or special threat situations—such as those involving barricaded gunmen and hostages—on an ad hoc basis, simply deploying as many officers as seemed appropriate to handle the situation in whatever way seemed appropriate at the time. This practice proved (tragically) ineffective several times during the tumultuous 1960s—such as when sniper Charles Whitman launched a murderous rampage in Austin, Texas, claiming forty-five victims in 1966—and police agencies began to develop specialized units to handle crisis situations in a systematic fashion. These specially equipped units were trained to employ tactics that would not typically be used in other realms of police work. Carrying armaments such as rifles and tear gas, and trained to work as a team to contain, control, and de-escalate the various crises they would be called to encounter, these units were christened Special Weapons and Tactics (SWAT) Teams. Over the years, police agencies have assigned a variety of appellations—such as TAG (Tactical Action Group) and ERT (Emergency Response Team)—to their crisis response units, but the title commonly associated with these specialized units is SWAT.

Since their inception, SWAT teams across the United States have taken a variety of forms, have been organized in a variety of ways, and have been called upon to handle a variety of types of crisis and special threat situations. Some agencies employ full-time teams, while others structure their SWAT units as part-time entities wherein team members have a primary assignment in some other detail (e.g., patrol) and come together for training and crisis response, while still other agencies have teams that include both full- and part-time SWAT officers. Many larger agencies have their own SWAT team, while many smaller ones participate in multi-jurisdictional teams that include officers from several different agencies. SWAT teams may handle a myriad of assignments apart from hostage and barricaded subject situations. These chores include dignitary protection, responding to civil disturbances, stakeouts, and the service of search and arrest warrants in situations that pose a greater than normal risk of injury to the police. Indeed, the first major shootout involving a SWAT team in the United States occurred when a group of Los Angeles Police Department SWAT officers attempted to serve a warrant on the local headquarters of the Black Panther Party in December 1969.

Since the advent of SWAT in the late 1960s, the inventory of SWAT equipment has increased dramatically. Today the accouterments kept by these teams range from simple tools such as ladders and ropes to highly sophisticated surveillance and listening devices. In recent years, SWAT teams have added to their stores an array of nonlethal weapons, such as impact munitions (e.g., bean bags) that can be fired from shotguns and tear gas launchers, in order to capture combative subjects without severely injuring or killing them. In a related vein, the available evidence indicates that although contemporary SWAT teams are equipped with a variety of deadly weapons—including sniper rifles, submachine guns, and assault rifles—they rarely fire them outside of training. A recent study of forty SWAT units from agencies serving 250,000 or more people disclosed that these teams discharged firearms only in sixty-four of the several thousand incidents they handled from 1990 through 1996. Because the only shots fired in many of these sixty-four incidents were directed at nonhuman targets (such as vehicles and streetlights), it is apparent that the shooting of a citizen by a SWAT team is an extremely rare event.

This low rate of deadly force use may be at least partly attributable to the fact that early in the evolution of SWAT, verbal tactics emerged as a vital part of how the police sought to manage special threat situations. Rooted in the fundamental precept that most crises can be resolved by de-escalation, police agencies developed training programs to teach officers how to negotiate with hostile individuals, in hopes of talking them into surrender. Some agencies use SWAT team members as negotiators; others have separate negotiation units. Whatever the structuring of the tactical and negotiation components in a given agency, SWAT teams rely heavily on negotiations to help resolve special threat situations.

Despite the emphasis on trying to resolve crises peacefully, SWAT teams were involved in some mishaps during the 1990s. The two most notable cases both involved the F.B.I.'s Hostage Rescue Team (HRT). In one instance, an HRT sniper mistakenly killed the wife of a fugitive at Ruby Ridge, Idaho. In the other, scores of citizens died within the walls of a religious compound near Waco, Texas, when the building caught fire as HRT agents in armored vehicles moved to insert tear gas into it.

Episodes such as these—coupled with a recent upswing in SWAT activity aimed at enforcing drug laws (primarily by serving search warrants)—have led to calls from some quarters to reform SWAT teams and operations. Critics charge that SWAT teams have become "militarized," affecting a combat footing that flows from the "war on drugs" rhetoric that has animated U.S. drug policy in recent years, and also from other cultural forces that foster military posturing. The critics further argue that there are simply too many SWAT teams, singling out those from smaller jurisdictions, which rarely experience the sorts of crises that SWAT was created to handle.

This critical clamor reflects the basic tension about police powers that has existed in the United States since the first urban police departments were instituted on the east coast during the middle of the nineteenth century. Americans have always feared that tyranny could arise from the government agencies they devised to protect them from criminal assault. One hundred fifty years ago this was fear of ill-equipped, poorly trained individual policemen. Today it is fear of well-trained teams of officers who possess the latest in social control technology. Thus, although SWAT teams possess special weapons and employ specialized tactics, they operate in the same culture of ambivalence as the rest of American law enforcement.

DAVID A. KLINGER

See also POLICE: HISTORY; POLICE: COMMUNITY POLICING; POLICE: CRIMINAL INVESTIGATIONS; POLICE: HANDLING OF JUVENILES; POLICE: ORGANIZATION AND MANAGEMENT; POLICE: POLICE OFFICER BEHAVIOR; POLICE: POLICING COMPLAINANTLESS CRIMES; POLICE: PRIVATE POLICE AND INDUSTRIAL SECURITY; URBAN POLICE.

BIBLIOGRAPHY

KLINGER, DAVID. "Deadly Force in SWAT Operations: Evidence from Two National Samples." Paper presented at the 50th Annual Meeting of the American Society of Criminology, Washington, D.C., 1998.

KRASKA, PETER B., and KAPPELER, VICTOR. "Militarizing American Police: The Rise and Normalization of Paramilitary Units." *Social Problems* 44, no. 1 (1997): 1–18.

MCMAINS, MICHAEL J., and MULLINS, WAYMAN C. *Crisis Negotiations: Managing Critical Incidents and Hostage Situations in Law Enforcement and Corrections.* Cincinnati, Ohio: Anderson, 1996.

MIJARES, TOMAS C.; MCCARTHY, RONALD M.; and PERKINS, DAVID B. *The Management of Police Specialized Tactical Units.* Springfield, Ill.: Charles C. Thomas, 2000.

POLITICAL PROCESS AND CRIME

If politics is the authoritative allocation of values, then crime and politics are inextricably linked. Substantive criminal laws articulate, as do few others, the basic values of society. Agencies of law enforcement and the administration of criminal justice possess a near-monopoly on the legitimate use of violence, and exercise vast power in deciding whether and how to enforce the law. The criminal justice system is composed of a sizable set of government officials who together have an important impact on politics. The symbols of crime affect the nature of political promise and expectation.

Crime, morality, and public authority

Substantive criminal laws both reflect and reinforce the dominant morality in society. Many proscriptions of the criminal law are virtually universal and not politically problematic—for example, taboos against incest and prohibitions against murder and theft—yet consensual affirmation of these values reinforces existing structures of political authority. Other laws are not so widely accepted, and they reflect the power of dominant groups in society. But whatever the degrees of consensus about the substantive criminal laws, their administration is likely to be problematic and to pose problems requiring resolution through political processes.

At times, specific controversies in the criminal law are tied to larger concerns of political theory about the nature and function of the state. For example, classical liberal political theory (Mill) informs the position of those who oppose the prosecution of so-called victimless crimes, whereas another philosophical tradition embracing a broader role for the state underlies the arguments of those who would permit legislation proscribing victimless crimes (Devlin). For example, during a long period the common law accepted marriage and later the right to chastise as absolute defenses in criminal cases where men were charged with assault and battery of their wives. As such, these rules reinforced the dependence of women upon men. Similarly, the ways in which criminal laws were construed and enforced strengthened the institution of slavery and thwarted efforts to organize labor. Decisions to treat acts of political rebellion as "common crimes" rather than acts of conscience have also had the effect of defusing political opposition and reaffirming the authority of dominant elites (Balbus). The selection and administration of sanctions also reflect political considerations. In eighteenth-century England, policies to expand provisions for capital punishment, as well as nineteenth-century efforts to restrict them, were shaped by considerations of how best to enhance the authority of the Crown. In twentieth-century America, restrictions on capital punishment followed an increase in the political power of blacks. Criminal trials have also long been used to consolidate political power. Throughout history, and especially in the modern era, revolutionary regimes and military victors have mounted political trials to consolidate support and to brand opponents as common criminals (Kirchheimer).

The politics of law enforcement and administration

Law enforcement and administration are connected with politics on a number of levels. Dominant political theory and ideology affect the structure, organization, and expectations of a society's criminal justice institutions. In turn, these institutions affect the ways in which the criminal law is enforced and administered.

Political culture, theory, and ideology. Although the connection between political theory and ideology and concrete practice is neither direct nor always clear, the links are there, and to understand practices and institutional arrangements, one must appreciate the theoretical and ideological milieu that justifies and legitimizes them. Theories of authority and the nature and function of the state vary widely, and it is such factors that in part account for variations in concrete institutional practices in the criminal process. In this sense, social and political theory are at the root of the criminal process.

To illustrate, a major tradition in continental political theory and legal philosophy has emphasized the autonomous nature of the state and justified strong central authority (Hegel). This tradition stands in sharp contrast to the liberal democratic tradition of Great Britain and the United States, which has been intensely skeptical of authority, has celebrated pluralism, and has advocated the decentralization and fragmentation of power (Locke; Hartz). These differing traditions have influenced both the structure of and expectations about governmental institutions, including the criminal process (Tocqueville). The influences of American political thought on the criminal process are exemplified by the importance given to the rights of the criminally accused in the Bill of Rights, and by the tradition of local, decentralized administration of justice. The connections among ideology, political culture, and the criminal process in nonwestern and socialist countries are even more striking (Bayley; Li).

There are numerous other contrasts between Anglo-American and continental criminal justice that are related to the differing political traditions. A public criminal law as distinct from private tort law, public prosecutors in contrast to private prosecution by the victim, a national police force, and a comprehensive national judicial system—all signs of highly developed central authority—emerged much earlier and have evolved more fully on the Continent than in England and the United States. The American political tradition, in particular, has been intensely skeptical of central authority and strong positive government, and has resisted the penetration of remote political authority by means of the criminal law into the daily affairs of citizens. This has led to local control and local administration of criminal justice to a degree unheard of in Europe. In the United States, most major officials in the criminal justice system—judges, prosecutors, sheriffs, court clerks, and in a few jurisdictions, public defenders as well—are elected locally, a practice that is regarded by many conti-

nental observers as inconsistent with the ideals of evenhanded administration. Indeed, in the United States both the financing and the administration of criminal justice firmly remain a function of local (as opposed to even state) government. As a consequence, American criminal justice officials are expected not only to administer the law evenhandedly, but also to be responsive to their local publics, tasks that often foster irreconcilable tensions.

Contrasting continental with American views on plea-bargaining illustrates the importance of different traditions of theory and ideology in understanding the operations of the criminal justice system. In West Germany, for example, plea-bargaining is viewed with disdain as a practice that is only slightly short of corruption and one that would undermine the very authority and integrity of the state. In contrast, even though there is considerable debate over plea-bargaining, the practice is generally accepted in the United States as a valuable, if problematic, tool for flexible and efficient administration of justice. This and other practices, such as rules of evidence and the right to silence, must be understood in light of different traditions in political thought about the nature and authority of the state.

The administration of criminal justice. Because of its local orientation and the weakness of state and national governments, the administration of criminal justice in the United States has long reflected local political culture. Indeed, in America the history of the administration of criminal justice is primarily an aspect of the history of local governments. This history reveals how the styles, aims, and practices of the police and courts have varied according to local political influences. In the urban centers of the nineteenth and early twentieth centuries, such influence was direct and immediate. Those engaged in gambling, prostitution, loan-sharking, extortion, and the like often developed close ties with police and other public officials in order to ensure against investigation and arrest. Laws were also used selectively to control newly arrived immigrants, mediate tensions between contentious community groups, combat efforts to organize labor, and protect persons and property (Walker).

The distinguishing features of accounts of law enforcement officials in the nineteenth and early twentieth centuries are the unbridled use of discretion and the frequency of appeals to particularistic (as opposed to universalistic) values. Bribery, appeals to friendship, family and political influences, racism, and prejudice of all kinds served to lighten official responses to crime in some cases and to heighten them in others. Some accounts detail the routine and perfunctory nature of arrest and proceedings against the riff-raff of the "criminal classes" (Friedman and Percival).

But even with the decline of widespread corruption and the rise of a full-time professional criminal justice system in the mid-twentieth century, local political culture continues to shape policies of law enforcement and administration. Although there is now little direct political influence on the day-to-day activities of the police and courts in most American cities, the type of political culture dominant in a community still significantly affects what types of police officials are recruited and what policies they pursue. In one community, police might routinely arrest everyone for whom there is probable cause, whereas in another they may negotiate among disputants, overlook some offenses, and the like. Such differences are systematically related to differences in political cultures (Wilson). Similar patterns are found in courthouses. Courts in reformed "good government" communities are less likely to embrace plea-bargaining and are more inclined to hand down harsher sentences than are courts in communities where traditional political machines prevail. As with the police, this is because officials with different backgrounds and experiences are recruited in the various types of communities (Levin; Feeley). For example, the styles, policies, and practices of police, prosecutors, and courts in the older, ethnically mixed industrial cities with traditions of well-organized local party organizations are quite different from those in the newer cities of the West, which have neither the ethnic mix nor the tradition of tight-knit party organizations.

It is a general proposition that policies of public-service institutions are formed and significantly shaped by those at the lowest level of administration. This proposition applies to the administration of criminal justice. The criminal process is an overdetermined system—there are more rules to enforce than resources for enforcement, the same conduct can be variously defined, even the most carefully drawn rules permit considerable leeway of interpretation, decision-making takes place in settings of low visibility, officials are charged with contradictory tasks, and there are few organizational devices for overseeing and supervising subordinates. As a consequence, law enforcement and administration are selective and discretionary. One result is that actual policy, the law-in-action, is shaped to a considerable extent by the adaptation of formal rules to individual values and by the organizational exigencies of those who are charged with enforcement and administration. Such factors go a long way toward accounting for the patrol, investigation, and arrest practices of police (Wilson; Skolnick), decisions by courts (Feeley; Vera Institute), and policies of prison administrators (Sykes).

This inevitability of discretion fuels the politics of the administration of justice. In their broadest form, these politics require selecting from a number of competing and antagonistic values emphasized by various agents of law enforcement and administration. One writer has constructed ideal types of clusters of values that compete for attention: the "crime-control model" emphasizes maximization of public safety through swift and efficient proceedings and reliance on expertise; whereas the "due process model" emphasizes the protection of individual rights, is skeptical of fact-finding by public officials, and requires careful, contested proceedings at each stage of the criminal process. Debate over these values, reinforced as it is with community expectations, limited resources, and the semiautonomous and antagonistic nature of various criminal agencies, constitutes the politics of the administration of criminal justice (Packer).

Practical politics and the criminal process

Prosecutors, politics, and patronage.   In the United States, the criminal justice system serves direct practical political purposes as well. Owing to the salience of crime as a public issue and the visibility of their positions, many criminal justice officials use their offices as stepping-stones to higher public office. For example, a great many members of congress and governors have served as criminal prosecutors, and the mayors of a number of large American cities have been police chiefs.

To be effective, political organizations must have the ability to reward activists, and law enforcement and courthouse positions have traditionally been used for this purpose. These positions have been especially valuable because they provide security, high pay, and high prestige and often require little work. Studies of the classic urban political machines of the late nineteenth and early twentieth centuries reveal that various appointments in police forces and courthouses (from bailiffs to high court judges) were effectively used to reward supporters and induce loyalty to the local political organization. Although the expansion of civil service rules and the introduction of "good government" reforms have muted this practice, police and courthouse positions, which in many states are still exempt from merit selection rules, continue to be used as political patronage (Levin; Feeley).

Crime and symbolic politics.   Historically in Western democratic societies crime and crime policy have not been a highly salient political issue in electoral politics. However, for a variety of reasons crime does emerge as a major political issue from time to time. In the early twentieth century in the United States, crime emerged as a major concern on the national political agenda, and resulted in the passage of several new federal criminal statutes, including prohibition, the Mann Act (prohibiting "White Slavery") and laws making bank robbery a federal offense, the establishment of the Federal Bureau of Investigation (F.B.I.), and the establishment of a Presidential crime commission (The Wickersham Commission). In the latter part of the twentieth century, crime again emerged as a salient issue in the United States and throughout Western Europe, and again it had a significant impact on the political process. Judges began to impose longer sentences and legislatures provided for still tougher sentences under determinate sentencing, mandatory minimum sentencing, truth-in-sentencing, "three-strikes" sentencing laws, and the like. Similarly, courts began cutting back on rules of criminal procedure, making it somewhat easier to secure convictions and impose the death penalty, which was a resurgence in the United States in the 1980s and 1990s, after near de facto abolition in the 1960s and 1970s. Some of these responses were brought about by a steadily rising crime rate during the 1960s through the 1980s, but the changes were sought by specific groups that were organized to press for them. Since the 1970s in the United States, prison guards and law enforcement organizations have been potent forces in political campaigns, providing substantial sums and endorsements to candidates who support "law and order" proposals. This issue dynamic first emerged on the national political agenda in the 1964 presidential race between Lyndon Johnson and Barry Goldwater, and has periodically resurfaced in presidential races since then. One of the most significant aspects of this development has been the rise of victims' rights organizations. Throughout the 1980s and 1990s, victims rights groups formed, often spear-headed by the family member of a victim of a serious crime, and for the first time victims as a group became a powerful political force. This unprecedented development has led to changes in several areas of the criminal law. One of the first such groups to form was Mothers Against Drunk Driving (MADD), which organized court-watch groups that put pressure on judges to convict those charged with drunk driving (rather than downgrade the charge) and impose stiffer sentences. Others followed in their wake: victims groups sought and obtained the right of victims to address the court at sentencing (the so-called victims' impact statement) and at parole, successfully lobbied legislatures for sexual predator notification law, changes in criminal procedure and rules of evidence to reduce the trauma for child victims and victims of sexual assault to testify in court. And beginning in the 1980s, in the wake of the assassination attempt on President Ronald Reagan, groups supporting gun control were energized and combined with law enforcement agencies to successfully lobby for stricter gun control legislation on both the state and national levels.

There are two quite different explanations for the emergence of crime as an electoral issue in the United States, Great Britain, and Western Europe. One holds that as crime increased, segments of the electorate and politicians responded by pressing for new policies to address the problems. However, another view holds that the issue is more complicated. Although the fear of crime is widespread and deep-seated, most citizens have limited direct personal experience with crime and the administration of criminal justice. Some argue that crime must be understood in terms of "symbolic politics" (Edelman). They hold that it is the combination of intense concerns coupled with limited direct experience that makes crime such a potent symbolic issue. This can be termed the dramaturgy of law and order. To illustrate, crime is a valuable political opponent. It is a universally despised enemy that has no defenders. At a societal level, crusades against crime serve to reinforce dominant cultural values and social solidarity (Erikson). At an organizational level, the intense emotional arousal that is generated over crime policies can be an important factor in binding voluntary organizations together (Gusfield). This theoretical perspective is nicely illustrated by a careful study of those who supported a particularly tough version of a "three-strikes" law adopted by voters in an initiative that provided for sentences of twenty-five years to life for those convicted of a third felony (Tyler and Boeckman). The authors of this study interviewed a random sample of voters to identify factors that predicted support for or opposition to this law. Support for these dramatically increased sentences, they found, was not associated with a belief that the criminal justice system had been too lenient. Those who thought the system was too harsh were just as likely to support this law as those who thought it was too lenient. Rather, the best predictors of support for the tough new law were those who felt that there was too much racial and ethnic mixing and conflict in society, and those who felt that authority in the family was diminishing. In short, these findings are consistent with the perspective of those who hold that much of politics, and especially the politics of law and order, is symbolic politics in the sense that crime (and other issues) may be convenient "condensation" symbols and proxies for insecurities of a more personal and direct nature (Scheingold). The success of this strategy, or at least the continued salience of crime and crime policy as an important issue in national politics, has led one observer to suggest that modern politics is the practice of "governing through crime."

A more straightforward approach might counter with the observation that crime and public safety emerged as a salient issue on the political agendas of North American and European countries in the late 1960s as crime rates escalated, and that since the mid-1990s it has begun to recede, after about a decade of declining crime rates. Perhaps, but one of the big changes that has occurred since the 1970s is the emergence of organized interest groups—and particularly victims rights groups—which have crime policy as their central if not only focus. In countries where single-interest groups can easily organize and flourish, such as the United States and Great Britain, this may lead to deep and permanent changes.

Conclusion

Crime and the political process are linked on many levels. Political theory, ideology, and culture foster expectations about the substance and form of the criminal justice system. The structure of political institutions shapes the structure, and hence the substance and administration, of the criminal law. Discretion, inevitable in an overdetermined system, gives rise to the politics of administration. Local political organizations rely upon the criminal process for their support, and in turn the criminal process is shaped by them. The symbols of crime, law, and order shape political rhetoric and public expectation.

MALCOLM M. FEELEY

See also ASSASSINATION; BRIBERY; CRIME CAUSATION: POLITICAL THEORIES; CRIME COMMISSIONS; CRIMINALIZATION AND DECRIMINALIZATION; CRIMINAL JUSTICE SYSTEM; CRIMINOLOGY: MODERN CONTROVERSIES; FEAR OF CRIME; MASS MEDIA AND CRIME; PUBLIC OPINION AND CRIME; TERRORISM.

BIBLIOGRAPHY

BALBUS, ISAAC. *The Dialectics of Legal Repression: Black Rebels before the American Criminal Courts.* New York: Russell Sage Foundation, 1973.

BAYLEY, DAVID H. *Forces of Order: Police Behavior in Japan and the United States.* Berkeley: University of California Press, 1976.

DEVLIN, PATRICK. *The Enforcement of Morals.* New York: Oxford University Press, 1965.

EDELMAN, MURRAY. *The Symbolic Uses of Politics.* Urbana: University of Illinois Press, 1964.

ERIKSON, KAI T. *Wayward Puritans: A Study in the Sociology of Deviance.* New York: Wiley, 1966.

FEELEY, MALCOLM M. *The Process Is the Punishment: Handling Cases in a Lower Criminal Court.* New York: Russell Sage Foundation, 1979.

FRIEDMAN, LAWRENCE M., and PERCIVAL, ROBERT V. *The Roots of Justice: Crime and Punishment in Alameda County, California, 1870–1910.* Chapel Hill: University of North Carolina Press, 1981.

GUSFIELD, JOSEPH R. *Symbolic Crusade: Status Politics and the American Temperance Movement.* Urbana: University of Illinois Press, 1963.

HARTZ, LOUIS. *The Liberal Tradition in America: An Interpretation of American Political Thought since the Revolution.* New York: Harcourt, Brace, 1955.

HEGEL, GEORG W. F. *The Philosophy of History* (1881). Translated by J. Sibree. Prefaces by Charles Hegel and J. Sibree. New introduction by Carl J. Friedrich. New York: Dover, 1956.

KIRCHHEIMER, OTTO. *Political Justice.* Princeton, N.J.: Princeton University Press, 1961.

LEVIN, MARTIN A. *Urban Politics and the Criminal Courts.* Chicago: University of Chicago Press, 1977.

LI, VICTOR H. *Law without Lawyers: A Comparative View of Law in China and the United States.* Boulder, Colo.: Westview, 1978.

LOCKE, JOHN. *The Second Treatise of Government* (1690). Edited with an introduction by Thomas P. Reardon. New York: Liberal Arts Press, 1952.

MILL, JOHN STUART. *On Liberty* (1859). Edited with an introduction by Currin V. Shields. New York: Liberal Arts Press, 1956.

PACKER, HERBERT L. *The Limits of the Criminal Sanction.* Stanford, Calif.: Stanford University Press, 1968.

SCHEINGOLD, STUART. *The Politics of Law and Order.* New York: Longman, 1984.

SKOLNICK, JEROME H. *Justice without Trial: Law Enforcement in Democratic Society,* 2d ed. New York: Wiley, 1975.

SYKES, GRESHAM M. *The Society of Captives: A Study of a Maximum Security Prison.* Princeton, N.J.: Princeton University Press, 1958.

TOCQUEVILLE, ALEXIS DE. *Democracy in America* (1835). 2 vols. The Henry Reeve text (translation) as revised by Francis Bowen. Further corrected and edited with introduction, editorial notes, and bibliographies by Phillips Bradley. Foreword by Harold J. Laski. New York: Knopf, 1945.

TYLER, TOM, and BOECKMAN, ROBERT. "Three Strikes and You're Out, but Why? The Psychology of Public Support for Punishing Rule Breakers." *Law and Society Review* 31 (1997): 237.

Vera Institute of Justice. *Felony Arrests: Their Prosecution and Disposition in New York City's Courts.* Rev. ed. New York: Longman, 1981.

WALKER, SAMUEL E. *Popular Justice: A History of American Criminal Justice.* New York: Oxford University Press, 1980.

WILSON, JAMES Q. *Varieties of Police Behavior: The Management of Law and Order in Eight Communities.* Cambridge, Mass.: Harvard University Press, 1968.

POPULAR CULTURE

As anyone who has spent time watching television or going to the movies understands, crime and criminal justice occupy a prominent place in popular culture. The drama of the law violator brought to justice, the portrait of the lives and work of law enforcement officials, the stories of notorious, sometimes sensational crimes, and of justice done or justice denied are found every day as the common fare of the mass media. Crime and criminal justice live in culture as a set of images, as marvelous morality tales, as spectacles of the human effort to maintain "civilization" against the "forces of savagery." Indeed the semiotics of crime and punishment is all around us, not just in the architecture of the prison, or the speech made by a judge as she sends someone to the penal colony, but in both "high" and "popular" cultural iconography, in novels, television, and film.

Crime and criminal justice traditionally have been great subjects of cultural production, suggesting the powerful allure of the fall and of our responses to it. "The law," as Ewick and Silbey write, "seems to have a prominent cultural presence . . . , occupying a good part of our nation's popular media . . . . We watch real and fictitious trials on television, often unable to distinguish fact from fiction . . . . We hear reports of crime and criminals on the nightly local news. And . . . millions of us devote hours of our leisure time to reading stories about crime, courts, lawyers and law" (p. 16). In addition, since the early 1970s, politicians have made crime a salient, often dramatic part of American political culture. As a result, the Miranda warnings, or the rituals of interrogation and cross-examination in a criminal trial, or even the internal life of law firms, these and many more, have a rich and powerful vernacular life (Gaubatz; Friedman, 1999). Thus anyone interested in understanding these subjects must, sooner or later, attend to their complex cultural lives and the consequences of these cultural lives for citizens and for legal institutions.

Scholars traditionally have looked to portraits of crime, whether fictional or based in fact, as devices through which cultural boundaries are drawn, arguing that solidarity is created through acts of marking difference between self and other (Durkheim; Mead). Yet today research suggests a more complex picture of the place of crime in popular culture and of its consequences for the cultural life of criminal justice. Some of this work examines the treatment of crime in popular culture for what it says about the adequacy of our institutions, their capacity to accurately assign responsibility and do justice. Still other research examines the representation of crime and criminal justice in popular culture to assess its accuracy or comprehensiveness, with a view to trying to understand the sources of public attitudes toward crime and justice. Finally, scholars analyze the way images in the media contribute to the creation of folk knowledge and assess the impact of that folk knowledge on the criminal justice system.

Criminal justice as "spectacle"

Any account of contemporary scholarship on crime and popular culture must come to terms with Michel Foucault's account of public executions. Historically, Foucault writes, executions were "More than an act of justice"; they were a "manifestation of force" (p. 50). Public executions functioned as public theater; they were always centrally about display, in particular the display of the majestic, awesome power of sovereignty as it was materialized on the body of the condemned (Gatrell). Execution without a public audience was, as a result, meaningless (Spierenburg).

Following Foucault, scholars such as David Garland suggest that images of criminal punishment help "shape the overarching culture and contribute to the generation and regeneration of its terms" (p. 193). Punishment, Garland notes, is a set of signifying practices that "teaches, clarifies, dramatizes and authoritatively enacts some of the most basic moral-political categories and distinctions which help shape our symbolic universe" (p. 194). Popular culture treatments of punishment teach us how to think about categories like intention, responsibility, and injury, and they model the socially appropriate ways of responding to injury done to us.

One example of a study of the pedagogy of punishment as it is portrayed in popular culture is Sarat's treatment of the films *Dead Man Walking* and *Last Dance*. These films, and others like them, focus on the appropriate fit between crime and punishment. As is typical of most representations of crime and criminal justice in popular culture, neither of these films explores the social structural factors that some believe must be addressed in responding to crime; instead they are preoccupied with the question of personal responsibility. To the extent they contain an explanation of crime and a justification for punishment it is to be located in the autonomous choices of particular agents.

While building dramatic tension around the question of whether their hero/heroine deserves the death penalty, these films convey a powerful double message: First, legal subjects can, and will, be held responsible for their acts; second, they can, and should, internalize and *accept* responsibility. *Last Dance* and *Dead Man Walking* suggest that there can be, and is, a tight linkage between crime and punishment such that those personally responsible for the former can be legitimately subject to the latter.

In the way they address questions of responsibility, *Dead Man Walking* and *Last Dance*, as well as much film and television drama about crime and criminal justice, enact a conservative cultural politics, a politics in which large political questions about what state killing does to our law, politics, and our culture are largely ignored. They leave "audiences clueless about systematic inequities and arbitrariness" of the criminal justice system (Shapiro, p. 1145) and, in so doing, support existing mechanisms of criminal punishment.

Critique of criminal justice

However, other research on representations of crime in popular culture also calls attention to the fact that those representations are sometimes quite critical of the criminal justice system, reminding their consumers of the inefficiencies and inequities that plague the criminal justice system, and highlighting the place of extralegal forces in balancing the scales of justice (Hall et al.). One example of such research is Miller's analysis of Clint Eastwood's film *Unforgiven*.

Set in the "old west," *Unforgiven* depicts the quest of a group of prostitutes to buy justice for one of their number who was attacked by a customer. Clint Eastwood plays the reluctant hero who heeds their call. Yet throughout the film, while vengeance is presented as justified, as an equitable complement to law, it is not simply heroic. *Unforgiven*, Miller says, is at once a praise of revenge but also a caution about it, an invitation to do justice justly, to do it humbly, to do it no more than absolutely needs to be done.

Miller's work highlights the importance of revenge in popular representations of crime. Miller contends that our culture is deeply conflicted about the moral status of revenge. Nonetheless, revenge retains its appeal; it is a pervasive theme in "the movies most people pay to see, the TV they watch, or the novels they read" (p. 169).

"Implicit in stories of revenge," Miller argues, "is the suggestion that revenge is a criticism of state-delivered justice" (p. 174). This criticism is directed at law's technicality, its preoccupation with procedure. Miller's research shows how popular culture draws our attention to the failings and inadequacy of a legal order. Law may thus always be called to account by narratives that it cannot fully contain or control. Those narratives provide powerful reminders of the gap between the justice that law regularly provides and the justice that resonates most powerfully throughout our culture.

"Accuracy" of popular representations

Another strand of research on popular culture analyzes the treatment of crime and criminal justice on television, in film, and in political campaigns to assess its informational content, in particular to determine whether the images presented there adequately and accurately portray the realities of crime and justice in the United States (Sasson). Not surprisingly, most such studies note gaps between the accounts provided in the mass media and the "facts." As Friedman notes, "popular culture, as reflected in the media, is not, and cannot be taken as, an accurate mirror of the actual state of living law . . . Cop shows aim for entertainment, excitement; they are not documentaries . . . Crime shows . . . over-represent violent crimes; shoplifting is no great audience-holder, but murder is" (1989, p. 1588; also Graber).

This same concern for the accuracy of portraits of crime has been influential in studies of the treatment of crime in political campaigns. One famous example of the "manipulation" of images of crime for political purposes is provided by George Bush's use of the controversial "Willie Horton" TV ads in the presidential campaign of 1988. These ads created a narrative nightmare of escape from punishment that resonated with public fears of criminal violence. The Horton narrative did so by making a black man who senselessly brutalized a white couple the symbolic representation of Michael Dukakis's alleged criminal justice policy failure. This narrative has provided the bedrock for both political rhetoric and the consciousness of crime and punishment ever since.

The Horton advertisements blamed Dukakis for the occurrence of senseless, brutal crimes because of his alleged policy of letting serious violent offenders back into society far too soon. The first ad showed a revolving door with running text warning that 268 convicts escaped while on furlough and a voice-over stating that many leave prison early to commit crime again. The second ad provided emotional testimony about Dukakis's record of failed furloughs and vetoes of capital punishment.

Kathleen Hall Jamieson has demonstrated the substantial effect of these ads on the public's consciousness of crime and punishment. She describes, for example, how a nine-member Dallas focus group that favored Dukakis by five to four early in the campaign shifted support to Bush by a seven-to-two margin shortly after the airing of the Horton ads. Analyzing this change Jamieson notes that "the cues in the media have triggered a broad chain of associations" (p. 35). She observes that the Horton narrative—"murderer released to murder again"—had a powerful resonance with the public's fear of violent crime and desire for a commonsense explanation for why it occurs. In Jamieson's words, the Horton ad "completes in a satisfying manner a narrative that is already cast with a menacing murderer in a mug shot; anguished, outraged victims; and an unrepentant, soft-on-crime liberal" (p. 36).

The captivating character of the Horton narrative was evident in another aspect of public response. In particular, over time, focus group members became resistant to evidence that might debunk the accusations against Dukakis. Despite statistics documenting the overall success of the Massachusetts furlough program, as well as statistics from the federal government showing higher rates of early release and recidivism in California under Governor Ronald Reagan, one group member was provoked to respond, "You can't change my mind with all of that. . . ." Another focus group member dismissed statistical evidence: "We should ship all our criminals to the college liberals in College Station . . . or Austin. Crime's not statistics, honey" (Jamieson, pp. 31–32).

Jamieson blames the media as a willing, sometimes eager, accomplice in creating distorted perceptions. The media, she suggests, did little to disabuse the public of the misimpression that Dukakis promoted an irresponsible and failed policy of early release, or to get the details or context of the Horton story across. However, to the extent that the Horton ads hit home, it may have been because they tapped into, rather than created, the prevailing cultural commonsense. As Ericson notes, the relationship between the media and the public involves a "process of discursive struggle and negotiation" (p. 237).

Impact of popular culture

A final kind of work takes this idea of "discursive struggle and negotiation" seriously as it examines the impact of media accounts, whether on the news or in dramatic programming, on "folk knowledge," with a view to understanding not the accuracy of that knowledge but rather its impact on the criminal justice system itself.

Steiner, Bowers, and Sarat (2000), to take one example, describe the impact of representations of crime and justice in shaping folk knowledge concerning the punishment of murderers not given a death sentence. In particular they seek to understand how long people believe those sentenced to life in prison actually serve. They find that most people believe that convicted murderers sentenced to life in prison do not serve life, but are instead released early. The impression of leniency is conveyed best, perhaps, by news accounts of the recidivism of ex-convicts or persons on probation, parole, or furlough from prison (Hall et al.; Barak). Such cases easily become the focal points for public debate about the "crime problem" and how it should be dealt with (Roberts and Doob).

As a result, Steiner, Bowers, and Sarat contend most citizens give time-served estimates that fall below the mandatory minimum for parole eligibility for first degree murderers in their states. The single most common estimate of the amount of time convicted murderers who are given life sentences actually serve is "less than ten years." This relatively low estimate is consistent with the kind of narrative representation contained in the news media and in film and on television (Ericson, Baranek, and Chan).

Most importantly, Steiner, Bowers, and Sarat (2000) suggest folk knowledge has an important influence on how citizens behave when they are given decision-making power in the criminal justice system, namely when they serve as jurors in capital cases. They report that when jurors deliberate specifically about what the punishment should be, their specific release estimates become especially salient. In the context of group decision-making, folk knowledge of the timing of release is the currency of negotiation and decision-making. Jurors whose folk knowledge leads them to believe that murderers are less likely to be released early if given a life sentence may be more open to mitigating evidence and argument during sentencing deliberations. By contrast, believing that the defendant would soon be released may close jurors minds to mitigation, and hence to a sentence less than death. Thus folk knowledge of crime and punishment not only shapes individual judgments, but it also short-circuits existing legal procedures (in this case the requirement to consider mitigating evidence).

Conclusion

Examining the representation of crime and criminal justice in popular culture reveals that these representations are both ubiquitous and highly consequential. Whether they reinforce prevailing ideas of criminal responsibility or critique the adequacy of formal legal institutions or their capacity to do justice, whether conveying accurate information or helping to create a stock of folk knowledge about crime and punishment, these representations mean that crime is neither an esoteric subject nor one far removed from the consciousness of ordinary Americans.

Research on the images of crime and criminal justice available in popular culture suggests that those images empower citizens, giving them a conception of the crime problem and the state's response to it that has a source independent of those whose legal authority derives from formal training or official position. It means that law can, and does, live in society, in ways that cannot readily be confined or controlled by state law. It also means that citizens can and will judge the seriousness of the crime problem and the state's responses to it in terms of a widespread cultural common sense. Presented with what they regard as cultural nonsense, they make recourse to their own store of folk knowledge, their own repertoire of legal understandings. The result, as Yngvesson notes, is that popular consciousness of crime and criminal justice may become "a force contributing to the production of legal order rather than . . . simply an anomaly or a pocket of consciousness outside of law, irrelevant to its maintenance and transformation" (p. 1693).

AUSTIN SARAT

See also FEAR OF CRIME; LITERATURE AND CRIME; PUBLIC OPINION AND CRIME.

BIBLIOGRAPHY

BARAK, GREGG. "Between the Waves: Mass Mediated Themes of Crime and Justice." *Social Justice* 21 (1994): 133–147.

DURKHEIM, ÉMILE. *The Division of Labor in Society.* Translated by G. Simpson. New York: Free Press, 1933.

ERICSON, RICHARD V. "Mass Media, Crime, Law, and Justice." *British Journal of Criminology* 31 (1991): 219–249.

ERICSON, RICHARD V.; BARANEK, PATRICIA M.; and CHAN, JANET B. L. *Representing Order: Crime, Law, and Justice in the News Media.* Toronto: University of Toronto Press, 1991.

EWICK, PATRICIA, and SILBEY, SUSAN. *The Common Place of Law: Stories from Everyday Life*. Chicago: University of Chicago Press, 1998.

FOUCAULT, MICHEL. *Discipline and Punish*. Translated by Alan Sheridan New York: Vintage Books, 1977.

FRIEDMAN, LAWRENCE. "Law, Lawyers, and Popular Culture." *Yale Law Journal* 98 (1989): 1579–1606.

———. "On Stage: Some Historical Notes About Criminal Justice." In *Social Science, Social Policy and the Law*. Edited by Patricia Ewick, Robert Kagan, and Austin Sarat. New York: Russell Sage Foundation, 1999.

GARLAND, DAVID. "Punishment and Culture: The Symbolic Dimension of Criminal Justice." *Studies in Law, Politics, and Society* 11 (1991): 191–224.

GATRELL, V. A. C. *The Hanging Tree: Execution and the English People 1770–1868*. New York: Oxford University Press, 1994.

GAUBATZ, KATHLYN. *Crime in the Public Mind*. Ann Arbor: University of Michigan Press, 1994.

GRABER, DORIS A. *Crime News and the Public*. New York: Praeger, 1980.

HALL, STUART; CRITCHER, CHARLES; JEFFERSON, TONY; CLARKE, JOHN; and ROBERTS, BRIAN. *Policing the Crisis: Mugging, the State, and Law and Order*. London: Macmillan, 1978.

JAMIESON, KATHLEEN HALL. *Dirty Politics*. New York: Oxford University Press, 1992.

MEAD, GEORGE HERBERT. "The Psychology of Punitive Justice." *The American Journal of Sociology* (1918): 577–602.

MILLER, WILLIAM. "Clint Eastwood and Equity: Popular Culture's Theory of Revenge." In *Law in the Domains of Culture*. Edited by Austin Sarat and Thomas Kearns. Ann Arbor: University of Michigan Press, 1998.

ROBERTS, JULIAN, and DOOB, A. N. "News Media Influences on Public Views of Sentencing." *Law & Human Behavior* 14 (1991): 451–468.

SARAT, AUSTIN. "The Cultural Life of Capital Punishment: Responsibility and Representation in *Dead Man Walking* and *Last Dance*." *Yale Journal of Law & the Humanities* 11 (1998): 153–190.

SASSON, THEODORE. *Crime Talk*. New York: de Gruyter, 1995.

STEINER, BENJAMIN; BOWERS, WILLIAM; and SARAT, AUSTIN. "Folk Knowledge as Legal Action: Death Penalty Judgments and the Tenet of Early Release in a Culture of Mistrust and Punitiveness." *Law & Society Review* 33 (1999): 461–506.

SHAPIRO, CAROLE. "Do or Die: Does *Dead Man Walking* Run?" *University of San Francisco Law Review* 30 (1994): 1143–1166.

SPIERENBURG, PETRUS. *The Spectacle of Suffering*. Cambridge, U.K.: Cambridge University Press, 1984.

YNGVESSON, BARBARA. "Inventing Law in Local Settings: Rethinking Popular Legal Culture." *Yale Law Journal* 98 (1989): 1689–1710.

PREDICTION OF CRIME AND RECIDIVISM

In the *Protagoras,* Plato states that "he who undertakes to punish with reason does not avenge himself for past offence, since he cannot make what was done as though it had not come to pass; he looks rather to the future, and aims at preventing that particular person . . . from doing wrong again" (p. 139). Twenty-four hundred years later, preventing crime by predicting who is likely to commit it and intervening in their lives to deflect the prediction is ubiquitous in the legal system. Decisions as to who should go to prison (sentencing) and when they should be let out (parole) are in substantial part predictive decisions. Assessments of the probability of future crime influence the judicial choice of whether to grant release of an offender on bail pending trial and whether to treat a juvenile as a juvenile or to waive him or her to adult court. The U.S. Supreme Court has stated that it was permissible for a state to make the imposition of the death penalty contingent upon a prediction that a murderer, unless executed, would be likely to offend again. "It is, of course, not easy to predict future behavior," Justice John Paul Stevens wrote. "The fact that such a determination is difficult, however, does not mean that it cannot be made" (*Jurek v. Texas,* 428 U.S. 262 (1976)) (see Monahan and Walker for a review of caselaw in this area).

This prevention-through-prediction strategy can take the form of *changing* the people who are predicted to be criminal, for example, by subjecting them to treatment in order to lower the probability that they will commit a crime. Alternatively, prevention can take the form of *isolating* those who are predicted to be criminal by incapacitating them in an institution, so as to deprive them of potential victims. Reviewing the history of prediction in Anglo-American law, Alan Dershowitz concluded that "the preventive confinement of dangerous persons. . .who are thought likely to cause serious injury in the future has always been practiced, to some degree, by every society in history regardless of the jurisprudential rhetoric employed. . . . Moreover, it is likely that some forms of preventive confinement will continue to be practiced by every society" (p. 57).

Preventive confinement certainly is increasingly practiced in the United States. In *Kansas v. Hendricks,* 521 U.S. 346 (1997), the Supreme Court upheld a civil means of lengthening the detention of certain criminal offenders scheduled for release from prison. Kansas' Sexually Violent Predator Act established procedures for commitment to mental hospitals of persons who, while they do not have a "major mental disorder" (such as schizophrenia), do have a "mental abnormality" (such as, in Hendricks's case, the personality disorder of "pedophilia") which makes them "likely to engage in predatory acts of sexual violence" (p. 357). A "mental abnormality" was defined in the act as a "congenital or acquired condition affecting the emotional or volitional capacity which predisposes the person to commit sexually violent offenses in a degree constituting such person a menace to the health and safety of others" (p. 352). The Court stated:

A finding of dangerousness, standing alone, is ordinarily not a sufficient ground upon which to justify indefinite involuntary commitment. We have sustained civil commitment statutes when they have coupled proof of dangerousness with the proof of some additional factor, such as a "mental illness" or "mental abnormality." These added statutory requirements serve to limit involuntary civil confinement to those who suffer from a volitional impairment rendering them dangerous beyond their control. . . . The precommitment requirement of a "mental abnormality" or "personality disorder" is consistent with the requirements of these other statutes that we have upheld in that it narrows the class of persons eligible for confinement to those who are unable to control their dangerousness. (p. 358)

It was not until the twentieth century that attempts were made to systematize the crime prediction process. In 1928, E. W. Burgess examined the official records of several thousand former inmates of Illinois prisons and identified numerous factors, such as prior criminal record and age at release, that were associated with the commission of crime on parole. This "experience table," as he called it (which would now be termed "statistical" or "actuarial" prediction), was then used to assess the suitability of other offenders for parole release. "Thus began a criminological research tradition characterized by the production of increasingly sophisticated instruments for predicting criminal behavior. . . . Indeed, it may be said that most later work has been largely a refinement and elaboration of Burgess' basic method" (American Justice Institute, p. 7).

Prediction by means of statistical tables, however, has been only one of two approaches used in forecasting the occurrence of crime. The other approach is generally known as "clinical" prediction. This method involves experts examining an offender and rendering an opinion based upon their subjective weighing of the factors they believe relevant to the commission of future crime. Only since the 1970s have there been scientific attempts to evaluate the accuracy of clinical predictions.

This entry will selectively review the empirical literature on the prediction of criminal behavior that has been published since the report of the President's Commission on Law Enforcement and Administration of Justice in 1967. (Reviews of studies published between Burgess's work in 1928 and the report of the President's Commission can be found in Gottfredson.) This article will also place emphasis on the prediction of violent forms of criminal behavior, rather than of property offenses. First, however, it is necessary to review briefly four key concepts in predictive decision-making.

Predictor and criterion variables

The prediction process requires that a person be assessed twice. At Time One, he or she is placed into certain categories that are believed, for whatever reason, to relate to the behavior being predicted. If one is interested in predicting how well a person will do in college, the categories might be grades in high school, letters from teachers (rated, for example, as "very good," "good," or "poor"), and the quality of the essay written for the application (perhaps scored on a scale of 1 through 10). These are all *predictor variables*—categories consisting of different levels that are presumed to be relevant to what is being predicted. For criminal behavior, the predictor variables might include frequency of past criminal acts, age, or degree of impulse control.

At some specified later point, Time Two, another assessment of the person is performed to ascertain whether he or she has or has not done what was predicted. This entails assessing the person on one or more criterion variables. For predicting success in college, the criterion variables might be college grades, class rank, or whether or not the person obtained a job in the field that person wanted (scored simply as "yes" or "no"). For criminal behavior, the criterion variables may include self-report, either arrest or conviction for certain crimes, or involuntary commitment to a mental hospital as a person dangerous to others.

Outcome of positive and negative predictions

There are four statistical outcomes that can occur when one is faced with making a prediction of any kind of future behavior. One can either predict that the behavior, in this case crime, will take place or that it will not take place. At the end of some specified period, one observes whether the predicted behavior actually has taken place or has not taken place.

If one predicts that crime will take place and later finds that this has indeed happened, the prediction is called a *true positive*. One has made a positive prediction and it has turned out to be correct, or true. Similarly, if one predicts that crime will not take place and it in fact does not, the prediction is called a *true negative*, since one has made a negative prediction of crime and it turned out to be true. These, of course, are the two outcomes that one wishes to maximize in making predictions.

There are also two kinds of mistakes that can be made. If one predicts that crime will take place and it does not, the outcome is called a *false positive*. A positive prediction was made and it turned out to be incorrect, or false. In practice, this kind of mistake usually means that a person has been unnecessarily detained to prevent a crime that would not have taken place in any event. If one predicts that violence will not take place and it does, the outcome is called a *false negative*. In practice, this kind of mistake often means that someone who is not detained, or who is released from detention, commits a criminal act in the community. Obviously, predictors of violence try to minimize these two outcomes.

Decision rules. Decision rules involve choosing a "cutting score" on some predictive scale, above which one predicts, for the purpose of intervention, that an event will happen. A cutting score is simply a particular point on some objective or subjective scale. When one sets a thermostat at 68°, for example, one is establishing a cutting score for the operation of a heating unit. When the temperature drops below 68° the

heat comes on, and when it goes above 68° the heat goes off. The "beyond a reasonable doubt" standard of proof in the criminal law is a cutting score for the degree of certainty that a juror must have in order to vote for conviction. Conviction is to take place only if doubt is "unreasonable." In the context of parole prediction, one could state that if a prisoner has a higher than X probability of recidivism, he or she should be denied parole for a given period.

Base rate

The term *base rate* refers to the proportion of individuals in the group being examined who can be expected to engage in violent criminality. It is the average, or "chance," rate that prediction seeks to improve upon. Prediction schemes can be evaluated either in terms of how well they differentiate true and false positives or in terms of how much they improve on the base rates. Thus, in the Michigan parole prediction study discussed below, the base rate for violent recidivism among all persons released from prison was 10 percent. A prediction scale was devised that could identify one subgroup of which 40 percent committed a violent crime after release. This device, therefore, improved on the base rate by a factor of four, although 60 percent of the individuals predicted to be violent were still false positives.

Statistical prediction

Here we consider four studies representative of the best of actuarial prediction. Ernst Wenk, James Robison, and Gerald Smith in 1972 reviewed several massive studies on the prediction of violent crime undertaken in the California Department of Corrections. One study, begun in 1965, attempted to develop a "violence prediction scale" to aid in parole decision-making. The predictive items employed included commitment offense, number of prior commitments, heroin use, and length of imprisonment. When validated against discovered acts of actual violent crime by parolees, the scale was able to identify a small class of offenders (less than 3 percent of the total) of whom 14 percent could be expected to be violent. The probability of violence for this class was nearly three times greater than that for parolees in general, only 5 percent of whom, by the same criteria, could be expected to be violent. However, 86 percent of those identified as potentially violent were not, in fact, discovered to have committed a violent crime while on parole.

The State of Michigan Department of Corrections in 1978 introduced an actuarial prediction device, the Assaultive Risk Screening Sheet, for use in program assignment and parole decision-making. Data on 350 variables were collected for over two thousand male inmates released on parole for an average of fourteen months in 1971. Statistical analyses were performed on the data for half the subjects to derive an actuarial table relating to arrest for a new violent crime while on parole. The resulting factors were then applied to the other half of the subjects in order to validate the predictive accuracy of the scale. The six items in the table were: "crime description fits robbery, sex assault, or murder," "serious institutional misconduct," "first arrest before 15th birthday," "reported juvenile felony," "crime description fits any assaultive felony," and "ever married." Using combinations of these items it was possible to place the offenders into five discrete categories: very low risk (2.0 percent recidivism), low risk (6.3 percent), middle risk (11.8 percent), high risk (20.7 percent), and very high risk (40.0 percent).

A noteworthy advance in the development of actuarial risk assessment to predict violence in the community was reported by Quinsey, Harris, Rice, and Cormier. A sample of over six hundred men who were either treated or administered a pretrial assessment at a maximum security forensic hospital in Canada served as subjects. All had been charged with a serious criminal offense. A wide variety of predictive variables were coded from institutional files. The criterion variable was any new criminal charge for a violent offense, or return to the institution for an act that would otherwise have resulted in such a charge. The average time at risk after release was almost seven years. Twelve variables were identified for inclusion in the final statistical prediction instrument, including an offender's score on the Hare Psychopathy Checklist, alcohol abuse, and elementary school maladjustment. If the scores on this instrument were dichotomized into "high" and "low," the results indicated that 55 percent of the "high scoring" subjects committed violent recidivism, compared with 19 percent of the "low scoring" group.

Along these lines, a major meta-analysis of actuarial risk factors for crime and violence among mentally disordered offenders, (Bonta, Law, and Hanson) found those risk factors to be remarkably similar to well-known risk factors among the general offender population:

Criminal history, antisocial personality, substance abuse, and family dysfunction are important for mentally disordered offenders as they are for general offenders. In fact, the results support the theoretical perspective that the major correlates of crime are the same, regardless of race, gender, class, and the presence or absence of mental illness (p. 139).

Finally, Steadman and colleagues studied actuarial risk assessment among a sample of men and women discharged into the community from acute psychiatric facilities. Using 134 risk factors measured in the hospital, they were able to classify approximately three-quarters of the patients into one of two risk categories. "High violence risk" patients were defined as being at least twice as likely as the average patient to commit a violent act within the first twenty weeks following hospital discharge. "Low violence risk" patients were defined as being at most half as likely as the average patient to commit a violent act within the first twenty weeks following hospital discharge. Since 18.7 percent of all patients committed at least one violent act toward another during this period, this meant that high violence risk patients had at least a 37 percent likelihood of being violent and low violence risk patients had at most a 9 percent likelihood of being violent. The actual rate of violence observed in the high risk group was 44 percent and in the low risk group was 4 percent.

Clinical prediction

Despite its long history and obvious advantage of economy and reproducibility, a statistical approach is used in only a minority of predictive decision-making points in the criminal justice system. Primary reliance is placed on the use of intuitive human judgment in many situations calling for a prediction of future crime.

Many studies have attempted to validate the ability of psychiatrists and psychologists to predict violent behavior. Here we consider three of the best ones. Harry Kozol, Richard Boucher, and Ralph Garofalo conducted a ten-year study involving almost six hundred male offenders, most of whom had been convicted of violent sex crimes. At the Massachusetts Center for the Diagnosis and Treatment of Dangerous Persons, each offender was examined independently by at least two psychiatrists, two psychologists, and a social worker. These clinical examinations, along with a full psychological test battery and "a meticulous reconstruction of the life history elicited from multiple sources—the patient himself, his family, friends, neighbors, teachers, employers, and court, correctional and mental hospital record" (p. 383), formed the database for their predictions.

Of the 592 patients admitted to their facility for diagnostic observation, 435 were released. Kozol and his associates recommended the release of 386 as nondangerous and opposed the release of 49 as dangerous, with the court deciding otherwise. During the five-year follow-up period, 8 percent of those predicted not to be dangerous became recidivists by committing a serious assaultive act, and 35 percent of those predicted to be dangerous committed such an act.

In 1966, the Supreme Court held that Johnnie Baxstrom had been denied equal protection of the law by being detained beyond his maximum sentence in an institution for the criminally insane without the benefit of a new hearing to determine his current dangerousness (*Baxstrom v. Herold*, 383 U.S. 107 (1966)). The ruling resulted in the transfer of nearly one thousand persons reputed to be some of the most "dangerous" mental patients in the state of New York from hospitals for the criminally insane to civil mental hospitals. It also provided an excellent opportunity for naturalist research on the validity of the psychiatric predictions of dangerousness upon which the extended detentions were based.

In their classic 1974 study of careers of the criminally insane, Henry Steadman and Joseph Cocozza found that the level of violence experienced in the civil mental hospitals was much less than had been feared, that the civil hospitals adapted well to the massive transfer of patients, and that the Baxstrom patients received the same treatment as the civil patients. Only 20 percent of the Baxstrom patients were assaultive to persons in the civil hospital or the community at any time during the four years after their transfer. Furthermore, only 3 percent were sufficiently dangerous to be returned to a hospital for the criminally insane during a four-year period after the decision. The researchers followed 121 Baxstrom patients who had been released into the community, that is, discharged from both the criminal and civil mental hospitals. During an average of two and a half years of freedom, only 9 of the 121 patients (7.5 percent) were convicted of a crime, and only one of those convictions was for a violent act.

Lidz, Mulvey, and Gardner (1993) took as their subjects not prisoners but rather male and female patients being examined in the acute psy-

chiatric emergency room of a large civil hospital. Psychiatrists and nurses were asked to assess potential patient violence to others over the next six-month period. Violence was measured by official records, by patient self-report, and by the report of a collateral informant in the community (e.g., a family member). Patients who elicited professional concern regarding future violence were found to be significantly more likely to be violent after discharge (53 percent) than were patients who had not elicited such concern (36 percent). The accuracy of clinical prediction did not vary as a function of the patient's age or race. The accuracy of clinicians' predictions of male violence substantially exceeded chance levels, both for patients with and without a prior history of violent behavior. In contrast, the accuracy of clinicians' predictions of female violence did not differ from chance. While the actual rate of violent incidents among released female patients (49 percent) was higher than the rate among released male patients (42 percent), the clinicians had predicted that only 22 percent of the women would be violent, compared with predicting that 45 percent of the men would commit a violent act. The inaccuracy of clinicians at predicting violence among women appeared to be a function of the clinicians' serious underestimation of the base rate of violence among mentally disordered women (perhaps due to an inappropriate extrapolation from the great gender differences in rates of violence among persons without mental disorder).

Conclusions and implications

In no sense do the data on the prediction of criminal behavior compel their own policy implications. Given that the level of predictive validity revealed in the research has at least in the case of violent crime been rather modest, one could use the data to argue for across-the-board reductions in the length of institutionalization of prisoners: since society cannot be sure who will do harm, it should detain no one. Alternatively, and with equal fervor and logic, one could use the same data to argue for across-the-board increases in the length of institutionalization: since society cannot be sure which offenders will be nonviolent, it should keep them all in. Whether one uses the data in support of the first or the second of these implications will depend upon how one assesses and weighs the various costs and benefits associated with each, or upon the nonutilitarian principles for punishment that one adopts. In regard to the former approach, the principal impediment to developing straightforward cost-benefit ratios for predictive decision-making is the lack of a common scale along which to order both costs and benefits. For example, how are "years in a prison" to be compared with rapes, robberies, murders, or assaults prevented? John Monahan and David Wexler (p. 38) have argued in this regard that when a behavioral scientist predicts that a person will be "dangerous" to the extent that state intervention is needed, that scientist is making three separable assertions:

1. The individual being examined has certain characteristics.
2. These characteristics are associated with a certain probability of violent behavior.
3. The probability of violent behavior is sufficiently great to justify preventive intervention.

The first two of these assertions, Monahan and Wexler hold, are professional judgments within the expertise of the behavioral sciences—judgments that can, of course, be challenged in court. The third is a social-policy statement that must be arrived at through the political process, and upon which the behavioral scientist should have no more say than any other citizen. What the behavioral scientist should do, they argue, is to present and defend an estimate of the probability that the individual will engage in criminal behavior. Judges and legislators, however, should decide whether this probability of criminal behavior is sufficient to justify preventive interventions because they are the appropriate persons to weigh competing claims among social values in a democratic society.

Barbara Underwood has asserted that one cannot evaluate the usefulness of prediction from a policy perspective other than in the context of the feasible alternatives to prediction as a basis for making decisions. In the sentencing and parole context, the principal alternative to making decisions on the basis of prediction is making them on retributive grounds. There have been numerous proposals, based in part upon dissatisfaction with the research findings reviewed above, to abandon prediction altogether and limit criminal disposition to consideration of "just deserts" for the crime committed (von Hirsch). The chief difficulty here, however, lies in the assessment of what constitutes "just deserts" for a given criminal behavior. Although the relative ranking of deserved punishments for

given crimes is reliable (everyone agrees that murder deserves more punishment than jaywalking), the absolute punishment to be "justly" ascribed is determinable by social consensus only within a broad range. If for no other reason than the lack of any workable alternative, the prediction of criminal behavior is likely to remain an essential aspect of the criminal justice system.

JOHN MONAHAN

See also CRIME CAUSATION: BIOLOGICAL THEORIES; CRIME CAUSATION: PSYCHOLOGICAL THEORIES; CRIME CAUSATION: SOCIOLOGICAL THEORIES; CRIMINOLOGY: MODERN CONTROVERSIES; INCAPACITATION; PROBATION AND PAROLE: HISTORY, GOALS, AND DECISION-MAKING; PROBATION AND PAROLE: PROCEDURAL PROTECTION; PROBATION AND PAROLE: SUPERVISION; SCIENTIFIC EVIDENCE; SENTENCING: GUIDELINES; SENTENCING: PRESENTENCE REPORT: VIOLENCE.

BIBLIOGRAPHY

AMERICAN JUSTICE INSTITUTE, with the National Council on Crime and Delinquency. *Sentencing and Parole Release*. Classification Instruments for Criminal Justice Decisions, vol. 4. Washington, D.C.: U.S. Department of Justice, National Institute of Corrections, 1979.

BONTA, JAMES; LAW, MOIRA; and HANSON, KARL. "The Prediction of Criminal and Violent Recidivism among Mentally Disordered Offenders: A Meta-Analysis." *Psychological Bulletin* 123 (1998): 123–142.

BURGESS, ERNEST W. et al. *The Working of the Indeterminate Sentencing Law in the Parole System in Illinois*. Springfield: Illinois Parole Board, 1928.

DERSHOWITZ, ALAN M. "The Origins of Preventive Confinement in Anglo-American Law: The English Experience." *University of Cincinnati Law Review* 43 (1974): 1–60.

GOTTFREDSON, DON M. "Assessment and Prediction Methods in Crime and Delinquency." *Task Force Report. Juvenile Delinquency and Youth Crime*. Washington, D.C.: President's Commission on Law Enforcement and Administration of Justice, Task Force on Juvenile Delinquency, 1967.

KOZOL, HARRY L.; BOUCHER, RICHARD J.; and GAROFALO, RALPH E. "The Diagnosis and Treatment of Dangerousness." *Crime and Delinquency* 18 (1972): 371–392.

LIDZ, CHARLES; MULVEY, EDWARD; and GARDNER, WILLIAM. "The Accuracy of Predictions of Violence to Others." *Journal of the American Medical Association* 269 (1993): 1007–1011.

MONAHAN, JOHN. *The Clinical Prediction of Violent Behavior*. Rockville, Md.: U.S. Department of Health and Human Services, Public Health Service, Alcohol, Drug Abuse, and Mental Health Administration, National Institute of Mental Health, 1981.

———. "Clinical and actuarial predictions of violence." In *Modern Scientific Evidence: The Law and Science of Expert Testimony*. Edited by D. Faigman, D. Kaye, M. Saks, and J. Sanders. St. Paul, Minn.: West Publishing Company, 1997. Pages 300–318.

MONAHAN, JOHN, and WALKER, LAURENS. *Social Science in Law: Cases and Materials*. Westbury, N.Y.: Foundation Press, 1998.

MONAHAN, JOHN, and WEXLER, DAVID B. "A Definite Maybe: Proof and Probability in Civil Commitment." *Law and Human Behavior* 2 (1978): 37–42.

PLATO. *Protagoras*. Translated by W. R. M. Lamb. Loeb Classical Library, vol. 4. London: Heinemann, 1925.

President's Commission on Law Enforcement and Administration of Justice. *The Challenge of Crime in a Free Society*. Washington, D.C.: The Commission, 1967.

QUINSEY, VERNON; HARRIS, GRANT; RICE, MARNIE; and CORMIER, CATHERINE. *Violent Offenders: Appraising and Managing Risk*. Washington, D.C.: American Psychological Association, 1998.

State of Michigan, Department of Corrections. *Information on Michigan Department of Corrections' Risk Screening*. Lansing, Mich.: The Department, 1978.

STEADMAN, HENRY J. "A New Look at Recidivism among Patuxent Inmates." *Bulletin of the American Academy of Psychiatry and the Law* 5 (1977): 200–209.

STEADMAN, HENRY J., and COCOZZA, JOSEPH J. *Careers of the Criminally Insane: Excessive Social Control of Deviance*. Lexington, Mass.: Heath, Lexington Books, 1974.

STEADMAN, HENRY; SILVER, ERIC; MONAHAN, JOHN; APPELBAUM, PAUL; ROBBINS, PAMELA; MULVEY, EDWARD; GRISSO, THOMAS; ROTH, LOREN; and BANKS, STEVEN. "A Classification Tree Approach to the Development of Actuarial Violence Risk Assessment Tools." *Law and Human Behavior* 24 (2000): 83–100.

UNDERWOOD, BARBARA D. "Law and the Crystal Ball: Predicting Behavior with Statistical Inference and Individualized Judgment." *Yale Law Journal* 88 (1979): 1408–1448.

VON HIRSCH, ANDREW. *Doing Justice. The Choice of Punishments*. New York: Hill & Wang, 1976.

WENK, ERNST A.; ROBISON, JAMES O.; and SMITH, GERALD W. "Can Violence Be Predicted?" *Crime and Delinquency* 18 (1972): 393–402.

PRELIMINARY HEARING

The purpose of a preliminary hearing is to determine whether the prosecutor has enough evidence to justify further criminal proceedings against the accused. The preliminary hearing is held in open court before a judge or magistrate. After the prosecution has presented its evidence and the defense has been given a chance to respond, the judicial officer decides whether there is probable cause to believe that the accused committed the crime charged. If the court finds probable cause, or in some jurisdictions "prima facie case," it will "bind the case over" to the grand jury or the trial court for further proceedings. If the evidence is insufficient, the charges are dismissed. The goal is to ensure that weak cases are eliminated early in the process, to save the defendant the anxiety and expense of having to defend himself at a trial against unwarranted accusations.

A procedural overview

Within forty-eight hours of arrest, a suspect typically has a "first appearance" before a magistrate. At that hearing the magistrate will advise the arrested person of the charges, appoint counsel if the suspect is indigent, and set bail. In addition, unless the suspect was taken into custody pursuant to an arrest warrant or following an indictment, the magistrate will ensure that there is probable cause to believe that the suspect committed the offense so as to justify the suspect's continued detention or other restraints on the suspect's liberty. This probable cause determination is often based in whole or in large part on the sufficiency of the criminal complaint; the suspect normally does not have the chance to introduce contrary evidence.

Also at the first appearance, the magistrate will often schedule the preliminary hearing (also called a "preliminary examination"). In the federal system the hearing is to be held within ten days of the first appearance if the suspect is in custody, and within twenty days if he is not in custody. Many states have comparable time limits, or may simply require that the hearing be held within a reasonable period after arrest. These time limits may be extended by the court with the consent of the defendant, or on a showing of extraordinary circumstances that justify the delay.

In contrast to the first appearance, the preliminary hearing is adversarial. The prosecution has the burden to convince the magistrate that there is probable cause to believe that a crime was committed and that the defendant committed it. The prosecutor may present witnesses, physical and documentary evidence to satisfy this burden. The defendant has the chance to make responsive arguments, to cross-examine the government's witnesses, and to present witnesses and other evidence of his own in an effort to show that probable cause is lacking. The suspect also has the right to be assisted by counsel, since a preliminary hearing is a "critical stage" in the pretrial process. The right to counsel is provided for in all jurisdictions by statute or court rule, although some lower courts have held that the failure to provide counsel may constitute harmless error. Also in contrast to the first appearance, a finding of no probable cause at a preliminary hearing will result in the dismissal (without prejudice) of charges against the defendant, rather than merely the release of the defendant from custody.

The preliminary hearing has some of the attributes of a trial, but there are important differences. The most obvious difference is that the court does not decide guilt or innocence; it simply decides whether the case should proceed toward trial. In addition, the rules of evidence often do not apply, and in many states and the federal system, the use of hearsay is explicitly authorized. This means that the prosecution need not, and frequently will not, present the witnesses who will testify at trial, thereby limiting the value of the defendant's right of cross-examination. Evidence that was obtained illegally is also admissible at preliminary hearings in many jurisdictions. In its discretion, however, the court may require a showing that admissible evidence will be available at the time of trial.

Another important difference between a preliminary hearing and a trial is that the magistrate can limit the suspect's ability to present a defense. Defense counsel's cross-examination of the government's witnesses may be cut off if the magistrate believes that counsel is simply trying to obtain discovery of the prosecutor's case, or is trying to generate a credibility dispute. Because the purpose of the hearing is to weigh the sufficiency of the prosecutor's evidence, most courts will say that disputes about the facts, including questions of credibility, are the province of the trial jury and are not the proper subjects of questioning. These limits on the defense present no federal constitutional concerns, because the Supreme Court has ruled that the confrontation clause of the Sixth Amendment generally does not require that the accused be afforded the right of cross-examination at a preliminary hearing.

Under the same reasoning, magistrates may limit or prevent testimony or cross-examination that is designed to elicit information regarding affirmative defenses; while these defenses could lead to an acquittal at trial, in many jurisdictions courts will find that they do not negate the existence of probable cause. In other jurisdictions, however, magistrates will permit the suspect to present evidence of affirmative defenses, and may even make limited credibility findings. These courts reason that for the preliminary hearing to serve its intended role, charges that appear to have little chance of success at trial should be promptly dismissed.

At the close of the hearing, the magistrate decides if there is probable cause to continue the case. The precise meaning of probable cause in this context is unclear. Many courts use the same standard that is required to sustain an arrest, but others use a more rigorous standard. In the latter jurisdictions the magistrate will find probable cause only if the prosecutor establishes a prima facie case of guilt, that is, when the evidence presented, if unexplained, would warrant a conviction at trial.

If the magistrate finds probable cause, the case is "bound over." In jurisdictions where grand jury review is required, the case is bound over to the grand jury. Note that the outcome of the preliminary hearing has no effect on the grand jury's decision; even if the magistrate found probable cause, the grand jurors may choose to indict, not indict, or indict for a different offense.

Where the use of grand juries is not required, or when the defendant waives that right, a finding of probable cause results in the case being bound over for trial. The prosecutor files an information in the trial court, formally setting forth the charges on which the defendant will be tried. A defendant who wishes to challenge the magistrate's finding of probable cause normally may seek review by the trial judge having jurisdiction over the case.

If the magistrate finds that probable cause is lacking, the charges are dismissed and the suspect is discharged. Because jeopardy has not attached at a preliminary hearing, a defendant who is discharged is still subject to rearrest and reprosecution for the same offense. Although the prosecution may ask the trial judge to review the magistrate's decision not to bind the case over, it may also simply file new charges and seek another preliminary hearing—often presenting new and more detailed evidence—or bypass the preliminary hearing entirely and present the case to the grand jury, as described below.

The defendant's right to a preliminary hearing

At the first appearance, suspects in federal and some state cases are told that they have the right to a preliminary hearing. This right is statutory, for the Supreme Court has said that there is no constitutional right to such a hearing. As a result, the right can be, and typically is, subject to certain limits. Most importantly, if the prosecution obtains an indictment from a grand jury before the date of the preliminary hearing, the preliminary hearing is mooted. Thus, in judicial districts where grand juries are regularly convened, prosecutors have the ability to avoid preliminary hearings at will. Some jurisdictions also permit the filing of an information to moot the preliminary hearing, although the Supreme Court has cautioned that there must be some judicial finding of probable cause to justify prolonged detention of a suspect.

A suspect can waive his right to a preliminary hearing. If the evidence of guilt is strong enough to make the probable cause finding a foregone conclusion, a suspect might waive the hearing for several reasons. He may wish to avoid the adverse publicity associated with a public airing of the evidence; he may fear that once the prosecution presents the evidence, it will spot a curable defect in its case; or, he may worry that once the prosecution begins organizing the evidence to present at the hearing, it may realize that the initial charges against the suspect are too low. These risks lead large numbers of suspects (as many as 50 percent in some jurisdictions) to bypass the preliminary hearing.

Other functions of a preliminary hearing

Even in cases where probable cause will be easy to establish, a defendant may decide not to waive the preliminary hearing, despite the risks. There are several benefits he might derive from the hearing that are unrelated to screening the prosecution's case.

First, the preliminary hearing can serve as an informal means of discovery. Discovery in criminal cases is typically far more limited than in civil actions, and resource constraints may hamper defense counsel's ability to learn the substance of the prosecution's case on her own. At the preliminary hearing, however, the prosecutor often will have to reveal the names of key witnesses and the substance of their testimony, information that can be of great value in preparing a defense. The ability to cross-examine government witnesses also can be an effective discovery tool, although here the defense must proceed with caution. In an effort to uncover information, the defense questioning may signal to the prosecution what the defense theory will be at trial, may inadvertently reveal a gap in the prosecution's case, or may even show that the defendant played a more prominent role in the crime than the government originally thought. As a result, unless the preliminary hearing is the only viable method of obtaining crucial information, defense counsel may prefer to learn what it can from the prosecution's case-in-chief, and not pursue additional discovery through cross-examination.

A second benefit is that the defense can lay the groundwork for the future impeachment of witnesses. If a witness gives helpful testimony to the defense at the preliminary hearing, but then backs away from that position at trial, the defense can use the prior, under-oath testimony to show how the witness has changed her story. Having a witness commit to a certain version of events can be particularly important at this early stage in the process, since at that point the witness may not be as well prepared to testify as she will be at trial. Again, however, there are risks in trying to extract useful testimony from a witness. If the cross-examination of the witness is too sharp or confrontational, the witness may harden her position in favor of the prosecution. In addition, if defense counsel exposes a flaw in the witness's testimony at the preliminary hearing, the prosecution may have time to correct the problem or find another witness by the time of trial.

For the prosecution, the main benefit of the preliminary hearing is the chance to perpetuate testimony. Once a witness has testified at the preliminary hearing, that testimony can be introduced as evidence at trial if the witness later dies, disappears, or otherwise becomes unavailable. Although defendants have complained that this procedure denies them the right to cross-examine the witness at trial, these objections are often, although not always, unavailing. Courts have generally concluded that because the defense has the opportunity to cross-examine the witness at the preliminary hearing, its ability to challenge the testimony is adequately protected. An additional benefit to the prosecution is the ability to "lock-in" a witness' story. If the prosecution is concerned that a witness has a poor memory or will feel pressured to alter her testimony prior to trial, placing the witness under oath and on the record at the preliminary hearing reduces the chances that the witness will later change her story.

A third benefit of a preliminary hearing is that it can help educate the defense, the prosecution, and the court. The suspect may realize for the first time the strength of the prosecution's case, which may help her decide whether to seek a plea bargain. For the prosecution, the hearing is the first chance to present the case in a formal setting, which encourages early preparation of the case and helps reveal how witnesses will perform under cross-examination. Finally, if the suspect was not represented at the first appearance (as is often the case), the preliminary hearing is the first chance defense counsel has to bring certain information to the court's attention. Most notably, the defense may move for a reduction in bail or other changes in the pretrial release conditions based on information not previously available to the magistrate.

Effectiveness of preliminary hearings

The vast majority of cases presented at a preliminary hearing are bound over. This has raised the question whether these hearings serve as an effective screen against unfounded charges.

Critics have suggested that the high rate of bindover decisions show that the magistrate gives only superficial, deferential review to the prosecutor's evidence. On reflection, however, it is obvious that the question is more complicated than the simple bindover rate would suggest. Prosecutors know that the case will be subject to pretrial review, and have every incentive to eliminate weak charges before presenting the case to the magistrate. Thus, the high bindover rate might demonstrate that preliminary hearings are a great success; under this view, most of the screening is done by the prosecutor before the preliminary hearing even begins.

Whether preliminary hearings are an effective screen or simply a rubber stamp on the prosecutor's charging decision depends on the extent to which magistrates have the ability to spot weak cases when they are presented. The magistrate's ability in turn depends on the procedures that are followed at the preliminary hearing. In general, the more the hearing procedures replicate those that will be followed at trial, the more difficult it will be for the prosecutor to establish probable cause, and the more likely the magistrate to find that a case should be dismissed.

Scholars have identified a number of variations in preliminary hearing procedures that will effect the screening function. Among the more important: (1) the extent to which cases in the jurisdiction are plea bargained before the preliminary hearing; (2) the extent to which prosecutors carefully evaluate their cases before the preliminary hearing, rather than using the hearing itself as a means of evaluating the charges; (3) the time and attention magistrates give a preliminary hearing; in busy jurisdictions, the court may only be able to spend a short amount of time on each hearing, necessarily leading to more abbreviated consideration; (4) the extent to which the prosecutor can introduce hearsay and other evidence that would be inadmissible at trial; (5) whether defense counsel is permitted to introduce affirmative defenses at the preliminary hearing.

Conclusion

Preliminary hearings play a variety of roles in the criminal system. Despite the prosecutors' high success rate in establishing probable cause, the hearings may force the government to engage in self-screening before presenting the case, which helps ensure that innocent defendants are not required to endure the trauma of a trial. There are limits, however, on how stringent a screen the preliminary hearing can be. The lax evidentiary rules, the reluctance to usurp the trial jury by making credibility determinations, and the prosecutor's ability in many jurisdictions to circumvent the hearing by obtaining an indictment may constrain the magistrate's ability to dismiss all but the very weakest cases.

The high likelihood of a bindover also means, however, that many defense counsels will choose not to call witnesses or otherwise raise a defense for fear of revealing their evidence or strategy, and thus defendants will often either waive the hearing or attempt to extract other benefits from the proceeding. The chance to see the prosecutor's evidence and to lay the foundation for future impeachment through the cross-examination can play an important role in preparing the defense for trial or plea negotiations.

ANDREW D. LEIPOLD

See also ARRAIGNMENT; BAIL; COUNSEL: RIGHT TO COUNSEL; CRIMINAL JUSTICE SYSTEM; CRIMINAL PROCEDURE: CONSTITUTIONAL ASPECTS; CROSS-EXAMINATION; DISCOVERY; GRAND JURY; TRIAL, CRIMINAL.

BIBLIOGRAPHY

ARNELLA, PETER. "Reforming the Federal Grand Jury and the State Preliminary Hearing to Prevent Conviction without Adjudication." 78 *Michigan Law Review* 463 (1980): 476–484, 529–539.

Federal Rules of Criminal Procedure 5(c), 5.1.

LAFAVE, WAYNE R.; ISRAEL, JEROLD H.; and KING, NANCY J. *Criminal Procedure.* Sections 14.1-14.4. St. Paul, Minn.: West Group, 1999.

SUBIN, HARRY I.; MIRSKY, CHESTER L.; and WEINSTEIN, IAN S. *Federal Criminal Practice.* St. Paul, Minn.: West Group, 1992.

TORCIA, CHARLES E. *Wharton's Criminal Procedure.* 13th ed. Sections 138-141. Rochester, N.Y.: Lawyers Cooperative, 1989. Supp. 1999.

18 U.S.C. sec. 3060.

WHITEBREAD, CHARLES H., and SLOBOGIN, CHRISTOPHER. *Criminal Procedure.* Westbury, N.Y.: Foundation Press, 1993. Pages 536–544.

WRIGHT, CHARLES ALAN. *Federal Practice and Procedure.* 3d ed. Sections 83-87. St. Paul, Minn.: West, 1999.

CASES

Coleman v. Alabama, 399 U.S. 1 (1970).
Gerstein v. Pugh, 420 U.S. 103 (1975).
Goldsby v. United States, 160 U.S. 70 (1895).

PRETRIAL DIVERSION

Pretrial diversion is an informal feature of the American criminal process that emerged in the late 1960s with the trappings of a formal "program." In 1973, the National Advisory Commission on Criminal Justice Standards and Goals defined pretrial diversion as "halting or suspending before conviction formal criminal proceedings against a person on the condition or assumption that he will do something in return" (U.S. Department of Justice, p. 27). By this definition, the commission sought to distinguish formal diversion programs from the vast array of informal mechanisms by which cases are routinely removed from the criminal justice system. A police officer's decision to ignore an incident or to "reprimand and release," a prosecutor's decision to decline or discount a charge, and a judge's decision to dismiss a case before trial or plea are all informal pretrial diversion procedures founded on the broad discretion available to decision-makers in a system that disposes of most of its cases without trial.

Formal diversion programs grew in response to broad disaffection with the vagaries of these discretionary release mechanisms, as well as to the perceived failure of the traditional criminal process to affect the behavior of those who remained in the system. Deinstitutionalization, decriminalization, diversion, and community corrections were all parts of the general search for alternatives to traditional criminal sanctions. All retained the goal of rehabilitation but sought to achieve it by strengthening the offender's ties to the community and forging more explicit links between individual behavior and the response of the criminal justice system.

In its traditional forms, pretrial diversion typically placed the defendant out of the reach of criminal sanctions, making him, in the candid view of one observer, "technically free to tell the diverter to go to hell" (Cressey and McDermott, p. 6). In its elaborated form, pretrial diversion involved a formal bargain with the accused. After arrest, selected defendants charged with nonserious offenses were offered a postponement of court action if they agreed to participate in a program of employment or counseling services for periods ranging from ninety days to one year. Satisfactory completion of the program resulted in a dismissal of charges; "failure" meant the resumption of criminal proceedings. From its modest beginnings in 1967 as an outgrowth of proposals for community treatment advanced by the President's Commission on Law Enforcement and Administration of Justice, the diversion movement flourished with generous federal funding support and the endorsement of local officials eager to embrace a strategy that promised to move the accused away from the jurisdiction of overburdened criminal courts and into an effective treatment alternative. By 1978, almost every state claimed a diversion program in one or more jurisdictions, and many had been formalized through the enactment of statewide enabling legislation.

Even as diversion was gaining strength, however, doubts were voiced in the academic community. Although early evaluations created high expectations that formal diversion programs would resolve many of the problems of traditional criminal justice treatment, more dispassionate observers found little evidence to support these claims (Zimring; Morris; Mullen). Even when formalized as an official "program," diversion's treatment of due process issues also left constitutional scholars uneasy (Freed; Note). Eligibility standards were often highly restrictive, and termination procedures remained almost wholly discretionary. Moreover, regardless of the locutions employed, the imposition of a rehabilitative "sanction" prior to trial suggested a presumption of guilt and the prospect of a new form of pretrial sentencing. Perhaps most important, these early critical reviews advanced the notion that diversion strategies might inadvertently serve to "widen the net of social control"—a concept that would be rediscovered at every turn in the movement to develop community-based treatment alternatives. Likened by Norval Morris to George Orwell's nightmare of the benevolent state in *Nineteen Eighty-Four*, the perceived danger was that the mere presence of another form of sanction—in particular, one that avoided the punitive overtones of traditional sanctions—might lead to the diversion of defendants who would otherwise avoid official attention because their cases were too inconsequential or the prosecutor's case too weak to support formal conviction and sentencing. Thus, although intended precisely to constrain the reach of the criminal justice system, diversion threatened instead to extend the scope of official control.

Despite these notes of caution, popular support for the diversion concept persisted until the late 1970s. Throughout that decade, innovation or expansion in criminal justice programming had become virtually synonymous with a grant from the Law Enforcement Assistance Administration (LEAA). With the termination of the LEAA block grant program in 1980 and the proliferation of increasingly costly standards devised to protect the legal rights of diversion participants (National Association of Pretrial Services Agencies), the general diversion movement began to lose momentum.

At the end of the decade of the 1980s, however, diversion would be reinvented as a central component of a new movement to supervise and rehabilitate drug dependent defendants remanded to treatment by drug court judges. In this application, diversion or deferred prosecution was an important tool to compel drug abus-

ers to accept and remain in drug treatment. Stimulated by the rapid increase in felony drug cases that surfaced in the 1980s, the new drug courts gave the diversion concept new legitimacy. Fears of expanding the net of social control were less salient when the expansion enabled the court to do something more than nothing with a class of defendants who were clogging court calendars and promised to return again and again for drug-related crimes.

Goals and program procedures

Measured against any single pretrial reform effort, the multiple ambitions of the early pretrial diversion programs were extraordinary. The courts would gain flexibility in case processing, court congestion and costs would be reduced, and prison and jail populations would decline. Program participants would avoid the stigma of criminal prosecution and receive a variety of helping services that would enhance their community adjustment and decrease recidivism. In theory, there was something for everyone. In practice, no single program could hope to achieve such diverse aims.

At the outset, it proved difficult to reconcile the combined interests of intensive treatment and diversion of large numbers of cases from the criminal justice system. The diversion concept called for removal from the jurisdiction of the court those defendants who might not require a full criminal disposition—by the usual definition, minimum-risk cases. At the same time, the costs of treatment could hardly be justified unless programs served higher-risk clients whose criminal careers might be influenced by the delivery of services. In the context of the diversion process, the dilemma was irresolvable. To be considered for a pretrial diversion program, defendants were required to pass a number of screening tests. In most cases, the logic of this screening was either implicitly or explicitly the selection of minimum-risk defendants.

General diversion programs

A tremendous range of programs emerged in the 1970s under the aegis of probation agencies, prosecutors, community service groups, or independent contractors. Although specific client groups and service configurations differed accordingly, the mechanics of the diversion process were generally similar. Eligibility was first defined by entry standards that restricted participation by such variables as alleged offense, age, prior record, and history of substance abuse. Although a formal admission of guilt was strongly discouraged by professional standards, a few programs expected the defendant to acknowledge criminal responsibility. Once identified, a typical program candidate agreed to participate by waiving the right to a speedy trial and indicating some willingness to cooperate with the program. The prosecutor, presiding judge, or both were also required to concur with the project's choice of diversion candidates.

After entry, participants typically spent three to six months under project supervision, receiving direct or referral assistance in meeting their needs for personal and vocational counseling, training, job placement, remedial education, and a variety of supportive services. At any time after entering a program, defendants who violated their projects' conditions for diversion (generally by absconding, incurring new charges, or failing to cooperate with the treatment regime) were terminated from the project and returned to the court on their original charge. Those who satisfied their obligations were recommended for dismissal, and, with the cooperation of the prosecuting attorney or judge, their cases were dropped at the conclusion of the pretrial period.

Clearly, the entire process was designed to be highly sensitive to the motivation of the defendant, the discretion of the program staff, and the prerogatives of the court and prosecutor. Moreover, the need to establish official confidence in project efforts created substantial pressures to divert minimum-risk cases and to terminate and thereby avoid final responsibility for defendants who evidenced little or no progress. In most programs the inevitable result of this process was the delivery of intensive services to small numbers of low-risk defendants. If pretrial diversion had been conceived solely as a screening device for prosecutors, the systematic exclusion of higher risks could be considered a rational policy. If, however, it was conceived as a program designed to reduce recidivism through intensive treatment, then the inclusion of defendants least likely to recidivate could hardly be considered a wise use of scarce criminal justice resources. As Franklin Zimring has suggested, either the wrong group was receiving the right services or the right group was receiving the wrong treatment.

Diversion of drug abusers

Ironically, the group destined to become the most promising class of diversion cases—the drug dependent—was specifically excluded from most general diversion programs. Though some diversion programs accepted persons charged with minor drug-related offenses, most such programs lacked the resources to promote specialized treatment and, therefore, avoided defendants with known chemical dependencies. Despite the inability of general deferred prosecution programs to accommodate these defendants, there have been numerous attempts to address their needs for treatment. Approaches have ranged from compulsory institutional treatment programs to voluntary community-based treatment alternatives imposed as conditions of pretrial release, probation, or parole. Prior to the development of drug courts, the broadest attempt to use the arrest process to absorb unmotivated drug users into treatment was the TASC (Treatment Alternatives to Street Crime) Program developed in 1971 by the President's Special Action Office of Drug Abuse Prevention and funded in cities nationwide by the LEAA.

TASC itself operated solely as a referral mechanism, generally relying on existing community-based treatment facilities to provide the necessary supervision and services. Three functions were commonly performed by TASC staff: (1) screening arrestees, identifying abusers, and determining their eligibility for TASC; (2) diagnosing individual problems and locating appropriate treatment resources; and (3) monitoring participant progress and maintaining contact with the criminal justice system. Initially conceived as a pretrial diversion program for heroin addicts, in many cities the design was altered to include all drug abusers who were intercepted at a variety of points of entry and exit from the criminal justice system. Nonetheless, eligibility criteria were still fairly restrictive, resulting in the admittance of only a small proportion of drug users appearing before the courts. Moreover, because TASC generally operated solely as a referral agency, it was often difficult for TASC staff to monitor progress in treatment or to ensure the defendant's compliance with other court-imposed conditions.

The emergence of drug courts

The drug court approach improved on the TASC model in a number of ways, principally by forging a stronger role for the judiciary: specific courtrooms were dedicated solely to drug cases, the presiding judge was given a more proactive role in fashioning treatment plans, and drug court judges also became central figures in monitoring treatment and program compliance.

No longer an extralegal process managed by external social welfare programs, diversion became a fully integrated part of the criminal process for drug court cases, using the coercive power of the court to promote abstinence and compel participants to stay in treatment (Belenko, 1998). While many had been restive about the notion of compelling defendants to accept employment and social services under the threat of prosecution, when applied to the problems of drug use, "coerced treatment" was now viewed as the program's primary strength (Drug Strategies).

Most observers credit Miami's Dade County Circuit Court for developing the first treatment-oriented drug court in 1989. Within ten years the concept of drug treatment courts gained national prominence and estimates of the number in planning or operation ranged from four hundred to six hundred. During those ten years, an estimated 140,000 drug offenders had entered drug court programs (Belenko, 1999). Initially designed as a diversion program for less serious, primarily possession-offenders, by the year 2000 most had established probation and post-plea-based programs for more serious offenders with long histories of drug abuse (National Drug Court Institute).

The initial impetus for the extraordinary growth of drug courts can be traced to the volatile market for crack cocaine that developed in the 1980s, bringing with it a dramatic increase in the rates that young people (particularly African American males) killed and were killed (McDonald). Although crack cocaine use peaked in the mid-1980s, heroin made a comeback in the early 1990s and abuse of methamphetamines began to show sharp increases in the mid-1990s. During these years, the federal government responded with a "war on drugs" that provided a massive infusion of federal dollars for drug law enforcement (Brown). Beginning in the mid-1970s with the passage in many states of tough mandatory minimum prison sentencing laws for drug trafficking and moving to the passage at the federal level of anti-drug statutes in 1986 and 1988, the entire criminal justice system focused on the war on drugs. Annual arrests for drug crimes increased from 416,000 in 1970 to 1.6 million in 1998 with corresponding increases in the number of drug law offenders in state federal prisons (McDonald). Yet despite the unprecedented increases in arrests and incarcerations, it was clear that these traditional solutions had not materially affected levels of drug-related crime. The stage was set for introducing treatment into the adjudication process.

During the decade of the 1990s, the drug court movement also benefited from the endorsement of U.S. Attorney General Janet Reno (who had founded Miami's program when she served as Florida's state attorney for Dade County) and the substantial federal support provided by the Department of Justice. By 1995, a separate Drug Courts Program Office was established within the U.S. Department of Justice with $12 million to support drug courts, growing to $40 million by fiscal 1999.

Impact on recidivism

The fundamental ambivalence of the goals of diversion was reflected in a number of early evaluations. In addressing the issue of participant recidivism, many programs pointed to a low absolute level of rearrest as a measure of treatment success, seldom recognizing that in the absence of a comparison group this measure did not distinguish the effects of the selection process from actual behavioral change. Many quasi-experimental designs were scarcely more persuasive. Not surprisingly, project evaluators found positive results after comparing participants before and after they were designated as successful, comparing only the successful participant group with all members of an untreated group, or comparing the performance of failures with that of successes. Since each of these designs suffered the obvious bias, it was impossible to determine whether the observed difference was a change attributable to treatment or simply a confirmation that the successful group had been less inclined to criminality in any event.

Even the more comprehensive evaluative efforts were frequently forced to rely on matched group studies in lieu of random assignment procedures as a result of resistance by program personnel to the notion of withholding services from eligible participants. In these designs, defendants who—on paper—appeared to match the characteristics of eligible participants were selected retrospectively from closed case files. Since entrance criteria always required participants to volunteer for the program and to pass more than a paper screening, these matching exercises seldom survived careful scrutiny. In only one study of the Manhattan Court Employment Project, one of the nation's oldest and largest diversion programs, was a satisfactory, retrospective comparison-group selection methodology used. This 1974 reanalysis demonstrated no effect of treatment on recidivism (Zimring). Five years later, in 1979, the same project issued the first definitive experimental study of adult pretrial diversion, which also failed to find any significant effect on recidivism (Baker). Ironically, although resistance to random assignment procedures has typically been founded on legal and ethical objections to the denial of services to eligible groups, the evaluation did not find participants receiving more services or less exposure to the criminal justice system than did members of the control group.

Turning to the literature on the early diversion programs for drug cases, TASC evaluations often repeated the same mistakes observed in evaluations of general deferred prosecution programs. As a result the only firm conclusion that could be drawn is that costs were high and participant impact of any kind, hard to detect.

The drug court successors to TASC (many of which annexed TASC programs) have generated a substantial evaluation literature. A report issued by the U.S. General Accounting Office (GAO) in July 1997 reviewed the results of twenty evaluations of sixteen drug courts and concluded that while positive outcomes were reported, they were typically based on quasi-experimental designs that did not permit any definitive conclusions about impacts on recidivism or drug use. For example, many authors persisted in making invalid comparisons between program graduates and drop-outs, believing that these comparisons demonstrated a positive program effect (Brown). Subsequent reviews in 1998 and 1999 by Belenko were considerably more optimistic than the GAO report, although the author acknowledged the limitations of the available data. In his 1999 review of twelve evaluations that measured post-program recidivism of participants and a comparison sample, he found lower rates of recidivism in seven studies, comparable rates in three, and mixed results in two (Belenko, 1999).

Truitt and Rhodes (2000) examined seven of the most robust evaluations and concluded that even among the best available studies, outcomes ranged widely with four programs finding an impact on recidivism and three (including two based on true experimental designs) showing comparable rates of recidivism. A critical review of those showing positive effects suggested the results were confounded by selection bias that may have caused lower risks to enter drug court. Attempting to correct for that bias in a study of programs in Escambia County, Florida, and Jackson County, Missouri, Truitt and Rhodes found a strong treatment effect in Escambia County when recidivism is defined as an arrest for a felony but no demonstrable effect when both felonies and misdemeanors were considered. In Jackson County, the authors found a sizable treatment effect even when regarding felony and misdemeanor arrests as a single outcome measure.

In the end, however, the best that can be said is that while participants are under the supervision of a drug court (and subject to random drug testing and judicial oversight of their progress in treatment) recidivism appears to be held in check. Thereafter, the results are mixed with the most rigorous evaluations finding no effect on recidivism.

Results of drug treatment, employment, and social services

Many of the earliest diversion projects were funded initially by the U.S. Department of Labor as an extension of its mandate to assist hard-to-employ workers. Although many project goal statements posited a relationship between unemployment and crime, it was not entirely clear that program sponsors were eager to link the success of their employment services to prospects of reduced recidivism. In this view, pretrial diversion was simply a strategy to gain early access to the economically disadvantaged at a time when the crisis of arrest might promote their receptivity to employment assistance. At the same time, the provision for a dismissal of charges in successful cases would eliminate the conviction record, an acknowledged barrier to employment prospects of young adults.

At the outset, adding social performance criteria to definitions of criminal conduct raised serious questions about the proper limits of criminal jurisdiction. Did the results of program services justify this intrusion? Again, the absence of appropriate comparison groups was a major problem in evaluating program performance. In the single available experimental evaluation, some improvements were recorded, but these could not be attributed to the effects of program participation since similar improvements were found among members of the control group.

In the final analysis, the pretrial intervention design failed to provide a fair test of the notion that employment services could accomplish their manpower development objectives. In the context of a ninety-day period of pretrial supervision, it was not clear that projects could do much more than develop stopgap employment—jobs that were clearly necessary to meet program criteria for a dismissal recommendation, but not sufficient to support expectations of sustaining significant or lasting change. At best, another line was drawn in the conflict between the goals of diversion and treatment.

In contrast to the early manpower-based programs, the drug court diversion model recognized that treatment duration was related to treatment outcome and typically required a minimum time in treatment of one year. Belenko reported that approximately 60 percent of participants were still in treatment after one year—a significantly higher retention rate than most outpatient and residential drug treatment programs (Belenko, 1999).

Has the increased intensity of treatment allowed programs to succeed in breaking cycles of drug dependency? Again, while under court supervision—and "unlike a traditional court judge, drug offenders may appear before the drug diversion judge twenty to thirty times during the course of the treatment plan" (Brown, p. 85)—programs have shown some improvement in rates of abstention and less frequent periods of relapse. Mirroring the findings on recidivism, however, post-program results have been mixed.

A majority of drug courts have also acknowledged the difficulty of successfully treating participants' addiction without attending to other social and economic needs. Accordingly, most programs provide vocational, educational, manpower, and other rehabilitative services. Once again, available data on the impact of these services are too limited to draw conclusions.

Alleviating the burden on court and correctional system

Proponents of many of the first diversion programs often cited the opportunities to relieve congested court calendars and overburdened probation caseloads as a central rationale for the development of intensive pretrial service alternatives. However, although these benefits were freely announced, they were seldom carefully explored. In fact, on the strength of their numbers alone, few projects could have demonstrated any significant reduction in court or correctional caseloads. Moreover, the diversion process itself still involved calendaring cases, with at least one and frequently two court appearances during the period of deferred prosecution.

Demonstrating the cost savings of the diversion approach proved equally problematic. Many programs handled limited caseloads and maintained a fairly costly service apparatus, resulting in high per capita costs. Even the lower-cost programs emerged as relatively expensive alternatives when program budgets were adjusted for the additional costs incurred by the court in processing unsuccessful cases. If the programs were truly functioning as alternatives to incarceration, justifying the expense would not be difficult. In the absence of a diversion alternative, however, available evidence suggested that few project participants would have faced a jail sentence.

Notably, reducing court caseloads was not a goal of the drug court, which sought instead to increase the court's attention to drug cases with dedicated courtrooms and judicial officers. Although many analysts have compared these costs with the costs of incarcerating drug-involved offenders, more often diversion has been an alternative to doing nothing: Many diversion participants have been first-time felony drug possession cases who would typically be placed on probation with minimal to no treatment or supervision. Demonstrating savings therefore requires demonstrating lower recidivism among drug court participants. As we have seen, this measurement task has thus far produced ambivalent results.

Expanding the options for case processing

To the extent that many applications of diversion failed to replace postconviction remedies, they nonetheless succeeded in increasing the alternatives available to the court for differential case processing. This goal implied that even if formal prosecution were unwarranted for the majority of program participants, the availability of an alternative more onerous than no action might usefully serve the interests of law and order. In this view, the dangers of "expanding the net" were less ominous than the prospect of screening out cases simply because the system was too overloaded to pursue those charged with minor offenses. As expressed in the goals of one of the earliest prosecutor-based diversion projects, a legitimate and major need exists to process and treat persons who are lawbreakers but not criminals (Perlman). Although this version of the goal appeared to define diversion more as a convenience to prosecutors than as a rehabilitative tool, other statements emphasized the therapeutic value of early intervention and treatment—presupposing that, left unattended, today's lawbreakers were tomorrow's career criminals.

Then came the drug court, and the concept of therapeutic jurisprudence acquired new meaning. In drug cases, judges faced two equally unpalatable alternatives—probation or incarceration, neither of which could promise to do anything about the offender's underlying substance abuse problem. Here at last a clear and compelling case could be made for bringing together criminal justice and public health interests in a new, problem-solving approach to justice. In giving a clear voice to the premise that a collaborative approach is needed to solve medical-legal problems, drug courts may have achieved their most important victory.

Conclusion

By the close of the 1970s, the earliest pretrial diversion programs had failed to demonstrate much promise as a means for achieving rehabilitation or resource conservation. Diversion programs could be justified only by their utility in providing the prosecutor with another disposition option—and then only if sufficient resources were available to permit expenditures on cases not amenable to full prosecution. As a result diversion gave clear form to the threat of a widened net of social control.

The fact that the new control mechanisms were dressed in the benign guise of community treatment was hardly comforting to those who saw the specter of Orwell's dystopia, where far-reaching social controls replaced the narrow constraints of the criminal law. In defense of their treatment of those charged with minor offenses, zealous program sponsors only reinforced this vision by arguing that descriptions of their clients' legal problems often failed to reveal their more serious needs for social assistance. Few stopped to ask whether this enthusiasm for solving social problems under the aegis of the legal process might not result in "considerable dilution of the desirable pressures to reduce and

clearly define the scope and purposes of the criminal law" (Zimring and Frase, p. 395).

With the development of the drug court at the close of the 1980s, the diversion concept, called in its early days "a practice in search of a theory" (Vorenberg and Vorenberg, p. 151), found its strongest rationale. Diversion or deferred prosecution would be used to motivate participation in court-supervised drug treatment. Instead of simply turning over the case to treatment personnel, the judge would remain on point, holding frequent status hearings and reviewing urinalysis results and reports from treatment providers. Diversion now functioned not as an alternative to the traditional court process but as an integral part of a new treatment-oriented court process.

Those who embraced the new therapeutic jurisprudence looked forward to the development of other treatment-based specialty courts (for domestic violence, for DUI cases, or for offenders with mental health problems) and asked that law schools recognize the moral imperative of the court to treat and not simply adjudicate cases (Simmons). Others relived early warnings about the appropriate scope of the criminal law and asked whether justice and therapy could be combined without producing a "therapeutic state" even more flawed than the system it was designed to replace (Cohen).

Absent from this debate is any clear and compelling evidence that the new treatment-oriented court process has seriously affected the incidence of drug-related crime. We know the process has succeeded in interrupting drug use and related crime—at least for the length of time participants remain in treatment and are subject to random drug tests and close judicial supervision. The extent to which these results are sustained when participants leave the program is less clear. Yet even if post-program performance proves disappointing, it may still be said that significant reform has been achieved. Drug courts have engaged many offenders in their first treatment experience. They have also provided offenders with far closer supervision and accountability than they would have received under other forms of criminal justice intervention. In so doing, the credibility of enforcement agencies has been strengthened; a sense of humanity has been injected into a process not known for its helping orientation; and closer ties have been forged between the accused, the justice system, and the treatment community. A structure has been put in place for integrating a medical treatment with the criminal process and may now only await advances in treatment technology to prove its worth.

JOAN MULLEN

See also ALCOHOL AND CRIME: BEHAVIORAL ASPECTS; ALCOHOL AND CRIME: TREATMENT AND REHABILITATION; DISPUTE RESOLUTION PROGRAMS; INFORMAL DISPOSITION; MENTALLY DISORDERED OFFENDERS; REHABILITATION.

BIBLIOGRAPHY

AUSTIN, JAMES, and KRISBERG, BARRY. "Wider, Stronger, and Different Nets: The Dialectics of Criminal Justice Reform." *Journal of Research in Crime and Delinquency* 18 (1981): 165–196.

BAKER, SALLY HILLSMAN. *The Court Employment Project Evaluation: Final Report.* New York: Vera Institute of Justice, 1979.

BELENKO, STEVEN. *Research on Drug Courts: A Critical Review.* New York: National Center on Addiction and Drug Abuse, 1998.

———. "Research on Drug Courts: A Critical Review 1999 Update." *National Drug Court Institute Review* 2 (1999): 1–58.

BROWN, JAMES R. "Drug Diversion Courts: Are They Needed and Will They Succeed in Breaking the Cycle of Drug-Related Crime?" *Criminal and Civil Confinement* 23 (1997): 63–99.

COHEN, ERIC. "The Drug Court Revolution." *The Weekly Standard* 5, no. 15 (1999): 20–23.

CRESSEY, DONALD R., and MCDERMOTT, ROBERT A. *Diversion from the Juvenile Justice System.* Ann Arbor: University of Michigan, National Assessment of Juvenile Corrections, 1973.

Drug Courts Clearing Office. *Looking at a Decade of Drug Courts.* Washington, D.C.: American University, 1998.

Drug Strategies. *Drug Courts: A Revolution in Criminal Justice.* Washington, D.C.: Drug Strategies, 1999.

FREED, DANIEL J. "Statement on Proposed Federal Legislation Regarding Pretrial Diversion." In *Hearing before the Subcommittee on Courts, Civil Liberties, and Administration of Justice of the Committee on the Judiciary, U.S. Congress, House.* 93d Cong., 2d sess., 6–7 February 1974, p. 144.

LEMERT, EDWIN M. "Diversion in Juvenile Justice: What Hath Been Wrought." *Journal of Research in Crime and Delinquency* 18 (1981): 34–46.

MCDONALD, DOUGLAS, et al. *Chapter for DOJ Strategic Plan 2000–2005.* Cambridge, Mass.: Abt Associates Inc., 2000.

MORRIS, NORVAL. *The Future of Imprisonment.* Chicago: University of Chicago Press, 1974.

MULLEN, JOAN. *The Dilemma of Diversion: Resource Materials on Adult Pretrial Intervention Programs.* Washington, D.C.: U.S. Department of Justice, Law Enforcement Assistance Administration, National Institute of Law Enforcement and Criminal Justice, 1975.

MULLEN, JOAN, and CARLSON, KEN. *Pre-trial Intervention: A Program Evaluation of Nine Manpower-based Pre-trial Intervention Projects.* Washington, D.C.: U.S. Department of Labor, 1974.

National Association of Pretrial Services Agencies. *Performance Standards and Goals for Pretrial Release and Diversion: Diversion.* Washington, D.C.: NAPSA, 1978.

National Drug Court Institute. *Development and Implementation of Drug Court Systems.* Washington, D.C.: National Drug Court Institute, 1999.

Note. "Pretrial Diversion from the Criminal Process." *Yale Law Journal* 83 (1974): 827–854.

PERLMAN, ELLIS. "Deferred Prosecution in Criminal Justice: A Case Study of the Genessee County Citizens Probation Authority." In *A Prosecutor's Manual on Screening and Diversionary Programs.* Chicago: National District Attorneys Association Publications, 1972. Pages 7–183.

SIMMONS, PAMELA L. "Solving the Nation's Drug Problem: Drug Courts Signal a Move Toward Therapeutic Jurisprudence." *Gonzaga Law Review* 35 (2000): 237–263.

TRUITT, LINDA, et al. *Evaluations of Escambia County, Florida and Jackson County, Missouri, Drug Courts.* Cambridge, Mass.: Abt Associates Inc., 2000.

U.S. Department of Justice, Law Enforcement Assistance Administration, National Advisory Commission on Criminal Justice Standards and Goals. *Courts.* Washington, D.C.: The Commission, 1973.

VORENBERG, ELIZABETH W., and VORENBERG, JAMES. "Early Diversion from the Criminal Justice System: Practice in Search of a Theory." In *Prisoners in America.* Edited by Lloyd E. Ohlin. Englewood Cliffs, N.J.: Prentice-Hall, 1973. Pages 151–183.

ZIMRING, FRANKLIN E. "Measuring the Impact of Pretrial Diversion from the Criminal Justice System." *University of Chicago Law Review* 41 (1974): 224–241.

ZIMRING, FRANKLIN E., and FRASE, RICHARD S. "Focus Issue: Pretrial Diversion Programs." *The Criminal Justice System: Materials on the Administration and Reform of the Criminal Law.* Boston: Little, Brown, 1980. Pages 349–395.

PREVENTION: COMMUNITY PROGRAMS

Community crime prevention programs were founded upon a simple idea: that private citizens can and should play a critical role in preventing crime in their communities. The concepts *community* and *crime prevention* have fluid interpretations. Consequently, the range of programs popularly or officially labeled community crime prevention has included a virtually limitless array of activities, including media anti-drug campaigns, silent observer programs, and neighborhood dispute resolution programs.

While no consensual definition of the community crime prevention program concept has emerged, criminal justice scholars tend to restrict its application to activities that include residents of a particular locality who participate in efforts to stop crimes before they occur in that locality. Generally excluded from this categorization are (1) programs that serve only known offender populations; (2) programs that are designed and implemented only by professionals (e.g., social workers and probation officers); and (3) programs that may involve community residents but are principally based in formal social institutions like juvenile courts or schools.

The history of community crime prevention

The predominant models of community crime prevention have changed considerably throughout history with respect to the customary roles played by community residents, the choices of criminogenic conditions to target, and the manner of interaction between civilian program participants and representatives of public entities. Accounts of the history of community crime prevention describe how these elements are shaped by interrelated developments in the local and national political economy and in intergroup relations (e.g., class and race relations) as well as perceptions of the crime problem and the effectiveness of particular citizen mobilization and crime prevention strategies.

The belief that citizens have a duty to curb deviant behavior—the essence of community crime prevention—is at least as old as recorded history. Formalized community crime prevention, however, appears to have started in England during the eighteenth century when playwright and novelist Henry Fielding mobilized a body of citizen householders for the purpose of addressing the root causes of crime and apprehending criminals.

The idea that law-abiding citizens could prevent crime in their communities through nonpunitive means achieved popular resonance in the United States in the 1930s, owing in part to the work of the Chicago School of Sociology. These scholars cogently argued that the causes of crime reside largely in structural forces that operate on neighborhoods and families rather than in genetic dispositions. In part as a result of their work, urban researchers and policy makers showed a greater sensitivity to environmental factors that contributed to poor socialization of urban children such as ethnic heterogeneity, the strains of immigrant life, overcrowding, and a lack of structured activities for youth.

To address the perceived social disorganization and the lack of coordination among existing neighborhood agents of socialization in urban slums, some cities during the 1930s formed community commissions for crime prevention. For instance, citing the work of the Chicago School, the Crime Commission of New York State in 1930 called for the formation of neighborhood councils, that would consist of neighborhood service professionals and elites "whose concern would be the present and future needs of the neighborhood, based on fact-finding, and whose problem it would be to integrate all the forces in the neighborhood that are working for social welfare, into a harmonious program." (p. 16). The centrally coordinated, community-wide integration of programs based on scientific assessments forms the core of modern community crime prevention "partnership" schemes.

Chicago areas project

The coordination of existing community agencies was not ambitious enough for the likes of Chicago researcher Clifford Shaw. Shaw theorized that it was not social service personnel who play a crucial role in imparting conventional values to youth but rather youths' immediate and wider social circles found within their communities. Shaw believed that social programs can reduce delinquency in high delinquency areas only if they fully integrate the people and institutions that shape youths' lives on a daily basis, thereby strengthening the often strained social relationships between youth and adults.

Involving residents of high delinquency areas in crime prevention activities on a large scale was a daunting task. Shaw founded the Chicago Areas Project (CAP) with sociologist Ernest Burgess of the University of Chicago. To facilitate the recruitment of community members, the project, with the aid of government funds, hired local residents whose social network ties, personal investment, and knowledge of the community proved to be an asset to the recruitment process. These paid community leaders worked to organize more than forty community committees, which were composed of residents of the community. CAP granted these committees considerable autonomy in staffing decisions and in deciding the nature of their crime prevention activities. Delegating decision-making authority to community leaders was intended to increase their stake in the program and cultivate their capacity to form self-sustaining organizations.

From 1931 to 1944, CAP organizations launched recreation programs, deployed "detached workers" to counsel youth gangs, and sponsored limited educational/training programs for immigrants and others in need. While evaluations suggest that CAP had an ambiguous impact on delinquency and formed durable but not "self-sustaining" community organizations, it played a pivotal role in the history of community crime prevention programs. CAP established the feasibility of creating stable community organizations, even in areas with relatively high rates of poverty and heterogeneity. Additionally, it introduced the youth outreach worker approach that aims to blend service workers into the natural milieu of at-risk youth. Finally, CAP continues to offer a model to help bridge the disconnect between institutional agents of youth welfare and informal agents of socialization.

Political mobilization

The Chicago Area Project is a rare example of indigenous control over the design and implementation of sizable, though highly circumscribed, programs. Many grass-roots community organizations that succeeded CAPS, influenced in part by the confrontational tactics of organizer Saul Alinksy, recognized that social cohesion must be accompanied by economic and political resources to give communities a fighting chance against crime. As a result, more organizations adopted what Tim Hope calls *vertical strategies*, which focus on linkages between community life and decisions made at higher levels of power outside the community.

The emphasis on vertical strategies was strongest in the 1960s. President John F. Kennedy's administration sought to tackle racism, poverty, and delinquency by launching Mobilization for Youth, an effort in fifteen cities designed to provide youth more opportunities through empowering disadvantaged groups to challenge the unjust distribution of resources in their communities. Although crime prevention was the explicit aim of Mobilization for Youth, its concern with attacking what Cloward and Ohlin labeled the "differential opportunity structure" in America extended far beyond a concern for youth crime. In the end, Mobilization for Youth was deemed a failure, because its narrow emphasis on political activity antagonized local governments and failed to garner sufficient grassroots support.

The perceived failure of government programs, along with mass social protest during the 1960s, helped spark what Adam Crawford calls a "crisis of legitimacy" among government agencies, whereby social service programs and criminal justice agencies were perceived as out-of-touch with the preferences of those they served and incapable of affecting social structure. Relatedly, the emphasis on social structure in criminology yielded some prominence to a conception of rational offenders responding to incentives in the physical environment and to an emphasis on the victim's role in crime and crime control. Community defense activities allowed increasingly fearful and punitive citizens to protect themselves and their property against opportunistic offenders and to "fight back" through such actions as citizen patrols and property marking.

Community defense approaches also carried some appeal for public officials. Sharing responsibilities with community groups not only met the 1970s demand for fiscal restraint, but it also helped cultivate an image of local government as responsive to public concerns and only partially to blame for alarming crime rates.

Not surprisingly, then, community defense—at times combined with citizen mobilization for more city services—became the predominant paradigm of community crime prevention beginning in the 1970s. The federal government, for its part, sought to encourage the expansion of such programs by developing standards for citizen involvement set forth by the U.S. National Advisory Commission on Criminal

Justice Standards in 1973, and by sponsoring training for community organizations and law enforcement agencies interested in launching such programs. The *neighborhood watch* model, which emphasizes collective vigilance over neighborhood space, became the most popular form of collective activity against crime, with 7 percent participation among adults in 1984. The estimated 18.3 million Americans—approximately 14 percent of whom are African American—volunteering in block watches and other neighborhood public safety programs in 1996 attests to its enduring popularity among diverse segments of Americans.

The trend toward public/private and inter-agency cooperation has spread to other crime prevention modalities—particularly delinquency prevention. During the 1990s the United States, Great Britain, and other nations experienced the spread of efforts to coordinate crime prevention efforts system-wide. Predicated on public health models of the development of high-risk behaviors, the community partnership approach views delinquency as the product of multiple *risk* and *protective factors* operating in a youth's social system. Coordinated partnerships strive to tailor the amount and type of services in a community to cost-effectively reduce and enhance, respectively, the multiple risk and protective factors assessed to be operating in a particular community.

The major federally initiated and funded partnership approaches, including Weed and Seed, the Comprehensive Communities Program, and Title V Community Prevention Grants Program—all launched during the 1990s—channel their funds through policy boards formed in various municipalities. Residents of particular neighborhoods and their leaders generally play a limited role in the coordinating bodies, often ceding authority to leaders of units of local government (e.g., police chief and school superintendent), and major social service organizations. On the other hand, members and leaders of community organizations may still assume important roles by serving as consultants in the assessment and planning process and helping mobilize support for and to implement community initiatives. Community-wide partnerships vary in the extent to which they support grassroots initiatives and in the direct control they exercise over these neighborhood organizations' use of the funds.

Evaluations of community crime prevention programs

Evaluators in the field of community crime prevention have met more success at describing whether community programs and initiatives have met their *process* or intermediate objectives—like membership recruitment, consensus building, sustainability, and so on—than they have at demonstrating a causal impact of these programs on measures of public safety.

Process evaluations have revealed some of the factors that help launch and sustain participation in crime prevention initiatives. First, the involvement of extant multi-issue community organizations and of charismatic community leaders are strong determinants of program initiation, participation, and longevity. Activities initiated by and established within long-standing community organizations appear to outlast government-initiated programs, because these organizations can sustain the crime prevention network even as perceptions of the crime problems and funding and political support vacillate.

Instilling community cohesion is another important process aim of community crime prevention; some scholars even consider it the primary objective. While community organizations in general have clearly advanced this goal, scant statistical evidence supports the many anecdotal reports of a strong effect of community crime prevention on social interaction and mutual solidarity.

In addition to community-building, another process aim of community crime prevention is enhancing the political efficacy of a community. Through their activities, community members learn effective ways to act collectively, to cooperate with other organizations, and to strategically challenge policy proposals. Accordingly, a study by Grant, Lewis, and Rosenbaum observed an increase in civic participation following the institution of a large-scale block watch program in an area of Chicago and concluded that participation in crime prevention translated into greater political leverage for the community over "criminal justice, municipal, and even state institutions" (p. 381).

The outcomes of greatest interest to criminologists, however, are perceived and actual levels of crime and disorder, as well as fear of crime. Unfortunately, various characteristics of community crime prevention programs and the evaluation process have severely curtailed the frequency and quality of outcome-based assessments. Frequently cited obstacles to effective evaluation are the lack of available funds, of baseline and victimization data, of untreated equivalent communities for comparison, and of the required number of program sites needed to make reliable causal inferences. Insufficiently short follow-up periods and the reporting and recording biases of arrest and crime incident report data are additional impediments to assessment. Furthermore, the existence of so many multi-modality programs with flexible implementation plans impairs the ability of researchers to pinpoint the source of the apparent positive or negative effects.

At the risk of ignoring numerous striking counterexamples, the cumulative results of outcome-based evaluations can be summarized as follows:

1. Strategies centering on community organization and political mobilization have evidenced no consistent impacts on crime measures, but some modest reductions in fear of crime.
2. Programs integrating youth or gang outreach workers fail to decrease crime and may even increase arrests, although Malcolm Klein demonstrated a decline in gang arrests during and immediately following a program that works with gang members as individuals.
3. The best evidence, including one evaluation involving randomization, fails to find any long-term impact of neighborhood watch programs on crime, disorder, and fear of victimization. Programs that also include close police community collaboration and/or environmental modification components have yielded some encouraging results, however.
4. While evaluations of comprehensive community programs of the 1990s are explicitly encouraged, disappointingly few outcome-based evaluations are pending.
5. Programs that have produced favorable results on some indicators of delinquency are after school recreation programs, the Big Brothers/Big Sisters program, and localized citizen-initiated community anti-drug efforts.

Problems and prospects

Inadequate and inconsistent evidence renders premature the frequent conclusion that most forms of community crime prevention pro-

grams are ineffective. Knowledge of this fact, however, does not prevent numerous scholars and researchers from proposing factors that impede crime prevention programs from attaining their goals. Most importantly, programs have been criticized for not addressing the structural correlates of crime such as poverty, unemployment, and housing segregation. While crime prevention programs that attempt to seriously challenge the power structure are largely unsuccessful, the prevailing models of community crime prevention that involve community/government agency partnerships have been criticized for actually reinforcing structures of inequality. Neighborhood self-policing initiatives may effectively organize citizens and clean up signs of disorder in very localized areas, but do little to increase the resources of the larger community and sometimes merely relocate the problems to other neighborhoods. Furthermore, crime watch–oriented groups, when they are dominated by homeowners and landlords, often develop an "us versus them" mentality. These groups may reduce crime and disorder at the expense of excluding less privileged members from the organization and helping remove those they define as threats (e.g., gang members and the homeless) from the community—which can manifest and exacerbate race and class tensions.

Both community/police partnership and larger comprehensive partnership approaches have also been criticized for subverting the agendas of community groups. Whether community organizations initiate the partnerships or they are lured into partnerships by the promise of greater resources and services, they may find themselves with little or no power over politically-driven resource allocation and programming decisions and/or saddled with various administrative hassles. This, along with issues over turf, may explain why the program sites of the Comprehensive Communities Program report difficulty in eliciting and maintaining the support of community residents—support that Shaw and others have deemed essential to the effectiveness of interventions. Communities face a trade off between the efficient and research-based delivery of more needed resources into their communities and their power to respond collectively and autonomously to their self-defined needs, based on their own democratic processes.

The immediate future looks bright for federally funded large-scale community crime prevention. For instance, congressional allocations to Title V Community Crime Prevention doubled at the end of the 1990s. Thus many programs that work toward a community crime prevention vision of strong urban communities—through mediating conflicts within them, giving residents a greater voice within the context of collaboration, and providing opportunities for at-risk youth—will continue to balance the popular community defense approaches. At the same time, exclusionary trends in the social and political landscape, including gentrification, increased punitive criminal justice intervention, social welfare retrenchment, and pervasive fear and distrust, have led to calls for investment in alternative programs—fashioned after programs in Australia and elsewhere—that include excluded groups in integrative community actions that reduce fear as well as crime. Thus even in the face of steady declines in crime, the need for community crime prevention programs may continue to grow.

PAUL J. HIRSCHFIELD

See also CRIME CAUSATION: SOCIOLOGICAL THEORIES; DISPUTE RESOLUTION PROGRAMS; ECOLOGY OF CRIME; FEAR OF CRIME.

BIBLIOGRAPHY

BENNETT, SUSAN F. "Community Organizations and Crime." *Annals of the American Academy of Political and Social Science* 539 (1995): 72–84.

BROWN, MARK, and POLK, KENNETH. "Taking Fear of Crime Seriously: The Tasmanian Approach to Community Crime Prevention." *Crime and Delinquency* 42, no. 3 (1996): 398–420.

CLARKE, RONALD V., ed. *Situational Crime Prevention: Successful Case Studies.* New York: Harrow and Henson, 1992.

CLOWARD, RICHARD A., and OHLIN, LLOYD E. *Delinquency and Opportunity.* Glencoe, Ill.: Free Press, 1960.

CRAWFORD, ADAM. "Appeals to Community and Crime Prevention." *Crime, Law and Social Change* 22, no. 2 (1995): 97–126.

The Crime Commission of New York State. *Crime and the Community: A Study of Trends in Crime Prevention by the Sub-Commission on Causes and Effects of Crime.* Albany, N.Y.: J.B. Lyon Company, 1930.

DAVIS, ROBERT C., and LURIGIO, ARTHUR J. *Fighting Back: Neighborhood Anti-Drug Strategies.* Thousand Oaks, Calif.: Sage Publications, 1996.

DONNELLY, PATRICK D., and KIMBLE, CHARLES E. "Community Organizing, Environmental Change, and Neighborhood Crime." *Crime and Delinquency* 43, no. 4 (1997): 493–511.

DUNCAN, J. T. SKIP. *Citizen Crime Prevention Tactics. A Literature Review and Selected Bibliography.* Washington, D.C.: National Institute of Justice, 1980.

FARRINGTON, DAVID P. "Evaluating a Community Crime Prevention Program." *Evaluation* 3, no. 2 (1997): 157–173.

FRIEDMAN, WARREN. "Community Volunteerism and the Decline of Violent Crime." *Journal of Criminal Law and Criminology* 88, no. 4 (1998): 1453–1474.

GRANT, JANE; LEWIS, DAN; and ROSENBAUM, DENNIS. "Political Benefits of Program Participation: The Case of Community Crime Prevention." *Journal of Urban Affairs* 10, no. 4 (1988): 373–385.

HAWKINS, J. DAVID; CATALANO, RICHARD F.; and ASSOCIATES. *Communities That Care: Action for Drug Abuse Prevention.* San Francisco, Calif.: Jossey-Bass, 1992.

HOPE, TIM. "Community Crime Prevention." In *Building a Safer Society. Strategic Approaches to Crime Prevention. Crime and Justice: A Review of Research,* 19. Edited by Michael Tonry and David P. Farrington. Chicago, Ill.: University of Chicago Press, 1995. Pages 21–89.

HSIA, HEIDI M., and BOWNES, DONNA. *Title V: Community Prevention Grants Program.* Washington, D.C.: Office of Juvenile Justice and Delinquency Policy, 1998.

KELLING, GEORGE; HOCHBERG, MONA R.; KAMINSKA, SANDRA. L.; ROCHELEAU, ANN MARIE; ROSENBAUM, DENNIS P.; ROTH, JEFFREY A.; and SKOGAN, WESLEY G. *The Bureau of Justice Assistance Comprehensive Communities Program: A Preliminary Report.* Washington, D.C.: National Institute of Justice, 1998.

KOBRIN, SOLOMON. "The Chicago Area Project." In *The Sociology of Punishment and Correction.* Edited by N. Johnston, L. Savitz, and M. Wolfgang. New York: Wiley, 1962.

LURIGIO, ARTHUR J., and ROSENBAUM, DENNIS P. "Evaluation Research in Community Crime Prevention: A Critical Look at the Field." In *Community Crime Prevention: Does It Work?* Edited by D. P. Rosenbaum. Beverly Hills, Calif.: Sage, 1986.

PARK, ROBERT E.; BURGESS, ERNST W; and MCKENZIE, R. D. "Community Organization and Juvenile Delinquency." In *The City.* Edited by R. E. Clarke et al. Chicago: Chicago University Press, 1926.

SCHOLSSMAN, STEVEN; ZELLMAN, GAIL L.; and SHAVELSON, RICHARD J. *Delinquency Prevention in South Chicago: A Fifty-year Assessment of the*

Chicago Area Project. Santa Monica, Calif.: RAND, 1984.

SHAW, CLIFFORD R. *Delinquency Areas.* Chicago: University of Chicago Press, 1929.

SHERMAN, LAWRENCE W.; GOTTFREDSON, DENISE; MACKENZIE, DORIS; ECK, JOHN; REUTER, PETER; and BUSHWAY, SHAWN. *Preventing Crime: What Works, What Doesn't, What's Promising.* Washington, D.C.: Office of Justice Programs, 1997.

SKOGAN, WESLEY G. *Disorder and Decline.* New York: Free Press, 1990.

TIERNEY, JOSEPH P.; GROSSMAN, JEAN B.; with RESCH, NANCY L. *Making a Difference: An Impact Study of Big Brothers/Big Sisters.* Philadelphia: Public/Private Ventures, 1995.

U.S. National Advisory Commission on Criminal Justice Standards. *Community Crime Prevention.* Washington, D.C.: The Commission, 1973.

PREVENTION: DETENTION

See BAIL.

PREVENTION: ENVIRONMENTAL AND TECHNOLOGICAL STRATEGIES

For many social scientists the physical environment is simply the space in which activity occurs. Others see this arena as a factor in affecting the behavior that it contains, but in so doing assign the physical context widely different levels of causal importance. Some take a direct, environmental determinist position, and argue that like any other variable, the built environment actively affects attitudes, conditions, and behaviors. In contrast, others argue that although environmental variables may be correlates of behavior, they do not directly affect it. This perspective sees ethnicity, income, life cycle, lifestyle, and other sociocultural factors as the ultimate generators of action, and a voluntary or forced affinity for specific types of physical environments as well. Thus, this selection model accepts that there is a strong association between environment and behavior, but suggests that assigning causality to it is spurious. Finally, a compromise position acknowledges causal importance in the architectural context, but stops short of determinism. This Darwinian model portrays physical settings as varying in the extent to which they permit or prevent behavior but locates the moti-

vation for it elsewhere (see Michelson). All three of these positions can be found in explanations of criminal and delinquent behavior, and all have different implications for preventing it.

Environmental determinism and crime

Associations produced by post-factum analyses of rates of crime and delinquency and various aspects of the built environment, whether cities, neighborhoods, or types of dwelling, can almost always be explained by a selection argument. However, it is also possible that the physical environment causes those who inhabit it to feel and behave differently. Environmental sociologists and psychologists such as John Calhoun report a causal link between population density and social pathology, including sexual assault and extreme violence, among rats in laboratory experiments. Many social psychologists take the same position when they describe the impact of the urban environment on people, arguing that high population density can overload nervous systems, producing aggression or withdrawal (fight or flight) as a response. Debate on the extent to which population density affects criminal or other behavior continues (see Gove), but there is little doubt that density can affect humans. The real question is how high density has to go to produce specific results, especially criminal violence.

A more cognitive version of environmental determinism can be found in the argument that the physical setting provides "cues" to which actors will respond with either conforming or deviant behavior (see, for example, Brantingham and Brantingham, 1981). Graffiti, broken windows, and other signs of low surveillance in urban areas may elicit criminal behavior and stimulate out-migration of law-abiding residents as well. Philip Zimbardo's classic experiment, where a team of researchers timed how long it took for an unguarded automobile to be stripped on a New York City street, exemplifies this perspective. The study concluded that the car represents an opportunity as well as an indicator of social disorganization, motivating even normally conforming passers-by to engage in criminal behavior.

Earlier in the twentieth century, urban ecologists at the University of Chicago suggested that it is indeed social disorganization that links the urban environment to crime and delinquency. Louis Wirth, for example, argued that the size, density, and social heterogeneity of urban populations makes the city infertile ground for community, social organization, or control. This erodes traditional norms, and the freedom, anonymity, and hyperstimulation promote individual withdrawal as a defensive reaction, with bystander apathy as a consequence. (This urban indifference not only allows offenders to get away with pleasurable but illegal activities, but may even inspire individuals to engage in flamboyant nonconforming behavior in an effort to assert their individualism and be noticed.)

The Chicago School is not without its critics, and in other times and places urbanization is a negative not a positive correlate of crime (Gillis, 1989). However, recent cross-sectional research in North America shows that contemporary urban areas are indeed higher in rates of most types of crime than are rural regions. Further, urbanites are also more tolerant of differences and nonconformity, draw a sharper distinction between friends and strangers, and treat the latter with greater indifference than do their rural counterparts (see Gillis, 1995). Whether these variables actually intervene between the physical environment and crime is uncertain. Disorganization theory has been reformulated in terms of network analysis, and supported empirically with data from Great Britain (Sampson and Groves). However, this research does not support the optimism of the early 1960s that clearing slums and improving the physical environment will actually combat crime as well as urban blight. This cannot happen when criminogenic demographic, economic, and cultural conditions continue (see Wilson).

Selection

The idea that rates of crime and delinquency are concentrated in some spatial configurations is widely accepted, especially at the macro level (see Gillis, 1996). However, whether these associations between environment and behavior are causal, or the product of selection, is less clear. For example, cities depend on migration from rural areas for their survival and growth because of the relative infertility of urban populations. Since rural migrants to cities are not randomly selected, people in some types of circumstances are more likely to migrate than are those in others. It is possible that people who leave rural areas for the bright lights of the city are also less bound by family and other local ties, more inclined to take risks, and more likely to become involved in crime than are those who stay put. The effect of this selection would be to lower crime rates in rural areas while simultaneously increasing them in urban areas, producing a positive correlation between urbanization and rates of crime. In fact, cities or neighborhoods may even attract excitement seekers or criminals from rural areas who travel to cities only to engage in crime (Gibbs and Erickson).

The attraction to large urban areas of thrill-seekers and people in search of the unusual is easy to understand. Cities are not simply large versions of small towns. They are different. Small, dispersed populations, such as those in rural areas, villages, and towns cannot support markets for highly specialized goods and services. In contrast, the large, diverse populations of cities can harbor a wide range of atypical and criminal interests that merge as deviant subcultures. This may explain why cross-sectional analyses show that the rate of criminal activity in the U.S. not only varies between rural and urban areas, but directly with the current size of metropolitan populations as well (Fischer).

Moreover, once areas become known for the specialized goods and services which they provide, both short- and long-run migration patterns are likely to be affected, further enhancing the reputation of the area. Even Calhoun's rats who were able to nest in low-density sectors frequently ventured into the high-density areas of the site, apparently for excitement. This is consistent with the idea that specific environments not only operate as entertainment areas, but as "deviance service centers." Although they can be as large as states (e.g., Nevada, when it first legalized gambling, prostitution, and quick divorces), or metropolitan areas such as Atlantic City, deviance service centers are most often a section of a city, a peripheral neighborhood, or a suburb. One of the most famous of these centers was Southwark, directly across the Thames from London. In Shakespeare's time (the turn of the seventeenth century) he and his Globe Theatre were situated in Southwark, providing popular adult entertainment. For additional amusement, an abundance of drinking establishments, hotels, brothels, and prostitutes accommodated patrons who were unable or unwilling to make it back to London before curfew. Jails, including the original "Clink," housed more disruptive revellers, and Winchester Cathedral was not only available for repentance, but for licensing prostitutes. Thus, without being inside the physical, political, or moral boundaries of the city, Southwark provided both legitimate and illegitimate entertainment for the people of Elizabethan London (Gillis, 1995).

The out-migration of conformists can also distribute crime and delinquency differentially in urban areas. Some suburban neighborhoods are not only exclusive to those who can afford to live in them but, as "gated communities" with private security, even restrict access to residents and authorized visitors. Even entire suburban communities may be restricted, as "edge cities" near but off limits to the residents of core areas. On the other side, there are neighborhoods and even specific cities that have been not only abandoned by employable residents, but by industry and legitimate economic opportunities as well (Wilson). In this respect, the extent to which gated communities and edge cities enjoy low rates of crime is directly related to increasing crime rates in inner cities.

The policy implications here are both social and legal. Disorganized areas of inner cities require assistance at both structural and cultural levels to escape the downward spiral in which they are caught. Legitimate economic opportunities and the motivation and ability to take advantage of them are lacking. If employment opportunities exist, they are likely to be illegal, and this may or may not be viewed as a problem in neighboring jurisdictions. With respect to deviance service centers, activities that are considered deviant or criminal when committed in one section of a jurisdiction need not be prosecuted as such in others. Elizabethan London, contemporary Amsterdam, and other cities containing deviance service centers represent efforts to contain, rather than constrain, behavior that is regarded as undesirable in the wider population. This is accomplished by permitting bounded zones of the urban environment to contain outlets for both providers and consumers of disreputable activity. Whether life is better or worse for those within the service sectors is both an empirical and ethical question.

Opportunities, constraints, and defensible space

Interaction models specify conditional relationships, or scope limiters, whereby other variables soften the determinism of an independent variable. In the case of population density, for example, individuals can be seen as more or less equipped by their personalities or the capital provided by their cultures to cope successfully with crowding (Gillis, Richard, and Hagan). This

could account for the inconsistent results reported by more deterministic additive equations examining the relationship between population density and criminal behavior.

Newman's *Defensible Space* (1972) presented an interaction model applied to the impact of the architectural environment on crime, from an environmental opportunity/constraint perspective. Newman suggested that specific aspects of urban design create unsupervised locations by inhibiting or preventing surveillance and control in neighborhoods, and even within apartment buildings. High walls around buildings, underground parking areas, long corridors, and secluded spaces such as stairwells provide opportunity for deviant or criminal activity. This is because these locations are concealed from formal policing on streets. At the same time, since this space lies outside their own dwelling units, residents do not feel obliged to maintain surveillance on these areas either. Distance from home is inversely related to willingness to intervene (Gillis and Hagan, 1990). As with the perspective developed by the Chicago School, then, Newman's argument accounts for the location of criminal activity, and suggests that structural barriers (in this case architectural) can block the local social ties that are community, permitting increased rates of crime and delinquency. In this respect, Pruitt-Igoe, the infamous public housing project in St. Louis, exemplifies how not to design.

The scale of neighborhoods, projects, and buildings may also contribute to the degree of disorganization and rate of mayhem. Pruitt-Igoe contained a concentration of disadvantaged people. This may have also provided a critical mass of young, criminally disposed males, who were not only able to act as individual offenders, but who coalesced as gangs, creating criminal subcultures with a program of recruitment. In line with this, juvenile residents of high-rises report greater use of illicit drugs than do their counterparts in low-density housing (Gillis and Hagan, 1982). In any case, since the debacle and destruction of Pruitt-Igoe, many communities try to avoid large-scale public housing projects, and follow a program of dispersal instead of concentration.

Interestingly, Newman attaches great importance to the presence of graffiti as an indicator of lapsed control and portentous of future crime. Declines in crime in cities such as New York during the late 1990s are typically explained by civic officials as the result of acting against minor as well as major offenses, including graffiti. This suggests that environmental cues may elicit illegal activity, as noted earlier, but the actual causal sequence here is uncertain. It is also noteworthy that the interaction model can be interpreted as a statement that a causal sequence will not hold under all conditions. Thus, increasing the lighting on streets will not reduce mugging any more than a vault will reduce bank robberies if no offenders are present in the population. Similarly, changing traffic flow by establishing a one-way street will not reduce prostitution in areas where there are neither prostitutes nor johns. On the other side, if Pruitt-Igoe and its surroundings had contained older women instead of young, truly disadvantaged males, the project's crime rate would have been low. The interaction argument is that environmental design can discourage informal social control, and that this will in turn result in increased criminal activity, but only in populations with a propensity to offend in the first place. Thus, criminogenic architecture and planning will have no effect on the crime rate of a population of conformists. However, in a population of risk takers, a crime prevention strategy based on environmental design and increased informal surveillance would make a difference, especially in urban areas. In rural areas and small towns, traditional occupations for husbands and wives revolve around the home, where surveillance is maintained and passersby noticed. In contrast, occupations and routine cosmopolitan activities in modern urban areas frequently draw adults away from home, leaving an unattended store of valuable goods, which may attract burglars (Cohen and Felson), even from the hinterland. In this way, specific areas may produce criminal opportunity more than offender personalities, and by so doing inflate the rate of crime in those environments.

On a broad level, commercial neighborhoods containing too few residences must depend solely on policing for after-hours surveillance. The planning implication here is to avoid desertion after 6 p.m. by zoning for a mix of residential and commercial land use.

Social reaction and offensible space

Disorganization theory and the opportunity-constraint argument suggest that the built environment can reduce community control and inflate crime rates. Directly opposed to this, a social reaction perspective alerts us to the possibility that variation in official rates of crime and delinquency may measure different patterns of enforcement and recording of offenses more than in patterns of criminal behavior. In the case of the physical environment, the likelihood of detection, apprehension, and recording of offenses may be higher in some locations than in others. Rather than seeing cities as places to commit crime with impunity, then, the reaction perspective suggests that because of their high density and more extensive surveillance, urban areas may actually increase the likelihood of criminal activity being detected and apprehended than in the countryside. Although many urban neighborhoods may look disorganized, especially to middle-class social scientists, the communities which they contain may be alive and well, with strong patterns of surveillance and intervention. Moreover, police are more likely to patrol high-density areas and detect any offenses that occur within them. Juveniles in high-density locations in urban areas corroborate this by reporting higher levels of police contact than do adolescents in low-density neighborhoods (Hagan, Gillis, and Chan). This may also occur on the macro level. Historically, the ratio of police to population is higher in urban than in rural areas (Gillis, 1989). Further, bureaucratized urban police forces are more likely to process and record the offenses that they detect than are their rural counterparts. Between increased informal surveillance of residents and formal control of urban policing, then, higher official rates of crime in cities may reflect heightened bureaucracy more than higher rates of criminal activity. Thus, a feedback model may best capture the relationship between crime and space.

A. R. GILLIS

See also CRIME CAUSATION: SOCIOLOGICAL THEORIES; ECOLOGY OF CRIME; GUNS, REGULATION OF; POLICE: PRIVATE POLICE AND INDUSTRIAL SECURITY.

BIBLIOGRAPHY

BRANTINGHAM, PAUL J., and BRANTINGHAM, PATRICIA, eds. *Environmental Criminology.* Beverly Hills, Calif.: Sage, 1981.
CALHOUN, JOHN B. "Population Density and Social Pathology." *Scientific American* 206 (1963): 139–148.
COHEN, LAWRENCE E., and FELSON, MARCUS. "Social Change and Crime Rate Trends: A Routine Activities Approach." *American Sociological Review* 44 (1979): 588–608.
COHEN, LAWRENCE E., and MACHALEK, RICHARD. "A General Theory of Expropriative Crime."

American Journal of Sociology 94 (1988): 465–501.

FISCHER, CLAUDE S. *The Urban Experience*, 2d ed. New York: Harcourt, Brace, Jovanovich, 1984.

GIBBS, JACK, and ERICKSON, MAYNARD. "Crime Rates of American Cities in an Ecological Context." *American Journal of Sociology* 82 (1976): 605–620.

GILLIS, A. R. "Crime and State Surveillance in Nineteenth-Century France." *American Journal of Sociology* 95, no. 2 (1989): 307–341.

———. "Urbanization." In *New Society*. Edited by R. J. Brym. Toronto: Harcourt Brace, 1995. Pages 13–40

———. "Urbanization, Crime, and Historical Context." In *Criminological Controversies*. Edited by J. Hagan, A. R. Gillis, and D. Brownfield. Boulder, Colo.: Westview Press, 1996. Pages 47–74.

GILLIS, A. R., and HAGAN, JOHN. "Density, Delinquency and Design: Formal and Informal Control and the Residential Environment." *Criminology* 19, no. 4 (1982): 514–529.

———. "Delinquent Samaritans: Social Conflict, Network Structure, and the Willingness to Intervene." *Journal of Research in Crime and Delinquency* 27, no. 1 (1990): 30–51.

GILLIS, A. R.; RICHARD, MADELINE A.; and HAGAN, JOHN. "Ethnic Susceptibility to Crowding: An Empirical Analysis." *Environment and Behavior* 18, no. 6 (1986): 683–706.

GOVE, WALTER. "Review of *Household Crowding and Its Consequences* by Edwards et al." *American Journal of Sociology* 101, no. 4 (1996): 1137–1138.

HAGAN, JOHN; GILLIS, A. R.; and CHAN, JANET. "Explaining Official Delinquency." *The Sociological Quarterly* 19, no. 3 (1978): 386–398.

MICHELSON, WILLIAM. *Man and His Urban Environment*, 2d ed. Reading, Mass.: Addison-Wesley, 1976.

NEWMAN, OSCAR. *Defensible Space*. New York: Macmillan, 1972.

NEWMAN, OSCAR, and FRANCK, KAREN A. *Factors Influencing Crime and Instability in Urban Housing Projects*. Washington, D.C.: U.S. National Institute of Justice, 1980.

SAMPSON, ROBERT J., and GROVES, W. BYRON. "Community Structure and Crime: Testing Social Disorganization Theory." *American Journal of Sociology* 94 (1988): 774–802.

WILSON, WILLIAM J. *The Truly Disadvantaged: The Inner City, the Underclass, and Public Policy*. Chicago: University of Chicago Press, 1987.

WIRTH, LOUIS. "Urbanism as a Way of Life." *American Journal of Sociology* 44 (1938): 3–24.

ZIMBARDO, PHILLIP. "A Field Experiment in Auto Shaping." In *Vandalism*. Edited by Colin Ward. London: Architectural Press, 1973.

PREVENTION: JUVENILES AS POTENTIAL OFFENDERS

If a program prevents the first delinquent act, the social harm associated with subsequent delinquency can be avoided. To deliver on this promise, however, prevention programs must be effective and targeted to those most likely to offend. Evaluation research has challenged the effectiveness of prevention efforts, prompting one careful reviewer to conclude: "Prevention projects don't work and they waste money, violate the rights of juveniles and their families, inspire bizarre suggestions and programs, and fail to affect the known correlates of urban delinquency . . . it is time to get out of the business of attempting to prevent delinquency" (Lundman, p. 245). In contrast to this appraisal, another careful examination concludes that such efforts "show promise in their potential for helping participants and having positive spillover effects for other members of society" (Karoly et al., p. 107).

The differences in these assessments reflect the different programs, outcomes, and evaluation procedures examined. This entry critically examines prevention efforts and their evaluation, and identifies the most promising new approaches. Early attempts, such as the 1825 opening of the New York House of Refuge and sixteenth-century British Poor Laws, aimed to prevent delinquency by housing a population one would today characterize as "at-risk youth." Since this time alternative approaches have emerged, including individualized treatment, early childhood intervention, and programs targeting adolescents, low-income communities, and youths in the juvenile justice system.

Individualized treatments

In the early 1900s delinquency prevention was based on individualized case-by-case treatment (Healy). Progressive Era reformers launched well meaning but vague efforts that were ultimately undercut by administrators (Rothman). Individualized treatment was predicated on early identification, using instruments such as the Minnesota Multiphasic Personality Inventory (Hathaway and Monachesi), the Glueck Social Prediction Table (Glueck and

Glueck), and reports of teachers, police officers, and playground workers (Powers and Witmer) to identify future delinquents. These scales tended to "overpredict" delinquency, misclassifying many youths. This is especially problematic since empirical evidence suggests that intervention treatment for high-risk youths may result in harmful consequences (McCord). Although predictive accuracy has improved over the years, the high "false positive" rate of the assessment tools and the heterogeneous nature of delinquency continue to impede individualized prevention efforts.

Since the 1980s, Multisystemic Therapy (MST) has revived individualized approaches, using treatment teams to address problems in each of the key settings in which the youth is embedded. MST interventions include family treatment to help parents monitor and discipline their children, peer interventions to remove them from deviant peers, and school and vocational interventions to advance their future potential. Some evaluations show reduced arrest rates among MST participants relative to those receiving other services or no treatment (Henggeler).

Early intervention

In the 1960s, the Perry Preschool program combined weekly home visits by teachers with early education for disadvantaged African American children. Evaluations showed that program benefits (such as increased tax revenues and reduced social service and criminal justice expenditures) significantly outweighed program costs. Students enrolled in the program were 12 percent less likely to be arrested than the control group, with an average reduction of 2.3 arrests per student (Karoly et al., p. 139).

These findings and research on brain development in early childhood have spurred subsequent interventions with young children. For prevention researchers, early childhood provides a "window of opportunity" for intervention, as well as a "window of vulnerability" to poverty and dysfunctional homes (Karoly et al., p. xi). Strategies such as preschool programs, home visits, and parental training have all shown promise. Randomized evaluations of nurse home-visit programs show significant reductions in delinquency (Olds, Hill, and Rumsey). Family therapy with parental training may also be an effective early intervention, at comparatively low cost (Zigler, Taussig, and Black).

Older youths

Beyond early childhood, prevention programs for older, at-risk youths have also shown some success. Graduation incentives (cash and other benefits) to induce disadvantaged high school students to graduate may prevent more crimes per dollar spent than many early intervention efforts (Greenwood et al.). Although program results have yet to be evaluated against a meaningful comparison group, school-based Gang Resistance Education and Training (GREAT) may reduce gang activity among middle-school youths. GREAT participants engaged in 4 percent less delinquency and reported more negative attitudes about gangs than nonparticipants and program dropouts (Esbensen and Osgood).

Community

Some prevention programs operate at the neighborhood or community level, such as area projects (Shaw and McKay) and detached gang workers (Dixon and Wright). The Chicago Area Project (CAP), which began in 1932, was the first effort to organize local self-help groups in high-delinquency areas (Shaw and McKay). Although there is some evidence that CAP and other community-based programs may reduce delinquency rates (Schlossman et al. 1984), these programs have yet to be rigorously evaluated.

The Gautreaux project is also a neighborhood prevention program, although it involves moving families from low-income into urban or suburban middle-income neighborhoods rather than attempting to change low-income neighborhoods themselves. Compared to the urban movers, children of families moving into suburbs were more likely to complete high school, attend college, and work full-time (Duncan and Raudenbush). A similar intervention, the Moving to Opportunity (MTO) experiment, examined arrest outcomes. Boys whose families had moved from low-income to middle-income neighborhoods had 17 percent fewer arrests for violent offenses and 13 percent fewer "other" arrests as compared to a control group (Duncan and Raudenbush). Because of neighborhood differences in enforcement, however, these evaluations must be replicated with self-reported delinquency measures before firm conclusions can be drawn.

Juvenile justice

Many juvenile justice efforts aim to prevent minor offenders from escalating into more serious offenders. In the Scared Straight project, prison inmates confronted minor delinquents to threaten them with the consequences of illegal activities. This intervention failed to prevent crime and may have actually increased delinquent involvement by setting in motion a "delinquency fulfilling prophecy" (Finckenauer, p. 169). Other juvenile justice efforts with mixed results (often no better nor worse than institutionalization) include guided group interaction (Empey and Rabow) and diversion (Lemert). Drug courts combining treatment and rehabilitation are one promising system-based approach that may reduce reoffending among first-time drug offenders (Deschenes et al.).

Evaluation

The authors suggest that researchers consider the following questions in evaluating future delinquency prevention efforts.

1. Did the design randomly assign selection into treatment? If not, the results may be biased because program volunteers may be less delinquent than nonvolunteers.
2. Did the program target the right population? Its effectiveness may be age-graded or limited to certain groups, such as high-risk families (Karoly et al.).
3. What outcome is examined? Since few youths are institutionalized, significant program effects on incarceration are unlikely. Other benefits, such as reduced arrest or improved graduation rates, may be more appropriate.
4. How long is the follow-up observation period? Residential treatments, for example, may only prevent crime while youths are in residence (Mallar et al.).
5. Was the program fully implemented, or did cost or logistical problems dilute the treatment?
6. Do researchers have the ethical and legal licenses to intervene? "Predelinquents" have not yet committed crime and even apparently benign treatment could harm them. Conversely, if the treatment is beneficial, how can it be equitably withheld from low-risk children?

Conclusion

This review suggests that past disappointments have helped illuminate the limits of inter-

vention. Relative to the numerous events occurring in the everyday lives of juveniles, treatments are generally weak and must be acknowledged as such. Future research must build on the demonstrated success of early childhood interventions and strong treatments for adolescents. Randomized designs (or at least matched comparisons) are absolutely critical for identifying what works in preventing juvenile offending. Although several excellent evaluations have been completed, many programs have yet to be carefully evaluated. Beyond prevention, one emerging area of research is in studying desistance or cessation from crime among young offenders. Desistance programs for young offenders mitigate the practical problems of false positive predictions and the ethical problems of subjecting nonoffenders to treatment (Uggen and Piliavin).

Delinquency prevention efforts grew more informed and less naively optimistic in the 1980s and 1990s. Researchers no longer assume that children are more malleable than "hardened" adult offenders. We know today that some well-meaning prevention efforts are ineffective and that it is difficult to identify potential offenders. Nevertheless, several prevention efforts have demonstrated their effectiveness, most notably nurse home visits (Olds, Hill, and Rumsey), high school graduation incentives (Greenwood et al.), family therapy with parental training (Sherman et al.), and programs that move families from low-income to middle-income neighborhoods (Duncan and Raudenbush).

CHRISTOPHER UGGEN
MELISSA THOMPSON

See also EDUCATION AND CRIME; FAMILY RELATIONSHIPS AND CRIME; JUVENILE AND YOUTH GANGS; JUVENILE JUSTICE: HISTORY AND PHILOSOPHY; JUVENILE JUSTICE: COMMUNITY TREATMENT; JUVENILE JUSTICE: INSTITUTIONS; JUVENILE JUSTICE: JUVENILE COURT; JUVENILES IN THE ADULT SYSTEM; JUVENILE STATUS OFFENDERS; JUVENILE VIOLENT OFFENDERS; POLICE: HANDLING OF JUVENILES; PREDICTION OF CRIME AND RECIDIVISM; SCHOOLS AND CRIME.

BIBLIOGRAPHY

DESCHENES, ELIZABETH P.; TURNER, SUSAN; GREENWOOD, PETER W.; and CHIESA, JAMES. *An Experimental Evaluation of Drug Testing and Treatment Interventions for Probationers in Maricopa County, Arizona*. Santa Monica, Calif.: RAND, 1996.

DIXON, MICHAEL C., and WRIGHT, WILLIAM E. *Juvenile Delinquency Prevention Programs: An Evaluation of Policy Related Research on the Effectiveness of Prevention Programs.* Washington, D.C.: National Science Foundation, 1975.

DUNCAN, GREG J., and RAUDENBUSH, STEPHEN W. "Neighborhoods and Adolescent Development: How Can We Determine the Links?" Paper presented at Pennsylvania State University Symposium, 5–6 November 1998.

EMPEY, LAMAR T., and RABOW, JEROME. "The Provo Experiment in Delinquency Rehabilitation." *American Sociological Review* 26, no. 5 (1961): 679–695.

ESBENSEN, FINN-AAGE, and OSGOOD, D. WAYNE. "National Evaluation of G.R.E.A.T." *Research in Brief, National Institute of Justice.* Washington, D.C.: Government Printing Office, 1997.

FINCKENAUER, JAMES O. *Scared Straight! and the Panacea Phenomenon.* Englewood Cliffs, N.J.: Prentice-Hall, 1982.

GLUECK, SHELDON, and GLUECK, ELEANOR. *Unraveling Juvenile Delinquency.* New York: The Commonwealth Fund, 1950.

GREENWOOD, PETER W.; MODEL, KARYN E.; RYDELL, C. PETER; and CHIESA, JAMES. *Diverting Children from a Life of Crime, Measuring Costs and Benefits.* Santa Monica, Calif.: RAND, 1996.

HATHAWAY, STARKE R., and MONACHESI, ELIO D. *Adolescent Personality and Behavior: MMPI Patterns of Normal, Delinquent, Dropout, and Other Outcomes.* Minneapolis: University of Minnesota Press, 1963.

HEALY, WILLIAM. *The Individual Delinquent: A Text-Book of Diagnosis and Prognosis for All Concerned in Understanding Offenders.* Boston: Little Brown, 1915.

HENGGELER, SCOTT W. "Treating Serious Anti-Social Behavior in Youth: The MST Approach." Office of Juvenile Justice and Delinquency Prevention. Washington, D.C.: USGPO, 1997.

KAROLY, LYNN A.; GREENWOOD, PETER W.; EVERINGHAM, SUSAN S.; HOUBÉ, JILL; KILBURN, M. REBECCA; RYDELL, C. PETER; SANDERS, MATTHEW; and CHIESA, JAMES. *Investing in our Children: What We Know and Don't Know about the Costs and Benefits of Early Childhood Interventions.* Santa Monica, Calif.: RAND, 1998.

LEMERT, EDWIN. *Instead of Court: Diversion in Juvenile Justice.* Washington, D.C.: USGPO, 1971.

LUNDMAN, RICHARD J. *Prevention and Control of Juvenile Delinquency,* 2d ed. New York: Oxford University Press, 1993.

MALLAR, CHARLES; KERACHSKY, STUART; THORNTON, CRAIG; and LONG, DAVID. *Evaluation of the Economic Impact of the Job Corps Program: Third Follow-up Report.* Princeton, N.J.: Mathematica Policy Research, 1982.

MCCORD, JOAN. "A Thirty-year Follow-up of Treatment Effects." *American Psychologist* 33, no. 3 (1978): 284–289.

———. "The Cambridge–Somerville Study: A Pioneering Longitudinal–Experimental Study of Delinquency Prevention." In *Preventing Antisocial Behavior: Interventions from Birth to Adolescence.* Edited by Joan McCord and Richard E. Tremblay. New York: Guilford, 1992. Pages 196–206.

OLDS, DAVID; HILL, PEGGY; and RUMSEY, ELISSA. "Prenatal and Early Childhood Nurse Home Visitation." Office of Juvenile Justice and Delinquency Prevention. Washington, D.C.: USGPO, 1998.

POWERS, EDWIN, and WITMER, HELEN. *An Experiment in the Prevention of Juvenile Delinquency: The Cambridge-Somerville Youth Study.* New York: Columbia University Press, 1951.

ROTHMAN, DAVID J. *Conscience and Convenience: The Asylum and Its Alternatives in Progressive America.* Boston: Little, Brown, 1980.

SCHLOSSMAN, STEVEN; ZELLMAN, GAIL; SHAVELSON, RICHARD; SEDLAK, MICHAEL; and COBB, JANE. *Delinquency Prevention in South Chicago. A Fifty Year Assessment of the Chicago Area Project.* Santa Monica, Calif.: RAND, 1984.

SHAW, CLIFFORD R., and MCKAY, HENRY D. *Juvenile Delinquency and Urban Areas: A Study of Rates of Delinquency in Relation to Differential Characteristics of Local Communities in American Cities.* Chicago: University of Chicago Press, 1969.

SHERMAN, LAWRENCE W.; GOTTFREDSON, DENISE C.; MACKENZIE, DORIS L.; ECK, JOHN; REUTER, PETER; and BUSHWAY, SHAWN D. "Preventing Crime: What Works, What Doesn't, What's Promising." *Research in Brief, National Institute of Justice.* Washington, D.C.: Government Printing Office, 1998.

UGGEN, CHRISTOPHER, and PILIAVIN, IRVING. "Asymmetrical Causation and Criminal Desistance." *Journal of Criminal Law and Criminology* 88, no. 4 (1998): 1389–1412.

ZIGLER, EDWARD; TAUSSIG, CARA; and BLACK, KATHRYN. "Early Childhood Intervention, A Promising Preventative for Juvenile Delinquency." *American Psychologist* 47, no. 8 (1992): 997–1006.

PREVENTION: POLICE ROLE

Picture crime prevention as a leisurely river that flows toward the sea, fed by a network of streams, creeks, and other tributaries, some of which flow into the river alone, and others which first join with one another before reaching the river. In this analogy, we can think of the sea as the universe of formal and informal mechanisms used by society to deal with crime. Many rivers flow into this sea, including those that represent actions taken before, while, and after crime occurs. The crime prevention river contains all the mechanisms used by society to prevent crime before it occurs. The streams, creeks, and tributaries flowing into this river represent the many "streams of thought" about how to prevent crime, who should do it, and when it should be done. Crime prevention is not a single set of uniform tools; it represents a complex amalgam of ideas emerging from various academic disciplines like psychology, sociology, geography, and criminology. Current knowledge about effective crime prevention strategies comes from evaluation research and anecdotes about successful and unsuccessful programs and strategies used in the past. Some of these strategies have very little to do with the police, while others involve the police in important ways. Crime prevention efforts involving the police represent just one stream among many types of crime prevention efforts. This entry contains a brief overview of the methods used by the police to prevent crime, and how those methods have evolved in recent years.

Crime prevention has been one of the primary mandates of police organizations since the establishment of the first "modern" style police agency, the London Metropolitan Police, in 1829. Throughout much of the twentieth century, U.S. police agencies relied on three core operational strategies for preventing and controlling crime: random preventive patrol, rapid response to calls-for-service from citizens, and retrospective investigation of criminal offenses. Evaluation research in the 1970s cast doubt on the effectiveness of these strategies for preventing crime. The Kansas City Preventive Patrol Experiment, for instance, found that changing the level of patrol coverage had no effect on crime, citizen fear of crime, and several other outcome variables (Kelling et al.). Other evaluation research showed that rapid response to calls for service from citizens does not increase the likelihood of preventing a crime or apprehending an offender (Van Kirk; Spelman and Brown). Evaluations of the criminal investigation process demonstrated that the success of a criminal investigation depends in large part on the willingness

of witnesses to provide information to police (Greenwood and Petersilia). Finally, evidence from dozens of studies suggests that increasing the number of officers does not improve the ability of the police to reduce crime (Eck and Maguire). Research evidence on the ineffectiveness of traditional police strategies to reduce, control, or prevent crime led noted policing scholar David Bayley to declare boldly that:

The police do not prevent crime. This is one of the best kept secrets of modern life. Experts know it, the police know it, but the public does not know it. Yet the police pretend that they are society's best defense against crime and continually argue that if they are given more resources, especially personnel, they will be able to protect communities against crime. This is a myth. (p. 3)

Faced with alarming evidence on the ineffectiveness of their core strategies, police agencies have been experimenting with new methods and strategies for preventing crime. Furthermore, policing as an institution has adopted a much more open perspective toward evaluation research as a strategy for testing innovative strategies. This openness and curiosity on the part of police executives has led to a culture of experimentation among police practitioners and a profusion of studies by scholars on what works in policing. Two influential articles by noted policing scholars helped to fuel the fire of innovation.

In 1979, University of Wisconsin law professor Herman Goldstein published an article in the journal *Crime and Delinquency* (1979) entitled "Improving Policing: A Problem-Oriented Approach." In this article, Goldstein sketched the foundation for a new theory of police effectiveness. He argued that police agencies are so preoccupied with internal matters such as efficiency, equipment, technology, and operating routines, that they tend to lose sight of their purpose. Goldstein recommended that police agencies should stop treating "incidents" as their primary unit of work. Since incidents are often symptoms of one or more underlying problems, Goldstein argued, police should attempt to identify and solve problems rather than simply responding to incidents.

In 1982, James Q. Wilson and George Kelling published their famous article, "Broken Windows: The Police and Neighborhood Safety," in *Atlantic Monthly*. Wilson and Kelling claimed that the police had become so narrowly focused on serious crime that they tended to view other important community problems, such as disorder, as outside the scope of their responsibilities. Wilson and Kelling used broken windows as a metaphor for neighborhood disorder, arguing that unchecked disorder is an open invitation to further disorder and more serious crime. The implications for police strategy were clear: agencies need to reorient police resources toward maintaining order and preventing crime. Police officers around the world can now be heard talking about fixing "broken windows."

Both articles emerged at an important juncture in police history. Several contemporary evaluations of team policing and community relations units had been fairly pessimistic about the ability of the police to forge and sustain improved relationships with the community (Sherman et al., 1973). A spate of other evaluation research challenged the efficacy of traditional police practices such as random preventive patrol, criminal investigation, and rapid response to calls-for-service from the public (Bayley). These two articles served an important role, emerging at a time when scholars and practitioners were struggling to redefine the proper role of police in a democratic society. While there were clear differences between the two reform strategies, both made some similar prescriptions: first, police need to expand their mandate beyond crime to include disorder and other persistent community problems; second, in responding to these problems, police need to be proactive rather than simply reactive. Crime prevention played a significant role in each reform strategy. Together, these strategies combined with other forces (such as organizational change reforms in the public and private sectors) to accelerate the birth of the community policing movement.

Throughout the 1980s, these ideas were tested in several cities, including Baltimore County, Maryland, Madison, Wisconsin, and Newport News, Virginia. By the late 1980s, police agencies were beginning to take crime prevention seriously, experimenting with a number of crime prevention strategies as part of a broader effort to implement community-oriented and problem-oriented policing. By the early 1990s, community policing was quickly becoming a household term, playing a major role in President Clinton's 1992 presidential campaign and the 1994 Crime Act. Crime prevention is only one component of community policing. Other overlapping elements include community partnerships, problem-solving, and a variety of organizational changes designed to make police agencies more flexible and responsive. Nonetheless, crime prevention is a core element of community policing, and the degree to which police agencies now take crime prevention seriously is due in large part to the success of the community policing movement. Under community policing, preventing crime means working together with communities, learning about their problems, and designing unique solutions to these problems. Thousands of police agencies throughout the United States now claim to have adopted a proactive or preventive approach to crime (Maguire et al.). Researchers are still examining the validity of these claims.

Not all crime prevention activities involve the police, and of those that do, some did not emerge from the community policing movement. Next we explore two other streams of crime prevention thought: environmental criminology and community crime prevention. Both evolved independently of the police, but over time began to involve the police to some extent. Both also now occupy a role in the larger community policing movement.

Environmental criminology

Ecology is a branch of the biological sciences that studies the relationships between organisms and their environment. Robert Park was the first scholar to apply an ecological perspective to social science, studying the growth of cities in the United States (Bohm). The human, or social ecological, model was later applied to criminology by Clifford Shaw and Henry McKay, who described it as the "social disorganization" perspective. Shaw and McKay (1931) hypothesized that delinquency was not merely a product of inner personal conflicts, but of environmental factors particular to certain identifiable neighborhoods. They concluded that delinquency was the result of a "detachment from conventional groups" caused by social disorganization in certain areas of a city. Sampson and Groves (1989) retested this theory and found five indicators of social disorganization: (1) lower economic status of residents; (2) diverse ethnic backgrounds of residents; (3) frequent residential turnover; (4) high level of dysfunction in families; and (5) urbanization (Bohm, pp. 72–75). Shaw and McKay's work provided the theoretical roots of environmental criminology, which is based on the important role of the "place" or the environment in shaping crime.

In 1961, Jane Jacobs examined the relationship between physical environment and crime in her book *The Death and Life of Great American Cities*. Her thesis was that less anonymity and isolation would lead to a reduction in crime in urban residential areas. C. Ray Jeffrey's influential book, *Crime Prevention Through Environmental Design* (1971), argued that modifying specific features of neighborhood design will reduce crime. In 1972, Oscar Newman argued that communities need to establish "Defensible Space," the title of his book. According to Newman, defensible space "is a model for residential environments which inhibits crime by creating the physical expression of a social fabric that defends itself" (p. 3). Both Jeffrey and Newman suggested that modifying the architecture of urban neighborhoods would reduce crime. Given a more adequate environmental design, residents will change their behavior and defend their territory against criminals (Murray). By the mid-1970s, major demonstration projects were established to test these hypotheses. The Law Enforcement Assistance Administration funded a multimillion-dollar project to extend the concept of defensible space to other environments, such as a residential area, a transportation system, a commercial strip, and a school (Murray). In addition to their implications for architecture, engineering, and urban planning, both *Defensible Space* and *Crime Prevention Through Environmental Design* have also become well-known concepts in policing.

In 1979, Cohen and Felson proposed the "routine activities" theory of crime. They argued that crime results when three elements converge in space and time: (1) a motivated offender; (2) a suitable target; and (3) the absence of a capable guardian (Felson, 1998, p. 53). According to routine activities theory, crime is most likely to occur when these three conditions occur simultaneously in some time and place. For example, if the owners of a new car (a suitable target) leave their keys in the ignition while they run into the store (absence of a capable guardian) in a high-crime neighborhood (pool of motivated offenders), then the probability that the car will be stolen is increased. Routine activities theory has direct implications for crime prevention. To prevent crime, we must alter at least one of its "ingredients": the offender, the target, or the degree of protection or guardianship. The most effective crime prevention strategies will focus on all three of these elements.

In 1981, Paul and Patricia Brantingham combined the ideas of social ecology, social disorganization theory, crime prevention through environmental design, defensible space, and routine activities theory into a single theoretical framework with their book *Environmental Criminology*. According to the Brantinghams, a criminal event is the convergence in time and space of a law, an offender, and a target. Unlike most criminologists who focus on the "root causes" of crime, environmental criminologists are concerned with the criminal event itself. Environmental criminology has highlighted the significant role of the "place" in generating criminal events (Brantingham and Brantingham, p. 18).

While crime prevention strategies are implicit in the theory of environmental criminology, they are the explicit focus of situational crime prevention. Throughout the late 1970s and early 1980s, Ronald Clarke developed the situational crime prevention strategy. Rather than basing crime prevention strategies on traditional "root cause" theories, Clarke's crime prevention strategies represent an applied form of environmental criminology, focusing on practical strategies to reduce the likelihood of a criminal event. Situational crime prevention attempts to reduce the opportunity for specific crimes by permanently manipulating the immediate environment to increase the risk of crime while reducing its perceived rewards.

Situational crime prevention strategies abound. Airports installed metal detectors to prevent hijacking. Libraries and stores made it more difficult to steal books and other items by installing electronic access control inserts. Caller ID programs reduced the number of obscene phone calls by taking away the caller's anonymity (Clarke, p. 22). Observe that these practical strategies do not attempt to change the behavior of offenders; they focus solely on preventing the criminal event. Unlike many other crime prevention strategies, the police are not responsible for administering situational crime prevention. It is done by merchants, governments, architects, and others with a vested interest in reducing crime. Yet, as more police departments adopt problem-oriented policing strategies, they rely on situational crime prevention techniques to analyze and respond to various types of offenses. Environmental criminology and situational crime prevention emerged independently of the police, but both now have an important influence on the practice of policing.

Community crime prevention

Community crime prevention is based upon the premise that private citizens can play a major role in preventing crime in their neighborhoods. Community crime prevention programs focus on "increasing the participation of individual citizens, small groups, and voluntary community organizations in activities designed to reduce crime and to improve the quality of neighborhood life" (Rosenbaum, p. 324).

According to Rosenbaum, community crime prevention has consistently evolved since the 1960s, when most formal crime programs constituted little more than a "public relations tactic" by police to improve their image. In the mid-1970s, police departments began to instruct community members about individual and collective crime prevention techniques. However, police limited the scope of responsibilities they granted to citizens by only allowing them to act as "eyes and ears" for the police. Toward the end of the 1970s, two federal crime prevention initiatives allocated money to community programs rather than to police: the 1977 Community Anti-Crime Program and the 1980 Urban Crime Prevention Program. During the 1980s, many scholars put more faith in community efforts to prevent crime than in law enforcement. According to Rosenbaum, "we have learned since, however, that community groups are quite limited in preventing urban crime without the support of law enforcement, adequate funding, and considerable technical assistance" (p. 325).

Three programs (known as the "Big Three") have played a major role in citizen crime prevention in the United States: crime prevention security surveys, Operation Identification, and Neighborhood Watch. Security surveys have long been utilized as a tool for identifying targets that are vulnerable to crime, whether a poorly lit walkway or an unlocked window. Rosenbaum describes a security survey as "a detailed on-site inspection of the dwelling unit and the surrounding area by a crime prevention expert to identify deficiencies or security risks; to define the protection needs; and, to make recommendations to minimize criminal opportunity" (p. 341). Not surprisingly, local police are often the crime prevention experts called upon to conduct these surveys.

Operation Identification, first initiated in California in 1963, involves engraving and/or marking personal property with a unique code identifiable to the owner. Marking personal property is intended to deter potential burglars by reducing the value of the merchandise (marked property is worth less than unmarked property). An owner will also be able to recognize the marked property, which in turn can sometimes be used to link the burglar to the crime scene and increase the risk of apprehension (Rosenbaum). In 1994, Whitaker found that 25 percent of all U.S. households participated in Operation Identification (Whitaker).

Neighborhood watch programs are intended to reduce the opportunities to commit crime by increasing the guardianship exercised by local residents. Neighborhood watch meetings encourage residents to work together in making neighborhoods safer, watching each others' property, and creating a stronger sense of community. Garafolo and McLeod surveyed 550 Neighborhood Watch programs and found that most included property marking (81 percent), home security surveys (68 percent), meetings to plan and exchange neighborhood information (61 percent), and neighborhood newsletters (54 percent). In addition, more than one-third involved efforts to improve the physical environment (Garafolo and McLeod). Thus, Neighborhood Watch is sometimes a forum for combining separate crime prevention strategies.

Once again, community crime prevention has its own history that is at least partially independent of the police. Yet, as Rosenbaum reports, the community is only one element of the crime prevention equation. Working alone and without funding, citizens are likely to accomplish little. Working together with local police agencies, they have the capacity to prevent crime. That is one of the fundamental elements of community policing. Under a community policing philosophy, police agencies are expected to forge new relationships with the community, consulting, and mobilizing them to take partial responsibility for preventing crime in their own neighborhoods.

Conclusion

Modern police organizations were established to prevent and respond to crime. For several decades, evaluation research has cast doubt upon traditional strategies of policing. Police organizations around the world are now experimenting with new methods for controlling and preventing crime. Several crime prevention strategies have also emerged independently of the police. Throughout the 1980s and 1990s, police organizations turned to community policing as a method for reducing and preventing crime while improving relationships with their communities. During this period, several streams of crime prevention thought began to converge: environmental criminology, situational crime prevention, community crime prevention, and problem-oriented policing. As the community policing movement continues to spread, these perspectives have had more and more influence on police policy. While crime prevention has emerged from many sources, the police continue to play an important role in its implementation.

EDWARD R. MAGUIRE
KIMBERLY HASSELL

See also ECOLOGY OF CRIME; POLICE: COMMUNITY POLICING; POLICE: CRIMINAL INVESTIGATIONS; POLICE: HANDLING OF JUVENILES; POLICE: POLICE OFFICER BEHAVIOR; POLICE: POLICING COMPLAINANTLESS CRIME; POLICE: PRIVATE POLICE AND INDUSTRIAL SECURITY; URBAN POLICE.

BIBLIOGRAPHY

BAYLEY, DAVID H. *Police for the Future.* New York: Oxford University Press, 1994.

BENNETT, TREVOR. "Situational Crime Prevention from the Offenders' Perspective." In *Situational Crime Prevention: From Theory into Practice.* Edited by Kevin Heal and Gloria Laycock. London: Her Majesty's Stationery Office, 1986.

BOHM, ROBERT M. *A Primer on Crime and Delinquency.* Belmont, Calif.: Wadsworth Publishing Company, 1997.

BRANTINGHAM, PAUL J., and BRANTINGHAM, PATRICIA L. *Environmental Criminology.* Beverly Hills, Calif.: Sage, 1981.

CLARKE, RONALD V. *Situational Crime Prevention.* New York: Harrow and Heston, 1992.

COHEN, LAWRENCE K., and FELSON, MARCUS. "Social Change and Crime Rate Trends—A Routine Activity Approach." *American Sociological Review* 44, no. 4 (1979): 588–608.

ECK, JOHN E., and MAGUIRE, EDWARD R. "Have Changes in Policing Reduced Violent Crime? An Assessment of the Evidence." In *The Crime Drop.* Edited by Alfred Blumstein and Joel Wallman. New York: Cambridge University Press. Forthcoming.

FEELEY, MALCOM M., and SARAT, AUSTIN D. *The Policy Dilemma.* Minneapolis, Minn.: University of Minnesota Press, 1980.

FELSON, MARCUS. *Crime & Everyday Life.* Thousand Oaks, Calif.: Pine Forge Press, 1998.

GARAFOLO, J., and MCLEOD, M. *Improving the Effectiveness and Utilization of Neighborhood Watch Programs: Executive Summary.* Albany: State University of New York at Albany, National Institute of Justice, 1987.

GOLDSTEIN, HERMAN. "Improving Policing: A Problem-Oriented Approach." *Crime and Delinquency* 25 (1979): 236–258.

GREENWOOD, P., and PETERSILIA, J. *The Criminal Investigation Process.* Vol. 1, *Summary and Policy Implications.* Washington, D.C.; National Institute of Justice, 1975.

KELLING, GEORGE, et al. *The Kansas City Preventive Patrol Experiment: A Summary Report.* Washington, D.C.: National Institute of Justice, 1974.

MAGUIRE, EDWARD R.; KUHNS, JOSEPH B.; UCHIDA, CRAIG D.; and COX, STEPHEN M. "Patterns of Community Policing in Nonurban America." *Journal of Research in Crime and Delinquency* 34, no. 3 (1997): 368–394.

MAZEROLLE, LORRAINE GREEN; KADLECK, COLLEEN; and ROEHL, JAN. "Controlling Drug and Disorder Problems: The Role of Place Managers." *Criminology* 36, no. 2 (1998): 371–403.

MURRAY, CHARLES. "The Physical Environment." In *Crime.* Edited by James Q. Wilson and Joan Petersilia. San Francisco, Calif.: ICS Press, 1995. Pages 349–362.

NEWMAN, OSCAR. *Defensible Space: Crime Prevention Through Urban Design.* New York: Macmillan, 1972.

ROSENBAUM, DENNIS P. "Community Crime Prevention: A Review and Synthesis of the Literature." *Justice Quarterly* 5, no. 3 (1988): 323–395.

SAMPSON, ROBERT J., and GROVES, W. BYRON. "Community Structure and Crime: Testing Social Disorganization Theory." *American Journal of Sociology* 94 (1989): 774–802.

SAMPSON, ROBERT J.; RAUDENBUSH, STEPHEN W.; and EARLS, FELTON. "Neighborhoods and Violent Crime: A Multilevel Study of Collective Efficacy." *Science* 277 (1997): 918–924.

SHAW, CLIFFORD R., and MCKAY, HENRY D. *Social Factors in Juvenile Delinquency.* Washington, D.C.: Government Printing Office, 1931.

SHERMAN, LAWRENCE W.; MILTON, C.; and KELLY, T. "Team Policing: Seven Case Studies." Washington, D.C.: Police Foundation, 1973.

SHERMAN LAWRENCE W.; GARTIN, PATRICK R.; and BUERGER, MICHAEL E. "Hot Spots of Predatory Crime: Routine Activities and the Criminology of Place." *Criminology* 27, no. 1 (1989): 27–55.

SHERMAN, LAWRENCE W. "The Police." In *Crime.* Edited by James Q. Wilson and Joan Peter-

silia. San Francisco, Calif.: ICS Press, 1995.
Pages 327–348.

———. "Policing for Crime Prevention." In *Preventing Crime: What Works, What Doesn't, What's Promising*. University of Maryland, Office of Justice Programs, Research Report. Washington, D.C., 1997.

SPELMAN, W., and BROWN, D. *Calling the Police: Citizen Reporting of Serious Crime*. Washington, D.C.: National Institute of Justice, 1981.

VAN KIRK, M. *Response-time Analysis: Executive Summary*. Washington, D.C.: National Institute of Justice, 1978.

WALKER, SAMUEL. *The Police in America: An Introduction*. New York: McGraw Hill Book Company, 1983.

WHITAKER, C. J. *Crime Prevention Measures*. Washington, D.C.: National Institute of Justice, Bureau of Justice Statistics, 1986.

WILSON, JAMES Q., and KELLING, GEORGE L. "Broken Windows: The Police and Neighborhood Safety." *Atlantic Monthly* 249 (March 1982): 29–38.

PRISONERS, LEGAL RIGHTS OF

Americans live in a time of the greatest prison expansion in the modern history. By the close of 2000, almost two million adults were imprisoned at an operational cost that exceeds over $38 billion dollars a year. Minorities are represented in the prison population in percentages that far exceed their representation in the general population. African Americans comprise less than 13 percent of the U.S. population, yet 48 percent of the prison population is African American. With so many people in prison and with so much spent to keep them there, the rights of prisoners takes added significance. An additional factor is that every year more than a half million men and women prisoners are released. The treatment these people received in prison—whether it conforms to constitutional norms or not—will have consequences. It could very well mean the difference between having prisoners return to their communities embittered or having them return ready to begin law-abiding lives.

This entry will trace the history of prisoners' rights, and will provide a general description of the current state of the law. This review provides a context for considering the likely direction of future developments.

History of prisoners' rights

The history of the development of the rights of prisoners occurred over three distinct historic periods. The first, and longest lasting, was the period in which the "hands-off doctrine" prevailed. The second was the period of the civil rights era, which saw the evisceration of the hands-off doctrine and the birth of the idea that prisoners could have enforceable rights. The third, and current, period is one of retrenchment. During this period the U.S. Supreme Court, through a series of decisions, has both elaborated upon and diminished the rights of prisoners. In addition, Congress has intervened through the enactment of the Prison Reform Litigation Act (PLRA), a law that severely limits the ability of prisoners to seek vindication of their rights in court.

The hands-off period

During most of the history of the United States, prisoners had no legal right to humane conditions of confinement that could be judicially enforced. This view was so strong that one much-cited case even described a suing prisoner as a "slave of the state" (*Ruffin v. Commonwealth*, 62 Va. (21 Gratt) 790, 796 (1871)).

The hands-off doctrine precluded judges from determining what rights survived incarceration. Judges refused to intervene on the ground that their function was only to free those inmates illegally confined, not to superintend the treatment and discipline of prisoners in penitentiaries. The pull of the hands-off doctrine was so strong that claims of racial discrimination were not heard. Even safety issues were ignored. In one case, a federal court refused to hear from inmates whose lives were endangered by being held in overcrowded conditions in a firetrap. Even under these conditions, because of the hands-off doctrine, the judge declined to intervene (*Ex parte Pickens*, 101 F.Supp 285, 287, 290 (D.Alaska 1951)).

Underlying the hands-off doctrine were concerns about the appropriate reach of federal judicial power. Courts feared that separation of powers and federalism would be violated if courts intervened in the operation of state penal institutions. They would be using federal power to dictate to the states how to run their own institutions—the management and control of these institutions are generally viewed as executive and legislative functions. By adjudicating claims in favor of the state inmates, the federal courts also expressed concern that, contrary to principles of federalism, they would be intervening in state affairs. Finally, the courts doubted their ability to fashion meaningful relief when improvements in prison conditions required additional funding.

The attitude of the courts and the prison officials worked hand-in-hand to deny prisoners' rights. The courts believed that they lacked the expertise to become involved in prison management and the corrections officials perceived judicial review as a threat to internal discipline and authority. The specter of excessive workloads may have influenced judges also. With large numbers of prisoners willing to press a wide variety of claims, judges invoking the hands-off doctrine may have done so to avoid being inundated with prisoner petitions. Even if the petitions proved meritorious, a judge would have to spend a great deal of time handling the case. The hands-off doctrine served to ease the court's workload; once the court determined the claim was based on a prisoners' rights theory, the suit was automatically dismissed. But, the doctrine imposed costs, the most serious being that the merits of potentially worthy complaints were never reached. This meant that there was little judicial pressure to improve prison conditions.

The hands-off doctrine was eventually discredited. Courts and commentators began to recognize that the separation of powers does not foreclose judicial scrutiny when the legislature or executive acts unconstitutionally (Note). They also recognized that courts regularly invalidate laws that violate citizens' constitutional rights. In fact, a major function of courts in the U.S. constitutional system is to ensure that constitutional rights are preserved and protected.

The argument that courts lack expertise in prison management was also criticized. The argument is based on a misconception of the judiciary's role. The consideration of a particular practice on constitutional grounds rarely, if ever, requires a court to assume management of the penal institution. Even when it orders changes in policy a court does not have to engage in management of an institution. That can be left to prison officials who have the authority to find the best way administratively to implement the court's decision.

Further, arguments of counsel and the taking of testimony, including the testimony of expert witnesses, supply the expertise needed for accurate decision-making by the court. The courts have an additional supervisory resource—the use of appointed masters to assist in carrying out their orders. Finally, the possibility of "opening the floodgates" to frivolous petitions has always been the cost of operating a judicial system. This possibility has never been deemed a valid excuse for denial of constitutional rights. The courts have procedural means to control the filing of frivolous suits without refusing to entertain the meritorious actions. (Moreover, new restrictive methods of controlling this problem have been legislated through the Prison Reform Litigation Act, which is discussed below.)

The beginnings of prisoners' rights law—the civil rights era

In the 1960s and early 1970s, the growth of the civil rights movement rendered the "hands-off" doctrine increasingly vulnerable to attack. It was difficult to maintain the validity of the hands-off doctrine at a time of rising expectations for fair and equal treatment by government.

Several forces combined during the 1960s to increase the number of prison cases and shake the noninterventionist foundations of the doctrine. First, prisoners were becoming increasingly militant and assertive. The Black Muslims' successful First Amendment challenge to prison officials who ignored or punished their efforts to practice their religion represented some of the first courtroom victories for prisoners (*Pierce v. LaVallee*, 293 F.2d 223 (2d Cir. 1961); *Sewell v. Pegelow*, 291 F.2d 196 (4th Cir. 1961)). These victories opened the door to litigation on a variety of prison-related issues.

Second, the emergence and growth of a civil rights–civil liberties bar in the legal profession coupled with private foundation and public funding under the legal services program provided the expertise and funding for effective prisoner litigation. Overburdened courts that easily dismissed the complaints of pro se prisoners with limited education and little, if any, legal training could not so readily dismiss the same complaints properly filed by attorneys. Legal support of the cause was buttressed by public and media support as prison reform and the more humane treatment of prisoners became popular reformist themes after the release of a presidential crime commission report in 1967 (President's Commission). Finally, a new federal crime-control program, the Omnibus Crime Control and Safe Streets Act of 1968, was enacted, providing visibility and financial incentives for correctional reform.

Third, the judiciary was becoming more responsive to the plight of society's underprivileged. Nationally, the Supreme Court expanded the rights of the individual in relation to the state. These opinions began to establish the principles that federal courts have a special role in protecting the rights of "discrete and insular minorities" who are politically powerless. Prisoners are, by and large poor, minority persons whose needs command little respect in state legislatures—exactly the type of individuals that needed the protection of the courts. Supreme Court decisions helped prisoners assert their rights in two other ways: the Court's extension of most of the provisions of the Bill of Rights to the states allowed prisoners housed in state institutions to sue for violations of federal constitutional rights; and, the Court's resurrection of the Civil Rights Statute (42 U.S.C. § 1983) provided prisoners with an attractive procedural avenue for challenging prison conditions and practices in federal courts.

Finally, the public, including judges, became increasingly aware of the sordid conditions that often characterized prison life. Remote locations and highly restrictive visitation and mail policies complicated discovery of the activities behind prison walls. But prisoner strikes and riots, like the uprising in Attica, New York, in 1971 brought the reality of prisons to the attention of the public. Widely read books by prison authors like Eldridge Cleaver, Malcolm X, and George Jackson also helped raise the consciousness of the public. Likewise, these independent sources of knowledge about prison conditions may have raised the credibility of prisoner complaints in the eyes of judges. All these ingredients set the stage for the courts to begin the development of prisoners' rights law, as the hands-off doctrine declined.

Because of these factors, lower court judges began, almost for the first time, to consider the claims of inmates. Litigation, about conditions of confinement, whether in the horrendous prison systems of Arkansas, Alabama, and Mississippi or the infamous "Tombs" jail in lower Manhattan, New York, forced the lower courts of the 1970s to come face-to-face with the grimmest conditions of human confinement (See, e.g., *Rhem v. Malcom*, 371 F.Supp 594, 672 (S.D.N.Y.), *affd*, 507 F.2d 333 (2d Cir. 1974), *affd on remand*, 527 F.2d 1041 (2d Cir. 1975); *Holt v. Sarver*, 309 F.Supp 362 (E.D.Ark 1970), *affd*, 442 F.2d 304 (8th Cir. 1971); *Newman v. Alabama*, 559 F.2d 283 (5th Cir. 1997), *cert denied*, 438 U.S. 915 (1978)).

These cases established that judicial review of the complaints of prisoners for more humane treatment was the new reality—very much a "hands-on" approach. Indeed, prison conditions were so poor during this period and the courts so willing to consider prisoner complaints that by the middle of the 1980s prisons in some forty-five states plus the District of Columbia, Puerto Rico, and the U.S. Virgin Islands were operating under some form of court order to correct constitutional violations ("Status Report").

The hands-off doctrine formally ended with two decisions from the Supreme Court in the early 1970s. In the first decision, Justice Byron White explicitly sounded the death knell for the hands-off doctrine in a single line: "[T]here is no Iron Curtain between the Constitution and the prisons of this country" (*Wolf v. McDonnell*, 418, U.S. 539, 555-56 (1974)). At about the same time, Justice Lewis A. Powell, writing for the Court, stressed that when a prison regulation or practice offends a fundamental Constitutional guarantee the federal courts will exercise their duty to protect those rights (*Procunier v. Martinez*, 416 U.S. 396, 405-06 (1974)). Since then, the Supreme Court has continually asserted that the hands-off doctrine has no place in constitutional jurisprudence (See, e.g., *Thornburgh v. Abbott*, 490 U.S. 401, 407 (1989) ("[p]rison walls do not form a barrier separating prison inmates from the protections of the Constitution"); *Turner v. Safley*, 482 U.S. 78, 84 (1987)(same); *Rhodes v. Chapman*, 452 U.S. 337, 352 (1981) ("courts have a responsibility to scrutinize [prisoners'] claims. . ."); *Bell v. Wolfish*, 441 U.S. 520, 562 (1979)). It is now settled law that "hands-off" ends where the abridgement of constitutional rights begins.

But to say that inmates have rights is not to list the specific constitutional rights they retain nor is it to chart their boundaries. The elaboration of prisoners' rights that began during the civil rights era continues today, but the current period is also marked by retrenchment.

Elaboration and retrenchment

Beginning in the late 1970s and early 1980s the elaboration of prisoners' rights by the courts was characterized by a move toward retrenchment. This retrenchment was signaled by two significant developments. First, the Supreme Court under Chief Justice Warren E. Burger (1969 to 1986), and especially under William H. Rhenquist (appointed Chief Justice in 1986), grew increasingly unreceptive to the claims of "discrete and insular minorities." Second, the Congress, responding to critics who claimed that the lower courts had moved too far in protecting the rights of inmates, passed the Prison Reform Litigation Act, which restricted inmate access to the courts. While these developments did not return the law to the old and discredited "hands off" era, they did leave the law governing prisoners' rights far more restrictive than the law that governs the constitutional rights of free world citizens.

The Supreme Court

The key question for the Court once the hands-off doctrine fell became what standard to apply in determining prisoners' rights. A high standard will mean that more rights will be recognized in practice. A lax standard, placing a burden on prisoners that is difficult to meet, might mean that the rights are more theoretical than real. In a series of cases, the Supreme Court has marked out at least three distinct approaches to this question depending upon the nature of the specific right being asserted. While the tests differ, the similarities are greater than the differences. Regardless of the test, caution and considerable deference to prison administration is the hallmark of the Supreme Court's restrictive approach.

A prime illustration of this retrenchment is *Turner v. Safley*, 482 U.S. 78 (1987), a case that dealt with First Amendment rights of inmates to communicate with one another and to marry. Normally First Amendment rights are given the highest protection from infringement and cannot be abridged unless government has a compelling interest in the restriction. However, in *Turner* a closely divided court, by a vote of five to four, held that an application of this standard would seriously hamper the ability of prison officials to anticipate security problems and to adopt solutions to what it saw as the "intractable" problems of prison administration. Additionally, the court warned that applying this very high standard would mean that the courts would become the primary arbiters of what constitutes the best solution to every administrative problem. Accordingly, the Court chose a variation of a "reasonable relationship" test, the lowest level of constitutional justification, normally reserved for the analysis of governmental regulations that merely intrude on economic not political rights.

Using this standard the Court held that a prison rule that restricts First Amendment rights

of inmates to communicate with one another is valid if it is reasonably related to a legitimate penological interest. To make that determination the Court considered four factors: (1) whether there is a logical connection between the restriction at issue and the governmental interests invoked to justify it; (2) the availability of alternative means to exercise the restricted right; (3) the impact that accommodation of the right might have on other inmates, on prison personnel, and on allocation of prison resources generally; and (4) whether there are "obvious, easy alternatives" to the challenged policy that could be adopted at a minimal cost.

With this highly deferential and open-ended approach it is very difficult, but not impossible, for an inmate to show that restrictions are unconstitutional. The *Turner* approach has become the Court's most frequently used approach to determine whether restrictions imposed on inmates are unconstitutional. It has been used, for example, in cases involving religious liberties (*O'Lone v. Shabazz*, 482 U.S. 342 (1987)), and in cases involving communication and expression—"speech" between prisoners and the outside world (*Thornburgh v. Abbott*, 490 U.S. 410, 109 S.Ct. 1874 (1989)).

An even clearer illustration of the Supreme Court's policy of retrenchment is found in the Court's treatment of cases in which inmates claim that the conditions of confinement violate the Eighth Amendment's prohibition on "cruel and unusual punishment." In one of the earlier prison conditions cases the Supreme Court had intimated that the Eighth Amendment is violated whenever the conditions of confinement fall below "the minimal civilized measure of life's necessities" (*Rhodes v. Chapman*, 452 U.S. 337 (1981)). In the 1990s, however, the Court dramatically changed this standard by superimposing a new, and additional, test for determining whether conditions of confinement violate the Eighth Amendment. Under the new test, conditions that are objectively uncivilized will not be held unconstitutional unless there also is a finding that the prison officials' subjective intent was to subject an inmate to cruel and unusual punishment (*Wilson v. Seiter*, 111 S.Ct 2321 (1991)). Thus, a prison that is severely overcrowded may no longer violate the Constitution, even if conditions are shocking, unless the court finds that the prison officials intended to create these conditions.

A third example of retrenchment is the Court's procedural due process model for resolving issues relating to prison disciplinary decisions. Under this model, a prisoner is not entitled to a due process hearing—even if a sanction is imposed on the prisoner as punishment—unless the sanction imposes an "atypical and significant hardship" beyond that which is generally inherent in the "ordinary incidents of prison life." The Court adopted this vague and difficult test in part because it believed that prisons are different from larger society, more dangerous and more in need of the application of administrative discretion (*Sandin v. Conner,* 115 S.Ct 2293 (1995)).

What all three of the examples above have in common is that they utilize a very different scale for measuring whether an inmate's rights have been violated than the scale the Court uses for determining the constitutional rights of persons who are not in prison. The Court's deferential standards have been criticized on a number of grounds. They provide prison officials with broad discretion to curtail and abolish many basic rights of the incarcerated with minimal justification. The tendency of the Court to subject fundamental constitutional rights of prisoners to low standards suggests the Court does not recognize any hierarchy of values among constitutionally protected interests. This trivializes important constitutional rights by treating the First Amendment rights to go to church or read a book in the same manner as the right of an inmate to possess small items of personal property in his cell. Moreover, there is a substantial amount of ambiguity in the nature of judicial scrutiny called for by the Court's deferential tests. Perhaps most telling is the complaint that the Court has been inching the law back to the now thoroughly discredited hands-off doctrine.

The prison litigation reform act of 1995

Congress added to the barriers created by the Supreme Court when it passed the Prison Litigation Reform Act (PLRA), which was signed into law by President Clinton on 26 April 1996. A very long and complex act, it has been described by one leading commentator as a "comprehensive charter of obstructions and disabilities designed to discourage prisoners from seeking legal redress" (Boston). The act contains restrictions on prisoner litigation that are not imposed on any other people who sue for violations of their rights.

A major thrust of the act limits the ability of the courts to enter injunctive relief, that is to order prison officials to do something or to stop

doing something, to improve prison conditions. The act states that federal courts must not grant injunctive relief any greater than what is minimally necessary to correct the violations of law identified by the courts. In shaping the relief, the court has to give substantial weight to the impact of its relief on public safety or the operation of the criminal justice system.

The burgeoning prison populations spawned many overcrowding cases. The PLRA contains a specific provision governing release orders in overcrowding cases. No release order can be entered unless the court has previously tried a less restrictive remedy that has failed and the defendant prison officials are given a reasonable time period to comply with the orders of the court. No relief may be granted unless there is a finding that overcrowding is the primary cause of the violation of a federal right and no other relief will remedy the violation. Moreover, the named defendants or other government officials who have the responsibility to fund and operate and maintain the programs of the released prisoners or to prosecute them may intervene to oppose a release order. Accordingly, a broad variety of officials including district attorneys, local jail officials, and local politicians are eligible to participate formally in these proceedings—formidable opponents to prisoner actions.

Other limitations on the way in which courts have enforced constitutional rights in prison reform cases are contained in the PLRA. Special masters, who once played a major role in the cases, are now subject to new constraints including limitations on the hourly rate that they can be paid. Another provision provides a two-year "sunset period" on injunctive orders. Under this provision, the relief order is automatically terminated whether or not compliance has been achieved on the second anniversary of the issuance of the order unless the prisoners' attorney again proves that constitutional violations are occurring.

The act provides that no consent decree can be entered that does not comply with certain spelled-out limitations. Consent decrees that go beyond the minimum necessary to correct the violation of the federal right in the least restrictive manner cannot be approved. Parties that do reach agreements without these findings cannot have these agreements enforced by the courts. Such agreements, called "Private Settlement Agreements," can merely provide that in case of noncompliance, the plaintiff may restart the case.

The scores of existing consent decrees already entered in prison-conditions cases were subject to immediate termination unless the district court found retroactively that the stringent requirements of the act had been meet. The relief under the consent decree is automatically stayed thirty days following the filing of the motion to terminate the decree until the court rules on the motion. At the discretion of the court the thirty-day period can only be extended for an additional sixty days. This ninety-day maximum imposes an almost impossibly brief time on the district court to make findings necessary to continue the decree. If the timetable is not met, the consent decree will not be enforceable for the period needed to reach a decision.

The PLRA's far-reaching provisions, which limit the powers of the federal courts to enforce the rights of prisoners, raise numerous constitutional issues. Lower courts found one aspect of the act, the automatic stay provision, unconstitutional (*United States v. Michigan*, 91 F.3d 144 (6th Cir. 1996), and *Hadix v. Johnson*, 933 F. Supp. 1362 (W.D. Mich. 1996)). However, in an important PLRA decision, *Miller v. French*, 120 S.Ct 2246 (2000), the Supreme Court upheld the automatic-stay provision. Writing for the five-member majority, Justice O'Connor held that the automatic-stay provision of the PLRA did not violate the constitutional requirement of separation of powers.

Other evidence of the restrictive nature of the PLRA on prisoner suits and its deference to prison administration includes the exhaustion requirement, the "three strikes, you're out" provision, and the physical injury requirement.

Under the exhaustion requirement, inmates may not sue in federal court until they have used all administrative remedies available to them. At first blush this may not seem unfair. However, it is questionable whether, in many cases, an inmate will receive a fair and complete hearing from a potentially hostile administration. Thus, the exhaustion requirement becomes a test of endurance and delay to which no other civil rights plaintiffs are subjected.

Perhaps the most draconian provision of the PLRA is the so-called "three strikes, you're out" section which deprives an inmate of the right to litigate as a poor person (that is, the right of qualifying pro se plaintiffs to have court filing fees waived) after three previously dismissed actions. There is only one exception where the inmate is in imminent danger of physical injury. There are many reasons for dismissal of a case, beyond the fact that the claim is without merit. An inexperienced, uneducated pro se inmate plaintiff is as likely to have his case dismissed on procedural grounds of which he has little knowledge, as for legitimate legal reasons.

The PLRA also purports to limit recovery by providing that no federal civil action may be brought "for mental or emotional injury suffered in custody without a prior showing of physical injury." Physical injury itself requires proof of resulting disease or other adverse consequences. The courts have eased the harshness of this provision by holding that the physical injury provision of the PLRA only applies to actions for mental or emotional injuries and not to claims of violations of constitutional rights that inflict injuries that are neither physical nor mental or emotional.

Balanced against the restrictions of the PLRA is the Civil Rights on Institutionalized Persons Act (the CRIPA), another act of Congress passed before the PLRA but not repealed by it. The CRIPA gives the Attorney General of the United States the authority to investigate conditions in prisons and jails and file suit or intervene in a pending action if a pattern or practice of unlawful actions by prison officials is found by the Attorney General to deprive inmates of their constitutional rights. The Attorney General has delegated day-to-day responsibility for enforcement of this Act to the Special Litigation Section of the Civil Rights Division of the Justice Department.

This act contains none of the restrictions that the PLRA imposed on private litigation. Thus, it allows the government to be a vigorous enforcer of the constitutional rights of inmates. However, this assumes that the government is controlled by politicians who place a value on the rights of inmates and who are willing to commit resources to the enforcement of those rights.

In the last administration, the Justice Department did use its authority under the act to some extent. In fiscal year 1997, for example, the Department reported activity under the act in cases involving 164 facilities in 30 states and the District of Columbia, as well as Puerto Rico, Guam, and the Virgin Islands. However, with two million people housed in thousands of prisons and jails throughout the United States that effort, while important, is not enough to realistically monitor and enforce the rights of all inmates.

Conclusion

Despite the cutbacks just described, we no longer live in a "hands off" era, nor are we likely to return to one in the future. Courts, even the Burger and Rehnquist Courts, have indicated time and again that the judiciary has an important watchdog role to play in ensuring that fundamental rights are not denied even to a group as politically powerless as prisoners. Yet, it is reasonable to wonder whether the courts and Congress went too far in cutting back on inmates' rights in the 1980s and 1990s. The deference that is reflected in both the Supreme Court opinions and in the PLRA is unlike that given to any other department of government. Ironically, deference has been granted to the very institution that, because of its all-controlling nature, poses a greater risk of abuse than virtually any other institution of government. The opposition to the current deferential doctrine was well expressed by Justice Brennan who wrote that a high level of deference to prison officials is not justified. Justice Brennan explained, "The Constitution was not adopted as a means of enhancing the efficiency with which government officials conduct their affairs, nor as a blueprint for ensuring sufficient reliance on administrative expertise. Rather it was meant to provide a bulwark against infringements that might otherwise be justified as necessary expedients of governing" (*O'Lone v. Estate of Shabbaz*, 482 U.S. 342, 356).

In the years ahead, these factors might compel the courts and the legislative branch to extend greater protections to prisoners' rights than is the case currently. With so many hundreds of thousands of Americans going into and coming out of prison every year, the well-being of the larger society demands no less.

MICHAEL B. MUSHLIN

See also CAPITAL PUNISHMENT: LEGAL ASPECTS; CAPITAL PUNISHMENT: MORALITY, POLITICS, AND POLICY; CONVICTION: CIVIL DISABILITIES; CORPORAL PUNISHMENT; CORRECTIONAL REFORM ASSOCIATIONS; CRUEL AND UNUSUAL PUNISHMENT; INTERNATIONAL CRIMINAL JUSTICE STANDARDS; JAILS; PRISONS: CORRECTIONAL OFFICERS; PRISONS: PRISONERS; PRISONS: PRISONS FOR WOMEN; PRISONS: PROBLEMS AND PROSPECTS; PROBATION AND PAROLE: PROCEDURAL PROTECTION; SENTENCING: ALLOCATION OF AUTHORITY.

BIBLIOGRAPHY

American Bar Association. "Legal Status of Prisoner Standards." *Standards for Criminal Justice.* Washington, D.C.: ABA, 1981.

American Correctional Association, Commission on Accreditation for Corrections. *Standards for Adult Correctional Institutions.* Rockville, Md.: The Commission, 1977.

BRANHAM, LYNN. *The Law of Sentencing, Corrections, and Prisoners Rights in a Nutshell*, 5th ed. St. Paul, Minn.: West Group, 1998.

JACOBS, JAMES B. "The Prisoners Right Movement and Its Impacts, 1960–1980." *Crime and Justice: A Review of Research* 2 (1980): 429–470.

MAUER, MARC. *The Race to Incarcerate.* The New Press, 1999.

MUSHLIN, MICHAEL B. *Rights of Prisoners*, 2d ed.. St. Paul, Minn.: Westgroup, 1993. With annual supplements.

Note. "Beyond the Ken of the Courts: A Critique of Judicial Refusal to Hear the Complaints of Convicts." *Yale Law Journal* 72 (1963): 506, 515.

President's Commission on Law Enforcement and Administration of Justice. *The Challenge of Crime in a Free Society.* Washington, D.C.: The Commission, 1967.

Sentencing Project. "Facts About Prisons and Prisoners." Washington, D.C.: Sentencing Project (April 2000).

"Status Report: State Prisons and the Courts as of October 1987." *Journal of National Prison Projects* 13 (1987): 24.

U.S. Census Bureau. *Statistical Abstract of the United States: 1999* (119th edition). Washington, D.C.: Government Printing Office, 1999.

U.S. Department of Justice. *Bureau of Justice Statistics.* Available on the Internet at http://www.USDOJ.gov 2000.

———. *Federal Bureau of Prisons: Quick Facts.* http://www.bop.gov/fact0598.html. Last updated July 2000.

CASES

Bell v. Wolfish, 441 U.S. 520 (1979).
Estelle v. Gamble, 429 U.S. 97 (1976).
Lewis v. Lang, 116 S.Ct. 2174 (1996).
Newman v. Alabama, 559 F.2d. 283 (1977).
Rhem v. Malcolm, 371 F.Supp 594 (S.D. N.Y.) *aff'd.*, 507 F.2nd. 333 (1974), *affd on remand*, 527 F.2nd 1041 (1975).
Rhodes v. Chapman, 452 U.S. 337 (1981).
Turner v. Safley, 482 U.S. 78 (1987).
Williams v. Lane, 851 F.3d 867, 881 cert. denied, 488 U.S. 1047 (1989).
Wilson v. Seiter, 111 S.Ct. 2321 (1991).
Wolff v. McDonnell, 418 U.S. 539 (1974).

PRISONS: HISTORY

By the end of the twentieth century, the United States had nearly two million people confined in its prisons or jails, representing ten or twenty times more of its population behind bars than that of most other postindustrial nations. Although these numbers increased more than fourfold in the last thirty years, imprisonment in various forms has played an important role in the American experience for more then five hundred years, helping to determine its history and shaping the society. This history helps to explain the paradox of a country that prides itself on being the citadel of individual liberty yet imprisons more of its citizens per capita than any other nation in the world. It also provides a warning about the future, for even as the United States epitomizes and sanctifies democracy, it continues to build a huge and growing complex of durable totalitarian institutions. This massive use of imprisonment has made American society highly dependent on prisons both economically and politically as well as socially.

Early jails and workhouses

Prisons have existed in human society for thousands of years. A prison is any institution or device that holds a captive in custody. Among the most common types are jails, or closed structures that detain persons for shorter periods, often while they await trial, and state prisons or penitentiaries that hold persons serving sentences for crime. Other forms of imprisonment dating from antiquity have included slavery and involuntary servitude, both as a punishment for crime and as a form of exploitation. For as long as wars have occurred, some vanquished persons usually have been held as captives instead of being killed. American history has included all of these forms of imprisonment and more. Prisons have not simply been used as a recent punishment for crime.

The rise of the prisoner trade

From the time of Christopher Columbus, prisoners of various kinds figured in the exploration and colonization of the New World. Spain and Great Britain (among others) sent convicts to help settle North America; they also seized some indigenous peoples (Indians) to use as slaves. Starting with Portugal in the early sixteenth century, the major western European powers also imported African men, women, and children to serve as slaves in the Caribbean and American colonies.

Starting in the early seventeenth century, Britain carried out an international prisoner trade for more than one hundred and fifty years. After 1650, in fact, most emigrants to the American colonies went as prisoners of one sort or another. Some were forcibly kidnapped or arrested and shipped against their will; some were tricked or enticed into giving up their liberty; others bound themselves as indentured servants to work on foreign plantations. Throughout many ports in England and Ireland, persons nicknamed "spirits" illegally took up all the powerless persons they could entice to sign up as servants in America. In 1680 the Reverend Morgan Godwyn estimated that ten thousand souls were being spirited to the colonies each year. Oftentimes these recruits were held in private jails until their ships were ready to leave, to prevent them from changing their minds.

Starting in the early seventeenth century, Britain also started an organized system of *convict transportation*, which sent convicted felons to America as punishment for crime. In 1717 Parliament passed an act empowering courts to sentence noncapital offenders directly to transportation for seven years. Anyone who returned before his or her term expired or who helped a convict to escape was liable to be hanged. In addition, by 1723, more than fifty crimes in Britain were punishable, at least in statute, by the death penalty. Some of these offenses included poaching fish, damaging trees, or stealing a silver spoon. Yet many of those convicted of these capital crimes were allowed to escape the noose by agreeing to voluntary exile. As a result, the overwhelming number of those condemned to death were pardoned and shipped to America, where they were sold as servants for fourteen years. Between 1717 and 1775, Britain alone transported more than fifty thousand convicts to America. France also utilized transportation to its colonies throughout the eighteenth and nineteenth centuries.

Moreover, others were compelled to enter military service (*impressed*), some of them after being forcibly taken into custody by *press gangs*. Many of these persons were used to man the fleets that transported the human cargoes and other goods between the mother country and the colonies.

Some of the vessels used in the trade carried convicts or other servants as well as slaves, and some companies and agents involved in trafficking prisoners of various types. By the eighteenth century, General James Edward Oglethorpe, an English prison reformer and director of the Royal African Company, founded the colony of Georgia in 1732–1733 with colonists obtained from English prisons; South Carolina's Henry Laurens (later president of the Continental Congress) also trafficked servants and slaves. And many leading colonists, including George Washington, bought and sold both white convicts and African slaves.

Convicts and indentured servants often experienced a comparable crossing. Shipboard losses among convicts averaged fifteen to thirty percent during the seventeenth century, dropping to as low as 3 percent by the last quarter of the eighteenth. As many as five thousand convicts or more may have perished en route to America. Indentured servants were forced to endure most of the same conditions.

Being sold was a common experience of white convicts, indentured servants, and redemptioners, as well as black slaves. To the extent that American history is the story of immigration, then American colonial history is largely the story of the immigration of prisoners of one sort or another. On both sides of the Atlantic, prisons of various sorts were an essential part of the prisoner trade.

A land of prisoners

Jails were among the first public structures built in colonial America. Besides serving as a necessary receptacle and staging place for reluctant emigrants, jails were an integral part of the system of bondage that existed in America. Virtually every American city and county was legally required to establish its own jail at public expense. Over the years, these structures became more pervasive, more secure, and more permanent. Some were built of stone and brick, equipped with iron bars. Colonial America had more jails than public schools or hospitals—almost as many jails as churches and taverns. Massachusetts Puritans also used jails to detain Quaker heretics who challenged Puritan hegemony or witches who were awaiting public burning.

In the beginning of his novel *The Scarlet Letter* (1850), Nathaniel Hawthorne wrote: "the founders of a new colony, whatever Utopia of human virtue they might originally project, have invariably recognized it among their earliest practical necessities to allot a portion of the virgin soil as a cemetery, and another portion of the site as a prison . . . . In accordance with this rule . . . the forefathers of Boston . . . built the first prison house."

Moreover, some colonies were established as a haven for persons who had suffered imprisonment and other persecution in Europe, or as a receptacle for undesirables.

By the end of the seventeenth century a class system had developed in America. In addition to masters, a class of overseers was quickly developed to rule over the other inhabitants. Below indentured servants and convicts, who served for terms ranging from six to seven or fourteen years, black slaves occupied the lowest rung in perpetual slavery.

South Carolina authorized racial slavery from the early days of the proprietorship. So did Virginia. Even Puritan Massachusetts allowed slavery for a time. Connecticut never established slavery in law although it allowed it in practice. Rhode Island (sometimes referred to as "Rogue's Island") acted early to limit bondage to ten years, but that restriction was often flaunted. Slavery in New Hampshire was officially acknowledged in 1645. Shortly after the British took over New Netherlands from the Dutch, New York adopted hereditary slavery. So did Delaware. Pennsylvania employed slavery at its inception. Georgia lifted its ban against slavery in 1750 to become a major slave power.

All of those bound were subject to severe punishments that could be administered directly by their masters, or they could be punished by an authorized government. Many servants, convicts, and slaves attempted to run away or engaged in other acts of rebellion. Virtually every colony adopted its own slave code and control apparatus, including a system of slave patrols and networks of jails and other means to detain and punish runaway or recalcitrant slaves and servants. Under this arrangement, even free blacks were subject to tight controls and their movements were limited. In the South, the plantation system developed, creating a vast network of prisons without walls.

Enlightenment reforms

Criticism of the prisoner trade increased in America during the eighteenth century. Civil actions were brought against alleged spirits and other illegal servant traffickers; tracts decrying the slave trade appeared; and mobs in some cities violently resisted roundups by press gangs. After one of these riots resulted in the death of a military officer, Boston attorney John Adams defended some of the rioters. Another fracas over impressment resulted in the Boston Massacre.

When some American colonists (many of them slaveholders) increased their agitation to end convict transportation, London's Dr. Samuel Johnson complained: "Why, they are a race of convicts, and ought to be thankful for anything we allow them short of hanging!" By the third quarter of the eighteenth century, some of the New England colonies especially were the scene of frequent tumults, jail breaks, and protests. This unrest eventually culminated in the outbreak of the American Revolution.

American Revolution

The Declaration of Independence cited a list of abuses related to the prisoner trade, including complaints that the Crown had obstructed justice, sent swarms of officers to harass the people, deprived many of the benefits of trial by jury, transported persons beyond the seas for pretended offenses, and committed other offenses. However, Thomas Jefferson's clause protesting slavery was deleted at the request of Georgia and South Carolina.

During the War for Independence both the British and the rebels held large numbers of captured enemies in existing and makeshift prisons. The British held New York City throughout the war and converted it into a huge prison camp holding thousands of captives. Rebel churches, abandoned sugarhouses, and other structures were made into prisons. The British also employed several antiquated naval vessels as prison ships in New York harbor. As many as 11,500 persons perished on the H.M.S. *Jersey* alone—more than the total number of Americans who died in battle.

Captured British soldiers were kept in crowded dungeons, prison ships, and an abandoned copper mine in Simsbury, Connecticut, that was known as Newgate. The Americans also held many Tories (persons who were considered to have sided with the Crown), some of whom were Quakers who had disavowed violence and slavery. Several members of the Society of Friends in Philadelphia were exiled to the wilderness or hanged.

One of the effects of the war on Britain was to disrupt the prisoner trade to America, cutting off convict transportation, servant trafficking, and the African slave trade. As a result, English jails became terribly overcrowded, prompting one English prison reformer to conduct a comprehensive study of prisons throughout the kingdom. John Howard's treatise *The State of Prisons in England and Wales, with Preliminary Observations and an Account of Some Foreign Prisons* (1777) established an agenda for future prison reform.

Following the loss of the American colonies, Britain established Australia as a penal colony and withdrew from the international slave trade. Indentured servitude was also ended.

Ideological and social origins of the prison movement

The new United States struggled to determine what to do with its penal and slavery apparatus. Many British prisons were converted to American ones and new penal codes were implemented. Some states such as Pennsylvania and New York provided for the gradual emancipation of their slaves at the same time they adopted new criminal codes providing for the use of sentences of imprisonment as a punishment for crime.

In the South, however, efforts to eradicate slavery were blocked. The Northwest Ordinance of 1787 forbade slavery and involuntary servitude in the Northwest Territory (later the states of Ohio, Indiana, Illinois, Michigan, and Wisconsin), specifying: "There shall be neither slavery nor involuntary servitude in the said territory, otherwise than in the punishment of crimes whereof the party shall have been duly convicted: provided always, that any person escaping into the same, from whom labor or service is lawfully claimed in any one of the original states. Such fugitive may be lawfully reclaimed and conveyed to the person claiming his or her labor aforesaid."

Most states also adopted determinate sentencing laws that prescribed fixed prison sentences as a punishment for violent or property felony crimes. Capital punishment was retained for the most serious offenses. Often modeled in large part on the English prison reformer John Howard's blueprint for a humane prison, the new penal institutions separated male and female inmates, included walls to prevent escapes and assaults from without, and required inmates to labor making shoes, nails, and other goods. Pennsylvania's Walnut Street added a separate cell house for felons in 1790. Many of the leading prison reformers were Quakers who recently had tasted political persecution and imprisonment under vile conditions.

By 1800 new state prisons had been built in Pennsylvania, New York, New Jersey, Massachusetts, Kentucky, Vermont, Maryland, New Hampshire, Ohio, Georgia, and Virginia.

The Auburn plan

The establishment of a second New York state prison at Auburn in 1816 soon led to a new prison model and regime, designed to keep convicts separate and unable to communicate with each other even as they were forced to labor as penal slaves. "Industry, obedience, and silence" were the guiding principles of the new system. One of its chief proponents and rulers was Elam Lynds, who served for many years as warden of Auburn and other prisons.

By the early 1820s, the Auburn plan had resulted in the construction of tiny individual cells and workshops as well as a rigid system of enforced silence and harsh punishments. Each entering convict was assigned a prison number, which served as his or her identity. Movement to and from the workshops was performed in a regimented manner, known as the *lockstep*, which called for prisoners to march in a military-style human chain.

A Boston clergyman who visited Auburn in 1826 found it a shining example of what could be accomplished with proper discipline and design. "The whole establishment, from the gate to the sewer, is a specimen of neatness," he wrote. "The unremitted industry, the entire subordination and subdued feelings of the convicts, have probably no parallel among an equal number of criminals." The Reverend Louis Dwight and his associates from the Boston Prison Discipline Society pronounced Auburn a "noble institution" and said, "We regard it as a model worthy of the world's imitation." The institution seemed so successful that in 1825 Lynds was assigned to build a similar prison in Sing Sing.

Many Americans took such pride in what they seemed to have accomplished in their new model prisons that they encouraged visitors to tour the institutions in exchange for a small fee, to see for themselves what was being done with public funds.

In 1831 two young French magistrates, Gustave de Beaumont and Alexis de Tocqueville, were dispatched by their government to study the new American prison systems and report back on their possible application in France. Al-though Tocqueville was also interested in observing America's political system, which later would form the basis of his classic study *Democracy in America* (1835, 1840), he visited the United States in order to examine different penal approaches. The pair wrote in *On the Penitentiary System in the United States and Its Application in France* (1833) that "[w]hile society in the United States gives the example of the most extended liberty, the prisons of the same country offer the spectacle of the most complete despotism."

The Pennsylvania system

Unlike Auburn or Sing Sing, Pennsylvania's Eastern Penitentiary (1829) was intended to keep convicts separate even as they worked, in order to prevent any earthly contamination or distraction that might impede their repentance—hence the term *penitentiary*. Located on Cherry Hill, on the outskirts of Philadelphia, Eastern represented one of the most imposing and expensive architectural achievements in the United States to date, and it contained innovations such as running water and flush toilets in all the cells.

Although Beaumont and Tocqueville found it "incontestable that this perfect isolation secures the prisoner from all fatal contamination," they favored the more cost-effective Auburn plan, which seemed more likely to enable states to profit from convict labor.

Francis Lieber—the Prussian immigrant scholar who translated Beaumont and Tocqueville's work into English—hailed America's new penitentiary system as "monuments of a charitable disposition of the honest members of society toward their fallen and unfortunate brethren." Lieber coined the term *penology* to describe "that branch of criminal science which occupies itself . . . with the punishment of the criminal not with the definition of crime, the subject of accountability and the proving of the crime, which belongs to criminal law and the penal process."

Another prominent foreign visitor to Eastern Penitentiary was much more critical of the uncompromising solitary-confinement approach. After touring the institution in 1842, Charles Dickens, the English novelist, concluded in his *American Notes* (1842) that the Pennsylvania plan was "cruel and wrong," saying he found "this slow and daily tampering with the mysteries of the brain, to be immeasurably worse than any torture of the body."

Propenitentiary and antislavery

Another New England intellectual, physician Samuel Gridley Howe of Boston, published *An Essay on Separate and Congregate Systems of Prison Discipline* (1845) in which he defended the Pennsylvania system on the grounds that it was the purest approach. Like many persons involved in the propenitentiary movement, Howe also favored the abolition of chattel slavery in the South, which many condemned for its licentiousness and other abuses. Other social reformers in this circle included the Reverend Louis Dwight, Dorothea Lynde Dix, Isaac Hopper, and Horace Mann.

The system of chattel slavery, however, proved highly resistant to change. Although American involvement in the international slave trade had been ended in 1808, the domestic slave trade continued to flourish through the 1850s. Jails and slave pens were an integral part of both this continued slave trafficking and the relentless pursuit of fugitive and unruly slaves. Many slave auctions were held in jails and prisons. Abolitionists who had been caught trying to aid slaves to liberty were imprisoned alongside common criminals. In 1861, sectional conflict over slavery finally resulted in the bloody Civil War.

The Civil War and its aftermath

The prison camps of the Civil War proved to be incredibly lethal. According to official statistics compiled at the end of the war, the North held a total of 220,000 Confederates and the South held 126,000 Unionists. Estimates placed the number of prison dead at 30,212 for the Confederate prisons and 26,774 in the Union prisons. To put matters in perspective, roughly two and a half times as many soldiers were imprisoned as were involved in the Battle of Gettysburg, yet the prison camps claimed nearly ten times as many lives as did the battle.

Following Abraham Lincoln's Emancipation Proclamation (1863), the Thirteenth Amendment to the Constitution of the United States was finally ratified in 1865. In language that mirrored the provisions of the Northwest Ordinance of 1787, the article outlawed slavery and involuntary servitude "except as punishment of crime whereof the party shall have been duly convicted." Consequently, although chattel slavery was finally abolished after more than two hundred and fifty years, penal slavery was formally embedded in the Constitution. The Thirteenth Amendment still stands.

After the war, the victorious federal government initiated the policy known as Reconstruction in the vanquished South. Four million slave men, women, and children throughout the South had suddenly been freed, without compensation or support. Lawmakers in several southern states adopted so-called Black Codes that called for vagrants and other minor criminals to be imprisoned and put to work on public projects.

During slavery days, most southern prisons had remained predominantly white—the slaves being held on plantations—but after the war many institutions suddenly became overcrowded with newly freed blacks. States passed laws enabling convicts to be leased out to private companies. By the end of Radical Reconstruction, Georgia, Tennessee, North Carolina, Florida, Texas, Arkansas, Alabama, Mississippi, South Carolina, Louisiana, and Kentucky were leasing convicts. Soon conditions in southern prisons resembled those under chattel slavery.

Reform and individualized treatment

The Civil War had profoundly altered America's system and rationale for imprisonment. Millions of slaves had been let loose, chattel slavery was ended, and penal servitude expanded. Thousands of inmates had perished in deadly prison camps kept by their own countrymen. Many more were badly scarred by what they had experienced.

Many Americans increasingly recognized that the previous reformers' expectations for model prisons, based on isolation, hard labor, and severe punishments, had not been achieved. "Institutions . . . so strongly built, so richly endowed . . . cannot be rid of so easily," Samuel Gridley Howe observed in 1865. The institutions were severely overcrowded and deteriorating, their administration was often corrupt and abusive, and their fixed sentencing schemes proved unwieldy and excessive. Convicts had no incentive to reform. The old enthusiasm for the existing system was gone.

In 1867 two prominent reformers, Enoch C. Wines and Theodore Dwight, reported to the New York State legislature: "There is no longer a state prison in America in which the reformation of convicts is the one supreme object of the discipline." Based on their review they concluded there was no prison system in the country that was not seriously deficient. To remedy this sad state of affairs, Wines and Dwight recommended that reformation of the offender should be the primary aim of imprisonment. This approach mirrored the nation's developing posture toward the South.

Wines helped to organize the National Congress on Penitentiary and Reform Discipline in Cincinnati in 1870. This gathering adopted a detailed "Declaration of Principles," which called for sweeping prison reforms, including the acceptance of reformation; sanitary improvements; an end to political appointments of prison administrators; greater participation of women in prison management; the progressive classification of prisoners based on character; rewards for good conduct and industry; expanded prison education; the end of physical punishments; and other radical changes. To facilitate improvement of the offender, the reformers advocated long indeterminate sentences that could be adjusted depending on an individual's progress.

Starting in 1876, Warden Zebulon Brockway helped to put some of these ideas into practice at the Elmira Reformatory in New York state's southern tier, near the site of a former Civil War prison camp. The Elmira system included a combination of military training and education with a system of indeterminate sentencing. It held sway for more than twenty years. But the training school approach was mostly limited to juvenile offenders.

Elsewhere, most adult prisons continued to follow their existing regimes. Southern states still resorted to prison farms and convict leasing, while prisons in the North continued to operate contract labor systems in industrial pursuits. Both approaches were rife with abuses, including torture and rampant corruption. But changing them would not prove easy.

Prisons as social laboratories

Starting in the 1880s or so, prisons increasingly were used as social laboratories for controlled scientific research on a host of subjects, including eugenics, psychology, intelligence testing, medicine, drug treatment, criminology, physical anthropology, and birth control. Elaborate identification and classification techniques were devised that ranged from phrenology, which categorized people by their skull shapes, the Bertillon method of uniform body measurement, and fingerprinting to Lombrosian theories about "born criminals" and somatotypes (which purported to link body physique with criminal proclivities). Vasectomies, lobotomies, and other surgical procedures were developed using captive human subjects. Theories about feeblemindedness and defective delinquency were propounded based on experiments conducted on prisoners. A few eugenicists recommended mass sterilization and even legal executions as a means of ridding society of undesirables. Some of these approaches were not fully repudiated and outlawed until the 1970s.

Some Progressive era reformers increasingly advocated on behalf of prisoners. Shortly after his appointment as warden of Auburn Prison in 1913, Thomas Mott Osborne ended the silent system and began to institute a system of inmate self-government, known as the Mutual Welfare League, which allowed prisoners to establish their own legal disciplinary apparatus. A year later he became warden of Sing Sing, where he also started to implement sweeping reforms. Although his reforms quickly achieved some impressive results, such as decreasing the rate of convict return to prison (recidivism), Osborne was attacked by political opponents and forced to resign. One by one, his reforms were overturned. The remaining vestiges of the Mutual Welfare League were ended in 1929 amid another clampdown on prison policies. In response to harsher sentencing laws, convicts at several New York prisons rioted later that year.

Modern prisons

The Great Depression of the 1930s resulted in greater use of imprisonment and different public attitudes about prisoners. From 1925 to 1939 the nation's rate of incarceration climbed from 79 to 137 per 100,000 residents. In large measure, this growth was driven by greater incarceration of blacks. Between 1930 and 1936 alone, black incarceration rates rose to a level about three times greater than those for whites, while white incarceration rates actually declined.

During the late 1930s, sociologists who were studying various prison communities began to report the existence of rigid class systems among the convicts. Donald Clemmer published *The Prison Community* (1940), based upon his research within Menard State Prison in Illinois. Clemmer described the inmates' informal social system or inmate subculture as being governed by a convict code, which existed beside and in opposition to the institution's official rules. He also outlined a process of socialization that was undergone by entering prisoners. Clemmer defined this *prisonization* as "the taking on in greater or less degree of the folkways, mores, customs, and general culture of the penitentiary."

By the late 1930s, the modern American prison system had existed for more than one hundred years. During that time, many penal institutions themselves had remained unchanged. Convicts lived in a barren environment that was reduced to the absolute bare essentials, with less adornment, private property, and services than might be found in the worst city slum. One aspect that had changed rather significantly, however, was the prison labor system. In 1929 Congress passed the Hawes-Cooper Act, which enabled any state to prohibit within its borders the sale of any goods made in the prisons of another state. By the time the act became effective in 1934, most states had enacted laws restricting the sale and movement of prison products. In 1935 the Ashurst-Sumners Act strengthened the law to prohibit the transportation of prison products to any state in violation of the laws of that state. In 1940 Congress enacted legislation to bar, with a few exceptions, the interstate transportation of prison-made goods. These developments contributed to decreased reliance on prison labor to pay for prison costs. More and more inmates became idle and were not assigned to jobs.

World War II brought plummeting prison populations but renewed industrial activity as part of the war effort. After the war, and with the onset of the Cold War, prison warehousing became more prevalent, making inmate control and discipline more difficult. Another round of prison disturbances occurred in the early 1950s at the State Prison of Southern Michigan at Jackson, the Ohio State Penitentiary, Menard, and other institutions.

Imprisonment became increasingly reserved for blacks, Hispanics, and Native Americans. By 1955 and the end of the Korean conflict, America's prison population had reached 185,780 and the national incarceration rate was back up to 112 per 100,000, nudged along by the "race problem." Drug law enforcement played a stronger role increasing the disproportionate imprisonment of blacks and Hispanics.

Although the United Nations adopted its Standard Minimum Rules for the Treatment of Prisoners, in 1955, justifying sentences of imprisonment only when it could be used to foster offender rehabilitation, American prisons generally continued to favor security and retributive or incapacitative approaches over rehabilitation.

Prisoners' rights

It was not until the 1940s, or so that the legal rights of prisoners gradually began to be expanded. A series of federal court decisions started to give inmates greater access to the courts, reversing a long-standing "hands-off" doctrine. From the late 1950s to the late 1970s, a pesky prisoners' rights movement growing out of the larger civil rights struggle significantly transformed the ability of prisoners to seek and obtain legal redress through the courts. In *Monroe v. Pape* (1961), the U.S. Supreme Court enabled attorneys to seek damages and injunctions in federal court against state abuses of an individual's constitutional rights. Under Chief Justice Earl Warren, the Court issued a series of opinions favorable to criminal suspects, which benefited many prisoners, but the Court made few decisions improving prison conditions. It was not until the 1970s, under Chief Justice Warren Burger, that the high tribunal intervened in a few cases affecting conditions of confinement, and more of the federal activism on behalf of prisoners occurred at lower levels within the federal court system. In 1975, for instance, U.S. District Court Judge Frank Johnson issued a comprehensive order mandating sweeping changes in Alabama's entire prison system. Similar orders were handed down in Texas and other states.

The bloodiest prison riot in American history occurred at New York's Attica Correctional Facility in September 1971, resulting in the death of forty-three persons, most of them inmates. All but one of the fatalities occurred during the police assault on the hostage-takers. The Attica rebellion was followed by massive federal and state funding of control technologies and programs, including heightened security, emergency control, public relations, program services, and inmate discipline.

But Attica did not put an end to major prison disturbances. In 1980 the New Mexico State Penitentiary at Santa Fe was the scene of horrific carnage among prisoners resulting in thirty-three deaths.

The "get tough" movement

Until 1963, the incidence of reported crime as measured by official crime statistics actually remained relatively constant. But then serious crime began to experience an upsurge. The nation's rate of incarceration also remained relatively stable until 1974, when it also began to shoot up. The total number of adults in prison custody on a census day in 1972 showed a rate of incarceration for the United States of 162 per 100,000 residents. By 1984 it had risen to about 318 per 100,000. By the end of 1995 it had skyrocketed to 600. From 1970 to 1994 the prison population of the United States doubled and redoubled. With some exceptions, most criminologists agreed there was little relationship between rates of crime and rates of imprisonment.

Studies showed that racial minorities were disproportionately affected by this rapid prison growth. A federal survey on 30 June 1994 found that nearly 7 percent of all black men nationwide were in prison or jail, compared with less than 1 percent of white men. Throughout the 1990s, most American prison inmates were serving time for drug crimes. The overwhelming majority of prison staff were white and most prisons were located in predominantly white rural areas.

By the end of the 1990s, the number of prisoners in custody approached two million, reflecting the greatest use of incarceration of any nation in the world. The enormous public costs of building and maintaining this multibillion-dollar prison complex already was exceeding that of public support for higher education in some states.

To reduce its prison costs while still resorting to high levels of incarceration, some states in the 1980s and 1990s began to turn to private, for-profit companies to build and operate their correctional institutions. Despite many of the problems associated with private prisons—some of them prevalent through imprisonment's painful past—such approaches appeared to be undergoing renewed popularity at the end of the twentieth century.

Likewise, the get-tough movement that started in the mid-1970s and escalated over the next two decades also seemed likely to continue for many years to come. Harsher mandatory prison sentences, increased use of capital punishment and life without parole, rollbacks of prison education programs and other rehabilitation efforts, as well as the increased development of maximum prisons and control units, all were on the increase. All this occurred despite the lack of public faith in prison effectiveness.

After being used for more than five hundred years, imprisonment still seemed to represent an integral but hidden part of the American experience—more than most citizens probably would like to admit.

SCOTT CHRISTIANSON

See also CORRECTIONAL REFORM ASSOCIATIONS; DETERRENCE; INCAPACITATION; JAILS; JUVENILE JUSTICE: INSTITUTIONS; PRISONERS, LEGAL RIGHTS OF; PRISONS: CORRECTIONAL OFFICERS; PRISONS: PRISONERS; PRISONS: PRISONS FOR WOMEN; PRISONS: PROBLEMS AND PROSPECTS; REHABILITATION; RETRIBUTIVISM.

BIBLIOGRAPHY

BEAUMONT, GUSTAVE DE, and TOCQUEVILLE, ALEXIS DE. On the Penitentiary System in the United States and Its Application in France. (1833). Translated by Francis Lieber. Carbondale: Southern Illinois University Press, 1964.
CHRISTIANSON, SCOTT. With Liberty for Some: 500 Years of Imprisonment in America. Boston, Mass.: Northeastern University Press, 1998.
CLEMMER, DONALD. The Prison Community. New York: Rinehart. 1940.
CRAWFORD, WILLIAM. Report on the Penitentiaries of the United States, 1835. Montclair, N.J.: Patterson Smith, 1968.
DICKENS, CHARLES. American Notes for General Circulation. London: Chapman and Hall, 1842.
FRANKLIN, H. BRUCE. The Victim as Criminal and Artist: Literature from the American Prison. New York: Oxford University Press, 1978.
GARLAND, DAVID. Punishment and Modern Society: A Study in Social Theory. Chicago: University of Chicago Press, 1990.
HOWARD, JOHN. The State of Prisons in England and Wales, with Preliminary Observations and an Account of Some Foreign Prisons. Warrington, U.K.: W. Eyres, 1777.
MORRIS, NORVAL, and ROTHMAN, DAVID J., eds. The Oxford History of the Prison: The Practice of Punishment in Western Society. New York: Oxford University Press, 1995.
"Nearly 7 Percent of Adult Black Males Were Inmates in '94, Study Says." New York Times, December 4, 1995.
ROTHMAN, DAVID J. The Discovery of the Asylum: Social Order and Disorder in the New Republic. Boston: Little, Brown, 1971.
———. Conscience and Convenience: The Asylum and Its Alternatives in Progressive America. Boston: Little, Brown, 1980.
WINES, ENOCH C., and DWIGHT, THEODORE W. Report on the Prisons and Reformatories of the United States and Canada. (1867). Albany: AMS Press, 1973.

CASE

Monroe v. Pope, 365 U.S. 167 (1967).

PRISONS: CORRECTIONAL OFFICERS

Correctional officers (C.O.s) are "people workers" who interact with prison inmates on an intensely personal level, in an environment of close physical proximity over long periods of time, while functioning as low-level members of a complex bureaucratic organization (Lombardo, 1981). C.O.s are the primary social control agents in the prison because they are responsible for regulating inmate behavior through direct supervision and the enforcement of rules and regulations. They function within a paramilitary organizational structure that requires them to wear military-type uniforms and carry firearms and other weapons during specific types of assignments. This organizational structure is autocratic in nature and C.O.s are required to follow loyally a rigid chain of command that is organized in terms of military ranks: officer, sergeant, lieutenant, captain, and major. These ranks form a command and control structure that has the power located at the top. Power and communication flow down the chain of command with every person in a subordinate position expected to obey without question the orders of their superior officer(s). The primary criteria for promotion in corrections is time in rank and job performance. Formal education is less of a consideration. The minimum requirement for employment as a C.O. continues to be a high school degree or a graduate equivalency diploma (GED). Therefore, most C.O.s have a limited formal education and the majority of supervisory (commissioned) officers are not college educated.

The correctional officer occupies the unique position of being both a manager and a worker. C.O.s are low-status workers, the lowest subordinates in the chain of command. However, they are also the primary managers of inmates. Because they occupy the lowest level in the correctional hierarchy C.O.s are under the constant scrutiny of commissioned officers in much the same way as inmates are under officer scrutiny. Because contraband is always a major security concern in a prison, C.O.s are subject to random searches as they enter the institution in the same way that inmates are subject to random searches as they go about their business. Officers are subject to administrative disciplinary action if they violate any of the rules and regulations contained in the code of ethics or conduct that managers use to define appropriate correctional employee behavior.

The C.O. and rule enforcement

The C.O. role of primary social control agent relies on enforcement of a multitude of rules. These rules are typically classified as major or minor. Major rules are prohibitions against violation of the crime code: murder, assault, rape, arson, escape, drug trafficking, drug use, and other felonies. Minor rules are prohibitions against the violation of institutional rules regarding horseplay, disrespect to employees, maintaining sanitary housing quarters, and not playing the radio too loud. Formal punishment of rule violations is initiated through the officer's filing of a written misconduct report that is reviewed during a semilegal proceeding that determines the inmate's guilt or innocence. If found guilty, the inmate is subject to sanctions imposed by the misconduct reviewer that may range from suspension of privileges to a recommendation that parole be denied. Increasingly, in an attempt to make decision-making impartial, this individual is a hearing examiner who is a correctional employee, but not an employee of the prison in which the misconduct has occurred. C.O.s no longer have the authority to determine guilt and sanctions.

Inmate rule violations are common. In 1986, 53 percent of the 450,000 state prison inmates received misconducts for at least one rule violation during the period of their confinement (Stephen). In 1997, state and federal C.O.s reported a total of 1,841,913 minor rule violations and 821,004 major rule violations (Camp and Camp, p. 28). However, there is evidence that the rule violations reported by C.O.s do not represent the total number of rule violations committed by inmates, or observed by C.O.s. Hewitt, Poole, and Regoli have reported that inmates engage in a much higher level of rule violation than official reports record because very few rule violations result in a misconduct report. This conclusion is supported by C.O.s reporting that they observe nearly the same number of violations claimed by inmates. C.O.s exercise a considerable amount of discretion in making the decision to report, or not report, inmate rule violations.

The ability of C.O.s to engage in discretionary rule enforcement is a matter of concern for researchers and practitioners alike because of the possibility that racial discrimination may be a source of differential rule violation reporting. For example, Carroll found that African American inmates were disproportionately reported for all levels of rule violations, especially serious violations, and were subjected to closer surveillance and control by white C.O.s than were white inmates. Held and others determined that African American inmates receive a disproportionately higher number of misconduct reports because white officers consider African American inmates to be more aggressive and dangerous than white inmates. This effect was most noticeable in minor rule violation situations in which the C.O.s had the most discretionary authority. Held and others concluded that the disproportionate number of misconduct reports written on African American inmates was the result of white officer perception of dangerousness, not inmate behavior. Poole and Regoli (1980) also reported that African American inmates were cited for more rule violations than were white inmates. Finally, in a review of fifteen studies Goetting found that seven reported higher rates of rule violation reports filed against African American inmates while seven found no significant difference in reporting rates by race.

Organizational culture

C.O.s are a numeric minority with a high potential for violent interactions with inmates (Brown). In 1997, inmates committed 14,359 assaults against correctional staff. Four of these staff members died (Camp and Camp, pp. 40, 153). The nature of the inmate population has changed since the late 1960s and the level of physical threat has increased dramatically in response to massive prison overcrowding and an influx of younger, more violent criminals (Hepburn). Because the inmate population views correctional officers as the enemy and may respond to their authority with hostile, dangerous, and unpredictable behavior (Poole and Regoli, 1981) the officer-inmate relationship is one of "structured conflict" (Jacobs and Kraft).

"Structured conflict" provides the foundation for an organizational culture dominated by three principles of officer-inmate interaction: (1) security and control are the highest priority; (2) officer-inmate social distance should be high; and (3) officers must be tough, knowledgeable, and able to control inmates (Welch). The officers' attitude toward inmates is composed of a mixture of suspicion, fear, contempt, and hostility (Jacobs and Kraft). New officers are taught to adhere to a subcultural code of conduct organized around group solidarity and mutual support. The values of this code include: (1) always go to the aid of an officer in distress; (2) never make

an officer look bad in front of inmates; (3) always support an officer in a dispute with an inmate; (4) always support another officer's sanctions against inmates; (5) show concern for fellow officers; (6) do not smuggle drugs for inmates' use; (7) do not be sympathetic to inmates; (8) maintain group solidarity against outside groups; and (9) never inform on another officer (Kauffman). This last value is central to the code of silence that prohibits C.O.s from testifying about other officers' corruption or brutality.

Changes in the correctional officer role

The organizational goals of American prisons define the role of the correctional officer (Hepburn and Albonetti). Prior to the 1960s the sole expectation for C.O.s was that they be custody-oriented. Recruitment standards were low or nonexistent. Applicants were required to have only a minimal level of education and, in many prisons, education was not a consideration in hiring. The primary incentive for prison employment was the security offered by civil service employment in a job that some found more appealing and lucrative than farming, mining, or manufacturing work. People were also forced into prison work by unfortunate circumstances, such as the unavailability of jobs (Jacobs and Retsky) or because of layoffs, injuries, or failure in their initial choice of occupation (Lombardo). As a result, the typical officer was a rural, white male possessing limited education, politically conservative, brutal, slow to accept change, who often came to corrections at a relatively late age after mixed success in civilian life or retirement from the military (Philliber).

Training was typically on the job and often involved nothing more than a new recruit being handed a set of cell block keys and being told to learn the job as quickly as possible. The custody-oriented C.O. role definition was unambiguous. They were to maintain security and control through enforcement of institutional rules. The ability to accomplish this goal was based on their unchallenged power to accuse and punish inmates for rule violations with no regard for due process or inmate rights. Inmate control methods relied on physical coercion and discipline, and C.O.s were called guards because guarding inmates was all that was expected of them. As a result there has always been a widespread public perception that C.O.s are low in intelligence, brutal, alienated, cynical, burned out, stressed, and repressors of minority individuals (Philliber).

However, beginning in the 1960s a broad range of inmate rehabilitation programs were introduced into prisons that had historically viewed custody and control as the sole organizational goal (Farmer). This new emphasis on rehabilitation also introduced the expectation that C.O.s were to move beyond the clearly defined security role and assume the much more ambiguous role of human service-oriented professionals who would assist highly educated treatment professionals in inmate rehabilitation (Jurik). The introduction of rehabilitation created an ambiguous social organization (Cressey, 1966; Brown) by introducing a set of contradictory goals. The goal of custody demands the maintenance of maximum social distance between C.O.s and inmates and the avoidance of informal relationships, affective ties, and discretionary rule enforcement (Cressey, 1965; Hepburn and Albonetti). However, the goal of treatment requires relaxed discipline, affective ties, informal relationships that minimize social distance, and the exercise of discretionary rule enforcement based on individual inmate characteristics and circumstances. Punitive control policies were subordinated to the expectation that C.O.s were to be human-oriented and flexible (Cressey, 1965).

Most correctional facilities today accept the dual roles of custody and treatment, and C.O.s are defined as agents of inmate change who are expected to use discretion to assist in the rehabilitation of inmates while simultaneously maintaining security through rule enforcement (President's Commission; Cressey, 1966; Poole and Regoli, 1981). Simultaneous performance of the dual roles of custody and treatment create role conflict characterized by uncertainty and danger because C.O.s can be disciplined for violating institutional policy even if that violation is meant to assist inmate rehabilitation (Hepburn).

The introduction of rehabilitation coincided with a series of U.S. Supreme Court rulings that provided inmates with increased civil rights and decreased the ability of correctional officers to rely on punitive control. The result was due process–oriented disciplinary hearings, restrictions on the use of isolation as a disciplinary sanction, and the creation of formal inmate grievance mechanisms. These significantly limited the power of C.O.s and provided inmates with a powerful countervailing power (Poole and Regoli, 1981). This shift in power created for correctional officers a perception of loss of control

and a belief that inmates possessed more power than officers (Fox; Hepburn). The product of this perception was a strained and unhealthy atmosphere (Duffee, 1974; Patterson) characterized by a perception that managers and treatment staff possessed more respect for inmates than for C.O.s. This perception of being treated unfairly has generated deeply ingrained C.O. feelings of frustration, anger, and lack of appreciation by superiors (Jacobs and Retsky; Huckabee; Wright and Sweeney).

One of the most significant consequences of the perception that correctional managers were no longer on the side of the officers has been unionization. In the early 1970s, federal law granted C.O.s the right to unionize and they quickly joined powerful national unions such as the American Federation of State, County, and Municipal Employees (AFSCME) whose leadership has effectively challenged numerous management policies viewed as not being in the best interests of the rank and file. Unions have the authority to successfully influence management's allocation of resources and salaries and benefits have risen dramatically as a result. Unions have been equally successful in leveling the playing field between officers and management through their ability to legally challenge management policies that are unfair, discriminatory, or arbitrary.

Changes in C.O. workforce demographics

In the 1970s, correctional managers recognized four fundamental challenges: high staff turnover; the growing lack of white applicants in the job pool; the lack of treatment-oriented officers; and minority inmate demands that the correctional work force be diversified (Philliber). The response to these challenges was a concerted effort to increase the number of women and minorities in corrections. The presence of female correctional officers in the men's prison was desired because they were seen as bringing a "normalizing" influence into prison. This perception was based on the assumption that women would rely more extensively on listening and communication skills than male C.O.s and develop personal relationships with inmates that could be used as a "technique of control" (Pollock, p. 111). Minority officers were sought because of a belief that minority inmates would be more amenable to rehabilitation if they were supervised by minority officers who could serve as role models. Minorities were viewed as constituting a more sympathetic work force with which minority inmates could identify (Jacobs and Kraft). The result was the creation of aggressive affirmative action programs.

Prior to the early 1970s, women in corrections worked as matrons in the women's prison or as clerical staff in the men's prisons. They were not hired as C.O.s in men's prisons because of male fears that women lack physical strength; are too easily corrupted by inmates; can not provide appropriate back-up in emergency situations; have a vulnerability to assault that jeopardizes facility security; are a disruptive influence because inmates will not obey them or will fight for their attention; and violate inmate privacy by being in a position to view inmate personal hygiene activities (Hawkins and Alpert; Alpert and Crouch). Because promotional criteria favored staff with direct supervision of male inmates, employees in clerical or matron roles had little hope of professional advancement (Chapman et al.).

The passage of amendments to Title VII of the 1964 Civil Rights Act in 1972 extended the prohibition of employment discrimination to government employers. Women used this amendment to file civil suits against correctional managers who would not hire them to work as officers in male prisons. As a result, women are no longer limited to supervising women inmates. In states such as Alabama where one-third of correctional officers are women, 89 percent work in men's prisons. In 1997, 14.8 percent of the Federal Bureau of Prison's new hires for the C.O. workforce were women. At the state level, 25.5 percent of the new hires, on average, were women (Camp and Camp, p. 144).

Thirty years of experience have found that male concerns about the unsuitability of women to be C.O.s in men's prisons are groundless (Walters; Wright and Saylor). Shawver and Dickover and Rowan reported that female officers are assaulted significantly less often than male officers and there is no relationship between the percentage of women officers and the number of assaults against male staff. Simon and Simon found that female C.O.s write approximately the same number of misconduct reports as male C.O.s, for the same types of violations. Jurik and Halemba found one significant difference between male and female officer perceptions of the job. The men wanted more discretion. The women wanted more structure. Both male and female C.O.s tended to believe that the majority of their work-related problems were caused by superiors, although women were more likely to express nega-

tive attitudes toward male coworkers and view them as the cause of many of their problems. Fry and Glasner (1987) found that female officers were more negative in their evaluation of inmate services.

However, male officer hostility to the hiring of female C.O.s has been a consistent problem in corrections and women are still a numeric minority in most men's prisons. Their appearance, demeanor, behavior, performance, and mistakes receive a disproportionate amount of attention (Zimmer). In addition, male supervisors often assign female C.O.s to low-risk assignments such as visiting rooms and control rooms, a practice that limits their opportunities for skills development and advancement and further antagonizes male C.O.s who resent working the dangerous jobs while women get the easy jobs (Zimmer; Jurik, 1985).

The decision to recruit minority officers through aggressive affirmative action programs was met with fierce resistance by white officers. Racism was prevalent and many white officers believed that nonwhite, urban C.O.s would be pro-inmate and less trustworthy (Irwin). The fear that minority officers would "go easy" on inmates has not been validated by research. In fact, Jacobs and Kraft found that African American C.O.s were more punitive than whites toward inmates. Klofas and Toch found that minority C.O.s expressed the need for high social distance between officer and inmate.

By the end of 1997, the percentage of minority hires in state departments of corrections was 26.9 percent of the total hired (Camp and Camp, p. 143). However, racism remains a powerful factor in corrections. Philliber notes the tendency of African American C.O.s to quit their jobs more often than whites, primarily because of conflicts with superior officers, and to express higher levels of job dissatisfaction than whites.

Correctional officer stress

A number of studies have documented that C.O.s experience higher levels of stress than most other occupational groups (Laskey, Gordon, and Strebalus; Lindquist and Whitehead; Honnold and Stinchcomb; and Wright). There are numerous stressors in the C.O.s' work environment. They live by a macho code that requires them to be rugged individualists who can be counted upon to do their duty regardless of circumstances. Both management and C.O.s expect that every officer will perform the functions of their assignment independently, and seek assistance only when it is absolutely necessary, as in the case of physical assault, escape, or riot. This macho code combined with the unpredictability of working with inmates, role ambiguity, and demographic changes in the work force create high C.O. stress levels.

In addition, C.O.s frequently complain of structural stressors associated with the traditional autocratic style of correctional management: feelings of being trapped in the job; low salaries; inadequate training; absence of standardized policies, procedures, and rules; lack of communication with managers; and little participation in decision-making (Philliber). The failure of managers to support line staff has been emphasized by Lombardo and Brodsky. There are also gender differences in stress perception. Zimmer and Jurik have found that female C.O.s report higher levels of stress than male C.O.s because of employee sexual harassment, limited supervisory support, and a lack of programs designed to integrate them into the male prison.

The consequences of stress include: powerful feelings of alienation, powerlessness, estrangement, and helplessness; physical symptoms such as high blood pressure, migraine headaches, and ulcers (Cornelius); twice the national divorce rate average; and high rates of suicide, alcoholism, and heart attacks. Cheek reports that C.O.s have an average life span of fifty-nine years compared to a national average of seventy-five years. The organizational consequences of stress include high employee turnover, reduced job productivity, high rates of absenteeism and sick leave use, and inflated health-care costs and disability payments (Patterson). Some C.O.s also respond to stress by engaging in corruption or inmate brutality.

Correctional managers have responded to these consequences by seeking to recruit and retain individuals who have the psychological resources to handle the stress of institutional life. Application selection methods rely on psychological testing, background checks, and rigorous interviews. Those applicants who are hired are required to complete a probationary period that is, on average, ten months in length and includes 232 hours of entry-level training (Camp and Camp, p. 146) before they can be assigned a permanent job within the correctional facility. This probationary period begins with standardized training in a correctional training academy whose instructors are qualified to provide oral instruction, written examination, and practical hands-on application of techniques. Training curriculums are designed to provide trainees with the knowledge necessary to become a human services–oriented professional who can assist inmates as they meet the challenges of incarceration and preparation for return to the community. The typical corrections curriculum includes instruction in such diverse areas as: the professional image; interpersonal communications; assertive techniques; development of observation skills; prison subcultures; classification of inmates; legal aspects of corrections; inmate disciplinary procedures; fire prevention; security awareness; stress awareness and management; control of aggressive inmate behavior; cultural sensitivity; emergency preparedness; HIV; report writing; suicidal inmates; mentally disturbed inmates and special behavior problems; principles of control; basic defensive tactics; standard first aid; use of the baton; firearms training; drug awareness; search procedures; use of inmate restraints; transportation of inmate procedures; and weapon cleaning and maintenance. Increasingly, academy curriculums include ethical behavior, cultural sensitivity, and awareness of diversity courses designed to help C.O.s adjust to a work environment that has become increasingly multicultured. State correctional systems now require C.O.s to annually participate in, on average, forty-two hours of in-service training designed to help them maintain high levels of professional efficiency and ethical behavior (Camp and Camp, p. 147).

In addition, correctional managers are increasingly adapting a participatory management style that emphasizes employee empowerment through shared decision-making and input solicitation, unit management, and formal mentoring programs (Cushman and Sechrest; Freeman). This management style is associated with higher levels of employee morale and job satisfaction than is the traditional autocratic management style (Duffee, 1989). As management and training philosophies become more sophisticated C.O.s will be better prepared to manage the stresses inherent in their critical role as human service professionals in an increasingly complex work environment.

ROBERT M. FREEMAN

See also CORRECTIONAL REFORM ASSOCIATIONS; DETERRENCE; INCAPACITATION; JAILS; JUVENILE JUSTICE: INSTITUTIONS; PRISONERS, LEGAL RIGHTS OF; PRISONS:

HISTORY; PRISONS: PRISONERS; PRISONS: PRISONS FOR WOMEN; PRISONS: PROBLEMS AND PROSPECTS; REHABILITATION; RETRIBUTIVISM.

BIBLIOGRAPHY

BRODSKY, CARROLL M. "Work Stress in Correctional Institutions." *Journal of Prison and Jail Health* 2, no. 2 (1982): 74–102.

CAMP, CAMILLE G., and CAMP, GEORGE M. *The Corrections Yearbook 1998.* Middletown, Connecticut: Criminal Justice Institute, Inc., 1998.

CARROLL, LEO. *Hacks, Blacks and Cons: Race Relations in a Maximum Security Prison.* Lexington, Mass.: D.C. Heath, 1974.

CHAPMAN, JANE R.; MINOR, ELIZABETH K.; RIEKER, PATRICIA; MILLS, TRUDY L.; and BOTTUM, MARY. *Women Employed in Corrections.* Washington D.C.: U.S. Government Printing Office, 1983.

CHEEK, FRANCES E. *Stress Management for Correctional Officers and Their Families.* College Park, Md.: American Correctional Association, 1984.

CRESSEY, DONALD R. "Prison Organization." In *Handbook of Organizations.* Edited by J. March. Chicago: Rand McNally, 1965. Pages 1023–1070.

———. *Contradictory Directives in Complex Organizations: The Case of the Prison Within Society.* Edited by Lawrence E. Hazelrigg. New York: Doubleday, 1966.

DUFFEE, DAVID E. "The Correctional Officer Subculture and Organizational Change." *Journal of Research in Crime and Delinquency* 11 (1974): 155–172.

———. *Corrections Practice and Policy.* New York: Random House, 1989.

FARMER, RICHARD E. "Cynicism: A Factor in Corrections Work." *Journal of Criminal Justice* 5 (1977): 237–246.

FOX, JAMES G. "Organizational and Racial Conflict in Maximum Security Prisons." Boston: D. C. Heath, 1982.

FRY, LINCOLN J., and GLASNER, DANIEL. "Gender Differences in Work Adjustment of Prison Employees." *Journal of Offender Counseling, Services and Rehabilitation* 12 (1987): 39–52.

GOETTING, ANN. "Racism, Sexism, and Ageism in the Prison Community." *Federal Probation* 49, no. 3 (1985): 10–22.

HAWKINS, RICHARD, and ALPERT, GEOFFREY P. *American Prison Systems: Punishment and Justice.* Englewood Cliffs, N.J.: Prentice-Hall, 1989.

HELD, BARBARA S.; LEVINE, DAVID; and SWARTZ, VIRGINIA D. "Interpersonal Aspects of Dangerousness." *Criminal Justice and Behavior* 6, no. 1 (1979): 49–58.

HEPBURN, JOHN R. "Prison Guards as Agents of Social Control." In *The American Prison: Issues in Research and Policy.* Edited by Lynne Goodstein and Doris Layton MacKenzie. New York: Plenum, 1989. Pages 191–206.

HEPBURN, JOHN R. and ALBONETTI, C. "Role Conflict in Correctional Institutions: An Empirical Examination of the Treatment-Custody Dilemma Among Correctional Staff." *Criminology* 17, no. 4 (1980): 445–459.

HEWITT, JOHN D.; POOLE, ERIC D.; and REGOLI, ROBERT M. "Self-reported and Observed Rule-Breaking in Prison: A Look at Disciplinary Response." *Justice Quarterly* 3 (1984): 437–448.

HONNOLD, JULIE A., and STINCHCOMB, JEANNE B. "Officer Stress." *Corrections Today* (December 1985): 46–51.

IRWIN, JOHN. "The Changing Social Structure of the Men's Correctional Prison." In *Corrections and Punishment.* Edited by D. Greenberg. Beverly Hills, Calif.: Sage, 1977. Pages 21–40.

JACOBS, JAMES B., and KRAFT, LAWRENCE. "Integrating the Keepers: A Comparison of Black and White Prison Guards in Illinois." *Social Problems* 25 (1978): 304–318.

JACOBS, JAMES B., and RETSKY, HAROLD G. "Prison Guard." *Urban Life* 4 (April 1975): 5–29.

JURIK, NANCY C. "Individual and Organizational Determinants of Correctional Officer Attitudes Toward Inmates." *Criminology* 23, no. 3 (1985): 523–539.

JURIK, NANCY C., and HALEMBA, GREGORY J. "Gender, Working Conditions and the Job Satisfaction of Women in a Non-Traditional Occupation: Female Correctional Officers in Men's Prisons." *The Sociological Quarterly* 25 (1984): 551–566.

KAUFFMAN, KELSEY. *Prison Officers and Their World.* Cambridge, Mass.: Harvard University Press, 1988.

KLOFAS, JOHN, and TOCH, HANS. "The Guard Subculture Myth." *Journal of Research in Crime and Delinquency* 19, no. 2 (1982): 238–254.

LASKEY, GARETH L.; GORDON, CARL B.; and STREBALUS, DAVID J. "Occupational Stressors Among Federal Correctional Officers Working in Different Security Levels." *Criminal Justice Behavior* 13, no. 3 (1986): 317–327.

LINDQUIST, CHARLES A., and WHITEHEAD, JOHN T. "Burnout, Job Stress, and Job Satisfaction Among Southern Correctional Officers: Perception and Causal Factors." *Journal of Criminal Science* 10, no. 4 (1986): 5–26.

LOMBARDO, LUCIEN X. *Guards Imprisoned.* New York: Elsevier, 1981.

PHILLIBER, SUSAN. "Thy Brother's Keeper: A Review of the Literature on Correctional Officers." *Justice Quarterly* 4, no. 1 (1987): 9–33.

POLLOCK, JOYCELYN M. "Women in Corrections: Custody and the 'Caring Ethic'." In *Women, Law and Social Control*. Edited by Alida V. Merlo and Joycelyn M. Pollock. Needham Heights, Mass.: Allyn and Bacon, 1995.

POOLE, ERIC D., and REGOLI, ROBERT M. "Race, Institutional Rule Breaking and Disciplinary Response: A Study of Discretionary Decision-Making in Prison." *Law and Society Review* 14 (1980): 931–946.

———. "Alienation in Prison: An Examination of the Work Relations of Prison Guards." *Criminology* 19, no. 2 (1981): 251–270.

President's Commission on Law Enforcement and Administration of Justice. *The Challenge of Crime in a Free Society*. Washington, D.C.: U.S. Government Printing Office, 1967.

SHAWVER, LOUIS, and DICKOVER, ROBERT. "Research Perspectives: Exploding a Myth." *Corrections Today* (August 1986): 30–34.

SIMON, RITA J., and SIMON, JUDITH D. "Female C.O.s: A Legitimate Authority." *Corrections Today* (August 1988): 132–134.

STEPHEN, JAMES. *Prison Rule Violators*. Washington D.C.: U.S. Government Printing Office, 1989.

WELCH, MICHAEL. *Corrections: A Critical Approach*. New York: McGraw-Hill, 1996.

ZIMMER, LYNN E. *Women Guarding Men*. Chicago: University of Chicago Press, 1986.

PRISONS: PRISONERS

The American public appears to have an insatiable fascination with what goes on inside prisons. Moviegoers flock to see Hollywood films about prison life (e.g., *Escape from Alcatraz*, *Murder in the First*, and *The Shawshank Redemption*). The news media is quick to cover lurid stories about prisons, including prison disturbances (escapes, prison riots, or the killings of inmates or staff members by inmates) and the executions of notorious killers. Media depictions often distort the realities of imprisonment, misleading the public about prison life. Average citizens stereotype prisons as either hell-holes filled with every imaginable evil, or country clubs (complete with swimming pools and golf courses) where inmates are sent to work on their tans. Neither of these stereotypes captures the central realities of incarceration for inmates: crushing routine and relentless boredom.

It is not just the general public that knows little about prison life; most policymakers and criminal justice practitioners are also poorly informed. State legislators authorize and pass bills that dramatically affect the conditions of confinement, but rarely tour prison facilities. Judges' names do not appear on the visitation lists of the criminals that they sentence to prison. Police officers regularly transport inmates to the gates of prisons without bothering to step inside. Trial judges and police officers often form their impressions of prison life based on the comments that they hear from ex-convicts (who are not the most reliable sources).

This essay discusses the factors that shape the experiences of prison inmates. It begins by reviewing a few facts and figures about the numbers and characteristics of prisoners in America. The official features and procedures of the formal organization of prisons that affect inmate life (e.g., the classification process, the security levels of prisons, and institutional programs) are discussed. The essay concludes by examining the informal organizational responses of inmates to these official procedures, through the development of a peculiar inmate subculture that has its own beliefs, rules, and statuses.

The characteristics of U.S. inmate populations

On 31 December 1985 there were 487,593 inmates confined in America's prisons; U.S. Department of Justice figures showed that as of 30 June 1998 there were 1,210,034 inmates incarcerated in the United States (Gilliard). This was an amazing rise in the prison population by 772,441 inmates in just over twelve years. Most of these increases can be attributed to tough new laws that give long prison sentences to career criminals (with multiple felony convictions) and drug offenders.

The overwhelming majority of those imprisoned in America in 1998 (1,102,653 inmates, or 91% of the prison population) were confined in state institutions, not federal prisons (Gilliard). This is because most felons—even those who have committed federal offenses—are prosecuted through state court systems. It is significant that most prisoners serve their sentences in state institutions because, for the most part, these facilities are more dilapidated and have fewer resources and programs than federal penitentiaries.

When considering incarceration rates (or the numbers of inmates imprisoned per 100,000 population, as of 30 June 1998) for different regions of the country, southern states had the highest rate of imprisonment (508 inmates per 100,000 population), followed by western states (411 inmates). The incarceration rates for midwestern and northeastern states were lower (respectively, 357 and 318 inmates per 100,000 population). Among individual states, California had the largest number of prisoners (158,742), followed by Texas (143,299). Both of these states had more incarcerated inmates than the entire federal prison system (118,408). The states with the smallest numbers of prisoners were North Dakota (883) and Vermont (1,312). Louisiana and Texas had the highest rates of imprisonment (respectively, 709 inmates and 700 inmates per 100,000 population); Minnesota and Maine had the lowest rates (respectively, 117 and 121 inmates per 100,000 population; Gilliard).

Among the 1,023,572 inmates incarcerated in state and federal prisons as of 31 December 1995, the overwhelming majority (961,210 inmates, or 94%) were male (Stephan). Between 31 December 1990 and 31 December 1995, however, the numbers of incarcerated women in the United States grew at a faster rate (a 56% increase) than the numbers of incarcerated men (a 42% increase; Stephan).

More minority group members are incarcerated in the United States than white, non-Hispanics. As of 31 December 1995, there were 488,222 African Americans imprisoned (48% of the prison population), compared to 363,918 white, non-Hispanics (36%) and 147,365 Hispanics (14%). There were very few incarcerated Native Americans (10,519, or 1%) and Asian Americans (8,436, or 1%; Stephan).

Relatively few inmates in America are incarcerated in high security prisons. As of 31 December 1995, 202,174 inmates (20% of the prison population) were imprisoned in maximum security institutions, compared to 415,688 inmates (41%) in medium security facilities and 366,227 inmates (36%) in minimum security facilities (39,483 inmates were confined in prisons with no specified security level classification; Stephan).

Almost half (46%) of the inmates serving time in state prisons in 1996 had current convictions for violent offenses (Mumola and Beck). Among the remaining inmates in these prisons, 24 percent were convicted for property offenses, 23 percent for drug offenses, and 7 percent for public order offenses (e.g., gambling and alcohol-

related crimes; Mumola and Beck). Trends since 1980 showed declines in the numbers of inmates incarcerated for violent and property offenses, with a sharp increase in the numbers imprisoned for drug offenses (Beck and Gilliard). These figures must be interpreted cautiously, because many inmates are versatile offenders who have committed other types of crimes than the ones for which they were convicted.

These statistics offer some general insight into the composition of prison populations. A more comprehensive understanding of prison life, however, requires consideration of the social organization of prisons.

Inmates and the formal organization of prisons

When sociologists study the effect of bureaucracies on their members, they make an important distinction between formal and informal social organization (Blau and Meyer). The *formal organization* of a bureaucracy includes its official hierarchy and functions, administered through a set of written rules that specify the responsibilities and obligations of members. The warden, the captain of the guard, and the director of vocational training are all examples of the positions within the official hierarchy of prisons. Sociologists use the term *informal organization* to refer to the casual associations, cliques, and friendships that form within a bureaucracy, affecting its operations. For example, longstanding disputes between several prisoners can significantly disturb peace and harmony within a cellblock. The informal organization includes covert norms, beliefs, and attitudes that may create expectations and practices at variance with official procedures.

The daily experiences of inmates are shaped by the formal and informal social organization of prisons. Some parts of the formal organization of corrections that affect inmates include the classification process, the security levels of institutions, confinement arrangements within the prison, program options and assignments, and special-needs placements. When criminologists discuss the informal organization among prisoners, they note the existence of a distinctive inmate subculture that thrives apart from the official prison hierarchy and procedures.

Upon arrival in prison following sentencing, inmates spend several weeks in a reception center that introduces them to the formal organization of the prison. During this time, they are *segregated* (i.e., kept apart) from other inmates, so they can be observed by the prison staff and informed about correctional rules and procedures. The most important purpose of the reception process is the *classification* of inmates, an essential feature of modern incarceration. Classification includes the *risk assessment* and *needs assessment* of inmates. Risk assessment involves some estimation of the threat that inmates pose to themselves or to others. Most correctional departments now use standard instruments that assign numerical scores to assess the risk level of inmates. In general, current and prior convictions for violent offenses result in high risk scores.

In needs assessment, prison staff evaluate the special problems of inmates that might affect institutional adjustment and the potential for treatment. Here, staff investigate such details as the physical and psychological health of inmates, their educational and occupational backgrounds and abilities, community support and the quality of inmates' family lives, and histories of drug abuse. Needs assessment affects the program assignments of prisoners once they complete classification. For example, inmates with little education will be encouraged to enroll in prison schools; those with few job skills will be targeted toward vocational training.

The purpose of classification is to assign prisoners to an appropriate level of custody (or institutional control). High-risk inmates with many needs must be supervised closely; low-risk inmates with few needs require minimal control. This *custody classification* assignment has immense consequences for an inmate, because it determines the *security level* of the institution where they will be confined once leaving the reception center.

The federal and most state correctional systems include an impressive array of institutions with different security level designations. Maximum security prisons operate as armed fortresses, complete with steel gates, high walls (sometimes extending many feet underground to prevent escapes through tunnels), perimeter fences (topped with multiple layers of razor-sharp concertina barbed wire), gun towers, and floodlights. Some of these prisons are marvels in advanced technology, containing a complex network of electronic surveillance that includes metal detectors, concealed video cameras, and heat and touch sensors in the walls, floors, and ceilings. Correctional officers in these prisons carefully supervise and control the every move of

inmates through detailed schedules and constant head counts.

Inmates in maximum security prisons have little freedom and autonomy; their lives are ruled by the same mind-numbing routines for months and years on end. These prisoners lead a depersonalized existence with little privacy; passersby can gaze into their cells to watch them eat, sleep, or use the toilet. They even shower together in large, open stalls that are closely monitored by correctional officers. In an effort to control the proliferation of drugs, weapons, and other contraband, there are frequent *shakedowns* (or random searches) of cellblocks in maximum security units. It is little wonder that inmates in these prisons often bitterly complain that they are displayed and managed like animals in a zoo.

While life in maximum security prisons is usually monotonous and boring, the tedium is sometimes broken by outbursts of violence. Threats, assaults, and killings are fairly commonplace in these institutions. For example, in 1995 there were 62 assaults reported per 1,000 inmates in maximum security prisons in the United States (Stephan). Reported assaults represent only the tip of the iceberg, since many inmates are highly skilled at concealing the beatings administered to settle disputes. The threat of violence is real enough in maximum security prisons to produce a constant undercurrent of tension, fear, and wariness among inmates and staff; smarter prisoners in these institutions make a habit of looking over their shoulders or standing with their backs to walls whenever they venture outside their cells (Hassine).

A more relaxed atmosphere prevails in most medium and minimum security prisons. Violence is much less common in these facilities: In 1995, there were 34 reported assaults per 1,000 inmates in medium security prisons, and 18 reported assaults per 1,000 inmates in minimum security institutions (Stephan). The conditions of confinement are usually much better in lower security prisons. For example, there are few fences and gun towers around medium security facilities; hidden electronic surveillance devices are often used to prevent assaults and escapes. Inmates in some minimum security institutions face virtually no visible physical restraints; the prison grounds may be encircled only by an easily scaled, low fence. Some lower security prisons have a cottage or campus design, with dormitories and individual rooms, rather than long cellblocks. Inmates have greater freedom of movement and autonomy in these prisons; they are also given more privileges and allowed to have more personal possessions in their cells. These prisons sometimes offer community release programs, where inmates leave the facility during the day to attend school or for work. Prison officials depend on effective classification to ensure that the inmates confined in medium and minimum security institutions are sufficiently responsible and dependable to be trusted with these freedoms. Of course, prisoners know that if they violate this trust, they can be reclassified and transferred to a maximum security prison.

Even within prisons, living arrangements vary considerably. Large maximum security penitentiaries usually have at least three forms of confinement: segregation units, the general population, and honor blocks. Inmates in segregation units are isolated from other prisoners, either for administrative purposes, for disciplinary infractions, or for protective custody. *Administrative segregation* is a special unit for inmates who need "greater attention and supervision than would be available in the general population" (Stinchcomb and Fox, p. 268). Examples might include older prisoners or those who are mentally retarded. *Disciplinary segregation* is a punishment unit where inmates who have violated institutional rules are locked in their cells all day, except for an hour or two of recreation time. *Protective custody* units confine prisoners who were threatened or attacked in the general population, usually because they owed debts, were involved in homosexual triangles, or offered staff members information about the misconduct of others.

Those confined in segregation units have much less freedom of movement and autonomy than the typical *mainline* inmate confined in the general population cellblocks of maximum security prisons. Unlike prisoners in segregation, those in the general population have unrestricted prison yard, gymnasium, and commissary privileges, and eat together in the prison cafeteria. Due to their exemplary behavior, honor block inmates (called *trustees*) have the most freedom of movement and autonomy: they usually are cleared through the prison control center to work as janitors in administrative offices, or even as caretakers of the grounds outside the prison. Despite their good institutional behavior, older trustees sometimes are stuck in maximum security prisons because they were convicted for murder.

Institutional programs are another important dimension of the formal organization of prisons. These programs are designed to improve the personal and social circumstances and skills of inmates. As a rule of thumb, a greater number and diversity of prison programs are found in larger institutions that confine inmates who scored high on needs-assessment instruments. In particular, this includes younger, drug-addicted, illiterate inmates with few job skills. It is believed that these prisoners' lives can be salvaged through effective remediation and treatment intervention. The hope is that this will reduce the *recidivism* (or repeat offending) rates of these prisoners following release. Certainly, the type and quality of programs available in a prison significantly affect the institutional experiences of inmates.

Perhaps the most important program is remedial and secondary education, aimed toward the goal of inmates completing high school or passing the GED examination (the high school General Equivalency Diploma). Basic education programs are essential in most prisons given the high illiteracy rate among inmates: a U.S. Department of Education study (1992) showed that 59 percent of all imprisoned adults were either functionally illiterate or completely illiterate. As of 31 December 1995, 87 percent of prisons nationwide offered remedial and secondary education programs (Stephan).

Many prisons also feature college programs (usually limited to two-year degrees, with the stipulation that inmates must pay for their own courses and books), work programs (including prison farms, prison industries, and facility support services, such as jobs in the prison cafeteria or the laundry), vocational training (teaching such skills as auto repair, small appliance repair, air conditioner and heating maintenance, and furniture making), recreational programs (including basketball, football, and softball leagues), and counseling services (ranging from drug counseling to marital, parenting, and employment skills training). Work programs and counseling services are found in almost all American prisons (in 1995, 99% contained work programs; 96% delivered counseling services). In contrast, college programs and vocational training are less common (in 1995, 38% of prisons nationwide had college courses offered on site; 64% had vocational training programs; Stephan).

Finally, the formal organization within correctional systems must accommodate special-needs populations. These inmates have unusual problems, because they are sick, weak, dependent, or infirm. This includes prisoners who are very young or very old, pregnant women, those who are mentally disturbed or retarded, prisoners with AIDS (acquired immunodeficiency syndrome) or other chronic diseases, and the physically impaired. For example, long prison terms coupled with the aging of the post–World War II babyboomer generation has resulted in the "graying" of inmate populations. (In 1990, 5% of prisoners nationwide were age fifty or older; by 1997, this figure rose to 7%; Camp and Camp.) Deinstitutionalization policies from the 1970s that discharged many patients from mental hospitals have inadvertently increased the numbers of mentally ill prisoners; approximately one-tenth of all inmates are diagnosed with significant to severe psychiatric abnormalities (Allen and Simonsen). There are no precise figures on how many inmates have AIDS, but it is estimated that the extent of infection is six to seven times higher in prison populations than on the streets (Allen and Simonsen). By the mid-1990s, one-third of the deaths in American prisons were attributed to AIDS (Stephan). Special-needs prisoners make convenient targets for all the bullies and predators roaming through the mainline; as a result, prudent correctional officials try to place the most vulnerable of these inmates in administrative segregation or protective custody.

Inmate subcultures and informal organizations

The day-to-day experiences of inmates are not only affected by the official, formal organization of prisons; an informal organization among inmates—known to criminologists as the inmate subculture—is equally influential. The inmate subculture is comprised of a peculiar language and a distinctive set of informal norms, attitudes, beliefs, values, statuses, and roles that give prisoners a different perspective from people on the outside (or as prisoners say, those of us in the *freeworld*).

To illustrate the existence of this unique subculture, prisons have an inverted status hierarchy that often honors behaviors and activities that are condemned by the law abiding. For most people, the cop killer is the ultimate symbol of a despicable criminal; confined in a men's maximum security prison, he is admired by other inmates as a *stand-up guy*, or congratulated for being an *outlaw* (the highest terms of respect in these institutions). Drug dealers and *gang bangers* (members of urban street gangs) are hated by society, but they occupy positions of importance

and power in the cellblocks. Even *strong-arm rapists* who sexually assault other inmates are grudgingly admired in prison for their ability to dominate the weak (Hassine).

Prisoners claim that an *inmate code* (or a set of values and beliefs distinctive to prisons) binds this subculture together. This code is the unofficial rule book for the informal organization of inmates. In particular, the code depicts prison as a chaotic, violent, and predatory jungle; inmates call penitentiaries *gladiator schools*, where only the strong survive (Abbott). The code admonishes *fish* (or newcomers to prison) to avoid entanglements and disputes with other prisoners, especially those that involve debts. One inmate's version of the code is: "Don't gamble, don't mess with drugs, don't mess with homosexuals, don't steal, don't borrow or lend, and you might survive" (Hassine, p. 52). Weaker inmates who ignore this advice often become *mules* for manipulative predators, using their body cavities to smuggle drugs into prison, or they may be *turned-out* as jailhouse prostitutes.

Academic accounts of the inmate code emphasize its oppositional values to conventional society in general and to prison authorities in particular (Ohlin; Sykes and Messinger). The cardinal sin is to cooperate with officials as a prison informer who *snitches, squeals,* or *rats* on other inmates in exchange for parole, favorable work details, or other considerations. (Incredibly gruesome and sadistical accounts of the torture and murder of snitches by other inmates during prison riots resonate throughout the *jailhouse grapevine,* or prison gossip network.) Other values in the inmate code noted by Gresham M. Sykes and Sheldon Messinger include "don't trust the guards," "maintain yourself' (as a tough *real man* who shows no sensitivity, emotion, or weakness), and "don't quarrel with fellow inmates" (*do your own time* by keeping your "nose out of other people's business") (pp. 6–8).

Another feature of the inmate subculture is the distinctive language used among prisoners. Examples of this slang (or argot) appear in italics throughout this essay. Some other colorful terms include *shank* or *shiv* (for prison knives or sharp weapons), *pruno* or *hootch* (homemade jailhouse alcohol), the *hole* or *jail* (disciplinary segregation), *brake fluid* (prescription tranquilizers used to calm antisocial inmates), *the man* (a term used with contempt for persons holding positions of authority), *hacks* (correctional officers), *rapos* (inmates who irritate others by constantly complaining that they were wrongly convicted), *old heads* (middle-aged or elderly inmates), *square johns* (middle-class, conventional inmates who identify with staff members), and *crazies* or *dings* (mentally disturbed inmates). The sentence "Bill's an old head square john gone crazy from drinking pruno; the man's got him on brake fluid" is incomprehensible to the average person, but would be immediately understood by almost any prisoner in America.

Prison slang that is used to refer to different types of inmates (e.g., ding or rapo) is indispensable in the identification of stable roles within the prison subculture. Inmates relate to each other based on these roles. In a classic study from the 1950s of inmate types in the New Jersey State Prison (a men's maximum security institution in Trenton), Sykes described numerous "argot roles" that he claimed offered a blueprint for the informal organization among inmates. For example, he found that the black market distribution of illegal goods and services in the prison was controlled by two inmate types: *merchants* and *gorillas*. Merchants bought and sold contraband using cigarettes for *script* (prison money). Gorillas preyed on the weak through theft and strong-armed tactics (extortion and robbery) to supply themselves and their friends with desired goods. Sykes discovered three inmate roles—*wolves*, *punks*, and *fags*—governing prison sexual relationships. Wolves were older, physically tough inmates who played the aggressive, masculine role; punks were their younger and weaker victims. Wolves and punks were heterosexuals before confinement; Sykes argued that their homosexuality was a situational adjustment to heterosexual deprivation within prison. Fags were homosexuals on the streets, and simply continued this behavior once incarcerated. The slang expressions that Sykes associated with homosexual roles are still used in contemporary men's prisons, although wolves are now often called *pitchers*, while punks and fags are generically called *catchers*. Similar inmate types relating to lesbianism exist in women's prisons between masculinized *butches* and the female role, played by *femmes*.

In prisons today, the illegal distribution of goods and services is controlled by gang members and *swag men*. Gang members dominate the most lucrative ventures in modern prisons—drug trafficking and gambling—through group intimidation and force. The swag man works alone as an inmate who buys, sells, and steals inexpensive commodities, often sandwiches from the prison cafeteria or snacks from the commis-

sary (among street criminals, the term *swag* refers to stolen goods).

John Irwin offered another well-known analysis of inmate types. From a study of 116 male parolees released from California state prisons in the mid-1960s, Irwin identified eight key inmate roles: *thieves* (professional armed robbers and burglars), *hustlers* (petty con artists), *dope fiends* (opiate addicts), *heads* (marijuana, acid, and methamphetamine users), *disorganized criminals* (a catchall category of criminal "screw-ups" who lack any discernible skills or specializations), *state-raised youth* (criminals who have spent most of their lives in prison since entering reformatories in their adolescence), *lower-class "men"* (conventional people from poor neighborhoods who find themselves in prison), and square johns.

There is a longstanding debate among criminologists about what causes inmate subcultures. In an important early sociological study of incarceration and its affect on prisoners completed in the mid-1930s at Menard State Penitentiary (a maximum security men's prison in southern Illinois), Donald Clemmer coined the term "prisonization" to refer to the learning or transmission of this subculture. Clemmer defined prisonization as "the taking on in greater or lesser degree of the folkways, mores, customs, and general culture of the penitentiary" (p. 299). He believed that the inmate subculture had its sources within the prison; later scholars referred to this as the "indigenous origin" theory. Clemmer argued that the beliefs, values, and behaviors of inmates grow more antisocial the longer they are exposed to this subculture.

What causes the inmate subculture to appear in the first place? Sykes greatly advanced Clemmer's argument by offering an explanation for the indigenous origin of inmate subcultures. From his study of the New Jersey State Prison, Sykes reasoned that the subculture develops to help inmates adjust to the deprivations of incarceration, or what he called the "pains of imprisonment." He noted five specific pains that incarceration imposes on prisoners, which include the loses of liberty, material goods and services, heterosexual relationships, autonomy, and personal security. Sykes claimed that particular argot roles within the subculture evolved to compensate for these loses. For example, merchants and gorillas provided inmates with goods and services forbidden in prison but easily acquired in the outside world. Likewise, wolves and punks are role adjustments to the loss of heterosexual outlets. To summarize, Clemmer and Sykes each argued that the "hardships of confinement lead to the development of a criminal subculture found only in prisons" (Wright, 1999, p. 162); this became known in criminology as *indigenous origin/deprivation* theory.

In the early 1960s, Donald R. and Irwin Cressey challenged indigenous origin/deprivation theory by proposing a radically different explanation called the *importation* model. This perspective considers preprison socialization experiences as crucial in shaping the development of inmate subcultures. Cressey and Irwin argued that the roles observed in these subcultures are not adjustments to the deprivations of confinement; rather, these roles are "composites of various criminal and conventional street identities" (Wright, 1999, p. 162). In 1970 Irwin presented data supporting this argument from his interviews with California parolees. The inmate roles identified in this study—for example, thieves, hustlers, dope fiends, and square johns—were produced by interaction and socialization that occurred outside the prison (state-raised youth were the only exception to this argument). Irwin claimed that the unusual features of inmate subcultures emerge through the association of peculiar criminal and conventional personalities imported into the prison.

In 1977, two studies independently appeared that strongly supported the importation explanation for inmate subcultures. Leo Carroll's 1977 analysis of inmates in Eastern Correctional Institution (his pseudonym for the men's maximum security prison in Rhode Island) showed that numerous recent correctional reforms (including more liberal visitation privileges, permission to wear street clothes and hairstyles, and permission to bring television sets and radios into prison) meant that inmates were no longer isolated from the outside world. Carroll concluded that these and similar reforms enabled "prisoners to retain their attachments to reference groups beyond the prison walls. And within the prison freedom to dress and to decorate their cells as they please. . .permits prisoners to interact on the basis of preprison identities, rather than solely as convicts" (1977, p. 45).

James B. Jacobs's mid-1970s study of changes in Stateville Penitentiary (a large men's maximum security prison in northern Illinois) showed that reforms introduced by liberal prison officials and federal court decisions relieved many of the pains of imprisonment, making it easier for prisoners to retain their criminal and conventional street identities and lifestyles. Jacobs observed that the recent liberalization of visitation, telephone, and mail privileges permitted inmates far greater contact with their relatives, friends, and associates from the outside world. For example, visitation rules in many prisons today allow limited physical contact between inmates and their spouses or lovers. These contacts make it easy to smuggle drugs into prison, enabling street addicts to continue using drugs behind bars.

Jacobs (1977) also examined how U.S. Supreme Court decisions in the 1960s and 1970s extended certain basic rights to inmates, allowing greater access to the freeworld. As one example, the 1964 *Cooper v. Pate* decision cleared the way for considerable freedom of religion in prisons. Following this decision, Nation of Islam ministers were permitted to conduct services in Stateville Penitentiary, enabling Black Muslims to practice their faith and retain their identities in prison. Other Supreme Court decisions—*Procunier v. Martinez* (1974) and *Wolff v. McDonnell* (1974)—virtually abolished the censorship of mail by prison officials. Furthermore, in the *Wolff* decision, the Court offered the opinion that although prisoners had "diminished rights," they could not be "wholly stripped of constitutional protections" and the due process of the law (Jacobs, 1983, p. 42). The cumulative effect of these and other court decisions has allowed influences from the outside world to stream into prisons: inmates today see the same television shows, hear the same music, and read the same magazines and newspapers as the general public.

In particular, prison reforms and federal court decisions have made it difficult to control the influx and activities of gang bangers in prisons. Jacobs showed that in the mid-1970s, four "supergangs" from the streets of Chicago dominated the inmate subculture in Stateville. Gang members brought into prison "intact organizational structures, highly charismatic leaders, support from the streets, and a long history of intergang warfare" (1977, p. 146). Stateville inmates interacted with each other based on these street-imported gang identities, rather than in terms of their statuses as prisoners. Furthermore, relaxed visitation, telephone, and mail restrictions kept gang members in prison informed about events on the streets, and gang members on the streets informed about developments in prison.

Most prison researchers concur that the importation theory more accurately explains inmate subcultures than the indigenous origin/

deprivation model (Cao et al.; McCorkle et al.; Wright, 1994). Correctional practitioners and scholars now recognize that the imposing walls that surround prisons are surprisingly permeable. "Prison walls, fences, and [gun] towers still prevent the inside world from getting outside, [but] they can no longer prevent the outside world—with its diverse attractions, diversions, and problems—from getting inside" (Wright, 1999, p. 164).

Despite this general conclusion, a number of factors since the 1970s have combined to increase the pains of imprisonment experienced by most inmates. Some scholars have claimed that the public and conservative politicians in America together have spearheaded a *penal harm movement*, with the intention of increasing the misery associated with incarceration (Clear; Cullen). Some aspects of the penal harm movement that have affected the conditions of confinement include the return of chain gangs and road crews in southern states, the decisions by some prison officials to keep known gang members permanently locked down in disciplinary segregation, the reintroduction of stripped uniforms as standard attire in some prisons, and legislation in several states that closes weight-training and conditioning rooms. A study by Todd R. Clear documented that every state since 1972 has "altered its penal policy in the direction of greater punitive severity" (p. 50) through such measures as the restriction or abolition of parole, the implementation of mandatory sentencing laws (that automatically require prison sentences for those convicted for particular offenses, often drugs and weapons violations), and "three-strikes-and-you're-out" laws (that mandate life sentences for a third felony conviction). These "get-tough" measures especially have targeted predatory street crime and the crack cocaine epidemic, filling American prisons with "minority-group, drug-addicted, urban-underclass offenders" (Wright, 1999, p. 164).

Rising prison populations and overcrowding have gone hand-in-hand with the penal harm movement. As noted earlier, prison populations have exploded since the early 1980s. From 31 December 1985 to 30 June 1998, there was a 148 percent increase in the number of convictees imprisoned in the United States (Gilliard). During this period, 57,795 new inmates were incarcerated each year. In practical terms, this means that every week in America, correctional officials must find space in existing institutions for over one thousand new inmates, or they must open a new prison with this capacity.

Not surprisingly, prison construction has lagged behind these increases in inmate populations. For example, figures from 1995 showed that the federal prison population was 24 percent over its maximum designed capacity (Stephan). Overcrowding forces prison officials to order the double-celling of inmates, or to introduce open, barracks-style sleeping arrangements in whatever space is available (e.g., gymnasiums or converted warehouses).

The deteriorating conditions of confinement, longer prison sentences, and overcrowding together have increased the suffering that inmates experience in prison. Levels of violence, fear, and hopelessness rise in crowded cellblocks that are saturated with drugs and overrun by gang bangers. This has led to the emergence of new, indigenous prison gangs organized for self-defense and for buying and sharing drugs (Hunt et al.; Hassine). In a study of men's prisons in California, Geoffrey Hunt et al. found that for every gang imported into prison from the streets, another gang forms inside for protection. Some of these new prison gangs will be exported into the freeworld once their members are paroled.

The turmoil in modern prisons means that inmate subcultures are in a precarious state. If prison conditions worsen, the pains of imprisonment could become severe enough to breed new values and roles among inmates, fundamentally altering the criminal and conventional personalities imported from the streets. This could signal a return to the "bad old days" in corrections where convicts were irreparably damaged through prisonization, or exposure to the inmate subculture. Some commentators already sense the growing unrest and despair in the cellblocks: Victor Hassine compares the modern prison to a "runaway train" filled with prisoners only concerned about "how they are going to survive this madness" (p. 156).

It is critical to reiterate that the experiences of prison inmates are a product of the complex interplay between the formal and informal organization of prisons. In the 1960s and the 1970s, the relaxation of strict rules by liberal prison officials and by federal court decisions were key forces that enabled the importation of criminal and conventional street identities into the inmate subculture. In the 1980s and the 1990s, the penal harm movement and prison overcrowding reversed these trends, threatening to restore the pains of imprisonment and prisonization. Changes in the official, formal organization of prisons inevitably reshape the informal inmate subculture. The fate of prisoners hangs in this delicate balance.

RICHARD A. WRIGHT

See also CORRECTIONAL REFORM ASSOCIATIONS; DETERRENCE; INCAPACITATION; JAILS; JUVENILE JUSTICE: INSTITUTIONS; PRISONERS, LEGAL RIGHTS OF; PRISONS: HISTORY; PRISONS: CORRECTIONAL OFFICERS; PRISONS: PRISONS FOR WOMEN; PRISONS: PROBLEMS AND PROSPECTS; RETRIBUTIVISM.

BIBLIOGRAPHY

ABBOTT, JACK HENRY. *In the Belly of the Beast: Letters from Prison.* New York: Vintage Books, 1982.

ALLEN, HARRY E., and SIMONSEN, CLIFFORD E. *Corrections in America: An Introduction,* 8th ed. Upper Saddle River, N.J.: Prentice-Hall, 1998.

BECK, ALLEN J., and GILLIARD, DARRELL K. *Prisoners in 1994.* Washington, D.C.: U.S. Department of Justice, Bureau of Justice Statistics, 1995.

BLAU, PETER M., and MEYER, MARSHALL W. *Bureaucracy in Modern Society,* 2d ed. New York: Random House, 1971.

CAMP, CAMILLE GRAHAM, and CAMP, GEORGE M. *The Corrections Yearbook 1997.* South Salem, N.Y.: Criminal Justice Institute, 1997.

CAO, LIQUN; ZHAO, JIHONG; and VAN DINE, STEVE. "Prison Disciplinary Tickets: A Test of the Deprivation and Importation Models." *Journal of Criminal Justice* 25, no. 2 (1997): 103–113.

CARROLL, LEO. *Hacks, Blacks, and Cons: Race Relations in a Maximum Security Prison.* 1974. Reprint, Prospect Heights, Ill.: Waveland Press, 1988.

———. "Race and Three Forms of Prisoner Power: Confrontation, Censoriousness, and the Corruption of Authority." In *Contemporary Corrections: Social Control and Conflict.* Edited by C. Ronald Huff. Beverly Hills, Calif.: Sage, 1977. Pages 40–53.

CLEAR, TODD R. *Harm in American Penology: Offenders, Victims, and Their Communities.* Albany, N.Y.: State University of New York Press, 1994.

CLEMMER, DONALD. *The Prison Community.* New York: Holt, Rinehart and Winston, 1940.

CRESSEY, DONALD R., and IRWIN, JOHN. "Thieves, Convicts and the Inmate Culture." *Social Problems* 10, no. 3 (1962): 142–155.

CULLEN, FRANCIS T. "Assessing the Penal Harm Movement." *Journal of Research in Crime and Delinquency* 32, no. 3 (1995): 338–358.

Escape from Alcatraz. Directed by Don Siegel. Paramount Pictures, 1979.

GILLIARD, DARRELL K. *Prison and Jail Inmates at Midyear 1998.* Washington, D.C.: U.S. Department of Justice, Bureau of Justice Statistics, 1999.

HASSINE, VICTOR. *Life without Parole: Living in Prison Today,* 2d ed. Edited by Thomas J. Bernard, Richard McCleary, and Richard A. Wright. Los Angeles: Roxbury, 1999.

HUNT, GEOFFREY; RIEGEL, STEPHANIE; MORALES, TOMAS; and WALDORF, DAN. "Changes in Prison Culture: Prison Gangs and the Case of the 'Pepsi Generation'." *Social Problems* 40, no. 2 (1993): 398–409.

IRWIN, JOHN. *The Felon.* 1970. Reprint, Berkeley: University of California Press, 1987.

JACOBS, JAMES B. *Stateville: The Penitentiary in Mass Society.* Chicago: University of Chicago Press, 1977.

———. *New Perspectives on Prisons and Imprisonment.* Ithaca, N.Y.: Cornell University Press, 1983.

McCORKLE, RICHARD C.; MIETHE, TERANCE D.; and DRASS, KRISS A. "The Roots of Prison Violence: A Test of the Deprivation, Management, and 'Not-So-Total' Institution Models." *Crime & Delinquency* 41, no. 3 (1995): 317–331.

MUMOLA, CHRISTOPHER J., and BECK, ALLEN J. *Prisoners in 1996.* Washington, D.C.: U.S. Department of Justice, Bureau of Justice Statistics, 1997.

Murder in the First. Directed by Marc Rocco. Warner Brothers, 1994.

OHLIN, LLOYD E. *Sociology and the Field of Corrections.* New York: Social Science Research Council, 1956.

The Shawshank Redemption. Directed by Frank Darabont. Castle Rock Entertainment, 1994.

STEPHAN, JAMES J. *Census of State and Federal Correctional Facilities, 1995.* Washington, D.C.: U.S. Department of Justice, Bureau of Justice Statistics, 1997.

STINCHCOMB, JEANNE B., and FOX, VERNON B. *Introduction to Corrections,* 5th ed. Upper Saddle River, N.J.: Prentice-Hall, 1999.

SYKES, GRESHAM M. *The Society of Captives: A Study of a Maximum Security Prison.* Princeton, N.J.: Princeton University Press, 1958.

SYKES, GRESHAM M., and MESSINGER, SHELDON. "The Inmate Social System." In *Theoretical*

Studies in the Social Organization of the Prison. Edited by Richard A. Cloward, Donald R. Cressey, George H. Grosser, Richard McCleary, Lloyd E. Ohlin, Gresham M. Sykes, and Sheldon Messinger. New York: Social Science Research Council, 1960. Pages 1–19.

U.S. Department of Education. *National Adult Literacy Survey.* Washington, D.C.: National Center for Education Statistics, 1992.

WRIGHT, RICHARD A. *In Defense of Prisons.* Westport, Conn.: Greenwood Press, 1994.

———. "Afterword." In *Life without Parole: Living in Prison Today,* 2d ed., by Victor Hassine. Edited by Thomas J. Bernard, Richard McCleary, and Richard A. Wright. Los Angeles: Roxbury Publishing Co., 1999. Pages 159–169.

CASES

Cooper v. Pate, 378 U.S. 546 (1964).
Procunier v. Martinez, 416 U.S. 396 (1974).
Wolff v. McDonnell, 418 U.S. 539 (1974).

PRISONS: PRISONS FOR WOMEN

Understanding the contemporary prison for women requires an examination of the historical development of this system of social control and the critical issues relating to the imprisonment of women in the modern era. These issues include the development of distinct subcultures within these institutions, the enormous rise in the numbers of women in prison beginning in the late 1980s, the characteristics of women prisoners, and the gender-specific concerns such as physical and sexual abuse, separation from children, substance abuse, and unmet program needs.

History

Throughout history, the female criminal has been cast as a "double-deviant"; first, because she violated the criminal or moral law and, second, perhaps more importantly, because she has violated the narrow moral strictures of the female role within society. In almost every Western society, women have been cast as second-class citizens, subservient to the will and wishes of men. Women who violated the law, then, also violated their subservient position and were seen as morally suspect as well as criminal. Prior to the development of prisons in the seventeenth and eighteenth centuries, punishment for women

and men took a variety of forms: Serious offenders were put to death by hanging or burning, or banished from their community or sold as slaves. Belknap notes that in the Middle Ages, for example, women who committed adultery or killed their spouses were commonly burned to death. Less serious offenders were subjected to physical punishments such as whippings, stocks and pillories, or branding; and social punishments including public humiliation and shame. For women, mask-like devices, called the brank or bridle, were used in England up until the 1800s and were designed to punish and control outspoken women who gossiped or disobeyed their husbands.

Although death and physical torture remained in use, Western society began to consider alternatives to them in the nineteenth century. Houses of correction, workhouses, and transportation to colonies were precursors of modern confinement and served to bridge the gap between the death penalty and the contemporary prison. The house of correction and the workhouse were designed to address the moral failings of the underclass. In their various forms, these institutions were used to confine less serious offenders, including penniless women and prostitutes. Women could also be sent to bridewells, poorhouses, or nunneries by fathers or husbands who wanted to punish the unruly, disobedient, or unchaste woman. These early modes of imprisonment attempted to combine punishment for past wrongdoing with attempts at reforming future behavior. Transportation developed in western Europe, most notably in England, as another alternative to the death penalty. In the 1700s, England transported over 60 percent of the convicted offenders to work as indentured servants in the colonies in America and Australia. Historians estimate that between 12 and 20 percent of those transported were women, who were typically convicted of crimes relating to poverty or sexual behavior. Ironically, women were transported to the colonies were often used as prostitutes or mistresses to meet the demand for sexual partners—willing or not—in these rough new worlds. Those escaping forced prostitution were indentured servants to the managerial class. About 24,000 women were transported to Australia between 1788 and 1852.

The penitentiary was the next step in the evolution of the prison. Dungeons, castles, and the like had been used for centuries to confine wrongdoers until physical punishment could be delivered. The penitentiary, however, was the first attempt to use confinement as the punishment itself. In England, one of the first models for the modern prison was intended to provide a place of penance for prostitutes. This radical experiment was based on principles of separation from the moral contagion of their former lives, religious contemplation, and rigid structure. Up until the late 1800s, women, men, and children were confined together in these attempts at correction, often with no provision for food, clothing, or bedding. Those without families or other means of support lived in brutal and unsanitary conditions. Women often resorted to prostitution with more propertied inmates or officials to survive. However noble in principle, most of these attempts at correction failed. Overcrowding, lack of adequate funding, a corrupt and untrained guard force, and little real commitment to the ideal of reforming the underclass contributed to this failure.

The history of prisons took a new turn in the American colonies. At the end of the American Revolution (1783), incarceration was relatively uncommon. The crimes committed by women were—and continue to be— fewer and less serious than those committed by men. For the female minor offender, public humiliations, such as the ducking stool, the stocks, and the "Scarlet Letter," were delivered to those behaving outside the authority of men as well as those breaking the law. Corporal and capital punishment continued to be the primary forms of punishment for serious crimes but new ideas about punishment and reform gained a foothold in the American colonies. By the 1820s, the American solution to crime was the American penitentiary. Based on the principles articulated in England, the American penitentiary flowered during the Jacksonian era. Two similar models took root between 1820 and 1840—the silent and the congregate systems. Both models used work, discipline, religious contemplation, and separation from the free world to attempt change in the convicted criminal.

Few women were confined in the emerging penitentiary system. While only about 4 percent of the U.S. prison population was female by 1950, most scholars agree that these few imprisoned women did not benefit from this experiment in reform. Robert Johnson states that women and minorities were "barely considered human" (p. 32), and thus not fit candidates for the penitentiary's regime. The few women imprisoned in the early 1880s were confined to traditional prisons that offered no plan for reform.

Pollock-Byrne (1986) describes these places of confinement as having little regard for the safety and health of the woman prisoner. Like the first houses of correction, prisons for women in America were dirty, crowded, unsupervised, and without adequate bedding, food, and other provisions. Women were often locked away in rooms above the guardhouse or mess hall of the male prison with little access to workshops and exercise yards. Often left without supervision, women were vulnerable to attacks by one another and the male guards. Male staff and prisoners alike sexually abused women in these early prisons. Freedman argued that women were subjected to the "worst debasement at the hands of prison officials and guards" (p. 60) and that sadistic beatings, rape, and illegitimate births combined to make the prison experience even more terrifying. Dobash, Dobash, and Gutteridge conclude that, "From the very beginning, women in prison were treated very differently from men, considered more morally depraved and in need of special, closer forms of control and confinement" (p. 1).

While Elizabeth Fry began her work to reform the conditions of English women's prisons in 1816, the reformatory movement in the United States developed later in the mid-nineteenth century. Prisons for women then diverged into two directions, custodial institutions and the reformatory (Rafter, 1986). The custodial model was the traditional prison, adopting the retributive purpose, high-security architecture, male-dominated authority and harsh discipline of the male prison (Rafter, 1985, p. 21). Many women remained confined to the male prison, with little regard to their gendered needs. The reformatory, in contrast, was a new form of punishment designed specifically to house women in entirely separate institutions, with female matrons and programs planned to reform women by promoting appropriate gender roles. Training in cooking, sewing, laundry, and other domestic arts were designed to return the woman prisoner to free society as either a well-trained wife or a domestic servant. The unwalled reformatories were built on large parcels of land, usually in rural areas with small cottages instead of cellblock structures. Rafter (1985) offers evidence that minority women were more likely to be sent to the more brutal custodial prison, whereas white women, particularly young, white women who had committed minor offenses, were more likely to be seen as ideal candidates for redemption in the reformatory. Alderson Federal Prison in

West Virginia and the California Institute for Women represent the reformatory model and were still in use at the end of the 1990s.

Ending in the 1930s, the reformatory movement established separate women's facilities with some recognition of the gendered needs of women. After the 1930s, the custodial and reform models merged, combining elements of their two styles with differing results throughout the United States. The legacy of these movements continues to shape prisons for women. First, with the exception of a relatively few "co-corrections" experiments that housed women and men together with common programming, most prisons in the 1990s were single sex. Second, vocational programming tends to reinforce gender stereotypes, although some innovative programs that offer training in welding, woodworking, and other male-identified trades are found in the contemporary prison. Third, women in prison continue to be subjected to the neglect that characterizes their history from the early houses of correction to the modern prison.

By the 1940s and 1950s, the medical model of corrections emerged as a new philosophy of punishment. Called "correctional institutions," these prisons moved away from the harsh discipline and work orientation of the custodial prison and instead attempted to introduce treatment to a newly defined inmate—rather than convict—population. "Correctional officers" replaced prison guards, and the inmates were introduced to a treatment regime that attempted to diagnose, classify, and treat the inmate prior to release. An indeterminate sentencing system rewarded those who appeared to conform to this treatment by release on parole. There is little evidence that this approach had any more success in rehabilitating women—or men—than other prior forms of punishment.

During this time, the social sciences "discovered" the prison and began investigating the way prisoners adjusted to and lived their lives in prison. While most of these studies of the prison focused on men, some of the classic work on the subcultures of women's prisons was conducted in the 1960s and early 1970s (Owen; Ward and Kassebaum; Giallombardo; and Heffernan).

The contemporary prison

Beginning in the 1970s, prison systems began to return to a custodial or "warehouse" model, with few prisons offering rehabilitative programs. This trend continued into the 1980s

and 1990s. In this period, the numbers of women in prison began to skyrocket, due primarily to enhanced and punitive sanctions against drug offenders. Prisons for women then became increasingly crowded as women were hard hit by this national trend. The female prison population increased disproportionately to the increase in women's involvement in serious crime (Immarigeon and Chesney-Lind). Some states began to build new prisons for women, again using designs based on male prisons. Many of the reformatory prisons remain in use, but the majority of modern prisons for women are now run as custodial rather than as rehabilitative institutions.

Most states have a relatively small number of prisons for women and thus house women prisoners at one or two geographically isolated locations. California, with the largest prison population in the United States (at almost 12,000 in 1999), is the exception with five prisons for women. Women are often housed far from home, friends, and their families and are distant from services more available in urban communities. While male prisoners are assigned to the more numerous facilities with a wider range of security levels, the majority of women in the United States are confined to prisons that encompass all classification and security levels in one facility. In the contemporary prison, security procedures often interfere with privacy. While privacy is eroded by crowded conditions, shared housing units, and the need for surveillance, the presence of male staff undermines a woman's ability to attend to personal hygiene and grooming without the scrutiny of men. In most prisons, between 50 and 80 percent of the custody staff is male. Male staff supervise housing units, monitoring women in showers, toilets, and in the rooms or cells where they dress. Most prison systems prohibit male staff from performing strip searches.

With the exception of newly arrived prisoners and the small number held in the more restrictive special housing units (such as administrative segregation or security housing units), most women prisoners remain in the general population. Most women prisoners work, attend school, and participate in other programs with all prisoners, whose classification may range from minimum to maximum custody. A very small number of women are housed in administrative segregation or security housing units. Movement within the institution, program participation, and other privileges are severely restricted in these housing units. Women in these units are confined to their cells an average of 23 hours a day, eat their meals in their cells, and are allowed very limited recreation and visiting privileges (Owens, 1998). Only a small percentage of all the women in prison are confined to special housing units but these conditions are often severe.

Co-corrections

Although most states began to build separate institutions for women during the reformatory era, some proportion of women remain confined to prisons with men. By the late 1980s, about 25 percent of the female prison population were held in "co-correctional" facilities. The Federal Bureau of Prisons pioneered the use of co-correctional facilities, but nationwide the number of co-correctional facilities dwindled in the 1990s. Most scholars agree that placing women in an environment with male prisoners creates a distinct disadvantage. While a sexually integrated prison appears to approximate "real world" social conditions and may offer more programs than found in female-only institutions, the research shows that women are more often subjected to more restrictive security and are less likely to take advantage of the increased program opportunities. In light of the move toward "gender-responsive" programming, the use of co-correctional facilities seems to have run its course.

Prison subcultures

The study of prison subcultures investigates the way prisoners adjust to prison, the way they learn to "do their time," and the resulting prison social structure. By the 1960s and 1970s, scholars began to study the subculture of women's prisons and found that it was much different than life in male prisons. The first two of theses important works (Ward and Kassebaum; Giallombardo) discussed a prison social structure based on family, traditional sex-roles, and same-sex relations. In *Women's Prison: Sex and Social Structure*, Ward and Kassebaum found the women in prison felt a loss of control over their lives and anxiety over the course of their prison term. In order to alleviate these feelings, women participated in a prisoner social system to regain a sense of control and belonging while in prison. Included in these feelings of loss were "affectional starvation" resulting from their loss of family and male partners. Ward and Kassebaum suggested women

prisoners developed the "pseudo family" and relationships with other prisoners to make up for this loss. Giallombardo's *Society of Women* also described the world of imprisoned women based on sex-role adaptation and family or kinship structures. She stated that the social order of women's prison is based on an adaptation of traditional feminine roles, such as mother, daughter, and wife. Masculine sex roles find expression in the prison social roles of the "stud." Giallombardo argued that the family or kinship structure of the women's prison is also based on this sex-role framework.

In a third classic study, *Making It in Prison: The Square, the Cool, and the Life*, Heffernan described how women prisoners organize their prison identities around two things: their pre-prison identities and their differential adaptation to the prison subculture. Women who did not define themselves as serious criminals prior to prison adopted "the Square" orientation to prison life, and continued to hold conventional behaviors and attitudes during their imprisonment. In contrast, women who adapted to prison life as "the Cool" became heavily invested in a prison-based identity and developed a form of doing time that was based on prison values. Finally, some women retained their street identity of the petty criminal and adopted "the Life" as their style of doing time. These three studies found remarkable similarities: Prison culture among women was tied to gender expectations of sexuality and family relationships and these expectations also shaped the way women developed their lives within prison.

Decades later, *In the Mix: Struggle and Survival in a Women's Prison* described the daily life of the women's prison, with an emphasis on the gendered nature of its social structure, roles, and normative frameworks. Owen also found that prison culture for women was tied directly to the role of women in society as well as to a dynamic social structure that was shaped by the conditions of women's lives in prison and in the "free world." Like Heffernan, *In the Mix* describes the lives of women before prison and suggests that these lives shape their adaptation to prison culture. Owen found that economic marginalization, histories of personal and substance abuse, and self-destructive behavior are defining features of inmate's lives prior to prison. She also saw that the amount of time women have to serve and their kinds of work and housing assignments affect the way women in prison "program," developing a pattern to their daily life and relation-

PRISONS: PRISONS FOR WOMEN   1195

ships that determines the way women adapt to prison. Since about 80 percent of the women in prison are mothers, great importance was placed on relationships with their children. Finally, Owen described "the mix" as part of prison culture that supported the rule-breaking behavior that propels women into prison. This study concluded that prison subcultures for women are very different from the violent and predatory structure of the contemporary male prison. Owen did not find the presence of gangs—a central feature of the contemporary male prison—at the prison she studied. Women experience "pains of imprisonment" but their prison culture offers them other ways to survive and adapt to these deprivations.

Population increases

Enormous increases in population characterize prisons for women since the mid-1980s. In 1980, 12,300 women were imprisoned in state and federal institutions, rising to 44,065 in 1990 and to 75,000 women in 1996. By 1998, this number had risen to 84,427, an almost fourfold increase in just under twenty years. In addition, approximately 64,000 women were incarcerated in local jails and over 700,000 were on probation, parole, or community supervision. In total, nearly 850,000 women were under some form of criminal justice supervision in the United States (Bureau of Justice Statistics 1999a, 1999b). In California alone, the female prison population rose dramatically from 1,316 in 1980, to almost 12,000 in 1999. During 1998, Texas incarcerated over 10,000 women, New York prisons held just under 4,000, and Florida over 3,500. In the federal system, the women's prison population almost doubled from 5,011 in 1990 to 9,186 in 1998. Between 1990 and 1998, the number of women in U.S. prisons increased 92 percent compared to 67 percent increase in the number of men (Bureau of Justice Statistics, 1999a).

This explosion in the women's prison population cannot be explained by looking at the crime rate of women only. Compared to men, women generally commit fewer crimes and their offenses tend to be less serious. A major gender difference is the low rate of violent crime committed by women. The offenses for which women are arrested and incarcerated are primarily nonviolent property and drug offenses. When women do commit acts of violence, it is most likely against a spouse or partner and in the context of self-defense. In analyzing data from the 1970–

1995 Uniform Crime Reports, Steffensmeir and Allan found that drug offenses have had the most significant impact on female arrest rates. Sharp increases in the numbers of women arrested for minor property crimes, like larceny, fraud, and forgery, have also contributed to the explosion in women's imprisonment. Many women resort to minor property crime in order to support their drug use. In addition to increased prosecution of drug offenses, the lack of viable treatment and alternative community sanctions for women has contributed to this unprecedented increase in women's population (Bloom, Chesney-Lind, and Owen). Most criminologists see that the war on drugs, a drug control policy started at the federal level in the 1980s, accounts for the unprecedented rise in the imprisonment of women.

The composition of women's prisons

The profile of women in prison has remained consistent: Female prisoners are primarily low income, disproportionately African American and Hispanic, undereducated, unskilled, and unemployed. They are mostly young and heads of households with an average of two children. At least two-thirds of incarcerated women have children under the age of eighteen. Substance abuse, compounded by poverty, unemployment, physical and mental illness, physical and sexual abuse, and homelessness also characterize the women's prison population (Owen and Bloom). Surveys conducted by the Bureau of Justice Statistics (1991b, 1994), the American Correctional Association (1990), and the Federal Bureau of Prisons (Klein), as well as individual state profiles (Owen and Bloom) provide information about the demographic characteristics of women in prison. These descriptions remain accurate even as the numbers of women in prison continue to surge upward. The following factors characterize this population.

Race and ethnicity. In addition to gender differences between male and female crime, women's arrest and incarceration rates vary by race (Chesney-Lind). Minority women are disproportionately represented in the U.S. prison population, with the percentage of African American women who are incarcerated growing at increasing rates. In 1991, African American women made up about 40 percent of the female prison population; by 1995, this population had grown to 48 percent. The percentage of Hispanic and Latina women is also growing at a somewhat slower rate (Bureau of Justice Statistics, 1997, 1994).

In spite of this disproportionate racial and ethnic composition, racial conflict has not been a primary feature of the social order of female prisons. While racial and ethnic identity is predominant in male prison culture, these conflicts do not shape the way women do their prison time. Women in prison generally live and work in an integrated environment and form personal relationships that often cross racial lines. Racial and ethnic gangs have not yet appeared in women's prisons to the extent they are found in male prisons. While a small number of women may enter the prison with some street gang or clique affiliation, the subculture of the women's prison offers little support for these pre-prison identities. Women seeking the personal and community ties found in street gangs are likely to find substitutes within the prison families or other personal relationships (Owen).

Race relations with staff, however, are potentially more antagonistic. The majority of correctional staff is both white and male in most U.S. prisons for women. Minority women prisoners have reported race-based instances of name-calling, job and program discrimination, and unfair disciplinary practices (Owen; Bloom). Faily and Roundtree (1979) found that African-American prisoners are more likely than other women to be cited for disciplinary infractions.

Age at first arrest and criminal history. The American Correctional Association (ACA) survey found that most women in prison were first arrested at a young age. One-third of those interviewed were first arrested between fifteen and nineteen years of age, and another quarter between twenty and twenty-four years old. Just over 9 percent were arrested prior to their fourteenth birthday and just over 10 percent were arrested after age thirty-five. According to the 1994 Bureau of Justice Statistics report, over half of the women in prison were serving their first prison term. This survey also found that most women serving a second term had been convicted in the past for only nonviolent offenses. Nearly two-thirds of all female inmates had two or fewer prior convictions. Almost three-quarters of all state female prisoners had served a prior sentence to probation or incarceration, including 20 percent who had served a sentence as a juvenile.

Drug use and drug arrests. In the 1990s, substance abuse played a key role in the imprisonment of women and contributed dramatically to the increasing numbers of women prisoners.

Women are more likely to use drugs, use more serious drugs more frequently, and be under the influence of drugs at the time of their crime than males (Bureau of Justice Statistics, 1994). In the national studies, over one-third of all female prisoners interviewed in 1991 reported being under the influence of some drug at the time of their offense. Around 40 percent reported daily drug use in the month before their offense. Almost one-quarter of the 1991 sample reported committing their crime to get money to buy drugs (Bureau of Justice Statistics, 1994).

Victimization. Women in prison have extensive histories of sexual and physical abuse. In the 1991 national surveys, an estimated 43 percent of women in prison reported previous physical or sexual abuse. Others found higher rates of abuse among women in prison (Owen and Bloom). Violent offenders were most likely to have previously experienced this abuse (Bureau of Crime Statistics, 1994). An estimated 50 percent of women in prison who reported abuse said they had experienced abuse at the hands of an intimate, compared to three percent of men. More than three-quarters of the female inmates who had a history of abuse reported being sexually abused. An estimates 56 percent of the abused women said that their abuse had involved a rape, and another 13 percent reported an attempted rape (Bureau of Justice Statistics, 1994). The 1990 ACA survey found that 50 percent of the women reported a history of physical abuse, with 35 percent reporting sexual abuse. This abuse was likely to be at the hands of husbands or boyfriends.

Other demographic factors. According to surveys conducted in the early 1990s, just over half of the women in prison at that time had been employed in the year prior to their arrest. Most were unmarried; 45 percent of the women prisoners had never been married and another third of female inmates were either separated or divorced. Just about 60 percent grew up in households without both parents present. Almost half (47%) had an immediate family member incarcerated at some time. About 35 percent had brothers and 10 percent had sisters who had been incarcerated. Eighty percent of the prisoners interviewed in a national survey reported incomes at or below the poverty level (Bureau of Justice Statistics, 1994).

Problems and unmet needs in the contemporary women's prison

Women in the contemporary prison face many problems; some resulting from their lives prior to imprisonment, others resulting from their imprisonment itself. Women in prison have experienced victimization, unstable family life, school and work failure, and substance abuse and mental health problems. Social factors that marginalize their participation in mainstream society and contribute to the rising number of women in prison include poverty, minority group member, single motherhood, and homelessness. While in U.S. prisons, women, like prisoners throughout the world, face specific pains and deprivations arising directly from their imprisonment. Criminologists have argued that the prison system is ill-equipped to deal with these problems and that theses issues are better managed outside the punitive environment of the prison (Owen and Bloom; Owen). Without attention to these issues, women are often released from prison unprepared to manage their preexisting problems as well as those created by their imprisonment. There are several critical problems faced by women in prison; most are unmet in the prison environment.

Separation from children and significant others. National surveys of women prisoners find that three-fourths of them were mothers, with two-thirds having children under the age of eighteen. Bloom and Chesney-Lind argue that mothers in prison face multiple problems in maintaining relationships with their children and encounter obstacles created both by the correctional system and child welfare agencies. The distance between the prison and the children's homes, lack of transportation, and limited economic resources compromise a woman prisoner's ability to maintain these relationships. Children of women in prison experience many hardships. Children may be traumatized by the arrest of their mother and the sudden, forced separation imprisonment brings. Emotional reactions such as anger, anxiety, depression, and aggression have been found in the children of incarcerated mothers. While most children of imprisoned mothers live with relatives—typically grandparents—a small percentage of these children are placed in the child welfare system. These conditions compound the problem of maintaining contact with children. Over half of the women responding to Bloom and Steinhart's 1993 survey of imprisoned mothers reported never receiving visits from their children.

An estimated 4 to 9 percent of women come to prison pregnant. Women who give birth while incarcerated are rarely allowed to spend time with their child after birth. Mother-infant bonding is severely undermined by this lack of contact after birth. Bedford Hills, a women's prison in New York, is the only program in the U.S. that allows women to keep their newborns with them in a special prison program. This humane response is more common in Britain and other European nations.

Most correctional systems do not take into account the importance of the mother-child relationship in designing policy for women in prison. Some states, such as New York and California, have begun innovative programs to address these problems. Coordinating visits to the prison and support services with child welfare agencies, providing special visiting areas, developing effective parenting classes, and developing community corrections programs for mothers and their children are examples of these innovations. Termination of parental rights also affect prison mothers. About half the states have policies that address the termination of parental rights of incarcerated parents. Advocates of women in prison and their children argue that family reunification, rather than termination of the mother's parental rights, should be a priority of correctional policy for women prisoners.

Lack of substance abuse treatment. Although women offenders are very likely to have an extensive history of drug and alcohol use, a relatively small percentage of women receive any treatment within the justice system. Insufficient individual assessment, limited treatment for pregnant, mentally ill, and violent women offenders, and a lack of appropriate treatment and vocational training limit the effectiveness of the few programs that exist (Wellisch et al.). These findings are supported by a 1998 study released by the National Center on Addiction and Substance Abuse. The report found that women substance abusers are more prone to intense emotional distress, psychosomatic symptoms, and low self-esteem than male inmates.

Physical and mental health care. In addition to requiring basic health care, women offenders often have specific health needs related to their risky sexual and drug-using behavior prior to imprisonment. Acoca has argued that the enormity of health care issues may in fact eclipse other correctional concerns as the female inmate population continues to grow. Women in prison are also at risk for infectious diseases, including HIV, tuberculosis, sexually transmitted diseases, and hepatitis B and C infections. Pregnancy and reproductive health needs are another neglected area of health care. Problems of pregnant inmates include lack of prenatal and postnatal care, inadequate education regarding childbirth and parenting, and little or no preparation for the mother's separation from the infant after delivery.

Mental health disorders are equally neglected in U.S. prisons. While the prevalence and incidence of these needs are still to be determined, estimates suggest that 25 percent to 60 percent of the female prison population require mental health services. Teplin, Abraham, and McClelland found that over 60 percent of female jail inmates had symptoms of drug abuse, over 30 percent had signs of alcohol dependence, and another third had post-traumatic stress disorder. Few prisons have adequate assessment or mental health treatment programs and often "overmedicate" women inmates in need of more intensive treatment.

The impact of physical, sexual, and emotional abuse found in the experience of women offenders also creates a significant need for counseling and therapy (Pollock). This abuse has implications for their emotional and physical well-being and may be tied to drug-abusing and offending behaviors.

Vocation and educational programs.   In addition to insufficient substance abuse and mental health services, educational and vocational programs are also in short supply. Several studies (Pollock-Byrne; Morash, Haarr, and Rucker) found that female prisons offered fewer vocational and education program opportunities when compared to those offered in male institutions. In general, women across the country lack training needed to obtain jobs that pay a living wage. One aspect of this inadequacy is that, like the training offered in the reformatories of the early 1990s, many vocational programs for female inmates emphasize traditional roles for women and work.

Sexual abuse.   The patterns of sexual abuse and coercion established in the early days of women's imprisonment continue in the contemporary era. Human Rights Watch examined this serious problem in their review of sexual abuse in selected U.S. prisons. The damage of the abuse itself is compounded by four specific issues: (1) the inability to escape one's abuser; (2)

ineffectual or nonexistent investigative and grievance procedures; (3) lack of employee accountability (either criminally or administratively); and (4) little or no public concern. The report bluntly states that the "findings indicate that being a woman in U.S. state prisons can be a terrifying experience" (p. 1).

Disparate disciplinary practices.   Although male prisons typically hold a much greater percentage of violent offenders, women tend to receive disciplinary action at a greater rate than men. Research has found that women prisoners were cited more frequently and punished more severely than males. These infractions committed by women in prison tend to be petty when compared to the more serious infractions committed by male prisoners (McClelland).

Gender-specific treatment.   Bloom and Covington have charged that the criminal justice system often fails to develop a diversity of options for dealing with the gender and culturally specific problems of female offenders. Gender-specific services should incorporate physical, psychological, emotional, spiritual, and sociopolitical issues in addressing these needs. Gender-responsive supervision and program approaches must focus on issues such as cross-gender supervision, appropriate relationships between staff and offenders, parity in programming, and appropriate interventions for women offenders. There is also a need for gender-responsive (and culturally relevant) classification tools, assessment instruments, treatment plans, and aftercare. Based on the characteristics of women offenders, their pathways to crime, how they differ from male offenders, and how the system responds to them differently, the need for gender-responsive treatment and services seems clear.

Conclusion

Women in prison are typically young, poor, from minority communities, and have experienced significant problems in their life prior to imprisonment. More simply, women in prison have been triply marginalized by race, class, and gender (Bloom).

Throughout history, women have been sent to prison for offenses that differ dramatically from those of male prisoners. While the increasingly harsh treatment of the drug offender leads to the incarceration of thousands of women and men into the contemporary prison, women have been sent to prison in rates far surpassing those of men. Women are usually incarcerated for nonviolent property and drug offenses and are very often serving their first prison term. Women also "do their time" in ways different from men: The "play family" and other personalized relationships structure prison culture for women; racial and ethnic differences are less pronounced; and children remain an important part of women's lives, even while imprisoned.

While scholarship in the 1990s provided more detailed description of women's prisons and those confined to them, significant gaps in our knowledge about women's prisons remain. There is insufficient information about programs and policies that address the gender-specific needs of women in prison (Bloom and Covington) and little criminological theory that explains why women come to prisons (Chesney-Lind). McQuiade and Ehrenreich have also argued that we know virtually nothing about the characteristics of women prisoners across racial and ethnic groupings.

From the beginning, prisons in the United States were designed to punish men, with little consideration for women and their specific needs. Although the numbers of women in U.S. prisons continue to grow, programs and policies responsive to the needs of women prisoners has not kept pace. This lack of policy and research attention only continues the tradition of neglect and inattention that characterizes the history of prisons for women.

BARBARA OWEN

See also CORRECTIONAL REFORM ASSOCIATIONS; DETERRENCE; INCAPACITATION; JAILS; JUVENILE JUSTICE: INSTITUTIONS; PRISONERS, LEGAL RIGHTS OF; PRISONS: HISTORY; PRISONS: CORRECTIONAL OFFICERS; PRISONS: PRISONERS; PRISONS: PROBLEMS AND PROSPECTS; REHABILITATION; RETRIBUTIVISM.

BIBLIOGRAPHY

ACOCA, LESLIE. "Defusing the Time Bomb: Understanding and Meeting the Growing Health Care Needs of Incarcerated Women in America." Crime and Delinquency 44, no. 1 (1998): 49–70.

American Correctional Association. The Female Offender: What Does the Future Hold? Washington, D.C.: St. Mary's Press, 1990.

BELKNAP, JOANNE. The Invisible Woman: Gender, Crime, and Justice. Belmont, Calif.: Wadsworth Press, 1996.

BLOOM, BARBARA. "Triple Jeopardy: Race, Class, and Gender as Factors in Women's Imprisonment." Ph.D. diss. University of California–Riverside, 1996.

BLOOM, BARBARA, and CHESNEY-LIND, MEDA. "Women in Prison: Vengeful Equity." In It's a Crime: Women and Criminal Justice. Edited by R. Muraskin. New York: Prentice Hall, 2000. Pages 183–204.

BLOOM, BARBARA, and COVINGTON, STEPHANIE. "Gender-specific Programming for Female Offenders: What Is It and Why Is It Important?" Paper Presented to the American Society of Criminology. Washington, D.C., 1998.

BLOOM, BARBARA; CHESNEY-LIND, MEDA; and OWEN, BARBARA. Women in California Prisons: Hidden Victims of the War on Drugs. San Francisco, Calif.: Center on Juvenile and Criminal Justice, 1994.

BLOOM, BARBARA, and STEINHART, DAVID. Why Punish the Children? A Reappraisal of the Children of Incarcerated Mothers in America. San Francisco: National Council on Crime and Delinquency, 1993.

Bureau of Justice Statistics. "Prisoners in 1989." Washington, D.C.: Department of Justice, 1990.

———. "Prisoners in 1990." Washington, D.C.: Department of Justice, 1991.

———. Women in Jail in 1989. Washington, D.C.: Department of Justice, 1992.

———. Women in Prison. Washington, D.C.: Department of Justice, 1994.

———. "Correctional Populations in the United States, 1986." Washington, D.C.: Department of Justice, 1999.

———. "Prisoners in 1998." Washington, D.C.: Department of Justice, 1999b.

CHESNEY-LIND, MEDA. The Female Offender: Girls, Women, and Crime. Thousand Oaks, Calif.: Sage, 1997.

DOBASH, RUSSELL; DOBASH, REBECCA; and GUTTERIDGE, SUE. The Imprisonment of Women. New York: Basil Blackwell, 1986.

FAILY, A., and ROUNDTREE, G. "A Study of Aggression and Rule Violations in a Female Prison Population." Journal of Offender Counseling, Service and Rehabilitation 4, no. 1 (1979): 81–87.

FREEDMAN, ESTELLE. Their Sister's Keepers: Women's Prison Reform in America, 1830–1930. Ann Arbor, Mich.: University of Michigan Press, 1981.

GIALLOMBARDO, ROSE. Society of Women: A Study of a Women's Prison. New York: John Wiley, 1966.

HEFFERNAN, ESTHER. Making It in Prison: The Square, the Cool, and the Life. New York: John Wiley, 1972.

HIRST, J. B. *Convict Society and Its Enemies.* Sydney, Australia: George Allen and Unwin, 1983.

Human Rights Watch. *All Too Familiar: Sexual Abuse of Women in U.S. Prisons.* New York: Human Rights Watch, 1996.

IMMARIGEON, RUSS, and CHESNEY-LIND, MEDA. *Women's Prisons: Overcrowded and Overused.* San Francisco: National Council on Crime and Delinquency, 1992.

JOHNSON, ROBERT. "Race, Gender, and the American Prison." In *Prisons: Today and Tomorrow.* Edited by Joycelyn Pollock. Gaithersburg, Md.: Aspen Press, 1997. Pages 26–51.

KLIEN, SUE. "A Profile of Female Offenders in State and Federal Prisons." In *Female Offenders: Meeting the Needs of a Neglected Population.* Baltimore, Md.: United Book Press, 1993.

KURSHAN, NANCY. "Women and Imprisonment in the U.S." In *Cages of Steel.* Edited by W. Churchill and J. J. Vander Wall. Washington, D.C.: Maisonneuve Press, 1992.

MANN, CORA MAE. "Women of Color in the Criminal Justice System." In *The Criminal Justice System and Women.* Edited by B. Price and N. Skoloff. New York: McGraw Hill, 1995. Pages 118–135.

MCCLELLAN, DOROTHY. "Disparity in the Discipline of Male and Female Inmates in Texas Prisons." *Women and Criminal Justice* 5, no. 2 (1994), 71–97.

MCQUIADE, S., and EHRENREICH, J.H. "Women in Prison: Approaches to Studying the Lives of a Forgotten Population." *Affilia: Journal of Women and Social Work* 13, no. 2 (1998): 233–247.

MORASH, MERRY; HAARR, ROBIN; and RUCKER, LILA. "A Comparison of Programming for Women and Men and U.S. Prisons in the 1980s." *Crime and Delinquency* 40, no. 2 (1994): 197–221.

National Center on Addition and Substance Abuse. *Behind Bars: Substance Abuse and America's Prison Population.* New York: Columbia University, 1998.

OWEN, BARBARA. *In the Mix: Struggle and Survival in a Women's Prison.* Albany, N.Y.: SUNY Press, 1998.

OWEN, BARBARA, and BLOOM, BARBARA. "Profiling Women Prisoners: Findings from National Survey and a California Sample." *The Prison Journal* 75, no. 2 (1995): 165–185.

POLLOCK-BYRNE, JOY. *Women, Prison, and Crime.* Pacific Grove, Calif.: Brooks/Cole, 1990.

POLLOCK, JOY. *Counseling Women in Prison.* Thousand Oaks, Calif.: Sage, 1998.

RAFTER, NICOLE. *Partial Justice: Women in State Prisons 1800–1935.* Boston: Northeastern University Press, 1985.

STEFFENSMEIR, DARRELL, and ALLAN, EMILIE. "The Nature of Female Offending: Patterns and Explanations." In *Female Offenders: Critical Perspectives and Interventions.* Edited by R. Zupan. Gaithersburg, Md.: Aspen Publishing, 1998. Pages 5–30.

TEPLIN, LINDA; ABRAHAM, KAREN; and MCCLELLAND, GARY. "Prevalence of Psychiatric Disorders among Incarcerated Women." *Archives of General Psychiatry* 53 (1996): 505–512.

WARD, DAVID, and KASSEBAUM, GENE. *Women's Prison: Sex and Social Structure.* Chicago: Aldine-Atherton, 1965.

WELLISCH, JEAN; ANGLIN, M. DOUGLAS; and PRENDERGAST, MICHAEL. "Treatment Strategies for Drug-Abusing Women Offenders." In *Drug Treatment and the Criminal Justice System.* Edited by J. Inciardi. Thousand Oaks, Calif.: Sage, 1994. Pages 5–25.

WATTERSON, KATHRYN. *Women in Prison: Inside the Concrete Womb.* Boston: Northeastern University Press, 1996.

PRISONS: PROBLEMS AND PROSPECTS

Most problems in prisons originate outside their walls. The police and courts leave varied groups of offenders at the gate, and prisons must do the best they can to sequester these persons. Prisons function as does one's stomach, digesting that which is often indigestible. If the police decide to arrest young gang members, the prison to which these young men are committed will experience a gang problem, consisting of drug trafficking, violent warfare, and the intimidation of nonaffiliated prisoners. If mental patients are jailed for disturbing the peace or annoying their neighbors, the prison must deal with serious mental health issues on an increasing scale. Mental health issues are subdivided into component challenges, such as having to arrange for psychiatric services, and having to enforce prison rules on persons whose symptoms include very sloppy housekeeping, sporadic suicide attempts or unprovoked assaults.

In the 1990s, the salient problems posed for prison systems included: (1) the waging of the war on drugs, which created an influx of drug-related offenders, (2) the advent of sentencing "reforms," which produced a proliferation of prisoners with long determinate sentences, and

(3) the increased use of adult courts for dealing with serious violent delinquents. All three of these developments contribute to the problems of prisons, but do so in different ways.

Prisons and the war on drugs

The influx of drug-related offenders is a key source of prison overcrowding, and it makes life behind walls difficult for inmates and the staff. Incarceration rates for murderers, robbers, and burglars have remained steady over the years, but the number of drug offenders who have been imprisoned has steadily escalated. At present, six of ten federal prisoners stand convicted of drug possession or drug use, and the federal prison system is operating at 19 percent over its capacity. State prisons are also overcrowded, though the proportion of drug offenders is not quite as high.

Since the early 1980s, prisons have increasingly become repositories of nonviolent felons, many of whom are addicted substance abusers. Such offenders pose limited risk to the community, and arguably are not the type of hard-core criminals for which prisons were invented or designed. Most nonviolent prisoners could benefit from serious supervised treatment programs that address their substance abuse problems. Such treatment is available in many prisons, but it would be much less expensive to treat the addicts without locking them up. Arizona diverts all its addicted offenders from prisons to probation, in line with the results of a referendum provision called the Drug Medicalization, Prevention and Control Act, which Arizona voters approved by a 65 to 35 percent margin. An appeals court judge has pointed out that compared to the typical Arizona offender who now gets probation and treatment, "the same guy in the Federal system is going to get a mandatory five-year sentence" (Wren, 1999). The difference in deprivation is appreciable, as is the burden to the system.

While Arizona is the only state that has implemented a policy of wholesale diversion, other states have experimented with drug courts, which steer addicts into community treatment. Several prison systems are also accelerating the release of their nonviolent offenders. The most popular strategy for early release involves the use of shock incarceration, which provides a short, intensive experience of treatment, education, physical exercise, and military discipline.

The war on drugs has generally contributed to prison congestion across the board, but it has particularly increased the proportion of women and minority offenders who are sent to prison. At the onset of the war on drugs, in the early 1980s, 4 percent of the prison population was female, but the proportion by mid-1998 was 6.4 percent and increasing. Women constitute over 10 percent of the U.S. jail population, and drug addicts make up the majority of the women who are jailed or sentenced to prison.

The proportion of minority prisoners has also escalated sharply as a result of the war on drugs. The Bureau of Justice Statistics has calculated that 82 percent of the prisoner increase in the federal system between 1990 and 1996 involved black offenders sentenced for drug offenses (the same held for 65% of whites). In state prisons, 30 percent of the increase among black prisoners was due to drug sentences, compared to 16 percent among white prisoners. These differences derive from the fact that street enforcement of drug laws has centered on open trafficking in the ghetto, and the majority of those arrested for drug trading are addicts who are supporting their own drug habits.

Differential effects of the war on drugs create differential problems in prisons beyond those that are immediately obvious. In the case of women, one such problem is that of family separation, since 75 percent of female prisoners are mothers. Small children of prisoners who are not cared for by family members frequently end up in foster care; mothers also lose contact with children where distance or other considerations make visitations difficult. Prisons for women try to mitigate such problems, but cannot do much beyond encouraging family visits. A few prisons provide nurseries for pregnant inmates to facilitate bonding of mothers and infants; many prisons offer courses in childcare and parenting, or sponsor support groups for mothers.

The influx of drug offenders has increased the demand for illicit drugs in prison despite the fact that drug use by inmates invites extended periods of solitary confinement. Given the nature of addiction as a compulsive or obsessive psychological disorder, considerable ingenuity is exercised by addicts to smuggle drugs into the prisons. Drugs arrive in prison visiting rooms in the face of systematic searches (including skin and cavity searches), close and continuous surveillance, and mandatory random drug testing. Short of strip-searching all prison visitors and totally prohibiting all contact visitation, there is no way of making a dent in this problem. No strategy can prevent the importation of drugs into settings that are inhabited by addicts who have supportive subcultural peer groups outside the walls.

A different consequence of the proliferation of addicted prisoners is the rate of infection with the human immunodeficiency virus (HIV) in the prisons. As of 1995, 2.4 percent of state prisoners were known to be HIV positive; the proportion reached 13.9 percent in New York state, where the war on drugs has been assiduously waged. The rate for women is higher than that for men, and African American inmates are disproportionately affected. But not all of the HIV infected prisoners are known to authorities, because HIV testing in most prisons is optional and the course of the disease is frequently asymptomatic. Many inmates do not know they are infected, and they can unwittingly infect other inmates—mostly by sharing needles, and sometimes through sexual contacts.

Active AIDS (acquired immunodeficiency syndrome) cases among prisoners call for expensive medical treatment, the costs of which are transferred from the community to the correctional system while the offenders are in prison. To their credit, prison physicians routinely prescribe costly drug combinations ("cocktails") that have sharply reduced fatalities among imprisoned AIDS patients. Between 1995 and 1996, AIDS–related deaths in state prisons decreased by 10 percent (from 1,010 to 907).

Female offenders incarcerated during the war on drugs have been disproportionate clients of medical services. Ross and Lawrence point out, for example, that "including the unique reproductive health problems of women, 28 percent of women admitted to state prison in New York in 1993 had medical problems requiring immediate and ongoing intervention" (p. 177). They noted that the illnesses of substance-abusing women "most often include asthma; diabetes; HIV/AIDS; tuberculosis; hypertension; unintended, interrupted, or lost pregnancy; dysmenorrhea; chlamydia infection; papillomavirus (HPV) infection; herpes simplex II infection; cystic and myomatic conditions; chronic pelvic inflammatory disease; anxiety neurosis; and depression" (p. 181).

Women prisoners need substantial care—including mental health services—but the dispensation of mood-modulating drugs is a controversial problem for women's prisons. Some critics of the system contend that medication is insufficiently available, while others charge that the inmates are overmedicated to control or re-

strain their behavior. Among women who live in prison, medical care is a common source of complaints, even where facilities appear to be adequate. One reason for the emphasis on physical complaints may be the monotony and boredom of prison life; another may have to do with addiction to prescription drugs.

The impact of draconian prison sentences

The war on drugs has led to prison congestion, but escalating sentences for other offenders as well as drug offenders are a clear contributing cause. One clue to this fact is that the number of inmates in prison is increasing more rapidly than the number who are being imprisoned or being released. To understand this difference, one must consider the fact that a prisoner serving a four-year sentence takes the same amount of space as two prisoners serving two-year sentences, because he occupies his cell twice as long. A prisoner serving a very long sentence multiplies the effect: A man serving twenty years eventually comes to occupy the same prison space as do ten two-year prisoners arriving consecutively. One twenty-year prisoner who enters the system today can therefore crowd it as much as do ten two-year prisoners, and ten two-year prisoners will leave the prison before the twenty-year man is discharged.

In the last decade the number of long-term prisoners has been increasing, and the cumulative effects are experienced at an accelerating degree. There are more long-term prisoners in the prison because there are countless sentencing provisions designed to ensure that convicted offenders are incapacitated. Ensuring the incapacitation of offenders has made political sense to legislators whose constituents know that an incarcerated offender can commit no new crimes. A protracted prison stay assures citizens that they will not have to face a particular offender late at night in a dark alley. By definition any recidivist has served a sentence that the public can argue was too short. Since this means that every prison sentence has the makings of being too short, such reasoning concludes that the simplest solution is to confine all offenders for as long as possible.

The National Institute of Justice reported in 1997 that:

By 1994 all 50 States had enacted one or more mandatory sentencing laws, and Congress had enacted numerous mandatory sentencing laws for Federal offenders. Furthermore, many State officials have recently considered proposals to enhance sentencing for adults and juveniles convicted of violent crimes, usually by mandating longer prison terms for violent offenders who have a record of serious crimes. Three-strikes laws (and, in some jurisdictions, two-strikes laws) are the most prominent examples of such sentencing enhancements. . . . For example, California's three-strikes law requires that offenders who are convicted of a violent crime, and who have had two prior convictions, serve a minimum of 25 years; the law also doubles prison terms for offenders convicted of a second violent felony. . . . A second frequently mentioned mandatory sentencing enhancement is "truth-in-sentencing," provisions for which are in the Violent Crime Control and Law Enforcement Act of 1994. States that wish to qualify for Federal aid under the Act are required to amend their laws so that imprisoned offenders serve at least 85 percent of their sentences. (Parent et al., p. 1)

Other provisions that have been introduced to lengthen periods of confinement involve prison terms—importantly including life prison terms—without possibility of parole. The offenders who are the unhappy recipients of such provisions face natural life sentences or inflexibly long prison careers. Such offenders tend to be classified as high-risk, in part because of their sentences. All of these long-term higher-risk inmates are sent to the traditional walled prison fortresses, which are designed to prevent escapes and control behavior. Such prisons are obviously inordinately expensive to build, and the supply has consequently not kept pace with the accelerating demand. The result has been extensive double or triple celling, program space converted into sleeping accommodations, shrinking program opportunities, and a lower quality of life for both staff and inmates.

The paradox is that long-term prisoners, who face the most painful terms of confinement, are subject to the most inhospitable prison conditions. (The paradox reaches its extreme in death rows, where amenities for condemned prisoners are even more sharply restricted.) Long-term inmates may in many instances be reclassified over time, but many years must pass before their conditions of confinement can improve. And if a long-term prisoner manifests behavior problems in confinement, he can be sent to an even more austere segregation facility where living conditions are often atrocious.

Insofar as prisons have provisions for educational and vocational training, these are apt to be designed for short-term inmates. The programs are delivered in self-sufficient modules over modest periods of time, so that they can be completed before the average prisoner is released. An inmate who serves a two-year sentence can leave prison with a certificate in plumbing or automobile repair, or a high school equivalency degree. He can also leave having attained basic literacy, or graduated from a term in a residential substance-abuse program.

Offenders who arrive in prison with long sentences of the kind that are increasingly prevalent are ill served by modular programming. Such inmates must be engaged in meaningful activities over long periods of time. Serving a long sentence should ideally provide a sense of progression, advancement, and hope, or at least an absence of hopelessness. If short-term program segments are employed, they must build sequentially one on another. For example, a course in automobile repair followed by a remedial literacy course does not qualify as a sequence. Educational experiences that are followed by opportunities for inmates to apply what they have learned, with chances of promotion thereafter, make more sense.

Many inmates who come to prison with mandated long terms are apt to be young violent offenders embittered by their draconian sentences. Others are mid-level narcotics offenders who know that they have been sentenced under provisions that are designed for drug kingpins; others are repeat nonviolent offenders charged arbitrarily as violent recidivists. Since fairness, equity, and justice are salient concerns in prison even in the ordinary course of events, such prisoners are bound to be bitter and resentful when they have finally exhausted their avenues of appeal and come to confront the full magnitude of their impending fate. Prisons are sensitive to this risk and to the fact that the absence of hope can leave some prisoners with "nothing to lose" when they act in anger. There is also concern about a "new breed of violent inmate" who may be serving a long sentence and presumptively poses dangers to other prisoners and to staff.

Concerns about potential violence in prisons have increased the managerial emphasis on security and disciplinary sanctions. One tangible manifestation of this emphasis is the proliferation of segregation settings that are earmarked for the "worst of the worst" inmates. Typically, the most brutal of these settings provide for unremitting isolation and a lack of contact with staff. The conditions in some of these segregation settings (called "maxi-maxi" prisons) have been challenged successfully in the courts. Cases have centered on allegations of brutality and the charge that experiences of solitary confinement exacerbate mental health problems.

If the response to the bitterness of alienated prisoners is custodial overkill, escalations of resentment and suppression can occur in the prison in which cycles of protest and punishment reinforce each other, and culminate in reciprocal violence. A sense of injustice among the prisoners combined with preemptive reactions by staff increases tension in prisons, which enhances the potential for confrontations, including prison riots. While no major disturbances have resulted from sentencing reforms, there is urgent need for prison officials to undertake defusing and deescalating moves. This need—which includes the need for expanding program opportunities—is obvious to most prison managers. Unfortunately, this realization coincides with well-publicized public sentiment—especially in the least liberal jurisdictions—that calls for curtailment of activities that can be defined as "amenities" for prisoners.

A desirable strategy for prison management would be to multiply opportunities for the peaceful expression of grievances and expanded avenues of redress where injustices are alleged or perceived. At present, an increased inhospitability of the courts to litigation by prisoners, and a tendency of judges to refrain from interfering with prison management decisions (unless deliberate neglect or brutality can be documented), creates a need for prison systems to multiply internal avenues of appeals, and to strengthen functions such as those of ombudsmen, inspectorates, or commissions charged with reviewing prison operations.

The old and the young

Different problems can arise—and have begun to manifest themselves—as long-term prisoners grow older and less resilient. The trend in prisoner age distributions points to a problem with incapacitative strategies, which is that offenders tend to be retained in confinement long after their capacity for offending has dissipated. Prison cells become occupied by "old cons" who spend a great deal of time locked in because they find their younger peers disturbing and irritating. Beyond self-insulation, the prisoners' contacts with significant others in the outside world becomes tenuous or nonexistent. Over time, the aging prisoners come to be less able to negotiate life if they are ever to be released.

Older prisoners develop multiple health problems, and they can eventually force the prison to set up gerontological units (or specialized institutions) for invalids and disabled senior citizens (Drummond, p. 60).

At the other end of the age spectrum, juveniles sentenced by adult courts have created a "kiddieland" problem. Institutions designed for younger offenders are at least partly equipped to provide for educational needs and to deal with lower-maturity clients, but prison crowding typically leads to "first come, come served" assignments, which has made age segregation (or age grading) less prevalent, leading to an admixture of adults and juveniles in the same settings. Despite the assumption that such admixtures can give rise to "schools of crime," misbehavior is negatively correlated with age, which means that the younger the inmate, the more troublesome he is likely to be, both for his peers and his custodians.

Young prisoners act out in a variety of ways, from noisy, carefree rambunctiousness to merciless predation. Violent juvenile gang behavior occurs in the prison, as does the bullying typical of reform schools. Young prisoners tend to have histories of negative experiences and resentments relating to authority; they react to imagined slights or indications of perceived disrespect, and lapses of deference. The more immature the delinquent, the more vociferously he may insist on being "treated like a man," and the more volubly he will resist guidance and instruction. Such behavior attenuates with age, but new generations are adjudicated by the courts as each cohort matures. The problem increases as age limits for transfer are lowered, because early onset of delinquency is related to the obduracy of violent offending. As more precocious offenders are sent to prison, the trouble they cause will become more chronic and persistent.

The juxtaposition of young and old prisoners is especially problematic. The older the inmate, the more susceptible he becomes to feeling invaded; the younger the inmate, the more prone he is to create a turbulent and disruptive environment. Such problems were fewer when age disparities among prisoners were narrower. Less congested prisons also allowed for better classification and sorting of the inmates, so that would-be victims could be separated from potential aggressors, and incompatible groupings could be avoided. Prisons in the past typically included institutions for "old timers" that offered quiescent and structured environments. They also offered educationally rich settings for youthful offenders, with experienced paternalistic staff.

Enhanced heterogeneity of prison populations has gone hand-in-hand with a decreased capacity for accommodating diverging requirements. The more complex the mix of prisoners, the less able prisons have become to sort and separate different groups of inmates.

The availability of employment in the prison

The most persistent management problem for prisons has been to find work for prisoners to do to occupy their time and prepare for release. A historical essay published in 1910 complained about outside opposition to prisoner industry and employment. The author Frederick Wines wrote:

The reasons assigned in support of the contention that an end should be put to the competition of convict labor with "free labor outside" are more specious than convincing. Prisoners cannot be allowed to rot in idleness. Apart from the demoralizing influence of idleness, its tendency is to mental deterioration, insanity and death. No form of labor can be devised, other than trade education, which does not result in competition. . . . Besides, the unconvicted man has a right, and it is his duty, to support himself; how does this change of status relieve him of that duty or deprive him of that right? (pp. 22–23)

Wines, a prominent turn-of-the-century prison reformer, asserts that "the opposition to constructive labor in prisons is irrational, cruel and wicked" (p. 22). He declared himself unsympathetic to the argument that cheap prison labor could cut into business and profits. "Even if it were proved," he writes, "that the supplies from prison labor tend to lower prices, that can hardly be deemed a calamity" (p. 23). His concerns, however, proved to be a minority view. As early as 1866, a bill was introduced in New York restricting prisoner competition with free-world manufacture. The following year, a declaration was promulgated that "no trades must be taught to convicts in prison."

The controversy has continued unabated to the present, with correctional officials chafing under restrictions that confine prison products to "state use" commodities, such as license plates, office furnishings, and clothing for in-house prison consumption. A perennial complaint of prison managers has been that there are not enough jobs for prisoners, and that an indecently high proportion of prison populations live in enforced idleness or are underemployed. Idleness creates disciplinary problems, and riots are said to have been instigated by a lack of jobs for prisoners who want to work.

Vocational training in prison has been similarly limited, and offenders who leave prison are said to be unemployable because they lack requisite skills, work habits, and motivation to work. Enforced leisure is also said to contribute to a propensity for crime, leaving time for offenders to compare notes about their offending attainments and the technology and available opportunities for committing antisocial activities. Moreover, the public is affronted by the notion of inmates spending their time playing checkers or watching television while law-abiding citizens engage in back-breaking disciplined labor.

Much ingenuity has been exercised by prison staff over the years to find productive work for prisoners that does not compete with work in the free world. The options, however, are limited, and the number of inmates who can be deployed in off-beat activities such as taming mustangs, manning switchboards, or caring for retired horses is infinitesimally small.

Restorative justice in corrections

A notion that is tied up with the issue of prison work is the presumption of profitability. It stands to reason that no outsider could object to prisoner contributions of a charitable nature. If the products of prison labor were items lovingly donated to the needy and disabled, no claim of unfair competition could easily arise. More importantly, such labor could humanize the inmates in the public's eyes, and raise prisons in the citizens' esteem, since prisons would be sponsors of the beneficent contributions of inmates.

Moneymaking in prisons has a disreputable history. Before the prison was invented, jailors turned a profit by running extortion rackets, charging detainees for room, board, leg irons, and custody services. In many early American prisons, inmates were routinely rented out as cheap labor. The prisoners became convenient and timely substitutes for slaves working in Southern plantations when slavery was abolished (Christianson). Contract labor therefore survived for many decades in the Deep South and dovetailed with prison-operated plantation systems.

The industrial revolution gave birth to the notion of the industrial prison, the concept of a factory behind walls that could be run at no public expense. This idea has been repeatedly revived in more recent debates, with the proviso that prisoners should be paid a free-world wage. At this juncture in the evolution of the world economy, the last suggestion smacks of particular irony, given the export of jobs to third-world countries in which labor costs compare unfavorably to American prison wages.

Nonprofit work by inmates, however, has acquired new stature, because it can be subsumed under the principle of *restorative justice*. Though this concept is abstract and somewhat vague, it has attracted some prison administrators because it has sounded like a goal with potential public appeal. Definitions of restorative justice vary, but they include the notion of a "process of reparation and rehabilitation," of "'a search for solutions which promote repair, reconciliation, and reassurance'" (Van Ness and Strong, p. 24). In the pursuit of reconciliation and restoration, "the offender is held accountable and [is] required to make reparation" (p. 25).

According to a study by the Office of Juvenile Justice and Delinquency Prevention, one of the key principles of restorative justice is that "accountability for the. . .offender means accepting responsibility and acting to repair the harm done. . .repairing the harm and rebuilding relationships in the community—is the primary goal of restorative justice. . . . Results are measured by how much repair is done rather than by how much punishment is inflicted" (p. 5). In other words, the offender has to substantially contribute to the public good to compensate for the public harm that he has caused.

The concept of restoration applies individually to encounters of contrite offenders and forgiving victims. It applies collectively to organized activities that benefit the community at large, paying the public back for harm that has been done, and generating goodwill and forgiveness. This objective is one that in practice applies to prisons because it can justify and undergird the voluntary contributions of prison inmates to communities and individuals within communities that adjoin prisons.

News releases by prison systems frequently detail extensive public service efforts of prisoners, especially those that benefit needy citizens and the disadvantaged. Descriptions in the news items also focus on assistance that has been rendered by inmate crews when emergencies and catastrophes occur in areas where prisons are located.

Corrections Today (the official journal of the American Correctional Association) has a section that describes community service activities by prison inmates. One issue in 1999 listed programs that focused on animals, senior citizens, and combinations of the two. Female offenders in a prison in Pennsylvania were described as having "contributed nearly 2,900 hours to the construction of a bird rehabilitation building, in which birds can learn to fly in a safe, controlled environment" (Tischler, 1999, p. 88). A more consequential construction project (in South Dakota) was described as supplying elderly citizens with "affordable, low-maintenance, energy-efficient, homes in their hometowns where they have friends and family ties." The homes in question were all constructed in the prison, and transported to small rural communities (Harry, 1999, p. 89). In Oklahoma inmates rescued dogs from animal shelters, trained them, and donated them as pets to the elderly. According to the program's director, "most of the recipients are alone. The pets help put meaning back into their lives." The official also testified that "I've been in corrections since 1976 and this is one of the only truly productive programs that I've seen" (Clayton, p. 87).

From a camp infelicitously called the Deadwood Corrections Camp, prison crews debarked to fight California forest fires. The correctional lieutenant running this program explained that "the inmates get a feeling of self-worth and a feeling of accomplishment," and "society is repaid." Some members of local society (a county board of supervisors) presented the inmate firefighters with a formal certificate of appreciation (Tischler, 1999, p. 84).

The June 1998 issue of *Corrections Today* described a Wisconsin program in which prisoners refurbished donated wheelchairs, "to supply mobility with dignity to those individuals who have no insurance or no financial means to acquire medical equipment" (Harry, 1998, p. 92). In a second Wisconsin program, inmates constructed birdhouses for endangered birds and "rocking horses and toys for Head Start and other community agencies." The warden of this institution explained:

We need to do what we can to give back to the community and offenders need to be a part of that, to provide some kind of restitution. The inmates feel good about doing this, and maybe for the first time in their lives they've gotten some positive feedback from. . .their communities. (Tischler, 1998, p. 84)

A prisoner-participant alluded to feedback as the "warmth in the smile of an elder and the spark of happiness in a child's eye over receiving something we've learned to take pride in" (p. 84). Similar sentiments were expressed in a program in Arizona in which prisoners transcribed children's books into Braille. According to the officer running this program, "the inmates receive satisfaction from their roles in shedding some light into the dark world of blind kids" (Harry, 1998, p. 93). A program in Iowa produced innumerable book-to-tape transcriptions for the disabled and educational institutions. In one instance, "a tutorial manual of Microsoft systems for Iowa's Commission for the Blind that was so well-received, the tape was posted on the Internet and has received inquiries from as far away as Japan and Ireland" (Harry, 1998, p. 86).

In some accounts, the accomplishments of the inmates and of prisons are meticulously quantified. The New York State prison system, for example, has reported that during a two-week ice storm "952 (prison) employees and 8,893 inmates worked for more than 68,000 hours clearing trees and other debris from roads. [One New York State prison] filled more than 21,100 sandbags. . .. By the end of the storm, [the prisons] had served 392,000 meals to shelters in neighboring towns" (Tischler, 1998, p. 87).

Projects such as these reflect correctional policies that may easily be in tune with public sentiments. The Vermont State Department of Corrections conducted consumers' surveys and reported the results of the study under the subheading "Market Research Finds Support for Restorative Justice" (Gorczyk and Perry). According to the authors—the Commissioner of the Department and the Director of Planning—"the public wants the process [of corrections] to be positive—one that adds value, not simply one that adds cost" (p. 79). The authors concluded that "the people want justice that is restorative rather than retributive. . . . They want us to provide offenders with the opportunities to improve the quality of life, not spend a small fortune to inflict pain on the offender" (p. 83).

Officials in Vermont claimed that "these findings have driven our policy and planning" (p. 83). If other states follow Vermont's lead, this development could significantly affect the prospects of constructive change in corrections.

The prospects for ameliorating prison problems

There are a number of reasons why the resolution (or nonresolution) of prison problems is hard to predict. The most important reason is that we cannot know whether prisons will become more or less crowded over time. In the past, the task of predicting prison populations appeared easy. The assumption was that as crime increases, more offenders would get arrested. As more offenders were arrested, more of them would be convicted and imprisoned. The extent of prison congestion could therefore be extrapolated from increases in the crime rate. The competing assumption was equally easy to advance. It was that as imprisonment rates go up, the definition of crime would get less stringent, and if prison cells were emptied, offense definitions would be relaxed. One would therefore predict that imprisonment rates would remain constant over time.

Prison populations in fact had been steady over a period of several decades. Then crime rates and prison populations escalated substantially. The standard prediction (crime drives prisons) therefore looked plausible, until crime rates began to decrease while prison populations continued to increase. One could, of course, then assume that crime rates had decreased because more offenders had been incapacitated, but the relationship (increasing imprisonment, decreasing crime) had not been in evidence on other historical occasions.

When prisons are very crowded some observers conclude that there are too many people in prisons, and others infer that the number of prisons is inadequate. The latter argument, however, becomes difficult to apply in practice because the cost of prisons begins to compete with the price of schooling and other valued services.

We now know that sentencing policies do matter. But the question then becomes, What is it that drives sentencing policies? It has been fashionable to blame public opinion (according to polls, the public wants offenders imprisoned) but retributive public sentiments have been voiced in earlier periods of time. Zimring and Hawkins note that "if negative public views caused increases in prison population, the population would be ceaselessly spiraling upward" (p. 129).

Moreover, public opinion does not endorse specific restrictive sentencing provisions. Zimring and Hawkins wrote:

The most significant element of public attitudes toward crime and criminals may operate principally at the symbolic level, so that what the public wants from participants in political debate is symbolic denunciations of criminals rather than concrete plans for action in the criminal justice system. If disapproval is the principal currency in the politics of crime and punishment, it need not have any fixed rate of exchange with factors like prison population. (p. 126)

Public opinion favors revised sentencing policies when "reform" advocates entice public opinion to support their cause. This has been the case most dramatically in gubernatorial campaigns, which have uniformly exploited the fear of crime (Davey). In 1994, the *New York Times* pointed out that "the governors were so united in seizing on crime that some tossed off the same applause lines." The governor of Mississippi, for example, said that "I will fight with every breath in my body to see that the criminals we take off the streets serve their time. And if that means that we have to build a bigger jail house, then hand me a shovel, stand back, and we'll get it built" (1994). Some governors advocated the return of chain gangs, which for a time made the United States a laughing stock abroad, and caused howls of outrage in the corrections profession.

Politicians have consistently undersold the fact—which has been repeatedly documented by studies of opinion in depth—that citizens approve of rehabilitation and have faith in its effectiveness (Toch). This public opinion is primarily targeted at the nonviolent offenders whose influx has been responsible for prison congestion. The diversion of such offenders from prison and the expansion of substance abuse programs and of educational offerings have thus been congruent with public opinion.

The moderate stance of the public has contributed to the proliferation of proposals for attenuating "get tough" provisions that are now on the books. But since there is also a fear among politicians of being cast as "soft on crime," it is impossible to predict how many ameliorative counterreforms will end up being enacted. And if one cannot predict the reform of sentencing reforms, one cannot extrapolate the effects of legislation on the prison population, and on programming in prisons.

The sentence-expanding trend may not have run its course, and "get tough" provisions can conflict with rehabilitative goals. In New York, for example, parole officers are now charged with case-managing substance abusers, while legislation is simultaneously pending to abolish parole for felons. The outcome of political battles that are still in progress will determine the probable future of prison systems.

Society has not resolved the question of the proper use of the criminal justice system, including prisons, in dealing with drug offenders. While decriminalization is not a likely option in the United States, a de-escalation of the war on drugs could occur, with greater emphasis on prevention programs. General Barry McCaffrey, who directed President Clinton's drug control policy, made this very point in a speech about sentencing policies—policies that he said "have caused thousands of low-level and first-time offenders to be incarcerated at high cost for long sentences that are disproportionate to their crimes." The general concluded:

It is clear that we cannot arrest our way out of the problem of chronic drug abuse and drug-driven crime. We cannot continue to apply policies and programs that do not deal with the root causes of substance abuse and attendant crime. What is needed is smart drug policy linked to a flexible and rational criminal justice system. What matters is whether our system works to end the cycle of drug abuse and crime. (Wren, 29 June 1999)

General McCaffrey's conclusion could head a roster of viable prospects for the amelioration of prison problems, which might include the following propositions:

1. Imprisonment could be reserved for drug offenders who require treatment in structured, institutional environments. Other substance abusers could be assigned to therapeutic settings in the community, under criminal justice auspices.
2. Special programming strategies could be developed for inmates who are long-term residents in the prison. Such strategies could involve sentence planning, sequences of progressive experiences or career steps, discriminable stages or phases of prison adjustment, and periodic reevaluations.
3. Provision could be made for the early release of long-term prisoners who no longer pose a danger to the community. Such provisions have to include combinations of risk assessment and inventories of coping capabilities, with bridging experiences to the challenges of community life preceding release.

4. Special settings in prison could be multiplied for prisoners with special needs. Such settings would have to include age-graded institutions and units for those prisoners who have limited coping competence. New settings would have to be established for inmates who are disruptive and emotionally disturbed and do not belong in conventional segregation settings.

5. It is essential for all prisoners to be meaningfully occupied. Meaningfulness of activities can be enhanced by multiplying opportunities for offenders to contribute to the community at large, such as by rendering services to the disabled and disadvantaged.

Finally, correctional facilities would have to live up to their name: prisons can be managed to be effective without being inhumane or gratuitously punitive. It has been an elementary assumption in corrections that offenders are sent to prison *as* punishment and not *for* punishment. Imprisonment must of necessity be uncomfortable, but this does not mean that it needs to be stultifying or destructive. The challenge for prisons is to find ways to ensure that inmates use the time they must spend in confinement to improve their chances of becoming law-abiding, well adjusted, and contributing members of society after serving their sentences.

HANS TOCH

See also CORRECTIONAL REFORM ASSOCIATIONS; DETERRENCE; INCAPACITATION; JAILS; JUVENILE JUSTICE: INSTITUTIONS; PRISONERS, LEGAL RIGHTS OF; PRISONS: HISTORY; PRISONS: CORRECTIONAL OFFICERS; PRISONS: PRISONERS; PRISONS: PRISONS FOR WOMEN; REHABILITATION; RETRIBUTIVISM.

BIBLIOGRAPHY

BERKE, RICHARD L. "Governors' 1994 Message: Crime, Crime and Crime." *New York Times* 24 January 1994.

Bureau of Justice Statistics. *HIV in Prisons and Jails, 1995.* Washington, D.C.: Office of Justice Programs, 1997 Bulletin.

Bureau of Justice Statistics. *Prison and Jail Inmates at Midyear, 1998.* Washington, D.C.: Office of Justice Programs, 1999 Bulletin.

CHRISTIANSON, SCOTT. *With Liberty for Some: 500 Years of Imprisonment in America.* Boston: Northeastern University Press, 1998.

CLAYTON, SUSAN L. "Friends for Folks." *Corrections Today* 61, no. 3 (1999): 87.

DAVEY, JOSEPH DILLON. *The Politics of Prison Expansion: Winning Elections by Waging War on Crime.* Westport, Conn.: Praeger, 1998.

DRUMMOND, TAMMERLIN. "Cellblock Seniors." *Time,* 21 June 1999, p. 60.

GORCZYK, JOHN F., and PERRY, JOHN G. "What the Public Wants: Market Research Finds Support for Restorative Justice." *Corrections Today* 59, no. 4 (1997): 78–83.

HARRY, JENNIFER L. "Bringing Iowans Together." *Corrections Today* 60, no. 3 (1998): 86.

———. "A 'Touching' Inmate Program." *Corrections Today* 60, no. 3 (1998): 93.

———. "Wisconsin on Wheels." *Corrections Today* 60, no. 3 (1998): 92.

———. "Affordable Senior Housing: Benefits Many." *Corrections Today* 61, no. 3 (1999): 89.

Office of Juvenile Justice and Delinquency Prevention. *Guide for Implementing the Balanced and Restorative Justice Model.* Washington, D.C.: Office of Juvenile Justice and Delinquency Prevention, 1998.

PARENT, DALE; DUNWORTH, TERENCE; McDONALD, DOUGLAS; and RHODES, WILLIAM. *Key Legislative Issues in Criminal Justice: Mandatory Sentencing.* Washington, D.C.: National Institute of Justice, Research in Action, 1997.

ROSS, PHYLLIS HARRISON, and LAWRENCE, JAMES. "Health Care for Women Offenders." In *Turnstile Justice: Issues in American Corrections.* Edited by Ted Alleman and Rosemary Gido. Upper Saddle River, N.J.: Prentice-Hall, 1998. Pages 176–191.

TISCHLER, ERIC. "Breaking the Ice." *Corrections Today* 60, no. 3 (1998): 87.

———. "Making Amends, Building Futures." *Corrections Today* 60, no. 3 (1998): 84.

———. "Learning to Fly." *Corrections Today* 61, no. 3 (1999): 88.

———. "Where There's Smoke, There's Fire." *Corrections Today* 61, no. 3 (1999): 84.

TOCH, HANS. *Corrections: A Humanistic Approach.* Guilderland, N.Y.: Harrow and Heston, 1997.

VAN NESS, DANIEL, and STRONG, KAREN HEETDERKS. *Restoring Justice.* Cincinnati, Ohio: Anderson Publishing Company, 1997.

WINES, FREDERICK HOWARD. "Historical Introduction." In *Prison Reform.* Edited by Charles Richmond Henderson. New York: Russell Sage Foundation, 1910.

WREN, CHRISTOPHER S. "Arizona Finds Cost Savings in Treating Drug Offenders: Probation Program, not Prisons, for Addicts." *New York Times,* 21 April 1999.

———. "White House Drug Official Fights Mandatory Sentences." *New York Times,* 29 June 1999.

ZIMRING, FRANKLIN E., and HAWKINS, GORDON. *The Scale of Punishment*. Chicago: University of Chicago Press, 1991.

PROBATION AND PAROLE: HISTORY, GOALS, AND DECISION-MAKING

Over five million people are under the supervision of the criminal justice systems in the United States. Approximately, 1.6 million are incarcerated in local, state, and federal institutions. The remaining, or almost 70 percent of those under the responsibility of the criminal justice system, are being supervised in the community on probation or parole. This means that at any one time a large number of U.S. citizens are in the community under correctional supervision. For example, nearly 2 percent or 3.8 million adult men and women in the United States were being supervised in the community on federal or state probation or parole in 1995 (Bureau of Justice Statistics, 1997).

While probation and parole are both considered community corrections and involve supervision in the community, they differ in other respects. Probation is a sentencing option available to local judges. Convicted offenders are released by the court to serve a sentence under court-imposed conditions for a specified period. It is considered an alternative to incarceration. In most cases the entire probation sentence is served under supervision in the community. The court retains the authority to supervise, modify conditions, cancel probation and resentence if the probationer violates the terms of probation. The responsible agency for overseeing probation can be either state or local. There are currently more than two thousand separate probation agencies in the United States.

In contrast to probation, parole is the early release of inmates from correctional institutions prior to the expiration of the sentence on the condition of good behavior and supervision in the community. It is also referred to as supervised release, community supervision, or aftercare. The parole board is the legally designated paroling authority. The board has the authority to release on parole adults (or juveniles) who are committed to correctional institutions, to set conditions that must be followed during supervision, to revoke parole and return the offender to an institution, and to discharge from parole. Thus, probation is a front-end decision that is made prior to incarceration in a jail or prison, while parole is a back-end decision to release inmates from jail or prison.

Community corrections includes traditional probation and parole as well as other sanctions such as intensive supervision, restitution, community service, correctional boot camps, and fines. Frequently these alternative punishments or intermediate sanctions come under the jurisdiction of the agencies responsible for the administration of probation and parole.

Origins of probation and parole

Despite the differences between probation and parole, there are many similarities between the two types of community corrections. Both were initially developed as methods to mitigate the severity of punishment.

The origin of probation. Probation as it is known today can be traced to the use of several judicial practices exercised in English and later, American courts. "Release on recognizance" or bail, for example, allowed defendants who agreed to certain conditions of release to return to the community to await trial. After setting bail, judges sometimes failed to take further action (Abidinsky). Thus, similar to modern-day probation, defendants were released to the community conditionally. If they failed to meet the condition of release, they were faced with the threat of revocation. And in some instances, they were spared further contact with the criminal justice system.

In English courts, judicial reprieve empowered judges to temporarily suspend either the imposition or execution of a sentence in order to permit a defendant to appeal to the Crown for a pardon (Abidinsky; Allen et al.). Although suspension was intended to be temporary, further prosecution of such cases was sometimes abandoned (Allen et al.). Judges in the United States exercised a similar power, enabling them to suspend the sentence of a convicted defendant if justice had in any way been miscarried. The use of judicial power to suspend a sentence was extended to cases in which there existed no miscarriage of justice. Sentences were suspended seemingly to give defendants another chance. Documentation of this practice in Boston dates back to 1830. Such suspensions were challenged near the turn of the twentieth century in a New York state court (1894) and later in the Supreme Court (1916). Both courts held that absent a legislative directive judges did not possess the authority to suspend sentences.

During roughly the same time period, a shoemaker-philanthropist in Boston, named John Augustus, began the practice of bailing offenders out of court and assuming responsibility for them in the community. Bailing hundreds of offenders between the years 1841 and 1859, John Augustus is most often credited as being the founder of probation in the United States. Augustus bailed the offenders out after conviction. As a result of this favor and with further acts of friendliness such as helping the offender obtain employment and aiding the offender's family in other ways, the offender was indebted to Augustus and was willing to abide by agreements. After a period of supervision in the community, the bailed offenders returned to court armed with Augustus's sentencing recommendations. Due to his efforts John Augustus's charges were typically spared incarceration.

John Augustus's probation bears much resemblance to probation as it is practiced today. Augustus took great care in deciding which prisoners were promising candidates for probation. He considered the person's "character," age, and factors that would impact the offender after release. In dubious cases, he required the offender to attend school or to be employed. Thus, Augustus's activities provided the origins for the presentence investigation as well as common conditions of present-day community supervision such as education or employment.

Not long after John Augustus published an account of his work in 1852, the Massachusetts legislature in 1878 passed a bill authorizing the city of Boston to hire a probation officer (Abidinsky). The practice of probation spread through the state of Massachusetts and was later adopted by numerous states around the turn of the twentieth century. Between 1897 and 1920, for example, twenty-six states and the District of Columbia passed adult probation statutes (Champion). By 1927, all states except Wyoming had adopted some type of probation law for juveniles. However, probation was not available for all adult offenders in the United States until 1956.

Regardless of whether the origins of probation are traced to judicial reprieve or to the work of John Augustus, it is clear that the guiding philosophy of probation was rehabilitation. John Augustus leaves no room for doubt, stating: "It became pretty generally known that my labors were upon the ground of reform, that I confined my efforts mainly to those who were indicted for their first offence, and whose hearts were not wholly depraved, but gave promise of better things . . ." (Augustus). Probation implies "forgiveness" and "trial," or a period during which offenders may prove themselves capable of obeying the law and abiding by society's norms. Court opinions as well as state statutes generally affirm that the overarching purpose of probation is rehabilitation (Brilliant).

Origins of parole. Prior to the mid-nineteenth century most offenders were sentenced to flat or *determinate sentences* in prison. Under this type of sentencing, an offender received a specific amount of time to serve in prison for a specific crime. This created a major problem when prisons became crowded. Governors were forced to issue mass pardons or prison wardens had to randomly release offenders to make room for entering prisoners.

Credit for developing early parole systems is usually given to an Englishman, Captain Alexander Maconochie, and an Irishman, Sir Walter Crofton. In 1840, Maconochie was appointed governor of the notorious English penal colony at Norfolk Island off the coast of Australia. At the time, English criminals were being transported to Australia and those sent to Norfolk Island were considered "twice condemned"; they had been shipped to Australia from England and from Australia to the island. Conditions were so bad that, allegedly, men who received reprieves from the death penalty wept. The first thing Maconochie did was to eliminate the flat sentence structure used in Norfolk at the time of his arrival. Instead of requiring convicts to serve their sentences with no hope of release until the full sentence had been served, Maconochie initiated a "mark system" whereby a convict could earn freedom by hard work and good behavior in the prison. The earned marks could be used to purchase either goods or a reduction in sentence. Prisoners had to pass through a series of stages beginning with strict imprisonment through conditional release to final freedom. Movement through the stages was dependent upon the number of marks accredited.

Like Maconochie, Sir Walter Crofton believed the length of the sentence should not be an arbitrary period of time but should be related to the rehabilitation of the offender. After becoming the administrator of the Irish Prison System in 1854, Crofton initiated a system incorporating three classes of penal servitude: strict imprisonment, *indeterminate sentences*, and tickets-of-leave. This indeterminate system or Irish system, as it came to be known, permitted convicts to earn marks to move from solitary confinement to a return to the community on a conditional pardon or ticket-of-leave.

Zebulon Brockway, a Michigan penologist, is usually credited with initiating indeterminate sentences and parole release in the United States. Similar to Maconochie and Crofton, Brockway believed inmates should be able to earn their way out of prison through good behavior. Thus, they should receive a sentence that could vary in length depending upon their behavior in prison. In his opinion, this had two advantages. First, it would provide a release valve for managing prison populations. Second it would be valuable in reforming offenders because they would be earning release by demonstrating good behavior.

Brockway had the opportunity to pioneer this proposal into practice in 1876 when he was appointed superintendent of Elmira Reformatory for youthful offenders in New York. Inmates at Elmira were graded on their conduct, achievement, and education. On the basis of their behavior in the reformatory, they were given parole. Volunteer "guardians" supervised the parolees and submitted written reports documenting their behavior in the community. A condition of the parole was that the offender report to the guardian each month.

Thus, by the turn of the century the major concepts underlying parole were in place in the United States: (1) a reduction in the sentence of incarceration based on good behavior in prison; (2) supervision of the parolee in the community; and (3) indeterminate sentences. By 1901, twenty states had parole statutes and by 1944, every jurisdiction in the United States had some form of parole release and indeterminate sentencing.

Changing goals of community corrections

Over the past thirty years, there have been major changes in the theoretical model guiding the practice of community supervision. During the twentieth century, most of the focus of probation and parole had been on the rehabilitation aspects of community supervision. However, since the 1960s, major changes have occurred in correctional philosophy and this has had a dramatic impact on the goals of community supervision.

Rehabilitation model. As described earlier, probation and parole were originally conceived in humanitarian terms—as a second chance or an opportunity for reform. Not surprisingly, the enactment of many community supervision statutes coincided with the Progressive period (1900–1920) in correctional history. Progressive reformers dismissed penal policies of the previous century as prohibitively rigid and advocated the adoption of the "medical model" (or "treatment" model) in conjunction with indeterminate sentencing. Deviant behavior was thought to be different for each offender. These individual differences were related to the particulars of an offender's life history either due to faulty environmental conditions or maladapted psychological mechanisms (Rothman). As a result, an attempt was made to individualize criminal justice procedures. In the presentence report the probation officer (social worker-expert) would diagnose the problems and this would be used to individualize the sentence.

Correctional practice was dominated by the rehabilitative ideal through much of the 1960s. During this period community supervision officers assumed the responsibility of changing offenders. Attention focused on the offender, not the offense, in an attempt to prevent future crimes. Officers possessed considerable discretion, as well as the power to utilize coercive means if deemed necessary, to further the process of rehabilitation (O'Leary). Consistent with the medical model, the presentence reports contained the "diagnosis" and prescribed the "treatment" necessary for a "cure." After sentencing, classification systems were used to identify and plan for the appropriate management and treatment of the offender. Parole boards would determine when the offender was "cured" and ready for release. It was the job of the supervising officer to counsel probationers and parolees as well as to ensure that the suggested interventions were in fact being realized.

The philosophy of the Progressive movement remained largely unchallenged until the early 1970s at which time it became the target of fierce attack. The assumptions of rehabilitation as a preeminent goal for sentence were questioned (Thomson). Critics such as Fogel (1975) and von Hirsch (1976) argued that the indeterminate sentences based on perceived offender characteristics and coerced involvement in rehabilitative programs were unethical and immoral.

In addition, empirical evidence widely disseminated in the mid-1970s cast doubt on the efficacy of rehabilitation (Thomson). In 1975, for example, Lipton, Martinson, & Wilks's evaluation of correctional treatment programs was published, leading to the oft-quoted, though overstated, claim that "nothing works." The demise of the rehabilitative ideal in theory resulted in modifications of probation practice, although by no means the wholesale abandonment of rehabilitative orientations. Empirical research argued that treatment programs were effective under certain conditions, for example, appropriate target groups, and properly implemented programs was published not long thereafter (see Ross & Gendreau) but such research did not overcome the popular cry of the period that "nothing works."

Neo-classical models

The immediate theoretical successors to the rehabilitation model of community supervision were grounded in the neoclassical assumptions of "volition, equity, proportionality, and fairness" (Thomson). Neoclassical models such as the "just deserts" model or the justice model emphasized the proportionality between crime and punishment, diverting attention from the offender back to the offense. Proponents opposed to the individualization of penal sanctions raised fundamental questions about the equity of the rehabilitation model. For example, Kay Harris, a justice model advocate, posed the question of whether it was fair to sentence one offender to three years of probation with the requirement to abstain from alcohol, earn a high school diploma, and obtain employment, while another offender guilty of the same offense but of higher socioeconomic status is given a shorter term with no special conditions.

In contrast to the rehabilitation model, offenders sentenced under a neoclassical sentencing scheme are punished for what they have done in the past, not for what they are likely to do in the future. The idea was to develop a system in which the exact, fair and just penalty for a crime is clearly articulated in advance and uniformly applied to all (O'Leary). Models of community supervision that fall under the rubric of neoclassicism include just deserts, retribution, commensurate deserts, and the justice model (Thomson).

Another important critique of the rehabilitative model articulated by justice model proponents is the tendency of the rehabilitative model to treat persons as if they were objects (Harris). The justice model views punishment as a kind of debt owed by offenders because of the crime they have committed; the treatment model sees it as a means of influencing offenders' future behavior.

While neoclassical reformers joined by other anti-Progressive groups have been largely successful in replacing indeterminate sentencing schemes with determinate ones, their impact on the actual practice of community supervision has been far less profound. Most supervising officers continue to do what they had always done. There were, however, changes in the sentencing process. Many jurisdictions passed laws to eliminate parole and return to the early flat or determinate sentences. Furthermore, to eliminate discretion and disparity many jurisdictions developed sentencing guidelines to be used by judges to determine appropriate sentences for offenders. Using the severity of the crime and the history of past convictions, the guidelines gave judges recommendations about the appropriate length of sentences.

Incapacitation/control models. The reluctance to implement models of probation grounded in neoclassical ideals may be attributed to several factors that contributed instead to the adoption of incapacitation or control models of community supervision in the 1980s. For example, according to David Rothman the neoclassical schemes were unpersuasive because they failed to address crime control concerns. The argument in support of the justice model focused on equity of sentences not on controlling crime in the community. Further, the exploding prison populations and skyrocketing correctional costs led to increasing numbers of felons being released early from prison or placed on probation caseloads (Petersilia, 1990). As a result, feelings of vulnerability to crime were intensified.

Empirically, one well-known study of felons sentenced to probation in California revealed that 65 percent of the sample (N=1,672) were rearrested and 51 percent were convicted of new crimes during a forty-month follow-up period (Petersilia and Turner). Replications of the study in other jurisdictions produced results that proved less cause for alarm, however (e.g., Clear et al.). Nevertheless, the movement to more effectively control offenders during community supervision gained considerable momentum throughout the 1980s.

Ultimately, the preeminent philosophical rationale for sentencing shifted from the neoclassical assumptions of the 1970s to a preference for incapacitation and control limited by the principle of just deserts. The just desert model failed to address crime control concerns and most likely this led to its demise as a widely accepted sole purpose of sanctioning. Another old-fashioned purpose for sentencing emerged—the notion of incapacitation. From this perspective, sanctions are used to control offenders so they cannot continue to commit crimes. Ideally, offenders would be locked away in prisons so they would be unable to commit crimes.

One obvious by-product of the new sentencing philosophy has been the reemergence of intensive supervised probation and parole programs (ISP). First implemented in the 1960s, the early ISPs were attempts at discovering the caseload size that would maximize the intensity of supervision. Intensity was assumed to be related to successful outcome. The second wave of ISPs surfaced in the mid-1980s despite the less than enthusiastic findings of the earlier movement.

Without doubt, the new ISPs clearly demonstrate the shift toward control-oriented probation. The Texas ISP manual is particularly illustrative with its focus on more surveillance, more control, and more contacts than traditional supervision. The emphasis of this ISP program is on offender control. Similarly, Harland and Rosen (1987) delineate the primary goals of ISP programs as minimizing the risk that probationers will reoffend or breach other conditions of their release, by restricting their opportunity and propensity to do so. ISP's goals are primarily incapacitation and deterrence through the intensive regulation and monitoring of offenders' whereabouts and conduct, and corresponding increased threat of detection and strict enforcement of consequences in event of violations.

The shift in the philosophy/practice of community supervision came at a time when the institution of probation was considerably demoralized (Tonry). Not only was probation publicly perceived as merely a "slap on the wrist" (as it has been by some since the days of John Augustus), faith in the ability of community supervision to rehabilitate had slowly eroded. The reemergence of ISPs and the control philosophy in general, therefore, seemed to have given probation and parole administrators a chance to rebuild the credibility, influence, and material resources for probation and parole (Tonry).

Probation and parole decision-making

Probation and parole agencies have always been responsible for two functions. First, the agencies must assist with the decision process. For probation officers this is the investigative aspect of their work and it involves assisting the court in the decision to sentence to probation in lieu of a prison sentence. For parole, the decision must be made to release an inmate from prison. The second responsibility of both agencies is to provide supervision for those offenders who are judged suitable for release to the community.

The decision to grant probation. The majority of individuals convicted of a crime are not given a prison sentence. Fifty-four of every one hundred felony arrests result in a conviction. Of those convicted, twenty-two are given a probation sentence, eighteen a jail sentence and fourteen are sent to prison (Boland, Mahanna, and Stones). Community corrections officials are critical players in these sentencing decisions. They must assess the level of risk offenders present to the public safety and make recommendations to the court about the appropriate sentence.

Probation officers often begin the investigative process during the pretrial period by examining an offender's background and history to assist in determining whether a defendant can safely be released on his own recognizance or bail. The report from the officer is frequently the primary source of information the court uses in this decision. At this point the court may *defer adjudication* or offer *pretrial diversion* and require probation supervision.

Once an offender is convicted, the probation officer prepares a *presentence investigation report* (PSI). The PSI is the major source of information on which courts base sentences. The primary function of the PSI report is to provide the sentencing court with timely, relevant, and accurate data about the offender. Such information is used to determine the sentence and classify offenders as to risk and therapeutic needs. The information is used to plan programming in institutions and in the community, to set conditions of supervision, and for release planning.

In determinate-sentencing jurisdictions the statutes specify similar sentences for offenders convicted of similar offenses. The PSI in these jurisdictions places the emphasis on offense-based reports where the dominant focus is on the offense and the offender's culpability in the offense. Where the court uses sentencing guidelines to determine the appropriate sentences the emphasis of the report is on providing verifiable information on the defendant's criminal record and *aggravating or mitigating* circumstances. Unlike the PSI provided by the indeterminate-sentencing jurisdictions, the primary focus is on the crime and not the criminal.

Typically, the PSI includes information on the seriousness of the crime, the defendant's risk for recidivism, the defendant's circumstances (living arrangement, employment, family), the legally permissible sentencing options, and a recommended sentence. Today with the increased concern with victim issues, the PSI may contain a *victim impact statement* that describes the impact of the offense on identifiable victims or the community.

Over 90 percent of all felony cases are eventually resolved through negotiated pleas so the major decision of the court is whether or not to imprison the offender. The PSI is critically important in this regard. Research has shown that the judge's knowledge of the case is limited to the information contained in the PSI. Furthermore, there is a high correlation between the recommendations provided by the probation officer in the PSI and the judge's sentence. Such recommendations are accepted between 65 and 95 percent of the time.

Eighty percent of all adults convicted of misdemeanors and 60 percent of all adults convicted of felonies are sentenced to probation or a combination of probation and jail. Thus, two-thirds of all convictions result in a sentence of probation. Research shows that people are less likely to be given probation if they: have more conviction counts, have more prior convictions, were on probation or parole at the time of arrest, were drug addicts, or used a weapon in the crime or seriously injured victims (Petersilia and Turner).

For those who receive probation, the court must also decide how to impose the sentence. Commonly, the judge gives a jail or prison sentence and then suspends the sentence in favor of probation. The jail or prison term is held in abeyance to be used if the offender fails to abide by the conditions of probation. About 50 percent of all probations sentences are suspended in this way (Latessa and Allen, 1997). The judge also imposes conditions that the probationer is required to follow during the community supervision.

Parole Release.   The parole board (or parole commission), an administrative body, is empowered to decide whether inmates shall be conditionally released from prison prior to the completion of their sentence. The board is also responsible for determining whether to revoke parole and to discharge from parole those who have satisfactorily completed the terms of their sentence. In most jurisdictions, once the parole board makes the decision to grant parole, the responsibility for supervision in the community is turned over to parole officers who are supervised by the department of corrections.

The decision to grant parole is usually based on a review of the individual offender's case file (including the PSI) and an interview with the inmate. Eligibility for parole is determined by statutory requirements and is usually based on the completion of the minimum sentence less any *good-time* credits earned during incarceration. Technically, parolees are still prisoners who can be recalled to serve the remainder of their sentence in prison if the parole board decides they have not fulfilled the terms of their release.

Parole boards have traditionally had great leeway in deciding when to grant parole. During the hearing stage when the board met with the inmate they were expected to observe whether the prospective parolee demonstrated his or her rehabilitation, a willingness to accept responsibility, and self-understanding. Decisions were not based on formally articulated criteria or policies but on subjective and intuitional judgments of the individuals on the board. Few courts have reviewed parole decision-making and those that have appear to agree with the contentions of paroling authorities that to impose even minimal due-process constraints on the decision-making process would interfere with the board's goals of diagnosis and prediction (Cromwell and Del Carmen).

Most parole boards appear to accept an incapacitation or a modified justice model when making release decisions (Petersilia, 1998). They reported that the single most important factor they considered in the release decision was the nature of the current offense (Runda, Rhine, and Wetter). Following this they considered any history of prior violence, prior felony convictions, and possession of a firearm during the crime. These indicators of dangerousness were used to determine how much time an offender should serve prior to parole. Board members did not consider any factors related to rehabilitation or program participation to be important to consider in making parole decisions.

Critics of parole release decisions characterize the system as arbitrary and capricious. This is one of the reasons some jurisdictions have abolished parole. Other jurisdictions have instituted guidelines to be used to structure decisions without completely removing discretion. The parole guidelines used by the U.S. Parole Commission for making parole release decisions served as a model for parole guidelines developed in many other jurisdictions. The commission developed a system for decision-making based on the seriousness of the offense and the risk of recidivism. An actuarial device, the Salient Factor Score, was used to determine the potential risk of a parole violation. Decision-makers then use the guidelines to determine the customary time to be served for a range of offenses based on the severity of the offense. Decision-makers may deviate from the guidelines but they are required to explain the specific factors considered in the decision to override the score. Other jurisdictions have developed "risk assessment" or prediction instruments to assist parole boards in making decisions about release.

The move toward the justice model of corrections and the use of incapacitation has led to questions about the viability of parole, but for different reasons. Justice advocates argue that the indeterminancy inherent in the parole system is unfair because the board must make decisions based on what will occur in the future. Furthermore, they assert it is impossible to tell when an offender is rehabilitated. Incapacitation advocates also argue against parole. From their point of view, a sentence to prison prohibits an offender from committing more crimes in the community; parole release does not. Both of these perspectives have been influential in changing sentencing in many jurisdictions, and in the past thirty years sentencing changes have dramatically affected the use of parole. Prior to 1975 sentencing codes of every state had some form of indeterminancy. Since then, every state in the nation has revised, replaced, or seriously considered determinate sentencing and the abolishment of parole (Petersilia, 1998). This has led to a dramatic decline in the percent of state prisoners released through discretionary parole (Bureau of Justice Statistics, 1996). In 1977 over 70 percent of offenders released from prison were released on parole. By 1994, this was reduced to 37 percent. An increasing percent of the releases were through mandatory release and expiration of sentence.

Recent trends

Increasing rate of revocations. There is some evidence that both the number and rate of revocations have increased and these have had a significant impact on prison and jail populations (Parent et al.). For example, in 1988 more than 60 percent of Oregon's prison admissions were due to probation or parole revocations. Furthermore, two-thirds of the prison admissions in

Texas in 1989, and 60 percent of California's prison admissions, were violators (Parent et al.).

Parent and colleagues note that while the increase in probation/parole populations alone might account for the increase in revocations, interviews with practitioners reveal that in some states the rate of revocations has increased as well. Increased rates of revocations have been attributed to many factors including: (1) the shift toward control-oriented practices of community supervision; (2) the law-enforcement background of new probation/parole officers (as opposed to the social work background of the past); (3) an increase in the number of conditions of probation; (4) improvement in the methods of monitoring violations; (5) the more serious offender placed on community supervision caseloads; and (6) an increase in probation and parole caseloads (Parent et al.).

Empirical data on technical violations. While data collected over time is not readily available, the largest follow-up study of felony probationers in the United States revealed that a substantial proportion of probationers fail to successfully complete their sentence (Langan and Cunnif). For example, within a three-year follow-up period, 62 percent of a sample of 79,000 felony probationers had been either arrested for another felony or had violated a condition of probation resulting in a disciplinary hearing (Langan and Cunnif). Thirty percent of those had both been arrested and had a disciplinary hearing, 13 percent had only been arrested, and 19 percent had only a disciplinary hearing. Furthermore, 46 percent of the sample were ultimately incarcerated. Of those probationers who were incarcerated, 35 percent were incarcerated for committing only a technical violation (Langan and Cunnif).

In contrast, however, Clear and colleagues' evaluation of 7,501 felony and misdemeanant probationers terminated from six probation agencies revealed that approximately one-quarter of the probationers committed violations, half of which were violations of technical conditions of supervision. Further, they found that most violators misbehaved only once. Therefore, the majority of probationers successfully completed their sentence without incident. In short, their study seemed to refute the assumption that due to early release and diversion from prison, the probation population has become increasingly dangerous.

The recidivism rates for parolees are even higher than the rates of probationers. Beck and

Shipley (1989) examined the recidivism rates of 108,580 men and women who were released from jail in eleven states. They found that 62 percent had been rearrested for a felony or serious misdemeanor within three years of release and 41 percent had been returned to prison.

Innovative responses. In response to the observation that increasing numbers of offenders are having parole revoked during community supervision, many jurisdictions are reexamining their revocation procedures (Parent et al.). A major development is the structuring of discretionary decision-making, consistent with the general trend in criminal justice. The goal of the structure is to give officers concrete guidance so that their choices become more certain and uniform without removing all discretion. Structure is incorporated into the decision-making by written policy giving the goals of revocation and specifying which violations are serious enough to result in revocation procedures. Behaviors that warrant alternative sanctions are also identified. Thus, agencies make it clear to officers that violations are a routine part of supervision that can be responded to in a variety of ways.

Some jurisdictions have expanded the range of sanctions available to officers so that officers are not forced to choose between sanctions that are too harsh (a return to prison) and sanctions that are too lenient. Other jurisdictions have developed intermediate sanctions specifically for probation or parole violators. For example, Georgia has developed a correctional boot camp for technical violators of supervision. The violators are required to complete ninety days in the boot camp before returning to the community.

Research assessing the effectiveness of community corrections

As noted above the recidivism rates for those on probation and parole are relatively high. According to the Bureau of Justice Statistics 43 percent of the felony probationers and 62 percent of the parolees will be rearrested within three years after beginning community supervision. The question is whether community supervision has any impact on reducing criminal activities. That is, would these offenders commit more crime if they were not being supervised in the community. Most research examining the effectiveness of probation and parole focuses on the effectiveness of increasing some component or condition of supervision, particularly the effectiveness of increasing different types of control. Disappoint-

ingly, the majority of these studies demonstrate no impact of the increased control; the recidivism rates for those who had the increased supervision or control over their behavior was approximately the same as the rates for the comparison groups (MacKenzie). In fact, frequently those who had more conditions requiring control had higher technical violation rates.

Several studies do give more hopeful signs. Most of the research examining the effectiveness of probation and parole has focused on the control aspects of community supervision; however, a few studies have examined the effectiveness of combining treatment and surveillance. The results of these studies are promising (MacKenzie). In several studies, the offenders who received increased supervision as well as increased treatment had lower recidivism than others who were not given the supervision and treatment. Many of these studies are exploratory and have not been replicated but they do present a hopeful sign that combinations of treatment and control may be effective in lowering recidivism.

Another indication that community supervision may have a positive impact on offenders comes from a self-report study completed by MacKenzie and her colleagues (1998). They asked offenders to report on their criminal activities during the year before arrest and during probation. Self-report criminal activity is important to study because few of the crimes committed result in an official record of arrest. The researchers found that the criminal activities of the offenders declined dramatically when the pre-arrest period was compared to the probation period. This suggests probation was effective in reducing the criminal activities of these offenders. Similarly, behaviors that constituted a violation of conditions of probation such as heavy drinking or illegal drug use were associated with increased criminal activity. The researchers found no evidence that increases in the intrusiveness of conditions, the agent's knowledge of misbehavior, or how the agent responded to misbehavior were associated with changes in criminal activity. Thus, while probation appears to be effective in reducing criminal activities and the violations of conditions signaled criminal activities, little else done during probation had a crime reduction effect.

The studies of the effectiveness of combinations of treatment and supervision and the findings from the self-report study of probation provide some encouragement that community supervision has the potential to be a valuable addition to the arsenal of activities criminal justice systems can employ to reduce crime in the community.

DORIS LAYTON MACKENZIE

See also PROBATION AND PAROLE: PROCEDURAL PROTECTION; PROBATION AND PAROLE: SUPERVISION.

BIBLIOGRAPHY

ABIDINSKY, HOWARD. *Probation and Parole: Theory and Practice.* Englewood Cliffs, N.J.: Prentice Hall, 1991.

ALLEN, HARRY E.; ESKDRIDGE, CHRIS W.; LATESSA, EDWARD J.; and VITO, GENNARO F. *Probation and Parole in America.* New York: The Free Press, 1985.

AUGUSTUS, JOHN. *John Augustus: First Probation Officer.* Montclair, N.J.: Patterson Smith, 1972.

BOLAND, BARBARA; MAHANNA, PAUL; and STONES, RONALD. *The Prosecution of Felony Arrests, 1988.* Washington, D.C.: U.S. Department of Justice, Bureau of Justice Statistics, 1992.

BRILLIANT, JON A. "The Modern Day Scarlet Letter: A Critical Analysis of Modern Day Probation Conditions." *Duke Law Journal* (1989): 1357–1385.

Bureau of Justice Statistics. *Probation and Parole Population Reaches Almost 3.8 Million.* Washington, D.C.: U.S. Department of Justice, 1996.

———. *Correctional Population in the United States, 1995.* Washington, D.C.: U.S. Department of Justice, 1997.

CHAMPION, DEAN J. *Felony Probation: Problems and Prospects.* New York: Praeger, 1988.

CLARKE, STEVENS H. "What Is the Purpose of Probation and Why Do We Revoke It?" *Crime and Delinquency* 25, no. 4 (1979): 409–424.

CLEAR, TODD R.; HARRIS, PATRICIA M.; and BAIRD, S. CHRISTOPHER. "Probationer Violations and Officer Response." *Journal of Criminal Justice* 20 (1992): 1–12.

CROMWELL, P. F., and DEL CARMEN, R. V. *Community-Based Corrections.* Belmont, Calif.: Wadsworth, 1999.

FOGEL, D. *We Are The Living Proof. . .: The Justice Model for Corrections.* Cincinnati, Ohio: Anderson, 1975.

HARRIS, KAY M. "Rethinking Probation in the Context of a Justice Model." In *Probation and Justice: Reconsideration of Mission.* Edited by Patrick D. McAnany, Doug Thomson, and David Fogel. Cambridge, U.K.: Oelgeschlager, Gunn & Hain, Publishers, Inc., 1984.

LANGAN, PATRICK A., and CUNNIF, MARK A. "Recidivism of Felons on Probation, 1986–1990." *Bureau of Justice Statistics Special Report.* Washington, D.C.: U.S. Department of Justice, 1992.

LATESSA, EDWARD J., and VITO, GENNORO F. "The Effects of Intensive Supervision of Shock Probationers." *Journal of Criminal Justice* 16 (1988): 319–330.

MACKENZIE, DORIS L. "Criminal Justice and Crime Prevention." In *Preventing Crime: What Works, What Doesn't, What's Promising.* Edited by Lawrence W. Sherman, Denise Gottfredson, Doris MacKenzie, John Eck, Peter Reuter, and Shawn Bushway. Washington, D.C.: U.S. Department of Justice, National Institute of Justice, 1997.

MACKENZIE, DORIS L., and SOURYAL, CLAIRE. "Probationer Compliance with Conditions of Supervision." In *Correctional Contexts: Contemporary and Classical Readings.* Edited by James W. Marquart and James Sorensen. Los Angeles, Calif.: Roxbury Publishing Co., 1997.

MACKENZIE, DORIS L.; BROWNING, KATHARINE; SKROBAN, STACY; and SMITH, DOUGLAS. "The Impact of Probation on the Criminal Activities of Offenders." *Journal of Research in Crime and Delinquency* 36, no. 4 (1999): 423–453.

O'LEARY, VINCENT. "Probation: A System in Change." *Federal Probation* 51, no. 4 (1987): 8–11.

PARENT, DALE G.; WENTWORTH, DAN; BURKE, PEGGY; and NEY, BECKI. *Responding to Probation and Parole Violations.* Washington, D.C.: U.S. Department of Justice, National Institute of Justice, 1992.

PETERSILIA, JOAN. "When Probation Becomes More Dreaded than Prison." *Federal Probation* 54, no. 1 (1990): 23–27.

———. "Probation and Parole." In *The Handbook of Crime and Punishment.* Edited by M. Tonry. New York: Oxford University Press, 1998.

PETERSILIA, JOAN, and TURNER, SUSAN. "Intensive Probation and Parole." In *Crime and Justice: A Review of Research,* Vol. 17. Edited by Michael Tonry. Chicago: University of Chicago Press, 1993.

———. *Prison Versus Probation in California: Implications for Crime and Offender Recidivism.* Santa Monica, Calif.: RAND, 1986.

ROSS, ROBERT. R., and GENDREAU, PAUL. *Effective Correctional Treatment.* Toronto: Butterworths, 1980.

ROTHMAN, DAVID J. "Sentencing Reforms in Historical Perspective." *Crime and Delinquency* 29 (1983): 631–647.

RUNDA, JOHN; RHINE, EDWARD; and WETTER, ROBERT. *The Practice of Parole Boards.* Lexington, Ky.: Association of Paroling Authorities, 1994.

THOMSON, DOUGLAS R. "The Changing Face of Probation in the USA." In *Probation and the Community.* Edited by John Harding. London: Tavistock Publications, 1987.

TONRY, MICHAEL. "State and Latent Functions of ISP." *Crime and Delinquency* 36, no. 1 (1990): 174–191.

TONRY, MICHAEL, and LUNCH, MARY. "Intermediate Sanctions." In *Crime and Justice: A Review of Research,* Vol. 20. Edited by Michael Tonry. Chicago: University of Chicago Press, 1996.

VON HIRSCH, ANDREW. *Doing Justice: The Choice of Punishments.* New York: Hill and Wang, 1976.

PROBATION AND PAROLE: GUIDELINES

See SENTENCING: ALLOCATION OF AUTHORITY.

PROBATION AND PAROLE: PROCEDURAL PROTECTION

Probation is a form of criminal sanction imposed by a court upon an offender, nearly always after a verdict or a plea of guilty or nolo contendere but without the prior imposition of a term of imprisonment. Probation may be linked to a jail term, known as a split sentence, where the judge sentences the offender to a specified jail term to be followed by a specified period of release on probation. Parole, on the other hand, is the conditional release of a convicted offender from a penal or correctional institution by an administrative agency: the parolee remains in the community within the continued custody of the state during the remainder of his previously imposed prison sentence.

Introduction

The differences between probation and parole are not very important in the analysis of the procedural protections afforded probationers and parolees. The procedural issues as to each may be conveniently analyzed within three categories: the decision to grant or deny probation or parole; supervisory issues particularly as they relate to the enforcement of the conditions of release; and the decision to revoke. Except in jurisdictions with legally binding sentencing guidelines, or parole guidelines, the decision to grant or withhold probation or parole is a highly discretionary one, with the candidate possessing few legal rights. While a number of laws will categorically deny probation or parole, usually based on the severity of the underlying offense, no law will require that probation or traditional parole be granted.

Once probation or parole is granted, however, the recipient receives a form of conditional liberty with important legal consequences both as to supervision in the community and to any effort to terminate—or revoke—this conditional freedom. One of the most significant developments in this area is the constitutionalizing of the revocation process and, to a much lesser extent, of the granting and community supervision process. In this connection, decisions of the U.S. Supreme Court and the lower federal courts will be discussed here; to complete the legal picture, statutory law and administrative regulations would have to be examined.

The dichotomy between the legal rights associated with the granting of probation or parole and termination of the grant is a general phenomenon that is pervasive in law. That is, persons who, for example, seek a license, employment, or entry to a university while not without rights, especially those related to antidiscrimination, have fewer rights than those faced with loss of a license, employment, or student status. Granting-type decisions, then, concede far more discretion to official decision-makers than termination decisions.

Lawyers are fond of problem solving by using analogical reasoning. For example, they note that the revocation of parole requires due process protection while a prison-to-prison transfer requires none. When an inmate is placed in a work release program and allowed to live at home or in a half-way house part of the time, if the release status is to be terminated, courts will ask if the program is more like parole or more like a prison-to-prison transfer. The closer the analogy to parole, the greater the chance for winning procedural safeguards.

Granting release

Parole. In *Greenholtz v. Inmates of the Nebraska Penal and Correctional Complex,* 442 U.S. 1 (1979), a closely divided Court rendered what was then a highly significant decision concerning parole release. The basic issue in *Greenholtz* was the extent to which the due process clause of the Fourteenth Amendment to the Constitution applied to discretionary parole release decisions in Nebraska. *Greenholtz* involved a challenge to the procedures employed by the board of parole in the exercise of its discretion to grant or withhold the release of an inmate who had reached the point of statutory eligibility. In Nebraska, as is the common practice, a prisoner's eligibility for release was established when he had served his minimum term, minus good-time credits.

Inmates were granted two types of hearings. At least once a year, initial review hearings were required regardless of eligibility. If the board determined from the file and from this initial review that the inmate was a likely candidate for release, a final hearing was scheduled. At the final hearing the inmate was permitted to give evidence, call witnesses, and be represented by retained counsel. The inmate, however, could not hear adverse testimony or engage in cross-examination. A tape recording of the entire hearing was made and preserved, and if denied parole, the inmate would receive a written statement of reasons.

In reviewing these procedures, the Supreme Court dealt a serious blow to the further evolution of due process procedures in this area. The majority found a critical distinction between the grant or denial of conditional freedom and the deprivation of such freedom after it is granted, thereby distinguishing *Greenholtz* from *Morrissey v. Brewer*, 408 U.S. 471 (1972), discussed below. An eligible inmate seeking parole was said to have no more than a desire for release, whereas the Constitution safeguards only legitimate expectations of liberty. The nature of the release-or-retain decision was characterized as being dependent on personal observation and prediction, rather than on a given set of facts that add up to a judgment of releasability.

In this analysis, the Court clearly gave constitutional sanction to decision-making either by intuition or expertise and also validated the characteristically vague statutes governing parole. More basically—and this is the crucial factor that divided the four dissenters from the majority—the existence of a parole system itself, despite the fact that at the time the vast majority of prisoners in this country achieved release by parole, was deemed not to create any constitutionally based claims to procedural fairness.

The majority did find that the somewhat unusual statutory language employed in Nebraska created an expectancy of release entitled to some constitutional protection. The Nebraska statute employed a "shall/unless" approach to parole release, stating that an eligible offender shall be released on parole unless parole is deferred for any one of four rather general factors; for example, if his release were to depreciate the seriousness of his crime.

The Court then concluded that Nebraska was providing the inmate with even more procedures than the Constitution required. Characterizing the function of legal process as being one of minimizing the risk of erroneous decision, the Court ruled that a full hearing is not necessary and that due process does not require the board of parole to specify the particular evidence relied upon. In conclusion, the Court stated: "The Nebraska procedure affords an opportunity to be heard, and when parole is denied it informs the inmate in what respects he falls short of qualifying for parole; this affords the process that is due under these circumstances. The Constitution does not require more" (p. 16).

It must be stressed that the above-stated procedural minima—an opportunity to be heard, and reasons for denial—were constitutionally required only when a given jurisdiction employed statutory language of the sort used by Nebraska. Where there is no such protected expectation, parole boards presumably need not provide even such minimal safeguards.

Release and *Sandin v. Conner*

With the decision in *Sandin v. Conner*, 515 U.S. 472 (1995), the Supreme Court may have overruled that aspect of *Greenholtz* finding a protected liberty interest in the shall/unless–type statutory language used in Nebraska. In *Sandin*, a federal appeals court found that a Hawaii prison regulation that required substantial evidence to support a finding of guilt to a charge of prison misconduct created a liberty interest in the prisoner. That is, without a finding of guilt by substantial evidence, held the lower federal court, the prison misconduct hearing was void as a denial of due process.

The Supreme Court used *Sandin* as the vehicle to re-examine a series of the Courts' decisions, including *Greenholtz*, where the verbal arrangement in the state law was used to find or reject a state-created liberty interest enforceable in federal court.

The Court stated it was time to shift the focus of the liberty (or protected) interest inquiry from the "language" of a regulation to the "nature" of the deprivation. One reason for doing so is to show deference to the states and further remove the federal courts from review of state correctional processes.

Henceforth, a state-created liberty interest depends on whether the state seeks to impose an "atypical and significant hardship on the inmate in relation to the ordinary incidents of prison life" (*Sandin v. Conner*, p. 484). Phrased differently, prisoners (including parolees in waiting) must suffer a very significant or grievous loss before they are entitled even to the rudiments of procedural due process. Post-*Sandin* inmates have been placed in disciplinary segregation for up to a year without even a rudimentary hearing, and the federal courts have found no grievous loss.

The Court describes *Greenholtz* as one of those decisions practicing the now disfavored "semantic due process," and while *Greenholtz* is not explicitly overruled, it is difficult to imagine that it is still breathing. After *Sandin*, paroling authorities may be constitutionally free to decide these cases simply on the written record.

Parole rescission

There are occasions when a parole authority may decide to grant parole and, in prison jargon, "give the inmate a date." Subsequent to the actual physical release the parole authority may come to believe that the inmate misrepresented certain facts or a serious disciplinary infraction may have occurred and the authority decides to rescind the previously extended offer of parole.

While state statutory law or administrative regulation may provide for a hearing, the general rule is that parole rescission may be accomplished unilaterally by the parole authority with no due process protections.

As for the competing analogies, rescission is treated as a part of the granting (no rights) process and not as a part of the revocation (due process rights) process.

Beyond parole: other decisions affecting release of prisoners

In *Connecticut Board of Pardons v. Dumschat*, 452 U.S. 458 (1981), the Court considered whether the Connecticut Board of Pardons's record of granting approximately three-fourths of all applications for commutation of life sentences had in fact created a constitutionally protected interest, calling at least for a statement of reasons when a particular application was denied. The Court held that in the absence of a statute or rule

imposing such an obligation on the board, and regardless of how frequently clemency had been granted in the past, no such constitutional protection exists.

In *Ohio Adult Parole Authority v. Woodard*, 118 S.Ct. 1244 (1998), a state prisoner challenged Ohio's clemency process as violating his due process rights. The Court stated:

Clemency proceedings are not part of the trial—or even of the adjudicatory process. They do not determine the guilt or innocence of the defendant, and are not intended primarily to enhance the reliability of the trial process. They are conducted by the Executive Branch, independent of direct appeal and collateral relief proceedings. *Greenholtz*, 442 U.S. at 7–8. And they are usually discretionary, unlike the more structured and limited scope of judicial proceedings. Wh'le traditionally available to capital defendants as a final and alternative avenue of relief, clemency has not traditionally "been the business of courts." (*Connecticut Board of Pardons v. Dumschat*, p. 452)

In *Meachum v. Fano*, 427 U.S. 215 (1976), the court held that there is no right to due process at an inmate's classification or reclassification (which determine eligibility for prison programs), or when an inmate is transferred from one prison to another.

In *Young v. Harper*, 520 U.S. 143 (1997), the Supreme Court held that the defendant's participation in due process was required to terminate Oklahoma's so-called preparole release program. The Court noted that the releasee kept his own residence; he maintained a job; and was generally free of the incidents of imprisonment.

Probation

Except in systems that have adopted legally binding sentencing guidelines, an offender has no legal "right" to receive a sentence of probation. Moreover, sentencing guidelines, mandatory minimum, and other "determinate" sentencing laws often limit the court's power to grant probation. These laws, as well as the general procedural requirements for sentencing, are covered in other entries and will not be further discussed here.

Assuming that an offender is legally eligible for probation, does he have the right to be fairly considered for probation? In one famous case, it was held to be error for a trial judge to refuse to consider for probation all defendants who stood trial (*United States v. Wiley*, 267 F.2d 453 (7th Cir. 1959), *on remand*, 184 F.Supp. 679 (N.D. Ill.

1960)). The sentencing judge in *Wiley* had stated this policy on the record. If he had remained silent, as is the common practice, the judge's sentencing discretion based on unarticulated factors would probably have prevailed. But other decisions support the proposition that it is an abuse of discretion, subject to reversal on appeal, for a judge simply to refuse to hear or consider an eligible applicant for probation.

While probation, like parole, is a form of conditional freedom in the community, its precise form has many variations. Probation may consist of little more than an admonition to commit no new offenses and maintain telephone contact with a probation officer, or it may be far more intensive and include spending some part of the day or evening in a residential facility, and/or specified frequent contacts with the probation officer, drug or alcohol tests, and so on.

An order of probation may also include a fine, restitution to victims, a period of "shock incarceration" (jail), home confinement with or without electronic surveillance, measures designed to shame the offender ("scarlet letter" conditions), substance abuse or sex offender treatment, community service, and various limitations on the offender's freedom of movement, activities, and associations.

For the most part, as long as these conditions do not violate some specific constitutional safeguard, for example, cruel and unusual punishment or First Amendment rights, courts give judges wide latitude in their imposition.

Supervision and conditions

The most fundamental point to be made regarding the legal status of the probationer and parolee while in the community is that he or she is a person who will have been deprived of certain civil rights by virtue of conviction of a crime. Precisely what rights are lost and for how long as a result of the conviction varies greatly from jurisdiction to jurisdiction.

As noted above, probationers and parolees suffer additional restrictions on their freedom as a result of conditions imposed by the sentencing judge or the parole authority. Once again, the discretion afforded the relevant authorities is enormous, although not without some legal limitations. The traditional view is that conditions will be upheld unless they are illegal, immoral, or impossible of performance (Cohen, 1969, p. 40); however, courts have been somewhat responsive to challenges regarding the breadth or ambiguity of conditions. For example, the probation condition of victim restitution has been frequently and successfully challenged where the judge failed to ascertain the offender's ability to pay, failed to limit restitution to proven damages, left ascertainment of the actual victim open, or caused the financial destruction of the offender (*Higdon v. United States*, 627 F.2d 893 (9th Cir. 1980)).

In determining the judge's or the parole authority's power with regard to probation or parole conditions, the starting point is the relevant statute. Thus, the federal probation law formerly provided for probation for such period of time and upon such terms and conditions as the court deems best.

Today, in an era of diminished judicial discretion in sentencing, the current federal probation law (18 U.S. Code § 3563) includes a list of "mandatory" conditions of probation, including the following: that the offender not commit further crime or use or possess illegal drugs; that he pay restitution and any fine that was imposed; and, in certain cases, that he enter a rehabilitation program or submit to random drug tests. However, the current law continues to list a wide variety of "discretionary" probation conditions that judges may chose to impose, provided such conditions are "reasonably related" to the offense and offender and to the traditional purposes of punishment, and are "reasonably necessary" to achieve those purposes. Thus, in addition to all of the traditional probation conditions previously mentioned, defendants may be required to support their dependents, "work conscientiously" (or avoid certain types of work), and refrain from "excessive use of alcohol" or the possession of any dangerous weapon.

The American Bar Association's 1970 *Standards Relating to Probation*, section 3.2(a), took the position that every sentence of probation should include a condition that the probationer lead a law-abiding life, that no other conditions should be required by statute, and that the sentencing judge should be free to fashion additional conditions to fit the circumstances of each case. This, of course, reflected an earlier view of the propriety of unregulated judicial discretion. (See also *The Model Adult Community Corrections Act* (American Bar Association, February 1992), which provides general guidance on the propriety, intensity, and content for what are termed community-based sanctions.)

Taking into account the so-called truth-in-sentencing laws that abolish traditional parole or diminish its availability, where parole in the form of discretionary release exists, the approach to parole conditions is similar to the rules governing probation as set out above. Typically, parole authorities impose certain "standard conditions" as well as "special conditions" related to the particular offense or offender.

Parole conditions are subject to challenge for their overbreadth and vagueness and as interfering with the individual's basic constitutional rights, or as having no relationship to the underlying offense. An example of a condition that was found to be impermissibly vague is that the individual "live honorably" (*Norris v. State*, 383 So.2d 691 (Fla. App. 1980)). Conditions that infringe upon First Amendment freedoms are among the most likely to be found void (Cohen, 1969, pp. 42–43). For example, a prior restraint on a parolee's desire to give a speech was held to be justified only by a showing that the speech entailed a clear and present danger of riot and disorder (*Hyland v. Procunier*, 311 F.Supp. 749 (N.D. Cal. 1970)).

The courts have also held that banishment from the state as a condition is void, either on constitutional grounds or on the basis of the pragmatic view that states which exile offenders will surely receive the exiles of other states (Cohen, 1969, p. 47). On the other hand, territorial restrictions on the movement of probationers or parolees are uniformly upheld.

Conditions may be imposed that are impossible of performance. For example, ordering a chronic alcoholic or a drug addict to refrain from drinking or drug use likely would be considered unlawful "impossible" conditions (*Sweeney v. United States*, 353 F.2d 10 (7th Cir. 1965)). However, requiring the individual to obtain or complete treatment, or to submit to reasonable tests in order to determine progress, would be upheld.

In the absence of legislative guidance, appellate courts have begun to construct some principles for assaying conditions challenged as unreasonable but not necessarily unconstitutional. An example would be a court's granting of probation to a person convicted of forgery and ordering that the probationer forego sexual intercourse with persons other than his wife. The above condition bears no reasonable relationship to the crime; it relates to conduct that is not inevitably criminal; and there is no apparent relationship between the condition and rehabilitation or future criminality. Such a condition would probably be found void (*Wiggins v. State*, 386 So.2d 46 (Fla. App. 1980)).

Conditions designed to shame offenders, so-called scarlet-letter conditions, are in vogue with some judges. The reported decisions disclose a probationer required to wear a T-shirt announcing he was on probation for theft; post a sign in the yard proclaiming the occupant a sex offender; place a bumper sticker on the car; wear a pink bracelet bearing the words "DUI CONVICT," or place an advertisement in the local paper with a mug shot and an apology.

Appellate courts continue to be reluctant to review such conditions even when offered proof that the probationer is harmed or put at risk by the condition; that First Amendment issues are created; and that little, if any, positive impact can be shown. Such conditions reflect the idiosyncratic whims of judges and should be reigned in by the legislature or appellate courts. (See Comment (1999) for a review of all these issues and citations to decisions.)

Convicted sex offenders are increasingly subjected to a number of intrusive conditions of supervised release. For example, such offenders are required to submit blood and saliva samples to a DNA bank, upheld in *Boling v. Romer*, 101 F.3d 1336 (10th Cir. 1996). In Ohio, eligibility for parole requires successful completion of a sex offender program while in prison, and that has been upheld. (See *Scott v. Ghee*, 68 F.3d 475 (6th Cir. 1995); *Schaffer v. Moore*, 46 F.3d 43 (8th Cir. 1995)). Indeed, where mandated sex offender treatment could not be obtained because the offender could not find a way to pay for it, one court upheld revocation of probation, (*State v. Morrow*, 492 N.W. 2d 539 (Minn. App. 1992)).

The Fourth Amendment: searches and seizures

An extraordinary array of conditions limit the freedom of probationers and parolees. As noted, almost all of those conditions are upheld by the courts. The Constitution itself is viewed as not being fully applicable to probationers and parolees whose constitutional identity is less than the ordinary citizen but more than that of a prisoner.

In *Griffin v. Wisconsin*, 483 U.S. 868 (1987), a probationer's home was searched by probation officers, accompanied by police, without consent, without a warrant, and without the semblance of probable cause. A handgun was found and introduced in evidence over objection at Griffin's felony trial.

The Supreme Court upheld the search as "reasonable" under the Fourth Amendment, stressing that the search was conducted under a state regulation authorizing probation officers to search a probationer's home when there were "reasonable grounds" to believe there was contraband in the home.

Plainly this search and seizure would have been illegal if Griffin had not been on probation or parole. The Supreme Court, without actually expressing this, had to choose between affording the probationer's home the traditional privacy protections extended the home or opting for the total lack of privacy protection afforded a prisoner's cell. (See *Hudson v. Palmer*, 468 U.S. 517 (1984)). The Court opted for the latter and in so doing diluted the privacy of other occupants of the home and also invited baseless searches.

In *Pennsylvania Board of Probation and Parole v. Scott*, 524 U.S. 357 (1998), the Pennsylvania Supreme Court had found that a search of a parolee's home without the owner's consent and not authorized by any state statutory or regulatory framework violated the Fourth Amendment and the evidence seized should not have been admitted at a revocation hearing. The U.S. Supreme Court reversed, in a 5–4 decision, holding that parole boards are not required by federal law to exclude evidence obtained in violation of the Fourth Amendment. The exclusionary rule was said to threaten the traditionally informal process of parole revocation and any marginal gains in deterrence would be offset by the significant restraints on the parole process.

The Court did not rule on the question of whether the actual search was unreasonable, noting that the case could be decided by ruling only on whether any such evidence must be excluded by a parole board. Thus, an open question from *Griffin* remains open: must there be reasonable suspicion to search a parolee's home where the parolee consents in advance as a condition of parole?

Revocation

***Morrissey* and *Gagnon*.** The term *revocation* at times refers to the act of imprisonment or reimprisonment, and at other times to the process of establishing a violation. Revocation is perhaps best viewed as a process resembling a cameo trial at which facts are alleged and proven to show a violation; that is, that the supervisee was at "fault" by committing a new crime or violating a condition of his release. After a violation is established, the judge or parole authority must then make a sentencing-like decision since a violation need not invariably result in incarceration.

Until the decision in *Morrissey v. Brener*, 408 U.S. 471 (1972), due process protections had often been denied at revocation by characterizing probation and parole as a privilege (an act of grace); as governed by contract (whereby the supervisee simply agreed to initial incarceration at the discretion of the court); or, in the case of parole, as a matter of continuing custody with reimprisonment argued to be simply the reassertion of full custody. *Morrissey* laid those arguments to rest by holding that the conditional liberty enjoyed by a parolee was within the compass of the liberty interests protected by the due process clauses of the Fourteenth and Fifth Amendments. In *Gagnon v. Scarpelli*, 411 U.S. 778 (1973), the Court applied the same analysis and reached the same result with regard to probation revocation. *Morrissey* held that procedural due process required that a parolee be accorded a hearing with an opportunity to be heard on the charge and the possible disposition, as well as to present evidence. *Sandin v. Conner* discussed earlier should not affect these decisions because the liberty interest at stake derives from the Constitution itself and not from any statutory formula employed by a state.

The Court further determined that there must be two hearings; a prompt preliminary hearing (conducted near the place of alleged violation or arrest) to determine probable cause that a violation occurred; and a final revocation hearing (which in fact most often takes place in a prison setting, for a parolee) to resolve contested relevant facts and determine whether those facts warrant imprisonment.

The minimum requirements of the preliminary hearing are as follows:

1. The hearing is to be conducted by an individual who is not involved in commencing the revocation proceedings. The state need not create a special hearing officer for these proceedings, and a parole officer other than the officer who recommended the revocation proceedings is considered sufficiently neutral.
2. Prior to the hearing the parolee is to receive notice of the facts upon which revocation is based.
3. The parolee is to be present at the hearing.
4. The parolee is entitled to be heard on his own behalf.
5. There is to be a written summary of the evidence and arguments presented.

6. The hearing officer shall make a written statement of his decision and reasoning, stating the facts upon which he relied.
7. During this hearing, the parolee is entitled to cross-examine any persons giving adverse information upon which revocation could be based, unless the hearing officer finds that revealing the identity of an informant may subject him to an unreasonable risk.

The final hearing is to be conducted by a neutral body or individual, and the parole board itself was held to qualify as such a body. This aspect of the decision has evoked strong criticism on the ground that parole officials tend to confirm the decision-making of their colleagues. In addition, *Morrissey* requires:

1. The hearing is to be held reasonably promptly; the Court found a period of two months to be reasonable.
2. Written notice is to be given the parolee of the claimed violations of parole.
3. The evidence against the parolee must be disclosed to him.
4. The parolee is to be afforded an opportunity to be heard on his own behalf, to present evidence, and to call witnesses.
5. The parolee is to be permitted to cross-examine adverse witnesses unless the hearing officer specifically finds good cause to deny cross-examination.
6. There is to be a written decision setting forth the facts and the reasoning upon which it is based.

In *Gagnon* the Court held that at a probation or parole revocation proceeding the alleged violator also has a qualified right to appointed counsel. The right exists if there is a substantial issue regarding whether the alleged violation occurred or, even if the violation is a matter of public record or is uncontested, there are substantial reasons—complex or difficult to develop—that justified or mitigated the violation and that make revocation inappropriate.

In the process of deciding the counsel-at-revocation issue, *Gagnon* also made clear that there is an absolute right to counsel at judicial sentencing, but only a qualified right at revocation. Thus, where a judge suspends the imposition of sentence (as in *Mempa v. Rhay*, 389 U.S. 128 (1967)) and grants probation, a subsequent revocation proceeding is also a sentencing proceeding for the purposes of right to counsel.

However, where the judge imposes a sentence (as in *Gagnon*) and suspends its execution, then the prison term is already fixed, the accused has been previously sentenced, and any right to counsel is governed by the above-noted *Gagnon* formula.

Other issues

Later cases have addressed several procedural questions left open in *Morrissey* and *Gagnon*.

In *Moody v. Daggett*, 429 U.S. 78 (1976), the Supreme Court held that a parolee has no right to an initial preliminary hearing before being confined to prison for a suspected parole violation when the parolee-inmate already has been convicted of the crime upon which parole revocation is based. The conviction, based on proof beyond a reasonable doubt, provides the requisite probable cause to believe there has been a violation. In addition, the Court clarified what it meant by a "reasonable time" for the final revocation hearing. Here, the parolee-inmate understandably wanted to serve his parole violation and new crime sentence concurrently. Thus, he argued for a speedy revocation hearing. The Court rebuffed this, finding that the right to a parole revocation hearing begins only when the parolee is taken into custody for the parole violation.

It is clear that *Morrissey* envisioned that, as the accuser, the government is obliged to present persuasive evidence of violation. In the face of almost total legislative and rule-making neglect, the courts have concluded that a violation need not be proved beyond a reasonable doubt, but only by a preponderance of the evidence (*State ex rel. Flowers v. Dep't of Health and Social Serv.*, 81 Wis. 2d 376, 260 N.W. 2d 727 (1978)), or an even lower standard of proof. (See *Relation v. Vermont Parole Board*, 660 A.2d 318, 320-21 (Vt. 1995)). This leads to the further conclusion that an acquittal on criminal charges will not bar a revocation of probation or parole based on the same grounds as the earlier acquittal.

In the opposite situation, where an unsuccessful revocation proceeding occurs before a criminal proceeding, some would argue that the government is estopped from going ahead with the criminal case. That is, if the facts underlying the alleged violation could not be convincingly shown to meet a preponderance (or lower) standard, then obviously they cannot meet the beyond-the-reasonable-doubt standard. But in

Commonwealth v. Cosgrove, 629 A.2d 1007, 1011 (Pa. Super. 1993), the court held that the informality of a revocation proceeding should not estop a subsequent criminal proceeding.

FRED COHEN

See also CRIMINAL PROCEDURE: CONSTITUTIONAL ASPECTS; PRISONERS, LEGAL RIGHTS OF; PROBATION AND PAROLE: HISTORY, GOALS, AND DECISION-MAKING; PROBATION AND PAROLE: SUPERVISION; SENTENCING: ALLOCATION OF AUTHORITY; SENTENCING: ALTERNATIVES; SENTENCING: DISPARITY; SENTENCING: GUIDELINES; SENTENCING: MANDATORY AND MANDATORY MINIMUM SENTENCES; SENTENCING: PRESENTENCE REPORT; SENTENCING: PROCEDURAL PROTECTION.

BIBLIOGRAPHY

American Bar Association, Advisory Committee on Sentencing and Review. *Standards Relating to Probation: Tentative Draft.* Chicago: ABA, 1970.

American Bar Association. *Model Adult Community Corrections Act.* Approved, February 1992.

BRANHAM, LYNN S., and KRANTZ, SHELDON. *Cases and Materials on the Law of Sentencing, Corrections, and Prisoners' Rights, In a Nutshell,* 5th ed. St. Paul, Minn.: West Publishing, 1997.

BRANHAM, LYNN S. *The Law of Sentencing, Corrections, and Prisoners' Rights,* 5th ed. St. Paul, Minn.: West Publishing, 1998.

COHEN, FRED. *The Legal Challenge to Corrections: Implications for Manpower and Training.* Washington, D.C.: Joint Commission on Correctional Manpower and Training, 1969.

———. "Sentencing Probation, and the Rehabilitative Ideal: The View from *Mempa v. Rhay.*" *Texas Law Review* 47 (1968): 1–59.

———. "Legal Issues and 'Treatment' in Community Corrections." *Community Corrections Report* I (1994): 1–27.

COHEN, NEIL P. *The Law of Probation and Parole,* 2d ed. New York: West Group, 1999.

Comment. "The Ideology of Shame: An Analysis of First Amendment and Eighth Amendment Challenges to Scarlett-Letter Probation Conditions." *North Carolina Law Review* 77 (1999): 783–864.

Community Corrections Report: On Law and Corrections Practice I, no. 1 (1993). A bimonthly newsletter published by Civic Research Institute of Kingston, N.J., that summarizes leading cases on probation and parole. 1993–.

HOFFMAN, PETER B. "History of the Federal Parole System: Part I (1910–1972)." *Federal Probation* 61 (1997): 23–31.

———. "History of the Federal Parole System: Part 2 (1973–1997)." *Federal Probation* 61 (1997): 49–56. These articles describe the gradual phase-out of the Federal Parole Commission along with some innovative programs on revocation, video hearings, and so on.

KILLINGER, GEORGE G.; KERPER, HAZEL B.; and CROMWELL, PAUL F., JR. *Probation and Parole in the Criminal Justice System.* St. Paul, Minn.: West Publishing, 1976.

MAUER, MARC. *Race to Incarcerate.* New York: New Press, 1999. For an overall perspective of the racial, political, and economic implications of increased imprisonment and the mechanisms of mandatory sentencing.

MERRITT, FRANK S. "Parole Revocation: A Primer." *University of Toledo Law Review* 11 (1980): 893–938.

PARISI, NICOLETTE. "Combining Incarceration and Probation." *Federal Probation* 44 (June 1980): 3–12.

President's Commission on Law Enforcement and Administration of Justice, Task Force on Corrections. *Task Force Report: Corrections.* Washington, D.C.: The Commission, 1967.

ROTHMAN, DAVID J. *Conscience and Convenience: The Asylum and Its Alternatives in Progressive America.* Boston: Little, Brown, 1980.

TRAVIS, LAWERENCE F., III, and O'LEARY, VINCE. *Changes in Sentencing and Parole Decision-making: 1976–1978.* Washington, D.C.: U.S. Department of Justice, Bureau of Prisons, 19.

U.S. Department of Justice. *The Attorney General's Survey of Release Procedures,* 5 vols. Washington, D.C.: The Department, 1939–1940.

———. Law Enforcement Assistance Administration, National Advisory Commission on Criminal Justice Standards and Goals. *Corrections.* Washington, D.C.: The Commission, 1973.

CASES

Boling v. Romer, 101 F.3d 1336 (10th Cir. 1996).
Commonwealth v. Cosgrove, 629 A.2d 1007, 1011 (Pa. Super. 1993).
Connecticut Board of Pardons v. Dumschat, 452 U.S. 458 (1981).
Greenholtz v. Inmates of the Nebraska Penal and Corrections Complex, 442 U.S. 1 (1979).
Griffin v. Wisconsin, 483 U.S. 868 (1987).
Higdon v. United States, 627 F.2d 893 (9th Circuit 1980).
Hudson v. Palmer, 468 U.S. 517 (1984).
Hyland v. Procunier, 311 F.Supp. 749 (N.D. Cal. 1970).
Meachum v. Fano, 427 U.S. 215 (1976).
Mempha v. Rhay, 389 U.S. 128 (1967).
Moody v. Daggett, 429 U.S. 78 (1976).

Morrissey v. Brewer, 408 U.S. 471 (1972).

Norris v. State, 383 So.2d 691 (Fla. App. 1980).

Ohio Adult Parole Authority v. Woodward, 118 S. Ct. 1244 (1988).

Pennsylvania Board of Probation and Parole v. Scott, 524 U.S. 357 (1998).

Relation v. Vermont Parole Board, 660 A.2d 318, 320-21 (Vt. 1995).

Schaffer v. Moore, 46 F.3d 43 (8th Cir. 1995).

Scott v. Ghee, 68 F.3d 475 (6th Cir. 1995).

State ex rel. Flowers v. Dep't of Health and Social Serv., 81 Wis. 2d 376, 260 N.W. 2dd 727 (1978).

State v. Morrow, 492 N.W. 2d 539 (Minn. App. 1992).

Sweeney v. United States, 353 F.2d 10 (7th Cir. 1965).

United States v. Wiley, 267 F2d 453 (7th Cir. 1959), *on remand*, 184 F. Supp. 679 (N.D. Ill. 1960).

Wiggins v. State, 386 So.2d 46 (Fla. App. 1980).

Young v. Harper, 520 U.S. 143 (1997).

PROBATION AND PAROLE: SUPERVISION

Probation and parole agencies share one particular and significant function: they provide supervision of offenders in the community. After an offender has been granted probation or parole, a probation or parole officer, hereafter referred to as "PO," is expected to supervise that offender in the community. The basic question remains: What is the purpose of supervision? To some, the function of supervision, drawn from the field of social work, is based upon the casework model. Based on this view, supervision forms the basis of a treatment program. The officer uses all the information available about the offender to make a diagnosis of that person's needs and designs a treatment plan. The treatment plan is an outline based on the needs of the offender (e.g., employment), and the PO's strategy for assisting the offenders in meeting their goal (e.g., enroll the offender in a job skills program).

Yet providing treatment is only one aspect of supervision. In addition, the PO is expected to maintain surveillance of those offenders who make up the case load. A classic definition of surveillance was provided by the National Conference of Parole: "Surveillance is that activity of the parole officer, which utilizes watchfulness, checking, and verification of certain behavior of a parolee without contributing to a helping relationship with him" (Studt, p. 65).

Although these statements indicate that the treatment and surveillance roles of the PO are almost diametrically opposed, many believe that they coexist as a part of probation or parole agency's mission. Many believe that the PO has two major responsibilities: to rehabilitate the offenders who are amenable to treatment, while simultaneously protecting society from those who prove to be dangerous.

Supervision of offenders usually involves both surveillance of offenders and assistance that will help the offender remain crime free in the community. While the term "surveillance" usually means simply watching in a police sense, it should be pointed out that a helping purpose can also occur. When surveillance is properly carried out, the offender can be continually sensitized to the possible results of a course of action that has made him or her vulnerable to breaking the law in the past. Just as an alcoholic or narcotics addict who is trying to change his or her life derives support from frequent contact with others who have successfully conquered their problems, so also can many offenders derive beneficial results from frequent meetings with the PO.

Social work or law enforcement?

The split between treatment and surveillance has attracted a great deal of attention, but very little in terms of empirical studies. Most authors seem to interpret role conflict as somehow tragic, intractable, and overwhelming. The most common solution has been to advocate that one orientation must be emphasized over all others. Simply put, is the role of the PO that of the helper or the cop?

The roots of role conflict often are attributed to inconsistencies that exist in the three main functions of supervision: to enforce the legal requirements of supervision (the "law enforcement" role), to assist the offender in establishing a successful community adjustment (the "social worker" role), and to carry out the policies of the supervision agency (the "bureaucrat" role). One critic of surveillance was John Conrad, who wrote:

We can hardly justify parole services on the basis of the surveillance model. What the parole officer can do, if it should be done at all, can better be done by the police. The pushing of doorbells, the recording of "contacts," and the requirement of monthly reports all add up to expensive pseudoservices. At best they constitute a costly but useless frenzy of activity. But more often than not, I suspect, they harass and humiliate the parolee without gaining even the illusion of control. (p. 21)

Certainly probation or parole officers have no monopoly on role conflict. Many feel that the true "professional" finds a way of integrating various role expectations, balancing them, and weighing the appropriateness of various expressions of the roles. It is probable that the treatment-surveillance dichotomy will remain forever. Recent developments suggest that surveillance is likely to become the primary emphasis, especially for offenders who constitute a demonstrable risk to society. Providing assistance to offenders can involve direct services by the PO, such as counseling in areas like employment, education, marital/family relationships, companions, and alcohol and drug usage. Often times POs do not directly provide services, but rather serve a referral function in which they refer offenders to other community resources for help or assistance.

Casework supervision versus brokerage supervision

In terms of community safety, the most significant responsibility of a probation or parole agency is supervising offenders. Underlying this duty are the dual objectives of protecting the community and helping the offenders. As we have already learned, these objectives are not always compatible.

Depending upon the jurisdiction in which the agency is located, offenders placed on probation or parole may have committed almost any type of criminal offense, and may range from first-time offenders to career criminals. The bulk of probationers and parolees are under regular supervision, although about one in nine are under some other management program, such as intensive supervision, electronic monitoring, house arrest, halfway house, or other programs.

In addition, there is likely to be variation among probationers or parolees with respect to the type and extent of conditions imposed upon them by the court or the parole board. Finally, individuals being supervised will vary considerably in the types of problems they face (family difficulties, educational or employment needs, mental illness, alcohol or drug abuse).

The two major orientations or approaches to supervision are *casework* and *brokerage*. We will briefly examine each approach. We are discussing "pure" types as though the approaches were mutually exclusive, as if a probation or parole department would adopt either a casework or a brokerage approach, but could not combine any feature of the two. In reality, the two approaches are so mixed that it would be unusual if any two departments exhibited precisely the same approach as extreme positions. Most departments adopt positions somewhere between the two.

Casework supervision

The traditional approach to probation and parole supervision has been the casework approach. Many definitions of casework have been offered. Bowers has provided a frequently cited definition: "[C]asework is an area in which knowledge of the science of human relations and skills in relationships are used to mobilize capacities in the individual and resources in the community appropriate for better adjustment between the client and all or any part of his total environment" (p. 127).

It is apparent that the basic element in casework is the nature of the relationship between the caseworker and the individual in trouble. It is also obvious from these definitions that casework emphasizes changing the behavior of the offender through the development of a supportive one-to-one relationship. Because of the closeness, this approach views the caseworker as the sole, or at least the primary, agent of treatment for the client.

Casework is so extensively used in probation and parole supervision that it is considered the "norm" as a service provision strategy. It basically follows the medical model of corrections in which the supervising officer, through a one-to-one relationship, diagnoses the offender, formulates a treatment strategy, implements that strategy and, finally, evaluates the offender in light of the treatment.

Following this approach, the probation or parole officer attempts to bring about a mutual interaction with the offender in an effort to promote a psychological and social atmosphere that will enable the offender to be more self-accepting and to interact more acceptably with others. In other words, through the use of this close, helping relationship, the officer attempts to change (positively) the behavior of the offender. Because of the close relationship required by the casework approach, the officer is the primary agent of treatment.

Brokerage supervision

Almost diametrically opposed to the case-work approach is the brokerage approach, in which the supervising officer is not concerned primarily with understanding or changing the behavior of the offender, but rather with assessing the needs of the individual and arranging for the probationer or parolee to receive services that directly address those needs. Since the PO is not seen as the primary agent of treatment or change, there is significantly less emphasis placed on the development of a close, one-on-one relationship between the officer and the offender. With the brokerage approach, the supervising officer functions primarily as a manager or broker of resources and social services that are already available from other agencies. It is the task of the PO to assess the service needs of the offender, locate the social service agency that addresses those needs, refer the offender to the appropriate agency, and make follow-up contacts to make sure the offender has actually received the services. Under the brokerage approach, it can be said that the officer's relationship with community service agencies is more important than the relationship with an individual client. With its emphasis on the management of community resources, the brokerage approach requires intimate knowledge of the services in the community and the conditions under which each service is available.

In addition to understanding the basic philosophical aspects of supervising offenders in the field, it is important to examine some of the alternative approaches and programs that are used by probation and parole agencies.

Intensive supervision

Offenders under correctional control in the community are generally given one of three general forms of supervision: (1) minimum, which requires little if any formal reporting; (2) regular, where the offender reports to a probation officer on a reoccurring basis; and (3) intensive, in which more stringent reporting requirements and other conditions are placed on the offender. An *intensive supervision* program (ISP) is most often viewed as an alternative to incarceration. Persons who are sentenced to intensive probation supervision are supposed to be those offenders who, in the absence of intensive supervision, would have been sentenced to imprisonment. Intensive supervision programs emphasize punish-

ment of the offender and control of the offender in the community at least as much as they do rehabilitation. Further, contemporary programs are designed to meet the primary goal of easing the burden of prison overcrowding. No two jurisdictions define intensive supervision in exactly the same way. However, one characteristic of all ISP programs is that they provide for very strict terms of probation. This increased level of control is usually achieved through reduced case loads, increased number of contacts, and a range of required activities for participating offenders that can include victim restitution, community service, employment, random urine and alcohol testing, electronic monitoring, and payment of a probation supervision fee. Intensive supervision programs vary in terms of the number and type of contacts per month, case load size, type of surveillance conducted, and services offered.

In an article summarizing the state of ISP, Fulton and others (p. 72) summarize what we know from the research concerning intensive supervision programs:

- ISPs have failed to alleviate prison crowding.
- Most ISP studies have found no significant differences between recidivism rates of ISP offenders and offenders with comparison groups.
- There appears to be a relationship between greater participation in treatment and employment programs and lower recidivism rates.
- ISPs appear to be more effective than regular supervision or prison in meeting offenders' needs.
- ISPs that reflect certain principles of effective intervention are associated with lower rates of recidivism.
- ISP does provide an intermediate punishment.

Shock probation

Shock probation is a program that allows sentencing judges to reconsider the offender's original sentence to prison and then recall the inmate for a sentence to probation within the community. It is presumed that a short term or imprisonment would "shock" the offender into changing their criminal behavior. With shock probation, an offender is sent to prison, and then within a specified period of time (usually between 30 and 120 days), a judge can bring that offender back out for community supervision.

The overall effects of shock probation remain unknown. Until more research is conducted, perhaps the best tentative conclusions is that it can reduce the cost of incarceration, and may be just as effective in preventing recidivism as prison.

Day reporting centers

Unlike many other supervision practices, *day reporting* is of recent vintage. While day reporting was used earlier in England, the first day-reporting program in the United States was opened in Massachusetts in 1986 (McDevitt). This inaugural program was designed as an early release from prison and jail placement for inmates approaching their parole or discharge date. Unlike traditional halfway houses, day reporting centers do not require the offender to reside in the program. Participants in day reporting programs are generally required to report to the center each day (hence the name), prepare an itinerary for their next day's activities, and report by telephone to the center throughout the day. The characteristics of these programs and the clients they serve vary considerably; however, most day reporting programs generally offer a variety of services to program participants. Most centers offer job skills, drug abuse education, group and individual counseling, job placement, education, life skills training, and drug treatment. Unfortunately, there have not been many empirical studies of day reporting centers, so their effectiveness remains an open question.

Home detention

House arrest, usually conjuring up images of political control and fascist repression, is court-ordered home detention in the United States, confining offenders to their households for the duration of the sentence. The sentence is usually in conjunction with probation, but may be imposed by the court as a separate punishment. Participants may be required to make victim compensation, perform community work service, pay probation fees, undergo drug and alcohol testing and, in some instances, wear electronic monitoring equipment to verify their presence in the residence. House arrest only allows the offender to leave her or his residence for specific purposes and hours approved by the court or supervising officer, and being absent without leave is a technical violation of conditions that may result in resentencing to jail or prison.

Home detention is a sentence that was designed in most cases to relieve institutional overcrowding. For many offenders it is their "last chance" to avoid being committed to jail or prison. The most significant critical argument against home detention is that many petty or low-risk offenders are brought under correctional control that would best be handled by diversion, fines, or other services or supervision. In general, such inclusive actions are viewed as "net widening," which occurs when offenders are sentenced to community control that might otherwise have received a lesser or even no sentence.

Electronic monitoring

Home detention has a long history as a criminal penalty but its new popularity with correctional authorities is due to the advent of *electronic monitoring*, a technological link thought to make the sanction both practical and affordable. The concept of electronic monitoring is not new, having been proposed in 1964 by Schwitzgebel and his colleagues as "electronic parole," and initially used to monitor the location of mental patients. The first studies of home detention enforced by electronic monitoring began in 1986, and by early 1992 there were at least forty thousand electronic monitors in use (Gowdy).

Electronic monitoring can be active or passive. In active monitoring, a transmitter attached to the offender's wrist or ankle sends signals relayed by a home telephone to the supervising office during the hours the offender is required to be at home. Under passive monitoring, a computer program is used to call the offender randomly during the hours designated for home confinement. The offender inserts the wristlet or anklet into a verifier to confirm her or his presence in the residence. There does not appear to be any difference in recidivism between those on passive or active systems. National surveys indicate that electronic monitoring was initially used for property offenders on probation, but since the 1900s a much broader range of offenders were being monitored than in the past. Monitoring has been expanded to include not only probationers but also to follow up persons after incarceration, to control those sentenced to community corrections, and to monitor persons before trial or sentencing. Recent evaluations in a number of jurisdictions indicate continuing support for electronic monitoring of correctional offenders; however, in terms of changing offender behavior, there is little evidence that electronic monitor without treatment and services, has much effect.

Community residential centers

Formerly known as "halfway houses," *community residential centers* (CRCs) are a valuable adjunct to community control and treatment services. Originally designed as residences for homeless men, they are now seen as a key nucleus of community-based correctional networks of residential centers, drug-free and alcohol-free living space, pre-release guidance centers, and private sector involvement with offenders who have multiple programs and who are in need of intensive services. They also serve as residence facilities for a number of different classes of offenders, most of whom are high-need individuals and pose medium to high risk to reoffend. CRCs are generally intended as an alternative to confinement for persons not suited for probation or for those who need a period of readjustment to the community after imprisonment. Some CRCs specialize by client or treatment modality: women only, abused women, drug-dependent, alcohol abusers, mentally ill, court diagnostic program, developmentally disabled, and so on.

As the foregoing discussion illustrates, it is not possible to describe the average residential facility. Diversity in population, program, size, and structure is the rule. It is, unfortunately, also not possible to know for certain how many such facilities are in operation today, or the number of offenders served by them.

Despite the long tradition of residential community correctional programs, the research literature is both sparse and inconclusive. Most research indicates that offenders in CRCs display greater needs than do regular probation or parole groups. Many of these needs, such as psychiatric and drug/alcohol counseling, are related both to positive adjustment and to new criminal convictions. Offenders in residential facilities are also more likely to receive a variety of treatment and counseling services. It can also be argued that CRCs are more humane that prisons and can serve to lessen the deprivations of incarceration. It appears that residential community correctional facilities will continue to grow and develop new programs. In large part this will be a response to the crowding of local and state correctional institutions.

Restitution

A court-ordered condition of probation known as *restitution* requires the offender to repair the financial, emotional, or physical damage done (a reparative sentence) by making financial payment of money to the victim or, alternatively, to a fund that provides services to victims. Restitution programs may also be ordered in the absence of a sentence to probation. Restitution is usually a cash payment by the offender to the victim of an amount considered to offset the loss incurred by the victim (medical expenses, insurance deductibles, time lost from work due to victim's injuries, etc.). Payments may be made in installments in most jurisdictions, and sometimes services directly or indirectly benefiting the victim may be substituted for cash payments. There is some evidence that restitution programs can serve a "restorative" purpose for victims and thereby reduce recidivism for offenders.

Use of volunteers

Community correctional programs operate under a basic philosophy of reintegration: connecting offenders with legitimate opportunity and reward structures, and generally uniting the offender within the community. It has become quite apparent that the correctional system cannot achieve this without assistance, regardless of the extent of resources available. Reintegration requires the assistance and support of the community. This concept is certainly not a new one. The John Howard Association, the Osborne Association, and other citizen prisoners' aid societies have provided voluntary correctional-type services for many years. The volunteer movement developed in this country in the early 1820s, when a group of citizens known as the Philadelphia Society for Alleviating the Misery of Public Prisons began supervising the activities of inmates upon their release from penal institutions. John Augustus, a Boston shoemaker, who worked with well over two thousand misdemeanants in his lifetime, later adopted this practice.

Volunteerism is alive and well in corrections. Although exact numbers are not known, it is safe to say that there are thousands of volunteers serving more than three thousand jurisdictions nationwide. Proponents of the volunteer concept consider it to be one of the most promising innovations in the field, claiming that it can help alleviate the problem of excessive probation and parole case loads, and contribute to rehabilitation and reintegration goals for the offender. Volunteers can range from student interns to older persons with time to devote. Some volunteers are persons that have a specific skill or talent to contribute, while others give their time and counsel.

Volunteerism generally refers to situations where individual citizens contribute their talents, wisdom, skills, time, and resources within the context of the justice system, without receiving financial remuneration. Volunteer projects operate on the premise that certain types of offenders can be helped by the services a volunteer can offer, and that such services can be provided at a minimal tax dollar cost and can result in significant cost savings. By drawing upon the time, talents, and abilities of volunteers to assist in service delivery, community supervision officers can serve to broaden the nature of the services offered. Any community consists of persons who possess a diverse supply of skills and abilities that can be effectively tapped by volunteer programs.

Effectiveness of community supervision

Despite the widespread use of probation, parole, and other community sanctions there remains debate over the effectiveness of many of these practices. The empirical evidence indicates that some correctional sanctions, such as intensive supervision, electronic monitoring, shock probation, and other control-oriented practices do not reduce recidivism. These sanctions may accomplish other goals, such as reducing prison crowding, but recidivism is usually the most important criteria by which community correctional programs are measured. Other options, such as halfway houses and day reporting centers can be effective in changing offender behavior, provided they deliver high-quality treatment programs and services.

EDWARD J. LATESSA

See also PROBATION AND PAROLE: HISTORY, GOALS, AND DECISION-MAKING; PROBATION AND PAROLE: PROCEDURAL PROTECTION.

BIBLIOGRAPHY

BOWERS, SWITHUM. "The Nature and Definition of Social Casework." In *Principles and Techniques in Social Casework.* Edited by Cora Kasius. New York: Family Services Association of America, 1950. Pages 126–139.

CONRAD, JOHN. "Who Needs a Door Bell Pusher?" *The Prison Journal* 59 (1979):17–26.
FULTON, BETSY; LATESSA, EDWARD J.; STICHMAN, AMY; and TRAVIS, LAWRENCE F. "The State of ISP: Research and Policy Implications." *Federal Probation* 61, no. 4 (1997): 65–75.
GOWDY, VONCILE. *Intermediate Sanctions.* Washington, D.C.: U.S. Department of Justice, 1993.
MCDEVITT, JACK. *Evaluation of the Hampton County Day Reporting Center.* Boston: Crime and Justice Foundation, 1988.
SCHWITZGEBEL, RALPH, K.; SCHWITZGEBEL, ROBERT. L.; PAHNKE, WALTER, N.; and HURD, WILLIAM S. "A Program of Research in Behavioral Electronics." *Behavioral Scientist* 2 (1964): 233–238.
STUDT, ELLIOTT. *Surveillance and Service in Parole.* U.S. Department of Justice: National Institute of Corrections, 1978.

PROSECUTION: COMPARATIVE ASPECTS

In the United States, the prosecutor is probably the most important decision-maker in the criminal process. The impetus to begin a criminal investigation usually emanates from a private complainant, and it is ordinarily the police who conduct the bulk of investigations; but the determinations whether to charge a suspect, what to charge him with, and what sanctions eventually to impose are made or substantially influenced by the prosecutor. The wide scope of American prosecutors' discretionary power has long remained undetected. It became the subject of scholarly discussion only in the 1970s, in the wake of seminal studies (Miller; Davis), and the debate about the need to limit and control prosecutorial discretion intensified in the 1980s when the introduction of limitations on judges' discretion in sentencing shifted even more power to the prosecutor (see Stith and Cabranes, pp. 130–142). Yet, even though express statutory authority is lacking, the existence of broad prosecutorial discretion is still widely accepted as part of the U.S. legal tradition. Several key features of the U.S. system of criminal justice are indeed dependent on prosecutors' freedom of action. Without it, selective enforcement of criminal laws and diversion of marginal offenders from the criminal process would be impossible, and plea bargaining would be likely to disappear. To demand the abolition or even a radical curtailment of prosecutorial discretion would thus not be realistic, and it would moreover not be desirable to have an overly rigid system of criminal justice lacking the prosecutor's office as a filter for those cases which are nominally criminal but, for various reasons, do not merit conviction and punishment.

This does not mean, however, that the American prosecutor's discretionary power should have to remain as broad and uncontrolled as it has traditionally been. In the United States, the fact that the great majority of state prosecutors are elected and thus responsible to the people is widely regarded as sufficient to control their powers. Although this form of control may be useful with respect to overall law enforcement policy, it has little impact on prosecutors' day-to-day decision-making and on their treatment of individual cases. The American prosecutor's political responsibility, which becomes effective only when and if the prosecutor seeks reelection, thus tends to mask the need for more direct limits on his discretionary powers as well as for controls upon decisions the prosecutor and his or her assistants make in individual cases. Foreign legal systems have developed various mechanisms in that regard. In some countries, statutes explicitly limit prosecutors' discretionary authority, and in many legal systems, the prosecutor is subject to various forms of control by courts, victims, or private citizens.

Restrictions on prosecutorial discretion of course do not exist in a vacuum. Their significance depends not only on the allocation of functions within the prosecutorial system but also on, for example, the general orientation of the criminal process ("truth-finding" versus conflict resolution), the relationship between prosecutors and courts, career structures within the prosecution service, case loads, crime rates, historical background, and popular expectations and conceptions of the criminal justice system. Before one makes changes based on a comparative perspective, one should therefore carefully assess the ramifications such changes may have for the system as a whole: even a slight reduction in the present scope of prosecutorial authority may lead to an unforeseen increase in some other agent's formal or informal powers. Only with that caveat in mind should recommendations be based on foreign ways of organizing prosecution, even when foreign models appear to be promising examples of more predictable and equitable ways of administering criminal justice.

This article focuses on the prosecutorial systems of four European countries: Austria, England, France, and Germany. Each of these countries has developed a different mode of organizing and controlling the prosecution function.

Who prosecutes?

In the United States, prosecution—except for the federal system—is organized locally; prosecutors are elected or appointed, frequently on the basis of political preference. By contrast, in Europe the prosecutorial corps is typically structured hierarchically on a nationwide or statewide basis. Prosecutors have the status of civil servants but lack judicial independence. Ultimate responsibility for the selection and appointment of prosecutors resides in a government-level official, usually the minister of justice. Appointment and advancement of local prosecutors are largely independent of political considerations and are based on performance in examinations and on merit in service. Young lawyers usually begin their prosecutorial career soon after completing their legal training, which includes some practical experience as an intern in a criminal court and/or prosecutor's office. Many prosecutors follow the prosecutorial career pattern until retirement. On the Continent, it is quite unusual for a prosecutor to become a private attorney, a law teacher, or a full-time politician.

According to legal theory, the prosecutorial function belongs to the executive branch of government. It is thus the minister of justice who is ultimately responsible for the organization of criminal prosecution. The minister also has the authority (rarely used) to issue general as well as specific instructions to prosecution personnel.

In marked contrast to American prosecutors, their continental counterparts display a strong affinity with the judiciary. They share attitudes and perceptions, and prosecutors see themselves more as detached officers of the law than as partisan advocates. In some countries, it is even customary for a career prosecutor to serve as a judge for a few years, and for a judge who aspires to higher office to do a stint as a prosecutor.

The proximity between the offices of judge and prosecutor in Europe has deep historical roots. In the traditional inquisitorial process, which prevailed on the Continent until the nineteenth century, the judge was responsible for investigating a criminal case as well as for deciding on the guilt or innocence of the defendant. He was thus called upon to determine the sufficiency of his own inquiry. The obvious conflict inherent in that dual role called for a separation of functions. In post-Revolutionary France, the procurator, who had since the Middle Ages represented the fiscal interests of the Crown, was entrusted with the prosecution of crime, thus leaving the trial judge to be a neutral arbiter. In the 1840s, this model spread from France to other European countries. The public prosecutor, who remained the sovereign's servant (and therefore continued to be regarded with due suspicion by many liberals), was created from the rib of the judge.

Several characteristics of the Continental prosecutor can be explained as part of that judicial heritage. In some countries, criminal procedure codes expressly require prosecutors to collect and consider exonerating as well as incriminating evidence (Strafprozessordnung 1960 in der Kundmachung der Wiederverlautbarung vom 9. Dezember 1975, Bundesgesetzblatt für die Republik Österreich 1975, stück 211 [Austrian StPO], para. 3; Strafprozessordnung vom 7. Januar 1975, Bundesgesetzblatt 1975 I, p. 129 [German StPO], para. 160, 2; Codice di procedura penale de 22 settembre 1988, Decreto del Presidente della Repubblica n. 447 [Italian CPP], art. 358), and under the French code the public prosecutor is described as a public officer who to it that justice is done (Code de procedure penale, Loi n. 57–1426 du 31 décembre 1957 [French CPP], art. 31). If it turns out in the course of the trial that the evidence does not support a conviction, the prosecutor is expected to withdraw charges or to ask the court to acquit the defendant. The prosecutor can (but rarely does) even file an appeal on behalf of the defendant if he regards a conviction or a sentence as unjustified (Austrian StPO, para. 282, 1; German StPO, para. 296, 2). The spirit of objectivity makes it easy for the continental prosecutor to assume a quasi-judicial role in pretrial proceedings (Brants and Field, pp. 144–145 [on Dutch prosecutors]; Frase, pp. 613–615: Goldstein and Marcus, pp. 249–250). Austrian and German prosecutors even assume the function of a judge in imposing noncriminal sanctions in return for refraining from pressing charges (see Austrian StPO, paras. 90a–90m; German StPO, para. 153a).

The English system differs strongly from the Continental approach. In theory, at least, any citizen can bring criminal charges (s. 6 (1) Prosecution of Offences Act 1985). In practice, however, it is the police who investigate the bulk of crime and initiate the prosecution by charging the sus-

pect. At that stage, the case is turned over to the Crown Prosecution Service who determine whether to go forward with the prosecution or to refrain from pursuing it further. The Crown Prosecution Service, which was introduced in 1986, bases its decisions on an independent evaluation of the evidence as well as on policy considerations. With respect to the former, prosecutors are limited to reviewing the written materials presented by the police; they do not themselves talk with victims or interrogate witnesses or the defendant (see Ashworth, pp. 160–172). The Crown Prosecutors' discretion in determining the public interest in prosecution is guided by paragraphs 6.4 and 6.5 of the Code for Crown Prosecutors, which offers two sets of legitimate considerations, one pointing toward prosecution, the other indicating a lack of public interest. Examples of factors suggesting nonprosecution are the lack of serious harm caused by the offense, a long delay since its commission, the old age or bad health of the defendant, and the fact that the offender has put right the loss or harm that was caused. As a rule, however, the Crown Prosecution Service go forward with the prosecution whenever there appears to be sufficient evidence to convict (Fionda, p. 24). Because the police will already have weeded out many cases that do not merit criminal sanction or can be resolved by merely cautioning the suspect, and because police files will reflect the police's assessment of the remaining cases as serious (see Brants and Field, pp. 140–143), public interest considerations do not frequently move the Crown Prosecution Service to drop convictable cases. In 1998–1999, the Crown Prosecution Service discontinued 12 percent of prosecutions in Magistrates' Court; in a further substantial percentage of cases, the prosecution did not offer any evidence, thus bringing about a directed acquittal of the accused (Ashworth, pp. 175–176; Sprack, p. 61).

Although the police, in conjunction with the Crown Prosecution Service, are responsible for prosecuting the majority of English cases, about one-quarter of prosecutions are brought by other agencies or by private individuals. The Inland Revenue Department, for example, investigates and prosecutes cases of tax fraud, and the Department of Health and Social Security prosecutes fraudulent benefit claims (see Lidstone, Hogg, and Sutcliffe, pp. 34–94). Prosecutions by individuals are rare except in cases of common assault. When a private individual brings a case before the criminal court, the Crown Prosecution

Service can at any time take over the prosecution, either in order to go forward with it or to discontinue it (ss. 6 (2), 23 Prosecution of Offences Act 1985). The private complainant has no legal recourse against such action (Sprack, p. 62).

Criminal investigation and the prosecutor

When one looks at the relevant law, the Continental prosecutor tends to play a leading role in the investigation process. His formal position depends on whether he is to share this role with the investigating magistrate (*juge d'instruction* in France, *Rechter-Commisaris* in the Netherlands), a judicial officer with a specific mandate to conduct pretrial investigations. But even when that is the case, the prosecutor is entrusted with the investigation of all but the most serious offenses. Although the law describes the prosecutor's role as "conducting" the investigation, the prosecutor generally delegates routine operations to the police. As a result, it is almost invariably the police who are in fact conducting the bulk of criminal investigation.

More specifically, legal arrangements in the three Continental countries treated here are as follows:

In Austria, police and all other public authorities are obliged to report to the prosecutor any suspicion of a criminal offense (Austrian StPO, para. 84). The prosecutor must then follow up on such reports by directing police or an investigating magistrate to obtain further information by interrogating witnesses and securing relevant physical evidence (Austrian StPO, paras. 87, 88). In the most serious cases, which are to be tried before a jury court, the prosecutor will then turn over the investigation to the investigating magistrate, who is responsible for determining whether there is sufficient evidence to make the defendant stand trial. Although the prosecutor is precluded from performing acts of investigation himself, he (as well as the suspect) can request the investigating magistrate to conduct particular acts of investigation (Austrian StPO, para. 97). The prosecutor can at any time terminate the magistrate's investigation by declaring that he no longer wishes to prosecute the case, and he can do so even when the magistrate has returned the file after closing the investigation with the indication that there is sufficient cause to proceed to trial (Austrian StPO, para. 112). The investigating magistrate, on the other hand, can dismiss the case even against the prosecutor's wishes (Austrian StPO, para. 109). The great majority of cases do not require involvement of an investigating magistrate. In these cases, it is the prosecutor who supervises and guides the investigation.

French procedure is similar in many respects. However, the French prosecutor can personally perform acts of investigation; he can, for example, interrogate witnesses and, if a suspect has been caught while committing the offense or soon thereafter, conduct searches and seizures on the spot (French CPP, arts. 54, 56). As is the case in Austria, investigations conducted by magistrates are in practice the exception rather than the rule (see Frase, p. 667), and it is thus the prosecutor who is in charge of investigating all but the most serious criminal cases.

Germany abolished the Office of Investigating Magistrate in 1975 and since that time places full responsibility for pretrial investigations in the hands of the prosecutor. Police are to undertake those investigative measures which are immediately necessary to avoid loss of critical evidence, but they must then report to the prosecutor without delay (German StPO, para. 163). The prosecutor conducts the investigation, calling upon the police for assistance to the extent necessary (German StPO, paras. 160, 161). As in other Continental legal systems, acts involving more serious intrusions into citizens' liberty or privacy (e.g., pretrial detention, wiretaps, and searches and seizures) require judicial permission prior to their execution or, if exigent circumstances made immediate action necessary, subsequent authorization by a magistrate.

The legal situation is somewhat different in England. According to English law, investigation is generally the task of the police, and the members of the Crown Prosecution Service are limited to requesting the police to undertake further investigatory acts if that is deemed necessary. The police are not compelled by law to honor such requests. The advantage of the English model is its clear separation of functions: the police investigate and initiate a prosecution, and the prosecutor makes all further determinations. The drawback of that model is that the prosecutor must accept the results of the investigation as presented to him and is dependent on the goodwill of the police for gathering further information he may regard as necessary for intelligent decision-making.

The Continental model avoids this problem by casting the prosecutor in the role of "conducting" the investigation as well as directing and supervising police activities. Continental laws describe the police in criminal proceedings as subservient to the prosecutor (see, e.g., French CPP, art. 41-2; German StPO, para. 161), and they are thus duty-bound to carry out all investigatory acts the prosecutor demands. The prosecutor's control over police is, at the same time, regarded as a guarantee of the police's adherence to relevant legal rules in pretrial proceedings.

In all Continental systems, however, reality differs from the statutory arrangement described above. In practice, the balance of powers established by the legislature is invariably tilted in favor of the police. At least in routine matters, the police clear up cases completely before even informing the prosecutor of their existence, and prosecutors typically defer to the police with respect to the investigation. This does not necessarily mean, however, that prosecutors always accept the findings of the police without further inquiry. In Germany, it has been found to be quite common for the prosecutor to request police to undertake further investigations if he or she is willing to press charges but perceives a need to obtain additional information to strengthen the position of the prosecution (Steffen, p. 183). Yet it is only in very serious or spectacular cases that the prosecutor actually directs the police investigatory activities or takes the investigation into his or her own hands. German prosecutors may sometimes personally interrogate the victim or an important witness—witnesses are under a legal duty to appear before the prosecutor but need not talk to the police (German StPO, para. 161a)—but even such limited involvement in the investigation usually occurs at the request of the police. According to one German study, prosecutors personally conducted parts of the investigation in only 1–5 percent of the cases (Blankenburg, Sessar, and Steffen, p. 99). The only area in which Continental prosecutors tend to investigate on their own is white-collar crime. Several prosecutor's offices have established departments staffed with lawyers, accountants, and other specialists, which have monopolized the investigation of serious economic crime.

The fact that Continental prosecutors largely abstain from investigation has a significant impact on the allocation of powers in the pretrial process. Although the police lack official authority to dismiss cases, there is strong evidence that they can and do predetermine prosecutorial decision-making by the amount of investigative effort they invest in particular types of offenses.

The police, moreover, collect and electronically store large amounts of information on crime and offenders, and they often shield this information even from prosecutors. As most Continental prosecutors are unable or unwilling to counteract such police strategies, prosecutors' impact on the case flow from detection of an offense to its adjudication is merely negative: they can screen out cases previously "cleared" by the police, but they cannot restore cases lost through strategic decisions of the police or through insufficient police work.

To a large extent, this state of affairs is inevitable because the police monopolize the manpower, expertise, information, and equipment necessary for successful investigation. Yet the possibilities of controlling police decision-making in the area of crime detection and investigation ought to be further explored. Because prosecution policy is heavily dependent on the allocation and deployment of police resources, these matters should not be left to ad hoc determination by police chiefs or individual officers. A thorough restructuring of decision-making and control processes in criminal investigations may well be necessary. Such reforms would have to start with accepting the fact that prosecutors do not conduct or even direct investigations. Shedding the fiction of prosecutorial domination of the investigation process might be the key to a realistic and feasible definition of the prosecutor's role. This role should primarily be supervisory. It could have the following features: police inform the prosecutor as early as possible of each prima facie plausible report or complaint of an offense; the prosecutor may give general or specific advice but leaves the conduct of the investigation to the police, who in turn make continuously available all relevant information to the prosecutor and confer with him when major strategic or tactical decisions have to be made. When the police deem the investigation complete, they submit their findings, and the prosecutor can demand further information if necessary. The decision whether to prosecute should be the prosecutor's alone.

The decision to prosecute

The crucial function of the prosecutor in any legal system is to determine which cases should be brought before the court for adjudication and which should be disposed of in other ways. In all legal systems, the prosecutor has some leeway in making this decision, yet the amount of freedom the prosecutor enjoys differs. American law grants the prosecutor almost unlimited discretion, whereas some European legal systems are considerably less liberal.

Discretion to dismiss. Because prosecutors do not in fact control criminal investigations, they receive from police many cases as "cleared" although the suspect's legal guilt is doubtful or sufficient evidence for establishing his responsibility in court is lacking. It would not only be a waste of judicial resources but would also be unfair to the suspect to make him stand trial if a conviction is unlikely. The prosecutor therefore has the important task of independently assessing the legal and factual circumstances of each case as well as the available evidence. He should dismiss as early as possible cases that cannot be successfully prosecuted. Standards of evidence required for preferring charges are formulated in different ways. A representative formulation might be that of the English Code for Crown Prosecutors, which proposes that charges should be brought only if there is a reasonable prospect of conviction, that is, if conviction is more likely than acquittal (Code for Crown Prosecutors, para. 5; see Ashworth, pp. 161–168).

Determining the chances of conviction implies predicting the behavior of decision-makers, that is, of the professional and/or lay judges comprising the court of first instance. Although the "prospect" test may be phrased objectively, that is, whether a "reasonable" court following the law would tend to convict, the prosecutor needs to make a prediction based on his or her personal assessment of the possible outcome of a trial—an assessment that is inevitably colored by the individual prosecutor's degree of confidence and willingness to take risks. This individual judgment on the strength of the prosecution case should, however, be distinguished from the concept of prosecutorial discretion. The prosecutor exercises discretion, in its proper sense, only when he or she regards the suspect's conviction as likely and yet refrains from filing charges. Discretion thus does not refer to the sufficiency of the evidence but is based on considerations of policy. The American system broadly permits discretionary dismissals of convictable cases and thereby casts the prosecutor in the role of an independent policymaker. In other systems, decisions on criminal policy are regarded as the exclusive domain of the legislature, and the prosecutor's task is consequently limited to determining the sufficiency of the evidence. One possible way of restricting or even eliminating prosecu-

torial discretion is adoption of the principle of "mandatory" prosecution. This principle, which is still recognized in a number of European systems (in Italy, the prosecutor's duty to file charges whenever there is sufficient evidence is even enshrined in art. 112 of the constitution), seeks to ensure the equal application of the criminal law by mandating its full enforcement. The law denies the prosecutor authority to make exceptions in individual cases, thus precluding favoritism or considerations of political partisanship. The source of this principle can be found in the nineteenth-century reformers' distrust of public prosecutors' impartiality—at that time, prosecutors were still regarded as obedient servants of the government, prone to abuse their power for political purposes.

Austrian law is an example of a system based on the principle of mandatory prosecution. The code of criminal procedure requires the prosecutor to do everything necessary to bring about the conviction of an offender whenever the prosecutor has received information of a criminal offense. Exceptions apply only to crimes committed abroad and to multiple offenses committed by one individual; in the latter case, the less serious charges need not be brought (Austrian StPO, para. 34). The law precludes the prosecutor from dismissing charges simply because he or she regards the case as unimportant or because the offender does not seem to merit punishment. Since 1999, the prosecutor can, however, withhold prosecution if the offender's guilt is not significant and the suspect made restitution to the victim or a payment to the state or did community service (Austrian StPO, para. 90a). This provision significantly limits the practical impact of the mandatory prosecution principle. Even before the introduction of the option of conditional dismissal, however, Austrian prosecutors did not in fact prosecute each and every criminal offense. One way to avoid wasting resources on trifles has been opened by a provision of the criminal code that permits the court to acquit the defendant when the offense does not merit punishment, especially in view of the fact that the offender had made restitution to the victim (Strafgesetzbuch der Republik Österreich of 1975, para. 42). If the conditions of this provision are met, the prosecutor can anticipate the court's decision and refrain from prosecution on the theory that the suspect would not eventually be convicted. In other cases, the prosecutor may conceal what is in effect a discretionary dismissal behind the label of "insufficient evidence"—he or she may cite doubts regarding the suspect's criminal intent or may decline to make the police follow up on an incomplete investigation (Driendl, pp. 254, 280–283; but see Nowakowski, pp. 272–275). Recognition of the principle of mandatory prosecution does thus, in effect, not preclude Austrian prosecutors from concentrating their resources on serious cases and from avoiding prosecution of even slightly doubtful minor offenses.

In Germany, the first nationwide Code of Criminal Procedure of 1877 (Strafprozessordnung vom 1. Februar 1877. Reichsgesetzblatt 1877) introduced the principle of mandatory prosecution, which can still be found in the actual version of the Code (German StPO, para. 152, 2). In the meantime, however, practical considerations led to the recognition of a growing number of exceptions (Frase and Weigend, pp. 337–339). The most important of these exceptions concerns "minor" offenses, that is, those with a statutory minimum sentence of less than one year imprisonment. With respect to these offenses—which comprise the great majority of cases reported to the police—the prosecutor can refrain from filing charges whenever the offender's guilt is "minor" and prosecution is not in the public interest (German StPO, para. 153). The prosecutor also has the option of imposing certain obligations on the suspect as conditions of nonprosecution; such obligations can be, for example, payments to be made to the victim or to a charitable organization (German StPO, para. 153a, see below). Further exceptions from the principle of mandatory prosecution exist for offenses committed abroad (German StPO, para. 153c), and for (even serious) offenses directed against interests of the state when prosecution and public trial might cause additional harm to these interests (German StPO, para. 153d). If the suspect is alleged to have committed more than one offense, the prosecutor can limit prosecution to the most serious charge and drop all others (German StPO, para. 154). Taken together, these exceptions almost seem to swallow the rule. German prosecutors are under an unqualified duty to prosecute convictable offenses only if the suspect has committed a serious felony with a statutory minimum penalty of one year imprisonment, such as murder, robbery, rape, or arson.

In fact, prosecutors make extensive use of their authority to dismiss cases on policy grounds. In 1996, prosecutors brought charges in only twenty-eight of one hundred cases in which the police were able to name a suspect. Twenty-seven out of one hundred cases were dismissed for lack of sufficient evidence, twenty-one cases were not prosecuted because there was no "public interest," and in six cases there was a conditional dismissal under para. 153a Code of Criminal Procedure (Statistisches Bundesamt, p. 118). (Eighteen out of one hundred cases were disposed of in other ways, for example, by referral to juvenile court or administrative proceedings.) Most German prosecutors nevertheless assume that prosecution should be the rule, at least with respect to non-trifle offenses. They actually welcome the principle of mandatory prosecution as a shield against pressure from outside. Yet they use their discretionary authority to get rid of the "small fry" that would only clog the court system without leading to significant sanctions.

The French Code of Criminal Procedure does not explicitly determine whether the prosecutor has discretion or is duty-bound to submit cases with sufficient evidence to the court. Yet Art. 40 CCP, which simply states that the prosecutor "receives complaints and denunciations and decides how to proceed," has generally been interpreted to confer broad discretion upon the prosecutor (Pradel, pp. 345–346). If the prosecutor does not wish to prefer charges, he or she simply lays the file aside, and prosecution can be resumed at any time. The code does not contain any guidelines on the exercise of prosecutorial discretion. Policy reasons that may prompt French prosecutors to dismiss convictable cases include restitution made to the victim, triviality of the offense, and availability of noncriminal sanctions (Frase, pp. 614–615). Prosecutors have formal authority to conditionally dismiss certain charges.

In England, both police and prosecutors have broad discretion whether to bring and sustain charges. Whereas police discretion is not formalized save by standing orders on a local level, the Code for Crown Prosecutors contains a list of considerations prosecutors are to take into account when determining whether to go forward with a case presented by the police. As a general guideline, the code states that prosecution in cases of any seriousness shall usually take place unless there are public interest factors against prosecution that clearly outweigh those tending in favor (Code for Crown Prosecutors, sec. 6.2). The list of factors suggesting a decision in favor of prosecution mainly contains criteria relating to the seriousness of the offense (for example, premeditation, a particularly vulnerable victim), whereas factors disfavoring prosecution include insignificant harm, expectation of a small penalty, negative effects of the prosecution on the victim's mental or physical health, and compensation paid by the defendant to the victim (Code for Crown Prosecutors, secs. 6.4, 6.5).

This brief overview shows that statutory rules and principles make little difference for actual prosecution practice. Prosecutors tend to follow simple rules of reason; they enforce the law vigorously with respect to serious crime, but they are selective in prosecuting minor offenses, giving due regard to characteristics of the offender and the victim as well as to noncriminal alternatives, most prominently restitution.

Informal sanctions. In many systems, prosecutorial discretion extends beyond the simple alternative between prosecution and complete inaction. Informal noncriminal sanctions are often imposed on suspects as a condition of nonprosecution. In the United States, such practices are known as pretrial diversion.

In the three Continental systems considered in this entry, the law authorizes the prosecutor to propose to the suspect that he fulfil certain obligations in exchange for having his case dismissed (Austrian StPO, paras. 90a–90m; French CPP, art. 41-1–41-3; German StPO, para. 153a). If the suspect consents and complies with these obligations, he will not be prosecuted. The theory of these provisions is that the suspect, by accepting and fulfilling the obligations, eliminates the necessity of punishment because the purposes of punishment (deterrence and/or rehabilitation) have already been met (see Burgstaller, p. 12). In the Austrian, French, and German systems, possible obligations include payments to the state or to a charitable organization (these are in practice imposed most frequently), restitution payments to the victim, and community work. In France, the suspect can also be required to give up his driver's license for a period of four months or less, or to turn over to the state objects that had been used in committing the offense (French CPP, art. 41-2). When the suspect has fulfilled the obligations he can no longer be prosecuted for the offense of which he had been suspected. While these features are identical in all three systems, rules differ as to the need for judicial consent to the prosecutor's disposition. In France, the president of the court has to ratify any agreement between the suspect and the prosecutor's office (French CPP, art. 41-2, 6); in Germany, judicial consent must be obtained (but is almost

never withheld) only when the offense is fairly serious; in Austria, the prosecutor can impose the statutorily authorized conditions for dismissal without involving the court.

When the option of "conditional dismissal" was first introduced in Germany in 1975, the new law was heavily criticized on the grounds that it shifted sentencing power from the judiciary to the prosecutor and that undue pressure was put on the suspect to comply with the prosecutor's offer even when he was in fact innocent or when his guilt could not have been proven at trial. This criticism has since subsided in view of the overwhelming practicality of this instrument. As noted above, prosecutors employ this diversionary tool on a regular basis (see Weigend) and have even extended its use to large-scale white-collar crime where required payments sometimes reach extremely high amounts. The fact that Austria and France have adopted similar models in 1999 seems to indicate that the idea of prosecutorial sanctioning, in spite of its interference with the traditional judicial monopoly on sentencing, has internationally been regarded as a sensible way of disposing of minor cases.

In England, conditional dismissal of charges has not yet been adopted for adult suspects. The widespread practice of police cautioning, which consists of giving the suspect a formalized warning that his or her criminal conduct will not be tolerated further (Sprack, pp. 65–66), does not imply any immediate consequences for the individual concerned. Introduction of cautioning plus informal sanctions has been discussed, but it seems that such practice would be acceptable only if it was placed in the hands of a public prosecutor, not the police (Brants and Field, pp. 139–143; Fionda, pp. 39–40).

Discretion to select charges. One important aspect of prosecutorial discretion in the common law systems is the prosecutor's power to select the legal charges he brings against the defendant. To most instances of criminal conduct, more than one section of the criminal code can be applied, and each section may provide for a different measure of punishment. By choosing the amount and nature of charges, the American prosecutor often predetermines to some extent the sentence the defendant receives if convicted. For that reason, the selection of charges frequently plays an important role in the prosecutor's negotiations with defense counsel about the conditions of a guilty plea.

The inquisitorial structure of Continental criminal procedure makes it impossible for the prosecutor to bind the court by his legal assessment of the case. The formal accusation filed by the prosecutor determines the scope of the court's inquiry only with respect to the factual situation (person of the suspect, time, and place of the conduct in question); that is, the court cannot punish the defendant for conduct on an occasion not mentioned in the formal accusation. But the court remains free to apply provisions of the law other than those cited by the prosecutor (Austrian StPO, para. 262; French CPP, art. 351; German StPO, para. 155, 2). Any "bargaining" that may occur in Continental systems thus cannot relate to the prosecutor's charge but must go directly to the sentence to be imposed by the court.

In England, courts are bound by the legal charges brought, yet they can convict for a lesser offense included (expressly or by implication) in the offense charged (Criminal Law Act 1967, sec. 6).

Control of discretion. The American system of prosecution relies almost exclusively on the political responsibility of prosecutors and provides few other checks on their discretionary powers. In Europe, two means of confining and controlling prosecutorial discretion exist: private prosecution and court supervision. Both are of interest especially insofar as they limit the prosecutor's inconspicuous power not to prosecute.

Private prosecution. Private prosecution has historically been the primary form of prosecution. In most legal systems, prosecution by an agent of the state has gradually superseded private prosecution. Yet the victim's (or any citizen's) right to bring criminal charges can serve as a check on the public prosecutor's inaction, and many modern legal systems provide for this possibility.

In England, private prosecution still forms the theoretical basis of the prosecution system. But in practice only a minuscule portion of prosecutions is actually brought by private citizens (see above). This is not surprising because private citizens typically lack the financial means and legal expertise necessary to launch successful prosecutions. Private prosecutions are further discouraged by the fact that the Crown Prosecution Service can at any time take the prosecution away from the private citizen and terminate it. The citizen has no legal remedy against this measure.

In Germany and Austria, some criminal offenses are labeled "private prosecution offenses" and can be brought to trial by the victim without any involvement of the public prosecutor. These offenses include slander, breach of confidentiality, and, in Germany, simple assault and trespass (Austrian StPO, paras. 2 and 46; German StPO, para. 374). In Germany, the public prosecutor can at any time take over the proceedings, and the court can dismiss the case if it deems the defendant's guilt to be minor (German StPO, paras. 377, 2 and 383, 2). For the same reasons as in England, private prosecutions in Austria and Germany are infrequently brought (in 1996, only 0.2 percent of German prosecutions were initiated by private individuals; Statistisches Bundesamt, p. 84), and even less often lead to conviction. The private prosecutor must gather and present evidence without assistance from the police, he must in some cases attempt reconciliation with the offender before he can bring charges (German StPO, para. 380), and he runs the incalculable risk of dismissal, with costs, in court. The public prosecutor, on the other hand, can remain inactive with respect to offenses subject to private prosecution, which is thus largely inefficient as a control mechanism.

A different approach is to accord the victim the right to request a judicial investigation. This model exists both in Austrian and in French law. In Austria, the victim can appear as a "subsidiary prosecutor" whenever the public prosecutor has declined to open a formal investigation or has closed it without filing charges, claiming lack of evidence. The victim can, however, not bring the case directly to trial but is limited to requesting an investigating magistrate to conduct or continue an investigation. The victim cannot insist on prosecution when the prosecutor has decreed a conditional dismissal (see above) (Austrian StPO, para. 48). French law goes one step further by permitting any victim personally harmed by the offense to declare himself or herself a "civil party" (*partie civile*) and to set in motion a public prosecution (French CPP, arts. 1,2 and 2). The victim can do so by requesting the investigating magistrate to conduct an investigation (French CPP, art. 85) or, with respect to less serious offenses within the jurisdiction of the correctional or police court, by directly submitting his or her claim to that court (French CPP, art. 388). In either case, the public prosecutor is compelled to join in the victim's suit. The victim can thus initiate the criminal process without bearing sole responsibility for collecting the evidence necessary for conviction. This far-reaching right was originally limited to individual victims; since the 1980s, the right to act as *partie civile* in criminal proceedings has been extended to a large number of organizations dedicated to supporting victims of crime.

Court supervision. The prosecutor's affirmative decision to file criminal charges is always reviewable by a court. In most legal systems, summary judicial review of the strength of prosecution evidence is available even before the defendant is required to stand trial; in the absence of such review, the truth of the accusation is in any event tested in the trial itself. The defendant cannot claim, however, that the prosecutor should have refrained from filing charges on the basis of his or her discretionary authority.

Judicial review is limited with respect to the prosecutor's decision not to act. German law gives a victim who had reported the offense to the police the right to appeal to the appellate court when the prosecutor has declined prosecution on evidentiary grounds. If the court finds, on the basis of the victim's brief and the prosecutor's file, that sufficient grounds for prosecution exist, it orders the prosecutor to bring charges. The complaining victim can then join the prosecution as a "supplementary prosecutor" (German StPO, paras. 171–175 and 395, 1). The court cannot, however, review a prosecutor's refusal to prosecute if it was based on policy grounds.

Such review may be available in England. In a number of decisions since the 1960s, the Court of Appeal indicated that it was willing to review decisions not to bring prosecutions if the victim could establish that the decision in question was unreasonable (Ashworth, pp. 188–189, citing cases).

Granting the victim access to the courts for the purpose of checking the appropriateness of a prosecutor's decision not to go forward appears to be a more effective control on prosecutorial decision-making than requiring victims to bring a private prosecution. Meaningful review would, however, require that the prosecutor state in writing the general rules that guide the exercise of his discretion.

THOMAS WEIGEND

See also ADVERSARY SYSTEM; COMPARATIVE CRIMINAL LAW AND ENFORCEMENT: CHINA; COMPARATIVE CRIMINAL LAW AND ENFORCEMENT: ENGLAND AND WALES; COMPARATIVE CRIMINAL LAW AND ENFORCEMENT: ISLAM; COMPARATIVE CRIMINAL LAW AND ENFORCEMENT: RUSSIA; CRIMINAL LAW REFORM: EUROPE; CRIMINAL LAW REFORM: ENGLAND; CRIMINAL PROCEDURE: COMPARATIVE ASPECTS.

BIBLIOGRAPHY

ASHWORTH, ANDREW. *The Criminal Process. An Evaluative Study.* Oxford, U.K.: Clarendon Press, 1994.

BLANKENBURG, ERHARD; SESSAR, KLAUS; and STEFFEN, WIEBKE. *Die Staatsanwaltschaft im Prozess strafrechtlicher Sozialkontrolle.* Berlin: Duncker und Humblot, 1978.

BRANTS, CHRISTJE, and FIELD, STEWART. "Discretion and Accountability in Prosecution." In *Criminal Justice in Europe.* Edited by Phil Fennell, Christopher Harding, Nico Joerg, and Bert Swart. Oxford, U.K.: Clarendon Press, 1994. Pages 127–148.

BURGSTALLER, MANFRED. "Über die Bedeutung der neuen Diversionsregelungen für das österreichische Strafrecht." In *Diversion. Ein anderer Umgang mit Straftaten.* Edited by Roland Miklau and Hans Valentin Schroll. Vienna: Verlag Österreich, 1999. Pages 11–18.

DAVIS, KENNETH C. *Discretionary Justice: A Preliminary Inquiry.* Baton Rouge: Louisiana State University Press, 1969.

DRIENDL, JOHANNES. "Staatsanwaltschaft und Strafverfolgung in Österreich." *Funktion und Tätigkeit der Anklagebehörde im ausländischen Recht.* Edited by Hans-Heinrich Jescheck and Rudolf Leibinger. Baden-Baden: Nomos, 1979. Pages 191–327.

FIONDA, JULIA. *Public Prosecutors and Discretion: A Comparative Study.* Oxford, U.K.: Clarendon Press, 1995.

FRASE, RICHARD S. "Comparative Criminal Justice as a Guide to American Law Reform: How Do the French Do It, How Can We Find Out, and Why Should We Care?" *California Law Review* 78 (1990): 539–683.

FRASE, RICHARD S., and WEIGEND, THOMAS "German Criminal Justice as a Guide to American Law Reform: Similar Problems, Better Solutions?" *Boston College International and Comparative Law Review* 18 (1995): 317–360.

GOLDSTEIN, ABRAHAM S., and MARCUS, MARTIN. "The Myth of Judicial Supervision in Three 'Inquisitorial' Systems: France, Italy, and Germany." *Yale Law Journal* 87 (1977): 240–283.

KOCK, GERALD L., and FRASE, RICHARD S. *The French Code of Criminal Procedure.* Translated from French by Gerald L. Kock and Richard S. Frase. Littleton: Rothman, 1988.

LIDSTONE, K. W.; HOGG, RUSSELL; and SUTCLIFFE, FRANK. *Prosecutions by Private Individuals and Non-Police Agencies.* Royal Commission on Criminal Procedure, Research Study No. 10. London: Her Majesty's Stationery Office, 1980.

MILLER, FRANK W. *Prosecution: The Decision to Charge a Suspect with a Crime.* Edited by Frank J. Remington. Boston: Little, Brown, 1970.

NOWAKOWSKI, FRIEDRICH. "Die Behandlung der Bagatellkriminalität in Österreich." *Zeitschrift für die gesamte Strafrechtswissenschaft* 92 (1980): 255–294.

PRADEL, JEAN. *Droit penal. Procedure penale,* 9th ed. Paris: Cujas, 1997.

SPRACK, JOHN. *Emmins on Criminal Procedure,* 8th ed. London: Blackstone Press, 2000.

Statistisches Bundesamt. *Rechtspflege. Fachserie 10, Reihe 2: Zivilgerichte und Strafgerichte 1996.* Stuttgart: Metzler-Poeschel, 1997.

STEFFEN, WIEBKE. *Analyse polizeilicher Ermittlungstätigkeit aus der Sicht des späteren Strafverfahrens.* Wiesbaden: Bundeskriminalamt, 1976.

STITH, KATE, and CABRANES, JOSE A. *Fear of Judging: Sentencing Guidelines in the Federal Courts.* Chicago: University of Chicago Press, 1998.

WEIGEND, THOMAS. "In Germany, Fines often Imposed in lieu of Prosecution." *Intermediate Sanctions in Overcrowded Times.* Edited by Michael H. Tonry and Kate Hamilton. New York: Oxford University Press, 1995. Pages 50–55.

PROSECUTION: HISTORY OF THE PUBLIC PROSECUTOR

There are several systems of criminal prosecution in the Western world, each distinguished in substantial part by the extent to which a public prosecutor decides whether crime should be charged. In England, any member of the public may prosecute but the attorney general has complete authority to dismiss the charge, and most prosecutions are conducted by the local police. In continental Europe, the initiative lies almost entirely with the state, acting through a public prosecutor or an investigating magistrate; charging discretion is said to be nonexistent or subject to judicial review. American criminal prosecution is a hybrid. Like continental systems, it is an institutionalized and public function; like its English ancestor, it places extraordinary emphasis on local autonomy and charging discretion.

It is misleading, however, to refer to *an* American system of prosecution because there are fifty-one and more such systems in the United States—one for the federal government and one for each of the states, with the state systems in turn comprised of many subsystems. Typically, state prosecution is organized along county lines under the direction of an elected and au-

tonomous prosecutor, variously designated as county attorney, district attorney, or state attorney. Only rarely is he part of a statewide department of justice. State police, too, have limited functions; the bulk of law enforcement is carried on by the cities and towns, each of which has its own police force. In these fragmented and non-hierarchical systems, the power of the county attorney to determine whether charges should be filed or dismissed has made him the critical link between the state's criminal code, its judicial system, and local police forces.

At first glance, the federal government has a structure that is more reminiscent of the national systems that are typical in continental Europe. The Attorney General of the United States is the chief federal prosecutor and heads the Department of Justice, which includes the Federal Bureau of Investigation and ninety-one United States attorneys, each supervising offices in a federal judicial district and prosecuting federal crime in that district. In practice, however, the United States attorney is independent of all but nominal supervision—the result of strong centrifugal elements that are rooted in the nature of the American federal system, the vast distances subject to federal criminal law, and the strong tradition of local law enforcement.

This entry will discuss how English and Western European patterns evolved in the United States into a distinctively American system of criminal justice, characterized in the states by an autonomous local public prosecutor endowed with virtually exclusive authority to prosecute and, in most places, elected by the people.

British and colonial origins

In the seventeenth and eighteenth centuries, a system of private prosecution prevailed in England. No public official was designated as a public prosecutor, either locally or nationally, although the local justice of the peace sometimes assumed the role. The attorney general of England could initiate prosecutions but did so only in cases of special importance to the Crown. He did, however, play an occasional part in controlling the excesses of private prosecution. By filing a writ of *nolle prosequi*, indicating his intention not to prosecute, he could dismiss any prosecution and his decisions in such matters were treated by the courts as entirely within his discretion.

Criminal procedure in the American colonies tended to follow this pattern. There was an attorney general in each colony, the first appointed in Virginia in 1643. Like their English counterparts, the American attorneys general could represent the Crown in both civil and criminal cases but left criminal prosecution largely to the victim. This system of private prosecution proved even more poorly suited to the needs of the new society than to the older one. Grand jurors were often in need of professional guidance and complainants were easily deterred by the difficulty and expense of conducting their own prosecutions, particularly when the distances to be traveled between settlement and colonial capital were great and communications rudimentary. Moreover, the severe criminal sanctions of the period were powerful spurs to abuse of the judicial system—by victims initiating prosecution to exert pressure for financial reparation, and by offenders avoiding criminal sanctions by settling their cases privately.

As population and crime increased, the single criminal court in each colony, and the sole attorney general, were replaced by county courts and by county attorneys attached to each court. This occurred as early as 1704 in Connecticut. These county prosecutors came to be regarded as local officials rather than as agents of a central colonial authority. In their counties, they were treated as if they were attorneys general and the prosecuting role of the colony's attorney general became a vestigial one.

While public prosecution was superimposed on private prosecution in most colonies, it emerged more directly in others, especially in areas that had been settled by the Dutch in the seventeenth century. In these settlements—constituting New Netherlands and counties of parts of what are now Connecticut, New York, New Jersey, Pennsylvania, and Delaware—the Dutch brought public prosecution with them. Prosecutions were conducted by an official called a *schout*. When the British took New York from the Dutch in 1664, criminal prosecution remained much as it had been under the Dutch administration, except that the *schout* was replaced by a sheriff.

In the British colonies of the Middle Atlantic seaboard, therefore, public prosecution was a practice that had been introduced either by a continental predecessor or was an expression of local self-government, replacing a system of private prosecution that was viewed as inefficient, elitist, and sometimes vindictive. It is impossible to say whether the movement to public prosecution reflected, in addition, a desire on the part of Scottish, French, and Swedish settlers to follow the systems they knew in their countries of origin.

In any event, by the time of the American Revolution, each colony had some form of public prosecution exercised on a local basis. In many instances, a dual pattern was established within the same geographical area, by county attorneys for violations of state law and by town prosecutors for ordinance violations. This pattern was carried over into the states as they became part of the new nation. The federal system of prosecution at first followed the state pattern with authority to "prosecute in each district" for federal crimes vested in local United States district attorneys appointed by the president. Not until the Civil War broke out in 1861 did Congress give the Attorney General of the United States "superintendence and direction of United States Attorneys" and lay the foundation for the United States Department of Justice.

The prosecutor as an elected local official

In the early years of the republic, the prosecuting attorney was a minor judicial official. Only five of the first thirteen state constitutions refer to an attorney general, and all include the office in the judicial, rather than the executive, article. Sometimes he was separately referred to in statutory provisions establishing a state's judicial system. The transformation of the prosecutor from a minor functionary of the local court to a powerful member of the executive branch began in the 1820s with the rise of Jacksonian democracy. During this period, the limited democracy of the early republic was supplanted by a system of extensive franchise and popular election of officials, including judges. With the election of local judges came the election of the local prosecutor. Today, there are only a few states in which prosecutors are appointed, usually by the governor. Although the attorney general in some states retains a theoretical right to prosecute, or to supervise or displace local prosecutors, the authority is so rarely exercised as to lose practical significance.

Local election of prosecutors originated as an incident of the election of judges, but it did not disappear when such elections were abandoned in most states. At the very time it was concluded that the need to stand for election could not be reconciled with "judicial" impartiality, local election was said to make the prosecutor more truly a "lawyer for the people." In time, his roots in local politics made him a more powerful figure than the local judge. Courts continued to describe him as a quasi-judicial official—more than a "mere adversary"—but he was viewed increasingly as an executive, rather than a judicial, figure. This perception was reflected in the new state constitutions, which now listed him as a member of the executive branch, along with other officials of local government.

This politically based and decentralized system was subjected to its most severe criticism in the 1920s and 1930s, when criminal laws proliferated in an effort to deal with increasingly heterogeneous populations, more complex societal phenomena, and more crime. Crime surveys of the period revealed that most prosecutors were elected for a short term, their assistants were usually underpaid political appointees, and many were employed only part-time. The office was found to suffer too often from incompetence, corruption, and political opportunism.

Nevertheless, there has been little inclination to abandon the system of elected local prosecutors. Direct accountability to the people has been treated as a virtue in an increasingly bureaucratic society. Reliance has been placed on other measures to improve efficiency and raise the level of accountability, chief among them the movement to full-time prosecutors and a greater emphasis on professionalism. In addition, criminal activity transcending county lines has led to greater efforts at coordination among local prosecutors, to vesting the attorney general of the state with specified prosecuting functions, and, on occasion, to the creation of statewide special prosecutors. The federal government, too, has expanded its role in dealing with "local" crime. Through statutes enacted under the commerce and other federal powers, many of which overlap state criminal laws, the local United States attorney can often step in to remedy grosser forms of local inaction, undercharging, corruption, or incompetence.

A monopoly of the power to prosecute

In the United States it is commonly assumed that the district attorney has exclusive authority to initiate the formal charge of crime. The police may not proceed to trial on their own, and only in the most extraordinary cases may grand juries do so. Even then, the prosecutor may ordinarily dismiss the charge. Nevertheless, vestiges of private prosecution remain on the statute books and in practice, as is to be expected in a system rooted in the English system of private prosecution.

During the colonial period, public prosecutors had no exclusive rights in the criminal courts, and judges did not hesitate to appoint counsel for the Crown when the attorney general refused or neglected to proceed. Even when public prosecutors began to displace private prosecution in the new nation, they were rarely given an explicit monopoly of the power to prosecute.

Gradually, however, the sense of a public stake in criminal prosecution grew larger. This was because private prosecutors were perceived as inherently partisan, criminal law was being used to serve regulatory purposes in which private parties might have only a limited interest, and public prosecutors were regarded as better qualified to make impartial evaluations of evidentiary sufficiency and public necessity. The issue took legal form in cases raising the question of whether a private party—for example, the victim—could conduct a prosecution if the public prosecutor refused or neglected to file a charge.

Several states have retained the private complainant's right to prosecute or to complain directly to a grand jury, but the trend has been toward placing control in the hands of the district attorney. However, some courts have adopted an intermediate approach. They permit a private attorney to assist the public prosecutor in preparation and trial if the court or the prosecutor consents and if the public prosecutor retains control. Appellate courts have invoked the fiction of "delegation" in order to sustain convictions in which public prosecutors have played little or no part. Especially in minor criminal cases, the concept of delegation has been stretched as public prosecutors facing crowded dockets have acquiesced in prosecution by private counsel.

The independence of the public prosecutor

The local district attorney enjoys an unusual degree of independence, not only from administrative superiors in a statewide system but from judges and grand juries as well. Over the years, the courts have reinforced his independence by allowing him a degree of "discretion" that contrasts dramatically with the control they have exercised over official action much less familiar to them. When victims have tried to compel prosecution on the ground that the district attorney was neglecting their and the public's interest, the courts have said the victims lack "standing," as in *Linda R.S. v. Richard D.*, 410 U.S. 614, 619 (1973). When statutes or court rules require judicial approval for dismissing or reducing a charge or accepting a guilty plea, matters have generally been left to the prosecutor.

The concept of an expansive prosecutorial discretion traces to the body of law that dealt not with the initiation of a charge by the prosecutor but with its termination by filing a writ of *nolle prosequi*. The writ had existed in England since the sixteenth century, but there it was the attorney general of England who could intervene and dismiss charges if they were frivolous or insubstantial, or if they might somehow interfere with a Crown prosecution. Though private prosecution has virtually disappeared in the United States, and the local district attorney has a virtual monopoly of the power to prosecute, the *nolle* has remained with him, on the assumption that he inherited the prerogatives of the attorney general of England. Through it, he has been able to dispose of criminal cases without trial and without review. If he could dismiss at will, it has been assumed that he alone could choose to initiate prosecution or not to do so.

The use of the *nolle* attracted relatively little attention until the early twentieth century. But in the 1920s, as the political nature of the office became evident, attacks were directed at the evils of selective prosecution and nonenforcement associated with the county attorney's unlimited power. By 1930, thirty-one states had responded to the criticism and had adopted some form of judicial control (*Criminal Procedure*, pp. 895–897). But the new statutes and rules, which required prosecutors to file motions for dismissal and which authorized courts to grant or deny the motion, have had remarkably little impact. The courts have not often asked for explanations or examined carefully those that were given.

Judicial reluctance to intrude on the dismissal power was based on several factors. The courts felt constrained by the constitutional doctrine of separation of powers. And they feared that they might be drawn into administrative considerations beyond their competence. Less often articulated but perhaps more important, the prosecutor's discretion played a critical role in producing the guilty pleas that accounted for most criminal convictions. If courts had pressed to the limit their authority to pass on the dismissal of charges, they would have had to begin a process of appraising the relation between charging discretion and guilty pleas, many of which are entered because the defendant expects he will gain some advantage from sparing the government the need to prove him guilty.

Until 1970, that course was not a viable option because the courts had left the guilty plea, and the practices underlying it, almost entirely to the parties. In 1970, however, the Supreme Court for the first time acknowledged the legitimacy of plea bargaining (*Brady v. United States*, 397 U.S. 742 (1970)) and set the stage for some judicial review of that hitherto invisible process. Since then, courts and law reformers have had to consider the implications of allowing a public prosecutor—caught up in the "competitive enterprise of ferreting out crime"—to administer virtually unchecked a system of charging, dismissals, and guilty pleas. This trend has been augmented by the emergence of a victims' rights movement that would restore to victims some role in controlling the degree to which public prosecutors act as their surrogates in these matters.

ABRAHAM S. GOLDSTEIN

See also ADVERSARY SYSTEM; CRIMINAL JUSTICE PROCESS; CRIMINAL PROCEDURE: COMPARATIVE ASPECTS; PROSECUTION: COMPARATIVE ASPECTS; PROSECUTION: PROSECUTORIAL DISCRETION; PROSECUTION: UNITED STATES ATTORNEY.

BIBLIOGRAPHY

AMERICAN LAW INSTITUTE. *Code of Criminal Procedure: Official Draft.* Philadelphia: ALI, 1931.
AMERICAN LAW INSTITUTE. *Criminal Procedure.* Philadelphia: ALI, 895–897.
Comment. "The District Attorney: A Historical Puzzle." *Wisconsin Law Review* (January 1952): 125–138.
Comment. "Private Prosecution: A Remedy for District Attorneys' Unwarranted Inaction." *Yale Law Journal* 65 (1955): 209–234.
CUMMINGS, HOMER S. *Federal Justice: Chapters in the History of Justice and the Federal Executive.* New York: Macmillan, 1937.
EDWARDS, JOHN L. *Law Officers of the Crown: A Study of the Offices of Attorney General and Solicitor General of England, with an Account of the Office of the Director of Public Prosecutions of England.* London: Sweet & Maxwell, 1964.
GOEBEL, JULIUS, JR., and NAUGHTON, T. RAYMOND. *Law Enforcement in Colonial New York: A Study in Criminal Procedure, 1664–1776.* New York: Commonwealth Fund, 1944.
GOLDSTEIN, ABRAHAM S. *The Passive Judiciary Prosecutorial Discretion and the Guilty Plea.* Baton Rouge: Louisiana State University Press, 1981.

HALL, DONALD J. "The Role of the Victim in the Prosecution and Disposition of a Criminal Case." *Vanderbilt Law Review* 28 (1975): 931–985.

JACOBY, JOAN E. *The American Prosecutor: A Search for Identity.* Lexington, Mass.: Heath, Lexington Books, 1980.

KRESS, JACK M. "Progress and Prosecution." *Annals of the American Academy of Political and Social Science* 423 (1976): 99–116.

LANGBEIN, JOHN H. "The Origins of Public Prosecution and Common Law." *American Journal of Legal History* 17 (1993): 313–335.

POUND, ROSCOE. *Criminal Justice in America.* New York: Holt, 1930.

REISS, ALBERT J., JR. "Public Prosecutors and Criminal Prosecution in the United States of America." *Juridicial Review,* New Series 20 (1975): 1–21.

SCOTT, ARTHUR P. *Criminal Law in Colonial Virginia.* University of Chicago Press, 1930.

SURRENCY, ERWIN C. "The Courts in the American Colonies." *American Journal of Legal History* 11 (1967): 253–276.

U.S. National Commission on Law Observance and Enforcement. *Report on Prosecution.* Washington, D.C.: U.S. Government Printing Office, 1931.

PROSECUTION: PROSECUTORIAL DISCRETION

The term "prosecutorial discretion" refers to the fact that under American law, government prosecuting attorneys have nearly absolute and unreviewable power to choose whether or not to bring criminal charges, and what charges to bring, in cases where the evidence would justify charges. This authority provides the essential underpinning to the prevailing practice of plea bargaining, and guarantees that American prosecutors are among the most powerful of public officials. It also provides a significant opportunity for leniency and mercy in a system that is frequently marked by broad and harsh criminal laws, and, increasingly in the last decades of the twentieth century, by legislative limitations on judges' sentencing discretion.

The grant of broad discretion to prosecutors is so deeply ingrained in American law that U.S. lawyers often assume that prosecutorial discretion is inevitable. In fact, some countries in Europe and Latin America adhere to the opposite principle of "mandatory prosecution," maintaining, at least in principle, that prosecutors have a duty to bring any charge that is supported by evidence developed by the police or presented by citizens. The extent to which that principle is actually followed in practice in these countries has been controversial. Some scholars have argued that practices analogous to American prosecutorial discretion and plea bargaining generally exist, more or less covertly, in such countries, or that the discretion exercised by prosecutors in the United States is effectively exercised there by the police instead.

The general acceptance of prosecutorial discretion in the United States is closely linked to our adversarial system of justice. The adversarial principle is generally taken to mean that judges in American courts are not commissioned to investigate cases, determine the truth, and provide justice. Instead, the courts are understood as dispute-settling institutions, in which judges take a more passive role, considering only such facts as are presented to them by the parties, and deciding only such issues as are necessary to resolve the disputes thus presented. Primary responsibility for defining the nature of the dispute, and presenting the relevant facts, lies with the parties and their lawyers. More specifically, criminal cases are seen as disputes between the government and individuals accused of crime. Just as a plaintiff in a civil suit has the option of withdrawing his claim, or settling it privately with the defendant—in which case the court has no further role—so in a criminal case, the prosecutor, as representative of the government, can decide that the interests of his client are best served by not taking any legal action at all, or by settling for relief short of what could in theory be available if litigation were pursued to its final conclusion. On essentially the same reasoning, the American system recognizes a formal plea of guilty by a criminal defendant as a conclusive resolution of the case that removes the need for judicial inquiry into the facts. If the plaintiff government and the defendant are essentially in agreement about whether the defendant should be punished, there is no dispute, and nothing for the courts to do. The authority of both prosecutor and defendant to waive or settle their potential differences thus gives rise to the potential for plea bargaining, in which the prosecutor agrees to waive some potential charges or sanctions in return for the defendant's agreement not to contest others.

The prosecutor thus plays a pivotal role in the administration of justice in America. To the extent that the prosecutor is the lawyer for the state, her client is not the police department or the individual victim of a crime, but society itself. As a practical matter, moreover, the prosecutor is not merely the attorney who represents society's interest in court, but also the public official whose job it is to decide, as a substantive matter, the extent of society's interest in seeking punishment. The prosecutor is thus not merely a barrister, exercising technical skill to advocate positions decided by someone else, but a significant public official, exercising political authority on behalf of the state to determine its substantive position. Consequently, the prosecutor is normally a politically responsible actor. In most states, the chief prosecutor of a district is elected, usually at the county level. (Often, the state attorney general, usually also an elected official, has some—generally limited—degree of authority over local district attorneys.) In the federal system, the chief prosecutor in a judicial district (the United States attorney) is appointed by the president, subject to confirmation by the Senate. While not directly elected, she is responsible to the people through the elected president and her Attorney General. As a practical matter, in both state and federal systems, the locally elected district attorney or the local United States attorney is usually the final authority on prosecutorial decisions in individual cases.

Varieties of discretion

The legal philosopher Ronald Dworkin has distinguished several senses in which the word "discretion" is used in legal discourse. Sometimes the word is used in a relatively weak sense, signifying that "the standards an official must apply cannot be applied mechanically but demand the use of judgment." (Dworkin, 1977, p. 31). For example, we might say that the lieutenant left the sergeant a great deal of discretion if she ordered him to select the five most experienced soldiers for a particular mission, since the criterion of experience could be applied in different ways. In a different weak sense, we sometimes say an official has discretion when we mean that his decision cannot be reviewed and reversed by a higher authority: although the rules of baseball clearly define the strike zone, the umpire could be said to have discretion over the call of balls and strikes, because no higher power can overrule his call, whether or not a videotape replay shows that the decision was inconsistent with the rule. We also sometimes use the word in a very strong sense, to mean that the official is sim-

ply not bound by any standard at all. If the university registrar is told simply to divide the students taking chemistry into two sections, she might have complete discretion to divide them alphabetically, or by pulling names from a hat, or by assigning the first students to register to the more popular instructor; there are no governing criteria by which her decision can be said to be wrong.

Even in this strongest sense, discretion is always conferred for a particular purpose, and operates within some limits. The registrar in our example has been given no authority to assign students who have *not* registered for chemistry to one of the two sections. Moreover, there may be some assumed or external constraints even on extremely broad discretion of this type: for example, the registrar might be in violation of law if she divided the sections by assigning students to sections according to their race.

Although prosecutorial charging discretion is extremely broad, there are some limits of this kind. First, prosecutors' discretion operates within the universe of cases in which the minimum requirements for legal punishment exist; while the prosecutor has a wide discretion *not* to bring charges that could be supported, she has no right to bring charges that are not supported by sufficient evidence, and legal checks are in place to absolve defendants of such charges. When a prosecutor decides to bring a charge, that decision is ultimately subject to a judge's authority to determine whether the legal elements of a crime have been alleged, and to a jury's ultimate power to decide whether the facts have been established beyond a reasonable doubt. Indeed, in the vast majority of U.S. jurisdictions, the prosecutor's assessment that the evidence warrants a felony charge must be submitted for review by a judge or grand jury before a trial or full judicial proceedings are instituted. (As a practical matter, however, such reviews are rarely a very significant check on the prosecutor. The evidentiary standard at this threshold stage is low, grand juries in particular operate under rules that permit prosecutors to dominate their proceedings, and in virtually every system, the pressure of case load requires that the review be cursory in most routine cases.)

Second, it is well established that a prosecutor's decision to bring charges against an individual may not be based on discriminatory grounds such as race, religion, or the expression of political opinion ("selective prosecution"), or as retaliation for the successful exercise of legal rights, such as the right of appeal ("vindictive prosecution"). The Supreme Court has ruled that when defendants claim to have been singled out for prosecution for discriminatory reasons, the prosecutorial decision is subject to the ordinary constitutional standard of equal protection. But this standard is extremely difficult to meet. It requires not merely a statistical showing that, for example, the vast majority of those prosecuted for a particular crime are members of minority groups, but also proof that prosecutorial decision-making was actually motivated by a discriminatory purpose. Even a statistical showing of disparate effect may well be difficult to establish, because the defendant must show not only that those prosecuted are members of a disfavored group, but also that there were cases in which members of favored groups were known to the authorities to have committed the offense, but were nevertheless not prosecuted. The latter information is not usually publicly available, the courts have resisted defendants' efforts to obtain discovery of statistical information from prosecutors about cases in which charges have not been filed, and it is difficult to control for the bewildering factual variations among different cases to eliminate possible nondiscriminatory explanations for suspicious patterns of results.

The Supreme Court has also held that the constitutional guarantee of due process protects a defendant against prosecutorial vindictiveness, that is, against a prosecutor increasing the charges in retaliation for a defendant's exercise of a statutory or constitutional right. For example, a prosecutor would be forbidden to bring a more serious charge in retaliation for the defendant's having appealed a conviction on a lesser charge. Indeed, in that situation, courts even apply a presumption of vindictiveness, requiring prosecutors to bear the burden of proving that the decision to increase the charge was *not* retaliatory. But the circumstances in which such a presumption is applied are extremely limited, and in the absence of a presumption, establishing that prosecutors acted from a deliberately vindictive motive is difficult. Moreover, the Supreme Court has held that the ordinary trade-offs of plea bargaining, in which a defendant forgoes a right in exchange for a reduction in charges, are legitimate, and do not constitute the equivalent of vindictively punishing those defendants who do choose to exercise their rights. Thus, the scope of this constraint also is more theoretical than practical.

Finally, it must be emphasized that even these limited legal constraints, even in theory, only permit a challenge to a charge that is brought for improper reasons; they do not provide a basis for requiring action by a prosecutor who has decided *not* to bring charges. Victims, police agencies, and members of the public have not been permitted, for example, to use selective prosecution arguments in an effort to force prosecutors to be more aggressive against favored groups.

Thus, when a prosecutor chooses not to bring a case, it can probably be said that he exercises discretion that has elements of all three of Professor Dworkin's types. Even where there is general agreement on the standard prosecutors should apply—for example, that a prosecutor should not bring charges where the evidence would be insufficient to support a conviction—the prosecutor exercises substantial discretion in Dworkin's first weak sense, since determining the quantity and quality of evidence necessary to convict requires the exercise of substantial experience and judgment, and similarly qualified lawyers might well disagree about the decision in a particular case. Similarly, like the baseball umpire, the prosecutor's decision not to proceed in a particular case is within her discretion in the second weak sense, because no court has the authority to reverse that judgment, however mistaken it might be. Finally, the prosecutor has, for the most part, discretion in the strong sense as well, because, outside the limited zones in which the prosecutor's judgment might in principle be regarded as unlawful, it is up to the prosecutor herself to decide what principles should influence the decision whether to proceed and how much weight should be given to each.

Subjects of prosecutorial discretion

The most significant aspect of the prosecutorial discretion is the decision whether to bring charges, and what charges to bring. As noted above, the prosecutor has virtually unlimited discretion not to proceed with a case, for any reason that she deems appropriate. This discretion is very frequently exercised, particularly in minor cases, where the prosecutor will often decide that a particular incident, or even a particular category of offenses, does not warrant the expenditure of resources or serious social sanction entailed by a criminal prosecution.

In more serious cases, the decision to withhold the criminal sanction entirely is less common. But this does not render prosecutorial discretion less important. American criminal codes frequently contain overlapping statutes bearing different penalties for the same actions, and a particular criminal scheme may include a number of acts, some of which may be independently chargeable as separate crimes. For example, a particular fraudulent scheme may permit prosecutors to bring charges of larceny, which may be differentiated into degrees, as well as less serious charges of forgery, impersonation, making false statements or falsifying business records. The prosecutor may elect to forgo the most serious charges, or to bring only a subset of the charges that may in theory be sustainable.

This discretion may be particularly important where some or all of the charges contemplated contain mandatory minimum sentences. In such a case, the prosecutor may in effect exercise significant control over the sentence to be imposed if the defendant is convicted. By choosing to bring the charge that carries the mandatory penalty, the prosecutor can guarantee that the judge has no power to impose a lesser sentence, while choosing a different applicable charge that lacks the mandatory penalty will free the judge to impose a more lenient penalty if she wishes.

Moreover, prosecutors can also influence defendants' fates by a variety of other decisions that fall within their discretion. Like the police, prosecutors have broad power to institute investigations, and can choose among different investigative tools, generally without judicial supervision or constraint. Indeed, because of their control of the broad investigative powers of the grand jury, prosecutors have much more power to institute intrusive investigations than the police. Potential witnesses can decline to cooperate with the police for any reason or for no reason at all, but the prosecutor can exercise the grand jury's subpoena power to require witnesses to attend and to answer, absent a legally valid privilege. Thus, the prosecutor, subject only to very limited judicial review, can require witnesses to undergo extensive and intrusive questioning, or to respond to burdensome and expensive demands for the production of documents, whenever he deems it desirable to further an investigation. By the same token, a prosecutor can decide that a case is not even worth investigating, or that a cursory inquiry will be sufficient.

After a charge is brought, the prosecutor decides how aggressively the case should be litigated. As already discussed, this includes the power to compromise or settle the case by accepting a lesser plea in satisfaction of the original charges. While courts have some authority to reject a plea bargain that is not in the public interest (in contrast to their lack of power to compel a prosecutor to bring a charge in the first instance), this power is exercised extremely rarely, out of deference to the executive branch's prerogatives and due to the impracticality of insisting that a prosecutor proceed to try a case to which she is no longer committed. Accordingly, the prosecutor for the most part retains throughout the case the discretion over charges that she had at the outset.

But even more routine litigation decisions, of the sort commonly entrusted to lawyers, can have a profound impact on a litigant, and as the state's lawyer, the prosecutor controls those decisions. The prosecutor's evaluation of the seriousness of the charges, and of the importance of securing a conviction, will determine whether a case is presented perfunctorily, or whether "hardball" tactics will be used. Will the resources necessary to call additional expert witnesses or to use expensive charts or computer graphics be devoted to the case? Will the office's best lawyers be assigned to work on it? Will the prosecutor resist motions for the suppression of evidence to the utmost, or agree not to present contested evidence to save time and effort? All of these decisions, and many more, rest in the prosecutor's power, and will significantly effect both the costs of presenting a defense and the likelihood that a particular defendant will be acquitted.

Even after conviction, discretionary choices by the prosecutor will have a significant effect on a defendant's fate. Even where mandatory sentences do not apply, and judges retain broad power to sentence anywhere within a broad range, the prosecutor's stance can influence the court. In a busy court operating under basic adversarial assumptions, judges will not often feel the need to impose a greater sentence than that recommended by the prosecutor. And the vigor with which a prosecutor advocates a severe sentence may influence a judge not only on the merits, but also by signaling to the judge the likelihood that her decision will be the subject of public criticism if the recommendation is rejected. Accordingly, the prosecutor's decision to recommend a sentence or to stand mute, the particular sentence the prosecutor chooses to advocate, and the aggressiveness with which that recommendation is pursued will all be important. Where the judge's sentencing decision is constrained by quasi-mandatory sentencing guidelines, moreover, the prosecutor's role can become even more potent. Just as the prosecutor evaluates whether the evidence will support a particular criminal charge and whether it is in the state's interest to pursue that charge, the prosecutor will evaluate whether the evidence justifies the application of a particular aggravating or mitigating factor, and whether the state's interest permits or demands expending resources to litigate its applicability. Since the applicability of these sentencing factors, like the presence of the elements of the crime itself, will often be controversial, the prosecutor generally will have considerable discretion to choose to litigate or compromise these issues. (Under current federal law, the prosecutor has yet another source of power over the sentencing process. Where a defendant has cooperated with the prosecution by providing substantial assistance with the investigation and prosecution of others, the judge is authorized to impose a sentence below the otherwise-applicable guideline range, and even below the statutory mandatory minimum—but only if the prosecutor specifically authorizes the departure from the norm.)

Standards of prosecutorial judgment

There are many reasons why a prosecutor would decline to prosecute a case that in theory could be brought, or to accept a guilty plea to lesser charges where a more serious charge could in principle be supported. First, the prosecutor might decide that the evidence in a case is simply not strong enough to justify prosecution. Evidence that is sufficient to justify the police in making an arrest is not necessarily enough to permit a finding of guilt. The prosecutor has the responsibility of reviewing the evidence developed by the police and determining whether a charge can be justified, and many charges brought by the police are dismissed at this stage. Of course, it is the prosecutor's duty to dismiss charges not founded on sufficient evidence, so that such cases might be seen as exercises of discretion only in the weaker senses.

In other cases, however, the evidence, while legally sufficient to permit a conviction, is still not strong enough to persuade the prosecutor himself of the suspect's guilt, or at least to create a reasonable likelihood of conviction. Most prosecutors believe that they have a moral obligation not to bring a charge where they themselves harbor doubts about the suspect's guilt. (This position is not universally held; some have argued that in some close cases, such as a victim's strong-

ly confident but potentially questionable identification of a perpetrator, the matter should be put to a jury regardless of the prosecutor's personal view.) Even where the prosecutor herself is confident of guilt, and the evidence is legally sufficient, the prosecutor might decide that it is unduly wasteful of limited law enforcement and judicial resources to pursue a case in which the difficult burden of proving guilt beyond a reasonable doubt to a unanimous jury is unlikely to be carried successfully. This is a prototypical question of prosecutorial discretion: where the seriousness of the crime or the dangerousness of the offender is believed to create a significant societal interest in punishment, the prosecutor is more likely to choose to invest resources at a relatively lower likelihood of success.

Second, the prosecutor might decide in a particular case that the interest of society is better served by exercising mercy than by imposing a criminal punishment on an offender. Perhaps the offense was an unusual instance of yielding to extreme temptation by a person of otherwise good moral character, or perhaps the offender acted under the influence of drugs or alcohol, and could better be rehabilitated by a noncriminal treatment program than by prison. Or perhaps the offender's action, while falling within the letter of a broad law, did not really cause the harm or create the risk of harm that the law was designed to avoid, and might well have been excluded from its coverage had the legislature anticipated the specific situation and considered its language more carefully. In such situations, the prosecutor might decide that a criminal conviction, and the stigma of a criminal record, would be excessive punishment even if the judge was permitted to, and chose to, impose probation or some other minimal punishment.

Third, as already mentioned in passing, the prosecutor in most jurisdictions has a heavy responsibility to marshal limited law enforcement resources. American crime rates in the last third of the twentieth century have been high; moreover, American criminal law subjects to potential criminal punishment a wide range of conduct not included in the F.B.I.'s "index" of crime rates, which comprises mostly serious, common law crimes against person and property. The budgets of police departments, investigative agencies, prosecutors' offices, courts, and prisons do not permit the full investigation, prosecution, and punishment of all crimes reported to the police. As a consequence, the prosecutor engages in a kind of triage, determining which categories of case receive priority; which types of offenses should be pursued aggressively, more passively, or not at all; and which cases should be brought only where easy convictions can be expected. Even cases that the prosecutor might choose to pursue if the institutions of justice were better funded will be sacrificed if the prosecutor thinks that the overall goal of minimizing serious crime would be better served by investing the necessary resources elsewhere. These decisions may be made on a case-by-case basis, or whole categories of crime may be relegated to a lower level of priority, or even not prosecuted at all.

Fourth, prosecutors frequently exercise discretion for tactical reasons. Leniency, or even complete immunity from prosecution, is commonly extended to criminals who "cooperate" with the authorities in the investigation or prosecution of more serious cases or more dangerous offenders. Although this practice is pervasive in the system, has deep historical roots, and is in principle justified, at least from a utilitarian standpoint, by the greater value to society of securing the testimony of minor offenders than of extracting full punishment, it remains controversial. Critics charge that serious offenders can escape prosecution based on the morally irrelevant degree to which they possess knowledge of others' crimes. Moreover, the availability of lenient treatment can create a strong incentive to criminals to implicate others falsely, or to fit their testimony to the theories of prosecutors regardless of the truth. Still more controversially, the potential for securing testimony against targets of investigation can lead prosecutors not only to be unduly generous to the dangerous criminal peddling information in return for leniency, but also to bring charges against marginal offenders who would not otherwise be charged, in order to pressure them to cooperate with investigators.

The prosecutor's control of this trade-off between prosecution and leniency, coupled with the prosecutor's authority to decide how much evidence is enough to proceed, and the need of the police for prosecutorial assistance in using certain investigative tools (such as the grand jury's power to compel testimony, the ability to provide statutory immunity to override a witness's invocation of his Fifth Amendment privilege, or formal legal applications to courts to authorize searches or electronic surveillance that require judicial approval), have expanded the role, and the discretion, of prosecutors beyond the courtroom into the investigative phase of the criminal process. In routine criminal cases, the traditional division of roles between the police, who investigate complaints and arrest offenders, and the prosecutors, who decide whether to bring formal charges and present the evidence in court, remains approximately in place. But in more complex investigations, such as those involving white-collar offenses, organized crime, and serious political corruption, the prosecutor is often an integral part of the investigative team, and is deeply involved in strategic decisions about the conduct of the investigation, from long before a case is ready to proceed to indictment and trial. The prosecutor's priorities, legal determinations, and sense of justice will thus be deeply implicated not only in ultimate decisions about the charges to be brought or the plea to be accepted, but also in the day-to-day control of the investigation.

Controlling prosecutorial discretion

There is a fairly extensive academic literature concerning the desirability of controlling or limiting prosecutorial discretion. The issues and suggested remedies to a considerable degree parallel those relating to judicial sentencing discretion. Critics of discretion argue that equal justice is best achieved by the application of formal rules that constrain official decision-makers. Laws, in this view, should be clear and relatively self-executing, to prevent officials from applying subjective and potentially biased standards. Discretionary decisions, moreover, are rarely transparent: unlike courts applying legal principles, officials making more subjective or intuitive choices operate behind closed doors, without an obligation to state reasons or to rationalize potentially conflicting decisions in different cases. These due process values are particularly important where the stakes are as high as they are in the criminal justice system.

Opponents of this view present both practical and conceptual arguments. The practical and contingent arguments are rooted in the actualities of the U.S. criminal justice system. This strand of argument concedes that it might be better in theory to have sharply defined rules that identify all and only that behavior that ought to be punished, and that leave little room for subjective choice. To achieve such a system, however, would require reform of much more in our legal system than simply the elimination of prosecutorial discretion. Our existing penal codes are filled with statutes that are unnecessary, overbroad, or poorly drafted, and the effort to enforce the law as written would be impossible without vastly expanded law enforcement and judicial resources, and intolerable if such resources were provided. Without thoroughgoing reform of the criminal law—a reform that may be impossible to achieve politically—the discretion of prosecutors and judges, it is argued, are necessary to avoid the injustice that would result from literal application of severe and ill-considered criminal statutes.

Other defenders of discretion take a stronger view, arguing that the need for discretionary systems of mercy and judgment are necessary and desirable in principle, and not only because our particular political or legal system is flawed. On this view, the aspiration to be "a government of laws, not men," is not an absolute value, to be pressed at all costs, but is a value that, like many others, would be intolerable if pressed to extremes. Criminal laws are often passed for expressive reasons, and not because the legislature expects or wants them to be enforced literally. From this perspective, that is not a regrettable failing of our political system, but a part of the function of the criminal law, that must in turn be moderated by sensible officials who understand that not every case that falls within the literal terms of the law is meant to be punished. No legal system can achieve a perfect congruence of formal rule and desired outcome, because the multiplicity and elusiveness of the factors that bear on the moral evaluation of human conduct cannot be captured without foreseeing and evaluating the infinite permutations of circumstances that might occur—a task perhaps beyond human wisdom, and certainly beyond the capacity of a body of legal rules that also aspires to be concise, clear, and understandable by the public.

Even if it were conceded that some measure of official discretion is necessary, however, it would not follow that prosecutors ought to be the officials exercising it, that the discretion should be exercised without public accountability, or that some form of review of the resulting decisions should not be permitted. Many have proposed schemes for regulating and reforming prosecutorial discretion, or for authorizing judicial review of prosecutorial decisions. It has been argued, for example, that prosecutors, like other administrative or executive agencies entrusted with substantial delegated power, should be required to adopt formal regulations governing their decisions, or that prosecutors should be required to state their reasons for particular actions. Victims' rights advocates have proposed that victims should be given at least a consultative role, and perhaps even a veto power, over prosecutors' charging and plea bargaining decisions.

Few of these proposals have proved sufficiently appealing to secure broad political support. If it is accepted that discretionary decision-making is to some degree inevitable, the quest for standards is to that extent quixotic—if the legislature cannot or will not capture in statutes the precise conduct it expects to lead to punishment, there is little reason to think that prosecutors or judges will be able to do a better job by way of regulations or common law articulation of standards. Nor is it clear that providing for additional levels of review will improve decision-making. The buck has to stop somewhere, and setting additional layers of review simply moves the ultimate decision to another official, without making that official's decision any more likely to be correct. Moreover, to the extent that the criteria for prosecution correctly include judgments about the social utility to be gained from the prosecution, as well as a moral evaluation of the wrongfulness of the defendant's conduct, the prosecutor—or at least some analogous, politically responsible official of the executive branch—is probably better placed, and has more political authority, to evaluate these factors than a judge. The recent unsatisfactory experience at the federal level with nonpolitically responsible independent prosecutors in high-visibility political cases has shown the importance of political accountability in making prosecutorial choices.

Published standards and internal review mechanisms

The U.S. Department of Justice, in its manual for United States attorneys and particularly in the section of the manual entitled "Principles of Federal Prosecution," has made a considerable effort to identify and articulate the factors that bear on the exercise of prosecutorial discretion, both in general and as applied to particular statutes. Moreover, both the department and the individual United States attorneys offices have established internal procedures requiring particular kinds of decisions to be reviewed or approved internally at higher levels of authority than individual prosecutors.

These efforts demonstrate both the promise and the limitation of such internal guidelines. On the one hand, efforts to articulate, even at a high level of generality, the considerations to be applied in making discretionary decisions provide guidance to prosecutors in approaching their responsibilities, and to defense counsel in couching arguments to persuade the decision-makers. By announcing these principles, the department contributes to public debate and accountability, and commits itself to apply its discretion in ways and for reasons the legitimacy of which can be defended or debated.

On the other hand, the standards are generally quite vague and admit of numerous and often subjective exceptions and qualifications. The principles are proclaimed for internal use only, and provide no rights of judicial enforcement. Even if they were enforceable, however, there would be little grip for judicial review. For example, in determining whether there is a "substantial federal interest" in a prosecution, the prosecutor is instructed to "weigh all relevant considerations," including, but evidently not limited to, federal law enforcement priorities, the nature and seriousness of the offense, the deterrent effect of prosecution, the person's culpability in connection with the offense, the person's history with respect to criminal activity, the person's willingness to cooperate in the investigation or prosecution of others, and the probable sentence or other consequences if the person is convicted. Though some might question one or another of these factors, most people would agree that these are relevant factors. Merely to list them, however, and to consider that these various incommensurable factors are somehow to be "weighed" against each other, is to demonstrate how complex, subtle, and subjective a judgment is being called for.

As the power of prosecutors relevant to other actors in the criminal justice system has grown, as sophisticated defense lawyers have come to appreciate that power, and as conscientious prosecutors have sought to define relevant standards and provide for internal review, an increasing proportion of criminal law practice has come to involve negotiations with or presentations to prosecutors, as opposed to arguments before courts and juries. For the vast majority of defendants—probably over 90 percent—the most important decisions affecting their fate are made in prosecutors offices rather than in courtrooms. Some observers have suggested that prosecutorial decision-making is so important that we have in effect created a criminal justice system that in reality is inquisitorial and administrative, rather than adversarial and judicial. It may be that the most important developments in American criminal procedure in the new century will involve the effort to render that system more public and accountable by regulating in various ways the procedure and substance of discretionary prosecutorial decisions.

GERARD E. LYNCH

See also ADVERSARY SYSTEM; CRIMINAL JUSTICE PROCESS; CRIMINAL PROCEDURE: CONSTITUTIONAL ASPECTS; DISPUTE RESOLUTION PROGRAMS; GRAND JURY; GUILTY PLEA: ACCEPTING THE PLEA; GUILTY PLEA: PLEA BARGAINING; INFORMAL DISPOSITION; PRETRIAL DIVERSION; PROSECUTION: COMPARATIVE ASPECTS; PROSECUTION: HISTORY OF THE PUBLIC PROSECUTOR; PROSECUTION: UNITED STATES ATTORNEY; SENTENCING: ALLOCATION OF AUTHORITY; SENTENCING: ALTERNATIVES; SENTENCING: DISPARITY; SENTENCING: GUIDELINES; SENTENCING: MANDATORY AND MANDATORY MINIMUM SENTENCES; SENTENCING: PRESENTENCE REPORT; SENTENCING: PROCEDURAL PROTECTION.

BIBLIOGRAPHY

DAVIS, KENNETH C. *Discretionary Justice: A Preliminary Inquiry.* Baton Rouge, La.: Louisiana State University Press, 1969.
LAFAVE, WAYNE R. "The Prosecutor's Discretion in the United States." *American Journal of Comparative Law* 18 (1970): 532–548.
LYNCH, GERARD E. "Our Administrative System of Criminal Justice." *Fordham Law Review* (1998): 2217.

PROSECUTION: UNITED STATES ATTORNEY

An United States attorney is the chief federal law enforcement officer in one of the ninety-four judicial districts in the United States (excepting Guam and the Northern Mariana Islands, which share a United States attorney). Appointed by the president, with the advice and consent of the Senate, United States attorneys work with grand juries and law enforcement agencies to investigate federal crimes, authorize or decline prosecutions, and determine the charges to be brought and the manner of prosecution. Overseeing a staff of assistant United States attorneys who conduct much of the day-to-day work of the office, the United States attorney is responsible for trying federal criminal cases on behalf of the United States, as well as negotiating guilty pleas and representing the United States in the appellate courts within the district. The United States attorney is also the principal litigator for the

United States within his or her district in civil matters.

United States attorneys differ from state and local prosecutors in several respects. First, unlike district attorneys who must rely principally upon state and local police for investigative assistance, United States attorneys can typically draw upon the national resources and personnel of federal law enforcement agencies like the Federal Bureau of Investigation and the Drug Enforcement Administration. (This is obviously useful in investigations and prosecutions that involve witnesses or evidence located in another district or even another country.) Next, while the legal authority of local prosecutors to investigate crime is generally limited to the state in which they work, the United States attorney can bring to bear the broader legal authority of the federal government. Working with a federal grand jury, which has nationwide subpoena power, the U.S. attorney can compel witnesses to appear in his or her district from wherever in the country they may be found. When a federal criminal defendant is arrested in another district on criminal charges brought by the United States attorney, there is no need for extradition; after a brief hearing to establish his identity, the defendant is simply transported from the district of arrest to the district where charges are pending.

Finally, and perhaps most significantly, most local prosecutors are elected to serve as the principal prosecuting authorities in their jurisdictions and, with their assistants, are broadly responsible to the electorate for the effective enforcement of criminal law. (There are roughly 25,000 to 30,000 state and local prosecutors nationwide; in 1996 these officials filed close to 998,000 felony charges.) The presidentially appointed federal prosecutor is somewhat different. Subject to removal by the president, he or she is responsible for protecting direct federal interests in the enforcement of certain laws—those reaching international terrorist activity, for instance, or prohibiting false statements to federal agencies or the counterfeiting of U.S. currency. More commonly, however, the federal prosecutor faces situations in which possible federal charges overlap with charges that could be prosecuted by state or local officials, who handle most criminal cases. (There were 4,773 assistant U.S. attorneys working in the ninety-three U.S. attorneys' offices as of August 1999; together, these offices have averaged about 35,000 cases annually since 1930.)

Because the U.S. attorney is not the principal prosecuting authority in a jurisdiction and is not viewed as such, a federal prosecutor may well decline prosecution in circumstances where potential criminal charges can be effectively handled by state or local authorities. On the other hand, the U.S. attorney may elect to prosecute—either to vindicate federal interests implicated in a case or to assist state and local authorities in addressing more local concerns. In practice, this means that the United States attorney probably exercises even broader prosecutorial discretion than most other prosecutors.

The Attorney General of the United States has statutory authority to supervise the work of the United States attorneys and the U.S. attorneys act generally within guidelines promulgated by the Department of Justice. In practice, however, the federal prosecutor has considerable autonomy. The daily operations and priorities of each U.S. attorney's office are largely under the U.S. attorney's control. And though the attorney general has the authority to take direct control of any case falling within the jurisdiction of the U.S. attorney, this authority is rarely invoked. As set forth below, the United States attorney's relative freedom from central authority derives not only from his or her distance from Washington, D.C., but also from the historical development of the position and the process by which each United States attorney is selected.

Origins of the United States attorney

The office of the United States attorney was created by the Judiciary Act of 1789, ch. 20, 1 Stat. 73, which provided for the appointment in each federal district of "a meet person learned in the law to act as attorney for the United States. . .to prosecute. . .all delinquents for [federal] crimes and offenses" (92). The same law established the office of the attorney general, but the attorney general's function at this time was limited to representing the United States in the Supreme Court and advising the president and the heads of the executive departments of the federal government on legal matters. The attorney general had no formal control over the United States attorneys charged with enforcing federal criminal law in their respective districts. Though proposals to grant the attorney general such control were introduced in Congress as early as 1791, legislation to this effect was not enacted until 1861.

In the interim, United States attorneys (or federal district attorneys, as they were then known) occasionally consulted with the attorney general on a voluntary basis. And in certain celebrated cases such as the treason trial of Aaron Burr, the attorney general did participate, at presidential request, in lower federal court proceedings. But the first official grant of supervisory power over U.S. attorneys, however, went to the Treasury Department, not the Justice Department. Any intervention into matters falling with the jurisdiction of the local federal attorneys, moreover, was infrequent. Even after Congress enacted legislation giving the attorney general supervisory authority over United States attorneys in 1861 (ch. 37, 12 Stat. 285 (1861)), it was not until a decade later (after Reconstruction and the Justice Department's creation in 1870), that federal prosecutors came under any meaningful national control.

The selection process

Both the Constitution and enabling legislation give the power to appoint United States attorneys to the president, subject to the Senate's "advice and consent." In practice, the senators of the president's political party from a given state often make the initial selection of a candidate for United States attorney. If both senators are from an opposing party, the state's congressional delegation or other state party officials may play a leading role. Each United States attorney is appointed for a term of four years, but generally continues in office at the expiration of his or her term until a successor is appointed. United States attorneys are subject to removal by the president. Assistant United States attorneys are appointed by the attorney general and are subject to removal by him or her, although in practice, the hiring and removal of assistant United States attorneys (who enjoy civil service protection) is handled at the local level. New U.S. attorneys will thus generally command a staff of assistants largely named by predecessors in office, but will themselves make the hiring decisions necessary to appoint new assistants.

The selection process for United States attorneys supports the traditional autonomy with which they have operated. Individuals who become United States attorneys typically do not view themselves as having obtained their appointment directly from the attorney general or the president. In congressional hearings in 1978, then–Attorney General Griffin Bell identified

this as a problem, arguing that because United States attorneys may not feel indebted to the attorney general for their positions, they are less likely to accede to supervision emanating from him or her. Bell supported legislation giving the attorney general the power to select and remove United States attorneys. Such legislation, however, was never enacted.

There may be merit in Attorney General Bell's observation that lodging the appointment power for United States attorneys in the Attorney General would produce United States attorneys more responsive to his or her concerns. Whether such increased responsiveness to national law enforcement officials is itself seen as a worthy goal of reform efforts, however, is likely to depend, at least in part, on the view one takes of the United States attorney's role. If the United States attorney's principal role is to implement national law enforcement priorities articulated by the president and the attorney general, the United States attorney should presumably be strictly accountable to these officers, and perhaps appointed directly by them. If, on the other hand, the United States attorney is to be responsive to local concerns—if it is a substantial part of the role to bring federal law enforcement resources to bear on local problems—it may be a strength of the current selection process that it often involves persons familiar with and directly responsible to the local electorate, such as senators and other locally elected officials.

It is also important that the United States attorney have and be perceived as having the independence necessary to enforce the law fairly— and particularly in those contexts where law enforcement policy and even individual prosecutions may have political overtones. The multiple influences brought to bear in the current selection process may help realize this end by securing for the federal prosecutor some measure of autonomy from any one of these influences.

Thus, the involvement of national political figures in the selection process helps to ensure the United States attorney's independence from the control of local officials. A federal prosecutor perceived as having obtained his or her appointment from a narrow circle of partisan politicians might well find his or her ability to discharge the functions of the office compromised. Similarly, however (and despite a tradition of nonpartisanship in the discharge of the functions of the office), attorney generals are not infrequently drawn into situations where there may be at least the perception of a conflict between their law enforcement obligations and their perceived personal and political loyalties to the presidents who appointed them. (It was the perception of the potential for such conflicts that resulted in the enactment of the Independent Counsel Statute, which Congress allowed to lapse only in the wake of the controversy surrounding Independent Counsel Kenneth Starr's investigation of President William Jefferson Clinton.) In such cases, it may be important that United States attorneys retain a measure of independence from the attorney general as well as local officials, lest the law enforcement activities of these federal prosecutors be influenced by or perceived as influenced by inappropriate national political concerns.

Some tradition favoring "merit," as opposed to purely "political" appointment of United States attorneys, also helps ensure their independence from narrow political control. This tradition manifests itself in a variety of ways. For example, senators not infrequently set up nominating commissions to submit names of suitable candidates for United States attorney slots. Some United States attorneys have remained in office through a change in administration—implicitly attesting to the relatively nonpartisan way in which these offices can function and can be perceived.

Daily operations

Although the Justice Department's supervision of United States attorneys has increased in recent years, the United States attorney retains substantial independence. As noted above, the United States attorney's daily operations remain largely free of centralized control by Justice Department officials in Washington, D.C. United States attorneys are explicitly vested with "plenary authority" over prosecutions in their districts. And even when the Justice Department establishes national prosecutorial priorities in the interest of allocating limited resources in such a way as to achieve an effective nationwide law enforcement program, United States attorneys may still establish their own priorities, "within the national priorities, in order to concentrate their resources on problems of particular local or regional significance" (U.S. Department of Justice, 1997).

To be sure, there are areas in which the Justice Department exercises more direct supervision. With regard to a handful of offenses, for instance, including the Racketeer Influenced and Corrupt Organizations Act, 18 U.S.C. §§ 1961 et seq., which is often used to prosecute organized crime, central approval to prosecute must be obtained in order to ensure some uniformity of charging standards. Tax prosecutions are also subject to more intense central control. The Solicitor General must authorize all appeals taken by U.S. attorneys. Any decision to seek or not to seek the death penalty must be approved by the attorney general. Justice Department officials in Washington also resolve interdistrict jurisdictional disputes that may arise among U.S. attorneys.

In addition, Congress has enacted legislation requiring more centralized control of some of the investigative tactics employed by federal prosecutors. Thus, high-ranking Justice Department approval is required before prosecutors may seek warrants for various forms of electronic eavesdropping. Applications for orders compelling the testimony of immunized witnesses must be signed by officials working more directly under the supervision of the attorney general. The Justice Department itself, as a matter of internal regulation, requires that central approval be obtained before an indictment is sought charging a person with a crime that has already been the subject of prosecution by local authorities. Central approval must also be obtained before subpoenas are issued to attorneys for information relating to the representation of clients.

Role in local law enforcement

This entry has suggested that United States attorneys are perhaps most distinguished from other prosecutors in the degree to which they must make significant judgments regarding how much of their efforts should be devoted to addressing local, as opposed to federal, interests in crime control. Indeed, United States attorneys must strike an important balance between devoting their offices' resources to the vindication of uniquely federal interests and using these resources, as well as the federal criminal law, to address local priorities and concerns.

The necessity for striking such a balance stems in part from the broad reach of federal criminal jurisdiction. Prior to the Civil War, federal criminal laws (at least outside those territories where the federal government had exclusive jurisdiction) were largely limited to acts threatening federal governmental processes or programs, such as the theft of government property, and misconduct by or against federal officers. The civil rights legislation enacted after the Civil War (namely, the Civil Rights Act of 1866, ch. 31, 14 Stat. 27, and the Civil Rights Act of 1870, ch. 114, 16 Stat. 140), extended federal criminal law beyond mere protection of national authority, involving federal prosecutors in the safeguarding of local citizenry and creating the potential for overlap between federal and state enforcement authority. The growth of an interdependent, national market at this time further stimulated Congress to criminalize various forms of fraud involving misuse of the mails and interstate commerce. The twentieth-century experiment in the prohibition of alcohol resulted in an unprecedented expansion in the scope of federal enforcement authority. After Prohibition's repeal, federal criminal jurisdiction continued to grow, extending to conduct like kidnapping, extortion and robbery affecting interstate commerce, bank robbery, securities fraud, and the interstate movement of stolen property.

Today, federal criminal jurisdiction is nearly limitless and reaches matters ranging from odometer tampering to the embezzlement of union funds; from street-corner narcotics distribution to local loan-sharking. Even violent crimes once thought to be entirely within the jurisdiction of states and localities have become subject to federal jurisdiction and increasing federal control. For example, in March 1991, the Justice Department instituted a national enforcement program known as "Project Triggerlock," in which each United States attorney was instructed to appoint a task force for the purpose of targeting violent street criminals who employed guns in their crimes. The purpose of this effort was to take advantage of federal statutes imposing "stiff mandatory sentences" for firearms offenses (Geller and Morris).

Even though much criminal conduct is subject to the dual jurisdiction of federal and state and local authorities, federal prosecutions comprise less than 5 percent of all the prosecutions in the nation (Strazzella). In practice, this means that United States attorneys significantly influence the effective reach of the federal law with decisions they make about the activities they will focus on. These decisions are often made in cooperation with local authorities, most frequently through informal consultations, but sometimes through formal mechanisms like the Law Enforcement Coordinating Committees, which were instituted to bring together federal, state, and local law enforcement agencies under the aegis of a United States attorney.

In some instances, a criminal case subject to dual jurisdiction may be handled by the United States attorney simply because it was investigated by federal agents and presented to the United States attorney for prosecution. In other cases, however, local law enforcement officials may specifically request a United States attorney to handle a given investigation or a resulting prosecution because federal law offers more advantageous rules for obtaining and presenting evidence than those in the affected locality. The remedies in federal criminal legislation can include asset forfeiture, which may offer state and local agencies both the enhanced ability to disable a criminal organization and the possibility of a share in forfeited assets. At any rate, and for a combination of reasons, there is a high degree of successful intergovernmental collaboration between United States attorneys and state and local law enforcement agencies.

Despite such successes, commentators have expressed the need for articulation of some principled basis for the exercise of federal prosecutorial discretion in cases of concurrent jurisdiction. The calls for principles to guide the exercise of federal power in this context, moreover, have grown more fervent since the federal Sentencing Guidelines went into effect in 1987. The Guidelines were promulgated in part to eliminate unjustified sentencing disparities within the federal system. Because the sentences they authorize are often more stringent than those commonly meted out in the discretionary sentencing regimes of many states, however, they can produce situations where similarly situated defendants may be subject to radically more stringent sentences simply because they are prosecuted in federal court. (The mandatory minimum sentences specified in some federal criminal statutes can have similar effects.) Given the relatively small number of federal prosecutions, this raises concerns that a small minority of defendants may be haphazardly "selected for federal prosecution and subjected to much harsher sentences—and often to significantly less favorable procedural or substantive standards—than persons prosecuted for parallel state offenses" (Beale, 1995). Though limited progress has been made on articulating standards for the exercise of federal prosecutorial authority in the context of concurrent jurisdiction, such concerns may point to the need for more efforts in this direction.

DEBRA LIVINGSTON

See also DRUGS AND CRIME: LEGAL ASPECTS; FEDERAL CRIMINAL JURISDICTION; FEDERAL CRIMINAL LAW ENFORCEMENT; JURISDICTION; PROSECUTION: PROSECUTORIAL DISCRETION; SENTENCING: GUIDELINES; SENTENCING: MANDATORY AND MANDATORY MINIMUM SENTENCES.

BIBLIOGRAPHY

ABRAMS, NORMAN, and BEALE, SARA SUN. *Federal Criminal Law and Its Enforcement*, 3d ed. St. Paul, Minn.: West, 2000.

BEALE, SARA SUN. "Too Many and Yet Too Few: New Principles to Define the Proper Limits for Federal Criminal Jurisdiction." *Hastings Law Journal* 46 (1995): 979.

———. "Federalizing Crime: Assessing the Impact on the Federal Courts." *Annals of the American Academy of Political and Social Sciences* 543 (1996): 39.

BRICKEY, KATHLEEN F. "Criminal Mischief: The Federalization of American Criminal Law." *Hastings Law Journal* 46 (1995): 1135.

CLYMER, STEVEN D. "Unequal Justice: The Federalization of Criminal Law." *Southern California Law Review* 70 (1997): 643.

CUMMINGS, HOMER S., and MCFARLAND, CARL. *Federal Justice: Chapters in the History of Justice and the Federal Executive*. New York: Macmillan, 1937.

EISENSTEIN, JAMES. *Counsel for the United States*. 1978.

GELLER, WILLIAM A., and MORRIS, NORVAL. "Relations between Federal and Local Police." In *Modern Policing*. Edited by Michael Tonry and Norval Morris. Chicago, Ill.: University of Chicago Press, 1992. Pages 231–348.

HUSTON, LUTHER A. *The Department of Justice*. New York: Praeger, 1967.

HEYMANN, PHILIP B., and MOORE, MARK H. "The Federal Role in Dealing with Violent Street Crime: Principles, Questions, and Cautions." *Annals of the American Academy of Political and Social Sciences* 543 (1996): 103.

JEFFRIES, JOHN C., JR., and GLEESON, HON. JOHN. "The Federalization of Organized Crime: Advantages of Federal Prosecution." *Hastings Law Journal* 46 (1995): 1095.

RICHMAN, DANIEL C. "Federal Criminal Law, Congressional Delegation, and Enforcement Discretion." *UCLA Law Review* 46 (1999): 757.

SEYMOUR, WHITNEY N. *United States Attorney: An Inside View of 'Justice' in America under the Nixon Administration*. New York: Morrow, 1975.

STRAZZELLA, JAMES A. Reporter. The Federalization of Criminal Law. Task Force on the Federalization of Criminal Law, American Bar Association, Criminal Justice Section, 1998.

U.S. Congress. House Committee on the Judiciary. "Selection and Removal of U.S. Attorneys: Hearings before the Subcommittee on Courts, Civil Liberties, and the Administration of Justice of the Committee on the Judiciary." House of Representatives, 95th Cong., 2d sess. Washington, D.C.: Government Printing Office, 1978.

U.S. Department of Justice. *Principles of Federal Prosecution*. Washington, D.C.: Department of Justice, 1997.

———. *United States Attorneys' Manual*. Washington, D.C.: Department of Justice, 1997.

PROSTITUTION

Prostitution as a legal category and as a social problem has undergone a reexamination in scholarly and policy debates since the 1970s. This rethinking of prostitution has relied upon a variety of historical and cross-cultural studies. Policy initiatives have increasingly turned to economic approaches, especially to transaction-cost analyses. New attention has been paid to the social position of the prostitute, especially to public health and other aspects of participation in prostitution, as well as to the gender politics of prostitution law and its enforcement. As a result of these studies, the earlier view that prostitution is a unitary and universal feature of human social life is no longer empirically or theoretically tenable. Rather, prostitution as we know it is a function of multiple sociocultural and historical processes, institutional structures, and interactional dynamics.

Social attribution and the construction of prostitution as a social problem

Prostitution as a category of crime and social identity is located at the intersection of sexuality and economics. Georg Simmel linked the "essence of prostitution" to the "nature of money itself" (p. 414). A more contemporary study has characterized prostitution as

a business transaction understood as such by the parties involved and in the nature of a short-term contract . . . . [T]o be a prostitute, one has to treat the exchanging of sexual gratification for an established fee as a business deal, that is, without any pretence to affection, and continue to do this as a form of financial occupation . . . . In other words, it must be clearly demonstrated that there is a buyer and a seller, a commodity offered and a contracted price. (Perkins and Bennett, p. 4)

The field of economics and the study of human sexuality have both gone through sharp internal polemics and revisions since the 1970s. Social and criminal justice policy toward prostitution has trailed along somewhat uncertainly in their wake. Indeed, prostitution policy has reacted to these scholarly developments in piecemeal fashion at best, as it has undertaken—in the absence of any single generally accepted conceptualization of the social problem of prostitution—a variety of ad hoc measures to mitigate prostitution's perceived negative social effects.

Universalist accounts of prostitution have maintained that it has existed throughout human history—the "oldest profession" canard—in all human communities, and even among some animal species. It is difficult to imagine that a historian writing after 1980 would undertake a project so grandiose and all-encompassing that it could be entitled *The History of Prostitution* (Bullough). Earlier scholars' claims that, for example, ancient Babylonian religious ritual sexual practices or the great variety of short term marital or quasi-marital relations (Islamic law temporary marriage, European morganatic marriage, East African *malaya* relationships) constitute prostitution seem now to reveal more about the writers' theoretical commitments than about the social institutions in question (see Bullough, pp. 17–30; Richards, p. 88; and for a critique Pateman, pp. 195–196). Instead, since the 1970s, a great many empirical studies of sexual exchange and of human sexuality in general have exhaustively demonstrated the historical, geographic, and ethno-cultural diversity of the forms of human sexual interaction, identity, and relations (e.g., Davis).

Prostitution as a crime of sexuality and commerce requires that an economy of market exchange exist within a particular social order and that certain forms of sexual interaction be normatively excluded from economic exchange by the force of criminal sanction. Following Ferdinand Tonnies's classic sociological analysis that posited an ideal-type distinction between *Gemeinschaft*, a community ordered by kinship and customary obligation, and *Gesellschaft*, a society organized by free economic exchange, we see that a crime of prostitution could logically exist in neither of them. In a community of reciprocal gift-obligation, nothing could be put on the market for sale to the highest bidder—sexual interaction perhaps least of all. Similarly, in a society of pure economic exchange, everything is understood as available for a price, so that the selling

of sexual services could hardly constitute a crime. It is only in a social order where some things are expected to be allocated by buying and selling in a market and other things are not to be sold at all that the selling of sexual interaction can be understood as a criminal offense.

This conceptual problem of how to distinguish between categories of licit and illicit sexual socioeconomic connection is an old issue in feminist thought that has attracted renewed attention since the 1970s. Two hundred years ago, Mary Wollstonecraft described a wife's status as "legal prostitution" (p. 247). To Emma Goldman in the early twentieth century, "it is simply a question of degree whether [a woman] sells herself to one man, in or out of marriage, or to many men" (p. 179). And for Simone de Beauvoir writing at mid-century, a wife is "hired for life by one man; the prostitute has several clients who pay her by the piece" (p. 619).

Since the 1970s many studies have focused closely on the gender politics of prostitution law and its enforcement. Although the Model Penal Code endorses gender neutrality by drawing no distinction between males and females accused of prostitution (section 207.12(1)), attention to prostitution as a two-sided economic transaction highlights a sharp gender asymmetry in the role of the consumer of sexual services. Markets in sexual services performed by men as well as women and directed toward male consumers are very widely attested. Yet, though it is easy enough to imagine a prostitution market aimed at female consumers, the virtual absence of reports of established markets selling sexual services to women is a robust sociological fact that has compelled a reconsideration of the gender effects of prostitution markets (Pateman).

A heightened concern over the public health aspects of prostitution followed the appearance of AIDS in the 1980s. This concern recalls the nineteenth-century furor over prostitution as path for disease transmission that achieved legal expression in the passage of Britain's Contagious Diseases Acts of the 1860s. In Carole Pateman's view, the compulsory public health registration of suspected prostitutes required by these acts was the precipitating factor for prostitution in our contemporary sense. This effect of compulsory registration was to "professionalize" a more or less permanent subclass of women as "common prostitutes" because of the difficulty of removing one's name once it had been added to the registry list and of subsequently finding other employment. Since the 1980s, public health concerns about AIDS and other sexually transmitted diseases have contributed to the expansion of risk management and transaction cost approaches to prostitution as a social problem. The case law of the 1980s and 1990s in many jurisdictions reflects a "prostitutephobia" (Davis, p. 114) in numerous instances of lengthened prison sentences for prostitution justified as a form of quarantine for public health reasons.

Transaction-cost approaches to prostitution: from repression to regulation

Along with many other domains of social life in Western societies, prostitution has increasingly been approached through the lenses of transaction cost economic analysis and risk management. The application of legal economic reasoning has been extended from the regulation of established markets to "informal" economies and, ultimately, to the "economics of crime." (The work of Nobel laureate Gary Becker is foundational here; see also Hellman, pp. 129–144; Posner, pp. 70–80.)

This widespread turn to economic approaches does not, however, imply any general agreement on prostitution policy. Some economic theorists have proposed quite classical Benthamite rational disincentives to deter prostitution as criminal conduct (Hellman). Others have followed Nobel laureate Ronald Coase's theory of the internalization of social costs ("negative externalities") in economic transactions (Coase; Posner, 1992). Still others have argued that prostitution should be promoted as a form of free economic exchange just like any other economic activity that increases aggregate social wealth (these two latter views are not inconsistent with one another; see the extremely influential work of Richard Posner (1992)).

Further, mutually opposing normative views of the labor economics of prostitution structure the debate between the social movements that seek, on the one hand, to advance prostitutes' rights as "sex workers" and, on the other, to "rescue" prostitutes from exploitation in unconscionable labor conditions (Jenness). Recognizing prostitution as a two-sided economic transaction between a sexual service provider and a consumer reframes the "prostitution question" away from focusing solely on the alleged criminality or sociopathology of the prostitute and redirects attention to the consumption behaviors of the customer.

Typology of prostitution

The usual taxonomy of "types" of prostitute thus becomes differently interpretable as a socially stratified array of sexual-market consumption niches. These "market segments" can be distinguished from one another by place, by manner of solicitation, and by price level (Reynolds). It is instructive that many of the most commonly identified markets for sexual services are ambiguously positioned between legal and illegal forms of commercial bodily interaction: massage parlors, studios for nude photography, strip clubs, stag parties, and other erotic dance venues. In such socially liminal spaces, the boundary line between licit and illicit encounters is permeable and negotiable on a flexible, occasional basis, and is therefore correspondingly difficult to study empirically or to police effectively.

A brief survey of common prostitution "types" or "market segments" illustrates the sorts of questions that confront both social scientists and criminal justice professionals.

Streetwalkers. Streetwalkers are prostitutes who make themselves visible and commercially available on urban streets. They solicit customers who are passing on foot or in automobiles. Services are performed in customers' cars, in nearby hotels, alleys, doorways, and so on. On average, these prostitutes command the lowest prices, they typically have the least bargaining leverage over condom use and choice of sexual practices, and they have the highest risk of harm from customers or others. They are generally considered to generate the highest levels of negative externalities in terms of diminished neighborhood property values, association with other criminal activities, and "curb-crawling" by their customers. Not surprisingly, they also run the highest risk of arrest.

Bar/hotel prostitutes. Some prostitutes solicit customers in bars, clubs, and hotels, especially those frequented by conventioneers and other likely customers. Prostitutes often collaborate, and must share their revenues, with either the manager of the bar or club or, in the case of hotels, a bellhop or desk clerk who refers clients to the prostitute. Services may be provided in the establishment, in a dark corner or back room of a club, or in a hotel room rented by either the prostitute or the customer. The prostitute's income varies from fairly low to quite high according to the prestige and price range of the establishment and its clientele. The prostitute's net income also varies according to the percentage of fees demanded by the manager or employee(s) of the establishment in exchange for referrals, protection, or simply for looking the other way. The prostitute's risk of harm and arrest are low to moderate as long as the collaborative relation with the establishment is maintained and the prostitute does not venture into unfamiliar territory.

Escort services and call girls/boys. Some prostitutes operate on an "outcall basis" and therefore, unlike streetwalkers and bar/hotel prostitutes, are not restricted to a specific site. However, their calls are most often to locations where there are well-to-do clients who prefer the insulation of an intermediary referral service. Customers are typically assigned to prostitutes by the escort agency, which first charges a fee to the customer. The prostitute then negotiates with the customer the price for specific services. Like escorts, call girls/boys also rely upon referral and screening either by an agent, by a restricted circle of other prostitutes in the same market, or by familiar clients. The prices in this market segment reach the highest levels. The prostitute has considerable bargaining leverage over condom use and sexual practices. The risk of harm or arrest is lessened by reliance on an intermediary, and by the fact that this market segment tends to be limited to upper-income customers whose need for the appearance of propriety minimizes negative externalities and diminishes the likelihood of violence or other reason for police intervention.

House or brothel prostitutes. The only legally tolerated prostitution in the United States is found in the brothels permitted in the rural counties of the state of Nevada, at the discretion of the individual county. Nevada's current legal regime dates to shortly after World War II (prostitution had been outlawed during the war to minimize sexually transmitted disease among the large numbers of troops undergoing training in Nevada). Typically, the prostitutes at Nevada brothels are women from outside Nevada who are brought in on short-term contracts, living at the establishments for two or three weeks at a time with one or two weeks off. They are expected to spend long shifts on display in a bar/lounge reception area where prices for services are posted, to accept any customer who chooses them, then to take the customer to another room to perform the services contracted. The customer typically pays the house and the prostitute later receives 40 to 60 percent of the revenue that she has generated, sometimes with deductions for room, board, and supplies. Prostitutes in this market segment enjoy the highest level of protection from their customers since they work in a highly controlled environment where condom use has been enforced since the late 1980s. However, they have little personal autonomy or bargaining leverage over working conditions with their managers. They are typically controlled by state and county regulations that require them to be fingerprinted and to undergo weekly medical examinations; other legal regulations (of doubtful constitutionality) frequently prohibit the prostitutes from joining or even mingling with the communities in which the brothels are located. In many other parts of the United States, various forms of house prostitution exist illegally, though not infrequently with the tacit tolerance of the authorities (sometimes purchased), as long as public visibility and negative externalities are kept to a low level.

Miscellaneous other markets. Since prostitution is a highly flexible segment of the informal economy a great variety of other prostitution arrangements exists. Many prostitutes move in and out of prostitution as their financial needs dictate. Some are seasonally active as they, for example, follow mobile encampments of migrant workers in agriculture, the lumber industry, summer and winter resort traffic, or even sports and music tours.

Regimes of prohibition, criminalization, and regulation

The 1980s and 1990s saw different faces of prostitution presented in American media. The 1980s case of Sydney Biddle Barrows, the "Mayflower Madam," and the 1990s case of Heidi Fleiss, the "Hollywood Madam," brought public scrutiny, even celebrity, to the world of elite call girls who earn thousands, even tens of thousands, of dollars per day for their services. Over the same period, the expansion of crack cocaine consumption in poor urban neighborhoods contributed to the appearance of the "crack whore." The "crack whore" has become an urban American social type, a persona that is at once a depiction of the most severely drug-addicted, impoverished street prostitutes as well as a rhetorical figure summoned up in policy debates over "welfare reform" and the "war on drugs." Socioeconomic studies of the lives and livelihoods of such drug-addicted prostitutes reveal that their income is often less than the federal minimum wage (Maher and Daly).

Academic, political, and criminal justice policy debates frequently hinge on whether one takes the "entrepreneurial call girl" or the "crack whore" as the paradigm case of prostitution, that is, whether the underlying "cause" of prostitution is free individual choice or socioeconomic and psychopharmacological compulsion. Arrest statistics showing that the vast majority of those charged with prostitution offenses are low-income urban ethnic-minority women are commonly cited to support the latter position. Yet, empirically, it is difficult or impossible to falsify the counterclaim that there exist large numbers of prostitutes who go about their business providing services and contributing to the economy in low visibility, informal market sectors and who are rarely or never arrested. Ultimately, there remains a lack of conclusive empirical findings and criminal justice policy is often mired in the politics of folk moralizing embodied in the warring media stereotypes of glamorous call girl versus pitiable crack whore. As a result, most American jurisdictions retain criminal statutes strictly prohibiting prostitution with little or no change from a century ago.

The legal prohibition in force in all U.S. jurisdictions except Nevada's rural counties is something of an anomaly in the global context. In most of Western Europe, India, Southeast Asia, Canada, Australia, the Pacific, and much of Latin America the policy regimes governing prostitution tend not to criminalize sexual commerce itself (which is usually not fully legal, but rather "decriminalized"). Instead, these countries generally criminalize prostitution-related activities such as solicitation, advertising, living off another person's earnings from sexual commerce, and recruiting and transporting persons to engage in prostitution (in the United States, most of these activities are also criminally sanctioned in addition to prostitution per se). The criminalization of activities associated with prostitution shades subtly into other regimes that are intended to regulate the conduct of prostitution while at least implicitly tolerating it (see Davis).

In Western Europe and certain other regions such decriminalization and regulatory approaches have led to a dual market in prostitution. Most European Union residents can engage in prostitution without criminal sanction, yet at the same time there also exists a widespread illegal secondary prostitution market made up of tens of thousands of migrants from Eastern Europe, Asia, and Latin America. These migrants practice prostitution in an underground economy, for lower earnings and in lesser conditions, fearing arrest, deportation, and coercive violence from their employers.

In virtually no country has prostitution been entirely accepted as a legitimate profession with the full social rights, worker protection, pensions, and other benefits accorded to other laborers and business enterprises. Whether legally prohibited, decriminalized, or regulated, wherever prostitution is practiced it remains a liminal social space subject to regimes of social control. Increasingly, no matter whether prostitution per se is legal or not, criminal justice and other social control strategies are directed toward minimizing the negative externalities (undesirable effects upon third parties or on society in general) that result from prostitution transactions.

A growing tendency is to make use of strategies for spatially segregating prostitution and activities associated with it in order to manage or minimize perceived externalities. This echoes the long-time practice in many cities where overt prostitution is de facto shunted into specific enclaves, often called "red light districts." These have usually been "low-rent" neighborhoods, that is, low-valued land-use urban zones, in or near ethnic minority or migrants' residential areas. It is illustrative of the spatial logic of minimizing the social costs of prostitution that the only place where it is legally tolerated in the United States are certain rural counties of Nevada—areas with very low population densities whose economic development alternatives include military weapons testing sites and toxic waste dumps.

In nearly all other American jurisdictions where prostitution is prohibited, it exists nonetheless and is in effect regulated through various spatially differentiated control strategies. Dallas, Texas, is an example of what has been called the "Control Model" (Reynolds). Here, police pressure is exerted to keep prostitution all but invisible in Dallas, except for some poorer neighborhoods. A certain amount of hotel and call girl/boy prostitution is tolerated as long as it remains confined to the convention trade and the more highly visible streetwalking is confined to poorer minority communities in the region.

San Francisco, a city that prides itself on its cosmopolitan tolerance, has been a long-time example of the "laissez-faire model" of prostitution regulation (Reynolds). One might describe this as a regime where nothing is legal but everything is permitted. Historically, overt street prostitution has flourished in the Tenderloin district and certain other lower-income neighborhoods. It is periodically suppressed by police pressure, just enough to minimize unsightliness that might offend the tourist trade. Much like Western European regulatory policies, San Francisco police strategy has often been to prosecute incidents of theft and violence associated with street prostitution but not to pursue the sexual offenses themselves. Call services and other less visible forms of prostitution are only rarely targeted by vigorous police enforcement.

In the 1970s, the city of Boston decided to use zoning law to localize de jure the city's "adult businesses" within a single neighborhood called the "Combat Zone." Although prostitution was not legalized, it was to a large extent effectively enclosed along with adult cinemas, pornography shops, and massage parlors. This extremely influential strategy has been called the "zoning model" (Reynolds). It sets up something rather like a sexual version of the "free trade zones" that exist in seaports and border towns, exempted from ordinary tariffs and regulations. Such spatial concentration of sex-oriented business may in fact lead to greater efficiency for sexual commerce because of lower search and transaction costs. However, the zoning model's greatest influence has been as a strategy for localizing and managing the risks and externalities associated with prostitution and other sexual commerce.

In the 1990s, other cities (notably Portland, Oregon) have employed zoning in a different fashion. Rather than quarantining sexual commerce by zoning it into a specific urban area like Boston's Combat Zone, now zoning is used to exclude prostitutes by establishing "prostitution-free zones." Drawing upon new urban strategies such as business improvement districts and area-specific gang-abatement injunctions, people who have been identified as known prostitutes are legally banned from whole sections of the city. The "cleansing" of New York City's Times Square in the 1990s is another example of such exclusionary strategies.

These adaptations of zoning law for the suppression, displacement, and spatial regulation of vice are part of a broader policy shift from strictly criminal repression to a flexible mix of criminal and civil sanctions in the crafting of new regulatory regimes. Although no jurisdiction has maintained customer-arrest levels equal to the arrest of prostitutes, there has been a new attention to this disparity. Some cities, notably San Francisco and Portland, have established programs modeled on so-called traffic schools for automobile driving infractions. Although these "therapeutic" programs are in principle available to prostitutes as well as to their customers, they are commonly referred to as "john schools" and have reportedly been little used by arrested prostitutes (Meier and Geis, pp. 52–53).

Conclusion

The fundamental problem of how to conceptualize prostitution—as sin, as crime, as enslavement, as productive work, as disease vector, as social risk profile—and of how to approach it in policy and practice became more acute in the 1980s and 1990s (Davis). The trends toward globalization in communications and the economy, in migrant labor flows, in international "sex-tourism," and in the spread of AIDS and other diseases have exposed the inadequacies of traditional, locally focused efforts to understand and to address prostitution (Truong, 1986, 1990). The conceptual incoherence of sociolegal theories is compounded by the radical complexity of global jurisdictional differences in legislation, in criminal justice policies, and in social consequences. Prostitutes from the most impoverished and disease-afflicted areas of the world walk the streets of the wealthiest countries as "sex-tourists" flow in the opposite direction. As media panics about disease epidemics and about the sexual exploitation and even enslavement of children as well as adults seize the short attention span of the global public, the dimensions of the problems are rapidly outpacing the authority and even the scope of vision of local and national governments.

International law instruments such as the 1949 UN Convention for the Suppression of the Traffic in Persons and of the Exploitation of the Prostitution of Others (only ratified by about one-third of the UN member states as of 1998) are still no more than tentative and rudimentary efforts. Nongovernmental organizations are considerably more in touch with the rapidly changing global facts of prostitution at the beginning of the twenty-first century, but they too suffer from the lack of any shared conception of the problems and they routinely expend their limited resources working at cross-purposes to one another. In few other domains of crime and justice is there a more urgent need for more and more rigorous empirical research on a worldwide scale and for a fundamental theoretical reorientation.

RICHARD WARREN PERRY

See also CRIMINALIZATION AND DECRIMINALIZATION; DE- VIANCE; GENDER AND CRIME; HOMOSEXUALITY AND CRIME; MASS MEDIA AND CRIME; ORGANIZED CRIME; PO- LICE: POLICING COMPLAINANTLESS CRIMES; RAPE: BE- HAVIORAL ASPECTS; RAPE: LEGAL ASPECTS; SEX OFFENSES: CONSENSUAL; SEXUAL PREDATORS; VICTIM- LESS CRIME.

BIBLIOGRAPHY

BECKER, GARY. "Crime and Punishment: An Eco- nomic Approach." *Journal of Political Economy* 76, no. 2 (1968): 168–217.

BULLOUGH, VERN L. *The History of Prostitution.* New Hyde Park, N.Y.: University Books, 1964.

COASE, RONALD. "The Problem of Social Cost." *Journal of Law and Economics* 3, no. 1 (1960): 1–44.

DAVIS, NANETTE J., ed. *Prostitution: An Internation- al Handbook on Trends, Problems, and Policies.* New York: Greenwood Press, 1993.

DE BEAUVOIR, SIMONE. *The Second Sex.* (1953). Translated and edited by H. M. Parshley. New York: Vintage, 1974.

GOLDMAN, EMMA. "The Traffic in Women." In *Anarchism and Other Essays* (1915). New York: Dover Publications, 1969.

HELLMAN, DARYL A. *The Economics of Crime.* New York: St. Martin's Press, 1980.

JENNESS, VALERIE. *Making It Work: The Contempo- rary Prostitutes' Rights Movement in Perspective.* New York: Aldine de Gruyter, 1993.

MAHER, LISA, and DALY, KATHLEEN. "Women in the Street-Level Drug Economy: Continuity or Change?" *Criminology* 34 (1993): 465–492.

MEIER, ROBERT F., and GEIS, GILBERT. "Prostitu- tion." In *Victimless Crime? Prostitution, Drugs, Homosexuality, Abortion.* Los Angeles: Roxbury Publishing, 1997.

PATEMAN, CAROLE. *The Sexual Contract.* Stanford: Stanford University Press, 1988.

PERKINS, ROBERTA, and BENNETT, GARRY. *Being A Prostitute.* Boston: Allen & Unwin, 1985.

POSNER, RICHARD A. *Sex and Reason.* Cambridge, Mass: Harvard University Press, 1992.

REYNOLDS, HELEN. *The Economics of Prostitution.* Springfield, Ill.: Charles C. Thomas, 1986.

RICHARDS, DAVID A. J. *Sex, Drugs, Death, and the Law.* Totowa, N.J.: Rowman and Littlefield, 1982.

SIMMEL, GEORG. *The Sociology of Georg Simmel.* (1908). Edited by Kurt H. Wolf. Glencoe, Ill.: Free Press, 1982.

TONNIES, FERDINAND. *Community and Society.* (1887). Translated and edited by Charles P. Loomis. New York: Harper and Row, 1963.

TRUONG, THANH-DAM. *Virtue, Order, Health, and Money: Towards a Comprehensive Perspective on Female Prostitution in Asia.* Bangkok: United Nations Economic and Social Commission for Asia and the Pacific, 1986.

———. *Sex, Money, and Morality: Prostitution and Tourism in Southeast Asia.* London: Zed Books, 1990.

WOLLSTONECRAFT, MARY. "A Vindication of the Rights of Men" (1799). In *A Mary Wollsto- necraft Reader.* Edited by Barbara H. Solomon and Paula S. Berggren.

PSYCHOPATHY

This entry covers the definition and scientific validity of psychopathy and related mental con- ditions and the criminal law's response to crimi- nals who manifest this condition.

What is psychopathy?

Although there is much dispute about the definition of and the criteria for the term *psychop- athy*, the best current conceptual and scientific understanding is that psychopathy is a mental disorder marked by affective, interpersonal, and behavioral abnormalities. In particular, people with psychopathy demonstrate an incapacity for empathy and guilt, impulsivity, egocentricity, and chronic violations of social, moral, and legal norms. (Because psychopathy is a mental disor- der, the preferred locution to describe those who suffer from it is "people with psychopathy," rath- er than to use the term *psychopath*, which improp- erly equates a person with the disorder. Nonetheless, the shorter locution is both com- mon in professional and lay usage and less un- wieldy, so this entry will use it.) Psychopaths can be found among all classes of the populations and in all professions. Not unexpectedly, their numbers among prison and jail populations are disproportionately large.

Historical development of the concept. The broad outlines of the condition and the begin- ning of the construction of a clinical diagnostic category date to the nineteenth century, but there has been little scientifically based agree- ment on the criteria for the disorder, leading some critics to maintain that the category is theo- retically or clinically useless and, even more ex- tremely, that it does not exist. Nonetheless, whether termed psychopathy, sociopathy, dysso- cial personality disorder, or some other term, the category has long been in use. The most influential modern clinical description of psychopathy was provided by psychiatrist Hervey Cleckley in a famous work, *The Mask of Sanity* (1976 [1941]). Cleckley observed that psychopaths, unlike people with major mental disorders such as schizophrenia, can seem quite normal and even charming, thus earning the descriptive term for the condition "mask of sanity." Psychopaths do not suffer from grossly psychotic symptoms, such as hallucinations or delusions, unless they also suffer from another major mental disorder. But people who lack empathy and guilt, who are willing to manipulate, lie, or cheat without hesitation or remorse to achieve their own ends, are so interpersonally and behaviorally abnormal that characterizing the condition as a disorder seems justifiable.

In 1968, a condition like psychopathy received the official imprimatur of the American Psychiatric Association by being included in the second edition of its *Diagnostic and Statistical Manual of Mental Disorders* (DSM-II), in which it was referred to as "antisocial personality" and characterized as a personality disorder. Unfortunately, DSM-II used vague criteria and researchers were unable to operationalize or to validate the construct, a problem that plagued DSM-II in general and psychopathy research in the 1970s in particular.

The next revision of the *Diagnostic and Statistical Manual of Mental Disorders*, DSM-III, published in 1980 and revised in 1987 as DSM-III-R, adopted a new approach to establishing the criteria for mental disorders, an approach that was retained in the next major revision in 1994, DSM-IV. Rather than using vague descriptive criteria for signs and symptoms and then providing no guidance about how many of the criteria had to be present and to what degree, DSM-III and later revisions tried to provide more specific criteria and inclusion and exclusion rules. The result was that independent observers could more readily agree about whether a disorder was present, but critics claimed that such an increase in reliability was accompanied by a loss in validity. That is, it was not clear that the more operationalized criteria of DSM-III that permitted diagnostic agreement among raters also accurately captured the true contours of the disorders it was attempting to define by those criteria.

Concerns about validity were a particular problem for the behavioral disorder under consideration, which was termed *antisocial personality disorder* (APD) and defined purely behaviorally in terms of chronic antisocial behaviors, such as stealing or failure to meet financial obligations. These behaviors could be objectively observed or discovered reasonably accurately and thus independent raters could agree about whether the person under consideration met the criteria, but the diagnostic criteria omitted the less observable, clinical inferential criteria, such as the ability to feel empathy or guilt, that many clinicians thought were the touchstone of the disorder. Such clinicians believed that antisocial behavior could certainly be a product of underlying psychopathology, but antisocial behavior could be produced by many other variables as well. Thus, DSM-III's behavioral definition apparently failed to distinguish true psychopaths, whose antisocial behavior was produced by the underlying clinical pathology, from people whose similar antisocial behavior might be produced by poverty, subcultural influences, or other potential causes. But until good operational measures of the underlying pathology could be developed, it was impossible to make conceptual and empirical progress.

Contemporary empirical research. In the 1980s, a Canadian researcher, Robert D. Hare, and colleagues developed an operationalized research instrument to measure psychopathy, ultimately termed the Hare Psychopathy Checklist Revised (or Hare PCL-R; a more easily administered, briefer screening version, the Hare PCL-:SV, has also been developed). Although many other estimable researchers have empirically investigated the behaviors associated with psychopathy and have developed other measures, it is fair to claim that Hare (and colleagues) and his measure have been the most influential. The PCL-R is a twenty-item rating scale that uses a semistructured interview to yield the data to be assessed. The subject's final score estimates the degree to which the subject appears to be like a classic psychopath as described by Cleckley. The PCL-R has excellent psychometric properties when used with male offenders and forensic patients, the groups with and for which it was originally developed, and in recent years its reliability and validity with female offenders and psychiatric patients has also been established. Because the PCL-R permits a continuous score on its scale, psychopathy may be considered a dimensional disorder rather than a clearly demarcated category. That is, psychopathy may be more or less marked. Which cut-off points are most useful for tasks such as the prediction of violence is an empirical question.

Although research demonstrates that the PCL-R appears to measure a unitary construct, there is also clear evidence that there are two distinct clusters of behavior that contribute to the total score. The first, which appears to measure "emotional detachment," includes primarily interpersonal or affective indicators of psychopathy, such as egocentricity or lack of remorse; the second, which appears to measure antisocial behavior and lifestyle, includes variables such as impulsiveness and antisocial conduct. High PCL-R scores are predictive of violence in both criminal and civil psychiatric populations, but it appears that the second, antisocial behavior factor, not the interpersonal, emotional detachment factor, accounts for most of the predictive efficacy. Critics believe that the PCL-R's predictive validity is produced by a nonspecific antisocial history, but research has shown that if one controls for such nonspecific factors, the PCL-R does increase predictive validity.

PCL-R scores are correlated with APD diagnoses in forensic populations, but the correlation is not perfect. In such populations, the base rate for psychopathy as measured by the PCL-R is much lower than the base rate for APD. Although most psychopaths meet the criteria for APD because APD criteria are similar to the antisocial behaviors that the second factor of PCL-R measures, most people with APD are not psychopaths because the criteria for APD do not include the affective and interpersonal variables that the first factor of PCL-R measures. In sum, psychopathy as operationalized by the PCL-R, which aims to measure the clinical construct described by Cleckley and others, is not identical to APD.

There are many causes of criminal behavior other than psychopathy (or APD). Indeed the prevalence of criminal and antisocial behavior is much greater than the prevalence of psychopathy. It thus appears that criminal behavior among psychopaths is produced by different variables than those that produce crime among nonpsychopaths. But psychopaths disproportionately engage in persistent and varied antisocial and criminal behavior. Furthermore, the risk of violence among violent psychopathic offenders does not seem to decrease with age, as it does with nonpsychopathic offenders.

Sexual psychopathy. "Sexual psychopathy" is not a technical term within psychiatry, psychology, and psychopathology. Although the normality of various sexual desires is a matter of debate, it is certainly the case that some unfortunate individuals have sexual desires that are widely considered abnormal, such as the persistent, intense desire for sexual contact with children, and acting to satisfy such desires is almost uniformly considered immoral and criminal. People with such desires do meet the criteria for a mental disorder in DSM-IV, although, once again, few manifest psychotic symptoms unless they suffer from another mental disorder. Some people with such abnormalities, often claiming that they cannot control their desires, persistently act to satisfy them, thus routinely violating the criminal law. Clear data are not available, but it is apparent that not all such offenders are psychopaths. They may behave antisocially, but they do not necessarily manifest the affective and interpersonal criteria of true psychopathy. They may feel guilt and remorse, for example. Disorders of sexual desire should be clearly distinguished from psychopathy although some individuals may suffer from both.

Causes and treatments. The causes of psychopathy are not well-understood. Biological, psychological, and sociological explanations have been proposed, but none has been confirmed. More recent advances in cognitive neuroscience appear to provide a potential neurophysiological explanation for the clinical observation that psychopaths lack emotional depth and understanding. Indeed, some hypothesize that brain dysfunction causes psychopathy. Such research is provocative and fascinating, but current data simply do not justify firm conclusions about the causes of this disorder.

Development of treatments for psychopathy among prison and forensic populations was hindered by the inability to distinguish psychopaths from other offenders. Nonetheless, various methods have been tried. It is fair to say, especially given the methodological limitations, that there has been little indication of success. It is now possible to distinguish psychopaths reliably and new treatment proposals have followed from better understanding of the clinical manifestations of the disorder. It is unfortunately still the case, however, that there are few hard data to demonstrate the efficacy of any proposed treatment program to reduce psychopathy in general or its antisocial behavioral manifestations in particular.

Continuing conceptual and clinical concerns. Despite the undoubted scientific advances in the measurement of psychopathy and provocative empirical findings concerning its causes, many remain skeptical of the validity of the category and fear its use in clinical and non-clinical settings. Some believe that available research does not confirm Hare's unitary model that amalgamates two factors and that there is no present, uncontroversially valid definition of the disorder. Others go further, claiming that psychopathy is little more than a label for a type of person that is both disliked and feared and that there is no good evidence that psychopathy is a genuine mental disorder.

There is some truth to all these criticisms. Available science is not perfect. In particular, psychiatry and psychology, unlike physical medicine, as yet have no physical "gold standard," such as underlying, objectively measurable anatomical or physiological abnormalities, with which to validate hypothesized discrete disorders. Moreover, it is too easy to "pathologize" those we do not like as a means of marginalizing and controlling them. Nonetheless, compared to other, less controversial psychiatric and psychological disorders, psychopathy has been better validated by a solid research base than most.

Psychopathy and the criminal law

Psychopathy provides a theoretical and practical challenge to criminal law and the criminal justice system in general because psychopaths are at disproportionate risk for persistent criminal behavior, their criminal conduct appears to be primarily the product of a mental disorder, and there seems little efficacious treatment.

Psychopathy and competence. Unless a psychopath who offends also suffers from a psychotic disorder, there is little if any likelihood that the offender will be incompetent to stand trial solely because the offender is a psychopath. Because psychopaths feel little hesitation about lying or manipulative behavior and are often adept at concealing such behavior, they may be difficult clients for their attorneys. Moreover, they may not understand that they have done anything wrong. Nevertheless, psychopathy per se does not undermine cognitive understanding to a degree that would meet the criminal law's requirements for incompetence to stand trial because psychopaths can understand the nature of the charges and are capable of assisting counsel. Psychopaths may be at risk for malingering incompetence if they believe that it would be in their interest to be found incompetent, but the risk of malingering is distinguishable from genuine incompetence to stand trial or from any other criminal law criterion related to mental abnormality.

Criminal responsibility. The most interesting theoretical and practical question psychopathy presents is whether psychopaths are morally and legally responsible for their criminal behavior. The criminal law's answer is doctrinally clear: psychopathy alone will not support a defense of nonresponsibility, such as legal insanity, and behavioral manifestations of psychopathy, such as the potential for danger or recidivism, are often aggravating factors in sentencing. Thus, convicted psychopaths are sent to prison like other convicted offenders and often they may face more severe penalties than nonpsychopathic offenders. But is the criminal law's response to psychopathy just and practically sound?

The argument for holding psychopaths responsible for their behavior begins with the observation that psychopaths are firmly in touch with reality. They know the factual nature of their conduct and they know the moral and legal rules and the consequences for violating those rules. Psychopaths might not understand the point of moral and legal rules because they do not understand any moral concern or any consequential concern that is not solely self-interested. Nonetheless, psychopaths have the capacity to feel pain and know that pain will be inflicted if they are convicted of a violation. Also, psychopaths do not appear to suffer from any traditional "volitional" problem. Consequently, it appears that the law can affect the behavior of psychopaths. Even generous application of the most forgiving insanity defense test would appear not to excuse psychopaths. Indeed, for many people, psychopaths seem especially immoral, especially evil, and thus deserving of enhanced punishment. Moreover, to the extent that psychopaths also present an enhanced risk of recidivism, there is good consequential reason to incapacitate them longer.

The argument that psychopaths should not be morally and legally responsible for criminal conduct concedes the truth of the psychopath's cognitive knowledge, but relies on a broader standard of responsibility that requires the capacity for empathy and moral understanding as fundamental to moral rationality. Psychopaths do not "get" the point of morality, of concern for others, of guilt or shame. They are entirely unable to use empathy, concern, or morality as reasons not to harm others, even though these are the best reasons to comply with moral and legal rules. They are "morally insane" and are incapable of being morally responsive agents. Psychopaths are simply not part of the moral community and do not deserve blame and punishment. Many might rebel at this conclusion because they fear psychopaths would then "beat the rap" and be released to harm others. An appropriate finding of legal insanity does not amount to wrongfully beating the rap, however. A person genuinely not responsible should not be blamed and punished.

Dispositional issues. What are the appropriate dispositional consequences of psychopathy? First, consider the standard case in which a psychopathic criminal is convicted and assume that the sentencing judge has some discretion to take psychopathy into account in imposing sentence. As we have seen, psychopathy is an apparently static condition that is not at present amenable to treatment and that increases the risk of recidivism. Psychopathy would then rationally be considered an aggravating factor that would warrant a harsher sentence and even death in jurisdictions that impose capital punishment. The justice of this result would depend entirely, however, on accurate identification of genuine psychopaths. Without such identification, psychopathy could be improperly used to impose unfair sentences based on prejudice or other irrational factors. Recidivism statutes are another means by which psychopathic criminals might receive enhanced incarceration. In this case, psychopathy would not be considered directly, but would produce the recidivism that triggers such enhanced sentencing statutes. Psychopathic criminals are perhaps at special risk for the application of such statutes, but they are not singled out by them.

If some psychopaths were found nonresponsible, as some propose, what should be the appropriate disposition? Most important, a finding of nonresponsibility does not necessarily entail immediate release. Much as people found legally insane may be involuntarily committed as long as they remain dangerous as a result of mental abnormality, psychopaths would be similarly committable. And again, because psychopathy is static and untreatable, dangerous psychopaths would have little hope for early release from involuntary confinement. Indeed, because post-acquittal commitment may be indefinite, there is substantial likelihood that some nonresponsible psychopathic offenders would be confined longer than if they had been convicted of the same crime. Although the outcome of a nonresponsibility finding might be as or more onerous than a conviction, it is still important that the law should clearly identify those who are not responsible and treat them as nonpunitively as possible.

The possibility of indefinite commitment does present a substantial risk to civil liberties. Even if psychopaths were not considered responsible, they do engender dislike and fear, thereby creating the potential simply to incarcerate them for life and without attempting to develop and apply treatments that might change the condition. Moreover, there is the risk that some people would be improperly labeled psychopaths in order to achieve otherwise unjustifiable indefinite incapacitation. Finally, because the risk of almost any harm may constitutionally satisfy the dangerousness component of post-insanity acquittal commitments, potentially lifelong commitment might result for psychopaths who have committed relatively nonserious crimes and are at risk only for such crimes. Careful substantive and procedural checks on findings of psychopathy would be necessary to avoid such various forms of unfairness.

Preventative measures. Are there sound and fair social and legal prophylactic measures to reduce the harms psychopaths might cause? Because the causes of psychopathy are so poorly understood, it will be difficult to devise and to implement social programs to prevent psychopathy or to identify and to treat psychopaths before a substantial antisocial career begins. Early identification of and intervention with children at risk would be especially desirable, but even if reasonably accurate identification were possible, it is not at all clear that efficacious treatment programs exist. Moreover, early identification is now problematic because many children exhibit disturbing, repetitive antisocial behavior, but not all of them are psychopaths and there is yet no clearly valid method for identifying psychopathy or potential psychopathy among children.

The most realistic possibility for limiting psychopaths' potential harms is therefore some form of pure civil commitment that does not depend on proving a charge of or a conviction for a criminal offense. Once again, however, this proposal raises substantial civil liberties concerns. Misidentification, prejudice, fear, and the like could lead to vast amounts of unwarranted deprivation of liberty. And even if proper cases for commitment could be identified, no efficacious treatment to facilitate release is available at present.

STEPHEN J. MORSE

See also CRIME CAUSATION: BIOLOGICAL THEORIES; CRIME CAUSATION: PSYCHOLOGICAL THEORIES; DIMINISHED CAPACITY; EXCUSE: INSANITY; MENTALLY DISORDERED OFFENDERS; PREDICTION OF CRIME AND RECIDIVISM; VIOLENCE.

BIBLIOGRAPHY

American Psychiatric Association. *Diagnostic and Statistical Manual of Mental Disorders*, 4th ed., text revision. Washington D.C.: American Psychiatric Association, 1994.

CLECKLEY, HERVEY M. *The Mask of Sanity*, 5th ed. St. Louis: Mosby, 1976. First published, 1941.

COOKE, DAVID J.; FORTH, ADELLE E.; and HARE, ROBERT D., eds. *Psychopathy: Theory, Research, and Implications for Society*. Dordrecht, The Netherlands: Kluwer, 1998.

HARE, ROBERT D. *Without Conscience: The Disturbing World of the Psychopaths among Us*. New York: Pocket Books, 1993.

———. "Psychopaths and Their Nature: Implications for the Mental Health and Criminal Justice Systems." In *Psychopathy: Antisocial, Criminal, and Violent Behavior*. Edited by Theodore Millon, Erik Simonsen, Morten Birket-Smith, and Roger D. Davis. New York: The Guilford Press, 1998, Pages 188–212.

LYKKEN, DAVID T. *The Antisocial Personalities*. Hillsdale, N.J.: Lawrence Erlbaum Associates, 1995.

MILLON, THEODOR; SIMONSEN, ERIK; BIRKET-SMITH, MORTEN; and DAVIS, ROGER D., eds. *Psychopathy: Antisocial, Criminal, and Violent Behavior*. New York: The Guilford Press, 1998.

MONAHAN, JOHN; STEADMAN, HENRY; SILVER, ERIC; APPELBAUM, PAUL; ROBBINS, PAMELA; MULVEY, EDWARD; ROTH, LOREN, GRISSO, THOMAS; and BANKS, STEPHEN. *Rethinking Risk Assessment: The MacArthur Study of Mental Disorder and Violence*. New York: Oxford University Press, 2001.

MORSE, STEPHEN J. "Excusing and the New Excuse Defenses: A Legal and Conceptual Review." *Crime and Justice: A Review of Research, Volume 23*. Edited by Michael Tonry. Chicago: University of Chicago Press, 1998, Pages 329–406.

QUINSEY, VERNON L.; HARRIS, GRANT T.; RICE, MANIE E.; and CORMIER, CATHERINE A. *Violent Offenders: Appraising and Managing Risk*. Washington, D.C.: American Psychological Association, 1998.

WOLF, SUSAN. *Freedom within Reason*. New York: Oxford University Press, 1990.

PUBLICITY IN CRIMINAL CASES

Media coverage of criminal cases poses a dilemma. Press attention in criminal cases sometimes has significant benefits. Publicity can cause unknown witnesses to come forward so that their information may be considered and the facts correctly determined. It can also help to ensure that those administering the criminal process will act fairly by subjecting their decisions to public scrutiny. Media attention can also provide the stimulus for needed changes in the criminal process or, alternatively, the information by which the public can conclude that the system operates appropriately. Nonetheless, press coverage may sometimes pose grave problems. Publicity may cause some judges or prosecutors, particularly those who must face reelection, to act out of political expediency rather than fairness. It may inappropriately expose witnesses or other participants to reputational damage, along with threats and even reprisals. It can disrupt courtroom proceedings. Also, and certainly not least important, it can bias jurors, usually against the criminal defendant.

The decision to solve this dilemma by restricting the press from publishing information it possesses has been favored in some countries. In England, and several other countries of the British Commonwealth, the press may only safely report before trial the essential facts of arrest and charge and, during trial, a balanced and objective account of the basic proceedings on the record. To do more will risk a contempt citation and fine or even imprisonment if the accounts are deemed to pose a reasonable chance of influencing the fact finder. In rare situations, the press may even be restricted by judicial order from reporting factually accurate material that would otherwise be published without sanction.

In the United States, the dilemma is not so easily solved because the arguments both for and against press coverage are often of constitutional proportions. On the one hand, the First Amendment guarantees the freedom of the press, which includes reporting on criminal cases. On the other hand, the Sixth Amendment and the due process clauses in the Fifth and Fourteenth Amendments guarantee the criminally accused the right to a trial by an impartial jury. It is also now established that these provisions limit the states as well as the federal government.

The problem of accommodating the public's right to a free press and the defendant's right to an unbiased jury has long existed. For example, during the 1807 trial of Aaron Burr for treason, Chief Justice John Marshall of the U.S. Supreme Court, sitting as a trial judge, was forced to contend with defense claims that jurors had been biased by pretrial press accounts. Likewise, both the trial of Sacco and Vanzetti in 1921, for murder, and the trial of Bruno Richard Hauptmann in 1935, for the kidnapping and murder of the Lindbergh baby, raised serious concerns about whether jurors had been unduly influenced against the defendants by publicity.

Nonetheless, the problem of prejudicial publicity for courts has increased since the middle of the twentieth century due to the expansion of federal constitutional rights, including their extension to state criminal justice systems, and the advent and growth of television as a powerful and widely observed medium for news reporting. The press coverage of the prosecution of O. J. Simpson for the 1994 killings of his ex-wife and one of her friends demonstrated the potential problem. The publicity in the Simpson case, particularly by the television media, was unrivaled in American history, and that coverage included much information that was damaging to Simpson that was not admitted as evidence at the trial. Likewise, in the prosecutions of Timothy McVeigh and Terry Nichols, for the 1995 murders of dozens of people from the bombing of a federal office building in Oklahoma City, serious questions arose about how to protect the defendants' constitutional right to an impartial jury in light of the intense and enduring television coverage not only in Oklahoma but throughout the country.

Despite the increasing magnitude of the problem of prejudicial publicity in criminal cases, the judicial response in the United States continues to reflect a high place for the First Amendment guarantee of a free press. Courts have gone far in assuming that biased jurors can be detected and excluded through the questioning process, called *voir dire*, that accompanies jury selection and, further, that those chosen as jurors can ignore publicity when told to do so by the trial judge. Where these protections are deemed insufficient, courts have also relied heavily on additional remedies designed to overcome prejudicial publicity rather than on remedies aimed at preventing publicity. Even where they have taken steps to limit publicity, courts have opted for measures that restrict the information flow to the press rather than measures that prevent the press from publishing information in its possession. The First Amendment has generally barred the use of direct limitations on the press's power to publish information it has obtained.

Difficulty for the trial judge in assessing prejudice

Evaluating whether publicity is prejudicial is a subjective endeavor. The problem arises in only a small proportion of all criminal prosecutions. The vast majority of cases spark no serious press interest. In larger urban areas, even murders are sufficiently common that many will receive relatively little attention. However, a few criminal cases attract intense media interest, usually because of the fame of the defendant, the fame of the victim, or the unusually gruesome or salacious nature of the crime. When a case has received publicity, there is always potential that the accounts have reached some of the jurors. Assessing whether the stories have rendered them biased can be difficult.

First, the legal standard of "impartiality" itself connotes a highly speculative determination. What does juror impartiality mean? It obviously does not signify that a juror must come to the courthouse as an empty cipher, without political leanings, moral beliefs, or views about crime. Impartiality also does not mean that a juror must be ignorant about the case or have avoided forming an impression about the defendant's guilt. The Supreme Court concluded long ago, in *Reynolds v. United States*, 98 U.S. 145 (1878), and has repeated many times, that an impartial juror is merely one who will base a verdict on the evidence presented at trial and the instructions of the trial judge. Prospective jurors who can put aside impressions about the defendant's guilt and can ignore external information to which they have been exposed are deemed impartial. Social science evidence reflects disagreement about whether juries will follow a trial court's instructions to ignore external information. Yet, many prospective jurors who have been exposed to external information, including powerful press accounts, will claim that they can abide by the impartiality standard. How should the trial judge decide when to believe them? Resolution of this kind of question involves much guesswork.

Measuring prejudice is particularly difficult when the assessment occurs weeks before trial, which is when claims of prejudicial publicity are typically first considered. At this stage, the trial judge often lacks good information about many factors that may bear on the prejudice inquiry. How many potential jurors may have seen or heard about the press accounts? With what level of interest have they followed the stories? Does the publicity reveal information that will not be admissible at trial? Does it give an undue emphasis to factors that would not be heavily emphasized at trial? Will the information in the news accounts accord with or conflict with a defense theory to be asserted? Assuming the publicity subsides, will the passage of time before the trial date cause jurors to forget much of the press accounts? The judge must often estimate the answers to these kinds of questions, because the prospective jurors have not been assembled for questioning, and the judge knows little about the trial evidence.

The determination involves much speculation even if delayed until the beginning of the trial. At this point, the judge can obtain information from potential jurors regarding the number who are aware of the publicity and the number who believe they could not ignore it. The judge still cannot easily assess, however, when jurors who assert that they can be impartial are being unrealistic. At this stage, the judge is also more likely to have ruled on the admissibility of some evidence subject to pretrial challenge, such as a confession by the defendant, and thus can know whether the press stories have exposed certain information that has been suppressed. However, the judge will likely remain only vaguely informed about much of the trial evidence and thus, will not know how much the press accounts will overlap with the government's case or conflict with the defense theory. To the extent that the external information is not covered by the evidence and collides with the defense, it may be more difficult for jurors to ignore. This means that, even at the start of trial, the judge's assessments of prejudice from publicity are imprecise.

Judicial rules governing prejudice assessments

The Supreme Court has dealt with the speculative nature of assessments of publicity through three rules that mean that the decision of the trial judge will usually be honored. First, the Court has held that juror-bias determinations are largely factual rather than legal so that the trial judge is in the best position to decide them; appellate courts have been directed to defer to a trial court's finding on juror impartiality except in cases of clear error. Second, the

Court has been grudging in its view of what constitutes evidence of prejudicial publicity. The Court has held that, except in extraordinary cases, publicity is not prejudicial unless a juror actually states an inability to ignore it. Third, the Court has held that trial courts need not ask potential jurors specifically about the content of relevant publicity to which they have been exposed, but rather may rely on more general questions about whether the jurors can be fair. These three rules together mean that a trial judge's conclusion that a jury is constitutionally impartial will rarely justify reversal.

The Supreme Court has long held that appellate courts should generally defer to the trial judge's finding on juror bias. The Court declared in *Reynolds v. United States*, 98 U.S. 145 (1878), that the factual nature of the inquiry justifies affirming the trial court's conclusion except in cases of "manifest error." In more recent times, in *Wainwright v. Witt*, 469 U.S. 412 (1985), the Court concluded that the impartiality question was purely factual, so that the trial court's finding should not be overturned unless the conclusion lacks support in the record.

The Court has also been reluctant to find evidence of juror bias from publicity unless a juror actually admits an inability to ignore it. Court opinions during the era of Chief Justice Earl Warren reflected the view that prejudice from pretrial publicity may sometimes be presumed, despite claims by jurors that they can remain impartial. More recent opinions, however, imply that the Court will rarely be willing to find prejudice unless a juror admits bias during voir dire.

The view of the Warren Court was embodied in the opinions in *Marshall v. United States*, 360 U.S. 310 (1959), and *Irvin v. Dowd*, 366 U.S 717 (1961). *Marshall* was decided under the Court's supervisory powers over the federal courts rather than as an interpretation of the Constitution. It held that jurors who have heard through the press of the defendant's previous criminal record are "presumed to be prejudiced," as this information would not typically be admissible in the government's initial case at trial.

In *Irvin*, the presumption of prejudice was grounded on the Constitution and was triggered by a combination of factors. The trial was held in a rural county adjoining the county in which the crime had occurred. The pretrial publicity in the trial county was intense and sustained throughout the six months before jury selection. For example, the press accounts revealed that Irvin had been convicted of previous crimes, that he had been identified from a police lineup as the murderer of six persons, that he had been placed at the scene of the charged murder, that he had confessed to the six murders, and that he had offered to plead guilty in return for a ninety-nine-year sentence. Also, many prospective jurors had been influenced by the stories. At the beginning of the trial, 268 of the 430 potential jurors were excused because they admitted having fixed opinions that Irvin was guilty. Almost ninety percent of the prospective jurors, including eight who were selected, admitted having some opinion that he was guilty. In these circumstances, the Supreme Court concluded that the jury should be presumed to have been prejudiced.

Three subsequent Warren Court decisions— *Rideau v. Louisiana*, 373 U.S. 723 (1963), *Estes v. Texas*, 381 U.S. 532 (1965), and *Sheppard v. Maxwell*, 384 U.S. 333 (1966)—confirmed that prejudicial press coverage could be found without an admission of bias by jurors In *Rideau*, local stations broadcast a twenty-minute film of the defendant confessing to the charged offenses three times about two months before the trial, and three members of the jury stated that they had seen it. In *Estes*, the press was allowed to create a "circus atmosphere" during the trial, sitting within the bar of the courtroom and overrunning it with camera equipment. In *Sheppard*, both the sensational nature of the pretrial publicity and the unrestricted presence of the media in the courtroom had produced a strong impression of the defendant's guilt. All three decisions applied the *Irvin* presumption of prejudice to cases based on the inflammatory nature of the press coverage, without statements by many prospective jurors that the media activity had biased them.

Supreme Court decisions after the era of Chief Justice Warren indicated, however, that the presumption of prejudice would not often be applied. The Court declined to apply the presumption in *Murphy v. Florida*, 421 U.S. 794 (1975), although extensive pretrial publicity had detailed the defendant's prior convictions for grand theft and murder, and 25 percent of the seventy-eight prospective jurors examined had been dismissed because they held a strong opinion about his guilt.

The use of the presumption of prejudice was also limited by the Supreme Court's decision in *Patton v. Yount*, 467 U.S. 1025 (1984). A high school teacher, Yount had been convicted in Pennsylvania state court after a second trial, held some four years after the crime, of the brutal murder of one of his female students. The crime had occurred in a rural county, and the publicity about it before the first trial had been intense and sustained. Even by the start of the second trial, only two of the 163 prospective jurors had not heard about the murder, and 126 of them stated that they would not be able to put aside their opinion that Yount was guilty. This was seventy-seven percent of the pool, an even higher figure than the similar group in *Irvin*. Five of the twelve jurors who heard the second trial also stated that they had previously formed an opinion that Yount was guilty, and one stated that he would require evidence of innocence to overcome his view. Nonetheless, the Supreme Court concluded that the trial judge had not erred in proceeding to trial with the jury. This decision means that prejudice from publicity is rarely a basis for constitutional challenge unless a juror has confessed to a bias. A presumption of prejudice will generally arise only where the media coverage has been exceptionally inflammatory and enduring and, except where the press has also overrun the courtroom, has caused the vast majority of prospective jurors to reach fixed opinions that the defendant is guilty.

A 5 to 4 majority of the Supreme Court also held, in *Mu'Min v. Virginia*, 500 U.S. 415 (1991), that a trial judge need not examine prospective jurors intensively about publicity. The media coverage in the case had been extensive and damaging to Mu'Min. He was charged with a murder committed after he had escaped from a prison work program. The publicity revealed that his prison sentence was for a prior murder and that he had been denied parole six times. It also indicated that he had confessed to the new murder. Sixteen of the twenty-six prospective jurors, and eight who made it onto the jury, stated in response to a general question that they had heard about the case. However, the trial judge declined a defense request to examine jurors specifically about what they had heard, relying on prospective jurors' general assurance that they had not formed opinions about guilt and could be impartial. While conceding that more specific inquiry could have helped in assessing whether jurors were impartial, the Supreme Court held that the inquiry was not constitutionally required.

Overcoming prejudicial publicity

Although trial judges are not often reversed in their rejection of constitutional claims of prejudicial publicity, they also often take steps to protect criminal defendants from publicity. Remedies protective of defendants can be grouped into two general categories. One group is designed to overcome publicity that has already appeared or that will be allowed to appear. The second group aims to prevent prejudicial publicity from appearing in the first place. This section covers the first category of remedies. The second category is covered subsequently.

Trial judges will often attempt to overcome potentially prejudicial publicity through the careful voir dire of prospective jurors and the use of forceful *instructions* provided to those who are selected to serve. During the voir dire process, the judge, or in some courts the lawyers, question prospective jurors about their views on matters that concern their general qualifications to serve and their impartiality regarding the particular case to be tried. Instructions are also given by the trial judge to jurors during the trial regarding their conduct while serving and regarding the information they are to consider in reaching a verdict. Although the Supreme Court's decision in *Mu'Min*, discussed earlier, indicates that the voir dire need not be particularly searching, the Supreme Court also has emphasized that a careful and probing voir dire to expose and exclude biased jurors, along with forceful instructions on the need to ignore external information, can go far toward remedying potentially prejudicial publicity in many cases.

Trial judges also sometimes order a *continuance* of the trial to help overcome potentially prejudicial publicity. With the passage of time, many prospective jurors may forget damaging details included in the media coverage and may soften or efface their opinions about the defendant's guilt. The Supreme Court acknowledged the importance of the passage of time between the publicity and the trial in *Patton v. Yount,* 467 U.S. 1025, 135 (1984), where it upheld the conviction over a claim of prejudicial publicity. At some point, this remedy involves a tension with the defendant's Sixth Amendment right to a speedy trial as well as with the benefits to victims, witnesses, the prosecution, and, ultimately, the public, from prompt adjudication of criminal charges. This remedy also will not help greatly in highly notorious cases where the local media interest can be expected to endure for a long period. Examples include the prosecution of Charles Manson for the 1969 Tate-LaBianca murders in Los Angeles, or the murder prosecution of Pamela Smart in New Hampshire for the 1990 killing of her husband by two fifteen-year-old boys, one

of whom she had been sexually exploiting. Nonetheless, it is commonplace for a trial judge to respond to a claim of prejudicial publicity by postponing the trial for several weeks, or even several months, particularly if the defendant requests this relief.

Sometimes a trial judge will grant a request for a *change of trial venue*, away from the location of the crime. Usually, the jurors will be selected from the area where the trial is occurring and will be less likely to have been influenced by local media coverage than persons from the original venue. If the jury is from the area of the new venue, this remedy can raise a conflict at times, particularly in federal court, with the defendant's Sixth Amendment right to be tried by a jury "of the State and district wherein the crime shall have been committed." However, the defendant can waive the right to a jury from the original state or district. Indeed, a change of venue, and a jury from the new venue, was imposed in the federal trials of Timothy McVeigh and Terry Nichols, for the 1995 bombing murders of scores of persons in the federal building in Oklahoma City. Although inconvenient to many, the federal judge took the extraordinary step of moving the trials from Oklahoma City to Denver.

To overcome prejudicial pretrial publicity, a judge may also use an *imported pool of prospective jurors*. A group of persons from a different, but still relatively nearby county, may be less influenced by publicity about a case. The trial judge used this approach in the 1979 trial in Chicago of John Wayne Gacy for the murder of more than thirty young men, whose bodies were found buried at his residence.

Where there is concern that publicity after the trial begins could influence jurors, the judge may also order *sequestration* of the jury. During sequestration, jurors are typically housed in a hotel and transported to the courthouse by court officials, so that their activities can be controlled and the possibilities for exposure to the media or other outside contacts greatly restricted. In the criminal trials of O. J. Simpson and Charles Manson, for example, the juries were sequestered. This remedy is not always popular, because it can be expensive and can impose a great personal burden on jurors.

Finally, a trial judge can sometimes *order a new trial* if it appears during or after trial that the jury was biased by publicity. In response to publicity that is deemed prejudicial to the defendant, a judge can stop a trial and order a new one at the defendant's request or, if the trial is completed and the defendant is found guilty, vacate the verdict and order a new trial. In the rare situation in which publicity prejudices the prosecution, double jeopardy law permits the judge to stop a trial and order a new one based on "manifest necessity," but does not allow a new trial once the defendant is acquitted. Although a new trial can sometimes be a backstop remedy for prejudicial press coverage, given the high costs of retrying a case, courts generally prefer to take precautions to ensure that the first jury sworn remains unbiased.

Preventing prejudicial publicity

Remedies designed to prevent potentially prejudicial press from occurring are also sometimes used to help ensure an impartial jury. However, the First Amendment imposes significant limitations on the trial judge's use of these approaches.

A *gag order* on the press, prohibiting publication of information that the press has secured, is rarely acceptable under the First Amendment. In *Nebraska Press Association v. Stuart*, 427 U.S. 539 (1976), the Supreme Court struck down such a gag order imposed by a state judge in connection with a notorious murder case being tried in a small Nebraska town. The Supreme Court concluded that such orders were presumptively unconstitutional, but not that they were always impermissible. Indeed, in connection with the federal trial of former Panamanian dictator Manuel Noriega, the United States Court of Appeals, in *United States v. Noriega*, 917 F.2d 1543 (1990), upheld a narrowly tailored gag order imposed by the trial judge on the Cable News Network, and the Supreme Court declined review. The order concerned certain tapes of purportedly private conversations between Noriega and his lawyers that the network had obtained. Arguably, these were unusual circumstances in which a gag order on the press was allowed by *Stuart*. However, the Supreme Court's denial of review does not necessarily indicate the Justices' view on the issue. Many legal commentators have concluded that the *Stuart* decision imposes a barrier to the use of gag orders on the press that can rarely be surmounted.

Likewise, the *imposition of civil or criminal penalties on the press* for the publication of information regarding criminal cases is generally impermissible. Tort law, particularly for defamation, may sometimes provide a sanction for the knowing publication of untruthful information

related to a criminal case. Supreme Court decisions suggest that the First Amendment would otherwise rarely allow civil or criminal sanctions for the publication of information about criminal cases. For example, in *Landmark Communications, Inc. v. Virginia*, 435 U.S. 829 (1978), the Court held unconstitutional, as applied, a state statute criminalizing the publication of information about proceedings conducted by a state judicial tenure commission. The Justices concluded that internal procedures within the commission could largely address the purposes of the statute. Moreover, in *Smith v. Daily Mail Publishing Company*, 443 U.S. 97 (1979), the Supreme Court struck down a state statute making it a misdemeanor for a newspaper to publish the name of a juvenile offender without written permission from a court. The Justices declared that such a sanction requires "the highest form of state interest" to sustain its validity and implied that the availability of alternative remedies should be considered. In light of the array of less draconian measures commonly employed to protect against prejudicial publicity in criminal cases, this option appears generally unavailable.

Because of the obstacles to preventing the media from divulging information it secures, courts sometimes try to cut off the media's sources by imposing *gag orders on attorneys and other participants* in the criminal case. In *Sheppard v. Maxwell*, (384 U.S. 333, 359 (1966)), the Supreme Court criticized the trial judge for failing to make efforts to "control the release of leads, information, and gossip to the press" and later asserted that the judge "might well have proscribed extrajudicial statements by any lawyer, party, witness, or court official which divulged prejudicial matters." The Supreme Court has also more recently held, in *Gentile v. State Bar of Nevada*, 501 U.S. 1030 (1991), that an attorney may be sanctioned, after the fact, for speech about pending litigation to the extent that the statements create a "substantial likelihood" of material prejudice to the case. However, the Court has not ruled on when a trial court may impose a prior restraint on attorney speech, and there has been substantial disagreement on this issue. The Supreme Court also has not ruled on whether a trial judge can impose a gag order on the speech of various other non-attorney participants, such as witnesses, to the same extent as that of attorneys, and, despite the language in *Sheppard*, the answer is not clear. It is also uncertain what authority the judge may have to impose a gag order on government officials, such as police officers, who are not participants in the criminal proceedings.

Courts also can order *closure of judicial proceedings* in limited circumstances, though the First Amendment generally protects the press's right of access to the courts. In *Gannett Co. v. DePasquale*, 443 U.S. 368 (1979), the Supreme Court held that the "public trial" provision in the Sixth Amendment confers no right on strangers to be present when the defendant waives a public trial. However, the Court subsequently held in *Richmond Newspapers v. Virginia*, 448 U.S. 555 (1980), and *Globe Newspaper Co. v. Superior Court*, 457 U.S. 596 (1982), that the First Amendment does confer a right of public access to the trial. The Court has also held in *Press-Enterprise Co. v. Superior Court*, 464 U.S. 501 (1984) ("*Press-Enterprise I*"), that there is a First Amendment right of access during the voir dire of the jury, which usually occurs immediately before the trial. In *Press-Enterprise Co. v. Superior Court*, 478 U.S. 1 (1986) ("*Press-Enterprise II*"), the Court also held that the First Amendment right of access extends to the preliminary hearing, a proceeding that comes shortly after arrest and well before the trial. It appears that this same right of access applies at all pretrial hearings, with the exception of grand jury proceedings, which historically have been secret.

The First Amendment right of access is not absolute. In *Globe Newspaper*, the Court held that denial of press access at trial is possible if it is shown "that the denial is necessitated by a compelling governmental interest, and is narrowly tailored to serve that interest." However, given the alternative of jury sequestration, this standard for closure of trial appears quite difficult to meet. For closure of a pretrial proceeding, the Court, in *Press-Enterprise II*, stated that a defendant must show a "substantial probability" of prejudice from an open proceeding and that other "reasonable" alternatives to closure will not protect the right to an unbiased jury. Commentators have indicated that trial courts may have more room under the First Amendment to order closure of pretrial hearings than of the trial itself.

Finally, courts have substantial authority to impose *limitations on media in the courtroom*. In *Sheppard v. Maxwell*, the Supreme Court stated that trial courts may limit the number of reporters in attendance. Likewise, courts may restrict the use of cameras. After criticisms raised by overwhelming media coverage in the trial of Bruno Richard Hauptmann in 1935, the American Bar Association House of Delegates adopted Judicial Canon 35, which recommended against photographic or broadcast coverage of court proceedings. Only a small number of states allowed the photographic broadcasting of trials through the 1960s. Since the 1970s, however, there has been a trend among the states toward allowing television cameras in courtrooms, although the circumstances in which they are permitted vary. This trend was so marked, that by 1991, the Courtroom Television Network began nationwide broadcasts on a full-time basis of more sensational trials from state courts across the country. Indeed, by the end of the century, only a tiny number of states, along with the federal government, still banned television cameras altogether from trial courtrooms.

Strong arguments for and against television cameras in the courtroom have been made on both the policy level and on the level of constitutional law. The policy arguments for cameras cover many of the same grounds as those for basic press coverage of the courts. Education of the public about the judicial process is an overriding theme. The arguments against cameras build on the view that they make the proceedings more politicized and less judicial. These arguments have taken on more credence in the wake of criticism that arose over the televised broadcasts of the O. J. Simpson criminal trial.

At the level of constitutional law, states and the federal courts appear to have substantial flexibility in deciding whether to permit and how to regulate cameras in their courtrooms. In *Estes v. Texas*, the Supreme Court reversed a conviction as a matter of due process based on prejudice resulting from the chaos surrounding the televising of the proceedings. However, after advancement in camera and lighting technology, the Court later upheld Florida's decision to allow cameras in the courtroom. In *Chandler v. Florida*, 449 U.S. 560 (1981), the Court ruled that, while the coverage should not compromise the defendant's right to a fair jury, cameras in the courtroom were not generally proscribed. The Court in *Chandler* did not suggest that the First Amendment creates a presumption favoring camera access. The Court's decision in *Nixon v. Warner Communications, Inc.*, 435 U.S. 589 (1978), rejecting a claim that the First Amendment required a court to relinquish subpoenaed tapes for copying, also raises doubt that the Court would reach such a conclusion. Commentators have argued that the press's right of access to the courts, first recognized in *Globe*, in 1982, should create such a presumption. However, at the end of the century, it remained up to each jurisdiction to decide whether to ban cameras from the courtroom or, instead, to permit them under regulations that would protect the criminal defendant's right to a fair proceeding.

Conclusion

The law regarding publicity in criminal cases is the outgrowth of efforts to protect competing rights, both of constitutional magnitude. Because freedom of the press holds a more cherished position in our constellation of values than in many countries, efforts to ensure that jurors in criminal cases are not biased by media coverage also require special and sometimes burdensome approaches. On the whole, however, trial courts in the United States have worked assiduously to accommodate both the First Amendment right to a free press and the Sixth Amendment and due process rights of criminal defendants to an impartial jury.

The most dramatic change in media coverage of criminal trials during the last quarter of the twentieth century has been increased televised coverage. Advances in camera technology have made the photographic broadcasting of court proceedings less physically intrusive than when the Supreme Court first addressed the issue in the 1960s. The development of cable television and the proliferation of networks devoted almost full time to news programming and, more specifically, to court matters, has also made the televising of courtroom proceedings common. In the long run, this trend will probably not be reversed. Although the Supreme Court may not find a presumptive First Amendment right for the press to bring television cameras into the courts, the Justices will also not likely ignore the benefits in the way of education of the citizenry about the judicial process that can result from televised coverage of criminal trials. Most jurisdictions will probably continue to confer substantial discretion on the trial judge regarding when to allow cameras. Given the accommodation to televising in many courts that has already occurred, it seems likely that the practice will continue to be common.

SCOTT W. HOWE

See also COUNSEL: ROLE OF COUNSEL; CRIMINAL JUSTICE PROCESS; CRIMINAL PROCEDURE: CONSTITUTIONAL AS-PECTS; JURY: BEHAVIORAL ASPECTS; JURY: LEGAL ASPECTS; TRIAL, CRIMINAL; VENUE.

BIBLIOGRAPHY

BUNKER, MATHEW D. *Justice and the Media: Reconciling Fair Trials and a Free Press.* 1997.

CHEMERINSKY, ERWIN. "Lawyers Have Free Speech Rights, Too: Why Gag Orders on Trial Participants Are Almost Always Unconstitutional." *Loyola of Los Angeles Entertainment Law Journal* 17 (1997): 311–330.

CHESTERMAN, MICHAEL. "O. J. and the Dingo: How Media Publicity Relating to Criminal Cases Tried by Jury is Dealt With in Australia and America." *American Journal of Comparative Law* 45 (1997): 109–147.

FREEDMAN, WARREN. *Press and Media Access to the Criminal Courtroom.* 1988.

HARDAWAY, ROBERT, and TRUMMINELLO, DOUGLAS B. "Pretrial Publicity in Criminal Cases of National Notoriety: Constructing a Remedy for the Remediless Wrong." *The American University Law Review* 46 (1996): 39–90.

KERR, NORBERT L.; KRAMER, GEOFFREY P.; CARROLL, JOHN S.; and ALFINI, JAMES J. "On the Effectiveness of Voir Dire in Criminal Cases with Prejudicial Publicity: An Empirical Study." *The American University Law Review* 40 (1991): 665–701.

KRAUSE, STEPHEN J. "Punishing the Press: Using Contempt of Court to Secure the Right to a Fair Trial." *Boston University Law Review* 76 (1996): 537–574.

LAFAVE, WAYNE R., and ISRAEL, JEROLD H. "Fair Trial and Free Press." *Criminal Procedure,* 2d ed.

LASSITER, CHRISTO. "TV or Not TV—That Is the Question." *Journal of Criminal Law and Criminology* 86 (1996): 928–1095.

LIEBERMAN, JOEL D., and SALES, BRUCE D. "What Social Science Teaches Us about the Jury Instruction Process." *Psychology, Public Policy and Law* 3 (1997): 589–639.

MINOW, NEWTON N., and CATE, FRED H. "Who Is an *Impartial* Juror in an Age of Mass Media?" *The American University Law Review* 40 (1991): 631–664.

SIMON, RITA J. "Does the Court's Decision in *Nebraska Press Association* Fit the Research Evidence on the Impact on Jurors of News Coverage?" *Stanford Law Review* 29 (1977): 515–528.

STACK, RICHARD. *Courts, Counselors & Correspondents: A Media Relations Analysis of the Legal System,* 1998.

WHITEBREAD, CHARLES H., and SLOBOGIN, CHRISTOPHER. "Fair Proceedings and Media Access." *Criminal Procedure: An Analysis of Cases and Concepts.* 1993. Pages 701–712.

WHITEBREAD, CHARLES H. "Selecting Juries in High Profile Criminal Cases." *Green Bag 2d.* 2 (1999): 191–198.

PUBLIC OPINION AND CRIME

Like the economy, politics, or religion, crime is a regular topic of national public opinion surveys, and journalists and social commentators often remark on the public mood when it comes to issues like the death penalty, police use of force, or fear of crime. For their part, criminologists have become increasingly interested in how the general public perceives or feels about matters related to crime and punishment, partly in recognition that some social consequences of crime (particularly fear of crime) depend on public perceptions of crime, but also in acknowledgment that public opinion can influence law and public policy.

Gathering data on public opinion about crime would seem to be an unobjectionable practice, particularly in a poll-obsessed culture like that of the United States. But there are serious and legitimate questions about the uses of public opinion data on crime, especially when those data are to be used to guide public policy. One of the very purposes of a criminal justice system is to protect accused persons from the coarser manifestations of public opinion (rumor, vigilantism, lynchings), and few scholars would claim that public opinion on matters of criminal justice is always informed opinion. To some social and legal analysts, the notion of linking criminal justice policy (e.g., sentencing or parole policy) to the shifting winds of public opinion is abhorrent to the very ideas of legality, precedent, and dispassionate justice.

At the same time, however, democratic societies like the United States grant a pivotal role to public opinion in many domains of life, and the thought of relinquishing social policy decisions to "experts" is repugnant to many citizens. Although legislators and judicial officials ought not be rigidly bound by public opinion, there are matters in which it may be legitimately consulted (for example, issues of expense or public safety). When it comes to understanding the causes and consequences of crime, many phenomena of deep interest to criminologists (e.g, the perceived certainty of punishment, the perceived serious-ness of crimes, the perceived risk of victimization) can only be measured through surveys of the general public because they are intrinsically subjective phenomena. And although critics are sometimes quick to dismiss public opinion on crime as coarse and unreflective, public opinion on some criminal justice issues is surprisingly thoughtful and nuanced (Warr, 1995).

However these competing positions may settle out, there remains the fact that a great deal of survey data concerning crime and punishment has accumulated in recent decades, and public opinion continues to figure heavily in political races and public policy. Accordingly, it is worthwhile to review some of the principal findings of survey research on crime and punishment.

Fear of crime

Fear of crime is not a perception or opinion about crime, but rather an emotion, a feeling of apprehension or dread caused by an awareness or expectation of danger. Public fear of crime in the United States has been a topic of enormous interest to criminologists since the 1960s, in large part because of the ability of fear to significantly alter behavior (where people go, when they go, how they go, and who they go with, for example) and to regulate or disrupt social life (Skogan and Maxfield; Skogan; Warr, 1994; Ferraro). Although it is difficult to quantify and easy to exaggerate, some social observers see in widespread fear of crime a general decline in quality of life in the United States, one that manifests itself in restrictions on individual freedom, a loss of community, deserted and decayed inner cities, and numerous intangible casualties to fear (ranging from loss of trust among strangers to restricted outdoor play for children).

To some, the preoccupation of criminologists with fear of crime might seem to miss the true issue, which is not fear of crime, but crime itself. That point of view, however, overlooks certain crucial facts. One of those is that the number of fearful individuals in our society during any particular period greatly exceeds the number of persons who will actually become victims of crime, often by orders of magnitude. People can be victims of fear, in other words, even when they are not actually victims of crime. Another important consideration is that public fear of crime is not necessarily proportional to objective risk. In fact, there is reason to believe that people often exaggerate the risk of rare, but serious, crimes (Warr, 2000). In American culture, where the ev-

1278   PUBLIC OPINION AND CRIME

eryday sensibilities of citizens are often acutely alert to danger, fear of crime merits attention as an object of study in its own right.

Fear of crime is ordinarily measured through social surveys, and the survey question most frequently used to measure fear of crime in the United States is this: "Is there any area near where you live—that is, within a mile—where you would be afraid to walk alone at night?" Since 1965, the question has been routinely included in surveys conducted by the Gallup Organization and (with minor wording differences) by the National Opinion Research Center (NORC). Following a modest rise in the late 1960s, the percentage of respondents answering "yes" to the question has remained relatively constant since that time, varying over a range of only about 10 percent (from approximately 40 to 50 percent). This relative invariance over time may surprise those who are accustomed to frequent media claims about "skyrocketing" fear in the United States.

The survey question used in the Gallup/NORC surveys is useful as a general barometer of fear in the United States, but it obscures the fact that different crimes are feared to very different degrees. One of the most enduring but mistaken assumptions about fear of crime is that the general public is most afraid of violent crimes, especially homicide. Homicide, however, is not among the most highly feared crimes in the United States, and the most feared crime—residential burglary when no one is home—is not even a violent crime. Why this seemingly strange state of affairs? The reason is that fear is not simply determined by the perceived seriousness of a crime, but by the interaction of perceived seriousness and perceived risk. To generate strong fear, an offense must be perceived to be both serious and likely. Americans do not greatly fear homicide because they regard it as a comparatively low-risk event, and they reserve their concern for a crime that is less serious (though hardly trivial) but far more likely—residential burglary (Warr and Stafford, 1983; Warr, 1994, 1995).

The death penalty

No area of public opinion galvanizes scholars and social scientists more than the death penalty, not only because of its moral and legal complexity and its life-and-death nature, but also because public opinion on the death penalty has exhibited one of the most dramatic shifts in public senti-

ment ever recorded. Two Gallup surveys from the 1930s (see Warr, 1995, for question wordings) attest to substantial public support for capital punishment in that decade (61 percent approval in 1936 and 65 percent in 1937), a level of support that was still evident in the early 1950s (68 percent in 1953). By the late 1950s, however, public support for the death penalty showed unmistakable signs of erosion, and by the middle of the following decade it had reached its lowest point in modern history (42 percent in 1966), having dropped some 26 percentage points from 1953. During the next two decades, however, public support for the death penalty increased in an unrelenting if uneven progression, and remained above 70 percent (and as high as 80 percent) from the mid-1980s through the 1990s.

Many explanations for this turnabout have been suggested (cf. Ellsworth and Gross). Some believe that large increases in crime rates during the 1960s renewed public demand for the death penalty. Others argue that the topic of crime and punishment became politicized for the first time in the 1968 presidential election. Whatever the reasons may be, there is extraordinary social consensus about the death penalty in the United States today. To be sure, that consensus is not monolithic—support for the death penalty is weaker among African Americans and among young people—but it remains unsurpassed in the history of survey research on capital punishment.

The police

Most Americans, it is fair to say, have reason to be ambivalent toward the police. On the one hand, the police contribute to crime prevention and offer the hope of protection and justice to victims of crime. On the other hand, they are symbols of authority (to some, oppressive authority) in our society. The most common contacts between the public and the police—traffic violations—are not often remembered as pleasant events by citizens. It may be somewhat surprising, therefore, to find that the public generally holds the police in very high regard. In repeated Gallup surveys, substantial majorities (70 percent in 1965, 77 percent in 1967, 60 percent in 1991) report that they have "a great deal" of respect for the police in their area. In 1994, 46 percent of respondents to a Gallup survey rated the honesty and ethical standards of the police as "very high" or "high," a rating that places police in the company of medical doctors and college teachers. And a national survey conducted by the National Victim Center revealed that the public rates the performance of the police above that of prosecutors, judges, prisons, and parole boards (Warr, 1995). Ultimately, it appears that any ambivalence that citizens feel toward the police is largely overcome by the fact that the police are the most visible element in our society's effort to insure public safety, and are the first persons to whom citizens often turn when they fall victim to crime.

Sentencing

One of the most intriguing areas of public opinion concerns public preferences with regard to criminal sentencing. Research in this area is unusually consistent in its findings and implications. First, having themselves invented the prison as a means for punishing criminals, Americans today regard imprisonment as the appropriate form of punishment for nearly all crimes, and other options (fines, restitution) are ordinarily viewed as supplements rather than substitutes for imprisonment. Second, the prison sentences preferred by citizens are, on average, considerably longer than those actually served by offenders in the United States. This preference for long sentences is quite evident in social surveys showing that enormous majorities of Americans (more than 80 percent in nearly every year since 1976) think that the courts in their area do not deal "harshly enough" with criminals. Still another finding from research is that the prison sentences preferred by the general public for different crimes are directly proportional to the perceived seriousness of those crimes, meaning that Americans endorse the notion that "the punishment must fit the crime" (Warr, 1994, 1995).

It is difficult to read into these finding anything other than a certain anger and punitiveness toward criminals on the part of the American public, combined with a very practical approach to crime control that emphasizes incarceration. At the same time, however, there is some evidence that Americans combine their insistence on strict punishment with a genuine concern for rehabilitation (e.g., Warr and Stafford, 1984), presumably on the knowledge that most offenders will eventually be released again into society. It is perhaps fair to say, then, that citizens of this country often approach matters of criminal justice with a tough, but not necessarily unthinking or hard-hearted, frame of mind.

The seriousness of crimes

When it comes to crime, few aspects of public opinion have been more thoroughly investigated than public beliefs about the seriousness of crimes. At first glance, the seriousness of a crime might seem to be an objective property of a crime (just as weight or mass are objective properties of an object), but seriousness is a perceptual or subjective property of crimes, one that can vary considerably across individuals, cultures, and over time. One need only consider behaviors like smoking marijuana or homosexual conduct to appreciate the range of public opinion when it comes to seriousness. Even when the seriousness of a crime can be quantified through some objective metric (e.g., the dollar value of stolen property), it does not necessarily correspond in any simple way with the perceived seriousness of the crime. For example, is an armed robbery that nets one hundred dollars twenty times as serious as one that nets five dollars? Few would say so (e.g., Wolfgang et al.).

Judgments about the seriousness of crimes seem to be critical to the way that most individuals think about crime, because seriousness is strongly related to many other public perceptions, judgments, and reactions, including beliefs about appropriate penalties for different crimes, perceptions of the frequencies of crimes, fear of crime, judgments concerning the likelihood of arrest, and other crime-related phenomena. Several large-scale surveys have been conducted in recent decades to precisely measure public opinion about the seriousness of crimes, and the results are both predictable and surprising (see Wolfgang et al.; Warr, 1994). In general, crimes against persons are perceived to be the most serious offenses, although some nonviolent acts (e.g., selling heroin) fall within the same seriousness range as violent crimes. The perceived seriousness of an offense can vary greatly depending on who the victim and offender are. Violence between strangers, for example, is perceived to be more serious than violence between intimates, even when the events are otherwise comparable. The physical vulnerability of the victim also affects seriousness judgments; striking an elderly woman is not the same as striking a young man. In general, there is a good deal of agreement about the seriousness of crimes within our society, although some behaviors (e.g., certain forms of drug use) remain contentious issues.

Some evidence indicates that individuals often differentiate between two elements of seriousness, the *harmfulness* of an act (i.e., the damage it inflicts) and its *wrongfulness* (moral gravity). Some offenses are perceived to be more wrong than they are harmful (e.g., stealing fifteen dollars from a close friend, shoplifting a pair of socks from a store), whereas others (disturbing the neighborhood with noisy behavior, killing a pedestrian while speeding) are perceived to be more harmful than they are wrong (Warr, 1989). In everyday life, it is clear that the seriousness attached to some acts (e.g., burning the flag or displaying the Swastika) has much less to do with their objective harmfulness than with the fact that they violate powerful social taboos.

Sources of information on crime

Some facets of public opinion pertain to matters of preference or moral judgment (e.g., beliefs about appropriate penalties for crimes) and cannot be properly characterized as "right" or "wrong," accurate or inaccurate. In other instances, however, public opinion bears on *objective* characteristics of crime: Is crime increasing? Is my city a safe place? How many burglaries occurred last year? In such cases public perceptions can be compared with objective data to assess the accuracy of those perceptions. Comparisons of this sort are of particular interest to some criminologists, who worry that the general public may be misinformed about crime and suffer needless fear, or may be insufficiently afraid of what are in fact substantial risks (see Warr, 2000).

Where does the general public get its information about objective characteristics of crime, such as the risk of victimization, the geography of crime in their city, or the relative frequencies of different crimes? When the public is asked where they obtain most of their information about crime, the resounding answer is the mass media, especially news coverage of crime. Graber, for example, reported that 95 percent of respondents in her survey identified the media as their primary source of information on crime, although 38 percent cited other sources as well (conversations or, more rarely, personal experience). Skogan and Maxfield found that more than three-quarters of respondents in the three cities they surveyed reported watching or reading a crime story on the previous day (44 percent had read a newspaper crime story, 45 percent had watched a crime story on television, and 24 percent had done both). The mass media are thus a very powerful mechanism for amplifying criminal events. Information initially known only to a few can within hours become known to many thousands or millions.

If the public relies on the mass media for information about crime, how do the media depict crime? Numerous forms of distortion in news coverage of crime have been identified and documented, distortions that tend to exaggerate the frequency and the seriousness of crimes. In the real world, for example, crimes occur in inverse proportion to their seriousness; the more serious a crime, the less often it occurs. Thus, petty thefts occur by the millions, robberies by the hundreds of thousands, and homicides by the thousands. In choosing stories for print or broadcast, the primary selection criterion used by the news media is "newsworthiness," and a key element of newsworthiness is seriousness—the more serious a crime, the more likely it is to be reported. By using seriousness as a criterion, however, the media are most likely to report precisely those crimes that are least likely to occur to individuals (Warr, 1994).

This "mirror image" of crime depicted in the media results in an extraordinary emphasis on violent crime. Investigators in one study (Skogan and Maxfield) reported that homicides and attempted homicides amounted to one-half of all newspaper crime stories in the cities they examined, even though homicides are only a minute fraction of all crimes in our society. Furthermore, they found, the number of homicide stories reported in city newspapers did not closely match the actual homicide rates in those cities, suggesting that the amount of space devoted to crime has more to do with editors' decisions about reporting crime news than with the true crime rate itself.

News coverage of crime has been criticized on other grounds as well, including the practice of using crime news as "filler" when other news is slow, the use of crime news to attract larger audiences ("If it bleeds, it leads"), and an unfortunate tendency to report crime trends using numbers rather than rates, thereby ignoring changes in population. With regard to the latter issue, observe that it is entirely possible for the number of crimes in a city to increase over time even as the rate of crime decreases. All that is required is that the population grow at a faster rate than crime itself. This sort of elementary statistical reasoning often seems to be lost on crime reporters.

The fact that the media present a distorted image of crime is no guarantee, of course, that the public believes or heeds what is sees, hears, and reads. Measuring the impact of media coverage on public opinion is a daunting task because of the difficulty of isolating media messages on crime from other sources of information (conversations with family and neighbors, personal experience, rumor). Still, it is difficult to believe that the media have little or no effect on public perceptions when the public itself cites the media as their primary source of information on crime and spends so much time attuned to the media. In addition, what seems to be a common error on the part of the public—a tendency to exaggerate rare risks and underestimate common ones—precisely corresponds with the way those risks are reported in the mass media (Warr, 2000).

Conclusion

Understanding public opinion on crime is of enormous importance to criminology. Some properties of criminal behavior (e.g., the perceived seriousness of crimes) are virtually meaningless without reference to public opinion, and some of the consequences of crime (e.g., public fear of crime) depend on public perceptions of the risk of victimization. It is not surprising, therefore, that criminologists have come to increasingly focus their attention on public opinion regarding crime and punishment.

That attention, unfortunately, is shared by people whose intentions are less noble. One of the more glaring and disappointing features of contemporary American politics is the tendency of political candidates to exploit and capitalize on public fear and anger over crime in an effort to win votes. Crime, in fact, has figured as a major issue in every presidential election since Richard Nixon took office, and may have been the pivotal issue in one or more presidential elections (recall the Willie Horton commercials in the Bush/Dukakis contest). At a more local level, crime regularly dominates political campaigns from the mayor's to the governor's office. The point is not that crime is not a legitimate subject of public discourse, but rather that efforts to garner votes using the issue of crime frequently transform what is an intrinsically complex subject matter into an object of sloganeering, bumper stickers, and specious efforts to demonstrate who is more "tough on crime." Rather than stimulate discussion, the transformation of crime into a political issue has acted to discourage sensible and reasoned public debate on critical issues of crime and punishment. The result, too often, has been

policies that possess superficial appeal but fail to address the real problems of crime and justice.

Mark Warr

See also Crime Commissions; Criminalization and Decriminalization; Fear of Crime; Mass Media and Crime; Political Process and Crime; Popular Culture; Publicity in Criminal Cases; Vigilantism.

BIBLIOGRAPHY

Dressler, Joshua; Thompson, Peter N.; and Wasserman, Stanley. "Effect of Legal Education upon Perceptions of Crime Seriousness: A Response to Rummel v. Estrelle." Wayne Law Review 28 (1982): 1247–1300.

Ellsworth, Phoebe C., and Gross, Samuel R. "Hardening of the Attitudes: Americans' Views on the Death Penalty." Journal of Social Issues 50 (1994): 19–52.

Ferraro, Kenneth F. Fear of Crime: Interpreting Victimization Risk. Albany: State University of New York Press, 1995.

Graber, Doris A. Crime News and the Public. New York: Praeger, 1980.

Maguire, Kathleen, and Pastore, Ann L. Sourcebook of Criminal Justice Statistics—1996. U.S. Department of Justice, Bureau of Justice Statistics. Washington, D.C.: U.S. Government Printing Office, 1997.

Robinson, Paul H., and Darley, John M. Justice, Liability and Blame. Boulder, Co.: Westview Press, 1995.

Skogan, Wesley G. Disorder and Decline: Crime and the Spiral of Decay in American Neighborhoods. New York: Free Press, 1990.

Skogan, Wesley G., and Maxfield, Michael G. Coping with Crime: Individual and Neighborhood Reactions. Beverly Hills, Calif.: Sage, 1981.

Warr, Mark. "What Is the Perceived Seriousness of Crimes?" Criminology 27 (1989): 795–821.

———. "Public Perceptions and Reactions to Violent Offending and Victimization." In Understanding and Preventing Violence. Volume IV: Consequences and Control. Edited by Albert J. Reiss, Jr. and Jeffrey A. Roth. Washington, D.C.: National Academy Press, 1994. Pages 1–66.

———. "Poll Trends: Public Opinion on Crime and Punishment." Public Opinion Quarterly 59 (1995): 296–310.

———. "Fear of Crime in the United States: Avenues for Research and Policy." In Crime and Justice 2000: Volume Four, Measurement and Analysis of Crime and Justice. Washington, D.C.: National Institute of Justice, 2000.

WARR, MARK, and STAFFORD, MARK C. "Fear of Victimization: A Look at the Proximate Causes." *Social Forces* 61 (1983): 1033–1043.

———. "Public Goals of Punishment and Support for the Death Penalty." *Journal of Research in Crime and Delinquency* 21 (1984): 95–111.

WOLFGANG, MARVIN E.; FIGLIO, ROBERT M.; TRACY, PAUL E.; and SINGER, SIMON I. *The National Survey of Crime Severity.* Washington, D.C.: U.S. Government Printing Office, 1985.

PUNISHMENT

Although punishment has been a crucial feature of every developed legal system, widespread disagreement exists over the moral principles that can justify its imposition. One fundamental question is why (and whether) the social institution of punishment is warranted. A second question concerns the necessary conditions for criminal liability and punishment in particular cases. A third relates to the form and severity of punishment that is appropriate for particular offenses and offenders. Debates about punishment are important in their own right, but they also raise more general problems about the proper standards for evaluating social practices.

The main part of this theoretical overview of the subject of legal punishment concentrates on these issues of justification. That discussion is preceded by an analysis of the concept of punishment and is followed by a brief account of how theories for justifying punishment can relate to decisions about the substantive criminal law and criminal procedures.

The concept of punishment

Punishment is not an exclusive province of the law. Parents punish their children, and members of private associations punish their wayward fellows. Like most concepts, "punishment" has no rigid boundaries. One useful way to understand its central aspects and uncertain borderlines is to identify the features of typical instances of punishment, and to inquire how far their absence would lead one to say that something other than punishment is taking place.

Typical and atypical instances. In typical cases of punishment, persons who possess authority impose designedly unpleasant consequences upon, and express their condemnation of, other persons who are capable of choice and who have breached established standards of behavior.

Responsible agents. Punishment is a practice that is performed by, and directed at, agents who are responsible in some sense. God and humans can punish; hurricanes cannot. People, but not faulty television sets, are fit subjects of punishment. A higher level of capacity is required to impose punishment than is minimally necessary to make one subject to it. To be subject to it, one need have only sufficient mental control over one's actions to refrain from disfavored behavior, a degree of control that quite small children and some animals possess. To punish, one must be able consciously to inflict harmful consequences because of a wrong that has been committed.

Unpleasant consequences. Punishment involves designedly harmful consequences that most people would wish to avoid. Medical treatment and other forms of therapy may also be painful, but their unpleasantness is an unfortunate contingent fact; pleasing or painless substitutes, if available, would be preferred. Unpleasantness is, on the other hand, part of the basic nature of punishment; if the response to those who break rules was to give them something they wanted, such as more money, one would not consider the response to be punishment, even if the aim were to reduce future violations.

Condemnation. The unpleasant consequences of punishment are usually preceded by a judgment of condemnation; the subject of punishment is explicitly blamed for committing a wrong. The close link between punishment and condemnation is attenuated in some instances. When a teacher punishes an entire class because one child has been naughty, he may not be condemning the other members of the class. The teacher's choice of collective punishment will reflect his belief either that the group as a whole is capable of constraining the actions of its members or that one student will hesitate to be the source of mischief for his classmates; but the teacher need not suppose that all the other members of the class are actually partly responsible for the particular naughty act. A similar analysis applies to vicarious punishment. Punishing one person for the sins of another may serve a purpose even if the victim of punishment is not condemned for the specific wrong.

For certain violations of law, condemnation may be wholly absent, except in the most formal sense. Some actions may be deemed antisocial and worth discouraging by unpleasant consequences even if no one really blames the persons who perform them. This is perhaps exemplified by the attitude American society now takes toward most parking violations. For a different reason, a reflective judgment of condemnation may be absent when very young children are punished. Parents may evince anger and impose simple penalties in the belief that this is the most effective way to teach acceptable behavior. They may thus treat their children as blameworthy, even though they doubt that the children are experienced enough actually to merit blame for performing the offending actions.

Condemnation is not in itself usually considered punishment. If members of a society regarded a formal condemnation as extremely shameful, one might think of that as a possible punishment in itself rather than merely a complement of more substantial consequences; this discussion will adopt the common assumption that punishment involves more than condemnation.

Authority. Punishment is imposed by people who have authority to do so—authority conferred by legal rule, associational standard, or social morality. A father can punish his own small children, but he cannot punish a neighbor's child unless the neighbor has given him power to do that. Only public officials can punish a thief for breaking the law. Authority may be conceived in a somewhat extended sense, whereby one can speak of a person's being punished by the community when his offensive behavior is met by the negative informal reactions of its members.

Standards. Punishment ordinarily follows some breach of established rules of behavior; the notion that people should have fair warning as to what behavior is punishable, and to what degree, is now an established principle of most legal systems. Yet, especially in informal family settings, people may be punished for doing things that they should have realized were wrong, even though they were not warned in advance about that specific sort of behavior. Even then, one can usually point to some relevant, more general standard that the children have been taught, such as taking care of family property, not harming brothers and sisters, and not disturbing parents. Many legal systems also contain some standards of misbehavior that are quite openended. Much more extraordinary is punishment of persons for actions they had no reason to suppose were wrong at the time they committed them.

Misperceptions. The assumption thus far has been that those who impose punishment, and the community at large, perceive circumstances as they really are. However, people may be woefully mistaken about critical facts. An innocent person may be punished because he is thought guilty, or all epileptics may be punished in the belief that having that disease evidences extreme moral fault. Misperceptions may also occur because of conscious manipulations by those aware of the actual facts. If officials successfully persuade others that a woman they know to be innocent is guilty, her condemnation and imprisonment will, in the public perception, constitute genuine punishment. Whether the knowledgeable officials should regard this as an instance of (unjust) punishment or something else is debatable. The crucial inquiry, in any event, is not whether what follows such deviations from the bases for imposing punishment can accurately be called punishment, but whether deviations of this sort can ever be morally justified, a matter analyzed below.

Legal punishment and the criminal law. Parts of the civil law authorize punitive consequences, but in advanced legal systems, legal punishment is linked to the criminal law. That law consists of prohibitions of antisocial behavior backed by serious sanctions. Not every criminal conviction is necessarily followed by punishment—alternative dispositions are often possible—but a set of mandatory rules that did not provide for punishing of violators would not be part of the criminal law. The meaning and possible justifications of legal punishment are, therefore, very closely related to the meaning and possible justifications of the criminal law.

Moral justifications and legal punishment

Since punishment involves pain or deprivation that people wish to avoid, its intentional imposition by the state requires justification. The difficulties of justification cannot be avoided by the view that punishment is an inevitable adjunct of a system of criminal law. If criminal law is defined to include punishment, the central question remains whether society should have a system of mandatory rules enforced by penalties. Relatively small associations of like-minded people may be able to operate with rules that are not backed by sanctions, and a choice by the larger society against authorizing legal punishment is at least theoretically possible. Moreover, actual infliction of penalties is not inextricably tied to authorization. A father who has threatened punishment if two daughters do not stop fighting must decide whether to follow through if the fight continues. Congruence between threat and actual performance on the scene does constitute one good reason for punishing. Future threats will be taken less seriously if past threats are not fulfilled, and parents usually wish to avoid the impression that they will not do what they say. Nevertheless, because he now sees that the punishment threatened is too severe, or understands better the children's reasons for fighting, the father may fail to carry out his threat.

In the broader society also, threatened punishments are not always inflicted on persons who have unquestionably committed crimes. The police or prosecutor may decide not to proceed, a jury may acquit in the face of unmistakable evidence of guilt, or a judge may decide after conviction not to impose punishment. A judge with legal authority to make such a decision must determine if punishment is appropriate; even if punishment is legally required to be imposed, the countervailing reasons may be so powerful that the court will not do so.

If actual punishment never or very rarely followed threatened punishment, the threat would lose significance. Thus, punishment in some cases is a practical necessity for any system in which threats of punishment are to be taken seriously; and to that extent, the justification of punishment is inseparable from the justification of threats of punishment.

The dominant approaches to justification are retributive and utilitarian. Briefly stated, a retributivist claims that punishment is justified because people deserve it; a utilitarian believes that justification lies in the useful purposes that punishment serves (the latter approach is sometimes also referred to as "consequentialist," or "instrumentalist"). Many actual theories of punishment do not fit unambiguously and exclusively into one of these two categories. Satisfying both retributive and utilitarian criteria may be thought necessary to warrant punishment; or utilitarian criteria may be thought crucial for one question (for example, whether there should be a system of punishment) and retributive criteria for another (for example, who should be punished); or the use of retributive sorts of approaches may be thought appropriate on utilitarian grounds. Beginning from rather straightforward versions of retributive and utilitarian theory, the analysis proceeds to positions that are more complex.

Retributive justification. Why should wrongdoers be punished? Most people might respond simply that they deserve it or that they should suffer in return for the harm they have done. Such feelings are deeply ingrained, at least in many cultures, and are often supported by notions of divine punishment for those who disobey God's laws. A simple retributivist justification provides a philosophical account corresponding to these feelings: someone who has violated the rights of others should be penalized, and punishment restores the moral order that has been breached by the original wrongful act. The idea is strikingly captured by Immanuel Kant's claim that an island society about to disband should still execute its last murderer. Society not only has a right to punish a person who deserves punishment, but it has a duty to do so. In Kant's view, a failure to punish those who deserve it leaves guilt upon the society; according to G. W. F. Hegel, punishment honors the criminal as a rational being and gives him what it is his right to have. In simple retributivist theory, practices of punishment are justified because society should render harm to wrongdoers; only those who are guilty of wrongdoing should be punished; and the severity of punishment should be proportional to the degree of wrongdoing, an approach crudely reflected in the idea of "an eye for an eye, a tooth for a tooth."

Close examination of this theory dispels much of its apparent simplicity, reveals some of the tensions between its implications and the practices of actual societies, and exposes its vulnerability to powerful objections. Taken as claiming an intimate connection between moral guilt and justified legal punishment, the retributive theory raises troubling questions about the proper purposes of a state and about any human attempts to equate reward and punishment to moral deserts.

Moral guilt and social judgment. One fundamental question is whether people are ever morally guilty in the way that basic retributive theory seems to suppose. If all our acts are consequences of preceding causes over which we ultimately have had no control, causes that were set in motion before we were born—if, in other words, philosophical determinism is true—then the thief or murderer is, in the last analysis, more a victim of misfortune than a villain on the cosmic stage. Although he may be evil in some sense and able to control his actions, his character has been formed by forces outside himself, and that ultimately determines the choices he makes. From this perspective, assertions that a vicious person should be punished simply because he deserves to be seem as anomalous as assertions that a vicious dog should be punished simply because he deserves to be. Unless one wishes to take the paradoxical position, analogous to certain religious doctrines of predestination, that people are guilty for qualities and acts they cannot help, the simple retributive theory is incompatible with determinism. It requires some notion of free will that attributes to humans responsibility for doing wrong in a way that is not attributed to other animals.

Acceptance of free will, which is certainly the undergirding for the ordinary sense of morality, does not remove all the obstacles to acceptance of retributivism. One human can rarely judge with confidence the moral guilt of others, and few doubt that among persons who commit similar wrongful acts, vast differences in moral guilt exist. Many of those who commit very serious crimes have suffered extreme psychological or social deprivation, and/or physical or psychological abuse. Moreover, a penalty supposed to redress a moral imbalance should perhaps depend upon an offender's overall moral record and how the good and bad fortunes of his life compare with that record; yet making such an evaluation with any accuracy is even more beyond human capacities than judging the moral guilt attaching to a particular act.

Finally, not all acts that reflect serious moral guilt are the subject of criminal punishment in a liberal society. Personal wrongs that members of families and acquaintances do to one another may be of greater magnitude morally than some petty crimes, even though they do not carry publicly imposed penalties. If the purpose of punishment were truly to redress moral guilt, justifying this variance in treatment would be difficult, but few people believe that a liberal society should make the punishment of all serious moral wrongs its business.

To some, the very idea that pain should be inflicted on a person simply because he has committed an earlier moral wrong may seem indefensible, whether the agent inflicting the pain is human or divine. Even those who believe that a just God would strike some such balance may think that restoring the moral order is not an appropriate human purpose, and is certainly not a proper purpose of the state, limited as the state should be in its capacities to learn about events and to dispose of people's lives.

The retributivist may resist this conclusion and maintain that the infliction of legal penalties for moral transgressions is a legitimate public purpose, one that happens to be outweighed by other values in certain circumstances. The retributivist can argue that the severity of an offense provides at least a rough indication of the magnitude of moral wrong and that a punishment proportioned to the offense, and perhaps tailored to some extent to other factors of moral relevance, can give the offender approximately what he deserves. These responses may save retributive theory from the attack of total irrelevance, but they do not provide a complete justification for practices of legal punishment as they exist or might exist.

Violations of social norms and fairness. A rather different retributive approach is that criminals deserve punishment because they violate norms established by society, the magnitude of the violation being measured by the seriousness with which society treats the offense. In this form, the theory sidesteps the objection that correcting moral wrongs is not the business of the criminal law, and it does not impose upon officials the impossible burden of ascertaining subtle degrees of moral guilt. This version of the theory fits better with existing (and conceivable) practices of criminal punishment, but in doing so, it no longer connects moral guilt so strongly to justifiable punishment and does not resolve the question of why morality demands that society punish those who violate its norms simply for the sake of punishing them.

One answer to this question is that fairness to citizens who make sacrifices by obeying the law requires that violators be punished rather than reap benefits for disregarding legal standards. What is crucial and debatable about this view is the claim that law-abiding members of the community will suffer an actual injustice if the guilty go unpunished. The position is most persuasive in respect to crimes whose commission actually increases the overall burden on those who obey. Given steady revenue needs, a sufficient amount of tax evasion will increase the burdens of those who pay in full. Demanding that the evader pay back taxes does redress an injustice, but whether failure to send him to jail, if that is the only possible penalty, would be unfair to honest taxpayers is less clear. The unjust loss to the honest will not be made up in any event, but the jail term will at least offset the evader's unfair advantage. Some criminal activities, such as speeding and theft, would be engaged in more widely if it were not for the law's prohibition, but their commission does not increase general burdens as directly as does tax evasion. Because the ordinary law-abiding person has foregone some possible gain, the criminal may still be perceived as having attained an unfair advantage that should be offset by punishment. The claim about fairness to law-abiding citizens is least persuasive in respect to criminal activities (such as rape) that very few citizens would wish to undertake, no matter what the law said about them.

For these crimes, as well as others directed at individuals, fairness to victims, rather than (or as well as) fairness to all law-abiding citizens, might be thought to justify punishment. Fairness to victims undoubtedly requires redress of their injuries to whatever extent that can be effected, but whether and to what extent it requires harsh treatment of criminals that does not benefit victims is doubtful.

The general normative question about both fairness arguments above is this: If someone has achieved a comparative advantage over another by an unjust act, does fairness to the person suffering a comparative disadvantage require stripping the offender of his advantage, even when that would do nothing to improve the position of the disadvantaged person? So understood, the fundamental question about the fairness argument is close to the question about the intrinsic value of punishing wrongdoing, although emphasizing a comparative dimension. Many of those who believe that inflicting pain on the morally guilty is not worthwhile for its own sake will also conclude that such pain cannot be supported simply because it nullifies some comparative advantage.

A third fairness argument compares the offender to other, similar offenders. Retributive or *just deserts* theories of punishment usually seek to promote not only proportionality of punishment relative to culpability, but also uniformity in the treatment of equally culpable offenders. A sentence less severe than that given to other, similar offenders is unfair to those offenders; a more severe sentence is unfair to the defendant. However, since equality norms do not require that offenders receive any particular degree of punishment (or indeed, any punishment at all), such norms are more properly seen as limiting, rather than justifying, the imposition of sanctions.

Utilitarian justification.   Utilitarian theories of punishment dominated American jurisprudence during most of the twentieth century. According to Jeremy Bentham's classical utilitarianism, whether an act or social practice is morally desirable depends upon whether it promotes human happiness better than possible alternatives. Since punishment involves pain, it can be justified only if it accomplishes enough good consequences to outweigh this harm. A theory of punishment may make the balance of likely consequences central to justification without asserting, as Bentham did, that all relevant consequences are reducible to happiness and unhappiness. It may even claim that reducing future instances of immoral violations of right is itself an appropriate goal independent of the effect of those violations on the people involved. In modern usage, *utilitarianism* is often employed to refer broadly to theories that likely consequences determine the morality of action, and this usage is followed here.

The catalogs of beneficial consequences that utilitarians have thought can be realized by punishment have varied, but the following have generally been regarded as most important.

1. *General deterrence.* Knowledge that punishment will follow crime deters people from committing crimes, thus reducing future violations of right and the unhappiness and insecurity they would cause. The person who has already committed a crime cannot, of course, be deterred from committing that crime, but his punishment may help to deter others. In Bentham's view, general deterrence was very much a matter of affording rational self-interested persons good reasons not to commit crimes. With a properly developed penal code, the benefits to be gained from criminal activity would be outweighed by the harms of punishment, even when those harms were discounted by the probability of avoiding detection. Accordingly, the greater the temptation to commit a particular crime and the smaller the chance of detection, the more severe the penalty should be.

Punishment can also deter in ways more subtle than adding a relevant negative factor for cool calculation. Seeing others punished for certain behavior can create in people a sense of association between punishment and act that may constrain them even when they are sure they will not get caught. Adults, as well as children, may subconsciously fear punishment even though rationally they are confident it will not occur.

2. *Norm reinforcement.* For young children, the line may be very thin between believing that behavior is wrong and fearing punishment. Adults draw the distinction more plainly, but seeing others punished can still contribute to their sense that actions are wrong, helping them to internalize the norms society has set. Practices of punishment can thus reinforce community norms by affecting the dictates of individual consciences. Serious criminal punishment repre-

sents society's strong condemnation of what the offender has done, and performs a significant role in moral education.

A person's feeling of moral obligation to obey rules may depend considerably on his sense that he is treated fairly under them. If others profit with impunity from violations of the law, a law-abiding person may develop a sense of unfairness, wondering if he too should break the law to obtain similar advantages. Punishment helps assure citizens that the laws as administered deal fairly with their interests. Whether or not the law-abiding citizen actually has some individualized moral claim to have wrongdoers punished, punishment will probably contribute to his willing acceptance of legal constraints. Similarly, if an offender sees that other offenders received less severe punishment, his feeling of having been treated unfairly may diminish his respect for and willingness to conform to the law. All of these considerations constitute the utilitarian side of fairness arguments for punishment.

3. *Individual deterrence.* The actual imposition of punishment creates fear in the offender that if he repeats his act, he will be punished again. Adults are more able than small children to draw conclusions from the punishment of others, but having a harm befall oneself is almost always a sharper lesson than seeing the same harm occur to others. To deter an offender from repeating his actions, a penalty should be severe enough to outweigh in his mind the benefits of the crime. For the utilitarian, more severe punishment of repeat offenders is warranted partly because the first penalty has shown itself ineffective from the standpoint of individual deterrence.

4. *Incapacitation and other forms of risk management.* Imprisonment temporarily puts the convicted criminal out of general circulation, and the death penalty does so permanently. These punishments physically prevent persons of dangerous disposition from acting upon their destructive tendencies. Less drastic forms of risk management include probationary or parole supervision, and accompanying requirements (for example, random urine tests to detect use of illegal drugs) and prohibitions (use of alcohol or firearms, association with certain persons, contact with the victim, and so on). As with individual deterrence, more severe risk-management measures are warranted for repeat offenders because such offenders are statistically more likely to commit further crimes. However, incapacitation of a high-risk offender may nevertheless fail to prevent further crimes. This would be the case

if such an offender were to be immediately replaced by another offender (for example, on a street corner well-suited for selling drugs). It would also be the case if the offender, when released from prison, had become more dangerous than he was before (so that the crimes he commits after release are more numerous or more serious than those which were prevented while he was imprisoned).

5. *Reform.* Punishment may help to reform the criminal so that his wish to commit crimes will be lessened, and perhaps so that he can be a happier, more useful person. Conviction and simple imposition of a penalty might themselves be thought to contribute to reform if they help an offender become aware that he has acted wrongly. In that case, punishment acts as a form of norm reinforcement operating at the individual rather than the community level; the importance of promoting the offender's awareness of wrongdoing is also cited by those who stress the "communicative" aspects of punishment. However, reform is usually conceived as involving more positive steps to make offenders less antisocial by altering their basic character, improving their skills, or teaching them how to control their crime-producing urges (for example, their tendency to abuse drugs or alcohol, or to commit sex crimes). Various psychological therapies, medications, and even drastic interventions such as psychosurgery, are designed to curb destructive tendencies. Educational and training programs can render legitimate employment a more attractive alternative to criminal endeavors. These may indirectly help enhance self-respect, but their primary purpose is to alter the options that the released convict will face.

6. *Vengeance.* The utilitarian, in contrast to the retributivist, does not suppose that wrongful acts intrinsically deserve a harsh response, but utilitarians recognize that victims, their families and friends, and some members of the public will feel frustrated if no such response is forthcoming. Satisfying these desires that punishment be imposed is seen as one legitimate aim in punishing the offender. In part, the point is straightforwardly to increase the happiness, or reduce the unhappiness, of those who want the offender punished, but formal punishment can also help increase their sense of respect for the law and deflect unchanneled acts of private vengeance.

7. *Community or victim restoration.* Another utilitarian sentencing goal that began to receive much greater emphasis toward the end of the twentieth century is to repair the damage that

the offense has caused, by requiring the offender to make restitution or perform compensatory service for the victim or the community. *Restorative justice* goals are also sometimes defined to include acceptance of responsibility or repentance by the offender, forgiveness by the victim, and victim-offender or community-offender reconciliation, for example, by means of mediation or an apology. Since some of these goals and measures may also benefit the offender, and depend heavily on his cooperation, they might not seem sufficiently unpleasant or stigmatizing to qualify as punishment; however, the same could be said for many measures designed to promote reform or manage the offender's risk of re-offending. Indeed, the broadest goals of restorative justice overlap with several previously mentioned punishment goals, in particular, norm reinforcement, risk-management, and reform. Restorative measures can also be seen as a means of deflecting the desires of victims and the public for vengeance, and providing a more constructive outlet for such feelings.

Unlike a basic retributive theory, the utilitarian approach to punishment is compatible with philosophical determinism. Whether or not human acts are completely determined by prior causes, punishment can be an efficacious prior cause. A determinist can support even the "condemnation" component of punishment on utilitarian grounds, believing that condemnation and feelings of guilt are useful instruments in guiding human behavior.

From the utilitarian perspective, the acts for which criminal punishment should be authorized are those with respect to which the good consequences of punishment can outweigh the bad; the persons who should be punished are those whom it is useful to punish; and the severity of punishment should be determined not by some abstract notion of deserts but by marginal usefulness. Each extra ingredient of punishment is warranted only if its added benefits outweigh its added harms and costs. (Of course, in real life such a fine scale cannot be developed, but legislators and those administering punishment should be guided by this principle.) The utilitarian does not start with the premise that penalties of equal severity should go to those with equal blame. For general deterrence, roughly equal penalties for the same offenses may be appropriate, but goals relating to individual offenders may support individuation of treatment, leading, for example, to long confinement for those judged irredeemably antisocial, and to rehabilitation and prompt release for those whose character can be positively transformed (or already has been, at the time of sentencing).

Philosophical objections to utilitarianism. Utilitarian programs for systems of punishment are subject to two kinds of objections: those which challenge basic philosophical premises, and those which claim that different systems would better accomplish social aims. When existing practices are attacked, disentangling the theoretical from the practical complaints often is not simple, but the following discussion tries to separate the two, dealing first with basic attacks on utilitarian theory and indicating what modifications may be needed to accommodate valid criticisms.

The most fundamental objection is to treating the criminal as a means to satisfy social purposes rather than as an end in himself. This objection bears on why, and how, guilty offenders may be punished; but the most damaging aspect of the attack is that utilitarianism admits the possibility of justified punishment of the innocent. The retributivist asserts that such punishment is morally wrong even when it would produce a balance of favorable consequences.

Various responses have been made by utilitarians. One is that since the term *punishment* implies guilt, the innocent cannot logically be punished. The terminological point is highly doubtful in cases in which innocent people are portrayed as guilty and given harsh treatment on that basis. In any event, even if the point is sound, it merely requires the retributivist to restate his worry, now objecting that utilitarian theory countenances subjecting the innocent to harms that have the appearance of punishment. The utilitarian may answer that his theory will certainly not support any announced practice of punishing the innocent. The purposes of punishment would not be served if people knew a person was innocent, and even to establish a general policy that officials would at their discretion occasionally seek punishment of those they know are innocent would cause serious insecurity.

One version of utilitarianism, called "rule" utilitarianism, makes the standard of moral evaluation the rules that would, if publicly announced, accepted, and applied, produce the best consequences. Under this version, punishment of the innocent may cease to be a problem, since no rule authorizing such punishment should be accepted. Suppose, however, that an official or citizen is sure that surreptitiously promoting the punishment of someone he knows to be innocent will be very useful. The rule-utilitarian account avoids the dilemma, but only by presupposing that proper moral decisions must be defensible in terms of rules that can be publicly announced. "Act" utilitarians, who judge the rightness of a particular action by its own likely consequences, do not have this escape. They might, however, also try to foreclose intentionally punishing the innocent as a practical alternative, pointing to the severe insecurities that would be caused by knowledge of such punishment and the difficulties of maintaining secrecy. Alternatively, they might concede that punishing the innocent would be appropriate if the balance of likely consequences were favorable, arguing that such a conclusion conflicts with moral intuitions only because those are developed to deal with ordinary situations.

Many people will feel that none of these utilitarian responses adequately accounts for the unacceptability of punishing the innocent, which is regarded as inherently wrongful. Similarly, many regard it as intrinsically unfair and morally wrong to impose severe punishment on those who commit minor crimes, however useful that might be; to give widely variant punishments to those who have committed identical offenses with similar degrees of moral guilt; or to count the interests of an offender as having as much intrinsic weight as the interests of a victim or ordinary law-abiding person.

Mixed or hybrid theories. Given these problems with unalloyed utilitarian theory, some mixture of utilitarian and retributive elements provides the most cogent approach to punishment. The basic reasons for having compulsory legal rules backed by sanctions are utilitarian; these reasons should dominate decisions about the sorts of behavior to be made criminal. Moral wrongs should not be subject to legal punishment unless that is socially useful, and behavior that is initially morally indifferent may be covered by the criminal law if doing so serves social goals. Notions of deserts, however, should impose more stringent constraints on the imposition and severity of punishment than pure utilitarianism acknowledges.

Relevance of deserts. Every practical system of punishment must admit the possibility that mistakes will lead to innocent persons being punished, but knowingly to punish an innocent person is to violate an independent moral norm. Wrongdoing alone may not be a sufficient basis to justify punishment, but the wrongful act creates a right of society to punish that does not exist with innocent persons.

Considerations of deserts should also be relevant to the severity of punishment. One possible position is that someone should never be punished more severely than could be justified both by utilitarian objectives and by the degree of his wrongdoing. Under this principle, a person would not receive more punishment than he deserves, even when that might be useful (a concept sometimes referred to as "limiting" retributivism), and he would not receive unproductive punishment, whatever his degree of guilt (a utilitarian principle sometimes referred to as "parsimony"—punishing agents should impose the least severe sanction necessary to achieve all relevant social purposes). The latter principle, however, might be seen as too rigid in some circumstances. One such circumstance involves violent offenders whose mental condition, while not excusing them altogether, does make them less blameworthy, but also renders them more dangerous and less amenable to being deterred or rehabilitated. Perhaps in an exquisitely precise system such offenders would be given a moderate criminal sentence and an extended form of civil commitment, but in the absence of such fine lines, most observers would support a criminal penalty somewhat greater than the offender really deserves. For a different reason, more severe penalties may also be warranted when those who rationally decide to commit certain crimes are very difficult to apprehend. To have a deterrent effect, the penalties may need to be greater than would be justified by the guilt of the individual offender who happens to be caught. If he has been forewarned and has chosen to take the risk, the punishment may not be unfair to him, but it may be out of proportion to the blameworthiness of his action.

In other kinds of situations, retributive concerns may make it justifiable to inflict punishment even when a balance of favorable consequences is not expected. Under an ordinary utilitarian approach, each person's welfare counts equally, but perhaps the welfare of those who intentionally commit crimes should not be given as much weight in some respects as the welfare of law-abiding citizens. The wrongdoers may, by their acts, have forfeited a right to count equally. Suppose, for example, that every one hundred executions of murderers could save seventy innocent lives. Putting aside all other relevant considerations, one might believe that those who are innocent simply have a greater claim to have their lives protected than those who have knowingly taken the lives of others, and thus, one might accept that saving seventy innocent lives is worth taking a hundred guilty ones.

As noted above, a cardinal principle of the utilitarian approach is that useless punishment should be avoided. Applying that principle may lead on occasion to selective or exemplary punishment—that is, choosing one of a number of offenders for the imposition of penalties. Imposing unequal punishments on similar offenders, however, has an element of unfairness about it, and may violate norms of uniformity or equality in the treatment of equally culpable offenders. Although punishing many people well beyond what is necessary is not warranted solely to achieve equality, when the principle of equality and the principle of parsimony (keeping punishment to the minimum necessary) come into conflict, application of the latter principle may appropriately be tempered to some degree to reduce unfairness.

Possible limits on utilitarian aims. Independent moral standards may be thought to limit not only the absolute and comparative severity of punishments, but also the nature of punishments and the utilitarian purposes that can properly be promoted by them. Torture, for example, may be ruled out on moral grounds no matter how effective it could be in particular instances. A similar position on capital punishment is taken by those who think it absolutely wrong for the state intentionally to take the lives of its members. Such a position can be consistently maintained by a thoroughgoing pacifist, but someone who accepts intentional killing in wartime and intentional killing by the police to stop terrible crimes cannot persuasively argue that execution is an unjustified punishment, however useful it is in saving lives, whatever its side effects, and however fairly it may be administered.

Some writers have urged that imposing penalties on people because of predictions of how they will act in the future is unjust. Given the impossibility of knowing whether a particular individual requires individual deterrence, incapacitation, or reformation, they note that punishment grounded on those rationales will lead to some false positives—that is, people punished unnecessarily. The existence of some false positives in itself, however, does not warrant abandoning those utilitarian aims of punishment unless all utilitarian aims, including general deterrence and norm reinforcement, are indefensible. For each of these aims, one person is

suffering punishment to protect the welfare of others. No difference in moral principle exists between punishing a person to deter other potential offenders and punishing him because he is a member of a class many of whose members will commit subsequent crimes, so long as the class is fairly defined and genuinely dangerous members cannot be more precisely determined.

A more plausible attack has been made on reformation as a permissible basis for compulsory measures. The contention is that the state should not force changes in people's character and that to do so violates their right to respect as persons. The offender has, however, already violated the rights of others, and his doing so may give the state more authority to tamper with him than it would otherwise have. Insofar as the offender's difficulty is lack of skills, compulsory efforts to remedy the defect do not represent a fundamental impairment of his personality. Compelled therapy or more extreme measures, such as surgical intervention, may do so. Although one cannot rule out on absolute principle every compulsory technique designed to alter an offender's basic character, measures that would change him radically against his will do violate moral limits on what the state can properly do.

Vengeance has been thought by some to be an unacceptable basis for punishment. Taking the view that people ideally would not seek to hurt those who have done harm simply for the sake of hurting them, this view asserts that morally unworthy human desires should not be satisfied even when that will cause happiness. Whether or not the satisfaction of malicious motives should generally count positively in a utilitarian calculus, the response can be that the state legitimately satisfies feelings of vengeance both because these feelings are linked to the maintenance of healthy moral opinion (a claim discussed below) and because such feelings will find socially damaging outlets if disregarded.

Theories and practices of punishment. During the mid-twentieth century, sentencing practices in the United States were largely consonant with utilitarian premises, although also consistent with important retributive limits on severity. General deterrence and more individually focused aims were given weight, in legislative enactments as well as theoretical analyses. Because individuals committing similar offenses have different characteristics and because circumstances of offenses vary, judges were typically given considerable latitude to set initial sentences. Judicial sentences to prison tended to be indefinite (for example, two to six years), so that the time of actual release could be determined according to a parole board's estimation of the offender's progress toward rehabilitation and of his level of dangerousness prior to release.

Reformation as the keystone.   One attack on this system came from those who were highly skeptical about the usefulness of condemnation and imprisonment and who placed hope instead in scientific reformation of the individual criminal. Most extreme were proposals to abolish punishment in favor of a medical model that would consider the antisocial individual as an ill person needing treatment. Appearing at first glance more humane than traditional attitudes and practices, the model's emphasis on treatment could give the state open-ended authority to achieve a cure of the antisocial person—however long that might take, however radical the necessary therapy, and whatever his original wrong. Full acceptance of the model might also lead to compulsory treatment of those identified as socially dangerous before they commit harmful acts, a prospect of social intervention that many people perceive as a denial of human dignity and autonomy. Because of the medical model's potential for sweeping intrusion into citizens' lives, and because few people with political power have been willing to give up the possible benefits of condemnation and fear of penalties, proposals for abolition of punishment have never won wide acceptance.

A more moderate reformist position was that within a system of punishment, heavier concentration should be placed on reform, with the length of sentence to depend even more on the rate of rehabilitative progress. The movement to emphasize reform had already influenced American sentencing practices, promoting more flexibility in prison terms than had previously existed and more attention to the quality of programs within prison; but some believed that genuine change had not gone nearly far enough.

Just deserts.   During the 1970s there was a sharp reaction against the emphasis on rehabilitation. Despairing over achievement of earlier reformers' goals, critics of existing practices argued that rehabilitation had largely proved a failure, that prison was more likely to harden criminals than to cure them of antisocial tendencies, and that parole boards were almost wholly unable to judge which prisoners were fit to be set loose on society. Flexible sentences, it was said, caused prisoners acute anxiety over their future, encouraged them to feign attitudes and emotions

they did not feel, made them prey to the arbitrary dictates of prison officials and parole boards, and engendered in them a sense that the system was unfair in fundamental respects. Critics also contended that in practice, reliance on individual predictions to imprison persons was unjust, since many of those considered dangerous would not commit crimes if released, and since many of those viewed as apt candidates for individual deterrence or reformation are not rendered more law-abiding by confinement. Broad discretion and unequal treatment of similar offenders were challenged because they were intrinsically unfair and because disparities failed to contribute to utilitarian objectives and caused deep resentment among those convicted.

Although not rejecting general deterrence as a proper aim of punishment, proponents of the "just deserts" model urged that sentencing should seek to achieve the goals of proportionality and uniformity: penalties for particular offenses should depend mainly on the severity of the offenses, and those who commit similar offenses should be given equal, or nearly equal, treatment. Terms of imprisonment would be squarely fixed at the time of sentence. In-prison efforts to help convicts should continue, but participation in therapy or job training would no longer be relevant to the timing of release.

In certain respects the just deserts model seems obviously overdrawn. Whatever the uncertainties of individual prediction, confining those whose dangerousness is attested by repeated violent crimes must be acceptable, and the plausibility of rejecting this ground rests on the implicit assumption that some other basis for imprisonment will be available for these persons. (One such alternative in fact began to be used with increasing frequency at the close of the twentieth century: indefinite civil commitment of sexually dangerous persons.) Moreover, making penalties equal for similar offenders would disregard both the significant differences between those who commit the same offense, and the value of avoiding useless punishment (sentencing "parsimony").

Nevertheless, in their positive emphasis on the values of equality and perceived fairness, in their distaste for arbitrary discretion, in their skepticism about rehabilitation induced by the implicit promise of release, and in their realism about the effects of prison life, just deserts theorists and other critics of highly discretionary sentencing systems have made a substantial contribution to thought about punishment. They have also encouraged reforms in many states (in particular, the enactment of sentencing guidelines or other determinate sentencing laws) that have reduced judicial discretion and reduced or eliminated parole board discretion to determine date of release. However, even in those states, such as Minnesota, whose reformed sentencing systems were strongly influenced by the just deserts model, individualized sentencing based on the goals of rehabilitation and risk management continues to play a very substantial role in the design of formal rules and, especially, in actual practice.

Utilitarian bases for retributive perspectives.   The modern debate over sentencing practices raises a more general theoretical question: May official decisions based on retributive premises be socially useful? The idea is that since people naturally think in retributive terms, they will be disenchanted and eventually less law-abiding if the law does not recognize that offenders should receive the punishment they "deserve." Although love for one's enemies may be a moral ideal, perhaps most people cannot feel strongly committed to a moral code without also wanting to see those who break that code punished. If the complex psychological and sociological assumptions that underlie this view are accurate, utilitarianism and retributivism may subtly blend. The ultimate philosophical justification offered for punishment would be promotion of human good, a utilitarian justification; but a retributive outlook among citizens would be welcomed and the operating official standard for punishment would be retributive. This apparent paradox is but an example in the context of punishment of an idea that has often been discussed in connection with utilitarian theory—the possibility that human welfare will be best advanced if people subscribe to a more absolutist morality than one which makes the promotion of good consequences the test of an act's rightness.

Justifications for punishment and the criminal law

In a rational system of penal law, a close connection will exist between accepted theories of punishment and both the boundaries of the substantive criminal law and the procedures by which criminal guilt is determined. The justifications obviously touch on sentencing policies and the sorts of activities that should be made criminal ("criminalization" decisions), but they are much more pervasive.

As far as criminal procedure is concerned, a dominant theme is avoidance of conviction of the innocent. The system of determining guilt is thus responsive to a view that such convictions are very bad, a view that is shared by both retributivists and utilitarians. In addition, concern over comparative desert is evidenced by worry about the unfairness of executing those whose behavior has been no worse than that of many others who receive only prison sentences. This worry has led to judicial and legislative reform of procedures for imposing capital punishment and has strengthened support for abolition of that penalty.

Definitions of guilt in the substantive criminal law place great emphasis on intentional, knowing, or reckless wrongdoing, largely eschewing criminal treatment for those who have the misfortune to be the accidental instruments of harm. Again the retributivist and the utilitarian largely unite, the retributivist claiming that punishing those who are not morally culpable is simply wrong and the utilitarian suggesting that such punishment is unproductive. There is, however, a point of significant difference. The retributivist may reject strict liability offenses, and perhaps even criminal liability for negligence (inadvertent, careless wrongdoing), on the basis of absolute principle; the utilitarian will remain open to the argument that in special settings such liability is warranted.

Similarly, justifications and excuses can be related to theories of punishment. For example, a person who acts in necessary self-defense is not morally culpable, nor will punishment serve any significant purpose. Such a person need not be reformed or deterred, others acting in self-defense should not be deterred, and punishment is much too high a price for a slight addition to the deterrence of those not acting in self-defense. Self-defense is made a justification for intentional assault that would otherwise be criminal. The insanity defense excuses those who are not blameworthy; it also reaches roughly to the class of those who are not deterrable by the sanctions criminal punishment can provide. Persons judged insane require incapacitation and need rehabilitation, but both can be accomplished by a mandatory civil commitment.

The conclusion that these and other major features of the substantive law are consonant with each of the two major theories of the justification of punishment should not be too surprising. Theories of justification are often built with existing practices in mind and do not usually stray too far from the reflective moral views of ordinary citizens. The fact that sharply divergent philosophical theories can have closely similar implications across a broad range of actual practices is less a startling coincidence than a product of the existential basis on which those theories are constructed.

KENT GREENAWALT

See also CAPITAL PUNISHMENT: MORALITY, POLITICS, AND POLICY; COMPARATIVE CRIMINAL LAW AND ENFORCEMENT: PRELITERATE SOCIETIES; CONVICTION: CIVIL DISABILITIES; CORPORAL PUNISHMENT; CRIMINALIZATION AND DECRIMINALIZATION; CRUEL AND UNUSUAL PUNISHMENT; DETERRENCE; INCAPACITATION; PRISONS: PRISONERS; PRISONS: PRISONS FOR WOMEN; PRISONS: PROBLEMS AND PROSPECTS; PROBATION AND PAROLE: HISTORY, GOALS, AND DECISION-MAKING; PROBATION AND PAROLE: PROCEDURAL PROTECTION; PROBATION AND PAROLE: SUPERVISION; REHABILITATION; RESTORATIVE JUSTICE; RETRIBUTIVISM; SENTENCING: ALLOCATION OF AUTHORITY; SENTENCING: ALTERNATIVES; SENTENCING: GUIDELINES; SENTENCING: MANDATORY AND MANDATORY MINIMUM SENTENCES; SENTENCING: PRESENTENCE REPORT; SENTENCING: PROCEDURAL PROTECTION; SHAMING PUNISHMENTS.

BIBLIOGRAPHY

ALLEN, FRANCIS A. *The Decline of the Rehabilitative Ideal: Penal Policy and Social Purpose.* New Haven, Conn.: Yale University Press, 1981.

ALEXANDER, LAWRENCE. "The Doomsday Machine: Proportionality, Punishment, and Prevention." *Monist* 63 (1980): 199–227.

ANDENAES, JOHANNES. "The General Preventive Effects of Punishment." *University of Pennsylvania Law Review* 114 (1966): 949–983.

BEDAU, HUGO A. "Concessions to Retribution in Punishment." In *Justice and Punishment.* Edited by Jerry B. Cederblom and William L. Blizek. Cambridge, Mass.: Ballinger, 1977. Pages 51–73.

BENN, STANLEY I. "Punishment." In *The Encyclopedia of Philosophy,* vol. 7. Edited by Paul Edwards. New York: Macmillan and Free Press, 1967. Pages 29–36.

BENTHAM, JEREMY. *An Introduction to the Principles of Morals and Legislation.* Edited by James H. Burns and H. L. A. Hart. London: Athlone Press, 1970.

BRANDT, RICHARD. "Retributive Justice and Criminal Law." In *Ethics and Public Policy.* Edited by Thomas Beauchamp. Englewood Cliffs, N.J.: Prentice-Hall, 1975. Pages 66–84.

DUFF, R. ANTHONY. "Penal Communications: Recent Work in the Philosophy of Punishment." *Crime and Justice: A Review of Research* 20 (1996): 1–97. Chicago: University of Chicago Press, 1996.

EZORSKY, GERTRUDE, ed. *Philosophical Perspectives on Punishment.* Albany: State University of New York Press, 1972.

FEINBERG, JOEL. *Doing and Deserving: Essays in the Theory of Responsibility.* Princeton, N.J.: Princeton University Press, 1970.

FRASE, RICHARD S. "Sentencing Principles in Theory and Practice." *Crime & Justice: A Review of Research* 22 (1997): 363–443.

GOLDMAN, ALAN H. "Can a Utilitarian's Support of Non-utilitarian Rules Vindicate Utilitarianism?" *Social Theory and Practice* 4 (1977): 333–345.

———. "The Paradox of Punishment." *Philosophy and Public Affairs* 9 (1979): 42–58.

GREENAWALT, KENT. "'Uncontrollable' Actions and the Eighth Amendment: Implications of *Powell v. Texas.*" *Columbia Law Review* 69 (1969): 929–979.

GROSS, HYMAN. *A Theory of Criminal Justice.* New York: Oxford University Press, 1979.

HALL, JEROME. *General Principles of Criminal Law.* 2d ed. Indianapolis: Bobbs-Merrill, 1960.

HART, H. L. A. *Punishment and Responsibility: Essays in the Philosophy of Law.* New York: Oxford University Press, 1968.

KANT, IMMANUEL. *The Philosophy of Law: An Exposition of the Fundamental Principles of Jurisprudence as the Science of Right.* Translated by W. Hastie. Edinburgh: T. & T. Clark, 1887.

MORRIS, HERBERT. *On Guilt and Innocence: Essays in Legal Philosophy and Moral Psychology.* Berkeley: University of California Press, 1976.

MORRIS, NORVAL. *The Future of Imprisonment.* Chicago: University of Chicago Press, 1974.

PINCOFFS, EDMUND L. *The Rationale of Legal Punishment.* New York: Humanities Press, 1966.

ROSS, W. D. "The Ethics of Punishment." *Journal of Philosophical Studies* 4 (1929): 205–224.

TONRY, MICHAEL. "Proportionality, Parsimony, and Interchangeability of Punishments." In *Penal Theory and Penal Practice.* Edited by Anthony Duff and Sandra Marshall. Manchester, U.K.: Manchester University Press, 1994.

TYLER, TOM. *Why People Obey the Law.* New Haven: Yale University Press, 1990.

VON HIRSCH, ANDREW. *Censure and Sanctions.* Oxford, U.K.: Clarendon Press, 1993.

MACCOLD, PAUL E. *Restorative Justice: An Annotated Bibliography.* Monsey, N.Y.: Criminal Justice Press, 1997.

WALKER, NIGEL. *Why Punish?* Oxford: Oxford University Press, 1991.

WASSERSTROM, RICHARD. "Some Problems in the Definition and Justification of Punishment." In *Values and Morals*. Edited by Alvin Goldman and Jaegwon Kim. Dordrecht, Holland: Reidel, 1978. Pages 299–315.

WILSON, JAMES Q. *Thinking About Crime, Second Edition*. New York: Basic Books, 1983.

WOOTTON, BARBARA, with SCOL, VERA G., and CHAMBERS, ROSALIND. *Social Science and Social Pathology*. London: Allen & Unwin, 1959.

ZIMRING, FRANKLIN E., and HAWKINS, GORDON. *Incapacitation: Penal Confinement and the Restraint of Crime*. New York: Oxford University Press, 1995.

R

RACE AND CRIME

The relationship between race and crime has been a primary concern among sociologists and criminologists since the beginning of the disciplines in America. Various racial and ethnic minorities in the United States have consistently been associated with higher rates of criminality, including peoples of Italian, Polish, Irish, German, Hispanic, and African descent, among others. Throughout history, most of the "high crime groups" have been newly immigrated populations. However, at the turn of the millenium, most of these groups seem to be distinguished predominantly by their skin color, residential location, and socioeconomic status. Hispanics and African Americans living in impoverished ghetto neighborhoods are subject to disproportionate police attention, and are overly represented in court dockets, jail and prison populations, media accounts of crime, street crime victims, and public fear of crime.

Data sources and meaning

There are two main sources of crime-related data that are typically analyzed to support the various race/crime explanations: the Uniform Crime Reports (UCR) and the National Crime Victims Survey (NCVS). Each tells us something slightly different about crime and its relationship to race. The UCR are prepared by the Federal Bureau of Investigation from official police department statistics, and therefore vary in reliability and validity depending on the type of crime (data are generally better for serious street crimes and violent crime). The UCR necessarily exclude all unreported crime (the "dark figure of crime") and crime not typically addressed by law enforcement, particularly white collar, corporate, and governmental crimes (Walker, Spohn, and DeLone). Analysis of the UCR tells much about police behavior while variously underestimating the amount of most crime types.

In general, the UCR demonstrate that racial minorities are much more likely to be arrested compared to whites, and other criminal justice data clearly demonstrate disproportionate representation in each successive part of the criminal justice system. Indeed, near the close of the 1990s, African Americans constituted 12 percent of the U.S. population yet 32 percent of those arrested for property crimes and 41 percent for violent crimes. The greatest disproportionality among Part 1 or Index crimes were for murder/non-negligent manslaughter and robbery, where African Americans account for 56 percent and 57 percent of all arrests, respectively. Two less serious offenses (included in the UCR as Part 2 crimes) for which African Americans are particularly overrepresented among arrestees are gambling (67 percent) and vagrancy (46 percent), both highly associated with poverty (U.S. Department of Justice, 1998). The UCR does not detail any rates for Hispanics (Walker et al.).

Studies of the relationship between race and criminal sentencing have produced conflicting results (Walker et al.). While racial minorities tend to receive longer sentences overall compared to whites, these differences are usually explainable by factors such as prior record and seriousness of the offense. The argument has been made, however, that such indicators were themselves the result of racial discrimination on the part of the police, judges, and juries, thus leading to a greater likelihood of an African

American or Hispanic defendant having a longer prior record, or that the socioeconomic position of most minorities increases the likelihood of committing an offense considered more serious by the courts. Regardless of the possible explanations, it is clear that the end result of the court process was the increasingly disproportionate incarceration of racial minorities in U.S. jails and prisons throughout the twentieth century (Irwin and Austin; Walker et al.).

Prisons throughout the nation are disproportionately occupied by African Americans and Hispanics. Although these trends hold true across most geographical areas, the rates of disproportionality tend to be higher in the South and in state correctional systems (Irwin and Austin). Indeed, African Americans represent 38 percent of inmates in federal prisons and 55 percent of those in state prison systems. Hispanics represent 28 percent and 17 percent of federal and state correctional populations, respectively (U.S. Department of Justice, 1999).

The second major source of crime data is the NCVS, administered by the Bureau of the Census for the Bureau of Justice Statistics. By sampling the general population about criminal victimization, the NCVS is able to uncover unreported crimes and describe the characteristics and relationships between victims and offenders. Overall, while the NCVS also indicates disproportionate involvement of racial minorities in street crime, the gap between minorities and whites is typically smaller than is apparent in the UCR (Walker et al.). African Americans account for 52 percent of all personal victimizations, including 49 percent of all violent crimes (excluding homicide, which is not determined by the NCVS). Hispanics account for nearly 49 percent of all victimizations, including 43 percent of violence. Although the vast majority of most crimes are committed intraracially (that is, white on white or black on black), respondents in the NCVS perceived that only 25 percent of violent offenders were African American (Bureau of Justice Statistics). These data, together with the much higher arrest rates of minorities for violent crimes, suggest that minorities probably commit fewer crimes than their arrest rates would suggest but are disproportionately caught and punished for the crimes they do commit.

Finally, one major explanatory factor that must be taken into consideration when studying disproportionate minority representation in crime is the socioeconomic status of minorities in American society. Despite legislative and judicial decisions over the past several decades, African Americans and other racial minorities remain as much or more residentially segregated at the turn of the millennium as before the monumental changes in the 1950s and 1960s (Massey and Denton). The ghetto experience is typical for most African Americans, including the entrenched poverty, unemployment, poor schools, and lack of social opportunities that are associated with such transitional and "disorganized" neighborhoods (Hagan; Wilson). Indeed, the various inequalities that exist within ghetto communities have been linked to numerous crimes, particularly homicide (Kovandzic, Vieraitis, and Yeisley).

Combined, these sources indicate that racial minorities (particularly African Americans and Hispanics) are disproportionately involved in street crime, victimized by street crime, and brought under the control and supervision of the criminal justice system. Furthermore, street crimes are more characteristic of impoverished, inner city, and ghetto neighborhoods; and occur more often among the nonemployed, young, and male. These same groups also appear to be more likely to penetrate deeper into the criminal justice system, with racial disproportionality increasing at each successive step into the system.

There is a near complete absence of valid or reliable white-collar, corporate, and governmental crime statistics in the UCR and NCVS measurements. This is an extremely important void when considering the relationship between race and crime, because by even the most conservative estimates street crimes account for only a fraction of all crimes. Nonetheless, American media, politicians, public, and even criminologists tend to focus on street crime, thereby dramatizing and potentially exaggerating the real racial over-representations of racial minorities in crime and the criminal justice system.

The nature and direction of the race and crime relationship

Official crime measures indicate that certain races are disproportionately represented in crime statistics and the criminal justice system. While there is legitimate cause to question official crime measures, a relationship between race and crime nonetheless exists. Two theoretical models explain the relationship between race and crime. The first explanation is the *disproportionality hypothesis*, which states that certain races, namely African Americans and Hispanics, are disproportionately represented in official crime statistics and the criminal justice system because these races are disproportionately involved in crime. This approach explains the relationship between race and crime as a product of legitimate, or legal, factors, such as offense severity and prior record. Obviously, if members of race A commit more crime than members of race B, then race A will be disproportionately represented in official crime statistics and the criminal justice system for legitimate reasons.

The second theoretical explanation is the *disparity hypothesis*, which states that multiple facets of society, namely the various stages of the criminal justice system, treat some races differently than others. In other words, there is disparity between how a member of one race and a similar member of another race are treated. This approach contends that extralegal factors play a role in affecting various parts of society and the criminal justice system. Rather than only considering legal variables, such as offense severity and prior record, when arresting or sentencing offenders, disparity theorists argue that society considers extralegal factors, such as race, ethnicity, social class, or lifestyle, when dealing with actual or potential offenders. According to the disparity hypothesis, members of some races are treated differently by the criminal justice system, and it is this pervasive disparity and discrimination that explains why some races are disproportionately represented in official crime statistics and the criminal justice system.

Bio-psychological theory

Several theoretical approaches justify the disproportionality hypothesis. Early research adopted an individualistic approach that focused on the biological and psychological differences of criminals and became known as biological positivism. Researchers believed criminals to be physically different from noncriminals, and considered criminals to be atavistic throwbacks that could be identified by certain biological features or physical stigmata. Many of these early biological studies singled out certain races as having more criminalistic features than others, and biological explanations of disproportionate involvement of certain races in crime were born. Many of the early biological studies have been written off as little more than pseudo-science; however, individualistic studies emphasizing biological and psychological differences between offenders and noncriminals have not disappeared. In

1939, E. A. Hooten, a Harvard anthropologist, stated that "criminals are organically inferior," and went on to propose that "the elimination of crime can be effected only by the extirpation of the physically, mentally, and morally unfit; or by their complete segregation in a social aseptic environment" (quoted in Vold and Bernard, p. 6). This belief that the causes of crime lie inside individuals has endured decades of criticism.

Biological and psychological positivism experienced somewhat of a revival in the 1970s, as a number of researchers began to look into biological and psychological factors associated with criminality. Biological and psychological factors, such as brain disorders, hormonal problems, biochemical effects, nerve disorders, chromosomal abnormalities, and intelligence deficiencies, have all been linked to criminal behavior. One of the most controversial biological/psychological positivistic perspectives is presented in *The Bell Curve* (1994) by Richard Hernstein and Charles Murray. Hernstein and Murray argue that Intelligence Quotient (IQ) determines success in life and that people with lower IQs are more likely to receive welfare, be unemployed, and commit crime. The authors argue that African Americans score lower on IQ tests than whites, that IQ is genetically determined and does not change throughout the life course, and that lower intelligence results in increased criminal offending. Critics argue that there is no such objective entity as "intelligence" and that IQ tests are culturally biased. Hernstein and Murray and their work have been largely discredited by the scientific community, but their approach to explaining the disproportionate criminal offending of particular races proved popular and has some advocates.

Biological and psychological studies have played an important role in shaping what is known about crime. However, their popularity has been more due to their controversial ideological nature that their scientific merit. Their treatment of complex behaviors as scientific byproducts of biological or psychological differences in persons is overly simplistic and woefully inadequate. Crime is a normative concept, and biological explanations tend to ignore the fact that what is deemed "criminal" in one place might be considered noble elsewhere. Despite the shortcomings of this vein of research, it has found a place in the disciplines of sociology, anthropology, and criminology, and remains as one approach to explain differential patterns of offending across racial categories.

Sociological theory

During the early part of the twentieth century, sociological explanations of crime causation grew in popularity. The sociological approach emphasized the environment and social interaction as causal factors in the study of crime and delinquency, rather than individualistic biological and psychological factors. A collection of social scientists in Chicago is credited with starting this trend, and their cohort of researchers came to be known as the Chicago School.

Members of the Chicago School accused existing individualistic theories of myopic reasoning, and proposed a broader approach acknowledging how societal factors play a role in causing crime and delinquency. The social landscape in the United States was changing rapidly, as people left rural farm communities for industrial urban centers. No place better represented this migration than the city of Chicago. The city's population grew rapidly throughout the latter half of the nineteenth century and the early part of the twentieth century, and virtually every racial and ethnic group came to be represented in the Chicago demographic. Members of the Chicago School saw this rapid change as a major factor in causing crime and developed a number of theories to explain the relationship between various societal factors and crime.

Clifford Shaw and Henry McKay are most clearly identified with starting this line of inquiry. Their work in the area of *social disorganization* explained how areas characterized by poverty and constant social change experience a breakdown in a number of social institutions, such as the family, employment, religion, education, and community. This breakdown results in a weakened value system, and the ability of disorganized communities to discourage deviant and criminal behavior is compromised. Once this disorganized environment, characterized by social instability and crime, takes hold, it is difficult to eradicate, as the compromised value system and resulting crime are passed along to subsequent generations. Many minority neighborhoods experienced social disorganization and increases in crime, which explains the disproportionate representation of certain races in official crime statistics and the criminal justice system.

In addition to social disorganization, *learning theory* and *differential association* explain how society plays a role in causing crime. Once the seeds of crime are planted in a community, delinquents and criminals either directly or indirectly teach others how to commit crime and the criminal substructure is passed on to future generations. Researchers, such as Edwin Sutherland, Donald Cressey, and Ronald Akers, have made profound contributions by explaining how crime is learned. Some minority communities seem to experience a disproportionate amount of crime, and communities with a lot of crime are rich in learning environments for future criminals. Therefore, learning theory plays an integral role in explaining why some races are disproportionately represented in crime statistics.

Anomie/strain theories are also helpful in explaining this phenomenon. Researchers, such as Robert Merton, Albert Cohen, Richard Cloward, Lloyd Ohlin, Steven Messner, and Robert Agnew, have made profound contributions in explaining why some societies experience more crime than others. Some societies like the United States place a relatively heavy emphasis on monetary success without emphasizing the merits of legitimate means of achieving this end, such as hard work, honesty, and education. These societies are said to suffer from anomie or normlessness, and indirectly encourage their citizens to seek monetary success without adhering to legitimate means. People who have limited access to the legitimate means of achieving monetary success have to disproportionately resort to illegitimate means. Society generates and conveys an expectation of what represents "success," but does not afford all its citizens the opportunities necessary to achieve "success" via legitimate means. This gap between the legitimate means and societal goals produces a strain in the lives of groups and individuals as they actively seek what is deemed "success" by society. This strain can cause people to employ illegitimate means in the search for monetary success, or indulge in other deviant and criminal behaviors as a way of rejecting the stated expectations of society. Anomie/strain explain why some races, who are often not afforded the same educational, employment, and social opportunities as other races, are disproportionately represented in crime statistics and the criminal justice system.

Control theory also plays a prominent role in explaining why some races are disproportionately represented in the criminal justice system. Control theorists, such as Travis Hirschi, Albert Reiss, Ivan Nye, and Walter Reckless, contend that numerous factors act to "control" human behavior. While control theories have been presented a number of different ways, the basic message is that some people, who have fewer or less effective controls, are more likely to indulge in unconventional behavior, which sometimes takes the form of crime and delinquency. Hirschi specified four types of control: *attachment* to others and caring about their perspective and well-being; *commitment* to conventional norms; *involvement* in conventional activities; and *belief* in the moral validity of conventional norms. Some people and some groups simply have more controls in their lives than others. Some groups seem to have fewer controls, which explains why some races are disproportionately represented in official crime statistics.

Out of the Chicago School blossomed numerous theories that explained how social factors play a role in producing crime and delinquency. Many of these social factors affect certain neighborhoods more than others, and as a result, affect certain groups disproportionately, so many neighborhoods are racially homogenous. The biological and psychological theories attempt to explain why some races are disproportionately involved in crime. Similarly, the sociological contributions go a long way in explaining what role environmental and social factors play in explaining this phenomenon. However, the approaches discussed thus far seem to ignore the pervasive economic and racial inequality that characterize the American experience.

Conflict theory

By simply researching what biological, psychological, or societal factors cause some groups or individuals to commit crime in a given society (the disproportionality hypothesis) implies that there is consensus among different groups about how society should operate, what laws should be enforced, and how justice should be carried out. The disparity hypothesis rejects this consensus approach in explaining why some races are disproportionately represented in official crime statistics and the criminal justice system.

The disparity hypothesis is based on a conflict theory perspective. The conflict perspective views the law as a tool used by dominant groups, those that have the social, political, and economic power, to maintain their privileged position over subordinate groups. Dominant groups include the white race, the wealthy, and the politically connected. Subordinate groups include minority races, the poor, and the politically neglected. These subordinate groups pose a threat, and the dominant groups use the legal code to keep the subordinate groups from usurping their power.

Behaviors often adopted by members of the subordinate groups are often criminalized in American society, while behaviors adopted by the dominant groups go unpunished. An excellent example is the disparity between federal sentencing guidelines for crimes involving powder cocaine and crack cocaine. Crack cocaine is the cocaine product of choice for poor and minority communities because it is less expensive than powder cocaine. Crack cocaine is made of powder cocaine and several benign substances, but it is less pure and therefore contains less pure cocaine than its powder counterpart. However, sentences for possession of crack cocaine are one hundred times as severe as sentences for possession of powder cocaine. For example, a person convicted of possessing five hundred grams of powder cocaine receives the same mandatory minimum prison sentence of five years as someone possessing five grams of crack cocaine. More than 90 percent of persons sentenced in federal courts for crack cocaine violations are African American (Walker et al.). This law, imposed by dominant groups, results in the arrest, conviction, and imprisonments of thousands of African Americans every year, and it is a clear illustration of how the law is used to control and suppress certain races.

Conflict theory rejects the consensus approach and contends that different groups do not necessarily share the same values, agree on what behaviors should be criminalized, and believe in the same penalty structure. Dominant groups determine what values should be favored, which laws should be enforced, and what penalties should be imposed, while the subordinate groups, often made up of minorities and the poor, are targeted, arrested, and punished unfairly. Conflict theory best explains and supports the disparity hypothesis, which is quite different than the disproportionality hypothesis. However, both perspectives are used in the disciplines of sociology and criminology to explain the disproportionate representation of certain races in official crime statistics and the criminal justice system.

Integrated theory

Most recently, integrated theoretical perspectives are offering a broader eclectic explanation of the association between race and crime, one that is capable of linking many other theoretical and empirical approaches in a variety of ways (Walker et al.). In general, most suggest that economic and racial segregation (ghetto inequality) contribute to crime primarily through their concentrated efforts on ghetto neighborhoods, as well as by isolating the extremely disadvantaged away from mainstream society (Massey and Denton). Cumulatively, these conditions impose severe deprivation on ghetto residents, eliminate opportunities for social and economic mobility, encourage deviant adaptations, and prevent structural change by provoking fear and condemnation of ghetto residents by mainstream society. Residents of ghetto neighborhoods are therefore more likely than most others to risk criminal justice sanctions by participating in illegal occupations such as drug dealing, gambling, and prostitution (Hagan). Drug markets, in particular, bring about a wide range of drug-related property and violent crimes as addicts scramble to obtain money to support their habits and dealers protect their illicit businesses (Chaiken and Chaiken). Such an integrated perspective unites social disorganization, social learning, anomie, control, conflict, and other theories while focusing on socioeconomic conditions as the base of the relationship. In addition, integration permits an understanding of the issue that acknowledges both disproportionality and disparity.

Conclusion

Clearly, a relationship between race and crime exists. It is less clear what accounts for this relationship. Research suggests that both disproportionality and disparity play a role; however, additional research is needed to better understand the complex nature of the race/crime correlation.

MARK YEISLEY
CHRISTOPHER P. KREBS

See also CLASS AND CRIME; CRIME CAUSATION: BIOLOGICAL THEORIES; CRIME CAUSATION: SOCIOLOGICAL THEORIES; UNEMPLOYMENT AND CRIME.

BIBLIOGRAPHY

Bureau of Justice Statistics. *Criminal Victimization in the United States, 1994*. Washington, D.C.: USGPO, 1996.
CHAIKEN, JAN, and CHAIKEN, MARCIA. "Drugs and Predatory Crime." In *Drugs and Crime*. Edited by Michael Tonry and James Q. Wilson. Chicago: University of Chicago Press, 1990. Pages 203–239.
HAGAN, JOHN. *Crime and Disrepute*. Thousand Oaks, Calif.: Pine Forge Press, 1994.
IRWIN, JOHN, and AUSTIN, JAMES. *It's About Time: America's Imprisonment Binge*. Albany, N.Y.: Wadsworth Publishing Company, 1997.
KOVANDZIC, TOM; VIERAITIS, LYNNE; and YEISLEY, MARK. "The Structural Covariates of Homicide: A Reexamination of the Effects of Income Inequality and Poverty in the Post-Reagan Era." *Criminology* 36, no. 3 (1998): 569–600.
MASSEY, DOUGLASS, and DENTON, NANCY. *American Apartheid: Segregation and the Making of the Underclass*. Cambridge, Mass.: Harvard University Press, 1993.
SIMON, DAVID, and EITZEN, STANLEY. *Elite Deviance*, 3d ed. Boston, Mass.: Allyn and Bacon, 1990.
U.S. Department of Justice. *Crime in the United States, 1997*. Washington, D.C.: USGPO, 1998.
U.S. Department of Justice. *Correctional Populations in the United States, 1996*. Washington, D.C.: USGPO, 1999.
VOLD, GEORGE B., and BERNARD, THOMAS J. *Theoretical Criminology*. 3d ed. New York: Oxford University Press, 1986.
WALKER, SAMUEL; SPOHN, CASSIA; and DELONE, MIRIAM. *The Color of Justice*, 2d ed. Australia: Wadsworth Publishing, 2000.
WILSON, WILLIAM JULIUS. *The Truly Disadvantaged*. Chicago: University of Chicago Press, 1987.
WOLFGANG, MARVIN E. "Cesare Lombroso." In *Pioneers in Criminology*. Edited by Hermann Mannheim. Chicago: Quadrangle Books, 1960. Pages 168–227.

RAPE: BEHAVIORAL ASPECTS

The National Victim Center and Crime Victims Research and Treatment Center reported in 1992 that 13 percent of all adult American women have been raped at some time in their lives. The NVC/CVRTC Report estimated that there were 683,000 forcible rapes during 1992, which translates to about 1,871 rapes per day. The American Psychological Association's Task Force on Male Violence Against Women concluded that between 14 and 25 percent of adult women have experienced rape (Goodman et al.). Although numerous methodological problems clearly preclude any definitive conclusions, a diverse cross-section of studies spanning several decades suggest that approximately 25 percent of adult women have experienced some form of sexual victimization and somewhere between 10 and 15 percent of women have been raped.

Classification of rapists

Sexual aggression derives from a complex amalgam of factors and typically reflects a chronic pattern of maladaptive behaviors. Those factors considered to be most importantly related to rape were reviewed by Prentky and Knight. These factors include: (a) impaired heterosexual relationships with peers; (b) relative lack of empathy; (c) poorly controlled and improperly expressed anger; (d) cognitive distortions, particularly around women and sexuality; (e) sexual fantasy that includes thoughts and images of coercion, force, and deviant or paraphilic acts; and (f) a highly impulsive lifestyle that often includes antisocial elements. Although all of these factors may be present in varying degrees, typically several of the factors predominate in a particular offender. When factors are sufficiently robust to differentiate among rapists, they may serve as the basis for classification.

To the best of the present author's knowledge, the only validated classification model for rapists is MTC:R3 (Knight and Prentky). The principal dimensions that are used for classifying rapists in MTC:R3 are (a) *Expressive Aggression* (nature, amount, and quality of expressed aggression in all known instances of sexually aggressive behavior); (b) *Pervasive Anger* (the presence of global, undifferentiated anger in the life of the offender, as reflected by a history of nonsexual assaults, fighting, and verbal aggression directed at men as well as women); (c) *Juvenile and Adult Unsocialized Behavior* (conduct-disordered, delinquent, and impulsive antisocial behavior); (d) *Social Competence* (as reflected by stability and quality of interpersonal relationships with peers, and stability and level of vocational achievement); (e) *Sexualization* (as evidenced by high sexual drive, sexual preoccupation, strong and frequent sexual urges, evidence of compulsivity in sexual assaults, evidence of paraphilias); (f) *Sadism* (evidence that pain, fear, or discomfort increases sexual arousal, preoccupation with sadistic fantasies, ritualization of violence, symbolic expressions of sadistic fantasy); and (g) *Offense Planning*. In addition to discriminating among rapists, these major dimensions reflect temporally stable behavioral domains that are targeted by most treatment programs.

These seven major MTC:R3 dimensions are used to classify an offender into one of nine subtypes: Type 1 (Opportunistic, High Social Competence), Type 2 (Opportunistic, Low Social Competence), Type 3 (Pervasive Anger), Type 4 (Overt Sadism), Type 5 (Muted Sadism), Type 6 (Sexualized, High Social Competence), Type 7 (Sexualized, Low Social Competence), Type 8 (Vindictive, Low Social Competence), and Type 9 (Vindictive, High Social Competence). The sexual offenses of the two Opportunistic subtypes are impulsive, unplanned, predatory crimes, controlled more by situational factors and immediately antecedent events than by any long-standing, recurrent rape fantasy. The sexual assaults of the Pervasive Anger type are driven by undifferentiated anger. These offenders are, in effect, "angry at the world." They are as likely to assault men as women. Their anger is not sexualized, and there is no evidence of protracted rape fantasy. The two Sadistic subtypes evidence poor differentiation between sexual and aggressive drives, and long-standing, frequent occurrence of sexually aggressive and violent fantasies. The two Nonsadistic, Sexual types evidence frequent sexual and sexually coercive fantasy that is devoid of the synergistic connection between sex and aggression that characterizes the Sadistic types. The fantasies and offense-related behaviors of these Nonsadistic, Sexual types are hypothesized to reflect an amalgam of sexual preoccupation, distorted attitudes about women and sexuality, and feelings of inadequacy. The Vindictive types harbor focal anger at women. Their attitudes and their behavior reflect this exclusive misogynistic focus. The sexual assaults of these rapists are marked by statements and behaviors that are intended to defile, demean, and humiliate the victims, as well as to physically injure. The MTC:R3 system represents the third version of ongoing programmatic research in this area. MTC:R3 is not a final "product," and will be revised in accordance with the results of current taxonomic research.

Serial rape

Serial rape is a "special" case that is defined in terms of repetitiveness (e.g., three or more known sexual assaults on adult women). There is no single classification that captures serial rape. Serial rapists may be any one of a number of different subtypes. A fantasy-based drive model for serial sexual homicide (cf. Prentky and Burgess) may be helpful in trying to understand serial rape. Simply stated, once the restraints inhibiting the acting out of internally generated, recurrent rape fantasies are no longer present, the individual is likely to engage in a series of progressively more accurate "trial runs" in an attempt to "stage" the fantasies as they were imagined. Because the trial runs can never precisely match the fantasy, the offender must restage the fantasy with a new victim. Although the number of serial rapists appears to be low, these offenders account for a very large number of victims. In one study of forty-one serial rapists, the collective sample of offenders was responsible for 837 rapes, over 400 attempted rapes, and over 5,000 "nuisance" sex offenses (Hazelwood, Reboussin, and Warren).

The theoretical model referred to above makes a number of implicit assumptions. First, the individual has created an inner world (i.e., a fantasy life) that is intended to satisfy, often in disguised or symbolic fashion, needs that cannot be satisfied in the real world. The inner worlds of serial rapists are dominated by a maelstrom of sexual and aggressive thoughts and feelings. Second, the mechanisms that drive the fantasies and the factors that permit the enactment and reenactment of the fantasies are at least as important as, if not more important than, understanding the specific content of the fantasies. This is critical, since it is commonly accepted that many nonoffenders have sexually deviant and coercive fantasies. Third, the content of the sexual fantasy derives from explicit, protracted sexually pathological experiences first sustained at a young age. Fourth, the parameters governing fantasy life in nonoffenders are different from the equivalent parameters in serial rapists. Rape fantasies in nonoffenders are not typically rehearsed and are not preoccupying. The fantasies are usually associated with an *exteroceptive* stimulus (e.g., movie) and diminish in intensity, or extinguish entirely, after the withdrawl of the stimulus. The rape fantasies of serial rapists, by contrast, are *intrusive* (distracting and preoccupying), *reiterative* (persistent and recurrent), and *interoceptive* (internally generated).

Etiology

Although there are, thus far, no unified, theoretical models for rape that are widely accepted, there has been clear progress in the development of such models. There has been a coalescence of ideas emerging from two methodologies: multidimensional linear models and taxonomic models. Both models use a path analytic approach, using multivariate analysis to examine the different life courses or "paths" leading to different outcomes (defined in the former case as the nature, severity, and frequency of sexual offenses, and in the latter case as different subtypes of offenders).

The input for these models are characteristics of familial, childhood, adolescent, and adult development. Childhood variables that are commonly examined include (a) caregiver instability resulting in impaired attachment, incapacity for attachment, empathy deficits, and distorted attitudes about intimacy; (b) developmental history of abuse, specifying the age of onset, duration, severity, and perpetrator relationship for emotional, physical, and sexual abuse; and (c) hypothetical biological factors (e.g., hypothesized biological substrates for psychopathy). These antecedent events from childhood and adolescence influence at least seven relevant adult outcomes: (a) impaired relationships with peers; (b) lack of empathy and callous indifference to others; (c) degree and nature of chronic anger; (d) cognitive distortions around women and sexuality; (e) deviant sexual arousal and high sexual drive; and (f) impulsive, antisocial behavior. These adult outcomes combine in a complex equation to predict the nature, severity, and frequency of criminal outcome (i.e., rape offenses). Since all of these factors throughout the life span interact in complex ways to influence the type of sexual crimes that are committed, the greatest clarity will be achieved by path models in which reliable combinations of events form unique developmental paths that lead to distinct outcomes.

Despite the evident complexity and multidimensionality of rape behavior, there has been noteworthy progress in developing and validating etiologic models using diverse samples of offenders.

Risk assessment

There are many risk factors that may be identified when conducting a clinical or forensic evaluation of an individual offender, for example, rape fantasy and urges to act on such fantasy; a long history of polymorphous and paraphilic sexual interests and behavior; multiple instances of coercive sexual behavior; a history of impulsive, antisocial behavior; clear, documented evidence of psychopathy; substance abuse; poor social and interpersonal skills; dominance and control needs; attitudes (e.g., anger toward victims, misogynistic attitudes, global anger, hypermasculine attitudes); denial of problems; poor community adjustment; and failure to comply with parole conditions.

Many of these factors, which may well be noteworthy when evaluating an individual offender, are not supported by empirical research on risk assessment with large samples of rapists. Generally speaking, those risk factors that consistently emerge in empirical research are: (a) impulsive, antisocial behavior; (b) psychopathy; (c) number of prior sexual offenses; (d) sexual drive strength; and (e) history of sexual coercion or documented evidence (using the penile plethysmograph) of arousal to such coercion or to rape fantasy. If we try to be even more reductionistic, we can distill the empirical research down to three basic, fundamental factors: (1) clinical traits associated with psychopathy (e.g., callous indifference to others, lack of empathy, emotional detachment, lack of affect, conning and manipulativeness, glibness, entitlement, and grandiosity); (2) a track record of impulsive, antisocial behavior; and (3) sexual coercion (a willingness to use force or manipulation to satisfy sexual needs). The last factor, referred to as "sexual coercion," has been variously described and conceptualized by different researchers and at the present time is the focus of considerable study. One element in this complex equation seems to be marked attachment deficits that permit, or increase the likelihood of, "impersonal" sex (i.e., sex in the absence of any emotional attachment). On a hypothetical interpersonal attachment continuum, we find, in addition to impersonal sex, many outlets for anonymous sex (e.g., phone and computer sex, strip clubs). If we put together these three elements, we have *emotional detachment*, leaving the offender relatively impervious to cues of victim distress and thus unempathic; *attachment deficits*, increasing the desirability and/or need for impersonal sex; and *coercion*, the willingness to use force to gratify personal needs.

Recidivism

In a recent meta-analysis of sixty-one follow-up studies of sexual offenders (N=23,393), the recidivism rate, on average, was low (13.4 percent) (Hanson and Bussiere). It would be impossible to abstract rates of recidivism specific to rapists, since the aggregated studies used highly heterogeneous samples. Hanson and Bussiere did identify, however, subgroups that recidivated at higher rates. These higher base-rate recidi-

vists were those offenders who evidenced clear deviant sexual preferences and those offenders with known prior sex offenses. To a lesser extent, offenders with greater criminal histories had higher recidivism rates. Sex offenders who failed to complete treatment had higher recidivism rates than those who successfully completed treatment. In one of the very few recent studies that examined sexual reoffense rates for rapists separately, the rate of sexual reconviction after an average of fifty-nine months was .20 (Quinsey, Rice, and Harris). Notably, there were only twenty-eight rapists in the Quinsey et al. study. In a subsequent twenty-five-year follow-up of 136 rapists, the failure rates for sexual charges and convictions were .19 and .11 at Year 5, .26 and .16 at Year 10, .31 and .20 at Year 15, .36 and .23 at Year 20, and .39 and .24 at Year 25 (Prentky, Lee, Knight, and Cerce). Can we conclude anything? As critical as recidivism rates are for risk assessment, for evaluating treatment efficacy, for drafting rape laws, and for social policy, we have no reliable estimates. The principal problem is the extraordinary variability of procedures and methods used to calculate recidivism among the extant studies (Prentky et al.). Studies differ considerably with regard to the composition of the samples (e.g., relative proportions of rapists, extrafamiliar child molesters, and exclusive incest offenders), the criminal behavior domains considered (e.g., only sexual offenses, all violent offenses, any new offense, etc.), the legal definition of what constitutes recidivism (e.g., a new arrest, a new conviction, a parole violation, etc.), the sources of outcome data gathered to assess recidivism (e.g., court records, public safety records, parole and probation records, F.B.I. records, etc.), and the length of the follow-up period (i.e., follow-ups range from twelve months to thirty years).

In addition, the most common method of estimating recidivism is to calculate the simple percentage or proportion of individuals who reoffended during the study period. This method will underestimate the rate of recidivism, because some of those individuals who were in the community for a briefer period of time may still reoffend (e.g., not everyone in a thirty-six-month follow-up will have been in the community for thirty-six months at the time the study ends; some individuals may have been in the community only for twelve months). This problem is addressed by using survival analysis.

Treatment

The rationale for the modification of any unwanted behavior stems from the informed consideration of those factors that are most importantly associated with the emergence and the sustenance of the behavior. In a relatively simple case, such as reactive or acute depression, we attempt to identify the precursors of the depression. Although sexual aggression derives from a substantially more complex amalgam of factors and typically reflects a chronic pattern of maladaptive behaviors, the principles remain the same. That is, before designing strategies for modifying sexually aggressive behavior, we first must identify those factors that are most importantly related to the behavior. The overarching model that is used to treat sex offenders is an adaptation of relapse prevention, with a practical emphasis on cognitive-behavior therapy as the modality of choice. Specific interventions are used to target each of the critical areas of deficit. Given limitations of space, only several of the most important target areas will be discussed.

Lack of empathy.   In all domains of interpersonal violence, a general lack of empathic relatedness for one's victim can be regarded as a powerful disinhibitor. Alternatively, the presence of empathic concern will serve to inhibit aggression. Although capacity for emotional relatedness and empathic concern have long been a focus of treatment for sex offenders, these issues have, until recently, been included in the larger topic of social skills deficits.

At this point most sex offender treatment programs include a separate component for increasing victim empathy. In addition to the standard exercises and tapes (video and audio) used in victim empathy training, expressive therapy may be used to increase the offender's emotional or affective response to the distress of the victim. Some programs introduce victim advocates, victim counselors, and occasionally victims to increase further the emotional ante. Moreover, increasing the offender's affective appreciation of his own childhood experiences of victimization can instill a greater awareness of his victim's experience of abuse.

Anger.   The recognition of the importance of anger as a driving force in sexual offenses has resulted in the inclusion of treatment techniques to reduce and contain anger. The most commonly employed of these techniques is anger management training, which uses cognitive-behavioral strategies to increase self-control as well as the timely and appropriate expression of angry feelings. In addition, relapse prevention, which also focuses on increasing self-management skills, and stress management can assist the offender to gain control over chronic and situationally induced anger. Lastly, early life experiences of victimization can fuel lifelong anger that is periodically triggered by real or imagined provocations. A group that focuses on childhood victimization can help the offender to cope more adaptively with these traumatic events.

Cognitive distortions.   Cognitive distortions are "irrational" ideas, thoughts, and attitudes that serve to: (a) perpetuate denial around sexually aggressive behavior; (b) foster the minimization and trivialization of the impact of sexually aggressive behavior on victims; and (c) justify and sustain further sexually aggressive behavior. Cognitive distortions are presumed to be learned attitudes that are instilled at an early age by caregivers, reinforced by peers during childhood and adolescence, and further strengthened in adulthood by the prevailing social climate.

The importance of cognitions in moderating sexual arousal has been repeatedly demonstrated. Moreover, clinical observations have suggested that most sexual offenders harbor offense-justifying attitudes and that these attitudes are importantly related to the maintenance of the "sexual assault cycle." Thus, the modification of irrational attitudes has been a major focus of treatment intervention. Although there are a variety of treatment modalities that may impact these distortions, the most commonly employed technique is cognitive restructuring. For cognitive restructuring to be most effective, it is critical that cognitive and affective components be addressed. That is, it is insufficient merely to confront the "distorted" nature of the attitudes, to discuss the role that such distortions play for the individual, or to provide accurate information about sexual abuse (all cognitive components). It is equally important to create discomfort by focusing on the victim's response (e.g., fright, pain, humiliation)—the affective component. This latter exercise is also integral to victim empathy training.

In addition to cognitive restructuring, a group that focuses on childhood victimization can also be very helpful. Since the origin of these distorted attitudes is often a primary caregiver who was an influential role model as well as exposure to peer role models, often in institutional settings, a group that focuses on these early life experiences can help to trace the cognitions to their source, thereby challenging their generality and diminishing their sense of "truth" or "reality."

Sexual fantasy and deviant sexual arousal. The frequent targeting of rape fantasies for therapeutic intervention reflects the widely held belief that deviant fantasies not only lead to and maintain deviant sexual behavior but also impede normal sexual adaptation. Behavioral techniques for modifying sexual arousal patterns are grouped into two categories, those that decrease deviant arousal (e.g., covert sensitization, aversion, masturbatory satiation, biofeedback, shame therapy) and those that increase appropriate arousal (e.g., systematic desensitization, fantasy modification and orgasmic reconditioning, "fading" techniques, exposure to explicit appropriate sexual material). Although over twenty different behavioral techniques have been reported in the literature, the most widely used method has involved some variant of aversive therapy.

In addition to the repertoire of behavioral interventions, organic treatment has become increasingly popular as a complement to psychological treatment. These organic or drug treatments consist primarily of antiandrogens and antidepressants (primarily the selective serotonin reuptake inhibitors such as fluoxetine).

Antisocial personality/lifestyle impulsivity. Clinicians have long recognized the importance of impulsivity for relapse and have introduced self-control and impulsivity management modules into treatment. In addition to groups that focus specifically on impulse control, most treatment programs include components of relapse prevention. Relapse prevention begins by identifying the chain of events and emotions that lead to sexually aggressive behavior. Once this "assault cycle" is described, two interventions are employed: (a) strategies that help the offender avoid high-risk situations; and (b) strategies that minimize the likelihood that high-risk situations, once encountered, will lead to relapse. There is also reasonable evidence in the literature that supports the efficacy of selective serotonin reuptake inhibitors for impulse disorders.

Conclusion. The verdict as to the efficacy of treatment for sexual offenders will inevitably be a complex one that addresses: (a) optimal treatment modalities for specific subtypes of offenders; (b) optimal conditions under which treatment and follow-up should occur; and (c) selection (or exclusion) criteria for treatment candidates. At the present time, the most informed and dispassionate conclusion must be that the jury is still out. The evidence submitted thus far, however, is encouraging. In a meta-analysis that included twelve studies of treatment with mixed samples of sexual offenders (N=1,313), Hall reported an overall effect size of .12 for treatment versus comparison conditions. The overall recidivism rate for treated sex offenders was .19, compared with .27 for untreated sex offenders. As Hall reported, these effect sizes were larger in studies with longer follow-up periods, studies with higher base rates of recidivism, studies that included outpatients, and studies that included cognitive-behavior and/or hormonal treatment. It is thus clear that treatment can work, and it is increasingly clear what factors lead to optimal treatment outcomes.

ROBERT PRENTKY

See also CRIME CAUSATION: BIOLOGICAL THEORIES; CRIME CAUSATION: PSYCHOLOGICAL THEORIES; FEMINISM: CRIMINOLOGICAL ASPECTS; FEMINISM: LEGAL ASPECTS; OBSCENITY AND PORNOGRAPHY: BEHAVIORAL ASPECTS; PRISONS: PROBLEMS AND PROSPECTS; RAPE: LEGAL ASPECTS; SEX OFFENSES: CHILDREN; SEX OFFENSES: CONSENSUAL; SEXUAL PREDATORS; VIOLENCE.

BIBLIOGRAPHY

GOODMAN, L. A.; KOSS, M. P.; FITZGERALD, L. F.; RUSSO, N. F.; and KEITA, G. P. "Male Violence Against Women. Current Research and Future Directions." *American Psychologist* 48 (1993): 1054–1058.
HALL, G. N. C. "Sexual Offender Recidivism Revisited: A Meta-Analysis of Recent Treatment Studies." *Journal of Consulting and Clinical Psychology* 63 (1995): 802–809.
HANSON, R. K., and BUSSIERE, M. T. "Predicting Relapse: A Meta-Analysis of Sexual Offender Recidivism Studies." *Journal of Consulting and Clinical Psychology* 66 (1998): 348–362.
HAZELWOOD, R. R.; REBOUSSIN, R.; and WARREN, J. I. "Serial Rape: Correlates of Increased Aggression and the Relationship of Offender Pleasure to Victim Resistance." *Journal of Interpersonal Violence* 4 (1989): 65–78.
KNIGHT, R. A., and PRENTKY, R. A. "Classifying Sexual Offenders: The Development and Corroboration of Taxonomic Models." In *The Handbook of Sexual Assault: Issues, Theories, and Treatment of the Offender.* Edited by W. L. Marshall, D. R. Laws, and H. E. Barbaree. New York: Plenum, 1990.

National Victim Center. *Rape in America. A Report to the Nation.* Arlington, Va.: National Victim Center, 1992.

PRENTKY, R. A., and BURGESS, A. W. "Hypothetical Biological Substrates of a Fantasy-Based Drive Mechanism for Repetitive Sexual Aggression." *Rape and Sexual Assault III: A Research Handbook.* Edited by A. W. Burgess. New York: Garland, 1991. Pages 235–256.

PRENTKY, R. A., and KNIGHT, R. A. "Identifying Critical Dimensions for Discriminating Among Rapists." *Journal of Consulting and Clinical Psychology* 59 (1991): 643–661.

PRENTKY, R. A.; LEE, A. F. S.; KNIGHT, R. A.; and CERCE, D. "Recidivism Rates Among Child Molesters and Rapists: A Methodological Analysis." *Law and Human Behavior* 21 (1997): 635–659.

QUINSEY, V. L.; RICE, M. E.; and HARRIS G. T. "Actuarial Prediction of Sexual Recidivism." *Journal of Interpersonal Violence* 10 (1995): 85–105.

RAPE: LEGAL ASPECTS

In the eighteenth century, William Blackstone defined rape as "carnal knowledge of a woman forcibly and against her will" (p. 210). This definition remains in effect in many American jurisdictions, and it has provided the starting point for revisions over the years. The legal aspects of rape include five topics concerned primarily with forcible rape—the purpose of rape law, the punishment for forcible rape, the elements of the offense, evidentiary issues, and practical concerns about enforcement. The sixth topic covered in this entry is nonforcible intercourse with a person under a statutory age of consent ("statutory rape").

Forcible rape: purpose of the law

Modern rape laws are conceived primarily as a means to protect women and men against physical harm, emotional injury, and interference with sexual autonomy (the right to choose the circumstances of sexual intimacy). Historically, the purposes of rape law were more limited, and the law's coverage was narrow. Rape law was long concerned, for example, with protecting the *chastity* of women. In practice, sexually experienced victims received far less protection, and the law often endorsed that perspective, for example, in its preoccupation at trial with evidence of a woman's prior sexual history.

In addition, rape law traditionally focused on protecting property-like interests of men—the interest of a father in the virginity (and thus the marriageability) of his daughter and the interest of a husband in exclusive sexual access to his wife. Thus, rape law did not apply when a woman was forced to have sex with her husband. Vestiges of these narrow conceptions of the law's purpose may survive today and may partially explain resistance to shedding traditional limits on the coverage of the offense.

The common complaint that rape law was (and perhaps still is) unfair to women is, at first glance, somewhat surprising because rape law traditionally protected *only* women; it afforded no protection at all to male victims of sexual assault. In what sense, then, is it plausible to think of rape law as discriminating *against* women?

Several points must be noted. First, the protection afforded to women was traditionally hedged with evidentiary restrictions unknown in other offenses. Second, rape law as traditionally administered provided fully effective protection only to certain women—those who dressed modestly, behaved properly, and did nothing to invite a sexual advance. By offering its primary protection *only* to such women, the law in effect favored (and perhaps still favors) some women over others.

This last feature of the law, moreover, arguably discriminates against *all* women, in that it may channel women into certain patterns of behavior and thus deny all women the freedom to choose a fully independent life. A nondiscriminatory law of rape arguably should protect the right of all persons, women and men, to freely choose the circumstances of sexual intimacy, without withholding protection from those who drink, walk alone at night, talk to strangers, or lead unconventional lives.

Forcible rape: punishment

At common law, rape, like all felonies, was punishable by death. By the early twentieth century, most American states had reserved the death penalty for cases of first-degree murder, but a substantial minority, primarily southern states, continued to authorize capital punishment for rape. There was intense concern, however, about racial discrimination, as the overwhelming majority of defendants executed for rape were black men accused of raping white women. Those concerns were in the background, though unmentioned, when the Supreme Court ruled capital punishment for the rape of an adult woman unconstitutional, on the ground that death was a penalty disproportionate to the severity of the offense (*Coker v. Georgia,* 433 U.S. 584 (1977)).

Where not subject to capital punishment, rape was typically punishable by long prison terms, including life imprisonment. In the 1950s reformers saw these severe penalties as an obstacle to effective enforcement. In date-rape situations and cases involving only implicit threats, juries often acquitted, or prosecutors refused to file charges, partly out of concern that authorized penalties were disproportionately severe. To combat this problem, the Model Penal Code recommended dividing rape into several distinct offenses, with the more severe penalties reserved for cases involving strangers and extreme forms of force. Today many states follow this approach, and many continue to authorize life imprisonment for the highest degree of rape.

Forcible rape: elements of the offense

The traditional offense of rape required proof of five elements: penetration, force and resistance, nonconsent, absence of a spousal relationship (the *marital exemption*), and a culpable state of mind (*mens rea*). This section explains these elements and the modern evolution that has led states to modify or abandon traditional requirements.

One feature of the modern evolution has been the abandonment of the term *rape* in many states and the use of a gender-neutral term such as *sexual battery* to describe the offense. In treating current law, this section discusses the statutes (however labeled) that apply to conduct traditionally called rape.

Penetration. The act of rape, described by Blackstone as "carnal knowledge," has always required sexual intercourse, in the sense of some penetration (however slight) of the penis into the vagina. Ejaculation is not required, but in some jurisdictions, penetration by objects other than the penis traditionally was insufficient, as was penetration of other parts of the body (e.g., the mouth or anus). The offense of rape was therefore gender-specific (only a woman could be raped) and was inapplicable to many serious sexual abuses, such as forcible sodomy. Other offenses partly filled this gap; such conduct could be prosecuted as sodomy or sexual assault. But neither offense was punished as severely as was rape.

The modern view of rape law as a means to protect physical integrity and sexual autonomy (rather than merely chastity and male control of sexual access) has led to change in the penetration requirement. Modern statutes typically punish as rape the forcible penetration—by any object—of a woman's mouth, anus, or vagina, and most rape statutes apply to penetration of a male victim as well. In states that limit the offense of rape to sexual abuse of a woman, an offense carrying a different label (but usually identical penalties) applies to analogous sexual abuse of a man.

Force and resistance. Under the traditional definition, a rape conviction requires proof that the sexual act was committed "forcibly and against [the victim's] will" (Blackstone, p. 210). Thus, there must be *both* force and a lack of consent. Except in three special situations, nonconsent alone is not sufficient.

The three cases in which intercourse traditionally has been equated with forcible rape, even in the absence of physical compulsion, are those in which the woman was unconscious, was mentally incompetent, or gave her consent under certain false pretenses.

The last category has a large history. Traditionally, a man who obtained consent by making a false promise of marriage was not considered a rapist, but he could be prosecuted for seduction. Other deceptive inducements were legally permissible, and in the 1930s most states abolished the crime of seduction. Thus, deceptive inducements can no longer lead to prosecution for any crime.

Deception can, however, support a rape prosecution when it involves "fraud in the factum"—that is, deception about the nature of the act agreed to rather than mere deception about the inducement for agreeing. Thus, it is considered rape for a doctor to penetrate a woman sexually on the pretext of examining her with medical instruments, or for a man to obtain a woman's consent by impersonating her husband. Apart from the three categories of unconsciousness, mental incompetence, and fraud in the factum—and consensual sex with a minor ("statutory rape," discussed below)—a rape conviction requires proof that submission was compelled by force.

The rationale for requiring proof of force is not self-evident, since many think that intercourse without consent should be an offense whether or not force was used. One rationale for the force requirement is that rape is considered a crime of violence, and penalties are severe. But this explanation implies that nonconsensual intercourse should qualify as a lesser offense, just as it is a crime to take property without consent by force (robbery) or without force (theft). But nonconsensual intercourse without force traditionally was not an offense at all, and this is still true in most states. Legally, force remains essential to distinguish criminal misconduct from permissible behavior.

The need for proof of force is sometimes explained on the ground that consent is too amorphous in sexual matters; it is argued that in the absence of force, genuine nonconsent is difficult to distinguish from "reluctant submission" or even from coy but voluntary participation. Others, however, argue that "reluctant submission" involves a harm the law should not ignore and that consent to sex is no more difficult to determine than consent in other important matters. Most fundamentally, critics of the force requirement argue that the law should protect not only physical safety but also sexual autonomy—the right to choose whether and when to be sexually intimate with another person. That right is denied not only by physical force but also by nonviolent actions that interfere with freely given consent.

These arguments for abolishing the force requirement have begun to make headway. Several states now punish all cases of intercourse without consent and treat force merely as a factor that aggravates the severity of the offense. But this remains a minority view, accepted in less than a dozen states. In most states force remains an essential element of the offense.

As traditionally interpreted, the force requirement could be met only by acts or threats of physical violence. In addition, as a corollary of the force requirement, the prosecution had to prove that the victim resisted. Absent resistance, courts assumed that the victim freely chose to acquiesce. One court, reflecting the view of early-twentieth-century male judges, stated, a woman "is equipped to interpose most effective obstacles by means of hands and limbs and pelvic muscles. Indeed, medical writers insist that these obstacles are practically insuperable in absence of more than the usual relative disproportion of age and strength between man and woman" (*Brown v. State*, 106 N.W. 536, 538 (Wis. 1906)).

Under the traditional resistance standard, courts required that the victim resist "to the utmost." Convictions were therefore difficult to obtain even in cases of extreme abuse. In addition,

the resistance rule in effect required the victim to fight her aggressor, even when that response could expose her to great danger.

Beginning in the 1950s courts and legislatures began to relax the resistance requirement, recognizing that resistance should not be required where it would be dangerous or futile. Today, most states still require resistance, but the requirement is less rigid than in the past. Courts require "reasonable" resistance, sometimes described as "resistance of a type reasonably to be expected from a person who genuinely refuses to participate in sexual intercourse" (former N.Y. Penal Law 130.00(8) (1977), repealed (1982)) or as "a genuine physical effort to resist as judged by the circumstances" (*State v. Lima*, 643 P.2d 536, 540 (1982)).

Many states, taking the next step, have in theory abolished the resistance requirement. In these jurisdictions, however, the prosecution still must prove actual or threatened force. As a result, the resistance requirement often resurfaces in practice, because it is difficult to show that a defendant compelled submission by force, unless there is evidence that the victim physically resisted his advances. Evidence of resistance also remains important because some jurors still believe that a woman who only protests verbally, not physically, is not really unwilling.

With or without a resistance requirement, nearly all states require proof of "force," understood to mean that the defendant compelled submission by physically overpowering the victim or by threatening to inflict bodily injury. Current interpretations of the force requirement are more flexible than in the past. Courts once insisted, in most cases, on proof of extreme brutality or an explicit threat of physical harm. Cases involving black defendants and white complainants were different; in those situations courts seldom insisted on proof of express threats or direct victim resistance. In cases involving white defendants or black defendants accused by black complainants, however, courts usually held that implicit threats and victim fears resulting from an intimidating situation were insufficient. Today, courts are more willing to find implicit threats sufficient. And even without an implicit threat, a complainant's fear can satisfy the force requirement, provided the fear is "reasonably grounded."

But nearly all courts insist that the injury feared must involve bodily harm; coercion by threats to inflict nonphysical injury is generally considered insufficient. In *State v. Thompson*, 792

P.2d 1103 (Mont. 1990), a high school principal allegedly compelled a student to submit to intercourse by threatening to prevent her from graduating. The court held that this threat, though clearly coercive, did not make the principal guilty of rape because he had not threatened any *physical* harm.

A few states have modified the strict rule that force must involve physical violence. The Pennsylvania Supreme Court has held that force includes "[any] superior force—physical, moral, psychological, or intellectual—[used] to compel a person to do a thing against that person's volition" (*Commonwealth v. Rhodes,* 510 A.2d 1217, 1225 (Pa. 1986)). This approach avoids the narrow strictures of the physical force requirement. But as it leaves unclear the line between compulsion and legitimate persuasion, there is concern about its potential vagueness. The Model Penal Code expands the concept of force in a less amorphous manner, permitting a conviction for "gross sexual imposition" when a man compels a woman to submit "by any threat that would prevent resistance by a woman of ordinary resolution" (Model Penal Code § 213.1(2)(a)).

The New Jersey Supreme Court has held that the force requirement can be met by the physical actions intrinsic to intercourse, whenever the complainant does not consent (*In re M.T.S.,* 609 A.2d 1266 (N.J. 1992)). This approach in effect eliminates force altogether and makes nonconsent sufficient to establish the offense. As a matter of statutory interpretation, this outcome is awkward because it equates violent and nonviolent rape for grading purposes and has the effect of imposing a high mandatory minimum sentence for both. Grading problems aside, *M.T.S.* achieves a significant result by criminalizing all intercourse without consent. Several states arrive at a similar outcome, with more tailored grading of penalties, through statutory reforms that require force for the most serious form of rape but create a lesser offense for nonconsensual intercourse without force.

To the extent that the criminal law should protect women and men not only from physical abuse but from all interference with sexual autonomy, this last approach seems best suited to a modern law of rape. Critics of this approach argue that nonviolent interference with autonomy is not sufficiently serious to warrant criminal sanctions, or that there is excessive danger of erroneous results when nonconsent alone is sufficient for conviction. Current law is far from static, with a slow but steady evolution in the direction of relaxing or eliminating the requirement of physical force.

Nonconsent. Even when a defendant has used force, his sexual conduct is not rape if the complainant consented; the act must be "against her will." A major drawback of this requirement, as administered in the past, was that it tended to encourage a focus on the complainant's state of mind, and evidence of her prior sexual experience was often used to insinuate that she wanted to have sex (or deserved whatever treatment she received). To prevent such tactics, many modern statutes eliminate the express requirements of unwillingness or nonconsent.

The reform effort to shift the focus away from victim consent has generally been unsuccessful, however. Courts assume that the legislature did not intend to impose severe sanctions on mutually consensual heterosexual sex; as a result courts hold that consent is a defense even when statutes do not say so explicitly. Thus, consent is always a potential issue, and it seems clear that the best means to prevent evidentiary abuse is through shield laws and other control of cross-examination, rather than through a futile attempt to eliminate the consent question entirely.

Recent developments on this point tend if anything to reverse the direction of earlier reform efforts. As illustrated by the *M.T.S.* decision above, courts have tended to place more weight on the consent question and to de-emphasize the requirement of force. The *M.T.S.* court took a statutory offense emphasizing force (with no mention of consent) and interpreted it so that the force requirement was in effect read out of the law and nonconsent was read in as the essence of the offense.

The meaning of "consent" is crucial and, both in law and culture, far from clear. One perspective is illustrated by the rallying cry that "no means no." Skeptics reply with equal vehemence that "no" does not mean no, at least not always. Empirical studies indicate that for most women, most of the time, "no" does mean no. But there is evidence that a substantial minority of contemporary women (35 to 40 percent in some studies) sometimes say "no" when they are willing to have intercourse and want their date to "try harder," "beg," or "get physical" (see Schulhofer, 1998, pp. 256–260).

Reflecting this view, most states treat consent as a question to be determined by the jury under all the circumstances. A jury is permitted to treat a woman's silence or passivity as indicating consent, and it may find consent from the context even when a complainant said "no."

It is not automatically proper, however, for the legal definition of consent to track the ambiguity of ordinary language. A crucial issue in formulating standards throughout law is the question of *comparative error costs*. Since no rule can perfectly capture objective reality, the problem is to minimize the harm caused by errors that will inevitably occur under any legal test. Many scholars argue that the harm caused when a man assumes consent and proceeds to intercourse with a woman who *was not* willing is far more serious than the harm caused when a man assumes nonconsent and desists from intercourse with a woman who *was* willing. As a result, it is argued, a legal presumption that "no means no" is preferable, even if that rule does not capture all the nuanced ways that language can be used.

Following this approach, some courts have ruled that "when a woman says 'no' to someone[,] any implication other than a manifestation of non-consent that might arise in that person's psyche is legally irrelevant" (*Commonwealth v. Lefkowitz*, 481 N.E.2d 277, 232 (Mass. App. 1985)). Legally, in other words, "no" always means no in these jurisdictions.

Even this relatively strict approach, however, leaves open the problem of determining consent when a woman's response to a sexual advance is vague or ambivalent. The "no means no" standard may imply that responses *short* of a firm refusal do not show nonconsent. Many argue, however, that the absence of a firm refusal should not be considered a sufficient ground for authorizing the sexual penetration of another person; in most contexts a serious physical intrusion requires actual permission, not merely the absence of an unambiguous protest.

Accordingly, a number of states now define consent as affirmative permission. One statute, for example, states, "'Consent' means that at the time of the act of sexual intercourse there are actual words or conduct indicating freely given agreement to have sexual intercourse" (Wash. Rev. Code 9A.444.010(6)(1981)). This approach reflects the view that rape law should not apply only in cases of active resistance and should fully protect sexual autonomy.

The marital exemption.   Traditionally, compelled intercourse could not constitute rape, no matter how much force was used, when the victim was the wife of the perpetrator. This "marital exemption" was originally based not on express statutory language but on a judicial presumption that the wife had irrevocably consented to sex with her husband. In the seventeenth century, Lord Matthew Hale wrote that "by their mutual matrimonial consent and contract, the wife hath given up herself in this kind unto her husband, which she cannot retract" (p. 629).

Until recently, the marital exemption was preserved in all American states. The Model Penal Code rape provisions likewise apply only when a man has intercourse "with a female not his wife" (Model Penal Code § 213.1(1)(2)).

Since the 1970s, the marital exemption has been under attack. The conclusive presumption that a wife always consents to sex with her husband, regardless of circumstances, is obviously untenable. Modern apologists for the exemption argue instead that in cases of marital discord, criminal sanctions represent an intrusion that could disrupt "the ongoing process of adjustment in the marital relationship" (American Law Institute, pp. 344–346). In addition, they argue, the harm of forced intimacy is less serious when the victim and the offender have "an ongoing relation of sexual intimacy."

Opponents of the exemption attack both claims. As to the first, they note that the marital exemption in its traditional form applies even when the parties are legally separated; moreover, when the parties are living together, legal sanctions for assault apply in cases of domestic violence, so there is no reason why other violent offenses within marriage should not be subject to punishment as well. As to the second claim, opponents of the exemption note that "wife rape can be as terrifying and life-threatening as stranger rape. In addition, it often evokes a powerful sense of betrayal, deep disillusionment, and total isolation" (Russell, pp. 190–191, 198–199).

Responding to these criticisms, many states have abolished their marital exemption completely, either by legislation or by judicial decision reinterpreting the common law. At least one court has ruled the marital exemption unconstitutional on equal protection grounds (*People v. Liberta*, 474 N.E.2d 567 (N.Y. 1984)).

Nonetheless, the exemption survives in modified form in most of the states. Though only fifteen states have abolished all distinctions between marital and nonmarital rape, many states still treat marital rape as less serious than other rapes or permit prosecution for marital rape only when aggravated force was used; some states permit prosecution only when the parties are legally separated or permit prosecution only when the parties are living apart (Shulhofer, pp. 43–44).

Mens rea. In addition to proving force and nonconsent, the prosecution must prove, as with any offense, that the defendant had a culpable state of mind. Generally in criminal law (and subject to many exceptions), culpability requires that the defendant had actual knowledge of the facts that made his behavior criminal or at least "recklessness"—an awareness that his conduct might cause a proscribed harm. As applied to rape, this principle would require proof that the defendant knew his victim did not consent, or at least that he knew this was possibly the case.

This standard culpability requirement takes on great practical significance when a rape defendant claims that he made a mistake about the victim's consent. Suppose, for example, that the victim repeatedly said "no." Even if the jury agrees that no means no and that the victim did not consent, the defendant may argue that he honestly thought she consented and that he therefore lacked culpability. When a defendant's *claimed* belief is patently unreasonable, a jury may conclude that he did not really hold the belief and that he is therefore culpable after all. But the pervasiveness of wishful thinking and sexist assumptions among men often makes it plausible to conclude that a defendant honestly thought he had consent, even under circumstances that make such a belief thoroughly unreasonable. The issue in such cases is to determine whether a defendant who holds an honest but mistaken belief in consent should be guilty of rape.

There was little attention to this question in the early case law, probably because the strict requirements for force and resistance would produce an acquittal in any situation where the defendant could plausibly claim a mistake about consent. When the issue was presented in Britain, the House of Lords ruled that the prosecution must prove mens rea in the traditional sense—either knowledge of nonconsent or reckless disregard of the woman's wishes (*D.P.P v. Morgan,* [1976] A.C. 182). Under this standard, also followed in a few American states, a belief in consent, however unreasonable, precludes conviction. Under the more prevalent American approach, negligence is sufficient; a defendant can be convicted whenever the asserted belief in consent is unreasonable. And a few American states impose a strict liability; if the jury finds nonconsent, an honest belief to the contrary, no matter how reasonable, is no defense.

The strict liability and negligence standards are often criticized on the ground that conviction for a major felony should require actual awareness of wrongdoing. But the latter standard creates a potentially serious loophole in rape enforcement because it provides no incentive for men to set aside their presuppositions and pay more attention to women's actual desires. And since carelessness is punished in other settings where it is important to encourage care (e.g., involuntary manslaughter), there is nothing unprincipled or unprecedented in imposing such liability for carelessness with respect to consent in rape.

These arguments suggest that rape liability can fairly be premised on unreasonable mistakes, provided that courts afford safeguards similar to those applied in manslaughter cases. Conviction should require proof of *criminal* negligence (a gross departure from the level of care reasonably expected) and the penalty imposed should be lower than that applied to intentional misconduct.

The mens rea standard applied in most American states is less demanding, in that ordinary negligence is sufficient, and it can lead to conviction for the highest grade of forcible rape. Many believe that a gross-negligence requirement is too strict and that conviction on the basis of ordinary negligence (or even strict liability) is necessary for adequate deterrence and fairness toward potential victims. There is some basis for this concern, because of continuing controversy within our culture about the ways that women express consent and continuing support for the idea that "no" does not always mean no. Against that background, some jurors might think that a defendant's mistake about consent was *not* unreasonable, even in the face of a woman's clear verbal protests. A strict liability standard would provide some women protection against that possibility.

But even a strict liability standard cannot fully counteract cultural attitudes of this sort. A juror who held such beliefs could conclude that the complainant in fact consented, despite her verbal protests, and hence that the defendant made no mistake at all. A legal response to inappropriate cultural assumptions might be more effective if addressed directly to defining what consent means, rather than leaving this crucial issue to be thrashed out by each jury according to its own values. Strict liability, moreover, poses a risk of unfairness to defendants who could face conviction and a mandatory prison term for conduct that was entirely reasonable by enlightened contemporary standards.

A preferable approach, therefore, might be to preserve traditional requirements of awareness of nonconsent (or gross negligence) but to *define* nonconsent as an absence of *affirmative* permission. With this definition, a defendant's belief that the complainant was subjectively willing would be irrelevant—even if sincere and even if deemed "reasonable"—when the complainant had said "no" or had remained silent, passive, or ambivalent. In such cases the defendant would *know* he did not have affirmative permission and therefore he would have a culpable state of mind even under strict traditional standards.

Forcible rape: evidentiary issues

The administration of rape law has long been influenced by judges' preoccupation with the possibility of false charges and erroneous convictions. For centuries, English and American courts were obsessed with the idea that a woman might fabricate a rape accusation because she feared the stigma of having consented to intercourse. Judges also worried that a woman might falsely accuse a man for reasons of blackmail.

American race relations heightened the traditional concerns. White society, especially in the South, strongly condemned interracial sexual relations, and racial fears fueled a myth that black men were driven to rape white women. In this climate, a white woman suspected of intimacy with a black man was under considerable pressure to claim rape, and ordinary requirements of proof beyond a reasonable doubt offered a black defendant little protection in a trial before an all-white jury.

The traditional and the specifically American concerns generated special evidentiary rules that were virtually unique to rape cases. Nearly all states required independent corroboration of the complainant's testimony, and many instructed their juries to examine that testimony with caution. These special rules have been challenged, however. Critics argue that false charges are no more likely in rape cases than in any others, that strict corroboration requirements can be virtually impossible to meet, and that the ordinary trial process offers sufficient protection against erroneous results. Responding to such criticisms, the law has changed dramatically. Currently, no American state requires corroboration in forcible rape cases, and very few continue to authorize special jury instructions questioning the complainant's credibility.

Defense tactics at trial posed a further problem. It was once common for defense attorneys to subject the complainant to searching cross-examination, with a particular focus on her private life and prior sexual relationships. Such background facts were considered relevant (and therefore admissible as evidence) on two theories—that a woman who had consented to sex in the past was more likely to have consented to sex with the defendant, and that a woman who had engaged in "immoral" conduct was less credible as a witness. These theories and the tactics exploiting them had the effect of humiliating many rape complainants at trial and prompted the comment that rape victims were "raped twice," once by the perpetrator and again in court.

Starting in the 1970s, states began to enact "rape shield" statutes to limit abusive cross-examination. Roughly at the same time, changing attitudes toward extramarital sex made such tactics less useful than in the past and more likely to backfire by discrediting the defense. Typically, rape-shield statutes permit cross-examination about prior sexual involvement with the defendant, on the theory that such involvement can be relevant to a claim of consent, but they prohibit most cross-examination about prior sexual contact with others.

The latter prohibition is not iron-clad, because there are unusual circumstances in which reference to prior sexual conduct may be essential for the defendant to present his defense effectively. Under the Sixth Amendment, a witness's legitimate desire for privacy must yield to a defendant's right to confront and cross-examine opposing witnesses when the subject of the questioning is relevant and essential to a fair trial. Accordingly, most rape-shield statutes contain exceptions for such situations; those that do not have been held unconstitutional in specific settings or interpreted to allow exceptions as needed to preserve the defendant's constitutional rights.

These limitations have made rape-shield statutes more porous than reformers initially expected, but the statutes have nonetheless had a major impact on rape trials. Empirical studies report that victims are much better treated than in the past and that efforts to limit the admissibility of sexual history evidence are usually successful.

Forcible rape: enforcement concerns

Specific legal doctrines were only one of the impediments to effectively protecting women from rape. Even in cases that met the legal definition of the offense, victims often refused to report it, fearful that officials would humiliate them and that the offender would avoid punishment in any event. In the relatively few cases in which a complaint was filed, police and prosecutors often ruled it "unfounded" on the ground that the victim knew the assailant; waited too long to report the crime; or had been drinking, hitchhiking, or wearing suggestive clothing. Officials often assumed that such facts proved the victim was lying or made conviction impossible even if she was not. Juries reinforced such expectations by acquitting with some frequency when there was a suggestion of "contributory fault" by the victim.

The rape reform movement changed many components of this picture. Police and prosecutors are far more sensitive in their treatment of rape victims. Victims accordingly are less hesitant to report their rapes, prosecutors are less quick to drop charges, and juries are less easily swayed by old stereotypes. There is a general impression that enforcement problems are less serious than in the past.

Empirical studies provide only limited confirmation of this impression, however. It remains unclear whether the legal system's greater receptivity to rape complaints and intangible improvements in the courtroom atmosphere have led to concrete differences in legal outcomes.

Statutory rape

Ever since the sixteenth century, intercourse, though fully consensual, has been classified as rape when the woman is under a specified age of consent. The earliest statute set the age of consent at ten, but modern American statutes typically set the age of consent at sixteen or eighteen.

Four features of traditional statutory rape law are contestible. The first is the refusal to require mens rea. No state requires proof that the defendant was aware of the possibility that his partner was underage. A few states permit a defense when a defendant's mistake was reasonable, but most jurisdictions treat this as a matter of strict liability. Thus, a defendant can be convicted even when he could not have known that his partner was underage, and courts often exclude as irrelevant any evidence offered to prove that it was reasonable for the defendant to think his partner was older.

Second, statutory rape laws typically apply only when the underage person is female; they afford no protection against the seduction of an underage male. In *Michael M. v. Superior Court,* (450 U.S. 464 (1981)), the Supreme Court upheld this discrepancy on the ground that such laws serve to deter conduct that can result in teen pregnancy, and "it is the female exclusively who can become pregnant" (p. 467). Even if the discrepancy is constitutionally permissible, however, the Court's point does not show that prosecution is an effective way to discourage teen pregnancy or, conversely, that the law should not also be concerned to discourage premature sexual activity between adults and young boys.

Third, if the law seeks to deter acts that can result in teen pregnancy, what is the justification for punishing only the male participant in those acts? The Court in *Michael M.* viewed the risk of pregnancy as an equivalent deterrent penalty for the female and said that punishing her would interfere with effective enforcement because females would then be less likely to report the offense.

Fourth, statutory rape laws are crude tools for preventing exploitation of minors, because they are typically triggered whenever the female is underage, even if the male is younger. Thus, if a seventeen-year-old girl seduces a thirteen-year-old boy, she would commit no offense, and he would be guilty of statutory rape.

A number of state statutes address these concerns. Though the traditional statutory structure remains in effect in most states, a minority now set two ages of consent. Sexual intercourse is made criminal for the older participant whenever the younger one (male or female) is under the first age level, usually thirteen or fourteen; intercourse is also made an offense when the younger participant is over the first age level but less than sixteen (or eighteen), provided that he or she is more than four years younger than the defendant. This approach avoids some of the anomalies of traditional statutory rape laws, while providing a means to protect boys and girls equally from exploitation and premature exposure to sexual activity.

STEPHEN J. SCHULHOFER

See also FEMINISM: CRIMINOLOGICAL ASPECTS; FEMINISM: LEGAL ASPECTS; RAPE: BEHAVIORAL ASPECTS; SCIENTIFIC

EVIDENCE; SEX OFFENSES: CHILDREN; SEX OFFENSES: CONSENSUAL; SEXUAL PREDATORS.

BIBLIOGRAPHY

AMERICAN LAW INSTITUTE. *Model Penal Code and Commentaries,* Part 2, Comment to §213.1. Philadelphia: American Law Institute, 1980.

BACHMAN, RONET, and PATERNOSTER, RAYMOND. "A Contemporary Look at the Effects of Rape Law Reform: How Far Have We Really Come?" *Journal of Criminal Law and Criminology* 84 (Fall 1993): 554.

BERGER, VIVIAN. "Man's Trial, Woman's Tribulation: Rape Cases in the Courtroom." *Columbia Law Review* 77 (January 1977): 1–103.

BLACKSTONE, WILLIAM. *Commentaries on the Laws of England* (1765), vol. 4. Chicago: University of Chicago Press, 1979.

BROWNMILLER, SUSAN. *Against Our Will: Men Women, and Rape.* New York: Simon & Schuster, 1975.

COOMBS, MARY. "Agency and Partnership: A Study of Breach of Promise Plaintiffs." *Yale Journal of Law and Feminism* 2 (1989): 11–13.

DENNO, DEBORAH W. "Sexuality, Rape, and Mental Retardation." *University of Illinois Law Review* no. 2 (1997): 315–434.

ESTRICH, SUSAN. *Real Rape.* Cambridge, Mass.: Harvard University Press, 1987.

HALE, MATTHEW. *The History of the Pleas of the Crown* (1736), vol. 1. Edited by W. A. Stokes and E. Ingersoll. Philadelphia: Small, 1847.

KALVEN, HARRY, JR., and ZEISEL, HANS. *The American Jury.* Boston: Little, Brown, 1966.

MACKINNON, CATHARINE A. *Toward a Feminist Theory of the State.* Cambridge, Mass.: Harvard University Press, 1989.

POSNER, RICHARD A., and SILBAUGH, KATHARINE B. *A Guide to America's Sex Laws.* Chicago: University of Chicago Press, 1996.

RAINE, NANCY VENABLE. *After Silence: Rape and My Journey Back.* New York: Crown, 1998.

RUSSELL, DIANA E. H. *Rape in Marriage,* 2d ed. Bloomington: Indiana University Press, 1990.

SCHULHOFER, STEPHEN J. "Taking Sexual Autonomy Seriously: Rape Law and Beyond." *Law and Philosophy* 11 (1992): 35–94.

———. *Unwanted Sex: The Culture of Intimidation and the Failure of Law.* Cambridge, Mass.: Harvard University Press, 1998.

SPOHN, CASSIA, and HORNEY, JULIA. *Rape Law Reform: A Grassroots Revolution and Its Impact.* New York: Plenum, 1992.

REHABILITATION

Each day in the United States, the correctional system supervises over six million of its residents. Approximately two million people are in prison or jail, while four million are on probation or parole. With so many people under its control, a central policy issue is what the correctional system hopes to accomplish with those it places behind bars or on community supervision. A simple response might be that the purpose of these correctional sanctions is to "punish" the criminally wayward. Since the inception of the American penitentiary in the 1820s, however, corrections has embraced as an important goal the transformation of law breakers into the law-abiding—that is, "rehabilitation" or "treatment." At times, the goal of reforming offenders has been dominant; at other times, its legitimacy and usefulness have been challenged and its influence on correctional policy diminished. But even today, after a period in the late 1900s of prolonged advocacy of "getting tough with criminals," rehabilitation remains an integral part of the correctional enterprise and continues to earn support among the public in the United States.

In this entry, we begin by exploring in more detail the concept of rehabilitation. We then use a historical perspective to examine the changing nature and support for rehabilitation as a correctional goal over time. Our attention next turns to the current treatment programs that are found within the correctional system. Perhaps the most important consideration is whether rehabilitation "works" to reduce the likelihood that offenders will "recidivate" or return to crime. Accordingly, we also review the latest research on the effectiveness of treatment interventions. We conclude this entry with comments on the future of rehabilitation as a correctional goal.

What is rehabilitation?

The concept of rehabilitation rests on the assumption that criminal behavior is caused by some factor. This perspective does not deny that people make choices to break the law, but it does assert that these choices are not a matter of pure "free will." Instead, the decision to commit a crime is held to be determined, or at least heavily influenced, by a person's social surroundings, psychological development, or biological make-up. People are not all the same—and thus free to express their will—but rather are different. These "individual differences" shape how people behave, including whether they are likely to break the law. When people are characterized by various "criminogenic risk factors"—such as a lack of parental love and supervision, exposure to delinquent peers, the internalization of antisocial values, or an impulsive temperament—they are more likely to become involved in crime than people not having these experiences and traits.

The rehabilitation model "makes sense" only if criminal behavior is caused and not merely a freely willed, rational choice. If crime were a matter of free choices, then there would be nothing within particular individuals to be "fixed" or changed. But if involvement in crime is caused by various factors, then logically re-offending can be reduced if correctional interventions are able to alter these factors and how they have influenced offenders. For example, if associations with delinquent peers cause youths to internalize crime-causing beliefs (e.g., "it is okay to steal"), then diverting youths to other peer groups and changing these beliefs can inhibit their return to criminal behavior.

Sometimes rehabilitation is said to embrace a "medical model." When people are physically ill, the causes of their illness are diagnosed and then "treated." Each person's medical problems may be different and the treatment will differ accordingly; that is, the medical intervention is individualized. Thus, people with the same illness may, depending on their personal conditions (e.g., age, prior health), receive different medicines and stay in the hospital different lengths of time. Correctional rehabilitation shares the same logic: Causes are to be uncovered and treatments are to be individualized. This is why rehabilitation is also referred to as "treatment."

Correctional and medical treatment are alike in one other way: they assume that experts, scientifically trained in the relevant knowledge on how to treat their "clients," will guide the individualized treatment that would take place. In medicine, this commitment to training physicians in scientific expertise has been institutionalized, with doctors required to attend medical school. In corrections, however, such professionalization generally is absent or only partially accomplished.

The distinctiveness of rehabilitation can also be seen by contrasting it with three other correctional perspectives that, along with rehabilitation, are generally seen as the major goals of corrections. The first goal, *retribution* or *just deserts*, is distinctive in its own right because it is nonutilitarian; that is, it is not a means to achiev-ing some end—in this case, the reduction of crime—but rather is seen as an end in and of itself. The purpose of correctional sanctions is thus to inflict a punishment on the offender so that the harm the offender has caused will be "paid back" and the scales of justice balanced. In this case, punishment—inflicting pain on the offender—is seen as justified because the individual used his or her free will to choose to break the law. The second goal, *deterrence*, is utilitarian and asserts that punishing offenders will cause them not to return to crime because they will have been taught that "crime does not pay." Note that deterrence assumes that offenders are rational, in that increasing the cost of crime—usually through more certain and severe penalties—will cause offenders to choose to "go straight" out of fear that future criminality will prove too painful. This is called *specific deterrence*. When other people in society refrain from crime because they witness offenders' punishment and fear suffering a similar fate, this is called *general deterrence*. Finally, the third goal, *incapacitation*, makes no assumption about offenders and why they committed crimes. Instead, it seeks to achieve the utilitarian goal of reducing crime by "caging" or incarcerating offenders. If behind bars and thus "incapacitated," crime will be impossible because the offender is not free in society where innocent citizens can be criminally victimized.

In comparison, rehabilitation differs from retribution, but is similar to deterrence and incapacitation, in that it is a utilitarian goal, with the utility or benefit for society being the reduction of crime. It fundamentally differs from the other three perspectives, however, because these other goals make no attempt to change or otherwise improve offenders. Instead, they inflict pain or punishment on offenders either for a reason (retribution in order to "get even" or deterrence in order to "scare people straight") or as a consequence of the penalty (incapacitation involves placing offenders in an unpleasant living situation, the prison). In contrast, rehabilitation seeks to assist both offenders and society. By treating offenders, they hope to give them the attitudes and skills to avoid crime and live a productive life. At times, this attempt to help offenders exposes rehabilitation to the charge that it "coddles criminals." This view is shortsighted, however, because correctional rehabilitation's focus is not simply on lawbreakers but also on protecting society: by making offenders less criminal, fewer people will be victimized and society will, as a result, be safer.

Rehabilitation across time

As "deconstructionists" often remind us, important meanings are embedded in the words we select and voice; what we call things, in short, reveals our values and ideologies. It is instructive, then, that in the United States our history is not sprinkled with terms like "punishment institutions" and the "Ministry of Justice." Instead, a look to the past uncovers words such as the "penitentiary," "reformatory," "correctional institution," and "Department of Rehabilitation and Correction." This language shows an important feature of the response that the U.S. system of control has made to criminals across time: there has been, at least in the ideal, a belief that state interventions with offenders should be transforming, turning the wayward into the law-abiding. The question of how such rehabilitation should be achieved, however, has varied across time. Although dividing history into periods truncates reality and leaves out many details of the story, it is useful to see correctional rehabilitation as having three separate eras that can be distinguished by the way in which reformers believed offenders should be transformed. We review these below, and then discuss a fourth period in which rehabilitation came under unprecedented attack.

Reform by regimen: the penitentiary. Although various types of institutions had previously existed, the United States is generally credited with—or blamed for, depending on one's perspective!—the invention of the state-administered, modern prison system (Barnes; Eriksson; McKelvey). Before the 1820s and 1830s, prisons as we think of them today did not exist. Local counties operated jails, but these facilities often had the architecture of a house (with the jailer and his family living on the premises) and were used to detain offenders awaiting trial or punishment. Offenders were typically fined, publicly embarrassed by being placed in the pillory, whipped, banished, or executed, but they were not incarcerated for the purpose of punishment or reform. Indeed, the notion that locking up offenders could serve a larger purpose would have struck colonial Americans as odd (Barnes).

By the 1820s, however, ideas about criminals and what to do with them had changed. As David Rothman (1971) points out, Americans increasingly came to view crime as a product of the "social disorder" that was gripping their communities—communities that were growing larger and more diverse. People did not fully relinquish their religious views and the tendency to equate crime with sin, but they were increasingly persuaded that families and communities were less able to impart the moral fiber needed to resist the criminal temptations that now seemed widespread. Importantly, attributions of crime causation make certain responses to offenders appear more "sensible." Simply put, if social disorder was at the root of the crime problem, then the solution to crime was to place the wayward in an orderly environment.

Such environments, however, had to be created. With idealistic visions of stable colonial communities still fresh in mind, reformers argued that such orderly environments should be based on a clear set of principles—ones they believed reigned a generation or two before: obedience to authority, religion, hard work, and separation from all criminal influences. Bordered by high, thick walls, prisons—or what they tellingly called "penitentiaries"—would provide the ideal setting for this utopian community. The obvious problem, of course, was how to stop offenders from commingling and contaminating one another when they were being concentrated into a "society of captives." In Pennsylvania, reformers solved this problem through the "solitary system," placing offenders in a single cell under what amounted to perpetual solitary confinement. In New York, a "congregate system" was favored in which inmates would sleep alone but eat, work, and attend religious services en masse. Inmate-to-inmate contact was ostensibly prevented through the rule of absolute silence; those who dared to speak were harshly dealt with through the whip.

Advocates of the "solitary" and "congregate" designs engaged in a bitter feud over which approach should be the blueprint for the American penitentiary. From today's vantage point, such disputes might seem excessive, given that the principles underlying each model were identical. But for the 1820s reformers, the details were what mattered. For they were convinced that if they could perfect the daily regimen of the penitentiary—if they could create that orderly community they believed could have amazing curative powers—they could reform inmates and thus rid their society of recidivists. It was, they held, the day in and day out routines that would break the will of offenders and open them up to a spiritual renewal that would prove transforming.

In retrospect, we would deem enforced solitary confinement and silence for years on end cruel and unusual punishment; such practices would be virtually unthinkable by today's standards. Further, some commentators have questioned the motives of these early reformers, noting that under the guise of "benevolence" they applied their disciplinary techniques mainly to the poor, not to those of their own class (see, e.g., Foucault). Still, we should be careful not to be too smug in hindsight. The founders of the penitentiary—whatever their errors in judgment and inability to move beyond their class interests—genuinely believed that they were ushering in a reform that would sweep away the barbarous and demonstrably ineffective punishments of the past. They also were able to rise above feelings of vengeance—feelings that often rear their head today—to articulate an ideal that remained vibrant for the next two centuries: that the reformation of lawbreakers is a worthy goal to undertake (McKelvey).

Reform by individualized treatment: the new penology and beyond. Notions of how best to rehabilitate offenders are dynamic, not static. Three decades or so after the penitentiary was initiated, the idea that the internal design and daily regimen of the prison would have transforming powers could no longer be sustained. In the aftermath of the Civil War, prisons began to fill to the brim, rendering obsolete any hopes of bunking inmates in solitary confinement and of maintaining total silence. Beyond such practical limitations, observers believed the penitentiary's blueprint had a fatal flaw: no matter what offenders did while in prison, they were released when their sentence expired. What self-interest, they wondered, did inmates have to better themselves while under lock and key? It was clear that the earlier theory of reforming offenders was bankrupt.

In 1870, the leading correctional leaders and thinkers—they were often the same in those days—met in Cincinnati to consider this state of affairs at the National Congress on Penitentiary and Reformatory Discipline. One possibility was to declare that prisons were not instruments of rehabilitation and/or that offenders were not changeable. After all, with social Darwinism and biological theories of crime available, they could have agreed with other commentators that the immigrant masses now behind bars were a "dangerous class." In this scenario, they could have argued that the best use of prisons was to employ them to incapacitate the innately wicked. But they did not. Instead, their belief in rehabilitation remained unshakable. In the face of failure

and with prisons in crisis, they affirmed that "the supreme aim of prison discipline is the reformation of criminals, not the infliction of vindictive suffering" (Wines, p. 541).

For many of the Congress's participants, prison administration remained a sacred enterprise. Their Christian ideals prompted them to believe that saving offenders was within their mission; they also were convinced that of "all reformatory agencies, religion is first in importance, because most potent in its action upon the human heart and life" (Wines, p. 542). But proclaiming the power of faith to change lives was not novel. Some other ideas had to emerge to excite correctional leaders—to move them to devise and embrace a "new penology."

As mentioned above, members of the Congress believed they had detected the fatal flaw in the penitentiary design: the use of "determinate" sentences—that is, prison terms whose lengths were determined or specified by judges before an inmate entered prison. Such a system, they argued, provided no incentive for offenders to better themselves. In contrast, the "indeterminate" sentence meant that the date of an inmate's release from prison would be unknown to him or her upon entering an institution. Release would now be contingent on the inmate showing correctional officials that he or she was reformed, something that could only be assessed during the course of the offender's incarceration. With freedom thus hanging in the balance, the system would be arranged to maximize the inmate's commitment to change. As Congress declared, the "prisoner's destiny should be placed, measurably, in his own hands.... A regulated self-interest must be brought into play, and made constantly operative" (Wines, p. 541).

Many other features of the Congress's "new penology" were so forward-looking that they would not be foreign to current-day penal discussions of correctional reform. Thus, the Congress favored the "progressive classification of prisoners"; the use of "rewards, more than punishments"; "special training" in order "to make a good prison or reformatory officers"; access to "education" and "industrial training"; and efforts to reintegrate offenders into society "by providing them with work and encouraging them to redeem their character and regain their lost position in society" (Wines, pp. 541–544).

Pregnant in this set of principles was the conclusion that rehabilitation should be individualized. This idea, however, was expressed more clearly and forcefully closer to the turn of the century. At this time, the Congress's "new penology" was being elaborated by the emerging insights from the nascent social sciences of psychology and sociology. These disciplines brought a secular perspective to the enterprise of reforming offenders. They suggested that it was possible to study the causes of crime scientifically. For any given offender, however, the causes were likely to be multifaceted and found in a unique combination. Two people might commit the same crime—for example, robbery—but the reasons for their acts could be widely divergent (e.g., emotional problems as opposed to exposure to gang influences). Once this premise was accepted, it led logically to the conclusion that successful rehabilitation depended on treating offenders on a case-by-case basis. A single treatment would not fit all lawbreakers because, again, they were all different. Instead, interventions had to be individualized (Rothman, 1980).

What kind of system should be set up to deliver individualized rehabilitation? Above all, individualization required that criminal justice officials have the *discretion* to fit correctional interventions to the *offender* and not base it on the offense. Indeterminate sentencing, of course, was essential because it meant that inmates would be released from prison only when they had been cured of their criminal propensities. To determine who should be released and when, a *parole board* would be necessary. The idea of parole in turn mandated that released offenders be supervised in the community by *parole officers* whose task it was to counsel parolees and, when necessary, to return to prison offenders who failed to go straight.

Reformers, however, also argued that incarceration was not the appropriate intervention for all lawbreakers; many could be rehabilitated in the community. This belief led to the creation of *probation*, a practice in which *probation officers* would both help and police offenders released to their supervision. These officers, moreover, would assist judges in deciding who to imprison and who to place in the community by amassing information on each offender. This portrait was compiled in a "presentence report" that would detail not just the offender's criminal history but also his or her employment record, family background, and personal characteristics.

Because juveniles differed from adults, it also made sense to create a separate *juvenile court*. This special court most fully embodied the ideals of individualized treatment. Wayward youths were not to be punished by the state, but rather "saved" from a life in crime (Platt). The court would act as a "kindly parent" who would, in essence, step in and help not only youths already involved in illegal acts but also those at risk for a criminal life. The jurisdiction of the juvenile court thus was not limited to youths who had committed a crime. Instead, the court claimed jurisdiction over youths who engaged in deviant acts seen as precursors to crime (i.e., *status offenses* such as truancy, running away from home, and sexual promiscuity) and over those who were neglected or abused by their parents.

The paradigm of individualized treatment offered a persuasive rationale for reform. This proposal offered to improve the lives of offenders and to protect society by curing criminals who could be cured and by locking up those whose criminality proved intractable. Science and religion, moreover, meshed together to suggest that offenders could be transformed and that mere vengeance would be counterproductive. But in advancing a seemingly enlightened correctional agenda, advocates remained blind to the potential dangers of individualized treatment. First, they assumed that judges and correctional officials would have the expertise to administer this new system—such as knowing what caused an individual's criminality and knowing what intervention would work to effect the offender's reform. Second, they assumed that the officials' discretion would be exercised to advance the cause of rehabilitation. They did not consider that the unfettered discretion given to judges and officials might be abused or used mainly to control, not help, offenders. These problems would later play a role in undermining the legitimacy of individualized treatment, but for the moment they either did not come to mind or were dismissed as naysaying.

Persuasive paradigms do not always translate into concrete policy reforms. By 1900, however, the United States had entered the Progressive Era, which came to be called the "age of reform" because of the diverse social and governmental reforms undertaken in this time span. Thus, at a particularly receptive historical juncture, the "new penology" ideas—ideas that had been embellished since the Cincinnati Congress—presented a clear blueprint for renovating the correctional system. The time was ripe for individualized treatment to be implemented. As is well known, the first juvenile court was initiated in 1899 in Cook County, Illinois. Two decades or so later, all but three states had a special court for hearing juvenile cases, and every state permitted probation for youths. For adults, two-thirds of the states had begun probation and forty-four states had initiated parole. Meanwhile, in little over twenty years, the number of states that allowed indeterminate sentencing had risen from five to thirty-seven (Cullen and Gilbert; Rothman, 1980).

Reform by corrections. By the end of the Progressive Era, then, the notion of individualized treatment had emerged as the dominant correctional philosophy and the basic contours of the modern correctional system—probation, parole, juvenile justice, and all the policies and practices they entail—were in place. As Rothman (1980) painfully details, the ideals of effective rehabilitation were infrequently realized. Shortages of knowledge, trained staff, resources, and institutional commitment often resulted in treatment that was poorly delivered or absent altogether. Still, confidence abounded that rehabilitation was possible and, with sufficient support, could be effective.

This continuing commitment to rehabilitation was embodied in a third period of reform that spanned, roughly, the 1950s to the late 1960s. During this time, prisons were relabeled "correctional institutions," with the name *corrections* suggesting that the core task of working with offenders was to change or "correct" them. Corresponding to this new vocabulary, a range of treatment programs was introduced into institutions. These included, for example, individual and group counseling, therapeutic milieus, behavioral modification, vocational training, work release, furloughs, and college education (Cullen and Gendreau; Rotman). Especially in the 1960s, "community corrections" became fashionable, as a movement emerged to "reintegrate" inmates into society through halfway houses and other community-based treatment programs. Reflecting the tenor of the times, the Task Force on Corrections, part of a presidential commission studying the nations crime problem, asserted in 1967 that the "ultimate goal of corrections under any theory is to make the community safer by reducing the incidence of crime. Rehabilitation of offenders to prevent their return to crime is in general the most promising way to achieve this end"(p. 16).

Reform rejected: the attack on rehabilitation. The apparent invincibility of rehabilitation as the dominant correctional philosophy was shattered in less than a decade. Treatment programs did not suddenly disappear, and faith in rehabilitation did not vanish. Even so, a sea change in thinking occurred seemingly overnight and policy changes followed close behind. Suddenly it became fashionable to be against "state enforced therapy." Beginning in the mid-1970s, states began to question indeterminate sentencing and call for sentencing in which judicial and parole board discretion was eliminated or, in the least, curtailed. About thirty states still retain some form of indeterminate sentencing, but this is down from a time when every state had this practice. Further, over the last quarter of the twentieth century, every state passed mandatory sentences, "truth-in-sentencing" laws, "three-strikes-and-you're-out" laws, or similar legislation aimed at deterring and/or incapacitating lawbreakers (Tonry). Meanwhile, state and federal prison populations ballooned from 200,000 in the early 1970s to over 1.36 million in 2000 (and to about 2 million counting offenders in local jails). Within the community, the treatment paradigm was challenged by programs that sought not to "correct" offenders but to "intensively supervise," "electronically monitor," or otherwise control them. Even the juvenile justice system did not escape the diminished confidence in rehabilitation. By the end of the 1990s, seventeen states had changed the legal purpose of the juvenile court to de-emphasize rehabilitation, and virtually every state had passed laws to make their juvenile justice systems harsher (Feld; Snyder and Sickmund).

Major shifts in correctional thinking are usually a product of changes in the larger society that prompt citizens to reconsider beliefs they had not previously questioned. The mid-1960s to the mid-1970s was a decade of enormous social turbulence. This period was marked by the civil rights movement, urban riots, the Vietnam War and accompanying protests, the shootings at Kent State University and Attica Correctional Facility, Watergate and related political scandals, and escalating crime rates. As the central state agency for controlling crime and disorder, the criminal justice system—including its correctional component—came under careful scrutiny. It was often seen as part of the problem—as doing too much, too little, or the wrong thing.

For conservatives, the reigning chaos in society was an occasion to call for "law and order." To them, it was apparent that the correctional system was teaching that "crime pays." Under the guise of rehabilitation, criminals were being coddled; judges were putting dangerous offenders on probation; and parole boards were releasing predators prematurely from prison. We needed to toughen sentences—make them longer and determinate—in order to deter the calculators and incapacitate the wicked.

For liberals, however, rehabilitation was not the source of leniency but of injustice and coercion. The prevailing events contained the important lesson that government officials could not be trusted—whether to advance civil rights, be truthful about why the nation was at war, act with integrity while in political office, or rehabilitate the wayward. In this context, judges and correctional officials were redefined as "state agents of social control" whose motives were suspect. Thus, judges were now portrayed as purveyors of unequal justice, using their discretion not to wisely individualize treatments but to hand out harsher sentences to poor and minority defendants. Similarly, correctional officials were accused of using the threat of indeterminate incarceration not to achieve the noble goal of offender reform but to compel offenders to comply obediently with institutional rules that had little to do with their treatment; maintaining prison order thus displaced rehabilitation as the real goal of indeterminate terms. In the liberal critics' minds, it was time to forfeit rehabilitation and embrace a "justice model" that would limit incarceration to short sentences and would grant offenders an array of legal rights to protect them against the ugly power of the state (Cullen and Gilbert). Notions of "doing good" were relinquished and replaced with the hope of creating a correctional system that would "do no harm."

Thus, both liberals and conservatives opposed rehabilitation, albeit for different reasons: conservatives because they thought it victimized society, and liberals because they thought it victimized offenders. These two groups also agreed that the discretion of correctional officials should be eviscerated and determinacy in sentencing implemented. They both embraced the punishment of offenders. They parted company, however, on how harsh those sanctions should be. Given the "get tough" policies that have reigned in recent times, it is clear that the conservative alternative to rehabilitation prevailed most often and in most jurisdictions (Cullen and Gilbert; Griset).

The story about the attack on rehabilitation has one additional chapter to be told. In 1974, Robert Martinson published an essay in which he reviewed 231 studies evaluating the effectiveness of correctional treatment programs between 1945 and 1967 (see also Lipton, Martinson, and Wilks). Based on this assessment, Martinson concluded that "With few and isolated exceptions, the rehabilitative efforts that have been undertaken so far have had no appreciable effect on recidivism" (p. 25). This rather technical conclusion might have been open to different interpretations—for example, that treatment programs were being implemented incorrectly or that inappropriate interventions were being used. But Martinson then proceeded to ask a more provocative question: "Do all these studies lead irrevocably to the conclusion that *nothing works*, that we haven't the faintest clue about how to rehabilitate offenders and reduce recidivism?" (p. 48, emphasis added). He stopped short of claiming that "nothing works," but it did not take a deconstructionist to deduce that this was the message he was conveying.

Researchers make many bold assertions, but most are forgotten or subjected to critical scrutiny; neither occurred in Martinson's case: his research immediately received national attention among academics and the media, and his findings were accepted by most observers as obviously true. A few scholars rose up in opposition, such as Ted Palmer, who demonstrated that nearly half of the treatment programs reviewed by Martinson actually reduced recidivism. But given the tenor of the times, people were ready to hear Martinson's "nothing works" message and unprepared to question empirical findings that reinforced what they already believed. With scientific findings on their side, they now could declare that "rehabilitation was dead."

Correctional programs in the United States

Rehabilitation, however, did not die. There have been reports that the commitment to treatment programs has diminished over the past quarter century. The dearth of systematic data, however, leaves open the question of whether the retreat from rehabilitation is extensive or applicable mainly to some types of programs (e.g., college education courses) and to some jurisdictions. Regardless, even a cursory examination of correctional institutions reveals the presence of a diversity of programs. Why these *treatment programs* have persisted in the face of the attack on, and apparent bankruptcy of, rehabilitation is open to question, but at least three possible reasons can be suggested: institutional inertia, which made eliminating programs and firing staff more work than keeping them; their functionality—treatment programs reduce inmate idleness and thus contribute to institutional order; and a continuing commitment among corrections leaders to rehabilitation (see Lin).

Education and work programs. Perhaps the two most extensively used modes of treatment in American prisons are education and work programs (Silverman and Vega). Undoubtedly, the prevalence of these programs reflects the abiding belief that educational and work skills—and the good habits learned in acquiring these skills—are integral to securing employment and being a productive citizen. Although the results are not unequivocal, the existing research generally suggests that the programs do have a modest impact in reducing postrelease recidivism, especially when targeted at certain inmates (e.g., those with low skills) and when part of a broader strategy—a *multi-modal* approach—to rehabilitating offenders (Adams et al.; Bouffard, MacKenzie, and Hickman; Wilson, Gallagher, and MacKenzie).

A 1995 survey of state and federal prisons revealed that nearly one-fourth of inmates were enrolled in some kind of educational program (Stephan). It is estimated that U.S. prisons spend over $412 million annually on educational programs ("Survey Summary"). Over fifty thousand inmates are enrolled in "adult basic education," which involves learning in such core areas as mathematics, literacy, language arts, science, and social studies. General Equivalency Development—usually knows by its acronym, GED—is a high school equivalency degree. In 1996, over thirty-seven thousand inmates earned their GEDs ("Survey Summary"). About four-fifths of U.S. prisons offer the GED, while three-fourths provide basic education courses (Stephan). College education courses are available in about one-third of institutions. However, because inmates were legally excluded by 1994 federal legislation from securing Pell Grants to fund their education, participation in college degree programs has declined (Tewksbury, Erickson, and Taylor). In 1996, one survey reported that 14,532 inmates received a two-year associate's degrees and 232 received a bachelor's degree ("Survey Summary").

Inmates also often have access to another form of education: life-skills training. These programs, which are sometimes seen as counseling interventions, are predicated on the notion that upon release to society, many offenders may not have the kind of basic understandings that are integral to functioning in American society. Thus, courses will teach such varied skills as how to apply and interview for a job, how to manage one's money and household, how to live a healthy life, how to parent and be a spouse, and how to secure a driver's license (Silverman and Vega).

Finally, to prepare inmates for employment, many correctional institutions offer vocational education. A 1994 survey of forty-three correctional systems found that over sixty-five thousand inmates were enrolled in programs aimed at training them in vocational skills that could be used to find employment upon release from prison (Lillis, 1994). It is also estimated that nearly two-thirds of all inmates are given a work assignment (Stephan). This duty may include institutional maintenance, working in a prison industry, or laboring on a prison farm. The assumption is that the discipline of working while incarcerated—regardless of whether marketable skills are learned—will translate into steady employment once the inmate is released. This assumption is tenuous and remains to be confirmed. Instead, it seems that the major function of most work programs is to reduce inmate idleness and, in turn, to keep institutions orderly.

Psychological/counseling programs. Beyond programs that attempt to furnish inmates with the skills to live productively in the community, other prison programs attempt to change underlying problems causing, or implicated in, an offender's criminality. Perhaps the most common interventions are drug abuse programs. As many as half of all offenders entering prison report having used drugs in the month before their arrest. One-third of state prison inmates and over 20 percent of federal inmates report being on drugs at the time of their offense for which they were subsequently incarcerated (Maguire and Pastore, p. 508). Further, the *war on drugs* from the 1980s onward has increased the number of people in prison on drug-related offenses. Between 1979 and 1991, the proportion of drug offenders in state and federal prisons rose from 6 percent to 21 percent (Sabol and Lynch). Not surprisingly, during this same period, it is estimated that the proportion of inmates participating in drug treatment programs rose from 4.4 percent to 32.7 percent (Silverman and Vega).

Some institutions have programs—sometimes called *therapeutic communities*—that house drug-addicted inmates in a separate unit. In 1994, the federal government began offering funding to states for its RSAT program—Residential Substance Abuse Treatment—which provides drug treatment in such a separate unit

("Reducing Offender Drug Use"). Other inmates live in the general offender population but participate in group or individual counseling. Despite the availability of drug counseling, it still appears that the demand for programming outstrips its supply. "A significant percentage of inmates with drug abuse histories," observes Arthur Lurigio, "are still without treatment" (p. 511).

Correctional institutions frequently provide individual and group counseling aimed at having offenders forfeit their criminal way of life. Over the years, various treatment modalities have been tried. However, a method of increasing appeal—in large part due to growing empirical support for its effectiveness—is *cognitive-behavioral* treatment (Van Voorhis, Braswell, and Lester; see also Andrews and Bonta). Although they come in various forms, these programs target the criminal attitudes and ways of thinking that foster illegal behavior. The intervention might involve, for example, counselors modeling prosocial conduct and also reinforcing inmates when such conduct is exhibited. Especially for juveniles, "token economies" are sometimes set up in which conforming offenders are given tokens that can purchase privileges. Counselors also focus on the content of offenders' thinking and reasoning. They challenge inmates' antisocial attitudes, rationalizations supportive of criminal behaviors, attempts to externalize blame, and failure to confront the harm they have committed.

Prisons house offenders who are *mentally ill*. In 1998, an estimated 283,800 inmates were mentally ill, which comprised 16 percent of the state prison population and 7 percent of the federal prison population (Ditton). About 45 percent of these offenders received counseling or therapy while incarcerated; half were taking a prescribed medication; and about a fourth had been in a mental hospital or treatment program (Ditton).

Another large group of offenders who receive special services in prison are *sex offenders*. There are over 100,000 sex offenders in state and federal prisons. In one survey of correctional systems, more than half reported special facilities for sex offenders (e.g., therapeutic communities, diagnostic centers). Most often, sex offenders receive some form of individual or group counseling (Wees).

We should also note another source of counseling and programming in prisons: chaplains and religious volunteer groups. Part of the for-mal role of prison chaplains is to provide counseling to inmates. Such counseling often moves beyond religious issues to other problems in the offenders' lives (Sundt and Cullen). Further, various types of "faith-based" programming are found within virtually every correctional system. These might include Bible study, prayer and meditation sessions, peer mentors, and worship services ("Religion Behind Bars"). In Texas, there is a unit within a correctional institution that is, in essence, a "faith based prison" where religious volunteers provide inmates with both religious and support programs (Cullen, Sundt, and Wozniak).

Finally, although most of the focus has been on adult offenders, we should note that many of the programs used in prisons are found as well in juvenile facilities. A survey in 1993 found that a majority of states offered these programs to *juvenile offenders:* "academic education, vocational training, vocational counseling, organized recreation, substance abuse counseling, mental health counseling, sex offender treatment, abuse counseling, and positive peer culture" (Lillis, p. 14).

Community-based treatment.   Although the main focus of this section has been on prison-based programs, some mention should be made of treatment programs conducted in the community. Only two states do not supervise offenders released from prison. Otherwise, inmates returning to the community are placed on parole or *mandatory supervised release*, and they are monitored by parole officers. Probation is an alternative to incarceration. Convicted offenders who are not sentenced to prison may be placed on probation and, if so, are monitored by probation officers. In some states probation is centralized and thus is a state function; in most states, however, probation is decentralized and is administered by local jurisdictions, such as counties and cities. There are over two thousand probation agencies. In contrast, parole is always administered by a central agency that is part of state government. The federal government, which runs its own correctional system, also supervises offenders in the community. In the United States, there were approximately 700,000 offenders on parole and over 3.2 million on probation in 1999 (Petersilia, 1997, 1999).

Traditionally, probation and parole officers have been given the dual role of surveillance and treatment—surveillance to detect any signs of continued criminality and treatment to help the offender to overcome criminal propensities and become a solid citizen. The notion of these officers as treatment providers evolved into the *social casework* model, in which officers would, in essence, be primarily responsible for the rehabilitation of offenders assigned to them. The shortcomings of this model, however, soon became clear. First, heavy caseloads restricted the time that officers had to devote to any one offender; in fact, today the average caseload for probation officers is 124 and for parole officers is 67 (Camp and Camp). Second, officers often lacked the expertise to address the diverse needs of offenders (e.g., drug addiction). Thus, while officers still provide individual counseling—and occasionally run group sessions—they mainly fulfill their treatment function by being a *service broker*. In this model, their role is to assess offenders and to direct them into programs in the community. Most often, these programs are administered by nonprofit, community-based agencies.

We should note, however, that starting in the 1980s, there was a trend to transform probation and parole from a treatment-surveillance model into a model that sought exclusively to control and punish offenders (Cullen, Wright, and Applegate). Increasingly, officers have been required to conduct drug tests on, secure restitution payments from, and intensively supervise offenders (what one officer called the "pee 'em and see 'em" model). These extra duties, as well as the philosophy underlying their performance, have served in a number of jurisdictions to limit the treatment services provided by probation and parole officers (Petersilia, 1999).

When undertaken, community correctional programs vary in the degree to which they envelop an offender's life. Some programs are residential, lasting from 30 to 120 or more days; some programs offenders report to during the day for treatment; and some programs are attended a few hours each week. A wide range of services are delivered through these various programs. Some programs provide specialized treatment services, such as drug and alcohol counseling, sex offender counseling, psychiatric services, domestic violence counseling, family counseling, vocational and employment counseling (including job referrals), and life skills education. Other programs, especially those that are residential, tend to be multimodal, offering several services aimed at supporting offenders' attempts to "go straight."

Quality of treatment services.   Several problems plague efforts to provide effective treatment services to offenders. First, the very existence of program options can vary greatly across correctional institutions and across communities (e.g., large counties have many more treatment options). As a result, programs may not exist to address the specific needs of certain offenders. Second, the availability of places in treatment programs does not always match the supply. Take, for example, the needs of parolees in California. As Joan Petersilia notes, "there are only 200 shelter beds for more than 10,000 homeless parolees, four mental health clinics for 18,000 psychiatric cases, and 750 beds in treatment programs for 85,000 drug and alcohol abusers" (1999, p. 502). Third, the quality or "integrity" of treatment programs varies widely. For example, a prison classroom may be a place where offenders are motivated to learn and secure degrees or a place where they sit impassively, doze off, or read the newspaper (Lin). Fourth, even if designed with the best of intentions, treatment programs may not be based on scientific criminological knowledge and thus may target for change factors that are not related to recidivism (i.e., much like a physician giving a patient medicine for the wrong disease).

Does correctional rehabilitation work?

As noted previously, Martinson's 1974 review of the research on correctional programs poignantly raised the question of whether correctional interventions "work." Harboring negative sentiments toward rehabilitation, many policymakers and criminologists embraced Martinson's critique of rehabilitation and embraced his conclusion that "nothing works" on corrections. Now that more than a quarter of a century has passed, we can provide a more balanced assessment of the question posed by Martinson. The evidence tells us that the heady optimism of early reformers was not warranted, but neither, it appears, is the pessimism of current-day critics of rehabilitation. Simply put, we know more now about what does, and does not, work to reduce offender recidivism (for a summary, see Cullen and Gendreau).

In recent years, correctional interventions have, at times, become more punitive and have sought to achieve recidivism by deterring offenders rather than by changing them. These intervention strategies, for example, have involved the intensive supervision of probationers and parolees, the electronic monitoring of offenders in the community, boot camps for those beginning a life in crime, and "scared straight" programs for juveniles. After considerable research, the evidence is clear: these deterrence-oriented programs do not work to reduce recidivism (Cullen and Gendreau; Cullen et al., 1996; Petersilia and Turner).

In contrast, it is now apparent that rehabilitation programs generally reduce recidivism and, when conducted according to the "principles of effective treatment" (Gendreau), cut re-offending substantially (Andrews and Bonta; Cullen and Gendreau; Lipsey and Wilson; Lurigio). Evidence favorable to rehabilitation has been generated by a statistical technique called *meta-analysis*. Traditionally, criminologists such as Martinson would read over a group of studies evaluating treatment programs. They would then either describe what the studies found—a *narrative review*—or try to count how many studies showed that offender treatment worked or did not work—the "ballot box" method. A meta-analysis, however, essentially computes a batting average across all studies, calculating the average impact of treatment on recidivism. Using this method, the existing research, which now involves hundreds of evaluation studies, shows that rehabilitation programs reduce recidivism about 10 percentage points. Thus, if a *control* group had a recidivism rate of 55 percent, the *treatment* group's rate of re-offending would be 45 percent.

A group of Canadian psychologists interested in crime—Don Andrews, James Bonta, and Paul Gendreau being its most prominent members—have taken the analysis of effective rehabilitation one step farther. They had two important insights. First, they believed that treatment should focus on changing those factors that are most strongly associated with or "predict" recidivism (e.g., antisocial values and peer associations, low self-control). Second, they hypothesized that rehabilitation programs that "worked" to reduce recidivism should share common features. Thus, it made sense to investigate what distinguished programs that decreased re-offending from those that did not.

Based on meta-analyses of treatment studies, they found that in rehabilitation programs that conformed to the *principles of effective intervention*, recidivism was about 25 percentage points lower in the treatment as opposed to the control group (Andrews and Bonta; Cullen and Gendreau). These principles include: (1) target the known predictors of recidivism for change; (2) use cognitive-behavioral treatments that reinforce pro-social attitudes and behavior, seek to challenge and extinguish criminal thinking patterns, and provide alternative, prosocial ways of acting; (3) focus treatment interventions on high-risk offenders; (4) try to take into account characteristics of offenders (e.g., I.Q.) that might affect their responsivity to treatment; (5) employ staff that are well trained and interpersonally sensitive; and (6) provide offenders with aftercare once they leave the program (Gendreau).

The future of rehabilitation

In the early 1970s commentators asked, "Is rehabilitation dead?" Attacked by both liberals and conservatives and with seemingly scant empirical support, offender treatment appeared ready to be relegated to the correctional dustbin. Rehabilitation programs, however, did not go away, even if this was often because it was more convenient to keep them than to get rid of them. Indeed, programming continued inside and outside prisons, even though the United States was in the midst of an unprecedented campaign to "get tough" on crime that has resulted in approximately a sevenfold increase in the prison population since the early 1970s (Currie; Mauer). Honest debates can take place over whether the increased imprisonment was necessary and/or effective, but it is clear that merely locking up offenders is not the full answer to America's crime problem. The question thus arises, what else can we do to reduce recidivism and protect public safety?

At least part of that answer will involve attempts to rehabilitate offenders. It is noteworthy that contrary to the claims often made in the media, study after study shows (1) that a sizable minority of the American public believes that rehabilitation should be the main goal of corrections and (2) that a substantial majority believes that treating offenders is an important goal of corrections. To be sure, citizens want dangerous offenders locked away and are not reluctant to support harsh sentences. Still, they also are open to community-based options for nonviolent offenders, and they believe that rehabilitation should be a core part of corrections inside and outside prisons (Cullen, Fisher, and Applegate). In short, the often-stated idea that the "public won't support rehabilitation" simply is not true.

In an age when politicians seem at times to govern by what the polls say, the receptivity of the public to rehabilitation is significant. Still, the question of effectiveness—does rehabilitation reduce recidivism?—will remain central to rehabilitation's future. It is clear that rehabilitation is not a panacea capable of saving every criminal from a wayward life. But it is equally clear that treatment programs are more effective than doing nothing with offenders and more effective than punitively oriented programs. Further, in the last decade or so, criminologists have made important strides in uncovering how best to reform offenders, including those who are serious chronic criminals. This knowledge about the principles of effective intervention is likely to grow and be refined in the future immediately ahead.

Perhaps the largest challenge for the field of corrections is whether the emerging knowledge base on effective rehabilitation will be used or ignored. Implementing effective programs can be daunting when resources are limited, when staff training is poor and not conducted according to any professional standards, and when leaders of correctional systems and agencies are antagonistic to research knowledge. Even so, there are clear signs in numerous jurisdictions around the United States that a "what works" movement is under way. As criminologists articulate a more precise blueprint for how to intervene effectively with offenders, it becomes increasingly attractive to do what works rather than to do what fails. Further, the press for accountability and to use public monies responsibly may well place pressures on even reluctant correctional officials to replace failed practices with "best practices" (Rhine).

There is a final reason why rehabilitation is likely to reassert itself as a correctional philosophy: it appeals to a core theme in American culture—one present across time—that offenders, especially young ones, are not beyond redemption. We are, after all, the very people who founded the "penitentiary," reaffirmed rehabilitation in the "new penology," and chose to call our prisons "correctional" institutions. We are perhaps more skeptical than our predecessors about the extent to which criminals can be reformed. Even so, we share their vision that we lose something as a people when we reduce the correctional enterprise to inflicting pain, warehousing offenders, and depleting the system of all hope and compassion (Clear). There is, in the end, something ennobling about rehabilitation—something that calls us to do good for offenders not because we must but because such action

symbolizes the kind of individuals and nation we wish to be (Cullen and Gilbert).

FRANCIS T. CULLEN
SHANNON A. SANTANA

See also CORRECTIONAL REFORM ASSOCIATIONS; DETERRENCE; INCAPACITATION; JAILS; JUVENILE JUSTICE: INSTITUTIONS; PREDICTION OF CRIME AND RECIDIVISM; PRISONERS, LEGAL RIGHTS OF; PRISONS: HISTORY; PRISONS: CORRECTIONAL OFFICERS; PRISONS: PRISONERS; PRISONS: PRISONS FOR WOMEN; PRISONS: PROBLEMS AND PROSPECTS; PROBATION AND PAROLE: HISTORY, GOALS, AND DECISION-MAKING; PROBATION AND PAROLE: PROCEDURAL PROTECTION; PROBATION AND PAROLE: SUPERVISION; RETRIBUTIVISM; SEXUAL PREDATORS.

BIBLIOGRAPHY

ADAMS, KENNETH; BENNETT, KATHERINE J.; FLANAGAN, TIMOTHY J.; MARQUART, JAMES W.; CUVELIER, STEVEN J.; FRITSCH, ERIC; GERBER, JURG; LONGMIRE, DENNIS R.; and BURTON, VELMER S., JR. "A Large-Scale Multidimensional Test of the Effect of Prison Education Programs on Offenders' Behavior." *The Prison Journal* 74, no. 4 (1994): 433–449.

ANDREWS, D. A., and BONTA, JAMES. *The Psychology of Criminal Conduct*, 2d ed. Cincinnati, Ohio: Anderson Publishing Co., 1998.

BARNES, HARRY ELMER. *The Story of Punishment*, 2d ed. Montclair, N.J.: Patterson Smith, 1972.

BOUFFARD, JEFFREY A.; MACKENZIE, DORIS LAYTON; and HICKMAN, LAURA J. "Effectiveness of Vocational Education and Employment Programs for Adult Offenders: A Methodology-Based Analysis of the Literature." *Journal of Offender Rehabilitation* 31, nos. 1–2 (2000): 1–41.

CAMP, CAMILLE GRAHAM, and CAMP, GEORGE M. *The Corrections Yearbook 1999: Adult Corrections.* Middletown, Conn.: Criminal Justice Institute, 1999.

CLEAR, TODD R. *Harm in American Penology: Offenders, Victims, and Their Communities.* Albany, N.Y.: State University of New York Press, 1994.

CULLEN, FRANCIS T.; FISHER, BONNIE S.; and APPLEGATE, BRANDON K. "Public Opinion About Punishment and Corrections." In *Crime and Justice: A Review of Research, Volume 27.* Edited by Michael Tonry. Chicago: University of Chicago Press, 2000. Pages 1–79.

CULLEN, FRANCIS T., and GENDREAU, PAUL. "Assessing Correctional Rehabilitation: Policy, Practice, and Prospects." In *Criminal Justice 2000—Volume 3: Policies, Processes, and Deci-*

sions of the Criminal Justice System. Edited by Julie Horney. Washington, D.C.: National Institute of Justice, U.S. Department of Justice, 2000. Pages 109–175.

CULLEN, FRANCIS T., and GILBERT, KAREN E. *Reaffirming Rehabilitation*. Cincinnati, Ohio: Anderson Publishing Co., 1982.

CULLEN, FRANCIS T.; SUNDT, JODY L.; and WOZNIAK, JOHN F. "The Virtuous Prison: Toward a Restorative Rehabilitation." In *Contemporary Issues in Crime and Criminal Justice: Essays in Honor of Gilbert Geis*. Edited by Henry N. Pontell and David Shichor. Saddle River, N.J.: Prentice-Hall, 2000. Pages 265–286.

CULLEN, FRANCIS T.; WRIGHT, JOHN PAUL; and APPLEGATE, BRANDON K. "Control in the Community: The Limits of Reform?" In *Choosing Correctional Interventions That Work: Defining the Demand and Evaluating the Supply*. Edited by Alan T. Harland. Thousand Oaks, Calif.: Sage Publications, 1996. Pages 69–116.

CURRIE, ELLIOTT. *Crime and Punishment in America*. New York: Metropolitan Books, 1998.

DITTON, PAULA M. *Mental Health and Treatment of Inmates and Probationers*. Washington, D.C.: Bureau of Justice Statistics, U.S. Department of Justice, 1999.

ERIKSSON, TORSTEN. *The Reformers: An Historical Survey of Pioneer Experiments in the Treatment of Criminals*. New York: Elsevier Scientific Publishing Co., 1976.

FELD, BARRY C. *Bad Kids: Race and the Transformation of the Juvenile Court*. New York: Oxford University Press, 1999.

FOUCAULT, MICHEL. *Discipline and Punish: The Birth of the Prison*. New York: Pantheon Books, 1977.

GENDREAU, PAUL. "The Principles of Effective Intervention with Offenders." In *Choosing Correctional Interventions That Work: Defining the Demand and Evaluating the Supply*. Edited by Alan T. Hardin. Thousand Oaks, Calif.: Sage Publications, 1996. Pages 117–130.

GRISET, PAMELA L. *Determinate Sentencing: The Promise and the Reality of Retributive Justice*. Albany, N.Y.: State University of New York Press, 1991.

LILLIS, JAMIE. "Survey Summary: Youth Count Drops by 15%; Overcrowding Remains." *Corrections Compendium* 18 (December 1993): 7–14.

———. "Survey Summary: Education in U.S. Prisons—Part Two." *Corrections Compendium* 19 (April 1994): 10–16.

LIN, ANN CHIH. *Reform in the Making: The Implementation of Social Policy in Prison*. Princeton, N.J.: Princeton University Press, 2000.

LIPSEY, MARK W., and WILSON, DAVID B. "Effective Intervention for Serious Juvenile Offenders: A Synthesis of Research." In *Serious and Violent Juvenile Offenders: Risk Factors and Successful Interventions*. Edited by Rolf Loeber and David P. Farrington. Thousand Oaks, Calif.: Sage Publications, 1998. Pages 313–345.

LIPTON, DOUGLAS; MARTINSON, ROBERT; and WILKS, JUDITH. *The Effectiveness of Correctional Treatment: A Survey of Treatment Evaluation Studies*. New York: Praeger, 1975.

LURIGIO, ARTHUR J. "Drug Treatment Availability and Effectiveness: Studies of the General and Criminal Justice Populations." *Criminal Justice and Behavior* 27, no. 4 (2000): 495–528.

MAGUIRE, KATHLEEN, and PASTORE, ANN L., EDS. *Sourcebook of Criminal Justice Statistics—1998*. Washington, D.C.: Bureau of Justice Statistics, U.S. Department of Justice, 1999.

MARTINSON, ROBERT. "What Works? Questions and Answers About Prison Reform." *The Public Interest* 35 (Spring 1974): 22–54.

MAUER, MARC. *The Race to Incarcerate*. New York: The New Press, 1999.

MCKELVEY, BLAKE. *American Prisons: A History of Good Intentions*. Montclair, N.J.: Patterson Smith, 1977.

PALMER, TED. "Martinson Revisited." *Journal of Research in Crime and Delinquency* 12 (July 1975): 133–152.

PETERSILIA, JOAN. "Probation in the United States." In *Crime and Justice: A Review of Research, Volume 22*. Edited by Michael Tonry. Chicago: University of Chicago Press, 1997. Pages 149–200.

———. "Parole and Prisoner Reentry in the United States." In *Prisons: Crime and Justice—A Review of Research, Volume 26*. Edited by Michael Tonry and Joan Petersilia. Chicago: University of Chicago Press, 1999. Pages 479–529.

PETERSILIA, JOAN, and TURNER, SUSAN. "Intensive Probation and Parole." In *Crime and Justice: A Review of Research, Volume 17*. Edited by Michael Tonry. Chicago: University of Chicago Press, 1993. Pages 281–335.

PLATT, ANTHONY M. *The Child Savers: The Invention of Delinquency*. Chicago: University of Chicago Press, 1969.

"Religion Behind Bars: Survey Finds Variety of Religious Beliefs, Activities within Correctional Institutions." *Corrections Compendium* 23 (April 1998): 8–21.

RHINE, EDWARD E., ed. *Best Practices: Excellence in Corrections*. Lanham, Md.: American Correctional Association, 1998.

ROTHMAN, DAVID J. *The Discovery of the Asylum: Social Order and Disorder in the New Republic.* Boston: Little, Brown and Co., 1971.

———. *Conscience and Convenience: The Asylum and Its Alternatives in Progressive America.* Boston: Little, Brown and Co., 1980.

ROTMAN, EDGARDO. "The Failure of Reform: United States, 1865–1965." In *The Oxford History of the Prison: The Practice of Punishment in Western Society.* Edited by Norval Morris and David J. Rothman. New York: Oxford University Press, 1995.

SABOL, WILLIAM J., and LYNCH, JAMES P. *Crime Policy Report: Did Getting Tough Pay?* Washington, D.C.: Urban Institute, 1997. Also available through the Internet at http//www.urbran.org/crime/ crime.htm.

SILVERMAN, IRA J., and VEGA, MANUEL. *Corrections: A Comprehensive Review.* Minneapolis, Minn.: West Publishing Co., 1996.

SNYDER, HOWARD N., and SICKMUND, MELISSA. *Juvenile Offenders and Victims: 1999 National Report.* Washington, D.C.: Office of Juvenile Justice and Delinquency Prevention, U.S. Department of Justice, 1999.

STEPHAN, JAMES J. *Census of State and Federal Correctional Facilities, 1995.* Washington, D.C.: Bureau of Justice Statistics, U.S. Department of Justice, 1997.

SUNDT, JODY L., and CULLEN, FRANCIS T. "The Role of the Contemporary Prison Chaplain." *The Prison Journal* 23, no. 3 (1998): 271–298.

"Survey Summary: Education Opportunities in Correctional Settings." *Corrections Compendium* 22 (September, 1997): 4–16.

Task Force on Corrections, President's Commission on Law Enforcement and Administration of Justice. *Task Force Report: Corrections.* Washington D.C.: U.S. Government Printing Office, 1967.

TEWKSBURY, RICHARD; ERICKSON, DAVID JOHN; and TAYLOR, JON MARC. "Opportunities Lost: The Consequences of Eliminating Pell Grant Eligibility for Correctional Education Students." *Journal of Offender Rehabilitation* 31, nos. 1–2 (2000): 43–56.

TONRY, MICHAEL. *Reconsidering Indeterminate and Determinate Sentencing: Research in Brief.* Washington, D.C.: National Institute of Justice, U.S. Department of Justice, 1999.

U.S. Department of Justice. Bureau of Justice Statistics. http://www.ojp.usdoj. gov/bjs.

U.S. Department of Justice. National Institute of Justice. http://www.ojp.usdoj. gov/nij.

VAN VOORHIS, PATRICIA; BRASWELL, MICHAEL; and LESTER, DAVID. *Correctional Counseling and Rehabilitation*, 3d ed. Cincinnati, Ohio: Anderson Publishing Co., 1997.

WEES, GREG. "Survey Summary: Sex Offenders in State and Federal Prisons Top 100,000 Mark." *Corrections Compendium* 21 (May, 1996): 10–25.

WILSON, DAVID B.; GALLAGHER, CATHERINE A.; and MACKENZIE, DORIS L. "A Meta-Analysis of Corrections-Based Education, Vocation, and Work Programs for Adult Offenders." *Journal of Research in Crime and Delinquency* 37, no. 4 (2000): 347–368.

WINES, E. C., ed. *Transactions of the National Congress on Penitentiary and Reformatory Discipline.* Albany, N.Y.: Weed Parsons and Co., 1871.

RELIGION AND CRIME

Claims and findings pertaining to the relationship between religion and crime in American society are conflicted. In the early 1940s Middleton and Fay concluded that religion may cause crime and delinquency, an outcome that Schur later linked to religious beliefs and moral codes supporting the legal regulation of practices such as alcohol consumption and sexual behavior. Kvaraceus (1944), on the other hand, reported that religion had no effect on criminal behavior. A few years later, Glueck and Glueck argued that religion was a significant deterrent of crime and delinquency. Taking stock in the 1960s, the President's Commission on Law Enforcement and the Administration of Justice (1967) observed that the relationship between religion and crime in American society had not been established. Influential scholars agreed (Sutherland and Cressey).

Fitzpatrick adduced a reason for the confusion. He noted that early criminological research had paid attention to the relationship between religion and crime, but by the 1960s many social scientists considered it irrelevant. Secular trends in American society had obscured—at least for the moment—the study of the relation between religion and crime and, thereby, precluded closure on questions raised by earlier criminological research. Reflecting the spirit of the times, Schur—not without irony given his conclusion that religion may sometimes play a role in causing crime—consigned the religious factor to the category of questionable crime theories.

"Hellfire and Delinquency" and beyond

Social scientists in the 1960s questioned the relevance of examining the effects of religion on crime. Their position was consistent with the view of many academics and intellectuals that religion in American society was not a major source of operative norms, values, and beliefs (Glock and Stark). Hirschi and Stark's widely cited article, "Hellfire and Delinquency," led to conclusions supporting that perspective.

Elaborating Hirschi's social control theory, Hirschi and Stark forged theoretical links between religiosity and internalized intrapersonal sources of conformity to the normative sociolegal order. They predicted that church attendance would have a direct negative effect on crime and would affect intervening variables that were associated with criminal/delinquent activities: amoral attitudes ("to get ahead, you have to do some things that are not right"; "suckers deserve to be taken advantage of"); disdain for the law ("it is all right to get around the law if you can get away with it"); rejection of a positive view of the police ("I have a lot of respect for the police"). They also predicted that church attendance would be associated with beliefs in supernatural sanctions that could deter delinquency: "there is a life beyond death"; "the devil actually exists." Hirschi and Stark assessed their hypotheses with data from a survey (Richmond Youth Study) of over four thousand students from a working-class town in the San Francisco Bay Area. Self-reports of delinquency (property crimes and violent offenses) were validated using official or police data.

The results of the empirical tests of the predicted effects can still be surprising to many people. Church attendance had no significant direct effect on delinquent activities nor did it affect the social control variables (endorsement of conventional moral principles and positive attitudes toward the law and the police). Church attendance was positively associated with beliefs about supernatural sanctions, but no significant relationships were found between these beliefs and criminal activity.

Where conventional religiosity had no effect on the measured indicators of social control, respondents who claimed a high level of respect for the law and the police were, indeed, much less likely to be delinquent than chiselers and those with contempt for the police. Likewise, those who believed in fair and just treatment of others were much less likely to be involved in delinquent activities than those who, for example, agreed that "suckers deserve to be taken advantage of."

Given its theoretically based argument, the analysis of data gathered from a large, carefully drawn sample of respondents, and the cross-validation of self-reported delinquency with police records, "Hellfire and Delinquency" seemed to be the final word about the relationship between religion, crime, and delinquency in American society. Translated into general theoretical language, Hirschi and Stark's results led to the conclusion that religion in an advanced industrial society such as the United States was differentiated or decoupled from the forces of social control that were thought to affect crime and delinquency. The strong tie between religion and social control that philosophers and sociological theorists from Feuerbach, Marx, Nietzsche, and Freud to Durkheim and Parsons had assumed to be the case was missing according to Hirschi and Stark. But was it?

Over the next decade, a number of studies examined the effect of religion on crime and delinquency. Some of Rhodes and Reiss's findings were consistent with those reported by Hirschi and Stark. There were no significant differences in delinquency rates across denominational lines in either Hirschi and Stark or Rhodes and Reiss. On the other hand, although it was not highlighted by them, the data in Rhodes and Reiss did show a negative relationship between church attendance and delinquency thus contravening Hirschi and Stark.

Burkett and White found that while church attendance had no effect on delinquent acts such as property crimes and assault, it did tend to curb status offenses (drinking and smoking). Albrecht, Chadwick, and Alcorn reported negative correlations among church attendance, religious beliefs, and delinquency, as did Higgins and Albrecht. In each case, relationships between religiosity and delinquency were stronger for victimless offenses than they were for crimes with victims.

Major studies of the link between religion and crime in the 1970s concluded with Jensen and Erickson's analysis of the Arizona Community Tolerance Study and their reanalysis of the Richmond Youth Study. The Arizona study gathered data from over three thousand high school students attending schools in metropolitan and small town contexts in southern Arizona. Church attendance had a significant impact on thirteen of eighteen delinquency items. The effects of involvement in church-related youth activities and beliefs were less pronounced. Among serious offenses, church attendance had the most impact. Among less serious offenses, both church attendance and youth activities had the most impact.

Jensen and Erickson also found that religious affiliation (Roman Catholic/Protestant/Mormon) had an effect on delinquency. Mormon youths, in particular, were more likely than Protestants or Roman Catholics to report low levels of smoking, drinking, and drunkenness. These denominational differences were more pronounced in the small towns sampled by Jensen and Erickson than in the metropolitan context.

Where church attendance and denomination were controlled, Jensen and Erickson (1979) suggested that the pattern of effects on delinquency could be explained by variation across denominations in the salience of offenses as moral deviations. Serious offenses, they argued, may be interdicted by all denominations, but minor offenses such as smoking may only be negatively sanctioned by groups that value personal asceticism. Finally, in comparing predictors of crime and delinquency, Jensen and Erickson found that measures of religion were of moderate importance, being more predictive than participation in secular activities (including sports and school clubs) but less important as predictors than various measures of attitudes toward the law, including respect for the police.

Jensen and Erickson also reanalyzed the Richmond Youth Study data. They found that church attendance was significantly related to drinking, smoking, and truancy. (Drinking and smoking had been omitted from Hirschi and Stark's delinquency index.) They also found differences between more and less "ascetic" denominations: Personal moral strictness tended to interact with church attendance to curb delinquency.

In the early 1980s, Stark, Kent, and Doyle developed a contextual explanation regarding the effects of religion on crime and delinquency. Stark and colleagues distinguished so-called moral communities from secular communities, arguing that religion in the former is a more prominent feature of daily life than in secular communities. Moral communities are characterized by relatively high rates of church attendance and church membership. Religiously based community activities for youth and adults are relatively common in moral communities compared with secular communities.

Stark and colleagues compared the effects of church attendance on delinquency in a "moral community" with a high rate of church membership (in Provo, Utah) with the effects of church attendance in a so-called secular community (Seattle, Washington, which had an exceptionally low rate of church membership compared with other cities in the United States). They report that the correlation between church attendance and delinquency was stronger (gamma =.45) in Provo than in Seattle (gamma =.13).

Instead of conceptualizing the effects of religion on crime and delinquency in a strictly individualistic manner, it is conceivable that the social context may mediate the effects of religion on individual behavior. However, in subsequent research by Cochran and Akers, the moral communities hypothesis received only limited support. Only when offenses are morally ambiguous (as, for example, marijuana use seems to be) does religion have a substantial effect according to Cochran and Akers. They also conclude that the effects of religion are limited primarily to instances where religious norms condemn certain acts (such as the Mormon church proscription regarding alcohol). Linden also concludes that the deterrent effects of religion seem limited to morally ambiguous offenses such as marijuana use.

In the 1980s, some additional articles contributed to the empirical research literature on religion and crime (see, e.g., Elifson, Petersen, and Hadaway; Tittle and Welch; and Peek, Curry, and Chalfant). Tittle and Welch concluded that individual religiosity deterred deviance most in relatively secular communities or areas with a relatively high percentage of religious nonaffiliates. In a subsequent analysis, Welch, Tittle, and Petee concede that their data have several limitations (such as measuring projected or potential, rather than actual, deviant behavior in a data set including only adult Catholics). Stack and Kanavy report that areas with relatively high proportions of Catholics have lower rates of sexual assault. Hadaway, Elifson, and Petersen conclude that church attendance and religious salience have a significant deterrent effect on drug use, including alcohol and marijuana. Peek, Curry, and Chalfant conclude that there is evidence of a decline in the deterrent effect of religiosity on delinquency as the time span between the measures of delinquency and religiosity increases.

In the 1990s, a series of studies has demonstrated that measures of religion are significantly correlated with measures of drinking and drug use (Cochran et al.; Brownfield and Sorenson; Stark; Benda and Corwyn, 1997; Lee et al.). For example, Cochran and others examine the influence of religious stability and homogamy among a sample of Protestant respondents. Their data were taken from the national General Social Surveys conducted between 1977 and 1989. Although Cochran and colleagues report that some measures of religion are not significantly related to alcohol use (e.g., frequency of prayer, belief in an afterlife, and level of confidence in the clergy), they did find significant negative correlations between drinking and church attendance, strength of religious identification, and holding a literal interpretation of scripture. Cochran and others find that religious stability and homogamy in marriage tend to increase the negative relationship between personal religiosity and alcohol use.

Brownfield and Sorenson, in an analysis of the Seattle Youth Study, examined the effects of religion on several types of drug use, including alcohol, marijuana, amphetamines, barbiturates, and cocaine. Using three measures of religion (religious affiliation, church attendance, and religiosity), Brownfield and Sorenson find that all three are significant, inverse correlates of all types of drug use measured.

Bainbridge concludes that individual religiousness can deter larceny and similar crimes within so-called moral or religious communities, while the correlations between religion and drug offenses are not significantly affected by religious context. Benson also concludes that the deterrent effects of religion on drug use are persistent (though occasionally modest) across a variety of settings or contexts. Benson points out that there is a need for more theoretical work on precisely how religion affects substance use.

Benda and Corwyn (1997) analyzed data collected from two southern states to assess the relationship between religion and drug use among adolescents. They conclude that church attendance is inversely correlated with drinking, controlling for demographic factors such as race, social class, age, and family structure. Lee and others conducted a large-scale survey of Seventh-Day Adventist youth in grades six to twelve. More than seven thousand completed questionnaires were obtained from a stratified random sample of the United States and Canada. Lee and colleagues report that youth who did not follow worship practices were most likely to report higher levels of alcohol and drug use.

Theoretical perspectives

All three of the "grand master" theorists in sociology—Marx, Weber, and Durkheim—predicted that religion would have significant effects on human behavior in general and on conformity and deviance in particular (Jensen and Rojek). Marx's famous dictum that religion is the "opium of the masses" meant that he regarded religious beliefs in a hereafter as a suppressor of discontent and revolt among the proletariat. The property of capitalists is protected, according to Marxists, by diverting the attention of the working class to the hereafter rather than to their exploitation on earth (Liska and Messner, 1999).

Weber argued that there are more subtle effects of religion and religious doctrine on human behavior and institutions. The Protestant ethic, most importantly perhaps, served to legitimate social changes that preceded the transition from feudalism to capitalism. Besides innovations in banking practices, which allowed for the necessary accumulation of capital for investment, the Protestant ethic encouraged individuals to engage in a lifestyle of hard work, sobriety, and saving.

Durkheim's classic monograph on suicide, however, probably details most clearly the normative and integrative role of religious institutions. Egoistic suicide would be prevented, Durkheim argued, when individuals participated in social institutions and rituals such as those sponsored by religion. Durkheim's theory of social integration might be simplified or reduced to the basic idea that we are moral beings to the extent we are social beings. The more that individuals become involved in community life, particularly though the family and religious institutions, the less likely that they will become self-centered and inclined to commit criminal or deviant acts.

Most of the traditional or causal criminological theories have yielded predictions that religion should deter crime. The three traditional, causal criminological theories—control, strain, and subcultural theories—may be derived from Durkheim's classic typology of suicide. Control theory, for example, has many parallels in Durkheim's concept of "egoistic" suicide, wherein individuals lacking social ties (to family and religion, for example) are predicted to be more self-centered and prone to commit suicide than individuals who have strong social ties. A more recent version of control theory, the "self-control" theory, predicts that crime is likely to result from poor socialization by institutions such as the family that fail to control impulsivity and inclinations to risk-taking. Individuals who lack self-control also are characterized by poor cognitive skills, inability or unwillingness to plan for the future, and a lack of compassion for others.

"Anomic" suicide referred to suicide caused by disruptions in the normative order (or "anomie") that are exemplified by extreme changes in the business cycle (Liska and Messner). Suicide rates were predicted to rise during both times of economic depression and economic expansion or growth.

Subcultural criminological theory parallels Durkheim's concept of "altruistic" suicide, in that both conformity and deviance are conceived of as adherence to the particular norms and values of various subgroups. Thus, the disgraced military officer may feel obligated to commit suicide, just as a gang member may feel compelled to join in acts of theft and violence with fellow gang members. Conventional social groups such as the family and the church, in contrast, can promote obedience to the law by advocating conventional norms and values.

Although strain theorists have not emphasized the role of religious institutions in promoting conformity, the logic of the theory is compatible with predictions that religion should inhibit crime and delinquency. Merton argued that cultures which became so focused on economic goals and values to the exclusion of non-economic institutions and values (e.g., linked to child rearing and the family) were more likely to have higher crime rates (Liska and Messner). Religious institutions that might foster greater emphasis on the acceptable or legitimate means to become financially successful should help reduce crime. So-called malintegrated cultures that legitimate an ethical standard of the "ends justify the means" have long been predicted by strain theorists to have high rates of crime.

Assessing whether effects of religion are spurious

A few studies have attempted the difficult task of determining whether any significant effects of religion on crime and delinquency are spurious. This is a difficult task because it can require identifying very specific non-spurious causes of crime and delinquency that help to eliminate all significant effects on religion. Further, even if certain variables can be identified that eliminate all significant effects of religion, such variables may be measures of intervening mechanisms that explain how religion might affect crime and delinquency. For example, if individuals who are religious refrain from alcohol and drug use because they define such activity as sinful, such definitions of drug use as sinful would be better interpreted as intervening variables that might explain how religion affects drug use.

In a 1995 study, Benda reports that the effects of religiosity on so-called antiascetic behaviors (such as alcohol use) are not mediated by other dimensions of social control. We might hypothesize that the effects of religiosity are mediated through factors such as parental supervision, but Benda does not conclude that this is the case. Similarly, in a 1993 study, Burkett reports that adolescent alcohol use remains directly affected by religiosity holding constant another measure of parental social control. Burkett concludes that drinking is still directly affected by religiosity, controlling for measures of conformity to parental wishes.

Cochran et al. conducted one of the most comprehensive examinations of whether religion is a spurious correlate of delinquency. They used measures derived from both arousal theory (a risk-taking theoretical perspective) and control theory. Cochran et al. conclude that religion still had a significant deterrent effect on tobacco and alcohol use, controlling for measures derived from both theoretical perspectives. The consensus among most researchers to date seems to be that the effects of religion, particularly on drug and alcohol use, are not spurious.

JOHN SIMPSON
DAVID BROWNFIELD

See also AGE AND CRIME; CLASS AND CRIME; CRIME CAUSATION: SOCIOLOGICAL THEORIES; ECOLOGY OF CRIME; GENDER AND CRIME; RACE AND CRIME.

BIBLIOGRAPHY

ALBRECHT, STAN L.; CHADWICK, BRUCE A.; and ALCORN, DAVID S. "Religiosity and Deviance: Application of An Attitude-Behavior Contingent Consistency Model." *Journal for the Scientific Study of Religion* 16 (1977): 263–274.
BAINBRIDGE, WILLIAM SIMS. "Crime, Delinquency and Religion." In *Religion and Mental Health.* Edited by John F. Schumaker. New York: Oxford University Press, 1992. Pages 199–210.
BENDA, BRENT. "The Effect of Religion on Adolescent Delinquency Revisited." *Journal of Research in Crime and Delinquency* 32 (1995): 446–466.

BENDA, BRENT, and CORWIN, ROBERT. "Religion and Delinquency." *Journal for the Scientific Study of Religion* 36 (1997): 81–92.

BENSON, PETER L. "Religion and Substance Abuse." In *Religion and Mental Health*. Edited by John F. Schumaker. New York: Oxford University Press, 1992. Pages 211–220.

BROWNFIELD, DAVID, and SORENSON, ANN. "Religion and Drug Use Among Adolescents: A Social Support Conceptualization and Interpretation." *Deviant Behavior* 12 (1991): 259–276.

BURKETT, STEVEN. "Perceived Parents' Religiosity, Friends' Drinking, and Hellfire." *Review of Religion Research* 35 (1993): 134–154.

BURKETT, STEVEN, and WHITE, MERVIN. "Hellfire and Delinquency: Another Look." *Journal for the Scientific Study of Religion* 13 (1974): 455–462.

COCHRAN, JOHN, and AKERS, RONALD. "Beyond Hellfire: An Exploration of the Variable Effects of Religiosity on Adolescent Marijuana and Alcohol Use." *Journal of Research in Crime and Delinquency* 26 (1989): 198–225.

COCHRAN, JOHN; BEEGHLEY, LEONARD; and BOCK, E. WILBUR. "The Influence of Religious Stability and Homogamy on the Relationship between Religiosity and Alcohol Use among Protestants." *Journal for the Scientific Study of Religion* 31 (1992): 441–456.

COCHRAN, JOHN; WOOD, PETER; and ARNEKLEV, BRUCE. "Is the Religiosity-Delinquency Relationship Spurious?" *Journal of Research in Crime and Delinquency* 31 (1994): 92–123.

ELIFSON, KIRK W.; PETERSEN, DAVID M.; and HADAWAY, C. KIRK. "Religiosity and Delinquency." *Criminology* 21 (1983): 505–527.

FITZPATRICK, J. P. "The Role of Religion in Programs for the Prevention and Correction of Crime and Delinquency." In *Juvenile Delinquency and Youth Crimes*. President's Commission on Law Enforcement and the Administration of Justice. Washington, D.C.: U.S. Government Printing Office, 1967.

GLOCK, CHARLES, and STARK, RODNEY. *Religion and Society in Tension*. Chicago: Rand McNally, 1965.

GLUECK, SHELDON, and GLUECK, ELEANOR. *Unraveling Juvenile Delinquency*. Cambridge, Mass.: Harvard University Press, 1950.

HADAWAY, C. KIRK; ELIFSON, KIRK W.; and PETERSEN, DAVID M. "Religious Involvement and Drug Use Among Urban Adolescents." *Journal for the Scientific Study of Religion* 23 (1984): 109–128.

HIGGINS, P. C., and ALBRECHT, G. L. "Hellfire and Delinquency Revisited." *Social Forces* 55 (1977): 452–458.

HIRSCHI, TRAVIS. *Causes of Delinquency*. Berkeley: University of California Press, 1969.

HIRSCHI, TRAVIS, and STARK, RODNEY. "Hellfire and Delinquency." *Social Problems* 17 (1969): 202–213.

JENSEN, GARY, and ROJEK, DEAN. *Delinquency and Youth Crime*. Prospect Heights, Ill.: Waveland Press, 1992.

JENSEN, GARY F., and ERICKSON, MAYNARD L. "The Religious Factor and Delinquency: Another Look At the Hellfire Hypothesis." *The Religious Dimension*. Edited by Robert Withnow. New York: Academic Press, 1979. Pages 157–177.

KVARACEUS, WILLIAM. "Delinquent Behavior and Church Attendance." *Sociology and Social Research* 28 (1944): 284–289.

LEE, JERRY; RICE, GAIL; and GILLESPIE, V. BAILEY. "Family Worship Patterns and Their Correlation with Adolescent Behavior and Beliefs." *Journal for the Scientific Study of Religion* 36 (1997): 372–381.

LINDEN, RICK. *Criminology*. Toronto: Harcourt Brace, 2000.

LISKA, ALLEN, and MESSNER, STEVEN. *Perspectives on Crime and Deviance*. Upper Saddle River, N.J.: Prentice Hall, 1999.

MIDDLETON, W., and FAY, P. "Attitudes of Delinquent and Non-Delinquent Girls toward Sunday Observance, the Bible and War." *Journal of Educational Psychology* 32 (1941): 555–558.

PEEK, CHARLES W.; CURRY, EVAN W.; and CHALFANT, H. PAUL. "Religiosity and Delinquency Over Time." *Social Sciences Quarterly* 66 (1985): 120–131.

RHODES, ALBERT LEWIS, and REISS, ALBERT J. "The 'Religious Factor' and Delinquent Behavior." *Journal of Research in Crime and Delinquency* 7 (1970): 83–89.

SCHUR, EDWIN. *Our Criminal Society*. Englewood Cliffs, N.J.: Prentice-Hall, 1969.

STACK, STEVEN, and KANAVY, MARY JEANNE. "The Effect of Religion on Forcible Rape." *Journal for the Scientific Study of Religion* 22 (1983): 67–74.

STARK, RODNEY. "Religion as Context: Hellfire and Delinquency One More Time." *Sociology of Religion* 57 (1996): 163–173.

STARK, RODNEY; KENT, LORI; and DOYLE, DANIEL P. "Religion and Delinquency: The Ecology of a 'Lost' Relationship." *Journal of Research in Crime and Delinquency* 18 (1982): 4–24.

SUTHERLAND, EDWARD, and CRESSEY, DONALD. *Criminology*. Philadelphia: Lippincott, 1974.

TITTLE, CHARLES R., and WELCH, MICHAEL R. "Religiosity and Deviance: Toward A Contingency Theory of Constraining Effects." *Social Forces* 61 (1983): 653–682.

WELCH, MICHAEL R.; TITTLE, CHARLES R.; and PETEE, THOMAS. "Religion and Deviance Among Adult Catholics: A Test of the 'Moral Communities' Hypothesis." *Journal for the Scientific Study of Religion* 30 (1991): 159–172.

RESTORATIVE JUSTICE

As the American criminal justice system enters the twenty-first century it continues to be faced with numerous unresolved problems. While some advocate greater retribution and harsher penalties, others continue to believe in the importance of rehabilitating criminals and preventing further crime. These conflicting views have led to an increasing lack of clarity about the basic purpose of sentencing. Is it meant to rehabilitate and change offender behavior? Are criminal sentences meant to deter others from committing crimes? Or should the purpose of sentencing be simply to incapacitate, by removing, the criminal from circulation in society for a set period of time?

Crime victims have traditionally been given virtually no legal standing in the process of doing justice in American courts, even though the justice system exists because individual citizens have been hurt by criminal behavior. Victims of crime feel increasingly frustrated and alienated by the current system of justice. The crime is against "the state" and state interests drive the process of doing justice. Individual crime victims are left on the sidelines with little, if any, input. Crime victims frequently feel twice victimized. First, by the offenders. Second, by the criminal justice system that their tax dollars are paying for. For many crime victims their encounter with the justice system leads to increasing frustration and anger as they are largely ignored, often not even provided with information about the process, court date changes, and the final disposition of the case. Rarely do criminal justice professionals take the time to listen to the fears and concerns of crime victims, seek their input, or invite their participation in holding an offender accountable.

Another problem facing the U.S. criminal justice system is that increasingly harsh punishments have failed to change criminal behavior. If severe punishment and incarceration were effective, America would be one of the safest societies in the world. Many citizens and politicians believe the United States is too lenient with criminals. The fact is, however, that more citizens are locked up in prisons in America, per capita, than in any developed nation in the world other than Russia. In a similar vein, sentences in the United States are far in excess of other democratic Western nations. The United States is the only developed nation to routinely advocate and carry out capital punishment.

Finally, the skyrocketing cost of corrections, and incarceration specifically, is driving a growing number of legislatures and policymakers to reconsider the wisdom of the current retributive system of justice, which relies so heavily upon incarceration, while largely ignoring the needs of crime victims.

The public debate around issues of crime and punishment is often driven by political leadership embracing the conservative or liberal solutions of the past. A significant new development in our thinking about crime and justice is the growing international interest in restorative justice theory (Bazemore and Umbreit; Galaway and Hudson; Van Ness and Strong; Zehr). Restorative justice offers a fundamentally different framework for understanding and responding to crime and victimization. Restorative justice emphasizes the importance of elevating the role of crime victims and community members, holding offenders directly accountable to the people they have violated, restoring the emotional and material losses of victims, and providing a range of opportunities for dialogue, negotiation, and problem solving, which can lead to a greater sense of community safety, conflict resolution, and closure for all involved.

In contrast to the offender-driven nature of our current systems of justice, restorative justice focuses upon three client groups: crime victims, offenders, and community members. It represents a growing international movement with a relatively clear set of values, principles, and guidelines for practice, although still lacking a comprehensive plan to fully replace our current systems of juvenile and criminal justice. This new theory is based upon many old-fashioned principles and it is gaining support among a growing number of correctional policymakers and practitioners, victim advocates, court officials, and law enforcement officials. At its best, restorative justice truly represents a unique way of responding to crime through more active involvement of crime victims and the community. It goes far beyond the traditional liberal and conservative positions of the past by identifying underlying truths and joint interests of all of those concerned about crime policy in a democratic society.

What is restorative justice?

Restorative justice provides an entirely different way of thinking about crime and victimization. Under previous criminal justice paradigms the state was viewed as the primary victim of criminal acts, and victims and offenders played passive roles. Restorative justice recognizes crime as first and foremost being directed against individual people. It assumes that those most affected by crime should have the opportunity to become actively involved in resolving the conflict. The emphasis is on restoration of losses, allowing offenders to take direct responsibility for their actions, and assisting victims in moving beyond their sense of vulnerability and achieving some closure. These goals stand in sharp contrast to those of traditional paradigms, which focused on past criminal behavior through ever-increasing levels of punishment (Bazemore and Walgrave; Umbreit, 1994; Wright). Restorative justice attempts to draw upon the strengths of both offenders and victims, rather than focusing upon their deficits. While denouncing criminal behavior, restorative justice emphasizes the need to treat offenders with respect and to reintegrate them into the larger community in ways that can lead to lawful behavior. It represents a truly different paradigm based upon the following values.

1. Restorative justice is far more concerned about restoration of the victim and victimized community than with ever more costly punishment of the offender.
2. Restorative justice elevates the importance of the victim in the criminal justice process, through increased involvement, input, and services.
3. Restorative justice requires that offenders be held directly accountable to the person and/or community that they victimized.
4. Restorative justice encourages the entire community to be involved in holding the offender accountable and promoting a healing response to the needs of victims and offenders.
5. Restorative justice places greater emphasis on the offender accepting responsibility for his or her behavior, and making amends whenever possible, than on the severity of punishment.
6. Restorative justice recognizes a community responsibility for social conditions that contribute to offender behavior.

The theory of restorative justice provides a blueprint for moving into the twenty-first century by drawing upon much of the wisdom of the past. In eleventh-century England, following the Norman invasion of Britain, a major paradigm shift occurred in which there was a turning away from the well-established understanding of crime as a victim-offender conflict within the context of community. William the Conqueror's son, Henry I, issued a decree securing royal jurisdiction over certain offenses against the king's peace (robbery, arson, murder, theft, and other violent crimes). Prior to this decree crime had always been viewed as conflict between individuals, and the emphasis was on repairing the damage by making amends to the victim.

Restorative justice also draws upon the rich heritage of many recent justice reform movements, including community corrections, victim advocacy, and community policing. The principles of restorative justice are particularly congruent with those of many indigenous traditions, including Native American, Hawaiian, Canadian First Nation people, and the Maori of New Zealand. These principles are also consistent with values emphasized by nearly all of the world religions.

Restorative justice can be expressed through a wide range of policies and practices directed toward offenders and crime victims, including: victim support and advocacy, restitution, community service, victim impact panels, victim-offender mediation, circle sentencing, family group conferencing, community boards that meet with offenders to determine appropriate sanctions, victim empathy classes for offenders, and community policing.

What does restorative justice look like in practice?

As communities move toward a more fully developed restorative justice system, juvenile and criminal justice practice would include the following characteristics, some of which are already in place.

- Victims and families of victims receive support and assistance.

- If they wish, victims have the chance to help determine how the offender will repair the harm done.
- Restitution is more important than other financial obligations of the offender.
- Victim-offender mediation and dialogue is available for victims who want to have a mediation meeting with the offender to discuss how the crime affected them and how the offender can repair the harm. Victim-offender mediations are conducted by trained mediators who are sensitive to the needs of victims and their families.
- Community volunteers work with offenders.
- The community provides work for offenders so they will be able to pay restitution to victims.
- Offenders participate in community service projects that are valued by the community.
- Educational programs for offenders include becoming aware of how victims feel and learning to empathize with victims. Education also helps offenders see their responsibilities as members of a community.
- Offenders face the personal harm caused by their crime through victim-offender mediation, hearing panels or groups of victims or community members talk about their experiences with crime and how crime has affected their lives.
- Orders to repair the harm caused by crime are more important than orders imposed just for punishment.
- The courts and corrections provide annual reports on how reparation is made.
- Community members advise the courts and corrections by being on advisory boards.
- Business and community groups work with offenders to bring them back into the community as the offenders make good on their obligations.
- Faith communities sponsor support groups for offenders trying to change their lives, or for crime victims during the initial crisis stage.
- Offenders end up with greater skills than when they entered the corrections system.
- Community members become involved in reparative probation boards, panels, or peacemaking circles, in which they become directly involved in holding the offender accountable for the harm caused, serving the needs of victims, and strengthening bonds within the community.

How widespread is interest in restorative justice?

The initial conceptualization of restorative justice began in the late 1970s and was first clearly articulated by Howard Zehr. At that time, the discussion of this new paradigm was based largely in North America, with a small network of academicians and practitioners in Europe. Restorative justice was not being considered seriously by mainstream criminal and juvenile justice policymakers and practitioners.

By 1990, an international conference supported by NATO funds was convened in Italy to examine the growing interest in restorative justice throughout the world. Academicians and practitioners from a wide range of countries (Austria, Belgium, Canada, England, Finland, France, Germany, Greece, Italy, Netherlands, Norway, Scotland, Turkey) presented papers related to the development and impact of restorative justice policies and practice. International interest in restorative justice has continued to grow. In 1995, the New Zealand Ministry of Justice issued a working paper on restorative justice for serious consideration as a federal policy. During 1996 and 1997, a group of scholars in North America and Europe interested in restorative justice met in the United States and Belgium to further examine this emerging practice theory. Additional and much larger international conferences have been held in the United States and in Germany. The Council of Europe endorsed the concept of restorative justice through victim-offender mediation in 1999, and a subcommittee of the United Nations has also been examining the concept.

Interest in the United States grew extensively during the mid- to late 1990s. Representing one of the oldest and most visible expressions of restorative justice, the practice of victim-offender mediation (Umbreit, 1995c; Zehr) in which the actual victim and offender meet each other, talk about the impact of the crime, and develop a plan for repairing the harm, is now occurring in more than three hundred communities throughout the United States and at more than one thousand locations in Europe (Umbreit and Greenwood).

Perhaps the strongest indication of how the restorative justice practice of victim-offender mediation is entering the mainstream is seen in the actions of one of its most powerful former skeptics. The American Bar Association has played a major leadership role in the area of civil court mediation for over two decades. After many years of little interest, if not skepticism, the A.B.A. in the summer of 1994 fully endorsed the practice of victim-offender mediation and recommended its development in courts throughout the country.

Another clear expression of the growing support for restorative justice is seen in the National Organization for Victim Assistance's endorsement of "restorative community justice." During the early years of this movement, most victim advocacy groups were quite skeptical. While some still are, however, there is a growing number of victim support organizations actively participating in the restorative justice movement.

Where have restorative justice practices been implemented?

In contrast to many previous reform movements, the restorative justice movement has major, system-wide implications for how justice is done in American society. While initiating restorative justice interventions such as victim-offender mediation, family group conferencing, restorative community service, victim panels, and other forms of victim-offender dialogue or neighborhood dispute resolution is important, restorative justice places a heavy emphasis upon systemic change. Already there are twenty states that have introduced and/or passed legislation promoting a more balanced and restorative juvenile justice system. Thirty other states have restorative justice principles in their mission statements or policy plans. There are individual restorative justice programs in virtually every state, and a growing number of states and local jurisdictions are dramatically changing their criminal and juvenile justice systems to adopt the principles and practices of restorative justice.

An example of systemic change

In 1994, the Vermont Department of Corrections embarked on one of the most ambitious system-wide restorative justice initiatives. Following a public opinion poll that indicated broad dissatisfaction with the criminal justice system and openness to more restorative and community-based responses to nonviolent crime, the department "took a wrecking ball" and demolished a one-hundred-year-old correctional system built upon the options of either prison or probation. They were able to identify up to 50 percent of the current probation caseload that they be-

lieved could be held accountable by Reparative Probation Community Boards made up of citizen volunteers. Instead of traditional probation supervision, a wide range of property offenders would be referred directly to a Reparative Community Board. In dialogue with the offender, the board determines a community-based restorative sanction, oftentimes including victim offender mediation, community service, or meeting with a victim panel. The Department is now encouraging crime victims to be represented on each Reparative Probation Community Board. Few other restorative justice initiatives in the United States represent such a major structural change that clearly elevates the role of community volunteers and crime victims in the process of holding offenders accountable to the community they violated.

An example of a widespread restorative justice program

Victim-offender mediation is a process that provides interested victims of (primarily) property crimes the opportunity to meet the offender, in a safe and structured setting, with the goal of holding the offender directly accountable for their behavior while providing importance assistance and compensation to the victim (Umbreit, 1995b). With the assistance of a trained mediator, the victim can tell the offender how the crime affected them, receive answers to questions they may have, and be directly involved in developing a restitution plan holding the offender accountable for the losses incurred. The offender is able to take direct responsibility for his or her behavior, learn the full impact of what they did, and develop a plan for making amends to the person(s) they violated. Some victim-offender mediation programs are called "victim-offender meetings" or "victim-offender conferences."

While many other types of mediation are largely "settlement driven," victim-offender mediation is primarily "dialogue driven," with the emphasis upon victim healing, offender accountability, and restoration of losses. Contrary to other applications of mediation in which the mediator would first meet the parties during the joint mediation session, in victim-offender mediation a very different process is used based upon a humanistic model of mediation (Umbreit, 1997). This model involves reframing the goal of mediation from settlement to facilitating dialogue and mutual aid; scheduling separate premediation sessions with each party; connecting with the parties but building rapport and trust, while not taking sides; identifying the strengths of each party; using a nondirective style of mediation that creates a safe space for dialogue and accessing the strengths of participants; and recognizing and using the power of silence.

Most victim-offender mediation sessions do in fact result in a signed restitution agreement. This agreement, however, is secondary to the importance of the initial dialogue between the parties; such a dialogue addresses the emotional and informational needs of victims that are central to their healing and to development of victim empathy in the offender, which can reduce future criminal behavior.

Since 1975 when the first victim-offender mediation program was established in Kitchener, Ontario, many criminal justice officials have been quite skeptical about victim interest in meeting the offender. Victim-offender mediation is clearly not appropriate for all crime victims or offenders; practitioners are trained to present it as a voluntary choice for the victim and the offender. With more than twenty years of mediating many thousands of cases throughout North America and Europe, experience has shown that the majority of victims presented with the option of mediation choose to enter the process.

What have we learned from research?

Little empirical data is available on most restorative justice policies and practices, although a growing number of studies are being initiated. For present purposes, findings that have emerged from the study of the oldest and most well-developed restorative justice intervention throughout North America and Europe will be highlighted. The practice of victim-offender mediation with juvenile and adult offenders has been the subject of forty studies in the United States and Europe (Umbreit, 2000). A cross-national study of victim-offender mediation in four states (Umbreit and Coates), four provinces of Canada, and two cities of England (Umbreit, Coates, and Roberts) found high levels of victim and offender satisfaction with the mediation process and outcome. Victims who met the juvenile offender were significantly more likely to have been satisfied with how the justice system handled their case than similar victims who did not participate in mediation, and they also were significantly less fearful of being revictimized, after the mediation session. Offenders in mediation were significantly more likely to successfully

complete restitution than were similar offenders who did not meet their victim. A large study of nearly thirteen hundred juvenile offenders (Nugent, Umbreit, Wiinamaki, and Paddock, 2000) found a 32 percent reduction in recidivism among those juvenile offenders who participated in a mediation session with their victim.

Conclusion

The restorative justice movement is having an increasing impact upon criminal justice system policymakers and practitioners throughout the world. As a relatively young reform effort, the restorative justice movement and the practice of victim-offender mediation, as its oldest empirically grounded intervention, hold great promise as we enter the twenty-first century. By drawing upon many traditional values of the past, and from many different cultures, we have the opportunity to build a far more accountable, understandable, and healing system of justice that can lead to a greater sense of community through active victim and citizen involvement in restorative initiatives.

MARK UMBREIT

See also AMNESTY AND PARDON; COMPARATIVE CRIMINAL LAW AND ENFORCEMENT: PRELITERATE SOCIETIES; INFORMAL DISPOSITIONS; PUNISHMENT; REHABILITATION; RETRIBUTIVISM; SENTENCING: ALTERNATIVES; VICTIMS' RIGHTS.

BIBLIOGRAPHY

BAZEMORE, G., and UMBREIT, M. S. "Rethinking the Sanctioning Function in Juvenile Court: Retributive or Restorative Responses to Youth Crime." *Crime & Delinquency* 41, no. 3 (1995): 296–316.

BAZEMORE, G., and WALGRAVE, L. *Restorative Juvenile Justice: Repairing the Harm of Youth Crime.* Monsey, N.Y.: Criminal Justice Press, 1999.

BRAITHWAITE, JOHN. "Restorative Justice." *Crime & Justice: A Review of Research* 25 (1999): 1–127.

GALAWAY, B., and HUDSON, J. *Restorative Justice: An International Perspective.* Monsey, N.Y.: Criminal Justice Press, 1996.

NUGENT, W. R.; UMBREIT, M. S.; WIINAMAKI, L.; and PADDOCK, J. B. "Participation in Victim-Offender Mediation and Re-Offense: Successful Replications?" *Journal of Research on Social Work Practice* 11, no. 1 (2000): 5–23.

UMBREIT, M. S. *The Handbook on Victim Offender Mediation: An Essential Guide for Practice and Re-*

search. San Francisco, Calif.: Jossey-Bass Publishers, 2001.

———. *Victim Meets Offender: The Impact of Restorative Justice & Mediation*. Monsey, N.Y.: Criminal Justice Press, 1994.

———. "The Development and Impact of Victim-Offender Mediation in the United States." *Mediation Quarterly* 12, no. 3 (1995): 263–276.

———. *Mediating Interpersonal Conflicts: A Pathway to Peace*. West Concord, Minn.: CPI Publishing, 1995.

———. "Humanistic Mediation: A Transformative Journey of Peacemaking." *Mediation Quarterly* 14, no. 3 (1997): 201–213.

UMBREIT, M. S., and COATES, R. B. "Cross-Site Analysis of Victim Offender Mediation in Four States." *Crime & Delinquency* 39, no. 4 (1993): 565–585.

UMBREIT, M. S.; COATES, R. B.; and ROBERTS, A. W. "The Impact of Victim-Offender Mediation: A Cross-National Perspective." *Mediation Quarterly* 17, no. 3 (2000): 215–229.

UMBREIT, M. S., and GREENWOOD, J. "National Survey of Victim Offender Mediation Programs in the United States." *Mediation Quarterly* 16, no. 3 (1999): 235–251.

VAN NESS, D., and STRONG, K. *Restoring Justice*. Cincinnati, Ohio: Anderson Publishing Company, 1997.

WRIGHT, M. *Justice for Victims and Offenders*. Philadelphia, Pa.: Open University Press, 1991.

ZEHR, H. *Changing Lenses, A New Focus for Crime and Justice*. Scottsdale, Pa.: Herald Press, 1990.

RETRIBUTIVISM

Retributivism is first and foremost a theory of punishment. It answers the question, Why do we have punishment institutions? The answer it gives is very simple: for the retributivist, we are justified in punishing persons when and only when they deserve to be punished. To avoid question-begging circularity, "deserve to be punished" in the above definition cannot simply mean "ought to be punished." Rather, to deserve punishment means to be morally blameworthy. The retributivist thus believes that the sole just end of punishment is to make the morally blameworthy suffer the sanctions we call punishment.

Contasting theories of punishment are the utilitarian and the rehabilitative theories of punishment. Typically, the utilitarian regards punishment as an evil but justifies it by the achievement of the greater good of crime prevention; punishment achieves this greater good through deterrence or incapacitation of would-be criminals (Bentham). Rehabilitationists are often merely utilitarians with a kinder, gentler crime prevention program, reform and education substituting for deterrence and incapacitation; as a truly distinct theory, however, the rehabilitationist regards crime as a disease that is not the fault of the criminal and punishment becomes a cure justified by duties of *distributive* justice to those unfortunate enough to suffer this disease (Menninger).

In addition to these three dominant theories justifying punishment institutions, there are also "mixed theories" that combine two of these three theories (Moore, 1984). The most widely embraced mixed theory holds that punishment must achieve both the utilitarian goal of crime prevention and the retributive goal of punishing those who deserve it in order to be justified (von Hirsch). Because the desert of the offender is a necessary condition of a just punishment under the mixed theory, this theory is sometimes called "weak" or "negative" retributivism (Mackie). These are misnomers because what is essential to retributivism is that the desert of the offender to be a *sufficient* reason to punish; a theory that regards such desert as only *necessary* leaves out what is so distinctive (and so troubling to many) about retributivism.

As a "theory of punishment," retributivism is said to answer the question, Why punish anyone? The question is best interpreted to be a very general one, asking after the justification for the entire criminal law and the institutions that serve it. Retributivism is thus, first and foremost, a theory about the legitimate end served by penal institutions. Retributivism, like other theories of punishment, is a theory about why we should have the criminal law (Moore, 1997). As such, retributivism also purports to answer more discrete questions about criminal law, such as questions about the correct doctrinal triggers for liability and questions about how much offenders should be punished for certain crimes when done with certain levels of culpability. Retributivism also has strong implications for the question of what should be prohibited by penal law; with certain suitable assumptions, a retributivist theory of punishment yields the legal moralist theory of criminal legislation according to which all and only morally wrongful behavior should be forbidden by the criminal law (Moore, 1997). On this latter theory, if a certain sort of behavior is morally wrong, that is a prima facie reason to criminalize it (although other factors may ultimately bar criminalization); if behavior is not morally wrong that is a very good reason not to criminalize it (for no retributive justice is achieved by the punishment of those who do good or at least do no wrong).

There have been famous attempts to restrict the range of questions properly answerable by a retributivist theory. John Rawls (1955) and H. L. A. Hart (1968) urged that retributivism answered the judge's question, Why should this offender be punished? but that the more general questions of why we punish anyone or what should be made criminal were to be answered on the basis of another theory, utilitarianism. The problem for this view was that no good reason can be given for restricting the range of properly answerable questions for either theory. If utilitarianism is a good theory of why and what we should punish, why is it not similarly a good theory of how punishment should be distributed in particular cases? If retributivism is a good theory for why some judge should punish poor old Jones, why is it not an equally good theory for why we should punish anyone like Jones in the relevant respects (namely, equally deserving of punishment)? The fact is that the questions answered by a theory of punishment like retributivism refuse to be cabined in this artificial way. Retributivism is both a general theory of punishment and also a theory about all the more discrete questions about the criminal law, right down to the question of whether and how much each particular offender should be punished.

For a variety of reasons retributivism has probably been the least understood of the various theories of punishment. Part of the bafflement about retributivism stems from its stark simplicity: it essentially asserts that we should punish because and only because culpable wrongdoers deserve it. This simplicity has lead many to seek to divine some other good that giving just deserts causes, inasmuch as this seems to make the theory more satisfyingly complex. For example, it is said that if the state punishes those who deserve it, that prevents vengeful citizens from taking the law into their own hands. This prevention of vigilante justice is then presented as the real good of the retributivism (Marshall). Alternatively, it is urged that if the state punishes those who deserve it, this will satisfy citizens' need for feeling that they are not dupes in restraining themselves from criminal actions. Such punishment thus serves the goods of satisfying a widespread preference that the guilty be punished and it keeps down dissatisfactions (about

unpunished free riders) arising among the law-abiding (Stephens).

Retributivism is inconsistent with all of these theories. Essential to retributivism is the thesis that punishing those who deserve it is an intrinsic good, that is, something good in itself and not good because it causes something else. All of these theories make punishment of the guilty merely instrumentally good, that is, good only because it causes: the diminishment of vigilante violence; the satisfaction of citizen preferences for punishment; the maintenance of a sense of social cohesion; or the prevention of crime by those not angered at the sight of others breaking the social contract with impunity. One cannot hold that punishing the guilty is good only because doing so produces these other goods, and still remain a retributivist. Retributivism is a much simpler theory: punishment is justified by the simple moral fact that culpable wrongdoers deserve it.

Retributivism is also sometimes confused with a family of theories that urge that punishment of the guilty is justified because it expresses society's moral outrage at what was done, because it denounces the crime and the criminal or because it communicates to the criminal society's disapproval (Feinberg; Hampton in Murphy and Hampton). On their face, these theories are doubly puzzling: first, why is it plausible to hold that expressing, denouncing, or communicating is much of a good, indeed, so good that the catharsis achieved could justify something as harmful as punishment administered to the offenders? Second, if these are plausible goods, their justification remains unclear since we could as easily undertake dramatic shaming ceremonies where the message is given but the harsh treatment and suffering of offenders is not (Feinberg). In any case, to the extent that these implausible theories reduce the punishment of the guilty to a mere instrumental good in the service of social expression, they are not to be equated with retributivism.

Closer to retributivism are theories that turn punishment into an instrument of victim revenge. Such theories urge that the desert of offenders gives the state the right to punish them, but it is only the desire of the victims for revenge that justifies the state in doing what it has a right to do, namely, punish the guilty. Often adherents of these theories urge that it takes very little to justify the state in punishing those who deserve it, and the slightest satisfaction provided the victim of a crime by punishment of her wrongdoer is reason enough (Murphy, 1990).

Such a view of punishment as an engine for victim-directed vengeance is not utilitarian, but neither is it retributive. A retributivist believes that justice is served by punishing the guilty and thus, the desert of an offender not only gives the state the right to punish him but also the duty to do so. Making victims feel good is no part of retributive justice, although the retributivist may regard it as a welcome side effect of punishment along with crime prevention. Retributive justice is achieved by punishing the guilty even if the victims of such guilty offenders all wish forgiveness and mercy upon their offenders.

How is retributivism to be justified?

Once the essential simplicity of retributivism is fully grasped, it may seem that little can be done in order to justify belief in it (Bedau). Indeed, if justification of some practice as right must consist in showing how the practice produces good consequences, the retributivism cannot be justified (Benn and Peters). In this retributivism and utilitarianism are ultimately alike, for once the utilitarian has shown how a practice maximizes utility there can be no further good that utility causes that makes utility good. It is essential to both theories that retribution and utility be intrinsic goods, and the moment one reduces them to instrumental goods—goods only because productive of other states of affairs—then the resulting theory can no longer be retributive or utilitarian.

It is thus no criticism of retributivism that it cannot be justified instrumentally, for ultimately all ethical theories are in the same boat; all ethical theories must hold something to be intrinsically good. Retributivism differs from utilitarianism in this respect only in what it regards as intrinsically good.

Fortunately none of this consigns either the utilitarian or the retributivist to some kind of irrationalism about their ethics. Fortunately instrumental modes of justification do not exhaust the possibilities with respect to justifying a moral principle. The trick is to show how retribution is good without relying on the consequences of retribution to make it good.

It is helpful to step away from retributive justice for a moment to see the possibilities here. Consider John Rawls's deservedly famous justification of his two principles of distributive justice (1971). Rawls urged that his two principles of justice were justified in two distinct ways. First, the principles are the best general expression of the mass of our "considered judgments" on more particular matters, such as the irrelevance of inherited wealth for distribution of benefits. Second, the principles are the ones that follow from other more general principles, what Rawls called principles of fairness. Neither of these modes of justification reduced distributive justice for Rawls into a merely instrumental good; this, because neither mode of justification relies on the capacity of distributive justice to produce some other states of affairs. Rather, the distributive principles are shown to be just in that they describe at a general level more particular considered judgments about what justice requires and in that they are the principles that would be chosen in a fair procedure.

Both of these modes of justification are open to the retributivist. Retributivists have long sought to rely on considered judgments in particular cases about what justice requires in order to show how only the retributivist principle can explain such judgments. Imagine, Kant urged, an island society about to dissolve with one vicious murderer yet unpunished. The dissolution of the society removes all of the obvious utilitarian reasons to punish, so that if the facts that make the killer so depraved move one to judge that he should be punished, such judgment can only be explained on retributivist grounds.

A variety of objections have surfaced about this mode of justifying retributivism (Dolinko). The most serious is the charge that our considered judgments in such cases are contaminated by irrational and unsavory emotions. Nietzsche cataloged these as the emotions of fear, resentment, cowardice, envy, sadism, and so on, all lumped under the French term *ressentiment* (Nietzsche). The objection is that such emotional origins of our retributive judgments make such judgments nonvirtuous to hold and thus unreliable epistemically, whereas our particular judgments of distributive justice can be relied on because stemming from the virtuous emotions of compassion, empathy, and fellow-feeling.

Retributivists have made two responses to this objection. About our third-person judgments about others' wrongful behavior, retributivists have sought to distinguish virtuous emotions of "moral hatred"—the hatred anyone should feel if she identifies both with other people who are victims and with morality itself—from the nonvirtuous emotions of *ressentiment* that Nietzsche described (Murphy and Hampton; Pillsbury). Our particular judgments about what punishment others deserve are then said to stem from these more virtuous emotions and thus to be reliable epistemically. Similarly, retributivists have sought to show how our first-person judgments about how we should be treated if we have culpably hurt another stem from the virtuous emotion of guilt and thus can be relied on in justifying retributivism (Moore, 1997).

Continuing the analogy to Rawls, the second mode of justification proceeds by showing how the retributive principle is part and parcel of some yet more general principle of justice or fairness. The history of retributivist literature is not reassuring on this matter, for much of what has been said of a general sort is too metaphorical to provide any real grounding for retributivism. Thus, retributivists have argued that unless the guilty receive their due: the blood guilt of the whole people will not be expiated; the moral order will not be restored; the offender's debt to society will remain unpaid; the control of the victim by the crime or the criminal will not be released; and so forth (Fletcher). If one presses these metaphors of blood guilt, moral orders out of whack, debt, control, and the like, they cash out to no more than that culpable wrongdoers deserve to be punished (Moore, 1999). They thus give no more support for that essential retributivist tenet than it gives itself.

The dominant contemporary exception among this mortuary of dead metaphors about retributivism is the attempt to justify the retributivist principle by reference to a general principle of fair play and unjust enrichment. Herbert Morris and others (Scher) have long argued that the prohibitions of the criminal law set a minimum of what is required for a scheme of social cooperation, that criminals unfairly appropriate to themselves the benefits both of their violation and of others' restraint, and that fairness demands some price (in the form of punishment) to be paid for this unjust enrichment. The aim is to show how the retributivist principle follows from a yet more general principle of fairness.

Whether either of these modes of justifying retributivism has succeeded, or can succeed, is not something on which there is any consensus. Issue had been joined at all points between retributivists and their critics, and it is safe to say that no resolution will be seen in the foreseeable future. What is surprising is how much retributivism has made a comeback among contemporary criminal law theorists, political philosophers, and lawmakers. For most of the twentieth century the standard educated view was that retributivism was moribund, but in the last three decades of that century the theory came very much alive.

The institutional implications of retributivism

Retributivism is often associated in the minds of many people with particular institutional arrangements, like the principle of *lex talionis* (an eye for an eye and a tooth for a tooth), or even more particularly, with the death penalty. While there certainly have been famous retributivists who favored such institutions, nothing essential to retributivism requires them. A retributivist is committed to the idea that the punishment must "fit the crime" in the sense of being proportionate to the degree of wrong done and to the culpability with which it is done; but he need not interpret such principle of proportionate punishment to require that a harm be visited on the criminal just like the harm he visited onto his victim. In addition, a retributivist can easily believe that no one deserves to be put to death at the hands of the state and thus be an opponent, not a proponent, of the death penalty.

Despite this, retributivism does give rise to a distinctive mode of justifying particular institutions within the criminal law such as the death penalty. The retributivist will urge, for example, that the debate about whether the death penalty deters crime is simply irrelevant to the question of whether the death penalty is justified. The only relevant question, according to retributivism, is whether one person can be so morally reprehensible as to deserve to die. If that question is answered affirmatively, then prima facie the death penalty is justified (because the state has the duty to give offenders what they deserve, according to retributivism).

Retributivism has similar implications for other institutions within the criminal law. Indeed, on every doctrinal issue, whether going to liability or to sanction, the retributivist will urge that the relevant policy is retributive, asking in each instance what such a class of persons deserve. Should intentional but nondeliberative killers be punished less than those who premeditate and deliberate about their killings? The relevant question, according to retributivism, is whether this factor makes such a difference in moral blameworthiness that intentional killers should be segregated into two classes (or "degrees") of murderers by this factor alone. Should those who kill under threats of serious harm to themselves be either wholly or partially excused? The relevant question, according to the retributivist, is the degree of moral courage we can fairly expect from people in those coercive circumstances; if we should each die rather than kill an innocent, then those whose behavior fails to live up to that standard are morally blameworthy and deserve punishment in proportion to the degree of their blameworthiness.

Much more determinate institutional implications than these can of course be spun out of retributive theory, but what those implications are depends on the kind of theory of moral responsibility that is accepted by the retributivist. Retributivists differ considerably among themselves on this issue, which is usually termed the "desert-basis" issue. There are three leading views on the touchstone of moral blameworthiness. One view is that there are two ingredients determining our moral blameworthiness, the kind of wrong we do and the culpable mental state in which we do it. On this view, the worse the consequences we bring about by our actions and the less the justification for bringing about such consequences, the more wrongful our actions. The more wrongful the action we either intend, foresee, or risk doing, and the less excuse we have for choosing to act nonetheless, the more culpable we are. The two together—wrongdoing and culpability—jointly determine an offender's overall moral blameworthiness.

A second view restricts blameworthiness to culpability alone. On this view what determines our blameworthiness is the degree of wrong we think we are doing in our own mind, not whether we actually succeed in doing such a wrong in the real world. Those who without justification or excuse shoot at another, trying to kill him, are as morally blameworthy if they miss as if they hit and kill their victim.

A third view regards character as the ultimate touchstone of moral blameworthiness. Character consists of our long-term traits, like generosity, courage, compassion. On this view what makes us morally blameworthy is bad character. Wrongful actions and culpable intentions usually evidence bad character, so these items are not irrelevant on this view; such items are merely evidential, however, for what is constitutive of blameworthiness is character and character alone.

The actual institutional implications of retributivism depends heavily on which of these three views of moral responsibility the retributivist adopts. In the Anglo-American penal system the first view has by and large predominated, but in the academic literature it has been seriously challenged by the other two views, particularly the second. All such views can properly be fitted within the retributivist theory.

MICHAEL S. MOORE

See also DETERRENCE; INCAPACITATION; PUNISHMENT; REHABILITATION.

BIBLIOGRAPHY

BEDAU, HUGO. "Retribution and the Theory of Punishment." *Journal of Philosophy* 75 (1978): 601–620.

BENN, S. I., and PETERS, R. S. *Social Principles and the Democratic State*. London: Allen and Unwin, 1959.

BENTHAM, JEREMY. *An Introduction to the Principles of Morals and Legislation (1823)*. New York: Hafner, 1948.

DOLINKO, DAVID. "Some Thoughts About Retributivism." *Ethics* 101 (1991): 537–559.

FEINBERG, JOEL. "The Expressive Function of Punishment." *Doing and Deserving*. Edited by Joel Feinberg. Princeton, N.J.: Princeton University Press, 1971.

FLETCHER, GEORGE. "The Place of the Victim in the Theory of Retribution." *Buffalo Criminal Law Review* 3 (1999): 51–64.

HART, H. L. A. *Punishment and Responsibility*. Oxford, U.K.: Oxford University Press, 1968.

KANT, IMMANUEL. *The Metaphysical Elements of Justice*. Translated by John Ladd. Indianapolis: Bobbs-Merrill, 1965.

MACKIE, J. "Morality and the Retributive Emotions." *Criminal Justice Ethics* 1 (1982): 3–10.

MARSHALL, THURGOOD. Concurring in *Gregg v. Georgia*, 428 U.S. 153 (1976).

MENNINGER, KARL. *The Crime of Punishment*. New York: Viking Press, 1968.

MOORE, MICHAEL S. *Law and Psychiatry: Rethinking the Relationship*. Cambridge, U.K.: Cambridge University Press, 1984.

———. *Placing Blame: A General Theory of the Criminal Law*. Oxford, U.K.: Clarendon Press, 1997.

———. "Victims and Retribution." *Buffalo Criminal Law Review* 3 (1999): 101–125.

MORRIS, HERBERT. "Persons and Punishment." *The Monist*. 52 (1968): 475–501.

MURPHY, JEFFRIE. "Getting Even: The Role of the Victim." *Social Philosophy and Policy* 7 (1990): 209–225.

MURPHY, JEFFRIE, and HAMPTON, JEAN. *Forgiveness and Mercy*. Cambridge, U.K.: Cambridge University Press, 1988.

NIETZSCHE, FRIEDRICH. *On the Genealogy of Morals (1887)*. Translated by Walter Kaufmann. New York: Vintage, 1969.

PILLSBURY, SAMUEL. "Emotional Justice: Moralizing the Passions of Criminal Punishment." *Cornell Law Review* 74 (1989): 655–710.

RAWLS, JOHN. "Two Concepts of Rules." *The Philosophical Review* 64 (1955): 3–32.

———. *A Theory of Justice*. Cambridge, Mass.: Harvard University Press, 1971.

SCHER, GEORGE. *Desert*. Princeton: Princeton University Press, 1987.

STEPHENS, SIR JAMES. *Liberty, Equality, Fraternity*. Cambridge, U.K.: Cambridge University Press, 1967.

VON HIRSCH, ANDREW. *Doing Justice*. New York: Hill and Wang, 1976.

RICO (RACKETEER INFLUENCED AND CORRUPT ORGANIZATIONS ACT)

The Racketeer Influenced and Corrupt Organizations Act (RICO) is a controversial and innovative federal penal statute. Adopted as part of the Organized Crime Control Act of 1970, RICO created several new crimes, revived the concept of property forfeiture as a punishment for crimes, and instituted a new civil cause of action that has generated a large volume of litigation.

Origins

RICO grew out of concern about the infiltration of legitimate institutions by organized crime. After this problem was highlighted in the 1967 report of a presidential commission on crime, a number of bills were introduced in Congress that would have prohibited the investment of money derived from criminal activities into a legitimate business. In addition to making such investment a crime, these bills used the model of the antitrust laws to permit civil law suits by businesses injured by such infiltration, and to divest criminals of their ill-gotten interests in legitimate businesses by requiring forfeiture of those interests to the government. Aspects of several such bills were eventually combined into what ultimately passed as RICO. The actual language adopted by Congress, however, was susceptible to much broader application.

Crimes

RICO's broadest and most-used section prohibits conducting the affairs of any "enterprise" (defined broadly to include just about any form of human endeavor) through a "pattern of racketeering activity" (defined as two or more criminal acts from an extremely broad list, that are related to each other, that do or threaten to persist over a period of time). This language makes it a crime for those with a significant role in operating any business, government office, labor union, social or political organization, or informal grouping to commit a series of crimes in furtherance of that organization's goals or by using the organization's resources. Indeed, since the Supreme Court has held that enterprises are covered whether or not they are legitimate (*United States v. Turkette*, 452 U.S. 576 (1981)), RICO permits the prosecution of members of an organized crime family or other criminal gang or association for conducting its affairs.

Other new crimes created by RICO, which have been rarely used by prosecutors, derive from the original concept of preventing criminal elements from gaining entry into legitimate business. The relevant provisions prohibit acquiring or maintaining an interest in any "enterprise" (other than by purchase of a trivial interest via the stock market), by investing the proceeds of loansharking or a pattern of racketeering activity (for example, investing the profits from narcotics dealing in a legitimate business), or by using such criminal means (for example, by the use of threats of violence to extort an interest in a business from its owner). In addition, RICO also prohibits conspiring to commit any of these new crimes.

Effects

One might wonder what is valuable or innovative about prohibiting actions that are by definition already crimes. The answer is largely procedural. By defining as a single offense the commission of a series of distinct crimes, RICO avoids a variety of traditional procedural, evidentiary, and jurisdictional rules that tend to discourage prosecuting separate offenses together. For example, RICO includes as "predicate acts" that may form part of a pattern of racketeering such crimes as murder, robbery, bribery, and arson, which normally are violations only of state law, thus permitting them to be investigated and prosecuted by federal officials in federal court.

When criminal organizations operate in several states, their offenses would normally have to be prosecuted separately in the states of federal judicial districts where the individual crimes occurred; however, by defining these offenses as part of a single pattern, the entire pattern can be prosecuted together as a single crime in any federal district where one of the predicate acts occurred. Procedural rules limiting the joinder of crimes or of defendants in a single indictment are inapplicable once the separate crimes or offenders are conceptualized as part of a single "racketeering enterprise" jointly committing the same crime. Evidentiary rules that seek to avoid "guilt by association" or easy conviction of the "usual suspects" by limiting reference to a defendant's prior convictions, other criminal acts, or associations with other criminals or criminal organizations are similarly inapplicable where the commission of a number of crimes, in association with other members of an enterprise, is the very crime to be proved. Where the statute of limitations precludes prosecution of crimes committed years ago, those crimes may often still be made part of a lengthy pattern of racketeering offenses, so long as at least one predicate racketeering act was committed within the limitations period. These and other effects of defining the RICO pattern as a single crime have facilitated the prosecution of cases involving members of the Mafia and other criminal groups. Critics of RICO have charged that the resulting "megatrials" of large numbers of defendants for a wide variety of separate crimes have diluted traditional protections against wrongful conviction, by complicating the task of jurors; making trials longer, more burdensome, and more expensive for defendants; and by permitting unfair "spillover" of inferences of guilt from one crime or defendant to other charges that are less well established, or to other defendants against whom the evidence is weak.

RICO has not been used only against organized crime groups. Because corporations, labor unions, and government offices are also "enterprises" as defined in RICO, the law has been used in cases of business fraud, labor corruption, and bribery of police or other government officials as well. In these cases, the criminal schemes are usually less wide-ranging than in the organized crime cases, and the cases typically could be brought within conventional procedural rules. However, the serious penalties available under RICO, including forfeiture remedies, and the increased stigma of a conviction for "racketeer-

ing," have made RICO an attractive tool for prosecutors in serious white-collar criminal cases. Critics of these prosecutions have pointed out that the expansive definition of a pattern of racketeering activity provides little if any definitional limitation on the kinds of fraud or corruption cases that can be brought under RICO, thus leaving the choice of which cases are "serious" enough to merit RICO penalties entirely to the discretion of prosecutors.

Penalties

RICO authorizes severe penalties of fine and imprisonment. The maximum punishment for an individual on a single RICO charge is imprisonment for twenty years (life if any of the predicate acts charged, such as murder, would permit such a punishment), and a fine of $250,000 or twice the proceeds of the offense. In addition, RICO revived the punishment of forfeiture of property, which before 1970 had been little used in American criminal law.

RICO imposes, as a mandatory penalty, a judgment of forfeiture to the United States government not only of any proceeds or property derived from the proceeds of the crime, but also of any interest the defendant holds in the enterprise, or any property of any kind that provides a source of influence over the enterprise. The latter provisions, rooted in the statute's original purpose of preventing criminal control of legitimate business, aim not only to punish the offender, but also to deny continuing power over an enterprise to anyone who has corrupted it to criminal ends.

Such forfeitures can be extremely harsh, and even disproportionate to the offense. For example, if an executive defrauds a number of customers of one division of a giant corporation, the forfeiture would encompass all of the offender's stockholdings in the company, whether the dollar value of those holdings was large or small in proportion to the losses caused by the fraud. In one Supreme Court case, the proprietor of an adult bookstore, convicted under RICO for selling a number of obscene books, forfeited to the government his entire store, including a large volume of nonobscene material. The Court held that since all the books were now property of the government, they could be destroyed, whether or not they were obscene (*Alexander v. United States*, 509 U.S. 544 (1993)).

A number of procedural provisions relating to forfeiture increase the impact of the forfeiture remedy. For example, RICO permits the government to obtain a restraining order in advance of trial, freezing any of the defendant's assets that are subject to forfeiture. Thus, before a jury has evaluated the case against the defendant, he can be deprived of the use of his property, and hampered from using that property to obtain legal counsel. Moreover, a judgment of forfeiture "relates back" to the time the property was obtained. Thus, if the court eventually finds that property was obtained by means of a RICO violation, the property is declared to have been the government's from the moment the violation occurred. Consequently, it can be recovered not only from the defendant, but also from anyone else to whom it had been transferred. Even someone who received a bona fide payment for legitimate goods or services from funds held to be racketeering proceeds would lose them to the government, unless he or she had no reasonable cause to believe that the property was forfeitable. Since defense lawyers in particular are on notice that the government has brought racketeering charges, legal fees paid to them could be recovered by the government. This possibility can complicate a RICO defendant's ability to retain counsel.

Civil remedies

In addition to these criminal law provisions, RICO also authorizes civil suits, both by the government and by private individuals who are economically injured by a RICO violation. (Somewhat curiously, no provision is made for suits by plaintiffs who were physically injured by racketeering acts.)

The government has found civil RICO to be a valuable tool against labor racketeering and other forms of criminal corruption. Once the government establishes that an enterprise has been the subject of RICO offenses, courts are permitted to enter wide-ranging equitable orders, including banning individuals from participating in the management of the enterprise, or reorganizing or even dissolving the enterprise itself. Unlike these provisions, corrupt labor unions have been ordered to democratize, and to operate under the supervision of court-appointed independent monitors with the power to investigate its affairs, and officials found to be corrupt or to have associated with organized crime have been banned from holding union office.

Private civil actions under RICO have become extremely common and extremely controversial. Unlike most ordinary civil suits, suits for violation of RICO permit recovery not merely of compensation for losses, but for treble damages and attorneys' fees. The attraction of these enhanced remedies, as well as of obtaining access to federal court, has led plaintiffs in ordinary business disputes to exercise considerable ingenuity to cast their claims not in ordinary terms of contract, tort, or common law fraud, but as violations of the federal mail, wire, bank, and securities fraud statutes, which are predicate acts under RICO. The broad coverage of these statutes permits many claims to be formulated in this fashion, leading to the escalation of many ordinary business disputes into "racketeering" cases. (Such claims became so widespread in the securities industry that Congress amended RICO in 1995 to prohibit civil suits based on securities fraud, except where the defendants had previously been criminally convicted.)

Civil RICO actions have also been brought against political activist groups, such as anti-abortion demonstrators and animal rights activists, whose tactics sometimes verge on or cross over into violence (*National Organization for Women, Inc. v. Scheidler,* 510 U.S. 249 (1994)). Critics of such actions argue that the potential for imposing extensive litigation costs and treble damages on activists who may have a tenuous connection to actual perpetrators of violence, poses a threat to legitimate dissent. Defenders point out the violent activity is as dangerous in pursuit of a political enterprise as of an economic one, and that RICO actions can be an effective tool against organizations that encourage terrorism.

Influences

RICO was little noticed, and little used, in the first ten years after its adoption. During the 1980s, however, as prosecutors and civil plaintiffs discovered its potential, the number of RICO cases increased dramatically. The many successful RICO prosecutions of organized crime figures and corrupt civil servants and businessmen, and the use of civil RICO as a tool of labor law reform, provided significant law enforcement benefits. Moreover, RICO has had an influence in the creation of other laws. The use of forfeiture as a punishment for crime, pioneered in RICO, has been extended more broadly to narcotics and money laundering offenses. The extensive use of RICO forfeiture also led to a renewal of interest in *civil* forfeiture remedies, which have also been greatly expanded. RICO's original concern with the introduction of criminal proceeds into the legitimate economy was developed further in the money-laundering statutes, which also follow the RICO pattern of using traditional crimes as the predicates for more complex prohibitions. Finally, the increased use of proactive investigative techniques, such as electronic surveillance and infiltration by undercover agents and informants, coupled with RICO prosecutions that present the results of such investigations in full context, has contributed to a more effective understanding of crime in terms of enterprises and criminal careers, rather than simply as isolated instances of illegal behavior.

On the debit side, RICO is complex and overbroad. The private civil action has generated excessive litigation, while having little effect on serious criminal conduct. Because RICO defines its prohibitions not in terms of specific behaviors, but in terms of differing relationships of broad abstract concepts like the "enterprise" and the "pattern of racketeering," its coverage is broad and somewhat elusive. In the area of fraud and corruption cases, the severe penalties and federal jurisdiction provided by RICO can be invoked or declined by prosecutors almost at will. Even with respect to criminal groups, the existence of an organized enterprise, as distinct from shifting combinations of loosely acquainted offenders who join and dissolve to commit ad hoc, opportunistic offenses, is sometimes in the eye of the beholder. It is hardly clear that the severe penalties and dangerous dilutions of traditional procedural rights are justified in all such cases.

GERARD E. LYNCH

See also BLACKMAIL AND EXTORTION; CIVIL AND CRIMINAL DIVIDE; CONSPIRACY; CRIMINAL CAREERS; FEDERAL CRIMINAL LAW ENFORCEMENT; GUNS, REGULATION OF; ORGANIZED CRIME; WHITE-COLLAR CRIME: HISTORY OF AN IDEA.

BIBLIOGRAPHY

BLAKEY, G. ROBERT. "Foreword to Symposium: The Twentieth Anniversary of the Racketeer Influenced and Corrupt Organizations Act: Debunkers RICO's Myriad Myths." *St. John's Law Review* 701, no. 64 (1990).

BLAKEY, G. ROBERT, and GETTINGS, B. "Racketeer Influenced and Corrupt Organizations (RICO) Basic Concepts—Criminal and Civil Remedies." *Temple Law Quarterly* 1009, no. 53 (1980).

BRENNER, SUSAN W. "RICO, LLE, and Other Complex Crimes: The Transformation of Criminal Law." 2 vol. *Bill of Rights Journal* 239 (1993).

COFFEY, PAUL E. "The Selection, Analysis and Approval of Federal RICO Prosecutors." *Notre Dame Law Review* 1035, no. 65 (1990).

LYNCH, GERARD E. "RICO: The Crime of Being a Criminal." Parts 1 and 2: *Columbia Law Review* 87 (1987): 661. Parts 3 and 4: *Columbia Law Review* 87 (1987): 920.

TARLOW, BARRY. "RICO Revisited." *Georgia Law Review* 291, no. 17 (1983).

RIOTS: BEHAVIORAL ASPECTS

Despite several decades of research on crowd behavior and collective violence, the definition of the term *riot* remains the subject of intense debate. The traditional view of rioting, and crowd behavior in general, formulated by scholars such as Gustave LeBon and others, suggests they are episodes of irrational destruction carried out by a few antisocial individuals and a relatively homogenous mass of followers. Rioting has thus been portrayed as a kind of collective madness. Such perceptions continue to be held by some law enforcement agents (Stott and Reicher) and are often echoed by the media as well, generating public support for police suppression of these events. By contrast, several contemporary researchers argue that riot behavior is not inherently irrational, nor are the crowds that characterize riots necessarily homogenous (Turner and Killian; McPhail). Furthermore, in light of the 1960s civil disturbances, scholars on the left have sought to redefine riots as the rational expression of grievances by the politically disenfranchised, considering them a form of protest (Fogelson; McAdam). In place of the term "riot," activists and their allies often substitute the words "rebellion" or "uprising," underscoring the protest nature of these events.

Riots display a unique combination of properties that distinguish them from other forms of crowd behavior such as protests and celebrations. First, riots are acts of collective violence. While protests and celebrations may take on a violent dimension, and thus become riots, most do not escalate to the level of widespread collective violence. Thus, violence is a key factor that sets riots apart from other forms of crowd behavior. Second, riots are generally unplanned. While protests and celebrations are typically slated to happen at some appointed time and place, riots most often emerge in haphazard fashion with the formation of an assembled crowd that then turns violent. Even if the assembling of the crowd is prearranged, such as a victory celebration or political protest, when violence results it is rarely part of an orchestrated script. All riots thus display some measure of spontaneity. Third, riots, unlike celebrations and protests, are never officially sanctioned. Rather, they frequently pose a challenge to the legitimacy of the social order. Yet, their scope generally remains local, stopping short of revolutions, which, by contrast, threaten the legitimacy of entire regimes. Nonetheless, riots have sometimes sparked full-fledged revolutions. Furthermore, while most riot activity has been undertaken by civilians against other civilians or the state, social control agents may also violate commonly held norms of conduct by engaging in widespread violence against civilians, thus constituting a "police riot" (Walker; Stark; Bergesen). Combining the above elements, here is an operational definition of riot activity: Riots are a form of collective behavior characterized by the spontaneous destruction of property and/or assaults on persons by members of an assembled crowd whose actions challenge the normative social order.

A brief history of rioting in America

Rioting has played a key role throughout American history. The American republic, for example, was born of rioting, with the Stamp Act riots, the Boston Tea Party, and the Boston Massacre paving the way for revolution against British rule. Political violence continued after independence, most notably in the form of election riots that occurred in Philadelphia (1834) and Baltimore (1856), followed by a series of disturbances regarding the legal status of slavery, such as those that took place in "bleeding" Kansas (1854–1861). During the late nineteenth century and early twentieth century, riots took on an economic dimension as worker efforts to organize labor unions led to skirmishes between strikers and company security forces, with violence enveloping entire towns such as Homestead, Pennsylvania (1892), Pullman, Illinois (1894), and Mattawan, West Virginia (1920). (For a more comprehensive historical overview of collective violence in America see Hofstadter and Wallace.)

During the twentieth century, the most common form of rioting in America involved members of different racial and ethnic groups contending for political power, economic resources, and social status. Race riots, as such, accompanied rapid demographic and social changes generated by waves of internal and international migration. Such riots took place in nineteenth-century New England, reflecting antagonism between those of English ancestry and recent Irish immigrants. Riots broke out in the North during the Civil War in which Irish laborers attacked newly emancipated blacks, and again during World War I and World War II when mostly foreign-born and second-generation white ethnics clashed with black migrants from the rural South. After World War II, whites began to move from cities to suburbs, leaving blacks increasingly segregated yet underrepresented on police forces and governance councils. Rising black militancy, combined with incidents of police brutality, sparked conflicts between urban residents and police forces throughout the 1960s. By the last two decades of the century, a new "multicultural" form of violence had emerged, with tensions developing among whites, African Americans, and recent immigrants, predominantly from Latin America and the Pacific Rim. These antagonisms, combined with continuing incidents of police brutality, gave rise to major riots in gateway cities such as Miami (1980) and Los Angeles (1992).

Types of riots

Given the extent of historical variation in riot activity, some scholars have sought to generate schema to distinguish certain kinds of riot events from other forms of riot violence. One such typology, developed by Morris Janowitz, focuses on the targets of riot violence. Whereas some riots predominantly involved personal assaults by members of one racial/ethnic group against members of another group, other riots were characterized primarily by attacks on property. Janowitz refers to the former as "communal," the latter as "commodity" riots. His typology is quite useful for distinguishing among race riots prior to and after World War II. Specifically, Janowitz noted a shift from prewar riots, which typically emerged at the borders of ethnic communities and reflected competition for turf, and postwar riots, which involved segregated African Americans seeking to challenge the white-dominated power structure by targeting government buildings and white-owned businesses. Employing this typology, Bergesen and Herman argue that we have recently witnessed a shift back from the commodity riots of the 1960s toward a communal pattern of violence in places like Miami and Los Angeles, where immigrants and blacks contend for jobs, housing, and turf. Yet, in contrast to Janowitz's typology, most riots, including those in Miami and Los Angeles, have involved some combination of property damage and personal assaults. As such it is best to think of communal and commodity riots as "ideal types" rather than mutually exclusive categories.

Like Janowitz, Gary Marx developed a typology of riots, but based his schema on two different dimensions: the presence of a guiding ideology or "generalized belief" and the perception that rioting would achieve some collective purpose. The first category of riots, incorporating both elements, roughly corresponds to the "commodity-type riot" with protest motivated by an antiregime ideology and a sense of collective purpose. This category also includes prison riots and bread riots. The second category corresponds to that of "communal riots," events that express a collective ideology but display no instrumental purpose other than venting animosity. By contrast, Marx suggested that some riots lack any motivating ideology, such as those that often follow sporting victories or are incited by police without provocation. These events, Marx states, are properly categorized as "issueless riots." Turner uses similar criteria to define the Miami and Los Angeles riots as "primitive rebellions" due to their lack of clear ideological or instrumental focus.

Precipating incidents and underlying conditions

As suggested by Janowitz's and Marx's typologies, the forms that riot events take are usually related to the particular incidents that spark them. In the case of communal riots, the most common sparks have involved perceived transgressions of racial/ethnic boundaries, either spatial, such as skirmishes that emerged over access to recreational facilities or religious sites, or sexual, such as accusations of rape made against a member of a minority racial/ethnic group by members of another group. In the case of commodity-type riots, the precipitants have ordinarily involved instances of police injustice, such as the excessive use of force against members of racial/ethnic minorities. Such was the spark of

many 1960s-era riots as well as more recent events in Miami and Los Angeles. In the latter cases, the degree of injustice was even more palpable after police officers were acquitted of beating black motorists. Yet the 1919 Chicago riot also developed in reaction to police activity, or in this particular case, the lack thereof, when a white police officer refused to arrest Irish teens who had stoned a black teenager swimming in the "white" section of Lake Michigan. So communal riots, like commodity riots, may also be sparked in part by police behavior and corresponding perceptions of injustice. In the case of Miami and Los Angeles, anger at police and civil authorities was diffused toward Asian business owners, indicating that the targets of violence need not correspond to the immediate event that sparked rioting. Thus, while precipitating incidents may offer valuable insight into the motives for riot participation, by no means do they supply a full explanation of the origins of these events. Rather than one decisive spark, most riots have been preceded by a series of smaller incidents rooted in the social structure of riot areas.

Prior to the "spark" or precipitating incident, riot events are foreshadowed by a gradual escalation of resentments or grievances held by people who live in the riot area. These feelings, correlated with the structural characteristics of riot communities, represent the underlying conditions of riot genesis—the fuel that feeds the fire when the appropriate spark is provided. There are three general sets of structural explanations for the origins of riot violence: economic, political, and demographic. The first of these economic explanations suggests that people riot in response to conditions of abject poverty. A second and related economic explanation is that people riot when they see themselves as deprived relative to members of higher economic strata. Relative deprivation may spark rioting among those whose economic fortunes are improving but not fast enough to fulfill their rising expectations. By contrast, riots may also develop as a response to political disfranchisement, breaking out in areas where particular groups are politically underrepresented and angry about their lack of access to institutional power. Similarly, riots may represent a reaction to racial/ethnic segregation, which often is combined with economic deprivation and political exclusion. By this measure, places with the highest levels of minority racial/ethnic population will be more riot-prone. Finally, the origins of rioting might also be discovered in processes of demographic change that alter the racial/ethnic composition of communities, affecting cultural control of institutions, and the psychic well-being of longtime residents who fear such changes. Thus rioting may be related to a general process of ethnic succession and competition.

Empirical studies using census data and statistical models to examine the association of structural conditions with riot activity have yielded widely varying results. Comparing cities that had riots to those that did not, Downes found support for an economic deprivation explanation. Poverty, unemployment, and the quality of housing were statistically related to the presence of rioting in cities during the 1960s. Using a similar technique but a larger and more diverse sample of riot events from 1913 to 1963, Lieberson and Silverman found that cities where riots took place had political structures that minimized minority participation on city councils and police forces. By contrast he found no association between unemployment or dilapidated housing and the presence of rioting. Nor did he find any effects of population change on rioting. Seymour Spilerman's influential empirical studies of riot violence found that neither economic deprivation nor population changes were able to account for the frequency or severity of rioting in his multicity sample. Rather, he found that the only significant predictor of riot frequency and severity among cities was the size of a city's black population (Spilerman, 1970, 1976). Later research utilizing more refined statistical modeling has challenged these results. Using Spilerman's data, studies by Olzak, Shanahan, and McEneany and by Myers both found interactive effects of racial/ethnic population change and economic factors on the likelihood of multiple riots in cities, providing evidence that racial/ethnic composition was a significant factor in the outbreak of riot violence. Finally, comparing census tracts within cities that experienced rioting, Bergesen and Herman and Herman found that rioting was associated with processes of ethnic succession and competition, confirming Olzak et al. and Myers's findings at a local neighborhood level. Summarizing these studies, there is a clear consensus that rioting is most likely to take place in predominantly black and poor communities, but black neighborhoods undergoing ethnic succession are even more prone to riot than stable segregated areas. Furthermore, it remains evident that rioting is also a joint product of political, economic, and demographic factors. Political exclusion cuts off channels for the redress of grievances, acting in concert with segregation, population change, and economic competition to foster violence.

The behavior of riot participants

Despite the extensive body of research on riot history, precipitating events, and structural preconditions, we still know relatively little about why or how individuals behave as members of riot gatherings. Most existing studies of riot participants were conducted by post-facto survey analysis or interviews with those arrested for rioting. After the actual riot events, participants were asked to indicate their reasons for participating. From these studies, some important findings have emerged. Perhaps the most significant finding is that riot participants share the same general attitudes as other members of their local communities (Moinat et al.; Ladner et al.). Furthermore, the demographic characteristics of rioters make them nearly indistinguishable from others members of the community who do not take part in riots. The U.S. National Advisory Commission on Civil Disorders failed to find any significant differences in employment status or income between riot participants and nonparticipants. In fact, those who were arrested during the 1960s civil disturbances were on average somewhat better educated and more politically aware than nonrioters. This evidence cuts against the traditional view that rioters represent a pathological element or the "riffraff" of their respective communities (Fogelson). By contrast, survey researchers have found that the same grievances were widely shared by rioters and nonrioters alike (Ladner et al.), with nonrioters often expressing tacit support for the activities of those who rioted.

Perhaps the main distinguishing factor of riot participants as opposed to nonparticipants is their age. Riot participants tend on average to be younger than those who do not participate. Yet even the age of riot participants may vary according to the day and time that they are arrested. As Quanterelli and Dynes found, rioters arrested later in the course of the riot event tended to be substantially older than those arrested at the beginning of rioting. Rioting thus tends to be initiated by teens and young adults, who engage in destruction of property, followed by slightly older opportunists who begin looting stores, and last by older community residents seeking to obtain a share of the loot.

In addition to age variation among riot participants, there are also differences in motivation among members of riotous crowds (Turner and Killian). Some people participate directly in rioting while others merely observe. Some lead, some follow, and some exploit the situation for their own personal advantage. Some individuals even act as counter-rioters, seeking to dissuade members of the crowd from further violence. Simply put, rioters are not a homogeneous group. When police officers treat riotious crowds as a mass rather than targeting leaders or looking to counter-rioters for assistance, this can lead to escalation of violence (Stott and Reicher). Rioters may act collectively or individually, but typically take their behavioral cues from family members or friends with whom they have assembled (Mc-Phail). Individuals are attracted to riot events in much the same way as they join other assemblies—through social network ties. During the looting phase of riot activity individuals often cooperate in locating and obtaining desired items. There is a considerable body of evidence that systematic vandalism of businesses occurs during most riots. These targets, typically owned by members of other racial/ethnic groups, are not randomly selected (Quanterelli et al.; Berk and Aldritch; Tierney; Rosenfeld). Finally, as Mc-Phail notes, riot activity ebbs and flows over space and time. Not all rioters are constantly engaged at any particular point or place. Even rioters go home to sleep, before resuming their activities elsewhere. Understanding the spatial and temporal dynamics of rioting is critical to the task of more effective policing.

The future of riot research

Riots are relatively rare and still unpredictable events. As such, opportunities for the ethnographic study of riot behavior have been few. Researchers have been limited to putting together the pieces after the event has passed. This has meant relying on surveys and census data, selecting variables for statistical analyses. Such analyses have been plagued by insensitivity to social and historical context, and have also failed to capture the spatial and temporal dynamics of riot behavior. Recent technological advances hold much promise for the future study of riot events. The increasing prevalence of videotaping may enable researchers to dissect riot activity frame by frame, while the use of Geographic Information Systems software will allow scholars to locate these behaviors in time and space. Layered with census demographics, survey data on community attitudes, and information on policing capabilities, riot-generated data will enable researchers to effectively link micro and macro units of analysis in a manner never before achieved. Such technology will help researches refine their predictions regarding where and when riots are most likely to occur. Like weather forecasting, however, the study of riot behavior will at best remain an imprecise science.

MAX HERMAN

See also PRISONS: PROBLEMS AND PROSPECTS; RIOTS: LEGAL ASPECTS.

BIBLIOGRAPHY

BERGESEN, ALBERT. "Official Violence during the Watts, Newark and Detroit Race Riots of the 1960s." In *A Political Analysis of Deviance*. Edited by Pat Lauderdale. Minneapolis: University of Minnesota Press, 1980.

BERGESEN, ALBERT, and HERMAN, MAX. "Immigration, Race and Riot: The 1992 Los Angeles Uprising." *American Sociological Review* 63 (1998): 39–54.

BERK, RICHARD, and ALDRITCH, HOWARD. "Patterns of Vandalism During Civil Disorders as an Indicator of Selection of Targets." *American Sociological Review* 37 (1972): 533–547.

DOWNES, BRYAN T. "Social and Political Characteristics of Riot Cities: A Comparative Study." *Social Science Quarterly* 49 (1968): 427–443.

FOGELSON, ROBERT M. *Violence as Protest: A Study of Riots and Ghettos*. Garden City, N.Y.: Anchor Doubleday, 1971.

HERMAN, MAX. "Fighting in the Streets: Ethnic Succession and Riot Violence in 20th Century America." Ph.D. diss., University of Arizona, 1999.

HOFSTADTER, RICHARD, and WALLACE, MICHAEL. *American Violence: A Documentary History*. New York: Vintage Books, 1970.

JANOWITZ, MORRIS. "Collective Racial Violence: A Contemporary History." *Violence in America: Historical and Comparative Perspectives*. Edited by Hugh Davis Graham and Ted Gurr. Rev. ed. Beverly Hills, Calif.: Sage Publications, 1979.

LADNER, ROBERT A.; SCHWARTZ, BARRY J.; ROKER, SANDRA J.; and TITTERUD, LORETTA S. "The Miami Riots of 1980: Antecedent Conditions, Community Responses and Participant Characteristics." *Research in Social Movements, Conflicts and Change* 4 (1981): 171–214.

Le Bon, Gustave. *The Crowd: A Study of the Popular Mind.* London: T. F. Unwin, 1903.

Lieberson, Stanley, and Silverman, Arnold. "The Precipitants and Underlying Conditions of Race Riots." *American Sociological Review* (December 1965): 887–898.

McAdam, Doug. "Tactical Innovation and the Pace of Insurgency." *American Sociological Review* 48 (1983): 735–754.

McPhail, Clark. "The Dark Side of Purpose: Individual and Collective Violence in Riots." *The Sociological Quarterly* 35 (1994): 1–32.

Marx, Gary. "Issueless Riots." In *Collective Violence.* Edited by James Short, Jr. and Marvin Wolfgang. Chicago: Aldine Atherton, 1972. Pages 47–59.

Moinat, Sheryl M.; Raine, Walter J.; Burbeck, Stephen L.; and Davison, Keith K. "Black Ghetto Residents as Rioters." *The Journal of Social Issues* 28, no. 4 (1972): 45–62.

Myers, Daniel J. "Racial Rioting in the 1960s: An Event History Analysis of Local Conditions." *American Sociological Review* 62 (1997): 94–112.

Olzak, Susan; Shanahan, Suzanne; and McEneany, Elizabeth H. "Poverty, Segregation and Race Riots, 1960–1993." *American Sociological Review* 61 (1996): 590–613.

Quanterelli, E. L., and Dynes, Russell. "Looting in Civil Disorders: An Index of Social Change." In *Riots and Rebellion: Civil Violence in the Urban Community.* Edited by Louis H. Masotti and Donald R. Bowen. Beverly Hills, Calif.: Sage Publications, 1968. Pages 131–141.

Rosenfeld, Michael J. "Celebration, Politics, Selective Looting and Riots: A Micro Level Study of the Bulls Riot of 1992 in Chicago." *Social Problems* 44, no. 4 (1997): 483–502.

Snow, David A., and Oliver, Pamela E. "Social Movements and Collective Behavior: Social Psychological Dimensions and Considerations." In *Sociological Perspectives on Social Psychology.* Edited by Karen S. Cook, Gary Alan Fine, and James S. House. Boston: Allyn and Bacon, 1995.

Spilerman, Seymour. "The Causes of Racial Disturbances: A Comparison of Alternative Explanations." *American Sociological Review* 35 (1970): 627–649.

———. "Structural Characteristics of Cities and the Severity of Racial Disorders." *American Sociological Review* 41 (1976): 771–793.

Stark, Rodney. *Police Riots: Collective Violence and Law Enforcement.* Belmont, Calif.: Wadsworth, 1972.

Stott, Clifford, and Reicher, Stephen. "Crowd Action as Intergroup Process: Introducing the Police Perspective." *European Journal of Social Psychology* 28 (1998): 509–529.

Tierney, Kathleen J. "Property Damage and Violence: A Collective Behavior Analysis." In *The Los Angeles Riots: Lessons for the Urban Future.* Edited by Mark Baldassare. Boulder, Colo.: Westview Press, 1994.

Turner, Ralph H., and Killian, Lewis M. *Collective Behavior.* Englewood Cliffs, N.J.: Prentice Hall, 1987.

Turner, Ralph H. "Race Riots Past and Present: A Collective-Cultural Behavior Approach." *Symbolic Interaction* 17 (1994): 309–324.

Walker, Daniel, ed. *Rights in Conflict.* New York: Grossett and Dunlap, 1968.

RIOTS: LEGAL ASPECTS

Introduction

In dealing with riotous or potentially riotous conduct, the common law developed several crimes, including breach of the peace, unlawful assembly, rout, riot, and disorderly conduct. Numerous statutory prohibitions exist today as well. For example, the California Penal Code offenses invoked in the Watts riots of 1965 included resisting officers (§ 69), riot (§ 404), unlawful assembly (§ 407), riot-rout-unlawful assembly (§ 415), remaining present after warning to disperse (§ 409), disturbing the peace (§ 415), drawing or exhibiting firearms (§ 417), arson (§§ 447(a), 448(a)), burglary (§ 459), theft (§§ 484–485), and malicious mischief (§ 594). The curfew provisions of the California Military and Veterans Code (Cal. Mil. & Vet. Code § 1600 (1955) (repealed 1970)) were invoked as well (Note, 1967, p. 122 n. 17).

Common law

Unlawful assembly. At common law an unlawful assembly was defined as a gathering together of three or more persons with the common intent to achieve a purpose, lawful or unlawful, in a riotous or tumultuous manner. The common purpose or intent could be formed either before assembling or after the gathering took place. A meeting could therefore start out as a lawful assembly but change into an unlawful one.

The states are divided as to whether there must be an intent to perform the planned activity in a violent manner. Many jurisdictions require the presence or threat of force or violence disruptive of public order. Other jurisdictions consider the nature of the assembly. If the purpose is unlawful, then an unlawful assembly exists.

Rout. *Rout* is generally defined as the moving forward of an unlawful assembly toward the execution of its unlawful design (*Follis v. State,* 37 Tex. Crim. 535, 537, 40 S.W. 277 (1987)). A rout is essentially an attempt to commit a riot. It requires a specific intent to riot and a situation that ultimately falls short of actual riot. Thus, if two or more persons have the intent to riot and if they commit an act that threatens further acts of force or violence, they could be guilty of rout. The crime of rout has usually been abandoned or merged with that of unlawful assembly.

Riot. The generally accepted common law definition of *riot* is the following: "A riot seems to be a tumultuous disturbance of the peace, by three persons or more assembling together of their own authority, with an intent mutually to assist one another, against any who shall oppose them, in the execution of some enterprise of a private nature, and afterwards actually executing the same in a violent and turbulent manner, to the terror of the people, whether the act intended were of itself lawful or unlawful" (Hawkins, p. 243).

Several elements are generally required for the crime of riot: there must be at least three persons participating in a common riotous purpose, although only one need perform the objectionable act; there must be an unlawful assembly and overt acts committed without authority of law; and there must be use of force and violence. For the necessary purpose or intent, there must be some evidence of concerted action toward the furtherance of a common goal. The requisite concert of action may be inferred from the manner in which the unlawful acts of violence are committed.

Since a common law riot was committed when those who were unlawfully assembled began the perpetration of their unlawful design, most states held an unlawful assembly to be a prerequisite to the offense of riot. Riot was committed under the common law when a mob employed force or violence to accomplish its illegal purpose. "Unlawful force or violence" is interpreted broadly, but is generally viewed as conduct more serious than loud noise or disturbance. Riot could occur even though the objective were lawful if the defendants' actions were carried out or attempted in a violent and

turbulent manner to the terror of the people. Persons charged with riot had to be present at the scene of the unlawful act.

In a few states, riot remains a common law crime (*Cohen v. State,* 173 Md. 216, 195 A. 532 (1937)). Most states have statutory definitions that follow the common law. Several states maintain the common law crimes as a supplement to their statutory enactments.

Statutory riot crimes

The first statutory riot act was the famous British Riot Act (An Act for preventing Tumults and Riotous Assemblies and for the more speedy and effectual punishing the Rioters, 1 Geo. 1, Stat. 2, c. 5 (1714) (Great Britain) (repealed 1973)), according to which a justice of the peace or other officer, when confronted with an "unlawful, riotous, or tumultuous assembly," was to approach as close as safety permitted and read with a loud voice the prescribed language: "Our Sovereign lord the King chargeth and commandeth all persons, being assembled, immediately to disperse themselves and peaceably to depart to their habitations or to their lawful business, upon the pains contained in the Act made in the first year of King George, for the prevention of tumults and riotous assemblies. God save the King" (143). The statute further provided that if twelve or more of the assembled persons failed to disperse within an hour, they were guilty of a felony.

Several American jurisdictions still have statutes requiring a command to disperse before local officials may move in to quell a riot. However, even under the British Riot Act, an unlawful assembly could be dispersed and arrests made for breach of the peace without the requirements for the act being fulfilled, since riot is a common law offense and so exists independently of the statute (*Commonwealth v. Frishman,* 235 Mass. 449, 126 N.E. 838 (1920)).

Three general approaches are followed in defining *riot.* The first is not to define it statutorily but simply to incorporate terms such as *riot, riotous, or persons unlawfully, riotously, or tumultuously assembled* into the statute. The second approach essentially codifies the common law definitions of *riot* or *violent and tumultuous* activity. A third categorization defines *riot* broadly as any use of, or threat to use, force or violence by a specified number of people. During the riots of the 1960s several states updated their own riot statutes, reflecting changes in social behavior and constitutional law. For example, one modern statutory definition of *riot* is "any unlawful use, by three or more persons acting together, of force or violence which seriously jeopardizes the public safety, peace or order" (Va. Code Ann. § 18. 2-405 (1999)).

Riot is usually classified as a misdemeanor, although several jurisdictions provide for "aggravated riot," which is a felony. Other states provide for increased punishment if the accused committed certain acts during the rioting, such as carrying a weapon, encouraging or soliciting others to commit violence, or wearing a mask or disguise. Most statutory schemes are more stringent when the offender also commits acts destructive of person or property.

Several jurisdictions distinguish between classes of riots. Under the New York statute, a riot in the second degree occurs when five or more persons have intentionally or recklessly engaged in "tumultuous and violent conduct" that results, or tends to result, in public alarm. If over eleven are involved and if physical injury or substantial property damage results to one not participating, then the offense is riot in the first degree (N.Y. Penal Law (McKinney) §§ 240.05, 240.06 (1999)).

Second-degree riot is a misdemeanor and focuses on riotous conduct that is terminated before actual injury results. First-degree riot conforms more closely to what is popularly understood as an urban riot, and is committed when the proscribed conduct results in personal injury or property damage. The phrase "tumultuous and violent conduct" includes "frightening mob behavior involving ominous threats of injury, stone throwing or other such terrorizing acts" (Hechtman, p. 251).

The number of persons necessary to constitute a riot varies among the states, some statutes requiring only two. Whereas the common law spoke in terms of three or more persons, modern statutes frequently require a larger minimum number. A few statutes specify "any number of persons" unlawfully or riotously assembled.

Related statutory offenses

Several statutory crimes exist that are offshoots of riot, including inciting riot, conspiracy to riot, failing to disperse upon command, and failing to render assistance upon lawful order. Under the British Riot Act, one who incited others to riot was guilty of simple riot, a felony with the same penalty as that attached to riot. Some jurisdictions make inciting to riot a felony, while treating simple riot as a misdemeanor.

The crime of inciting to riot, both at common law and by statute, deals with a critical stage of a riot. It is well known that the conditions for a riot may exist but need a spark to set them off. The inciting-to-riot statutes attempt to prevent the spark from being struck by focusing on the instigator of the disorder rather than on the potential participants. The statutes require a specific intent to cause a riot; an act or conduct that urges a riot; and a time, a place, and circumstances that constitute a clear, present, and immediate danger. A riot need not materialize for the violation to exist, nor need the defendant participate in the riot if it ensues.

A major problem with both inciting-to-riot statutes and riot statutes involves defining the crime so as to avoid offending the free-speech guarantees of the Constitution. The statute should be broad enough to encompass inflammatory conduct and specific enough to give warning to an offender of the nature of the violation, but it should also be narrow enough to survive constitutional attack.

Riot statutes have generally been upheld against constitutional attacks. It would seem that those statutes which adhere closely to the traditional common law definitions of *riot* are less susceptible to such attack. Moreover, most arrests for riot have been made during large-scale mass disorders in which little question arises about suppression of First Amendment rights.

Several jurisdictions, such as that of New York, have a separate offense of conspiracy to riot. For a conspiracy, only two or more persons are necessary, and the defendant need not cause or participate in the riots. A New York case upheld a conviction for conspiracy to incite riot (*People v. Epton,* 19 N.Y. 2d 496, 227 N.E. 2d 829 (1967)). Other frequently invoked statutory and common law crimes in riot situations are breach of the peace and disorderly conduct, but these have an application much broader than riot situations.

The federal Riot Act

On April 10, 1968, Congress enacted the Riot Act of 1968, 18 U.S.C. §§ 2101, 2102 (1999), which made it a federal crime "to use any facility of interstate commerce to incite or participate in a riot." The federal act thus focuses on the individual who crosses a state line for the purpose of creating public disorder. One of the underlying assumptions was that outside agitators play a role in causing modern urban disturbances. The act provides:

> (1) Whoever travels in interstate or foreign commerce or uses any facility of interstate or foreign commerce, including, but not limited to, the mail, telegraph, telephone, radio, or television, with intent—
>
>> (A) to incite a riot; or
>> (B) to organize, promote, encourage, participate in, or carry on a riot; or
>> (C) to commit any act of violence in furtherance of a riot; or
>> (D) to aid or abet any person in inciting or participating in or carrying on a riot or committing any act of violence in furtherance of a riot;
>
> and who either during the course of any such travel or use or thereafter performs or attempts to perform any other overt act for any purpose specified in subparagraph (A), (B), (C), or (D) of this paragraph—
>
> Shall be fined under this title, or imprisoned not more than five years, or both [§ 2101].

The act treats those who attempt to commit the offense, as well as aiders and abettors, as principals. Neither presence at (or participation in) a riot nor imminent threat or harm is required. In *National Mobilization Committee to End War in Vietnam v. Foran*, 411 F. 2d 934 (7th Cir. 1969) and *United States v. Dellinger*, 472 F. 2d 340 (7th Cir. 1972), the constitutionality of the act has been upheld on the ground that the First Amendment does not protect rioting or incitement to riot.

DENIS BINDER
DAN M. KAHAN

See also JUSTIFICATION: LAW ENFORCEMENT; RIOTS: BEHAVIORAL ASPECTS.

BIBLIOGRAPHY

Casenote. "Criminal Law—Riot: What Constitutes." *Oregon Law Review* 18 (1939): 254–259.
Comment. "The Michigan Revised Criminal Code and Offense against Public Order." *Wayne Law Review* 14 (1968): 986–1006.
Comment. "Wisconsin's Disorderly Conduct Statute: Why It Should Be Changed." *Wisconsin Law Review* (1969): 602–626.
DUCHARME, GERALD D., and EICKHOLT, EUGENE H. "State Riot Laws: A Proposal." *Journal of Urban Law* 45 (1968): 713–734.
HAWKINS, WILLIAM. *A Treatise of the Pleas of the Crown; or, A System of the Principal Matters Relating to That Subject, Digested under Proper Heads.* 2 vols. 8th ed., rev. and enlarged by John Curwood. London: S. Sweet, 1824.
HECHTMAN, ARNOLD D. Practice Commentary on Section 240.04. *New York Penal Law (McKinney).* St. Paul: West, 1980, pp. 250–251.
Note. "California's Urging to Riot Law." *San Diego Law Review* 4 (1967): 118–140.
Note. "The King's Peace: Riot Law in Its Historical Perspective." *Utah Law Review* (1971): 240–258.
Note. "Legislation and Riots: Interaction." *Brooklyn Law Review* 35 (1969): 472–485.
Note. "Virginia's Legislative Response to Riots and Their Underlying Causes." *Virginia Law Review* 54 (1968): 1031–1063.
ROBINSON, PAUL. "Riot Responsibility." *New York State Bar Journal* 66 (1993): 6–8.
Survey. "The Long, Hot Summer: A Legal View." *Notre Dame Lawyer* 43 (1968): 913–1016.

ROBBERY

Robbery is a form of theft that is accomplished by the use or threat of violence.

Legal definition

In modern English and American law the crime of robbery is generally defined by statute. The definitions used are primarily of two kinds: those that are closely derived from the older English common law, and those that have adopted modifications of the type recommended by the American Law Institute's Model Penal Code. The California statute is typical of the common law approach. Borrowing language almost word for word from Edward East's text of 1803, it defines robbery as "the felonious taking of personal property in the possession of another, from his person or immediate presence, and against his will, accomplished by means of force or fear" (Cal. Penal Code Ann. (West) § 211 (1999)). Other statutes of this kind go into greater detail, while a few states, such as Virginia, leave the definition almost wholly to the common law.

Under the older definitions, robbery requires proof of *larceny*, the principal common law form of theft, plus two additional factors: (1) that the taking be by means of force or fear; and (2) that the theft be from the person of the victim or from his immediate presence.

Particular requirements

Use of force or fear. The central requirement of robbery is that the taking be by means of either force or fear. One common type of robbery involving force is mugging, in which the robber grabs the victim around the neck from the rear and forcibly removes his wallet or other valuables. Other common kinds of force involve striking a victim with the fists, a gun, or a blunt object.

Like any other category of crime, robbery presents a number of situations in which it is difficult to determine whether or not there is in fact a robbery. In these boundary situations, if there is no robbery there is generally some other crime rather than no crime at all. If the victim's purse is snatched, for example, it is often difficult to determine whether the force necessary for robbery has been used. If the purse is snatched quickly so that the victim offers no resistance, the common law and many American states find that there has been no robbery and that the crime is instead larceny from the person. If the victim struggles to hold on to the purse, however, so that the thief must jerk it loose, the common law and virtually all the American states find that a robbery has been committed.

Historically, these lines were drawn at a time when robbery was a capital crime and common law judges were reluctant to paint with too broad a brush, and the distinctions consequently emphasize formal logic more than the actual or potential harm. The elderly women who are often the victims of purse-snatchings tend to be badly shaken by the experience even if "force" is not used, but this has not as yet caused any widespread change in the distinctions made.

Picking a victim's pocket is generally not considered robbery because there is no use of fear and because robbery requires more force than that necessary simply to remove the property. However, if the thief jostles the victim in the taking, or if the victim notices the attempt and resists, the crime is robbery.

Fear or intimidation is an alternative to the use of force. The most common situation is the holdup, in which the robber threatens to shoot if valuables are not turned over. The threat may be implied rather than stated verbally, but it generally must be to do immediate rather than future harm. The threat may concern the property holder, members of his family, or another person who is present, and must generally concern death or bodily injury of some kind rather than an injury to reputation. Other threats—to prosecute the victim, to do future harm, or to expose the victim's sordid past if he fails to pay—may constitute blackmail or extortion but are not robbery.

Most American states do not require that the victim actually be afraid. If the victim is not frightened, it is enough that he be aware of the impending harm. Even a slight threat is enough to constitute robbery, however, if it causes the victim to part with money or valuables.

It is sometimes said that robbery is a crime that combines both larceny and assault, but this is not strictly true. Some threats that are not sufficient to constitute an assault are sufficient for the crime to be robbery.

Another definitional problem involves thefts from persons who are unconscious because of their own acts of drinking or drug-taking. If money is simply removed from the person of such a victim, the crime is not robbery because there is no force or fear. If force is used to move the victim in order to find his money or to gratuitously inflict harm, however, as is often done in skid-row drunk rolls, the definition of robbery under most statutes would appear to be met, despite the lack of awareness on the part of the victim. If the victim is either drugged or knocked unconscious by the thief in order to secure the victim's property, it is clear that the crime is robbery.

At common law, force or fear had to precede or coincide with the theft in order for the crime to be robbery. If force or fear was used only in the escape, the crime was considered to be larceny because there was no force or fear in the taking. From the point of view of the danger involved, however, the escape creates as much risk as the taking, and the Model Penal Code (§ 222.1) and some states have dropped the requirement that force or fear must be used in the taking.

Taking from person or presence. The second common law requirement for robbery is that the taking be from the person or the immediate presence of the victim. Property is considered taken from the victim's person if it is taken from his hand or clothing or from a place where it was discarded while the victim was in flight from the robber. The victim's "presence" is considered to be his area of immediate control. Property is not generally found to be taken from the victim's person or presence if it is located some distance away. Consequently, if a victim held by a gunman directs by telephone that property in a remote warehouse be delivered to the gunman's confederate, the crime, under the traditional rule, is not robbery. Taking the real issue to be the use of force or fear, however, the Model Penal Code, the Theft Act, 1968, c. 60 (Great Britain), and a number of states have dropped the requirement that property be taken from the person or presence of the victim. This solves some problems but leaves open the question as to how close in time and place the use of force or fear must be to the taking for the crime to be robbery.

Larceny problems. Because larceny is a component of robbery, all the problems that exist in defining larceny are also problems in defining robbery. The common law rules that prevent the taking of real property or services from being larceny, for example, may also prevent the forcible taking of these things from being robbery. Similarly, since a taking that results from an erroneous but honest claim of ownership is not a theft because there is no intent to deprive the rightful owner, such a taking with force is not a robbery in most states because there is no theft.

If the older, more technical rules concerning larceny have been replaced with a single, more comprehensive concept of theft, there may be other problems. The wrongful failure to return borrowed property, for example, was not larceny under the older law but is included in many modern definitions. This raises the question as to whether a borrower who has wrongfully refused to return property commits a robbery if he threatens to beat up the owner for trying to recover his property. Similar questions may arise when the property was initially obtained by fraud or trickery and when force is used or threatened to keep the victim from regaining the property.

Unlike burglary but like other common law thefts, robbery requires that property actually be taken by the offender. If force or fear is employed but property not taken, there may be an assault or an attempted robbery, but at common law and in most states there is no robbery. The Model Penal Code and the statutes of some states have recognized that the harm to the person is the same whether the theft is completed or not, and have defined the crime to include the incomplete theft as well as the completed one.

Aggravated robbery. Many statutes provide stiffer penalties for particularly threatening robberies. Some factors that aggravate robbery in this way are use of a dangerous weapon, infliction of serious bodily harm, intent to kill, the presence of accomplices, or the choice of an especially vulnerable target such as a person on a train or bus, or an elderly person. In many of the newer criminal codes some of these same factors now serve as aggravating factors for crimes in general, as well as specific aggravating factors for robbery. This overlap sometimes raises the question as to whether the presence of an aggravating factor such as the use of a gun should result in one additional penalty or two—as aggravation under the robbery statute only, or under both the robbery statute and the general law.

Robbery is generally viewed as a crime against the person threatened. Consequently, if there is more than one victim, many states allow multiple charges to be filed and multiple sentences to be imposed.

Related crimes

Some crimes closely related to robbery are larceny, larceny from the person, assault, battery, kidnapping, extortion, and murder.

Larceny is the principal common law form of theft, and differs from robbery in that it involves neither the element of force or fear nor the requirement that the taking be from the person of the victim. Larceny from the person is an aggravated form of theft that does involve a taking from the person but that does not involve the use of force or fear. Originally created by an Elizabethan statute designed to deal with a cut-purse and pickpocket problem that was serious even then (An act to take away the benefit of clergy from certain offenders for felony, 8 Eliz. 1, c. 4, § 2 (1565) (repealed)), the most common forms of larceny from the person today continue to be purse-snatching, pick-pocketing, and thefts from sleeping or intoxicated persons.

Assault is a common law crime that involves putting another person in fear, and battery is an unlawful touching or hitting. These crimes thus involve force or fear, but do not involve theft.

Kidnapping for ransom involves an unlawful seizure of a victim and, in most states, a carrying away of that person for the purpose of gaining money or other valuables. Since such movement of the victim is present in almost every robbery, there is considerable potential for overlap in the two crimes. The courts have generally sought to avoid this by ruling that for a crime to be kidnapping, the movement of the victim must be greater than that necessary for robbery to be committed.

Extortion or blackmail is a statutory crime involving threats to expose a crime or other shameful deed perpetrated by the victim unless money is paid or some other act performed. In many states the crime also covers future threats of bodily harm. The crime developed largely to protect against harms not covered by the law of robbery.

If a robber intentionally shoots or seriously injures a victim and the victim dies, the robber is guilty of murder. In most states even an accidental shooting by a robber that ends in the death of the victim is also murder because of the felony-murder doctrine, which provides that killings in the course of a felony (or at least of a dangerous felony such as robbery) constitute murder.

The history of robbery

First listed as a plea of the Crown by Henry II in the twelfth century, robbery was one of the early crimes under English law to be made punishable by the state rather than through compensation of the injured party or through private vengeance. While not well defined at this time, robbery probably required a taking by actual force from the person of the victim, and was punishable by death or mutilation. It soon became a capital felony, however, and remained so in England—at least in theory—until the great reforms of the 1830s, when the list of capital crimes was sharply reduced. The last execution in England for simple robbery took place in 1836.

Although Roman law and other ancient codes recognized a crime similar to robbery, the older Anglo-Saxon law did not always include the concept. At one point the distinction between thefts done in the open (manifest) and thefts carried out in secret was more important. Unlike modern law, which emphasizes the potential for violence in robbery, this distinction appears to have been based on the greater certainty of proof available when the thief is caught red-handed.

In the United States, robbery was from colonial days a felony punishable by death. As late as the early 1960s, ten states made some forms of robbery punishable by death. The punishment was far from theoretical, as twenty-four persons were executed for robbery offenses between 1930 and 1962. Current constitutional doctrine would prohibit the execution of an offender convicted of robbery only. However, when his accomplice kills someone in the course of their crime, a robbery offender, under at least some circumstances, can be sentenced to death on a felony murder theory, even if he did not himself intend the killing (*Tison v. Arizona,* 481 U.S. 137 (1987)).

Robbery as a separate category embodying theft by violence is contained in the codes of many countries and cultures, both ancient and modern. This method of categorization is not universal, however, and some important legal systems have done without it. Thus, although German and Soviet law have long treated robbery as a separate crime, French law does not. Theft with violence is considered an aggravated form of theft but not a separate crime.

Types of behavior

Robbery includes a wide variety of behavior ranging from opportunistic schoolyard shakedowns to carefully planned multimillion-dollar thefts from Brink's or the London–Glasgow train.

In the United States about half of the robberies committed are never reported to the police. Of those that are reported more than half involve some kind of weapon, most commonly the handgun. As many as a fifth of all robberies may result in some injury. Most injuries are minor, however, and serious hospitalization is infrequent. Death is even rarer, occurring less than once in every 200 reported robberies. Even so, robbery is involved in about a tenth of all homicides.

In the United States about two-fifths of all reported robberies are of commercial enterprises, and the remaining three-fifths are of individuals. About a tenth of the total are robberies of persons in their residences. In some of these situations a burglar caught in the act uses force or fear against the householder; in others, a robbery was intended from the start, and force or fear was used to gain entry.

In the United States, men are robbed more often than women, partly because of the legal distinctions that place most purse-snatches in the category of thefts from the person rather than in that of robbery. This distinction is also relevant to the argument as to whether the elderly suffer disportionately from robberies. If measured by the total population, and with purse-snatches excluded, the elderly do not appear to be particularly vulnerable. If purse-snatches are included, however, the elderly (particularly in inner cities) do appear to be a high-risk group.

Two-thirds or more of the robberies in the United States are stranger-to-stranger crimes. In robberies involving friends or acquaintances, one party often attempts to resolve an argument over money or property by force, as when a poker player uses a gun to seize disputed winnings, or an employee forcibly demands extra pay. Although these situations are generally classified in criminal statistics as robberies, the taking is often made under a claim of right that is legally sufficient to negate the robbery charge. As a consequence, there are few convictions for robbery in these circumstances.

Other robberies arise out of brief relationships such as those engendered by hitchhiking, prostitution, and drug-dealing. In these situations both parties are vulnerable to attack, often with impunity, because the victim is reluctant to make his illicit purposes known to the police. Unreported robberies tend to be less serious than reported ones; significant numbers involve robberies of teenagers by other teenagers.

Robbery is largely an urban crime, and generally increases with the size of the city. Reported rates vary enormously from country to country. In the United States they are generally eight to ten times as great as in England or Europe, and thirty or more times greater than in Japan.

Characteristics of offenders

Most robbers are male, and in the United States approximately 60 percent are between fifteen and twenty-four years of age. Approximately 30 percent are under eighteen, and the peak years appear to be those between the ages of sixteen and nineteen. A high proportion of robbers, both as described by victims and according to arrest rates, are black. Abroad as well, minority and disadvantaged groups figure prominently in the statistics.

The majority of robbers have previously committed some other kind of crime, and many do not commit repeated robberies. The extent to which offenders progress from lesser to more serious forms of theft such as robbery is in dispute, but many do appear to follow this path. Most robbers devote little time to planning their offenses and give scant thought to the possibility of being caught. A high proportion carry out their robberies within their own neighborhood or city.

Some common kinds of robbers include first offenders, persistent thieves and hustlers, drug addicts, disorganized opportunists, violent robbers, habitual robbers, and skillful planners.

Probably the largest group is that of persons who commit a single robbery and then stop. This group includes persons who have committed other crimes but who choose not to continue with an active robbery career, as well as persons who for situational or other reasons commit robbery as a first offense.

Persistent thieves and hustlers tend to be drifters who seek to acquire money in any possible way. They are often involved in burglary, shoplifting, and other forms of theft, as well as in robbery.

Another category consists of narcotics addicts who support their habit in whole or in part through robberies. While it is clear that many addicts are not involved in robbery, those who are tend to commit the offense repeatedly.

Other offenders do not set out to commit a robbery but simply take advantage of passing opportunities. Many street robberies and many robberies committed by youths fall into this opportunist category.

Some persons who commit robberies seem more interested in violence than profit. These offenders often use far greater force than is necessary; the theft they commit sometimes seems almost incidental.

Certain robbers develop very specific habits, for example, robbing liquor stores on Tuesday or Thursday afternoons. Having mastered a technique that is at least initially successful, these robbers tend to repeat their pattern over and over again until caught.

A few robbers—the skillful planners—plan their crimes very carefully, often manifesting the qualities of a military tactician. They generally commit the most spectacular robberies, usually small in number but highly lucrative.

As might be expected, different kinds of robberies are committed by different kinds of robbers. Armed and commercial robberies tend to be committed by white older offenders. Street robberies, on the other hand, are most frequently committed by younger offenders from minority groups.

Because the crime is a forceful and direct one, robbers tend to be viewed favorably by other criminals. Even among the general public, robbers sometimes achieve folk-hero status: Robin Hood, Butch Cassidy, and the Brink's robbers are but a few of many examples.

FLOYD FEENEY
DAN M. KAHAN

See also ASSAULT AND BATTERY; BANK ROBBERY; THEFT.

BIBLIOGRAPHY

American Law Institute. *Model Penal Code: Proposed Official Draft*. Philadelphia: ALI, 1962.

BICKEL, BRUCE D. "Struggling with California's Kidnapping to Commit Robbery Provision."

Hastings Law Journal 27, no. 6 (1976): 1335–1367.

Bureau of Justice Statistics. *Sourcebook of Criminal Justice Statistics*. Washington, D.C.: USGPO, 1998.

CONKLIN, JOHN E. *Robbery and the Criminal Justice System*. Philadelphia: Lippincott, 1972.

EAST, EDWARD HYDE. *Pleas of the Crown* (1803), vol. 2. Reprint. London: Professional Books, 1972.

FEENEY, FLOYD, and WEIR, ADRIANNE. *Holdups, Muggings, and Pursesnatches*. Lexington, Mass.: Heath, 1982.

HUNT, MORTON. *The Mugging*. New York: Atheneum, 1972.

IRWIN, JOHN. *The Felon*. Englewood Cliffs, N.J.: Prentice-Hall, 1970.

LAFAVE, WAYNE R., and SCOTT, AUSTIN W., JR. *Handbook on Criminal Law*. St. Paul: West, 1972.

McCLINTOCK, F. H., and GIBSON, EVELYN. *Robbery in London*. London: Macmillan; New York: St. Martin's Press, 1961.

Note. "A Rationale of the Law of Aggravated Theft." *Columbia Law Review* 54 (1954): 84–110.

RURAL CRIME

This entry addresses the research literature exploring the nature and extent of rural crime in the United States, and theoretical explanations of rural crime. First, it is important to develop an understanding of what is meant by the term *rural*. The definition of a rural community has been debated by social scientists for quite some time, and differences in the definition of rural have implications for our understanding of rural crime.

Much of the criminological literature has ignored rural-urban differences in crime rates, and theories have commonly been tested using large cities as the unit of analysis. If crime were exclusively a large-city phenomenon, such a focus would be justified. However, the existence of rural crime, and differences in the rates and types of such crime, have important implications for criminological theories.

Rural-urban distinctions

Much confusion exists in the criminological literature over rural-urban distinctions. In most cases, theoretical distinctions by rural and urban sociologists have been ignored, and criminolo-gists have employed simple, arbitrary cutoff points to distinguish rural from urban areas. In some instances, in fact, commentators have designated entire states as rural or urban. For example, a report prepared for the U.S. Senate in the early 1990s, which claimed that crime rates in rural America were increasing, noted:

America's rural towns, villages, and small communities are suffering a plague of violent crime, drug trafficking, and drug abuse. The latest crime figures show that the violent crime toll is growing faster in rural America than large urban states; faster in rural states than in even America's largest cities. These reports document rural America's skyrocketing criminal violence—murders, rapes, robberies, and violent attacks are growing at an astonishing pace. (U.S. Senate Majority Staff Report)

This report reached these stunning conclusions by classifying some states as rural and then comparing percentage changes in Uniform Crime Report data for these "rural states" with two of the most populous states, California and New York. As Ronet Bachman points out, classifying a unit of analysis as large as a state as rural is flawed, because at least one urban area exists within virtually every state.

Of course, these problems are not unique to recent examinations of rural-urban differences in crime rates. In the 1880s, one commentator classified states as rural or urban on the basis of their primary economic activity, and argued that "rural (agricultural) communities have ever been distinguished for good order and stability" (Pickard, p. 460). Noting that the ratio of offenders committed to prison to the total population in "agricultural states" was much lower than in "manufacturing states," Pickard asserted that "the theory was founded in fact" (p. 461). In commenting on such gross distinctions that were prevalent in much of the literature, Sorokin and Zimmerman noted that the data brought to bear on empirical questions concerning rural and urban differences "often concern not the pure rural and urban groups, but groups which represent only a relative and remote approximation to them" (p. 37).

In the more contemporary context, Ralph Weisheit, David Falcone, and L. Edward Wells point out that the definition of rural utilized by researchers is an important consideration. In their review of over ninety studies on rural crime, the authors note that 62 percent gave no measurable definition of the term *rural;* they also note that some crime studies have even described cities with populations of up to 175,000 as rural or small town. As these authors suggest, despite the apparent simplicity of the concept of rural, there is nothing mechanical or straightforward about developing a working definition of it.

Weisheit et al. suggest, however, that there are four important dimensions of rural that need to be taken into account: (1) demographic; (2) economic; (3) social; and (4) cultural. The demographic dimension encompasses how many people are concentrated in an area, along with where they are located. Generally, one would expect rural areas to be geographically isolated, and physically removed from major urban centers. The economic dimension relates to the primary economic activity of an area; one usually thinks of rural areas as being predominantly agricultural. The social dimension of rurality relates to a variety of characteristics; rural areas are seen as having the defining characteristics of intimacy, informality, and homogeneity. The final aspect of rurality is related to cultural issues. Individuals who reside in rural areas are perceived as being more traditional and conservative in their political attitudes.

In short, given the considerable confusion in the literature surrounding how rural and urban areas are defined, we must treat the findings from studies of differences between rural and urban crime with caution.

Urban-rural crime differences

The murder which develops from a quarrel over the line fence, the seductions in the rural districts, and the marital infidelities on the farm do not make as dramatic stories for the sensational press as the activities of the gunmen of New York or the alleged immoralities of the so-called high society, but they are recorded in the census office. ("Rural Perfection a Myth")

A perusal of the literature on rural-urban crime differences in the United States during the nineteenth and twentieth centuries reveals considerable empirical and theoretical confusion regarding the seemingly straightforward question of whether crime in general, and violent crime in particular, is higher or lower in rural versus urban areas. For example, an early study of homicides for Massachusetts for the period 1871–1892 showed a greater prevalence of homicides in rural as compared to urban sections of that state (Cook). Although it did not represent

a particularly valid distinction between urban-rural areas, in 1910, the director of the U.S. census commented that "In general, the more serious the offense, the greater is the proportion of farmers and farm laborers among the total number of males committed (to prison) for it" (quoted in Sutherland).

The census director pointed out that while only 2.6 percent of those committed to prison for drunkenness were farmers, 18.6 percent of those committed for "grave" homicide and 19.8 percent of those committed for lesser homicide were farmers. At that time, farmers represented 18.6 percent of the male population ten years of age and older in the United States. Edwin Sutherland interpreted this comparative overrepresentation of farmers in homicide statistics as being due to the fact that "among the farmers are included the large number of Negroes in the South, with their high rate of homicide" (p. 95). Similarly, an article that appeared in the popular magazine *Literary Digest* ("Rural Perfection a Myth") noted that "the small cities of Kansas have a record of homicide four times as great as the large cities of New York; the small cities of Virginia seven times the rate of homicide than is credited to the large cities of Massachussets" (p. 34).

In contrast to the findings of higher homicide rates in rural areas, Dublin and Bunzel asserted that since the beginning of the twentieth century, federal statistics had demonstrated a consistently higher rate of homicide in urban as compared to rural areas. Although Dublin and Bunzel failed to describe their operational definition of rural, they claimed that the ratio of the urban to the rural homicide rate was two to one in 1900 and ten to seven in 1930. In attempting to explain these differences, Dublin and Bunzel noted that a large proportion of the murders and manslaughters in rural areas were "crimes of passion," while in urban areas economic incentives were probably more important factors in homicides.

On the other hand, Frankel noted that homicide rates in New Jersey's rural counties for the 1930–1934 period were not higher than in urban areas. George Vold argued that "in the case of murder, manslaughter, and serious sex offenses, there is little difference between rural and urban areas" (p. 40). Finally, in their classic text *The Principles of Urban-Rural Sociology*, Sorokin and Zimmerman argued that there was a tendency for rural areas to exhibit higher crime rates in offenses against the person, such as homicides, infanticides, and grave assaults, but a lower proportion of crimes against property.

There is also considerable confusion in the more contemporary literature regarding whether or not crime rates are higher or lower in rural areas, as measured by population size. Marshall Clinard found a relationship between city size and homicide rates, with smaller cities having lower homicide rates than larger cities. Wolfgang (1968) reported slightly higher homicide rates for rural areas in the United States in 1965 than for small cities. Similarly, Archer et al., examining the 1971–1975 period in the United States, found larger cities had higher homicide rates. Similarly, Kowalski and Duffield, using county level homicide data for 1979–1982, found that rural areas had lower rates of homicide than urban areas, and argued this was the result of reduced individualism and stronger group identification in rural areas. Mosher et al., using 1990 Uniform Crime Report data, also found that homicide rates were lowest in cities with populations under 2,500. In contrast to these findings, however, Kposowa and Breault used Uniform Crime Report and census data from over three thousand counties in their analysis of homicide for the years 1979 to 1981, and found that of the top thirty counties with the highest rates of homicide, twenty-three of them had populations below twenty thousand.

Focusing generally on violent crime and using national victimization data, Robert Sampson reported consistent and substantial differences in crime rates across units of different population size. He noted that rural crime rates are not only lower, but may in fact be the result of different causal factors. For example, Sampson found that while poverty was related to victimization in larger counties, in smaller areas the number of dwellings that contained multiple families was a more important predictor of crime victimization rates.

In order to examine the current relationship between population size and crime rates, Table 1 provides data on arrest rates per 100,000 population in 1996 for cities grouped according to their size, for a number of offenses. Murder rates are highest in cities with populations greater than 250,000 and decline for each decreasing city-size category, to a low of 3.0 per 100,000 for cities under 10,000. A similar pattern is seen for robbery, where arrest rates are over six times higher in the largest, as opposed to the smallest, cities. However, there are no clear differences in arrest rates across city size categories for the crime of larceny-theft. Although rural-urban distinctions based exclusively on size of place are not ideal, this pattern of a strong relationship between city size and violent crime rates and weaker relationships for property crimes generally holds for several different societies and in several different historical periods (Sacco et al.).

Similar relationships have been revealed in studies using victimization data. For example, Bachman analyzed data from the National Crime Victimization Survey for the years 1973 to 1990, and found generally that individuals living in central cities had the highest rates of criminal victimization for all types of crime, while those living in nonmetropolitan (rural) areas had the lowest rates. More specifically, on average, individuals residing in central areas experienced nearly twice as many crimes of violence as those living in nonmetropolitan areas, although Bachman noted that the gap in violent crime victimization had been decreasing over the 1973–1990 period.

The notable exception to the pattern of higher crime rates in urban as opposed to rural jurisdictions revealed in Table 1 is for the offense of driving under the influence of alcohol. For this offense, rates were lowest in cities with populations greater than 250,000, increasing to a rate of 833.4 per 100,000 in cities of less than 10,000. These differences are at least partially explained by the fact that alcohol use, particularly among young people, is more frequent in rural areas. This may pose a particular problem for rural dwellers who have to spend far more time on the road, traveling longer distances.

Theoretical explanations of rural-urban crime differences

A consideration of urban-rural crime rate differences has important implications for criminological theory and crime policies. As Weisheit and Wells note, the tendency has been for theories to be developed for urban crime problems and then to assume these have universal application—a perspective that has been called "urban ethnocentrism." Perhaps ironically, the earliest theories in criminology were characterized by a nonurban perspective, reflecting the predominantly rural backgrounds of the early theorists in sociology and criminology. But as Weisheit and Wells suggest, "contemporary criminology has come full circle from these origins and dramatically reversed this bias" (p. 383).

Table 1

Arrest rates (per 100,000 inhabitants) for selected offenses by size of place 1996

	Size of place					
Offense	250,000+	100,000-249,999	50,000-99,999	25,000-49,999	10,000-24,999	Under 10,000
Murder and non-negligent manslaughter	16.9	9.9	5.3	3.7	3.2	3.0
Robbery	154.8	85.4	60.8	45.4	35.5	25.5
Larceny/theft	658.6	760.5	752.9	725.3	727.4	657.6
Driving under the influence	298.6	390.8	432.3	488.1	579.5	833.4

SOURCE: Uniform Crime Report Data, 1996.

For example, several criminological studies assert that poverty is a cause of crime; however, it is important to note that poverty is a common problem in the rural United States where unemployment is generally higher, and for those who are employed, wages are generally lower. Therefore, theories of crime that invoke poverty as a potential cause have difficulty explaining the fact that crime rates are generally lower in rural jurisdictions.

Criminologists have also argued that the high rates of gun ownership in the United States are related to violent crime. However, Wright, Rossi, and Daly (1983) observed that gun ownership is much more prevalent in rural as opposed to urban areas—in rural areas over 75 percent of citizens are gun owners, while in large cities only 25 percent of citizens own guns. And while many rural gun owners are hunters who primarily use rifles, the percentage of citizens owning handguns is also higher in rural areas than in central cities. Interestingly, however, while rural residents are more likely to own guns, they are less likely to use them in the commission of crime (Weisheit et al.).

In 1941, George Vold argued that the higher crime rates of urban areas could be explained using two basic hypotheses. The first of these held that there had been a selective migration from rural areas to cities of the individuals who were most likely to commit crimes, thereby increasing crime rates in cities and decreasing those in rural areas. The second hypothesis was that the city itself has an influence on the life of its inhabitants that tends to promote and facilitate criminality. More recently, theorists have developed what are known as the "determinist" and "compositional" models in attempts to ex-

plain rural urban crime differences. The determinist argument asserts that urban residence itself contributes to crime in these areas; the compositional argument, on the other hand, suggests that urban residence itself has no significant effect on the risk of crime victimization. Instead, the differences in crime rates between rural and urban areas are better explained through reference to the social and demographic characteristics of the populations who reside in each type of place (Sacco et al.; Tittle).

Related to the compositional argument, it is commonly believed that rural areas are more governed by informal social control, which is facilitated by the fact that many residents of rural communities, including the police, know each other socially—as George Vold commented in a 1941 article, "in the open country... every person is a policeman" (p. 38). Rural populations are generally more stable, and the social networks in rural communities are largely overlapping rather than segmented, and characterized by a higher density of acquaintanceship (Freudenberg). In contrast, as Wirth contended, urbanism as a way of life promotes social estrangement and alienation, which allows urban dwellers to escape the regulatory influences of the informal social controls that tend to operate in less urbanized places. These differences in urban and rural lifestyles need to be considered when examining differences in crime rates.

Unique rural crime problems

It is also important to note that rural areas may have special or unique crime problems, including the organized theft of livestock, equipment, and other agricultural products. Weisheit et al. point out the potential for an increase in such crimes resulting from the trend toward larger farms in the United States. For example, an article in the *Los Angeles Times* reported on widespread thefts of bull semen from farms in the San Joaquin in California, which is apparently a multimillion-dollar enterprise. In addition, as Weisheit et al. point out, there are a number of ways in which rural and urban crime are interrelated. They note that rural areas are often used to produce drugs—in particular, marijuana and methamphetamine—for consumption in rural as well as urban areas. Further, rural areas are frequently used as transshipment points for illegal goods such as drugs and stolen automobile parts.

It is also important to note that some efforts to influence economic growth in rural areas can increase crime there. The recent development of labor-intensive industries such as meat and poultry processing in rural areas has attracted large numbers of (often illegal) immigrants. As Weisheit et al. point out, the presence of these immigrants in what were previously homogeneous small communities creates the potential for racial tensions and hate crimes. There is also the issue of the emergence of militia movements in several rural areas, and problems associated with ecological or environmental crime. As the problem of disposing of hazardous waste increases and the costs of disposing of such waste legally climb, it can be expected that the illegal dumping of waste in rural areas will increase, as will the risks to the health and welfare of residents of rural areas.

It is thus clear that while crime in rural areas is generally lower than in urban areas and different in type, criminologists need to be aware of these differences in order to further develop criminological theories and policies to deal with crime.

CLAYTON MOSHER
THOMAS ROTOLO

See also CRIME CAUSATION: SOCIOLOGICAL THEORIES; DEVELOPING COUNTRIES, CRIME IN; ECOLOGY OF CRIME; STATISTICS: HISTORICAL TRENDS IN WESTERN SOCIETY; URBAN CRIME.

BIBLIOGRAPHY

ARAX, MARK. "Rural Cops Battle Rising Crime in the Cropland." *Los Angeles Times,* 2 March 1998.
ARCHER, D.; GARTNER, R.; AKERT, R.; and LOCKWOOD, T. "Cities and Homicide: A New Look at an Old Paradox." *Comparative Studies in Sociology* 1 (1977): 73–95.
BACHMAN, RONET. "Crime in Nonmetropolitan America: A National Accounting of Trends, Incidence Rates, and Idiosyncratic Vulnerabilities." *Rural Sociology* 57 (1992): 546–560.
CLINARD, MARSHALL B. *Sociology of Deviant Behavior*. New York: Holt, Rinehart and Winston, 1974.
COOK, W. L. "Murders in Massachusetts, 1871–1892." *American Statistical Association* 3 (1893): 1893.
DUBLIN, LOUIS I., and BUNZEL, BESSIE. "Thou Shalt Not Kill." *Survey Graphic* 24 (1935): 127–139.
FRANKEL, EMIL. "One Thousand Murders." *Journal of Criminal Law and Criminology* 29 (1939): 672–688.
FREUDENBERG, WILLIAM R. "The Density of Aquaintanceship: An Overlooked Variable in Community Research." *American Journal of Sociology* 92 (1986): 27–63.
KOWALSKI, GREGORY, and DUFFIELD, DON. "The Impact of the Rural Population Component on Homicide Rates in the United States: A County-Level Analysis." *Rural Sociology* 55 (1990): 76–90.
KPOSOWA, AUGUSTINE J., and BREAULT, KEVIN D. "Reassessing the Structural Covariates of Homicide Rates: Are There Any Invariances Across Time and Social Space?" *Sociological Focus* 26 (1): 27–46.
MOSHER, CLAYTON; PHILLIPS, DRETHA; and ROTOLO, THOMAS. "Don't Forget the Small Places: Exploring Structural Covariates of Homicide Rates Across Cities of Varying Population Size." Paper presented at the annual meeting of the American Sociological Association, Chicago, 1999.
PICARD, J. L. "Why Crime Is Increasing." *North American Review* 140 (1885): 456–463.
"Rural Perfection a Myth." *Literary Digest* 29 March 1919, pp. 33–34.
SACCO, VINCENT F.; JOHNSON, HOLLY; and ARNOLD, ROBERT. "Urban-Rural Residence and Criminal Victimization." *Canadian Journal of Sociology* 18 (1993): 431–451.
SAMPSON, ROBERT J. "The Effects of Urbanization and Neighborhood Characteristics on Criminal Victimization." *Metropolitan Crime Patterns*. Edited by Robert M. Figlio, Simon Hakim, and George E. Rengert. Monsey, N.Y.: Willow Tree Press, 1986. Pages 3–25.
SOROKIN, P. A., and ZIMMERMAN, C. C. *Principles of Rural-Urban Sociology*. New York: H. Holt and Co., 1931.

SUTHERLAND, EDWIN. *Criminology.* Philadelphia: J. B. Lippincott Co., 1924.

TITTLE, CHARLES. "Influences on Urbanism: A Test of Predictions from Three Perspectives." *Social Problems* 36 (1989): 270–288.

U.S. Senate Majority Staff Report. "Rising Casualties: Violent Crime and Drugs in Rural America." Washington D.C.: GPO, 1991.

VOLD, GEORGE. "Crime in City and County Areas." *Annals of the American Academy of Political and Social Science* 217 (1941): 38–45.

WEISHEIT, RALPH A., and WELLS, L. EDWARD. "Rural Crime and Justice: Implications for Theory and Research." *Crime and Delinquency* 42 (1996): 379–390.

WEISHEIT, RALPH A.; FALCONE, DAVID N.; and WELLS, L. EDWARD. *Crime and Policing in Rural and Small-Town America.* Prospect Heights, Ill.: Waveland Press, 1999.

WIRTH, LOUIS. "Urbanism as a Way of Life." *American Journal of Sociology* 44 (1938): 3–24.

WOLFGANG, MARVIN E. "Urban Crime." In *The Metropolitan Enigma.* Edited by J. Q. Wilson. Cambridge, Mass.: Harvard University Press, 1968. Pages 245–281.

WRIGHT, JAMES D.; ROSSI, PETER H.; and DALY, KATHLEEN. *Under the Gun: Weapons, Crime and Violence in America.* New York: Aldine, 1983.

ISBN 0-02-865322-X